T0391026

The Lonka Project

THE POWER OF LIFE

A PHOTOGRAPHIC TRIBUTE TO THE LAST
HOLOCAUST SURVIVORS AROUND THE WORLD

JIM HOLLANDER AND RINA CASTELNUOVO HOLLANDER
EDITORS

WITH A FOREWORD BY DAVID GROSSMAN

Copyright © Jim Hollander and Rina Castelnuovo Hollander
Jerusalem 2024/5784

All rights reserved. No part of this publication may be translated, reproduced, stored in a retrieval system or transmitted, in any form or by any means, electronic, mechanical, photocopying, recording or otherwise, without express written permission from the publishers.

Foreword (p. 17) by David Grossman © 2007. Used by permission.

All photographs © 2019, 2020, 2021, 2023 by the individual photographers.

Cover photograph: Dorothy Bohm in her London flat.
   Marissa Roth, USA, photographer
Back cover photograph: Tattoo number of Bat-Sheva Degan, Holon, Israel.
   Rina Castelnuovo, Israel, photographer

Cover Design: John Hubbard
Typesetting: John Hubbard

ISBN: 978-965-7801-52-9

1 3 5 7 9 8 6 4 2

Gefen Publishing House Ltd.	Gefen Books
6 Hatzvi Street	c/o Baker & Taylor Publisher Services
Jerusalem 9438614,	30 Amberwood Parkway
Israel	Ashland, Ohio 44805
972-2-538-0247	516-593-1234
orders@gefenpublishing.com	orders@gefenpublishing.com

www.gefenpublishing.com

Printed in Israel
Library of Congress Control Number: 2023952543

Lisa & Douglas Goldman Fund

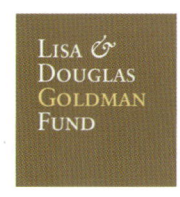

This first print edition is made possible thanks to the generosity of Lisa & Douglas Goldman Fund in San Francisco.

The Lonka Project is supported by philanthropists Yuval & Michal Rakavy and Debra Pell

The Lonka Project

FOUNDERS AND CO-DIRECTORS
Jim Hollander and Rina Castelnuovo Hollander

COORDINATING PRODUCER
Dr. Chagai Rot

TEXT EDITORS
Bradley Burston and Howard Goller

PHOTO EDITOR
Jim Hollander

BOOK DESIGN AND LAYOUT
John Hubbard | emks.fi, with Jim Hollander

PAGE 16: The wagon monument at Yad Vashem, Jerusalem, photographed by Jim Hollander, was designed by Moshe Safdie and is also known as the Memorial to the Deportee.

The Lonka Project logo was designed by Yuval Rakavy.

WWW.THELONKAPROJECT.COM

The Lonka Project book is dedicated to all Holocaust survivors around the world and their families.

With immense gratitude to all the participating photographers who volunteered their talents.

Yanek and Lonka Nass

Gino Hollander

Murray and Hana Greenfield

THE LONKA PROJECT is named after **Dr. Lonka (Eleonora) Nass** (1926–2018). Lonka survived with her mother Fella the years of the Holocaust in the Krakow Ghetto and the concentration and extermination camps Plaszów, Auschwitz, Bergen-Belsen and Terezin. Her father, a baby brother and extended family members perished. For 70 years she was married to **Dr. Yanek (Jerzy) Nass** (1927–2021). Yanek survived with his parents first in an underground bunker in the Polish town Jaworów, today Ukraine. He witnessed the atrocities committed by the Nazis and their Ukrainian collaborators. He was one of a small group of boys who fled briefly to the forests after joining Artek Hener. Most of the boys were killed. Lonka and Yanek immigrated to Israel, where they rebuilt their lives.

Gino (Eugene) Hollander (1924–2015) was an artist and a decorated American soldier in the original 10th Mountain Division ski troops. He fought in World War II in northern Italy, including at Riva Ridge and Lake Garda. He was awarded a Bronze Star for valor and two Purple Hearts for his service but never spoke of his war activities until well into his 70s, after living in Spain for 30 years and back in Aspen, Colorado, where he trained in the 10th Mountain as a teenager. The photo shows Gino at the Arno River and the Ponte Vecchio in Florence, Italy, during time off in World War II.

Their children, Jim Hollander and Rina Castelnuovo, initiated The Lonka Project in 2019 in memory and in honor of the Holocaust survivors scattered around the globe.

Hana Lustig Greenfield was born in 1926 in Kolin, Czechoslovakia. During the war, the Lustig family was relocated to the Terezin Ghetto. Hana was deported to Auschwitz and later sent to forced labor in Hamburg. She survived the death march from Hamburg to Bergen-Belsen and was liberated by the British Army on April 15, 1945. Hana and her sister Irene were the only survivors of their family. Hana immigrated to Israel in 1952. She married Murray Greenfield, a sailor who had volunteered to sail the ship *Hatikva* from the United States to Europe, smuggling survivors of the Holocaust to Mandatory Palestine in 1947. Hana and Murray created a family and established Gefen Publishing House in Jerusalem. Hana passed away on International Holocaust Remembrance Day, January 27, 2014.

Lydia Abramson 215
Trudy Album 103
Joseph Alexander 180
Yechiel Alexander 139
Andrea Anati 328
Paulette Angel 390
Naomi Applebaum 327
Simcha Applebaum 327
David Aptowitzer 418
Itzhak Arad 194
Shlomo Arad 365
Eva Arban 452
Haim Arbiv 339
Judith Ashriel 218
Sara Atzmon 389
Inge Auerbacher 340
Avraham Aviel (Lipkonsky) 277, 428
Colette Avital 416
Dr. Moshe Avital 105
Peter Bachrach 436
Yehuda Bacon 458
Saadia Bahat 459
Samuel Bak 157
Aharon Barak 117
Rachel Barda 465
Judith Barnea 48
Moshe Barth 293
Genia Basov 42
Esther Béjarano 326
Eugene Beko 152
Margie Beko 152
Itzchak Belfer 245
Samuel Beller 308
Feiga Belostotsky 463
Gisela Ben Yaacov 32
Fannie Ben-Ami 62
Pnina Berkowitch 438
Leonid Bernshtein 490
Zina Bernshtein 490
Stella Bichler 120

Michael Bieder 200
Aron Bielski 196
Naphtali Bilu 358
Walter Bingham 446
Itzchak Biran 172
Halina Birenbaum 45
Georgette Blajchmann 368
Jacob Blankitny 408
Elazar Gusty Blau 310
Zehava Blau 310
Motke Blum 50
Shmuel Blumenfeld 140
Hela Blumenthal 209
Dr. Wiktor Bodnar 442
Hedy Bohm 495
Dorothy Bohm cover, 166
Ted Bolgar 357
Ingrid "Inge" Boos 200
Aliza Bunzel 322
Irene Butter 64
Avraham Carmi 477
Herta Caspi 369
Janos Cegledy 386
Daniel Chanoch 260
Mordechai Chechanover 304
Isabelle Choko 283
Yitzhak Cohen 311
Henri Mass Coleman 252
Chana Copenhagen 480
Dr. Giselle Cycowicz 388
Bat-Sheva Dagan 440
Moshe Dagan 406
Hannie Dauman 264
Henri Dauman 24
Shoshana Sivron Davidman 381
Hannah Davidovich 462
Ester Erna Kaveson Debevec 232
Yosef Dekel 303
Yeshayahu Deutsch 438
Sheine Deyzh 399

The Survivors

Nina Dinar 130
Mellpomeni Dina 183
Barbara Drotow 200
Lord Alfred Dubs 84
Alice Eichenbaum 104
Zvi Eichenwald 267
Rachell Eisenberg 118
Uri Eshed 394
Arie Eshel 131
Moshe Eshel 172
Raphaël Esrail 163
Moshe Etzion 110
Eftychia Battinou Ezra 122
Mordechay "Motke" Faer 121
Emil Farkas 392
Dr. Helga Feldner-Busztin 298
Ben Ferencz 108
Reverend John Fieldsend 350
Ryfka Finkelstein 486
Ben Zion Fischler 161
Abraham Foxman 424
Yeshayahu Foyer 426
Harry J. Fransman 475
Arkady Frechenco 466
Henry Friedman 143
Ida Friedmann 398
Naftali Fürst 472, 473
Gera Gabriel 144
Edith Galai 294
Miriam Kato Galai 294
Wolf Galperin 223
Fortouni Politi Gani 179
Chaya Gantz 372
Bina Ganz 319
Joseph Ganz 319
Peter Gardosch 259
Alexander Gelman 385
Salomea Genin 352
Rachel Gera 127
Rachel Gidali 240

Zvi Gil 316
Kama Ginkas 375
Inge Ginsberg 302
Dalia Hofmekler Ginzburg 478
Grete Glotman 468
Edith Gluk 320
Arie Goldberg 250
Lea Goldberg 221
Israel Goldberger 438
Fishel Goldig 356
Paula Goldstein 200
Pearl Good 330
Dr. William Ze'ev Good 330
Charles Górlicki 69
Rachel Gottlieb 44
Eliezer Greenfeld 219
Rachel Greenfeld 219
Abraham Michael Grinzaid 147, 371
Simon Gronowski 378
Chaim & Aliza Grosbein 487
Alex Gross 190
Bernard Gross 213
Nikolaus Grünerwas 473
Luba Grungrass 36
Lily Gumbush 263
David Gur 347
Yaacov Guterman 460
Menachem Haberman 154
Dan Hadani 169
Moshe Haelyon 52
John Hajdu 324
Ralph Hakman 124
Yocheved Halperin 374
Adam Han-Górski 272
Jacob "Jackie" Handeli 128
Abraham Har Shalom 233
Ruth Haran 506
Anat Harpaz 262
Yehuda Havas 28
Horace Hecht 296

Mina Heilig 334
Eli Heineman 396
Rifka Helfand 303
Sir Ben Helfgott 230
Arek Hersh 496
Yechezkel Hershtik 492
Juliane Heyman 336
Gabor Hirsch 370
Hermann "Mano" Höellenreiner 280
Xaviera Hollander 91
Yaacov Holzman 395
Lia Hoover 48
Ryszard Horowitz 246
Niusia Horowitz-Karakulska 430
Jay Ipson 251
Fania Istovich 200
Leila Jabarin 301
Stephen B. Jacobs 174
Eddie Jaku 366
Anna Janowska 443
Madeleine Kahn 222
Nicole Kahn 287
Ellen Kaidanow 138
Jerry Kaidanow 138
Meir Kaiser 438
Goldie Szachter Kalib 118
Emmanuel Kalisch 75
Sonia Kam 264
Ray Kaner 266
Leon Kaner 268
Hana Kantor 433
Gabriella Karin 457
Ilana Karniel 177
Baruch Kasher 140
Hedva Katz 274
Joshua Kaufman 346
Agnes Keleti 158
Yehudith Kenigsberg 212
Eva Kepes 299
Margot Pins Kestenbaum 208

Henri Kichka 234
Max Kirschberg 323
Dr. Nicole Wittman Klapish 88
Gerda Weissmann Klein 134
Gershon Klein 290
Sonia Klein 100
Godel Kleinman 456
Martha-Miriam Kleinman 87
Yosef Kleinman 361
Juergen Kliger 417
Ibolya "Iby" Knill 343
Charlotte Knobloch 225
Solomon Kofinas 354
Ginette Kolinka 82
Gaby Koren 256
Moshe Kravitz 314
Dr. Robert Krell 338
Leonid Kret 453
Ella Rosenblatt Krzetowski 297
Marion Kunstenaar 469
Sheila Kuper 449
Shaul Paul Ladany 202
Dov Landau 125, 248
Lea Landsman 274
Anita Lasker-Wallfisch 332
Rabbi Yisrael Meir Lau 98
Esther Lavon 436
Dr. Renata Laxova 170
Gizella Lefkovits 488
Rabbi Mordechai Shraga Leibovitz 74
Sara Leicht 142
Nate Leipciger 497
David Dugo Leitner 274, 438
Claude Lelouch 244
David Lenga 376
Edouard Mendelsohn Lessel 148
Lia Lesser 349
Mona Levin 318
Asya Levit 150
Mirjam Bolle Levy 480

Regina Lewin 200
Krystyna Linden 182
Evelyn Lippman 401
Dov Livne 348
Jean Serge Lorach 90
Ernest Lorant 200
Frank Lowy 254
Shaul Lubovitz 63
Irena Danka Lustiger 431
Nachmann Magen 172
Yehuda Maimon 140
Lidia Maksymowicz 400
Igor Malickij 269
Leon Malmed 60
Gizella Schöner Man 432
Rabbi Nissan Mangel 419
Adela Manheimer 200
Esther "Stenia" Mannheim 198
Genia Manor 284
Nahum Manor 284
Harry Markowicz 288
David Marks 72
Yorek Maron 61
Rachel Masiach 484
Dr. Moshe Meron 241
Franz Michalski 188
Sheindi Miller 317
Sami Modiano 227
Gabriel Moked 56
Yossi Mor 183
Edgar Moran 412
Oleg Mortkovich 384
Ed Mosberg 59
Zoya Moyal 58
Salo Muller 278
Marie Nahmias 86
Abba Naor 476
Moshe Neumann 111
Danilo Nikolić 226
Bernard Offen 151

Ruth Oppenheim 93
Uri Orlev 214
Anna Ornstein 482
Aryeh Oz 172
Ruth Pardess 447
Peggy Parnass 236
Gad Partuk 229
Yossi Peled 498
Eda Pell 216
Joseph Pell 216
Victor Perahia 65
Irene Perbal 414
Shlomo Perel 220
Dr. Shaul Perlberg 362
Naomi Perlman 450
Mordechai Perlov 114
Veronica Phillips 46
Hannah Pick-Goslar 454
Roman Polanski 206
Ralph J. Preiss 502
Otto Dov Pressburger 483
Rena Quint 253
Assia Raberman 249
Fishel Rabinowicz 258
Ina Reinart Rakavy 137
Tomi Reichental 205
Shlomo Reichik 408
Mimi Reinhard 187
Renata Reisfeld 165
Miriam Reitzenstein 200
Malka Rendel 485
Moshe Ridler 504
Leila Romano 448
Sam Ron 383
Yosef Ron 95
Judith Rosenberg 54
Zeni Rosenstein 312
Maria Ross 200
László Roth 129, 500
Rabbi Yechezkel Roth 255

Gitta Ryle 96
Dov Sacajiu 470
Lt. Col. Sam Sachs 413
Diamantina "Tina" Vivante Salonichio 94
Dr. William Samelson 26
Svetlana Samilova 461
Irène Sapir 116
Léon Sapir 116
David Sarid 373
Leon Schagrin 70
Liese Scheiderbauer 364
Kathy Schenk 200
Moshe Schleifstein 195
Eva Schloss 80
Helga Schmitz 146
Eva Schneider 415
Rabbi Arthur Schneier 155
Batya Schon 445
Franco Schönheit 160
Paul Schwarzbart 85
Leon Schwarzbaum 292
Monika Sears 276
Charlotte Seeman 58
Arie Segal 126
Batya Segal 126
Senator Liliana Segre 344
Shelomo Selinger 404
Esther Senot 380
Tommy Schwartz Shacham 140
Hanoch Shacher 30
Nat Shaffir 210
Zehava Shamir 464
Sara Shapira 178
Eliezer Shefer 438
Sara Shefer 274, 438
Eliezer Shimoni 274, 438
Gusti Shoval 365
Vitzek Avi Shtembuj 238
Rabbi Roman Shvartsman 470
Michael Sidko 444

Al Silverstein 102
Hilda Simche 396
Rene Slotkin 168
Lili Lea Solzbek 43
Ruby Sosnowicz 132
George Soros 315
Ida Spektor 422
Vincent J. Speranza 346
Tibor Spitz 176
Walter Spitzer 156
Andrew Stefanski 434
Regina Steinitz 106
Zwi Steinitz 107
Andor Stern 306
Ben Stern 228
Rabbi Moshe Stern 309
Betty Helena Sternlicht 71
Motek Mordechai Szymonowicz 184
Arie Tabuch 68
Hessy Taft 76
Toby Tambor 200
Rabbi Menachem Mendel Taub 34
Hilda Tayar 38
Mordechai Teichner 97
Yehudith Teichner 97
Moshe Tirosh 321
Samuel Tirosh 321
Miriam Tobol 382
Dr. Viola Torok 305
Yitzchak Turner 300
Marian Turski 199
Magadi Unger 274, 438
Zvi Unger 335
Jacobus Mozes Van Ameringen 291
Selma van de Perre 437
Betty Van Essen 480
Dr. Herman van Norden 342
Yoka Verdoner 78
Ernst Verduin 149
Aliza Vitis-Shomron 286

Miriam Seidel Volk 402
Robert Wajcman 164
Frida Koh Wasserman 313
Tova Kupel Wasserman 313
Janine Webber 77
Jacques Weimann 427
Anne Hanke Weinbaum 136
Dr. Leon Weintraub 420
Yossi Weiss 66
Jakub Weksler 360
Jack Welner 37
Dr. Ruth Westheimer 112
Francisco Wichter 40
Hinda Wichter 40
Simon Lodewijk Wijnbergen 33
Ada Willenberg 204
Ada Winsten 113
Roza Fatter Winter 341
Irena Wodislavsky 51
Bolesław "Tarzan" Wojewódzki 89
Miriam Wolberg 274
Natalia Wolberg 29
Helmut Wolff 192
Yitzhak Wollach 224
Yanek Yakobovitz 186
Sarah Yanai 183
Dena Yarmus 58
Arthur Zicherman 200
Rochelle Zicherman 200
Miriam Ziegler 270
Harry Zipper 410
Bella 282
Edith 294
Gena 282
Irene 162
Judith 92
Leon 282
Riva 282
Sophie 100

Tsafrir Abayov 202, 286, 463
Mike Abrahams 77
Lori Adamski-Peek 217
Ronen Akerman 257
Artemis Alcalay 122, 123
Yoav Alon 194
Shay Aloni 313, 389
Yossi Aloni 61
Miriam Alster 182
Stephanie Alvarez-Ewens 102
Rafi Amar 358
Odd Andersen 220
Andy Anderson 108, 109
Ira Anner 498
Jean-Andre Antoine 266
Tomer Appelbaum 428
Shlomo Arad 365
Timothy Archibald 78, 79
Jane Evelyn Atwood 83
Reli Avrahami 369
Jonny Baker 290
Oded Balilty 198
Roger Ballen 114
Micha Bar-Am 131
Ittai Bar-Joseph 130
Daniel Bar-On 341
Shalom Bar-Tal 75
Simcha Barbiro 128
Leo Barizzoni 162
Rabia Basha 472
Eli Basri 426
Rustam Bayramov 208
Natalie Behring 402
"Koko" Meir Ben-Ari 294, 316
Oren Ben-Hakoon 28, 263, 317
Sara Bennett 486
Harry Benson 197
Tom Bickles 382
Harry Borden 350
Andrew Bordwin 240

The Photographers

Rodger Bosch 209
Karine Sicard Bouvatier 283
Christian Bruna 22
Jared Buckley 299
Dave Burnett 211
Mauricio Candela 132, 133
Rina Castelnuovo 112, 173, 282, 436, 441, 448, 450, 507
Emma Cattell 401
Chien-Chi Chang 298
Yuval Chen 120
Andy Clark 338
David Cohen 195, 255
Oren Cohen 493, 494
Gil Cohen-Magen 178
Roger Cremers 437
D-MO 69, 475
Jonny Daniels 461, 467
Marko Dashev 383, 419
Jono David 289, 387
Barbara Davidson 124
Leonardo DeGorter 342
Peter Dejong 91
Shaul Dishi 244
Moe Doiron 271
Meital Dor 374
Magali Druscovich 40, 41
Emmanuel Dunand 183
Thomas Dworzak 225
Jillian Edelstein 325
Nir Elias 233
Gil Eliayahu 373
Scott Elmquist 251
Kristen Joy Emack 482
Davis Factor 181
Sivan Farag 215
Michal Fattal 39
Stephen Ferry 340
Chuck Fishman 151
Olivier Fitoussi 427

Stuart Franklin 80
Ruth Fremson 449
Debra Friedman 136
Noga Friedman 285
Limor Friedmann 398
Yoav Gad 396
Yigal Gawze 177
Eldad Gershgoren 314
Milton Gevertz 306, 307
Karen Gillerman 204
Anne Helene Gjelstad 318
Shuka Glotman 468
Nimrod Gluckman 444
Shaul Golan 86
Sara Gold 319
Chaim Goldberg 309
Dana Goldstein 103
Mike Goldwater 84
Ancho Gosh 249, 473
Eyal Granit 363
Reza Green 469
Liz Gregg 349
Lori Grinker 176
Maria Gruzdeva 423, 453
Marcial Guillén 323
Robert Gumpert 60, 85
Galia Gur Zeev 460
Mika Gurovich 431
Amnon Gutman 305
Carol Guzy 118, 119
Yechiel Hakoen 248
Nati Harnik 157
James Marcus Haney 457
Erez Harodi 85
Blaine Harrington III 35
Seth Harrison 138
Ron Haviv 168
Eli Hershkowitz 262
Debbie Hill 165, 301
James Hill 422

Max Hirshfeld 174
Jim Hollander 16, 36, 92, 98, 154, 360, 440, 458, 484
Christopher Hopkins 320
Alvaro Hoppe 276
Madeleine "Maddie" Hordinski 434, 435
Emanuel Ilan 212
Edi Israel 470
Olga Izakson 385
Gadi Kabalo 275
Vardi Kahana 45
Bea Bar Kallos 159, 432
Kobi Kalmanovitz 221
Richard Kalvar 368
Cindy Karp 296
Ed Kashi 105
Reuven Kastro 300
Rick Katz 297
Nir Keidar 446
Alain Keler 164
Louise Kennerley 366
Uzi Keren 33
Corinna Kern 126
Friso Keuris 278
Quique Kierszenbaum 161
Yunghi Kim 101
Douglas Kirkland 376
Alex Kolomoisky 62, 63
Lauren Koplowitz 191
Rafi Koren 372
Ziv Koren 140, 141, 495, 496, 497
Witold Krassowski 199
Ofra Moran Kurnick 464, 465
Lois Lammerhuber 364
Eyal Landesman 310
Andrzej Lange 89
Tomasz Lazar 222
Franck Leclerc 206
Pascaline Lefin 234
Stéphane Lehr 90

Clifford Lester 411, 412, 413, 414, 415
Alex Levac 462
Heidi Levine 127
Amir Levy 303, 456
Ariane Littman 88, 388
Grzegorz Litynski 430, 442, 443
Kim Ludbrook 47
Tiffany Luna 331
John MacDougall 242, 243, 417
Seffi Magriso 439
Mark Mann 502
José Giribás Marambio 259, 269, 280
Gideon Markowicz 184, 185, 187
Ursula Markus 302
Vera Markus 370
Axel Martens 237
Steve Mason 113
Maya Maymoni 218, 334
Steve McCurry 264
Veronika Merkova 343
Omer Messinger 333
Moshe Milner 59
Moti Milrod 219
Roy Mizrachi 327
Lior Mizrahi 277
Oz Moalem 392
Stefano Montesi 227
John Myers 70
Tali Nachshon-Dag 418
Jonathan Nackstrand 421
Michael Nelson 170
Tomer Neuberg 487
Nadav Neuhaus 144, 146
Moran Ahdut Nissim 229, 452
Avichai Nitzan 335
Jorge Novominsky 238
Marlen Noy 250
Official Photographer 315
Yossi Gal Oliver 111
Cheney Orr 76

Tzachi Ostrovsky 129
Orestis Panagiotou 179
Hadas Parush 50
Judah Passow 54
Dor Pazuelo 311
Eyal Pe'er 397
Paolo Pellegrin 390
Gilles Peress 247
Or Perevoznik 394
Daniel Pilar 474
Ethan Pines 201
George Pirkle 213
John Pregulman 252, 253
Eldad Rafaeli 67
Yuval Rakavy 228, 445
Joyce Ravid 433
Regina Recht 287
Eli Reed 26, 27
Sarah Reingewirtz 58
Richard B. Ressman 96
Tamas Revesz 158
Natalya Reznik 150
Brandon Richardson 346
Moshe Ridler 504
Avi Roccah 223
Alon Ron 95
James Andrew Rosen 267, 356, 357
Ricki Rosen 490, 491
Oliver Halsman Rosenberg 268
Marissa Roth cover, 166
Yanai Rubaja 322
Raday Rubenstein 142
Atef Safadi 30, 31
Anat Saragusti 485
Howard Schatz 72
Liat Schnitman 339
Eric Schütt 292, 326
Kristian Schuller 353
Nissim Sellam 404, 405, 500, 501
Avishag Shaar-Yashuv 141

Amit Shabi 304
Avner Shahaf 488
Tal Shahar 347
Ariel Shalit 245
Ilana Shapira 260
Effi Sharir 241
Jonathan Sharlin 104
Anna Shmitko 375
Yaaqov Shofar 97
Nati Shohat 125
Enrique Shore 94
Michael Shubitz 476, 479
Chen Shuval 395
Yonatan Sindel 293, 361
Igal Slavin 139
Armin Smailovic 193, 226, 232
Roland Smith 25
Roni Sofer 328
Tomasz Solinski 321
Alec Soth 273
Thierry Soval 116
Stefano Spinelli 258
Amelia Stein 205
Harvey Stein 424
Ami Steinitz 106, 107
Brent Stirton 337
Shira Stoll 44
Abir Sultan 35
Eric Sultan 454, 477
Shabtai Tal 169, 186
Allan Tannenbaum 155
Daniel Tchetchik 416
Mario Tedeschi 160
Gali Tibbon 224
Sasson Tiram 42, 480
Perry Trotter 148, 291
David Turnley 64
Peter Turnley 65
Miri Tzachi 43, 51, 110
Marty Umans 308

Avigail Uzi 53, 70
Tom Vack 344
Roberta Valerio 380
Sébastien Van Malleghem 378
B.A. Van Sise 354
Vatican Media 400
Dusan Vranic 214
Oded Wagenstein 312, 371
Eyal Warshavsky 57
Noam Warshavsky 348
Todd Weinstein 143
Maurice Weiss 189
David H. Wells 93
Etienne Werner 149
Greg Williams 230
Pavel Wolberg 29
Kobi Wolf 147
Baruch Yaari 74, 399
Gili Yaari 121
Alfred Yaghobzadeh 156
Ilia Yefimovich 32
Itzik Yogev 447, 459
Yehoshua Yosef 409
Patrick Zachmann 135
Jegor Zaika 384
Daniella Zalcman 163
Yossi Zamir 117
Yossi Zeliger 254
Tatyana Zenkovich 21
Oren Ziv 381
Rafat Zrieq 483
Ronen Zvulun 152, 153
Ohad Zwigenberg 48

Jim Hollander USA

YAD VASHEM, JERUSALEM, 2019

Foreword BY David Grossman

Despite the close relationship between Israel and Germany today – and between Israelis and Germans, between Jews and Germans – even now there is a place in one's mind and in one's heart where certain statements must be filtered through the prisms of time and memory, where they are refracted into the entire spectrum of colours and shades. I was born and raised in Jerusalem, in a neighbourhood and in a family in which people could not even utter the word "Germany." They found it difficult to say "Holocaust," too, and spoke only of "what happened over there."

It is interesting to note that in Hebrew, Yiddish and every other language they speak, when Jewish people refer to the Holocaust, they tend to speak of what happened "over there," whereas non-Jews usually speak in terms of "what happened then." There is a vast difference between there and then. "Then" means in the past; "then" enfolds within it something that happened and ended, and is no longer. "There," conversely, suggests that somewhere out there, in the distance, the thing that happened is still occurring, constantly growing stronger alongside our daily lives, and that it may re-erupt. It is not decisively over. Certainly not for us, the Jews.

As a child, I often heard the term "the Nazi beast," and when I asked the adults who this beast was, they refused to tell me, and said there were things a child should not know. Years later, I wrote in *See Under: Love* about Momik, the son of Holocaust survivors who never tell him what really happened to them "over there." The frightened Momik imagines the Nazi beast as a monster that controlled a land called "over there," where it tortured the people Momik loves, and did things to them that hurt them forever and denied them the ability to live a full life.

When I was four or five, I heard for the first time of Simon Wiesenthal, the Nazi-hunter. I felt a great sense of relief: finally, I thought, there is someone courageous enough to fight the beast, even willing to hunt it down! Had I known how to write at the time, I might have written Wiesenthal a letter full of the detailed and practical questions that were preoccupying me, because I imagined that this hunter probably knew everything about his prey.

My generation, the children of the early 1950s in Israel, lived in a thick and densely populated silence. In my neighbourhood, people screamed every night from their nightmares. More than once, when we walked into a room where adults were telling stories of the war, the conversation would stop at once. We did pick up an occasional sentence fragment: "The last time I saw him was on Himmelstrasse in Treblinka," or "She lost both her children in the first Aktion."

Every day, at 20 minutes past one, there was a 10-minute programme on the radio in which a female announcer with a glum and rhythmic voice read the names of people searching for relatives lost during the war and in the Holocaust: Rachel, daughter of Perla and Abraham Seligson from Przemysl, is looking for her little sister Leah'leh, who lived in Warsaw between the years… Eliyahu Frumkin, son of Yocheved and Hershl Frumkin from Stry, is looking for his wife Elisheva, née Eichel, and his two sons, Yaakov and Meir… And so on and so forth. Every lunch of my childhood was spent listening to the sounds of this quiet lament.

When I was seven, the Eichmann trial was held in Jerusalem, and then we listened to the radio during dinner when they broadcast descriptions of the horrors. You could say that my generation lost its appetite, but there was another loss, too. It was the loss of something deeper, which we did not understand at the time and which is still being deciphered throughout the course of our lives. Perhaps what we lost was the illusion of our parents' power to protect us from the terrors of life. Or perhaps we lost our faith in the possibility that we, the Jews, would ever live a complete, secure life. And perhaps, above all, we felt the loss of the natural, childlike faith – faith in man, in his kindness, in his compassion.

About two decades ago, when my oldest son was three, his pre-school commemorated Holocaust Memorial Day as it did every year. My son did not understand much of what he was told, and he came home confused and frightened. "Dad, what are Nazis? What did they do? Why did they do it?" And I did not want to tell him. I, who had grown up amid the silence and fragmented whispers that had filled me with so many fears and nightmares, who had written a book about a boy who almost loses his mind because of his parents' silence, suddenly understood my parents and my friends' parents who chose to be mute.

I felt that if I told him, if I even so much as cautiously alluded to what had happened over there, something in the purity of my three-year-old son would be polluted; that from the moment such possibilities of cruelty were formulated in his childlike, innocent consciousness, he would never again be the same child.

He would no longer be a child at all.

When I published *See Under: Love* in Israel, some critics wrote that I belonged to the "second generation", and that I was the son of "Holocaust survivors." I am not. My father emigrated to Palestine from Poland as a child, in 1936. My mother was born in Palestine, before the state of Israel was established.

And yet I am. I am the son of "Holocaust survivors" because in my home, too, as in so many Israeli homes, a thread of deep anxiety was stretched out, and with almost every move you made, you touched it. Even if you were very careful, even if you hardly made any unnecessary movements, you still felt that constant quiver of a profound lack of confidence in the possibility of existence. A suspicion towards man and what might erupt from him at any moment.

In our home, too, at every celebration, with every purchase of a new piece of furniture, every time a new child was born in the neighbourhood, there was a feeling that each such event was one more word, one more sentence, in the intensely conducted dialogue with over there. That every presence echoed an absence, and that life, the simplest of daily routines, the most trivial oscillations over "Should the child be allowed to go on the school trip?" or "Is it worth renovating the apartment?" somehow echoed what happened over there: all those things that managed to survive the there, and all those that did not; and the life lessons, the acute knowledge that had been burned in our memory.

This became all the more pertinent when greater decisions were at stake: which profession should we choose? Should we vote rightwing or leftwing? Marry or stay single? Have another child, or is one enough? Should we even bring a child into this world? All these decisions and acts, small and large, amounted to a huge, practically superhuman effort to weave the thin fabric of everydayness over the horrors beneath. An effort to convince ourselves that, despite everything we know, despite everything engraved on our bodies and souls, we have the capacity to live on, and to keep choosing life, and human existence.

Because for people like myself, born in Israel in the years after the Holocaust, the primary feeling – about which we could not talk at all, and for which we may not have had the words at the time – was that for us, for Jews, death was the immediate interlocutor. That life, even when it was full of the energies and hopes and fruitfulness of a newly revived young country, still comprised an enormous and constant effort to escape the dread of death.

You may say, with good reason, that this is the basic human condition. It is so, but for us it had daily and pressing reminders, open wounds and fresh scars, and representatives who were living and tangible, their bodies and souls crushed.

In Israel of the 1950s and 60s, and not only during times of extreme despair, but precisely at those moments when the great commotion of "nation-building" waned, in the moments when we tired a little, just for an instant, of being a miracle of renewal and re-creation, in those moments of the twilight of the soul, both private and national, we could immediately feel, in the most intimate way, the band of frost that suddenly tightens around our hearts and says quietly but firmly: how quickly life fades. How fragile it all is. The body, the family. Death is true, all else is an illusion.

Ever since I knew I would be an author, I knew I would write about the Holocaust. I think these two convictions came to me at the same time. Perhaps also because, from a very young age, I had the feeling that all the many books I had read about the Holocaust had left unanswered a few simple but essential questions. I had to ask these questions of myself, and I had to reply in my own words.

As I grew up, I became increasingly aware that I could not truly understand my life in Israel, as a man, as a father, as a writer, as an Israeli, as a Jew, until I wrote about my unlived life, over there, in the Holocaust. And about what would have happened to me had I been over there as a victim, and as one of the murderers.

I wanted to know both these things. One was not enough.

Namely: if I had been a Jew under the Nazi regime, a Jew in a concentration camp or a death camp, what could I have done to save something of myself, of my selfhood, in a reality in which people were stripped not only of their clothes, but also of their names, so that they became – to others – numbers tattooed on an arm. A reality in which people's previous lives were taken away from them – their family, their friends, their profession, their loves, their talents. A reality in which millions of people were relegated, by other human beings, to the lowest rung of existence: to being nothing more than flesh and blood intended for destruction with the utmost efficiency.

What was the thing inside me that I could hold up against this attempt at erasure? What was the thing that could preserve the human spark within me, in a reality entirely aimed at extinguishing it?

One can answer these questions, only about one's self, in private. But perhaps I can suggest a possible path to the answer. In the Jewish tradition, there is a legend, or a belief, that every person has a small bone in his body called the luz, located at the tip of the spine, which enfolds the essence of a person's soul. This bone cannot be destroyed. Even if the entire human body is shattered, crushed or burned, the luz bone does not perish. It stores a person's spark of uniqueness, the core of his selfhood. According to the belief, this bone will be the source of man's resurrection.

Once in a while, I ask people close to me what they believe their luz is, and I have heard many varied answers. Several writers, and artists in general, have told me that their luz is creativity, the passion to create and the urge to produce. Religious people, believers, have often said that their luz is the divine spark they feel inside. One friend answered, after much thought: parenthood, fatherhood. And another friend immediately replied that her luz was her longing for the things and people she missed. A woman who was roughly 90 at the time talked about the love of her life, a man who committed suicide over 60 years ago: he was her luz.

The other question I asked while writing *See Under: Love* is closely related to the first, and in some ways even derives from it: I asked myself how an ordinary person – as most Nazis and their supporters were – becomes part of a mass-murder apparatus. In other words, what is the thing that I must suspend within myself, that I must dull, repress, so that I can ultimately collaborate with a mechanism of murder? What must I kill within me to be capable of killing another person or people, to desire the destruction of an entire people, or silently to accept it?

Perhaps I should ask this question even more pointedly: am I myself, consciously or unconsciously, actively or passively, through indifference or with mute acceptance, collaborating at this very moment with some process that is destined to wreak havoc on another human being, or on another group of people?

"The death of one man is a tragedy," Stalin said, "but the death of millions is only statistics." How do tragedies become statistics for us? I am not saying that we are all murderers. Of course not. Yet it seems that most of us manage to lead a life of almost total indifference to the suffering of entire nations, near and far, and to the distress of hundreds of millions of human beings who are poor and hungry and weak and sick, whether in our own countries or in other parts of the world.

With wondrous ease we create the necessary mechanisms to separate ourselves from the suffering of others. Intellectually and emotionally, we manage to detach the causal relationship between, for example, our economic affluence – in the sated and prosperous western countries – and the poverty of others. Between our own luxuries and the shameful working conditions of others. Between our air-conditioned, motorised quality of life and the ecological disasters it brings about.

These "others" live in such appalling conditions that they are not usually able even to ask the questions I am asking here. After all, it is not only genocide that can eradicate a person's luz: hunger, poverty, disease and refugee status can defile and slowly kill the soul of an individual, and sometimes of a whole people.

Perhaps it is only in this global reality, where so much of our life is lived in a mass dimension, that we can be so indifferent to mass destruction. For it is the very same indifference that the vast majority of the world displays time after time, whether during the Armenian genocide or the Jewish Holocaust, in Rwanda or in Bosnia, in the Congo, in Darfur, and in many other places.

And perhaps, then, this is the great question that people living in this age must relentlessly ask themselves: in what state, at which moment, do I become part of the faceless crowd, "the masses"?

There are a number of ways to describe the process whereby the individual is swallowed up in the crowd, or agrees to hand over parts of himself to mass control. I become "the masses" when I stop formulating my own choices and the moral compromises I make. When I stop formulating them over and over again, with fresh new words each time, words that have not yet eroded in me, not yet congealed in me, which I cannot ignore or defend myself against, and which force me to face the decisions I have made, and to pay the price for them.

The masses, as we know, cannot exist without mass language – a language that will consolidate the multitude and spur it on to act in a certain way, formulating justifications for its acts and simplifying the moral and emotional contradictions it may encounter. In other words, the language of the masses is a language intended to liberate the individual from responsibility for his actions, to temporarily sever his private, individual judgment from his sound logic and natural sense of justice.

To illustrate the encounter between one individual – a remarkably exceptional one, with a uniquely personal language – and "mass language," or between tragedy and statistics, I enlist the case of the Polish Jewish author Bruno Schulz. I am referring to the story of his murder during the Second World War, in the ghetto of his town, Drohobycz. It is a well-known episode, one that is probably inaccurate and may only be a legend, a fictional anecdote, which emerged during the years when the "Bruno Schulz myth" was being constructed by his admirers all over the world.

"Anecdotes are essentially faithful to the truth," writes Ernesto Sabato, "precisely because they are fictional, invented detail by detail, until they fit a certain person exactly." And so, even if this particular account of Schulz's death is untrue, what it evokes is essentially faithful to the truth, certainly to Schulz's own ironic, tragic truth, and to the horror of the encounter between "individual" and "mass." And so I will retell it the way I first heard it:

> In the Drohobycz ghetto during the war, there was an SS officer who exploited Schulz and compelled him to paint murals in his home. An adversary of this SS officer, a Nazi commander himself, who was involved in a dispute with him over a gambling debt, happened to meet Schulz on the street. He drew his pistol and shot Schulz dead, to hurt his patron. According to the rumour, he then went to his rival and told him: "I killed your Jew." "Very well," the officer replied, "now I will kill your Jew."

I learned of this tale soon after I had finished reading Schulz's stories for the first time. I remember that I closed the book, left my house, and walked around for several hours as if in a fog. My state was such that, quite simply, I did not wish to live. I did not wish to live in a world where such things were possible. And such people. And such a way of thinking. A world in which a language that enables such monstrosities as that sentence was possible.

"I killed your Jew." "Very well, now I will kill your Jew."

I wrote *See Under: Love*, among other reasons, to restore my will to live and my love of life. Perhaps also to heal from the insult I felt on behalf of Bruno Schulz – the insult at the way his murder was described and "explained." The inhuman, crude description, as if human beings were interchangeable. As if they were merely a part of some mechanical system, or an accessory, which can be replaced with another. As if they were only statistics.

Because, with Schulz, every sliver of reality is full of personality: every passing cloud, every piece of furniture, every dressmaker's mannequin, fruit-bowl, puppy or ray of light – each and every entity, even the most trivial, has its own personality and essence. And on every page and in every passage of his writing, life is bursting with content and meaning. Every line Schulz writes is in defiance of what he calls "the fortified wall that looms over meaning", and a protest against the terror of vapidity, banality, routine, stereotyping, the tyranny of the simplistic, the masses.

When I finished reading Bruno Schulz's book, I realised that he was giving me, in his work, one of the keys to writing about the Holocaust. To write not about the death and the destruction, but about life, about what the Nazis destroyed in such a habitual, industrial, mass-minded way.

I also recall that, with the arrogance of a young writer, I told myself that I wanted to write a book that would tremble on the shelf. That the vitality it contained would be tantamount to the blink of an eye in one person's life. Not "life" in inverted commas, life that is nothing more than a languishing moment in time, but the sort of life Schulz gives us in his writing. A life of the living. A life in which we are not merely refraining from killing the other, but rather giving him or her new life, revitalising a moment that has passed, an image seen a thousand times, a word uttered a thousand times.

The world we live in today may not be as overtly and unequivocally cruel as the one created by the Nazis, but there are certain mechanisms at work that have similar underlying principles. Mechanisms that blur human uniqueness and evade responsibility for the destiny of others. A world in which fanatic, fundamentalist forces seem to increase day by day, while others gradually despair of any hope for change.

The values and horizons of this world, the atmosphere that prevails in it and the language that dominates it, are dictated to a great extent by what is known as "mass media" or "mass communication." The term was coined in the 1930s, when sociologists began to refer to "mass society." But are we truly aware of the significance of this term today, and of the process it has gone through? Do we consider the fact that, to a large extent, "mass media" today is not only media designed for the masses, but that in many ways it also turns its consumers into the masses?

It does so with the belligerence and the cynicism that emanate from all its manifestations; with its shallow, vulgar language; with the over-simplification and self-righteousness with which it handles complex political and moral problems; with the kitsch which infects everything it touches – the kitsch of war and death, the kitsch of love, the kitsch of intimacy.

A cursory look would indicate that these kinds of media actually focus on particular persons, rather than on the masses. On the individual rather than the collective. But this is a dangerous illusion: although mass media emphasises and even sanctifies the individual, and seems to direct the individual more and more towards himself, it is ultimately directing him only towards himself – his own needs, his clear and narrow interests. In an endless variety of ways, both open and hidden, it liberates him from what he is already eager to shed: responsibility for the consequences of his actions on others. And the moment it anaesthetises this responsibility in him, it also dulls his political, social and moral awareness, moulding him into conveniently submissive raw material for its own manipulations and those of other interested parties. In other words, it turns him into one of the masses.

These forms of media – written, electronic, online, often free, highly accessible, highly influential – have an existential need to preserve the public's interest, to constantly stimulate its hungry desires. And so even when ostensibly dealing with issues of moral and human import, and even when ostensibly assuming a role of social responsibility, still the finger they point at hotbeds of corruption and wrongdoing and suffering seems mechanical, automatic, with no sincere interest in the problems they highlight. Their true purpose – apart from generating profits for their owners – is to preserve a constantly stimulated state of "public condemnation"

Belarussian soldiers at a cemetery with coffins containing the remains of 1,214 murdered Jews from a Jewish ghetto killed during World War II during a reburial ceremony in Brest on May 22, 2019. The remains together with personal belongings of the victims were discovered at a recent construction site in Brest and are interred in 120 coffins decorated with Stars of David.

Tatyana Zenkovich BELARUS

BREST, 2019

Vandalized photographic portraits of Holocaust survivors on display along the Ringstrasse in Vienna in May 2019. Some ten portraits made by Luigi Toscano had been vandalized and covered with Nazi swastikas in the previous week.

Christian Bruna AUSTRIA
VIENNA, 2019

or "public exoneration" of certain individuals, who change at the speed of light. This rapid exchange is the message of mass media. Sometimes it seems that it is not the information itself that the media deem essential, but merely the rate at which it shifts. The neurotic, covetous, consumerist, seductive beat it creates. The zeitgeist: the zapping is the message.

In this world I have described, literature has no influential representatives in the centres of power, and I find it difficult to believe that literature can change it. But it can offer different ways to live in it. I know that when I read a good book, I experience internal clarification: my sense of uniqueness as a person grows lucid. The measured, precise voice that reaches me from the outside animates voices within me, some of which may have been mute until this other voice, or this particular book, came and woke them. And even if thousands of people are reading the very same book I am reading at the very same moment, each of us faces it alone. For each of us, the book is a completely different kind of litmus test.

A good book – and there are not many, because literature, too, is subject to the seductions and obstacles of mass media – individualises and extracts the single reader out of the masses. It gives him an opportunity to feel how spiritual contents, memories and existential possibilities can float up and rise from within him, from unfamiliar places, and they are his alone. The fruits of his personality alone.

At its best, literature can bring us together with the fate of others, distant and foreign. It can create within us, at times, a sense of wonder at having managed, by the skin of our teeth, to escape those strangers' fates, or make us feel sad for not being truly close to them. For not being able to reach out and touch them. I am not saying that this feeling immediately motivates us to any form of action, but certainly, without it, no act of empathy or commitment or responsibility can be possible.

At its best, literature can be kind to us: it can slightly allay the sense of insult at the dehumanisation that life in large, anonymous, global societies gives us. The insult of describing ourselves in coarse language, in clichés, in generalisations and stereotypes. The insult of our becoming – as Herbert Marcuse said – "one-dimensional man."

Literature also gives us the feeling that there is a way to fight the cruel arbitrariness that decrees our fate: even if at the end of *The Trial* the authorities shoot Josef K "like a dog"; even if Antigone is executed; even if Hans Castorp eventually dies in *The Magic Mountain* – still we, who have seen them through their struggles, have discovered the power of the individual to be human even in the harshest circumstances. Reading – literature – restores our dignity and our primal faces, our human faces, the ones that existed before they were blurred and erased among the masses. Before we were expropriated, nationalised and sold wholesale to the lowest bidder.

When I finished writing *See Under: Love*, I realised that I had written it to say that he who destroys a man, any man, is ultimately destroying a creation that is unique and boundless, that can never again be reconstructed, and there will never be another like it.

For the past four years, I have been writing a novel that wishes to say the same thing, but from a different place, and in the context of a different reality. The protagonist of my book, an Israeli woman of about 50, is the mother of a young soldier who goes to war. She fears for his life, she senses catastrophe lurking, and she tries with all her strength to fight the destiny that awaits him. This woman makes a long and arduous journey by foot, over the land of Israel, and talks about her son. This is her way of protecting him. This is the only thing she can do now, to make his existence more alive and solid: to tell the story of his life.

In the little notebook she takes on her journey, she writes, "Thousands of moments and hours and days, millions of deeds, endless acts and attempts and mistakes and words and thoughts, all to make one person in the world."

Then she adds another line: "One person, who is so easy to destroy."

The secret allure and the greatness of literature, the secret that sends us to it over and over again, with enthusiasm and a longing to find refuge and meaning, is that literature can repeatedly redeem for us the tragedy of the one from the statistics of the millions. The one about whom the story is written, and the one who reads the story.

Mevaseret Zion, 2007

Henri Dauman was born in Montmartre in Paris in 1933. In 1940, his father Isaja enlisted with the French foreign regiment of volunteers, but after the defeat to Nazi Germany, he returned briefly home, only to be summoned by the Vichy regime in what is known as The Green Ticket roundup. On May 14, 1941, thousands of Czech and Polish Jews in and around Paris obeyed orders by the Nazi authorities and reported to police stations for "verification" of their status. They were all arrested upon arrival, as was Isaja. Henri and his mother escaped arrest and were able to stay in their Paris apartment. Isaja was deported to Auschwitz death camp in convoy no. 6. There he was murdered by the Nazis on September 4, 1942, 47 days after arrival in the camp. Henri's mother Chana, also known as Annette Blumenfeld, was able to keep Henri and herself safe and hidden separately throughout the war. While Henri was in hiding in the small community of Limay, living with the Morin family, a small German airplane attacked, shooting and missing Henri. Fearing for the Morin family as the Nazis tightened their grip, Henri and his mother escaped to Normandy, where he witnessed the arrival of the Allies after their landing on D-Day, June 6, 1944. The mother and son returned to their Montmartre apartment after the war, in 1946. But a tragedy occurred soon after, a homicide that made the front pages of French newspapers. A pharmacist on Rue Ramey poisoned six people with rat poison. Annette was one of the victims. Henri, then 13, was placed in an orphanage, where he would spend his teenage years. The orphanage got him a job processing photographs and also his first camera, a twin-lens Rolleiflex. Henri learned photography at an independent studio in 1949 and became an assistant to a fashion photographer. Before his departure for New York, he created his first portraits of celebrities in the fields of entertainment, cinema and music. At the end of 1950, Henri crossed the Atlantic onboard the liner *Liberté*, joining his uncle Sam who lived in the Bronx, New York. Throughout his career, Henri photographed for magazines such as *Life*, *Newsweek* and *Paris Match*, the Italian *Epoca* or *L'Express*. He also originated photographers' copyrights in the United States for the American Society of Media Photographers (ASMP). His photograph of Jacqueline Kennedy at the funeral of the assassinated President John F. Kennedy is an iconic photograph which has been widely re-published. This photograph was also used many times by Andy Warhol in his paintings. Henri became a father of two with his first wife, Denis, who passed away in 1985. He also helped raise a stepson with his second wife. It was at the age of 81 that Henri Dauman had his first major retrospective at the Palais d'Iéna in Paris in 2014. An American documentary film, *Henri Dauman: Looking Up* was released in 2018. A process was initiated in 2018 for the Morin family to be recognized as "Righteous Among the Nations." The honor was awarded them posthumously in February 2022. Henri Dauman passed away in New York City on September 13, 2023.

Henri Dauman by Roland Smith USA
NEW YORK CITY, NEW YORK, USA, 2018

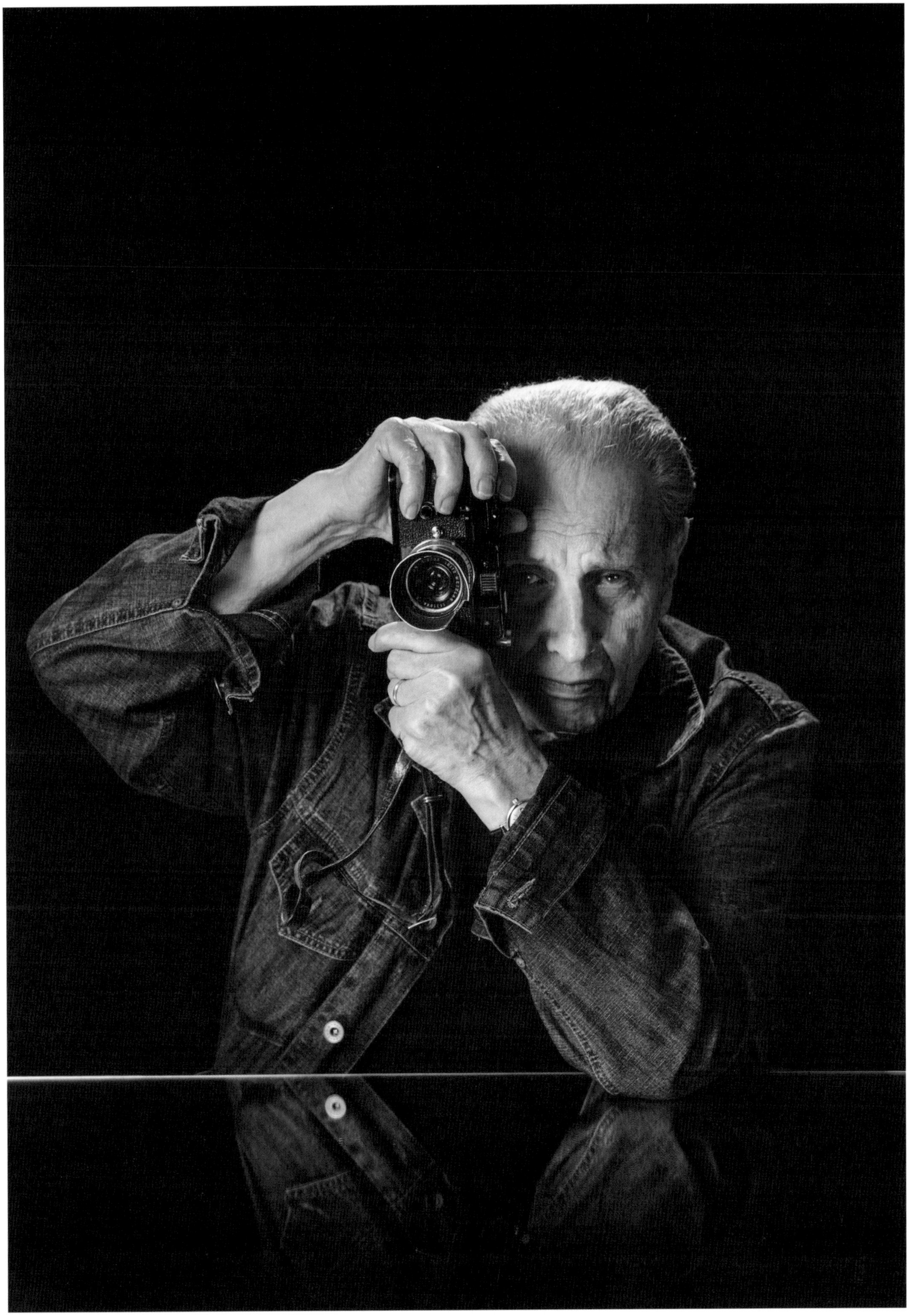

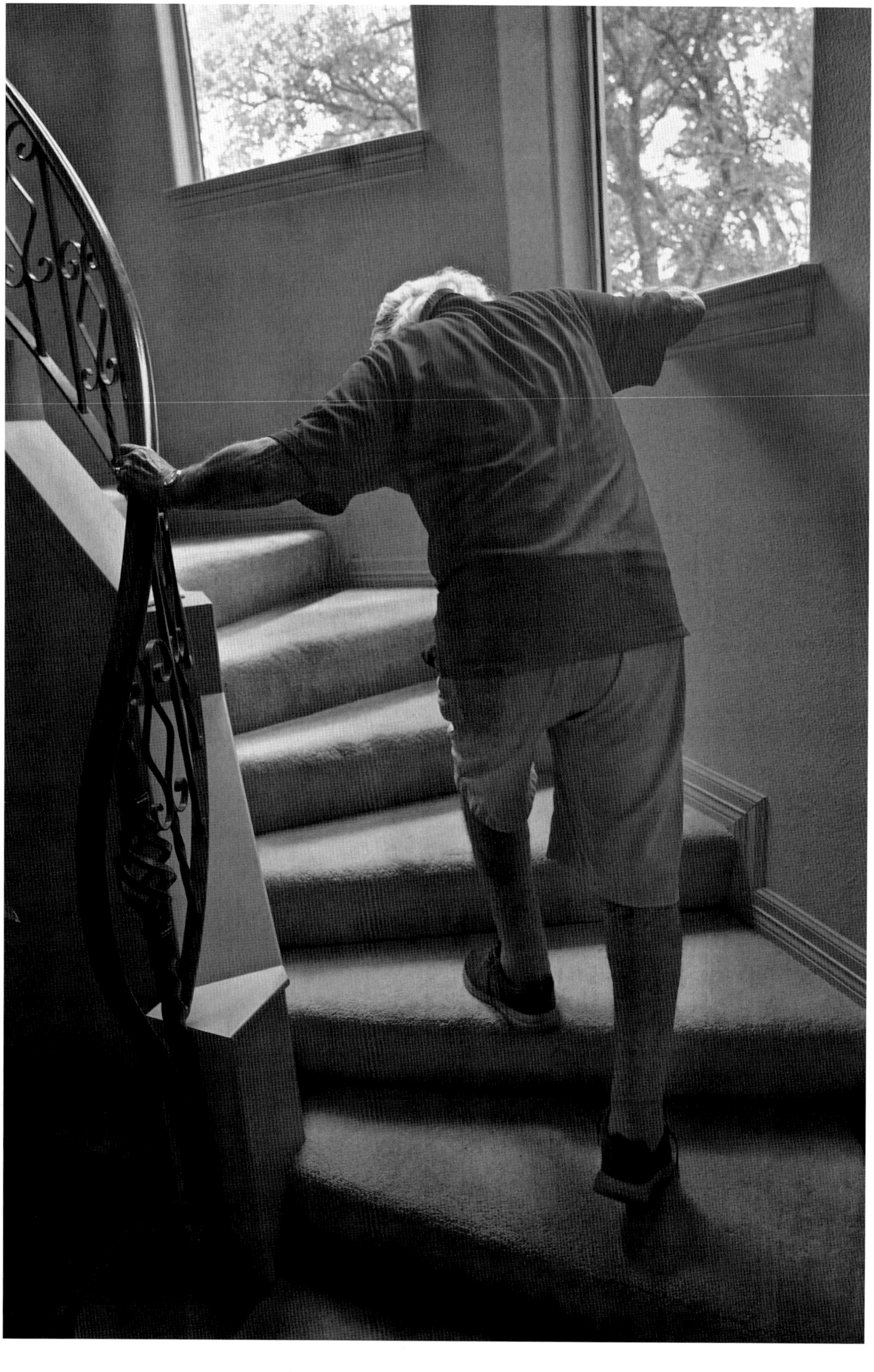

WILLIAM SAMELSON was born in Poland and lived there until the age of 10, when he was forced into various Nazi labor and concentration camps throughout Poland and Germany. He was a member of the Polish partisans at the age of 13. Captured by the Nazis, he was taken to the Buchenwald concentration camp where he spent three and a half years. William was known as 611441 in Buchenwald. 'Usually, when your number was called, you never returned,' William said. His mother was healthy, still in her 30s, but his little sister, only six, clung to the skirt of her mother. 'She opted to stay with the little one,' William recalled. 'The last time I saw her, she was climbing into a freight train.' He was liberated by the US Army in April 1945, and then spent six months recuperating in a hospital in Borna, Germany. William immigrated to the United States in 1948, following studies in Germany after the war. He was working on his M.A. degree in Germanic and Comparative Literature in 1951 when he was drafted into the US Army during the Korean War. William is an author and professor emeritus in the foreign languages department at the University of Texas in Austin.

Dr. William Samelson BY Eli Reed USA
AUSTIN, TEXAS, USA, 2019

Yehuda Havas was born in Hungary in 1925. When Nazi Germany invaded Hungary, there were already detailed plans for the rapid extermination of Hungarian Jewry, which then numbered close to half a million people. In April 1944, the Debrecen Ghetto was established. Yehuda, his brother and their parents were forced to relocate to the ghetto and were allowed to stock up on food for two weeks. The teens were immediately taken to forced labor. In June 1944, the ghetto residents were moved to a transport center on the city's outskirts. There was no food, tap water was scarce, and most were forced to sleep outdoors. Soon thereafter, 13,000 Jews from Debrecen and the surrounding area were sent to Auschwitz. Yehuda's parents were sent to their deaths in the gas chambers. Yehuda and his brother were held in Auschwitz for one year, then sent to Bavaria to work in a factory, where Jewish prisoners were required to build large bunkers for the production of fighter jets. Over 30,000 prisoners worked under inhumane and murderous conditions of imprisonment and labor. A third of them died. Yehuda and his brother were liberated by American soldiers. After the war, Yehuda volunteered to care for Polish Jewish orphans. This granted him a certificate to immigrate with orphan children to Mandatory Palestine in 1947. Upon his arrival, Judah was immediately drafted and fought in Israel's War of Independence.

Yehuda Havas BY Oren Ben-Hakoon ISRAEL

JERUSALEM, 2019

Natalia Wolberg was born in 1926 in Leningrad, the city that Hitler decided to starve to death. The Siege of Leningrad resulted from the German army's failure to capture the city. It lasted 900 days. Jews who remained in areas which had been occupied by the Nazis, were tortured and killed. Natalia remembers people looking like skeletons roaming the streets, as well as the constant air attacks which killed her closest friend and her family. Rosa, Natalia's mother, was working in fortifications in the bombarded and starving city and, fearing for her daughter's life, had instructed Natalia to always stay indoors. The starvation led to cannibalism and the murder of children, which was the final stage of the Nazi blockade. A total of 850,000 of the city's residents died. Natalia survived, and years later, in 1973, immigrated with her son Pavel to Israel. Natalia Wolberg passed away several weeks after her portrait was made by her son.

Natalia Wolberg BY Pavel Wolberg ISRAEL
TEL AVIV, ISRAEL, 2019

Hanoch Shacher BY Atef Safadi ISRAEL
SAFED, ISRAEL, 2019

Hanoch Shacher was born in Czechoslovakia in 1935. After Nazi Germany invaded Prague, Hanoch was taken to a monastery where he grew up in hiding as a Christian child for two years. Nazis were constantly raiding the monastery in search of Jews and his mother had to take him back. The family was deported to Theresienstadt concentration camp, which Nazis used in their propaganda to the world as a model camp for "normal life." Hanoch was able to keep a violin given to him by his neighbors whose child perished. Hanoch's parents and sister, with the majority of the Jews in the camp, were sent to extermination. Hanoch says that what saved him was his love of sports. 'What gave me the strength to live was the sport; in the camp, I organized competitions for the children. I would improvise jumps from the floor down and jumps from bed to bed.' On another transport of children to death, Hanoch hid with another child and his life was saved. 'A woman told me, "when you see people with high boots, you must hide, otherwise you will die." That's how I was saved.' After liberation, Hanoch was taken to an orphanage in Prague. Sport became his passion. Hanoch Shacher moved to Israel in 1949, and became an award-winning marathon runner. He lives in Safed in northern Israel and next to the dozens of trophies and medals, there is his most precious one, the violin of the child who died at the hands of the Nazis.

GISELA BEN YAACOV was born in Cottbus to a Jewish mother and a Christian father. When the Nazi Party came to rule Germany, she was forced to move to Berlin without her family. She strongly remembers wearing the yellow star, as well as the Allied forces' bombing of Berlin, where she had no shelter as a Jewish youngster. She remembers working in a factory without food or rest. But the hardest part was when the war ended and her family tried to escape Germany as the Russian Red Army and the American forces were dividing the territory of Germany. She lived in many refugee camps, both in Germany and in Holland, before, only a year after the war ended, she made her way alone to the shores of Haifa.

Gisela Ben Yaacov BY Ilia Yefimovich ISRAEL

JERUSALEM, 2019

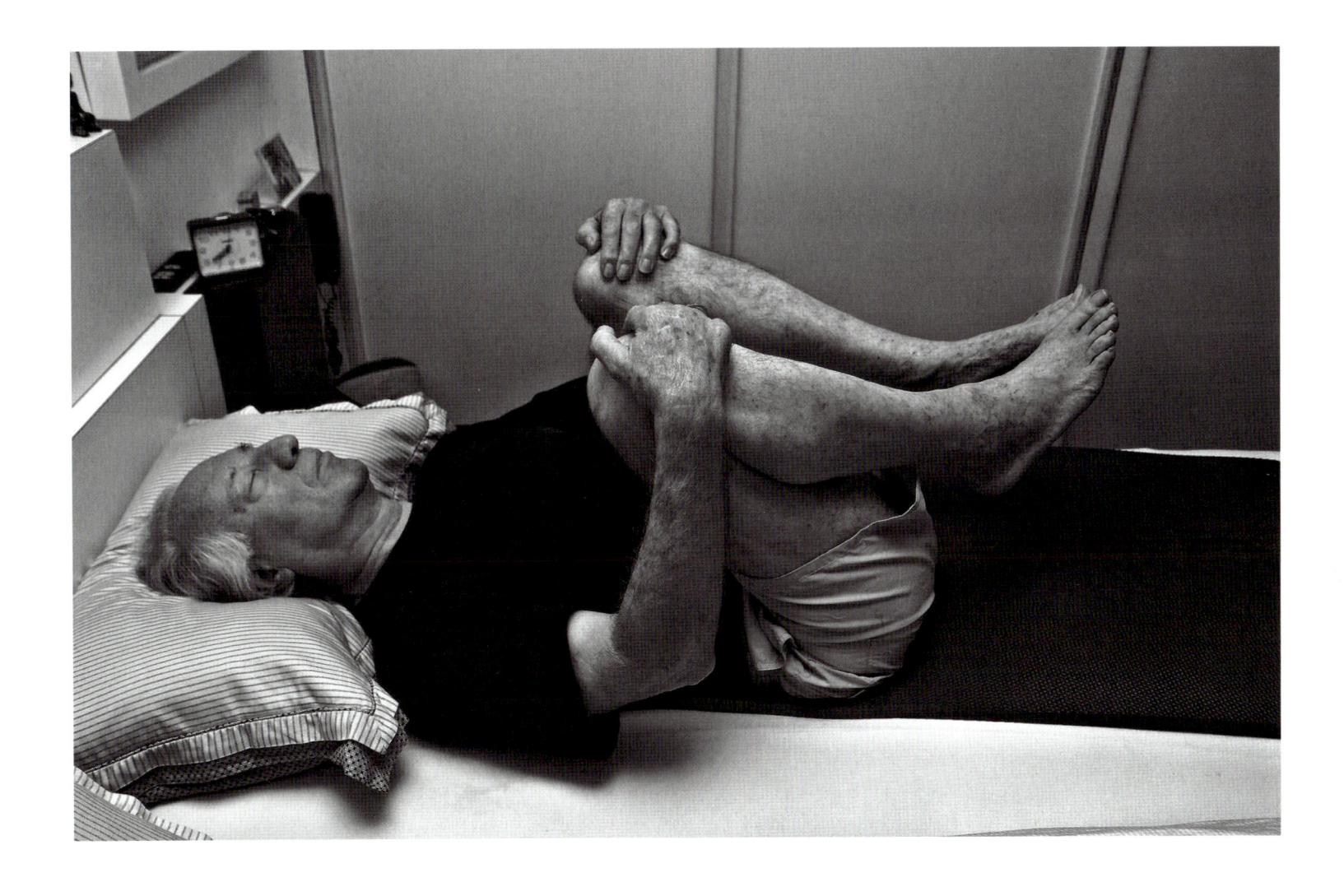

SIMON LODEWIJK WIJNBERGEN was born in Amsterdam, in 1940. Simon was three when he was captured by the Nazis with his family in 1943 and brought to the Ravensbrück death camp. At first, children arrived with mothers who were Romani or Jews incarcerated in the camp or were born to imprisoned women. Most of the children died of starvation. In 1943, almost all Jewish women from the Ravensbrück camp were sent to Auschwitz in several transports. In January 1945, prior to the liberation of the remaining camp survivors, an estimated 45,000 female prisoners and over 5,000 male prisoners remained at Ravensbrück, including children and those transported from satellite camps only for gassing, which was being performed in haste. Simon was smuggled by the Dutch underground and placed in a foster family under a false identity. Many of the hidden children were traumatized for life, including those whose parents never returned. Some children, whose parents managed to survive, were torn between remaining with their foster families or going back to their birth parents whom they scarcely remembered. Simon became a successful architect and lives in Tel Aviv, Israel.

Simon Lodewijk Wijnbergen BY Uzi Keren ISRAEL
TEL AVIV, ISRAEL, 2019

Rabbi of the Kaliv Hasidic dynasty and Holocaust survivor **Menachem Mendel Taub** (C) attends a prayer service in the Kaliv synagogue, Jerusalem, March 13, 2019. Rabbi Taub was born in 1923 in Marghita, Transylvania (today Romania), as the seventh in a direct paternal line of the Kaliv dynasty. He was a survivor of the Auschwitz extermination camp and of Bergen-Belsen camp. In Auschwitz he was experimented on by Dr. Joseph Mengele and was unable to grow facial hair, had an unusually high-pitched voice and was made sterile, unable to have children, following chemical burning experiments. After the war ended, he reunited with his wife in Sweden and immigrated to the US in 1947. In 1962 he immigrated to Israel and founded the Kaliv Yeshiva in Rishon LeZion. In 2004 he moved to Jerusalem. Rabbi Menachem Mendel Taub died on April 28, 2019, age 96, six weeks after the photograph was made.

Rabbi Menachem Mendel Taub by Abir Sultan ISRAEL
JERUSALEM, 2019

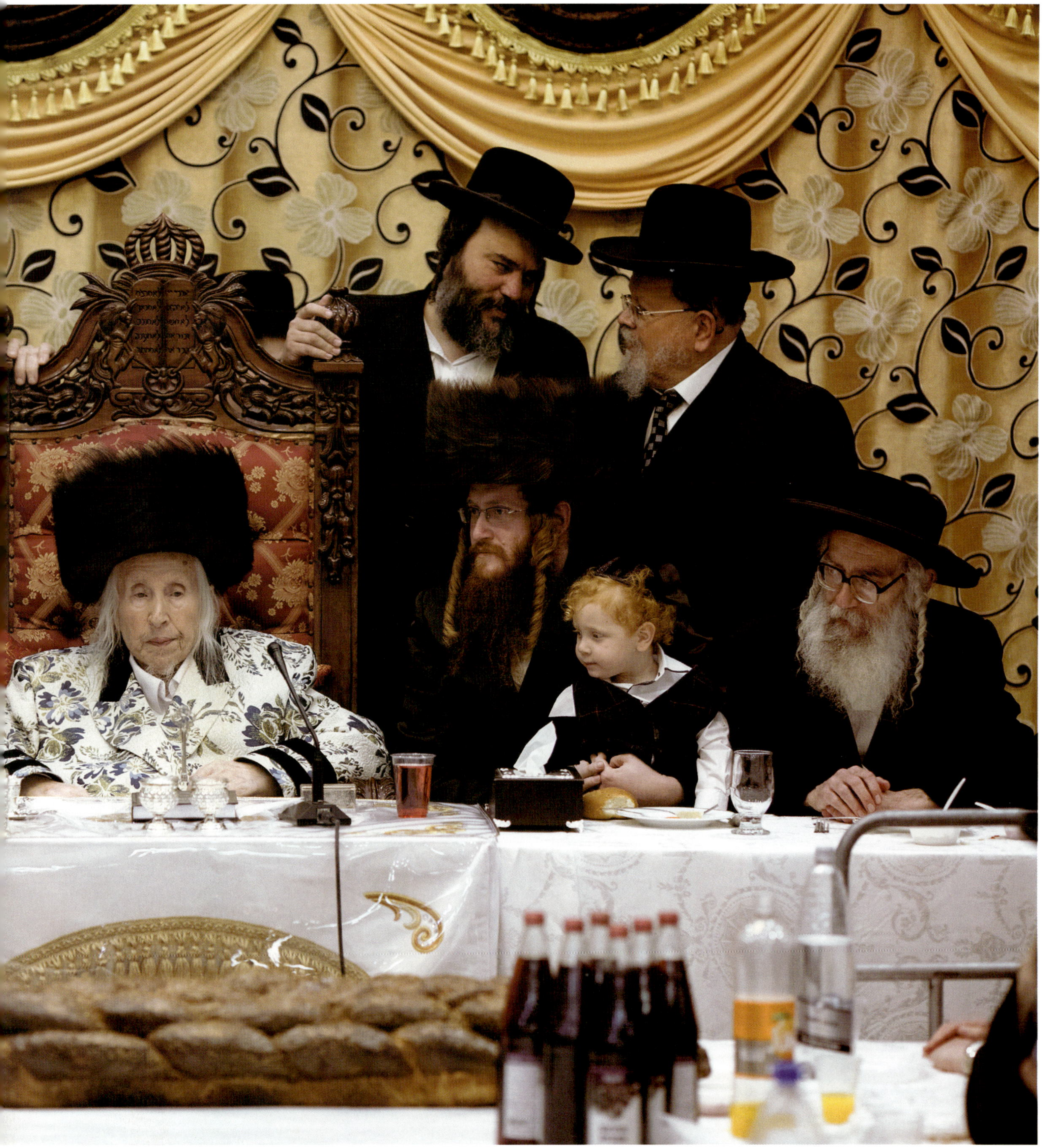

LUBA GRUNGRASS, age 95, a Holocaust survivor from Poland, dances in her Purim costume with other Holocaust survivors and a number of Israeli soldiers during a Purim party organized by the Israeli humanitarian aid organization Adopt-A-Safta (Hebrew for grandmother), in Tel Aviv, Israel, March 24, 2019. Grungrass spent four years in Nazi concentration camps including Auschwitz and Bergen-Belsen. She says the Nazis did not put her to death as she had lovely hair as a teenager.

Luba Grungrass BY Jim Hollander USA
TEL AVIV, ISRAEL, 2019

JACK WELNER, 98, a Holocaust survivor. Welner was interned in the Lodz Ghetto in Poland, where he faced hard labor and starvation before being transferred to Auschwitz and later to Dachau. In 1950, he came to Denver, Colorado, where he lived until the end of his life. He has a large family of grandchildren and great-grandchildren. His optimism helped him not only to survive but to thrive. He said, 'Never let hate take root in your heart.' Jack Welner passed away in August 2019.

Jack Welner BY Blaine Harrington III USA
DENVER, COLORADO, USA, 2019

Hilda Tayar (née Kraiser) was born in Köln, Germany, on March 14, 1924. Her parents were Polish, and the family left for Antwerp, where they had relatives in the diamond business. When Nazi Germany invaded Belgium, the family escaped by train. A ten-day journey brought them to Toulouse, France. There they were rounded up by Vichy government police and deported to the Rivesaltes concentration camp outside of Perpignan. 'Not better and not worse than the camps in Poland,' Hilda said. Her father was sent to a forced labor camp. Hilda offered her assistance to the camp's many children, who were helped by Secours Swiss, affiliated with the Red Cross. Hilda's work with the children saved her from deportation to death camps until 1942, when some 2,251 Jews, including 110 children, were transferred from Rivesaltes via the Drancy internment camp to Auschwitz, where they were murdered. Among them was Hilda's mother, deported to her death. 'Last time I saw my mother was in August 1942 during a big transport.' Hilda's life was saved as she was about to board the transport train to Auschwitz with her younger sister, Hannah. An Austrian nurse for whom Hilda worked, Friedel Bohny-Reiter, a member of the medical staff of the Secours Suisse, saved Hilda and her sister by hiding them in a shack for three days. Later she helped to provide Hilda with a fake ID card, and Hilda lived through the war under the false identity of Helene Rambaux. Friedel Bohny-Reiter saved many of the Jewish and Roma children she had looked after at the Rivesaltes camp, smuggling them out of the camp by hiding them with local families. For her bravery, Friedel was honored by Yad Vashem as a Righteous Among the Nations. After the war, Hilda and her sister Hannah traveled to Grenoble, a town to which many Jewish survivors came looking for the Emergency Committee to Save European Jewry. There Hilda met the son of the legendary Ze'ev Jabotinsky, Ari, who worked assisting survivors. Ari asked Hilda, "Why do you stay here? Come to Israel." Soon after, Hilda and her sister boarded a boat on their way to Mandatory Palestine. 'My sister was always with me.' After days at sea, 'The British stopped us, and we were redirected to detention in Cyprus for a year and a half.' In the camp in Cyprus, Hilda met Raoul Tayar, and they married in 1947. In 1948, two weeks before the declaration of the State of Israel, Hilda, her husband and her sister arrived at the port of Haifa. Hilda's husband Raoul later served as a member of the Israeli Knesset from 1964 to 1972. They created a family and a home, and Raoul became a lawyer. Hilda, who was widowed in 2011, says today, 'We are really the last people alive that can tell really what happened. People do not believe, I think. It is very important. Whenever I can, I tell my story, so people know that it really happened. The people here [in her old age home in Jerusalem] don't talk! They don't talk because it's painful. I know, but you have to tell!'

Hilda Tayar BY Michal Fattal ISRAEL
JERUSALEM, 2019

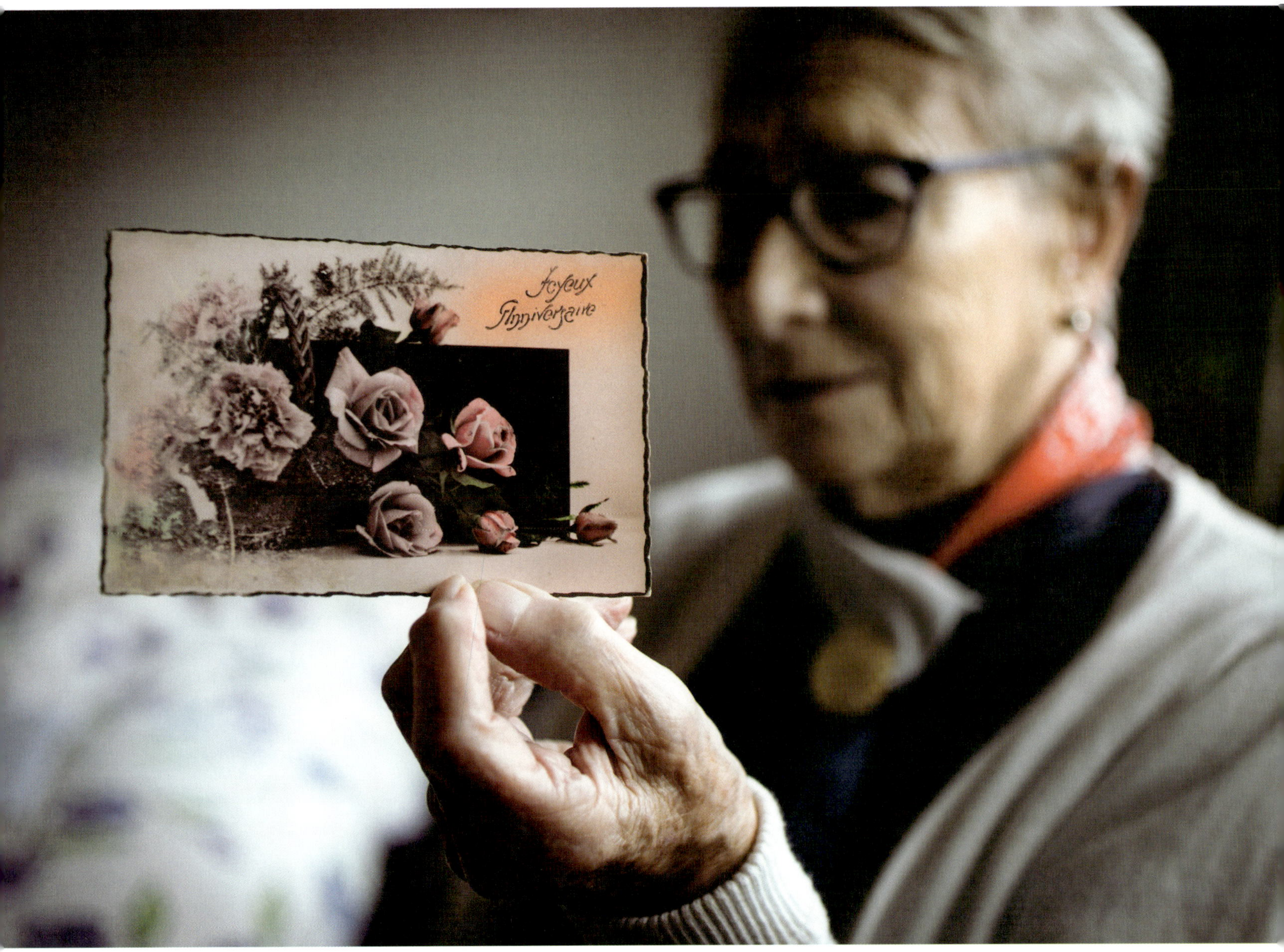
Joyeux
Anniversaire

Francisco & Hinda Wichter BY Magali Druscovich ARGENTINA
BUENOS AIRES, 2019

FRANCISCO WICHTER was born on July 25, 1926, in Markuszew, Poland. He was the eldest of six siblings. His father was killed at the beginning of the war in Poland in 1943. He saw his mother and sister for the last time at the beginning of Simhat Torah. All the family was in Belzitz, a town in Poland where the Nazis ordered everyone into the main park. Francisco's family decided to hide ten young people who could survive. He was one of them, and the only one who survived of the ten. After that, he was a prisoner in four concentration camps. The last camp was in Budzin, Germany. From there, Oskar Schindler took many people to work in his factory. This was the beginning of Schindler's List. May 8, 1945, Schindler turned on the radio and heard Churchill's voice speaking in English, followed by a translation in German. Everybody was in silence. The Second World War was over. Schindler said: "You are free." 'Free of what?' Francisco said. He went back to his town and everything was destroyed. He was living in the streets looking for someone from his family. No one survived. The attitude in Poland forced him to find a way elsewhere in Europe. He arrived in Rome where he found a cousin and friends. In one of those meetings outside the refugee camp, they went to the movies and he met HINDA. Since then, they never again separated. They got married on April 20, 1947, in Rome. Through the Joint, he contacted an aunt who was living in Argentina. She escaped after World War I. Francisco remembered her address because she was mentioned in a letter at his home. After she said she was going to receive them, they arrived illegally in Argentina in July 1947. They went through Paraguay, Brazil, and Uruguay in order to arrive in Buenos Aires, where his aunt was waiting for them. They have been together for 75 years, have two children, four grandchildren and six great-grandchildren.

Genia Basov (center with walker) was born in 1936 in Ukraine. In 1942, Nazi German troops rounded up all the residents of her small village, most of whom were Jews, and forced them to march to a nearby forest, where they were fenced off in what became known as Camp Kupai. Jews caught attempting to leave the camp were killed. Genia lived in the camp with her mother, two brothers, her sister and a baby. Genia's mother hid the baby, because babies and infants were forbidden in the camp and would have been killed. The family found a large tree with a hole in its trunk, where they would hide the baby. For two years they lived in famine, with little water, and facing freezing cold. 'We ate what we could find in the forest.' Every morning corpses were collected and transferred to one large pit. One day the baby, hidden in the tree, was bitten by ants and the cries were heard by the guards. Nazi soldiers arrived immediately and pulled the baby out of the hole. 'Luckily, she looked terrible with bites covering her body and one of the soldiers said: she will die anyway, no need to waste a bullet, and threw her on the ground.' The baby survived. In 1942, Romanians, having allied with Nazi Germany, recaptured the territories occupied by the Soviets in 1940. They "liberated" the forest camp and transferred those who survived to the Kopeigurod Ghetto, to be put to hard labor. Still, conditions in the ghetto were an improvement for Genia and her family, who survived until they were liberated by the Red Army. In 1997, all 150 survivors of Camp Kupai decided to immigrate to Israel together, and today most of them live in Be'er Sheva. They have erected a small monument in memory of the victims, and they meet there once a year on the anniversary of the day of their liberation.

Genia Basov BY **Sasson Tiram** ISRAEL
JERUSALEM, 2019

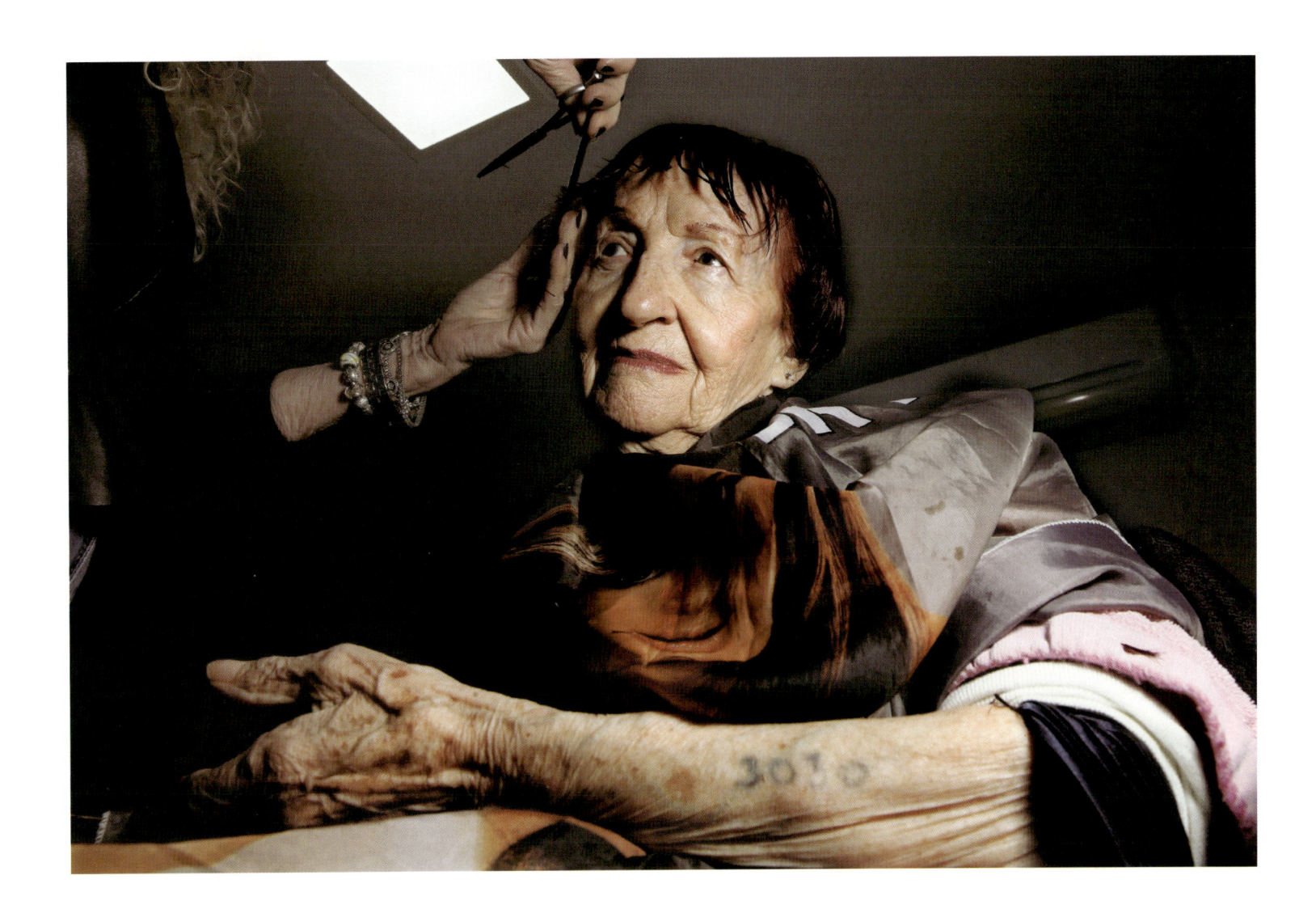

LILI LEA SOLZBEK was born in Czechoslovakia in 1927. In 1942, when she was 15 years old, she was expelled to the Auschwitz death camp. The imprisoned women were forced to have their hair shaved, Lili, with her long red hair, among them. For three years in Auschwitz she endured atrocities she was never able to share with anyone. Lili said she promised herself that, should she survive, she would be a redhead until her death. Lili passed away in 2019, a few months after she was photographed.

Lili Lea Solzbek BY Miri Tzachi ISRAEL
JERUSALEM, 2019

RACHEL GOTTLIEB was born in 1924. She was 20 years old when Hungarian police invaded her home in Rozavlea, Romania. She recalls having handed her father his prayer shawl and phylacteries, then Rachel, her parents and six brothers were shipped to Auschwitz. After the first Selektion (literally, selection; term used by the Nazis to denote the sorting of deportees or prisoners into two groups – those who were selected to do forced labor and for other purposes, and those who were to be killed), Rachel walked towards the crematorium with her mother. None of them knew they were sentenced to death. But there was a line of girls in their 20s, and her mother said "run after the girls." Rachel ran to join the line of the girls. No one stopped her. From afar, Rachel saw her mother walking into the crematorium. Her mother never came out. In October 1944, Rachel was sent to Bergen-Belsen, Lippstadt, and later to Leipzig, where she was forced on a death march. The Nazi guards shot those who collapsed on the march. After the war ended, she came home to Rozavlea and was reunited with the two of her six brothers who had survived. She also met her future husband, Maier, and in 1962, they settled in Borough Park, Brooklyn. Rachel passed away in early 2020, and a final note says the photographer, Rachel, who bore number 7564 from Auschwitz, had a motto and would always say, 'Who came back from the Holocaust can give you a blessing. Be well and live long.'

Rachel Gottlieb BY **Shira Stoll** ARGENTINA
STATEN ISLAND, NEW YORK, USA, 2019

Author **HALINA BIRENBAUM** was born in Warsaw in 1929. In 1943 she survived the Warsaw Ghetto Uprising and liquidation by the Nazis. She was transported to the Majdanek gas chambers with hundreds of women. 'We were obediently and silently undressed, knowing that there was no exit from here. We hung the clothes on the hangers and sat on the benches next to the walls with the greatest of tension, knowing when and how would death come.' A temporary malfunction saved her life. Halina's mother was murdered in Majdanek and her father perished in the Treblinka extermination camp. Halina had lived through Auschwitz, prisoner 48693, a death march and two camps in Germany. In 1945, she was liberated by the Red Army. After the war she returned to Warsaw and was reunited with her brother Marec, the only survivor of her family. In 1947, she arrived to Mandatory Palestine. In Israel she wrote her first book, *Hope Is the Last to Die*. Jacob Gilad, Halina's son, created lyrics inspired by his mother's life story to "Ashes and Dust," a music album composed by Yehuda Poliker.

Halina Birenbaum BY Vardi Kahana ISRAEL
TEL AVIV, ISRAEL, 2019

Veronica Phillips, living in Johannesburg, South Africa, was born in Hungary in 1926. She was arrested by the Arrow Cross militia in Budapest and deported on December 1, 1944, from Budapest to Ravensbrück. While there she was "by luck" selected as a laborer and taken to work in Penig (a sub-camp of Buchenwald), where she suffered inhumane conditions. She was taken on a death march. At Johanngeorgenstadt, the group was liberated by the Allies, but only after many had been killed, by either the Nazis, starvation or fatigue. She returned to Budapest in an emaciated physical condition to find her mother and brother. Veronica became a microbiologist and geneticist at Brunel University, eventually moving to South Africa, where she was a microbiology lecturer at the University of the Witwatersrand for 20 years. As a result of what she endured as a teenager under the Nazis, Veronica suffered eight miscarriages and could never have children. The only child she gave birth to survived less than two days. Veronica passed away in Johannesburg on February 24, 2021.

Veronica Phillips BY **Kim Ludbrook** SOUTH AFRICA
JOHANNESBURG, SOUTH AFRICA, 2019

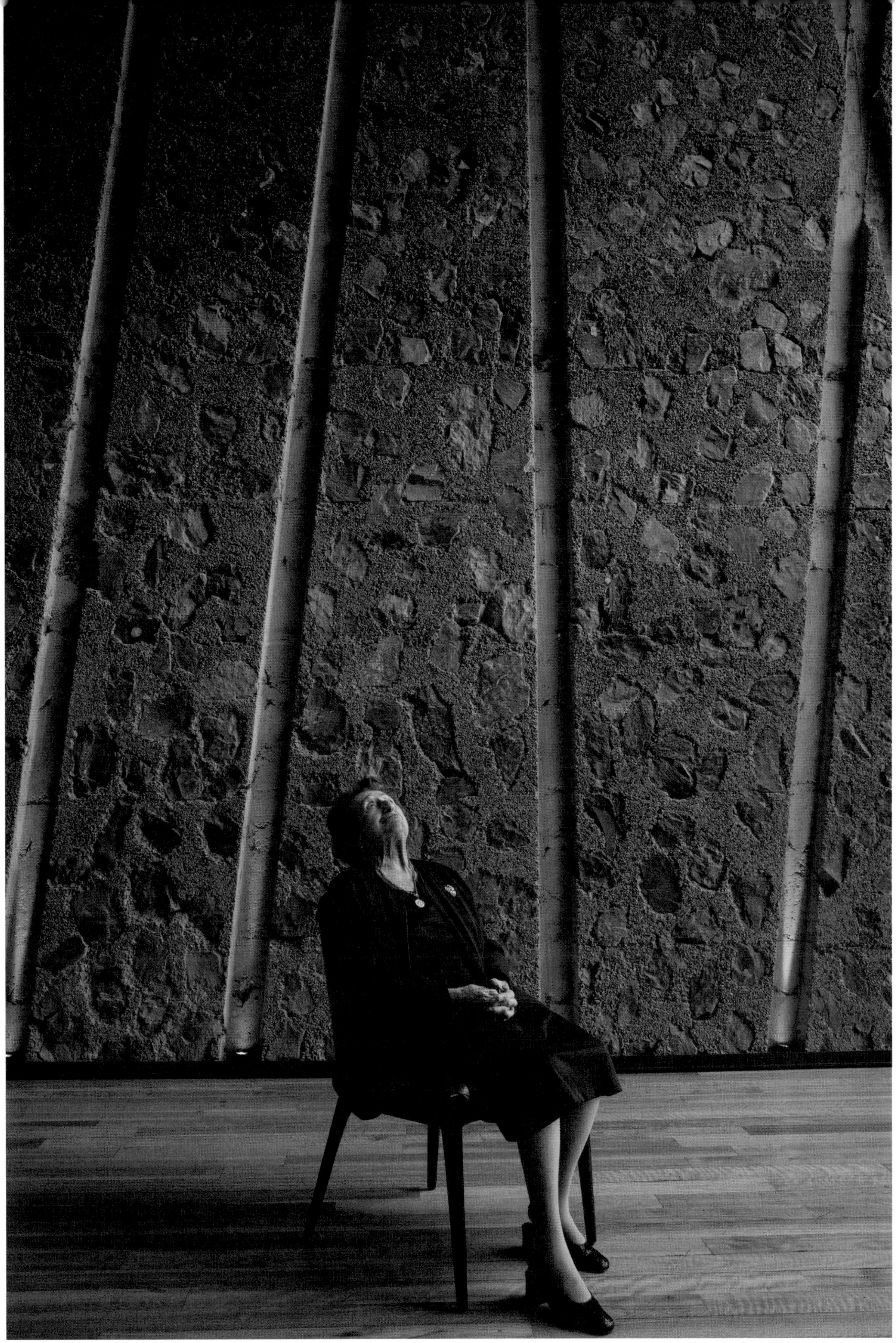

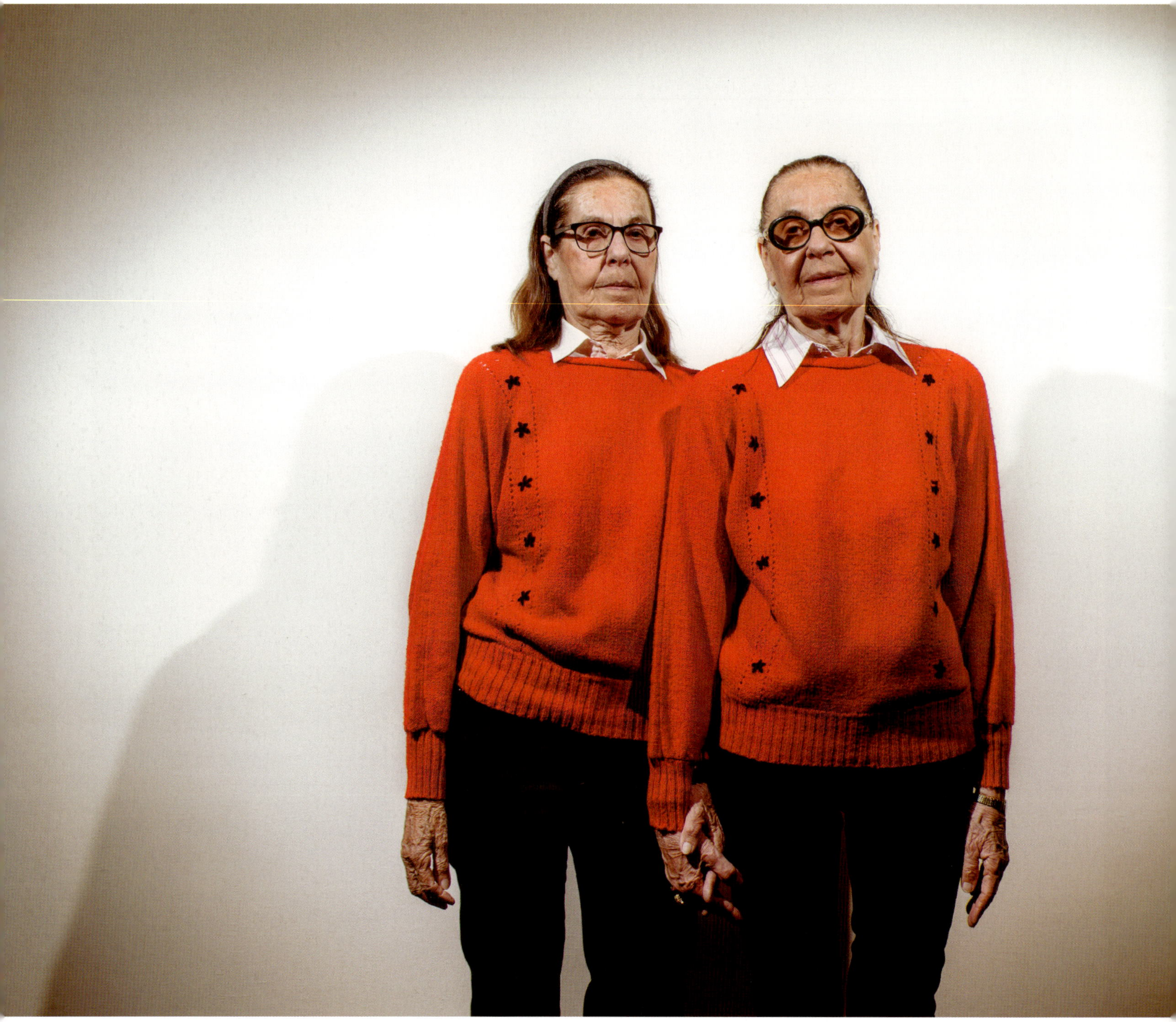

Lia Hoover and her twin sister, Judith Barnea, were born in 1937 in Silesia, Transylvania (Hungary). In 1942 their father Zvi was taken to a forced labor unit on the Russian front. In 1944, when the two were six years old, the family was deported to Auschwitz. The girls, identical twins, were selected for Josef Mengele's medical experiments. Mengele used to draw blood from Judith and Lia's bodies and, on one occasion, while he was conducting medical experiments on the girls, their mother burst into the shack and begged him to stop. In response, she was injected with a shot that made her permanently deaf. The three survived many Selektions until the camp's liberation. Their mother, Miriam-Rachel, would continue to sneak into the barracks where they were kept, and give them her slice of bread. The girls survived with their mother, and after the war they were reunited with their father.

Lia Hoover & Judith Barnea by Ohad Zwigenberg ISRAEL
RA'ANANA, ISRAEL, 2019

MOTKE BLUM was born in Racacun, Romania, in 1925. At the age of five he moved to Bucharest. In 1938, he was taken by the Romanian Iron Guard during the pogroms before the Germans invaded Romania. He is a survivor of the labor camps where his talent for painting often saved his life. Several years ago Motke Blum's grandchildren asked him to tell them about his experiences during the Holocaust. For the first time, the artist exposed his story in depth, but not in words. The result was a series of hundreds of paintings, mostly in black and black-and-white, depicting the symbols of evil, fear and horror experienced by groups of haunted people, who lost their identity and personality overnight, as Motke is trying to speak their voice. In 1944 he escaped from a labor camp, received a certificate and boarded an immigrant boat for Mandatory Palestine. He experienced the trauma of the sinking of the *Mefkure*, and arrived at Kibbutz Avuka. These harsh experiences are expressed in his paintings of boat skeletons and shipwrecks, barbed wire and faces filled with sorrow, which lead the observer through the stories. Throughout the years the artist swayed between light and darkness: from his innocent experiences as a child to a frustrating, harsh adolescence; between tragedies and hopes. After graduating from Bezalel Academy in Jerusalem, he was commissioned to restore mosaics and frescoes all over Israel. In 1969, he set up his permanent studio in Hutzot Hayotzer (the Artists' Quarter) outside the Jaffa Gate near the Old City of Jerusalem, where he works and sells his paintings, sculptures and mosaics to this day.

Motke Blum BY Hadas Parush ISRAEL
JERUSALEM, 2019

IRENA WODISLAVSKY was born in Zakopane, Poland, in 1936, an only child of a street photographer and a guesthouse maid living in the Polish ski resort. When she was about five, in the midst of the war, Irena's parents left Zakopane to their family home in Przemysl. 'We reached Przemysl where the Jews were already confined to a ghetto. We lived together with my grandmother, uncles and their children.' Her parents used to risk their lives and sneak into the Russian side of the city to buy food, until the day her mother did not return. 'I looked at the street for days, waiting for her. She was captured by the German Nazis and was killed.' Her father asked his close friend Veronica, a Christian Pole, to look after his child before he was taken by the Russians and sent to work in a coal mine. Veronica did not hesitate and went to save the child from the ghetto about to be liquidated. 'Veronica told me that she loved my father,' Irena recalls. 'I did not object leaving with her. She told me not to talk and not to cough, until we reached the other side.' Irena's fair skin and blonde hair made her look Polish, and Veronica took a job in a farm where nobody knew them. Veronica and Irena were feeding the farm livestock when one day Veronica asked Irena to bring food for a boy in the attic. 'I was so happy that there was another child on the farm. I ran upstairs, Abramek was hungry and I brought him food and played with him. One day Abramek was gone.' Only after the war Irena learned that Abramek was caught and killed. Veronica and Irena were denounced to the Gestapo, and the farm owner saved them both. 'I was growing up as a Christian, going to church and praying. I did not know what it means to be Jewish.' Veronica kept moving from farm to farm with Irena and saved her life time and time again. After the war, Irena met her father, who had survived forced labor, and the two stayed in Poland. Irena became a chemist and in 1958 immigrated to Israel where she met Kuba, a survivor of the Warsaw Ghetto. Kuba, her late husband, was a collector of WWII objects and they decided to establish a Holocaust memorial in the city of Ariel, north of Jerusalem, to raise awareness among the youth in the city. Irena is the director of the Holocaust Memorial of Ariel established in her home.

Irena Wodislavsky BY Miri Tzachi ISRAEL
ARIEL, 2019

Moshe Haelyon was born in Thessaloniki, Greece, in 1925. In 1943, Moshe and his family were transported in packed freight wagons to Auschwitz. 'In Auschwitz I met a friend who came from Birkenau. I told him, "Have you seen my mother? My sister Nina?" He told me that in Birkenau there were gas chambers and crematoriums, and from day one they killed everyone. I didn't want to believe it.' Moshe's mother and sister and his entire extended family were gassed upon arrival. Moshe was sent to forced labor, on a death march and to Mauthausen and its sub-camps, where the hunger was so atrocious that he ate carbon to survive. He was liberated by US troops May 6, 1945. In 1946, Moshe arrived to Mandatory Palestine and was imprisoned by the British in Atlit for one year. He later joined the IDF and fought in Israel's wars, retiring with the rank of colonel in 1976. He held an M.A. in humanities from Tel Aviv University and served on Yad Vashem's board. Moshe Haelyon passed away on November 1, 2022.

Moshe Haelyon by Avigail Uzi ISRAEL
TEL AVIV, ISRAEL, 2019

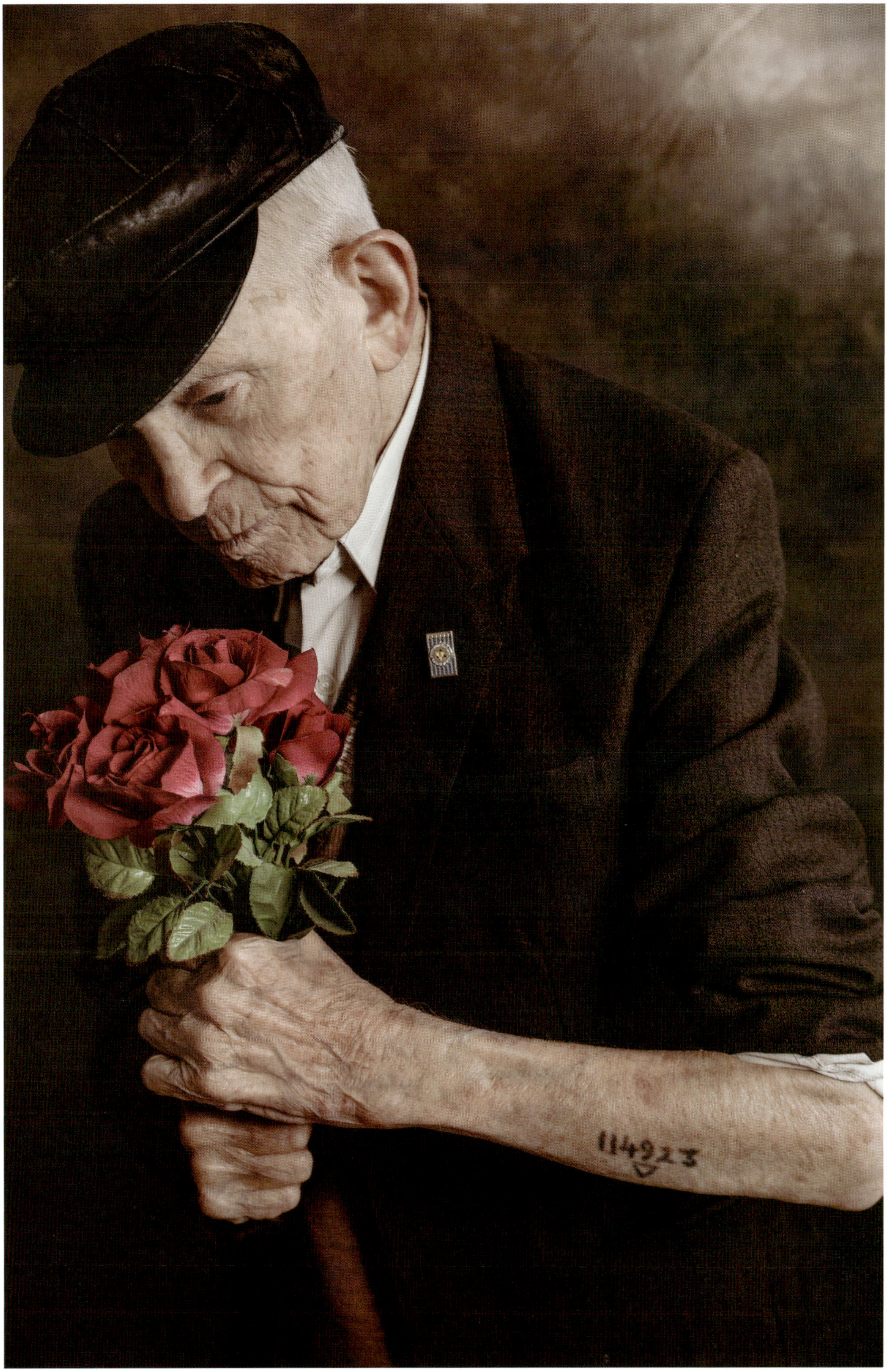
114923

Judith Rosenberg BY **Judith Passow** UK/ISRAEL

GLASGOW, SCOTLAND, UNITED KINGDOM, 2019

JUDITH ROSENBERG, at the age of 96, was the last living Nazi concentration camp survivor in Scotland, with a giant photographic cut-out of her late husband Harold, which she kept in her Glasgow apartment. Because of anti-Jewish quotas in Hungary, the land of her birth, Judith was not allowed to attend university, despite having excelled at high school. As a result, Judith became a watch repairer, a decision which would save her life, before being transported to Auschwitz at the age of 21 with the rest of her family in 1944. She was separated from her father on arrival at the Nazi concentration camp and never saw him again. Experiencing unimaginable disease, deprivation and hunger, Judith, her sister and mother were ordered to work in a munitions factory in Lippstadt in Germany, where she produced grenades. After she survived the death march from Auschwitz, Judith married the British Army Glaswegian lieutenant who had found her, and returned with him to Scotland. Judith passed away on January 22, 2021.

Gabriel Moked, Israel's famed professor of philosophy and one of the most important figures in Israel's literary world, was born in Warsaw on August 27, 1933. His father, a doctor whose friends included Janusz Korczak, managed to smuggle his wife and only son out of the ghetto but chose to remain behind and attend to patients. He died with them during the Warsaw Ghetto Uprising. From an attic where young Gabriel was hiding on the other side of the fenced-off ghetto, he saw the buildings go up in flames and heard the sounds of shooting. He was told to be quiet, to say no words, so he read every book he could find. For many long years it was he and the books, and the sound of war became distant – except, to this day, every knock on the door frightens the child in the attic.

Gabriel Moked BY Eyal Warshavsky ISRAEL
TEL AVIV, ISRAEL, 2019

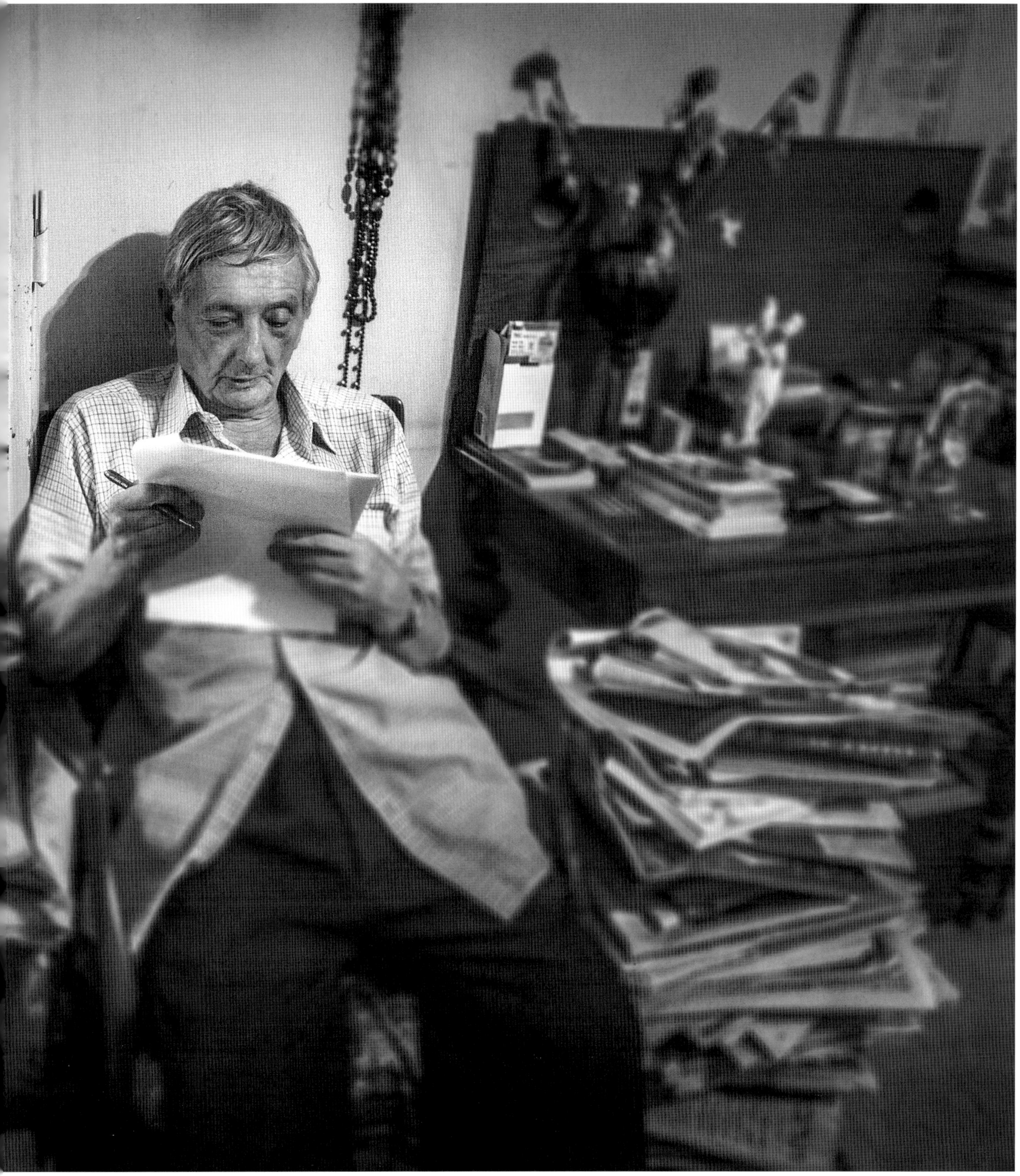

Holocaust survivors **Zoya Moyal** (L), 90, Dena Yarmus (C), and Charlotte Seeman (R), ages 90 to 99, speaking with Rabbi Ron Goldberg as high school students visit Holocaust survivors at the Los Angeles Jewish Home, to hear their stories and discuss antisemitism. Zoya Moyal's story began in Vilna, Poland, resumed in Israel, and endures in Reseda, California. As World War II began, Zoya moved into the Vilna Ghetto with her family at the age of 12. Before that she had spent some two years moving from one concentration camp to another. After the war, as the lone member of her family to survive, she languished even more in a Cyprus internment camp, after British forces intercepted her arrival to Mandatory Palestine on a ship from Europe organized by the Haganah, a pre-state Jewish paramilitary organization. At the Jewish Home for the aging, Zoya was among five of the center's 61 Holocaust survivors who outlined how the armed forces of Nazi Germany murdered their families and upended their young lives. In the wake of a national controversy stirred by a photograph of students with a Nazi swastika at a Costa Mesa, California, party, Zoya declared, 'I don't want this to happen again.'

Zoya Moyal BY **Sarah Reingewirtz** USA
RESEDA, CALIFORNIA, USA, 2019

EDWARD MOSBERG was born on January 6, 1926, in Krakow, Poland. He had two sisters, Halina and Karolina. In 1939, Ed and his family were forced to the Krakow Ghetto where Ed provided much-needed food. In 1943, the ghetto was liquidated and the Mosberg family was moved to the Płaszów camp near Krakow. As an office worker in the camp, Ed was able to provide ID papers and witnessed many atrocities committed by the infamous camp commander Amon Goeth, who would later be tried, convicted and hanged as a war criminal. The following year, Ed's mother and sister were taken to the Nazi death camp of Auschwitz in Poland. Ed was deported a few days later, first to Auschwitz and then to Mauthausen in Austria. After liberation, he briefly returned to Poland, then Belgium and later to the USA, where he became successful in real estate. Holocaust survivor Edward Mosberg participated in the 28th March of the Living at the entrance to the former Nazi concentration death camp Auschwitz I in Oświęcim, Poland, May 2, 2019. A few thousand people, mostly Jewish and Polish youth, will cross the three-kilometer "Death Road" between the former German Nazi death camp Auschwitz I to Auschwitz II Birkenau in Oświęcim, to honor Holocaust victims. Over 1.1 million people, mostly Jews, lost their lives in the Auschwitz death camp during World War II. He often wears a Nazi concentration camp uniform as he educates about the Holocaust. He was awarded Poland's highest medal, the Order of Merit, for what he has done so that the Holocaust will not be forgotten. Ed Mosberg passed way, surrounded by family, in New Jersey, USA, on September 21, 2022, at age 96.

Ed Mosberg BY **Moshe Milner** ISRAEL
OŚWIĘCIM–AUSCHWITZ, POLAND, 2019

Leon and his family were living in the town of Compiègne, occupied France, when the French police came for his parents. Leon was four and his older sister Rachel was 10. The downstairs neighbors told Leon's parents and the police that they would look after the children until the parents were released. They never returned. Leon's mother, Chana, died either on the way to Auschwitz or immediately upon arrival, as she was never tattooed. She was 31. His father Srul died in 1944 at age 38, a few months before the camp was liberated. The downstairs neighbors, Henri and Suzanne Ribouleau, became the childrens' second parents. Leon is holding portraits of the four people he considers his parents. In his left hand a portrait of his parents, last seen being taken away by the French police in 1942, and in his right, his second parents, the Ribouleaus, who took in Leon and his sister on that day, instead of letting the police take them away as well. "Papa Henri and Maman Suzanne" Ribouleau were honored as Righteous Among the Nations by Yad Vashem in 1977.

Leon Malmed BY Robert Gumpert USA
SOUTH LAKE TAHOE, CALIFORNIA, USA, 2019

YOREK MARON was born in Lvov in 1937. Neighbors gave Jews up to the Nazis, and they were thrown into the ghetto in Zlotzov. He remembers seeing people dying from hunger. Mostly he remembers being hungry. They were forced go on a death march three kilometers to a train. Whoever stumbled was shot and killed. He was pushed into a wagon with 300 people. The train went to the Belzec work camp. It stopped to connect more wagons. When the train was moving, one man was able to force open a door, but his coat was caught and he was cut in two, Yorek remembers. Then Yorek's mother pushed him out of the train and she herself jumped, grabbed him, and started to run. His mother was 29. They went into hiding in the woods in the Strassler bunker. They were saved when the Russians arrived in June 1944 and broke down the bunker. He fell in love with the speed of motorcycles. He returned to Warsaw and went to Israel in 1957 to find his father. At 82, Yorek refuses to separate from his motorcycle, and when he took his son to visit Auschwitz, he told him, 'It's good to come here on a motorbike and not a train.'

Yorek Maron BY Yossi Aloni ISRAEL

BAT YAM BEACH, ISRAEL, 2019

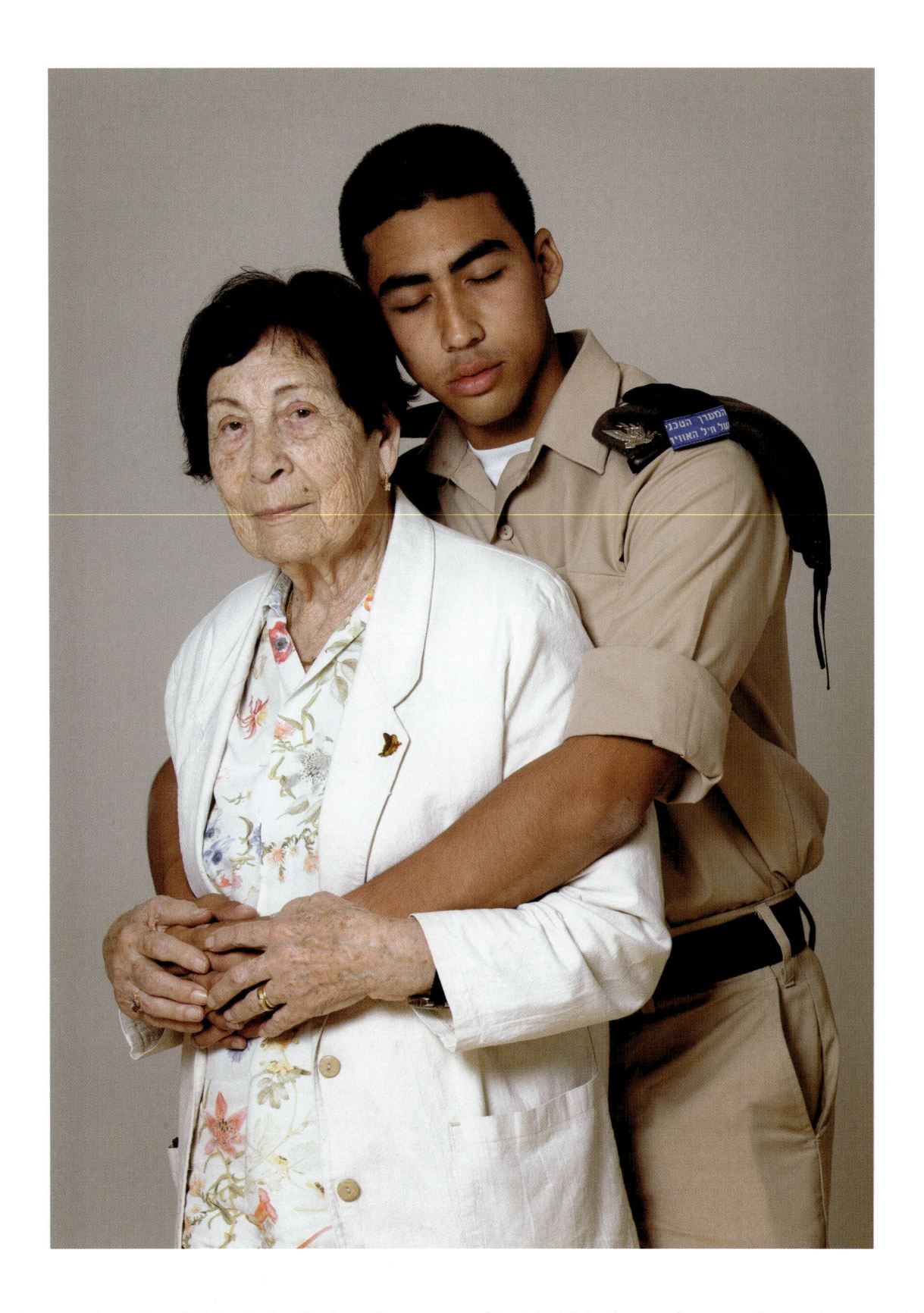

FANNIE BEN-AMI was born in 1930 in Baden-Baden, Germany. When Hitler came to power, the family fled to Paris. When war broke out, her parents were arrested, and Fannie was placed in a Jewish children's home with her sisters. The home was dismantled soon after the German invasion of France. Fannie led the dozens of Jewish children across forests to the border area with Switzerland, and all were smuggled in. After the war, Fanny learned that her parents had been murdered. Fanny was awarded the Legion of Honor for her bravery, but she refused to accept it.

Fannie Ben-Ami BY Alex Kolomoisky ISRAEL

JERUSALEM, 2019

SHAUL LUBOVITZ was born in 1934 in Braslav, today Belarus. In the summer of 1941, a few weeks after Nazi Germany invaded and occupied the area, his father Yitzhak was murdered during forced labor. Shaul, his mother and sister relocated to the ghetto with other relatives in April 1942. The day the ghetto was liquidated, they went into a hiding place under a barn. They were discovered, but some of those in hiding managed to escape. Shaul heard gunfire, and realized that his mother, Bluma, and his sister had been murdered. 'I understood that I was now alone in the world.' Shaul and other escapees roamed around for six months, sleeping in fields and ditches until a local farmer, Szakel, found them and brought them to his farm. Later they joined a group of partisans in the forest. 'We lived in a temporary shelter called a *zemlianka* with other families with children.' When Braslav was liberated in 1945, Shaul and his relatives returned to the city, which was under Soviet control. Antisemitism quickly made the group flee again. They fled to Poland, and then to Germany. They stayed in displaced persons camps, and reached Israel in 1949. Shaul was adopted by his uncles. Szakel was recognized as a Righteous Among the Nations. Shaul married Nechama, who was killed in a suicide bombing on a bus in Ramat Gan, Israel, in 1995. Photographed with his granddaughter Daria at Mount Herzl.

Shaul Lubovitz BY Alex Kolomoisky ISRAEL
JERUSALEM, 2019

IRENE BUTTER was born in Berlin in 1930. 'My family had lived in Germany for generations. My father had fought for Germany during the First World War.' With the growing Nazi threat, her family relocated to Amsterdam in 1937. In 1940, Germany invaded and once again they were under Nazi oppression. 'My grandparents in Germany were taken away to Theresienstadt in 1942, and we never saw them again.' Irene and her family were rounded up on June 20, 1943, and sent to Westerbork transit camp, a stopover for Dutch Jews before being sent to death. 'We managed to stay in Westerbork longer than most, because my father secured for us Ecuadorian passports. The passports didn't allow us freedom, but they did give us a different status until we were forced on a train in 1944 for Bergen-Belsen.' Irene recalls the starvation and slave labor that took its toll on the prisoners. 'My friend Hanneli Goslar from Amsterdam, and her closest friend, Anne Frank, were in Bergen-Belsen in neighboring sections of the camp. We met at the barbed wire fence and later Anne and her sister became gravely ill and so did my family.' Irene's father died in Bergen-Belsen just before Nazi Germany needed prisoners to trade for German prisoners held by the Allies. Irene, her mother, and brother were exchanged and they arrived in Switzerland. 'I was put on a train for Marseilles and then a ship for Algeria. The Swiss did what even the Nazis never did to me: they tore apart my family.' With the war's end, 'In the late fall I boarded an American Liberty ship and sailed for the United States, arriving on Christmas Eve, 1945.' Irene was reunited with her mother and brother six months later. 'I was told not to talk about my experience, so I focused on studying and becoming one of the first women to earn a Ph.D. in economics from Duke University.' Irene participated in a panel about Anne Frank and since the late 1980s, she has been teaching students about the Holocaust. 'My memoir, *Shores Beyond Shores*, details my journey. I'm a co-founder of the Raoul Wallenberg Medal & Lecture series at the University of Michigan, and one of the founders of Zeitouna, an Arab-Jewish women's dialogue group in Ann Arbor. Suffering never ends, so our work must continue.'

Irene Butter BY David Turnley USA/FRANCE
ANN ARBOR, MICHIGAN, USA, 2019

On July 15, 1942, at Saint-Nazaire, **Victor Perahia** and his parents were arrested by the Germans, transferred to Nantes and then to Angers. His father was deported from Angers to Auschwitz on July 20, by convoy no. 8. He would not return. Victor Perahia and his mother were transferred at the beginning of September to the Drancy camp, where they stayed 21 months. 'Mom was exceptionally courageous, she pretended we were a war prisoner's family.' They were deported by a convoy on May 2, 1944, to the Bergen-Belsen death camp. 'Those were three years of dehumanization, cold and hunger.' From there the young boy and his mother were transferred to Theresienstadt, where they were liberated. On June 29, 1945, Victor Perahia returned to Paris. 'When we were released, we had nothing left. It was up to us to rebuild ourselves.' He remembers every detail and every moment of growing up in the death camps, but it took Victor 40 years to be able to share his testimony with others.

Victor Perahia BY Peter Turnley USA/FRANCE
PARIS, 2019

Yossi Weiss, 82, was born in 1937 in Bratislava, Slovakia. He was transferred to the Zilina camp in 1941, and from there to a camp named Novaky, both in Slovakia. 'My parents and I went through inhumane conditions. We were separated, and I with my mother fled to the forests. For a year and a half we lived in hiding in the forests with the partisans, suffering cold and extremes. My father was killed in the camps, I was five when I last saw him. After the war, we returned to Topolcany. We lived in great poverty, moving from place to place.' At the age of 11, he was separated again from his mother, whom he would never see again. He immigrated to Israel alone. He enlisted to the Israeli Navy at the age of 17, later choosing a life on the sea as a sailor. He spent 64 years at sea, and only stopped in 2018. Yossi Weiss is married to Michal, and they have four children. They live in a rental apartment in Zichron Ya'akov, Israel. Photographed on a ship in Haifa port in May 2019.

Yossi Weiss BY Eldad Rafaeli ISRAEL
HAIFA, ISRAEL, 2019

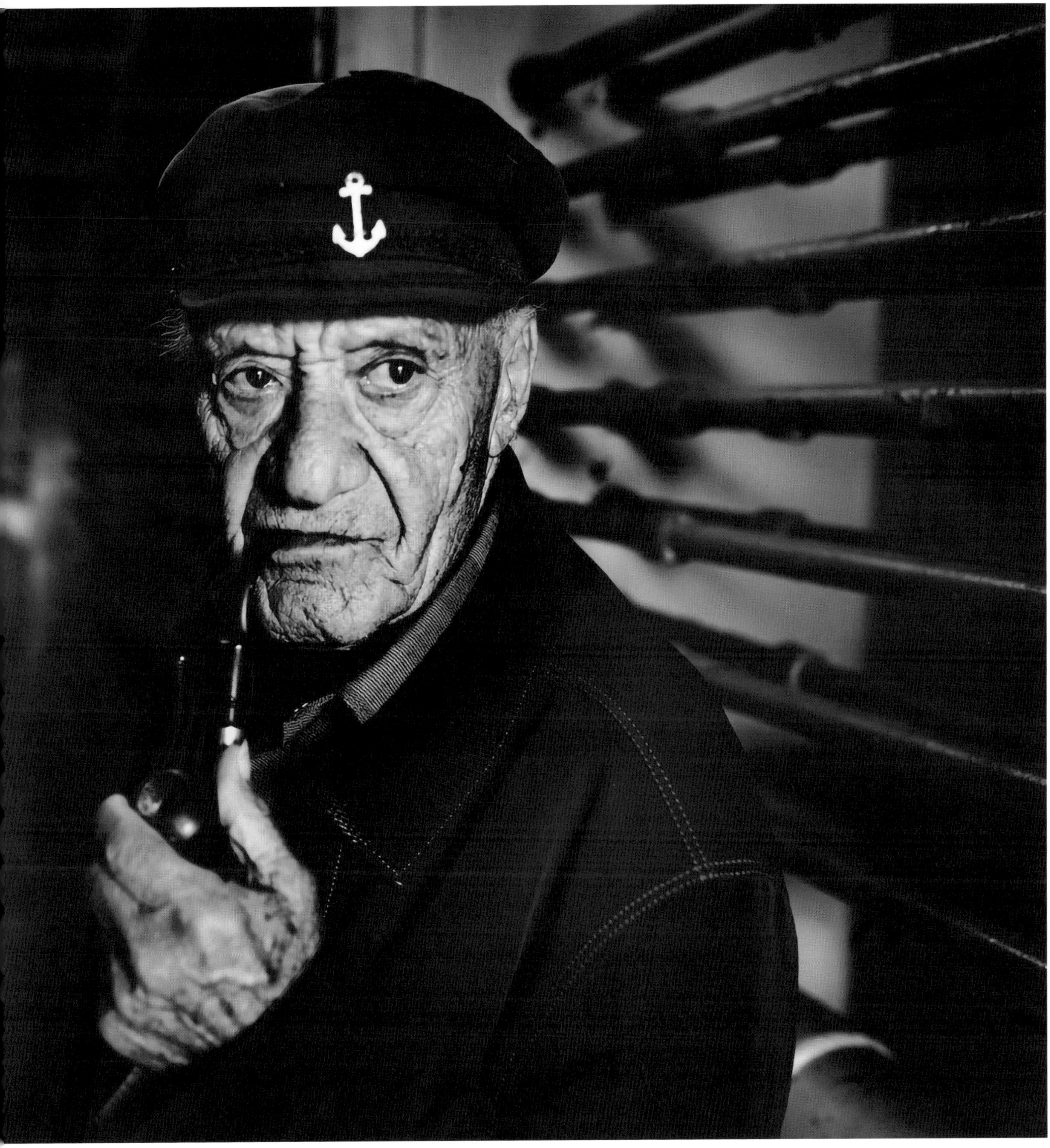

Arie Tabuch, 93, was born in Thessaloniki, Greece. He was sent to Auschwitz in March 1943. 'How can a 15-year-old young man live in this hell of Auschwitz?' he wrote about the first evening on the train to Auschwitz. 'Even the worst film, the worst in the world, cannot describe that humiliation, beatings and suffering. On arrival, there was right and left, who goes to a labor camp and who goes to the crematorium, you go to live, or you go to die. We were stripped of our clothes. It was March and it was snowing, freezing cold weather and we were naked, and the guards take buckets of ice water, splashing on us. For hours we stood crying, trembling, shouting. I was with my brother and my dad. My father didn't survive. Two weeks later they sent him to die. When the war was over, we were recovering in the camp. Suddenly a jeep arrived with Jewish Brigade members. We almost passed out. In the hell we lived to see Jewish officers.' In May 1945 Arie boarded a ship to Mandatory Palestine. The ship was captured by the British soldiers and he spent six months in a Cyprus detention camp before arriving in Israel.

Arie Tabuch BY **Avigail Uzi** ISRAEL
TEL AVIV, ISRAEL, 2019

Charles Górlicki was born on May 25, 1928, in Chmielnik, Poland. He was one of six siblings. Only he and his sister Hinda survived the war. From the Polish invasion in 1939 until his liberation in 1945, Charles was in forced labor camps, eventually ending up in Buchenwald. One of the child survivors of the camp, he was only 16 years old when the war was over. He was faced with the task of rebuilding his life. Initially, Charles went to Paris. He stayed three and half years and learned to be a clothing machinist. It was the quickest way to learn a profession, earn a bit of money and support himself. Charles took a chance, and on January 19, 1949, he arrived in Sydney, Australia, to start a new chapter in his life. Charles passed away on March 23, 2020.

Charles Górlicki BY D-MO AUSTRALIA
SYDNEY, AUSTRALIA, 2019

Leon Schagrin & Betty Helena Sternlicht BY **John Myers** USA
PARKLAND, FLORIDA, USA, 2019

LEON SCHAGRIN was born in Poland in 1926. Leon was 12 when Nazi Germany occupied his hometown Grybow. He grew up often assisting his father, a veterinarian, in tending to horses. In 1942, Leon's father, mother, four sisters and an infant brother were sent to their deaths in the gas chambers of the Belzec death camp. 'I became the buggy driver of the top Nazi official in the Ghetto Tarnow, SS Hermann Blache….' Leon also had to use the buggy to collect dead bodies during the liquidation of the Tarnow Ghetto. Leon was forced by SS guards to descend into the death pits to search for valuables among the thousands of bodies 'piled on top of each other.' Blache ordered the immediate transfer of the horse, named Maciek, and the horse's caretakers, Leon and another boy, Moshe Blauner, to the Szebnie labor camp, with a recommendation noting Leon's skills with horses. Leon had to break Maciek, a carriage horse, so that he could be ridden by the Nazi Camp Commander Grzimek. Grzimek later took the horse away from Leon, to Krakow's Plaszów death camp. Leon was deported to the Auschwitz-Birkenau extermination camp. For four months he witnessed tens of thousands murdered in gas chambers. The noted Italian author Primo Levi slept on the bunk next to Leon as both worked at the Buna Werke laboratory for synthetic rubber in the Auschwitz III camp. In August 1944, Leon was injured by shrapnel from intensive US Air Force bombing of the Buna factory. Later, when Allied forces were nearing the camp, Primo Levi was ill with scarlet fever, and Leon was suffering from severe malnutrition, weighing only 80 pounds. Their conditions saved both from the death march. On January 27, 1945, they were liberated by the Red Army. After the war, Leon went back to school, enlisted in the Polish Army, and was put in charge of a barracks with Nazi prisoners. Throughout his ordeals, Leon remembered his father's last words, "You will survive and tell the story of everything that happened." In the late 1950s, Leon obtained a permit to leave Soviet-controlled Poland. He traveled to Israel, where he met his future wife Betty, a survivor from Poland. The couple settled in the United States and decided not have children. Leon dedicated his life to completing his father's mission to tell the world what had happened. Betty recalled, 'Leon and I still wake up with night terrors… he jumps up in a sweat…I ask him what's the matter…he says he was being chased and running with his horse.' BETTY HELENA STERNLICHT, born in 1925 in Krakow, Poland, survived the Holocaust with the help of Oskar Schindler. She passed away on December 2, 2019.

David Marks BY Howard Schatz USA

SHERMAN, CONNECTICUT, USA, 2019

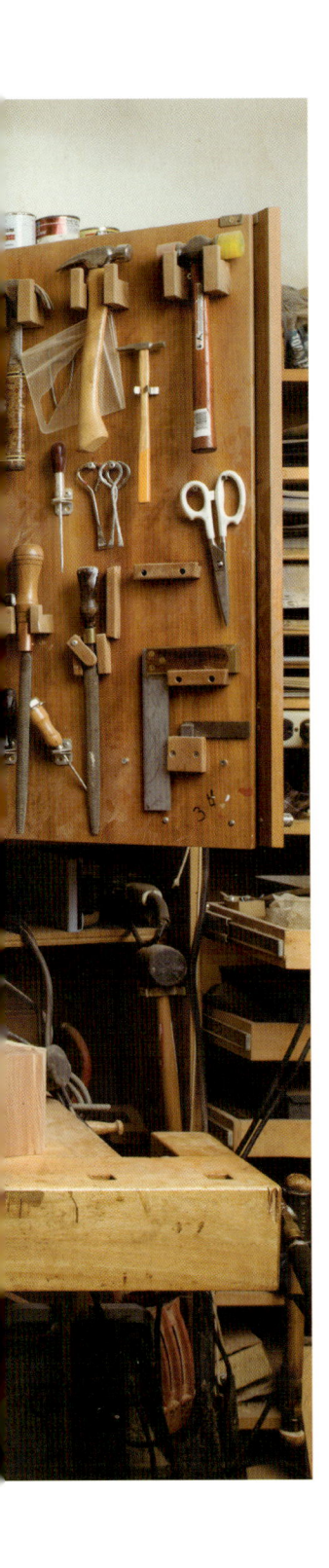

David Marks was born in 1928 in Szilágysomlyó, in the area of Transylvania that was annexed to Hungary in 1940. He was 16 when he was crammed into a cattle-car with thousands of others and brought to Auschwitz, the largest of the Nazi death and extermination camps. Thirty-five members of his immediate and extended family of Romanian Jews were killed in Auschwitz, including his father and brother on the day he arrived. David, on that same day, was selected for work. 'That same day, 35 members of my family were burned or cremated the same day, that Friday.' He returned to Auschwitz for the first time in January 2020 to mark the 75th anniversary of the liberation of Auschwitz by the Russian army, and also recounted there his story for the first time. 'I didn't talk about it with my children,' he said. 'I didn't want they should know what I went through.' He added, 'I would love Hitler should be alive to see what I accomplished – that I'm alive.' He still works every day in his woodworking shop. His sons now run the fine furniture and cabinetmaking business he founded in Brooklyn, NY. In 2020 David returned to visit the Auschwitz extermination and death camp for the first time since the war ended, marking the 75th year of its liberation by the Red Army. David Marks passed away on February 8, 2022, at the age of 93.

RABBI MORDECHAI SHRAGA LEIBOVITZ was born in the Ukraine in 1928. The family was sent to Auschwitz and he does not talk about those years, except losing first his father and later the rest of his family. He describes hiding from the SS guards in the filled sewers in Auschwitz, as they began the liquidation of Auschwitz and its sub-camps. SS units forced some 60,000 prisoners to march west with Soviet troops approaching. Thousands had been killed in the camps in the days before these death marches began. Tens of thousands of Jews were forced to march. SS guards shot anyone who collapsed because of the freezing temperatures or starvation. As many as 15,000 prisoners died during the evacuation marches from Auschwitz and the sub-camps. After the war, Rabbi Leibovitz was reunited with one brother who survived.

Rabbi Mordechai Shraga Leibovitz BY BARUCH YAARI ISRAEL
JERUSALEM, 2019

EMMANUEL KALISCH was born in 1921 in Poland. Emmanuel, a survivor of death camps, will not speak about the Holocaust. He is also a trumpeter, living in a shelter for Holocaust survivors in Israel. He was liberated from Bergen-Belsen concentration camp and all he is prepared to tell is that he was forced to play music by the Germans, and that is why he stopped. Musical ensembles of imprisoned musicians were formed in death camps, and were forced to play when Jews were being sent to extermination and until they entered the gas chambers; during the Selektions; in the organized marching of the prisoners to forced labor and on their return; and they also played at performances for the German staff. In 2018 Emmanuel received a gift, a trumpet, and at age 98, he is a trumpeter again.

Emmanuel Kalisch BY **Shalom Bar-Tal** ISRAEL
TZUR MOSHE, ISRAEL, 2019

Hessy Taft at home in her apartment on the Upper West Side, New York City. She stands by the piano which was prized by her parents, and poses with the photo of her as the "Aryan" baby who made the journey from Germany to Latvia and eventually to the United States. Hessy was selected at six months of age as the most beautiful Aryan baby, and was on the cover of this popular magazine by the Nazi Party, which appeared in the 1930s, in a photograph taken by Hans Blane, a well-known photographer in the German capital at the time. The picture was selected by Joseph Goebbels' office, which had approached German photographers and asked everyone to send a picture of a baby to compete in the competition of the most beautiful baby. This picture won the competition and was also published on postcards. Hessy, now 84 years old, lived in Berlin at the time, and one day the cleaning woman came and told her mother that she saw a picture of Hessy. After the mother saw the newspaper, she went to the photographer and asked him how it happened. The photographer explained that he had sent the picture in, and then the mother asked him, "Do you not know that we are Jews?" The photographer replied that he knew only that he wanted to mock them and make fun of them.

Hessy Taft BY Cheney Orr USA
NEW YORK CITY, NEW YORK, USA, 2019

JANINE WEBBER was born in July 1932 in Lvov, Poland (now Ukraine). The Nazis invaded in 1941, and during a Gestapo raid her father, Alfred, was shot dead, and her grandmother thrown down the stairs and dragged away to a fate unknown. Janine and her mother, Lipka, were moved to the ghetto. They hid in a dog kennel, then a rat-infested cellar. It was there that her mother Lipka died of typhus. Janine's uncle, Selig, found a Polish farmer willing to hide Janine and her younger brother, Arturo. But the two children were betrayed by the family's 20-year-old daughter, who brought an SS officer to the farmhouse. He ordered Janine to walk away but her seven-year-old brother was shot and then buried alive. By 1943, Janine was alone, finding occasional work as a shepherdess. Janine's life was saved by a Polish Catholic teenager named Edek whose name had been given to her earlier by her aunt. Janine recalls, 'He took me to a building. He put a ladder against the wall and told me to climb up. I opened the door and that's where I found my aunt and my uncle – all in all, 13 Jews.' They dug a bunker under the stable floor where Janine stayed underground for a year. There was no air and minimal food. Her uncle managed to get her false papers as a young Catholic girl. She ended up working as a maid for an elderly couple. Her Aunt Rouja found her there six months after liberation. Only in the 1990s was Janine to discover that "Edek" was Franciszek Rzottky, a member of the Polish underground who saved her and the Jews in hiding, and who did not disclose the bunker after he was captured by the Gestapo. After the war, Edek became a priest. He died in 1972. Janine immigrated to the UK in 1956 and still lives in London. In 2017 Janine was awarded the British Empire Medal by Queen Elizabeth for her contribution to Holocaust commemoration.

Janine Webber BY Mike Abrahams GREAT BRITAIN
LONDON, 2019

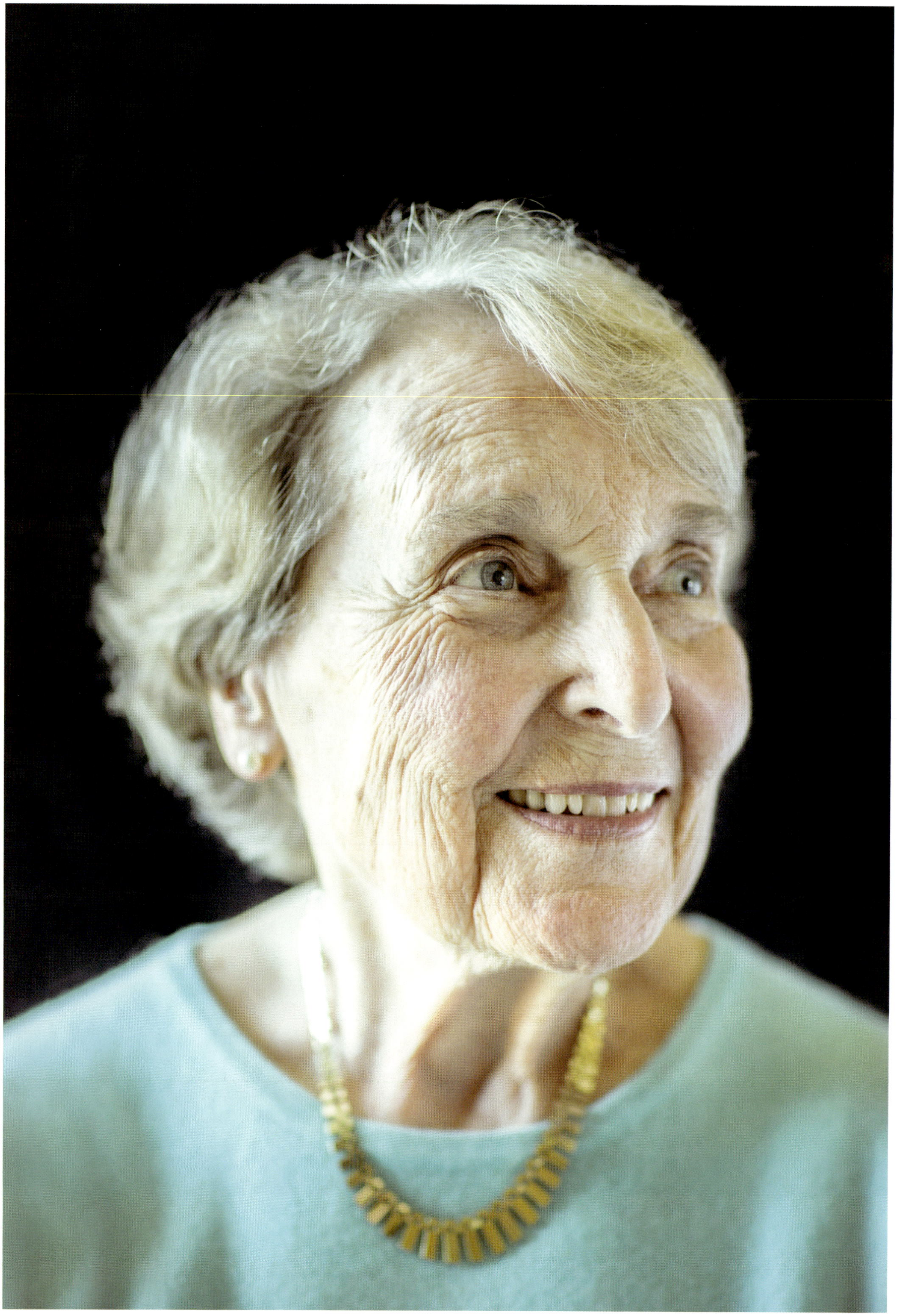

YOKA VERDONER was born in the Netherlands in 1934. After Nazi forces occupied the country, her mother, Hilde, was interned at Westerbork camp between December 1942 and February 1944, and then deported to Auschwitz, where she perished. Yoka was seven when she, her father, and her two siblings went into hiding, all separately. They were taken care of by foster families who risked death by looking after Jewish children. 'My younger sister was five, and she had no understanding of why she suddenly had to live with strangers. She suffered thereafter from lifelong depression.' Yoka moved to the United States, and is a retired teacher and psychotherapist in California. Yoka published her mother's last letters from Westerbork in a book titled *Signs of Life*. Her mother Hilde was 33 when she was captured by the Nazis. Hilde never tried to escape although she had the opportunity to do so, for fear of reprisals against her parents and brother, who were imprisoned with her. Hilde's letters, written before she was sent to Auschwitz and her death, ended with a final understanding of her fate. Yoka never recovered. 'I was never able to really settle down. I lived in different countries and was successful in work, but never able to form lasting relationships with partners. I never married. I almost forgot to mention my own anxiety and depression, and my many years in psychotherapy.'

Yoka Verdoner BY Timothy Archibald USA
SAN FRANCISCO, CALIFORNIA, USA, 2019

Eva Schloss BY Stuart Franklin GREAT BRITAIN

LONDON, 2019

Anne Frank's friend **Eva Schloss** celebrates her 90th birthday in London. Eva is the stepdaughter of Otto Frank, father of Anne Frank. Eva and Anne became friends after Eva's family fled Austria for Amsterdam. She lived in the same apartment block in Amsterdam as Anne Frank. The girls, a month apart in age, enjoyed simple childhood activities until that innocence was shattered after the Germans invaded in 1942, and the families went into hiding. In May 1944 they were betrayed, captured by the Nazis, and Eva and Anne were sent to Auschwitz-Birkenau death camp. Anne was later transferred to Bergen-Belsen, where she died. Eva's father and brother did not survive the war, and Eva and her mother were barely alive when Soviet troops freed them in 1945. After the war Eva and her mother renewed their friendship with Otto Frank, who was at that time contending with the loss of his wife and children, and the discovery of his daughter Anne's diary. In November 1953, Eva's mother Elfriede (1905–1998) married Otto Frank. Anne's father was the only member of his family to survive, though his daughter's diary continues to inspire and inform new generations. Eva did not talk about her experiences in the Nazi camps until after her stepfather's death in 1980. Eva felt compelled to take on the responsibility of keeping Anne Frank's name alive and began to recount her family's experiences during the Holocaust. As an author she has sought to preserve the memory of the Holocaust.

GINETTE KOLINKA was born in Paris on February 4,1925. She is a survivor of the Auschwitz-Birkenau concentration camp and has dedicated her life to the preservation of the memory of the Holocaust. On March 13, 1944, at the age of 19, Ginette Kolinka was arrested with her father, Léon Cherkasky, and other family members in Paris, by the Gestapo. One month later the family was deported by convoy no. 71 to the Auschwitz-Birkenau camp. As soon as the train arrived at the death camp, her father and brother were taken and gassed. Ginette Kolinka was selected for a job and joined the women's camp. In convoy 71 there was also Simone Veil and the director Marceline Loridan-Ivens. From October 1944 to April 1945, Ginette Kolinka was transferred to Bergen-Belsen and Theresienstadt. At the Theresienstadt camp, she worked in an aviation parts factory. She contracted typhus during this period. In May 1945, she was liberated by the Allies and returned to Paris.

Ginette Kolinka BY Jane Evelyn Atwood USA/FRANCE
PARIS, 2019

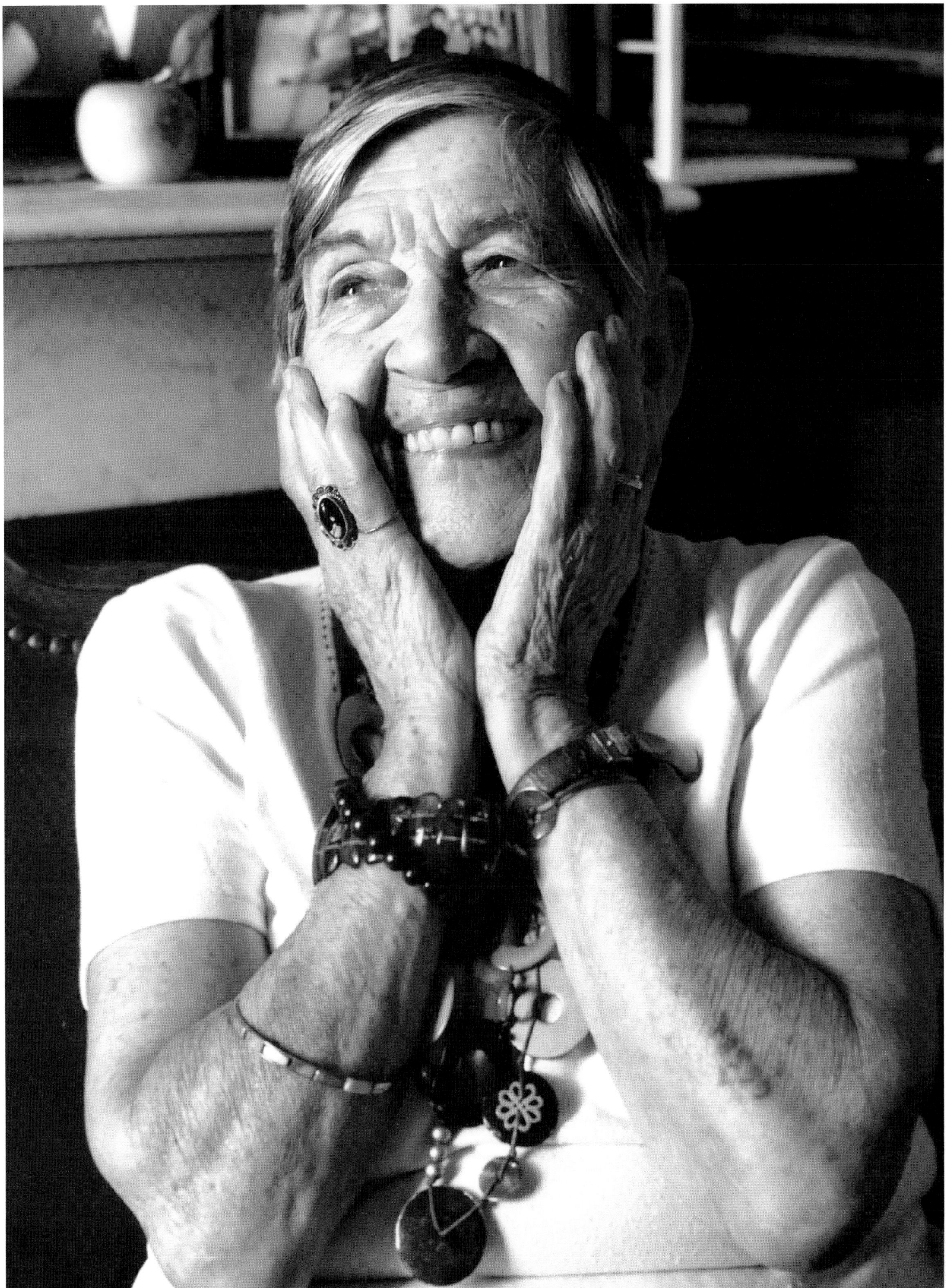

LORD ALFRED DUBS was born in 1932 in Prague. When Alfred was six, he was one of 669 Czech Jewish children rescued from the Nazis by British banker and humanitarian Sir Nicholas Winton, who organized the Kindertransport, bringing the children to the UK between March and September 1939. Alfred's father, who was Jewish, had fled to England the day the Nazis invaded Czechoslovakia in March of that year. 'In June, my mother, having been refused permission to leave, put me on a Kindertransport train with a knapsack of food for the journey – which I forgot to open. I can still clearly see my mother in my mind standing on the platform waving me off, surrounded by Nazis in uniforms and swastikas. My mother was later able to escape and join us. We all had dog tags to identify us. For many of the children it was the last time they ever saw their parents, who perished in the Holocaust.' Lord Dubs became a politician and member of parliament. In 2016, Lord Dubs sponsored an amendment to the Immigration Act 2016 to offer unaccompanied refugee children safe passage to Britain amidst the European migrant crisis.

Lord Alfred Dubs BY Mike Goldwater GREAT BRITAIN
LONDON, 2019

PAUL SCHWARZBART was born in Vienna, Austria, in 1933. Paul, his father Friedrich (Fritz) Schwarzbart, and his mother Sara Ryfka (Sidi) Schneider Schwarzbart, fled Austria in 1938 for Belgium, a country which was taking refugees, if they could make it across the border without being caught. If caught, they would be returned. Paul's father preceded them in crossing the border. After being caught once, mother and son reunited with the father and began life in Brussels. In 1940, Paul's father was arrested and sent to a French forced labor camp, from which he was then shipped to one of the death camps sometime between 1942 and 1943. He survived until the early months of 1945, at which time he was murdered. In 1943, a man came to the Schwarzbart apartment in Brussels with news that if Paul's mother wanted her son to live, she would have to send him away with this stranger, who they later learned was a member of the underground. Paul was given an assumed name and a new religion, and put on a train with instructions to get off when he saw the sign for Jamoigne. There he was met on the platform by a man in a Boy Scout uniform and taken to a chateau, in fact a Catholic boarding school. He lived there, studied, and even became an altar boy, never disclosing his true identity (known only to the headmaster and headmistress). After the liberation by the Americans, he made his way back to Brussels and found his mother. After three years of waiting for a visa for the United States, he and his mother boarded a freighter and made the nine-day crossing to New York.

Paul Schwarzbart BY Robert Gumpert USA
SAN RAFAEL, CALIFORNIA, USA, 2019

MARIE NAHMIAS was born in Tunis in 1926. When the Nazis invaded Tunisia, Marie suffered persecution which remains a part of her to this day. The Jewish community in Tunisia was obligated to provide human resources for forced labor in support of the German occupiers. Marie escaped arrest on the night of her engagement while Nazis conducted house-to-house searches and deportations of Jews, sending them to the 20 labor camps they had established in Tunisia. The German defeat by the Allies in 1943 saved the Jews of Tunisia from the same fate as the European Jews. Marie immigrated to Israel in 1950 and was initially housed in immigration camps. She is known for being a foster parent to 52 abandoned children in Israel.

Marie Nahmias BY Shaul Golan ISRAEL
RAMAT HASHARON, ISRAEL, 2019

MARTHA-MIRIAM KLEINMAN was born in 1938 in Warsaw, Poland. Only after the death of her husband Haim did she find the strength to face her past. The Holocaust took her mother and father when she was four, and all of her extended family a year later. A Polish family rescued her, but also later abandoned her, according to her own perspective as a child. Her Aunt Tusia raised her for a magical year in Poland, until she handed the child to a group of orphans of the Holocaust. Miriam never shared her story with her friends at Kibbutz Ein Shemer, where she found a home after a painful voyage on the illegal immigration ship *Exodus*. She spent a year of wandering among displaced persons camps after the *Exodus* was turned back by British soldiers to Germany. When she arrived at Kibbutz Ein Shemer, she put up a screen on her past, and built her new successful life.

Martha-Miriam Kleinman BY Erez Harodi ISRAEL

KIBBUTZ EIN SHEMER, ISRAEL, 2019

Dr. Nicole Wittman Klapish was born January 30, 1936, in Neuilly-sur-Seine, France. When the war broke out, Nicole and her mother left for Auch in the Free Zone of Southwestern France and moved into a farm owned by friends. Her father, a dental surgeon, looked for work although Jews were forbidden to practice. Nicole remembers 'the blue steel artichoke fields where a bee stung me and how my father cured me with vinegar.' This would be the last time Nicole Klapish, age five, would see her father. In 1941, David Wittman was arrested in Paris and deported to Auschwitz, where he was put to death. Moving often, and changing their family name, mother and daughter eventually found refuge in a preventorium, an institution for sick and weak children. They were there until the end of the war. After the war they returned to their apartment in Neuilly-sur-Seine, still under seal because it had been occupied by German troops. In 1970, she made aliyah to Israel with her husband and their two children, becoming both a psychiatrist and a psychoanalyst.

Dr. Nicole Wittman Klapish BY Ariane Littman ISRAEL
JERUSALEM, 2019

BOLESŁAW WOJEWÓDZKI was born in Poland in 1928. He was sixteen when he volunteered to take part in the 1944 Warsaw Uprising, the single largest military effort undertaken by resistance forces to oppose the Nazi German occupation during World War II. Bolesław volunteered on August 4, 1944, and served in the "Baszta" regiment - VI Battalion. Upon joining the fighting forces, Bolesław was given the pseudonym "Tarzan." 'I took part in the uprising with my two brothers Jerzy and Stasio. Jerzy was 19 when he was struck with a burst from a German machine gun and was killed. The Germans started shelling with cannons, artillery, tanks, infantry, and planes. It was hell.' On August 1, 1944, the Polish Home Army (Armia Krajowa, AK), a resistance movement, initiated the Warsaw Uprising to liberate the city from the Nazi Germany occupation and reclaim Polish independence. The Western Allies dropped ammunition and supplies as the Soviet army was approaching and within sight of the city. The uprising lasted 63 days and was crushed by the Nazis on October 2. The Germans then deported civilians to concentration and forced labor camps while reducing Warsaw to ruins. A few months before passing away, Bolesław met with world heavyweight boxing champion Mike Tyson from the United States, who called him a hero. During their meeting Bolesław told Tyson how he could not forget the scenes of death and described Warsaw: 'The walls of the houses were streaming with blood.' Bolesław passed away in October 2019, several months after the portrait was made.

Bolesław "Tarzan" Wojewódzki BY Andrzej Lange POLAND
WARSAW, 2019

JEAN SERGE LORACH was born in June 1939 in Belfort, France. In February 1944, at the age of four, Jean Serge was deported first to Drancy with his grandfather and mother Denise and, from there, with 240 women and 80 children, to the death camp of Bergen-Belsen. He remembers even as a child the hunger and death everywhere. 'My family was considered by the Nazis hostages – because my father was a captain in the French army and a prisoner of war in Germany.' His grandfather, a former French soldier, was sent to Auschwitz, where he was executed on the day of his arrival, March 11, 1944. 'Adolf Eichmann arrived in person to establish trains loaded with 1,000 people each. We were the bargaining chip, to be exchanged for German prisoners of war. After 10 days on the train tracks, we were liberated by Cossacks on horseback from the Red Army at Trobitz. There we rediscovered antisemitism; for them we were stateless Jews. I was almost seven years old when war was over and reunited with my father Jacques. I have chosen to become a lawyer like he was to "fight against injustices and antisemitism." My mother Denise created the Museum of Resistance in Besançon, July 17, 1971, dedicating her life to the preservation of the memory of the Holocaust. Despite my many legal activities I was unable to relive those terrible years of my childhood and was not involved in trials against criminals like against Barbie and Touvier who committed crimes against humanity. At the age of 80, I have a peaceful life surrounded by a beloved family.'

Jean Serge Lorach BY Stéphane Lehr FRANCE

PARIS, 2019

Born in June 1943 to a Dutch Jewish physician father and a mother of French and German descent, in Surabaya, Japanese-occupied Dutch East Indies, which later became Indonesia, Xaviera "Vera" de Vries spent the first years of her life in a Japanese-run internment camp. In her 20s, she moved from Amsterdam to Johannesburg and later to New York City. She was a secretary of the Dutch consulate in Manhattan but left and became a call girl and a madam under the name Xaviera Hollander, making some $1,000 a night. She opened her own brothel and soon became known as New York City's leading madam. She was arrested for prostitution in 1971 and left the US for Canada. Her book *The Happy Hooker* was published in 1971. She went on to write many other books, including *Child No More: A Memoir*, in 2002, and she penned a monthly advice column in *Penthouse* magazine entitled Call Me Madam. She has been married twice and has had many lovers. She runs a bed-and-breakfast in her Amsterdam home and has produced and directed many theatrical productions in Amsterdam.

Xaviera Hollander BY Peter Dejong THE NETHERLANDS
AMSTERDAM, 2019

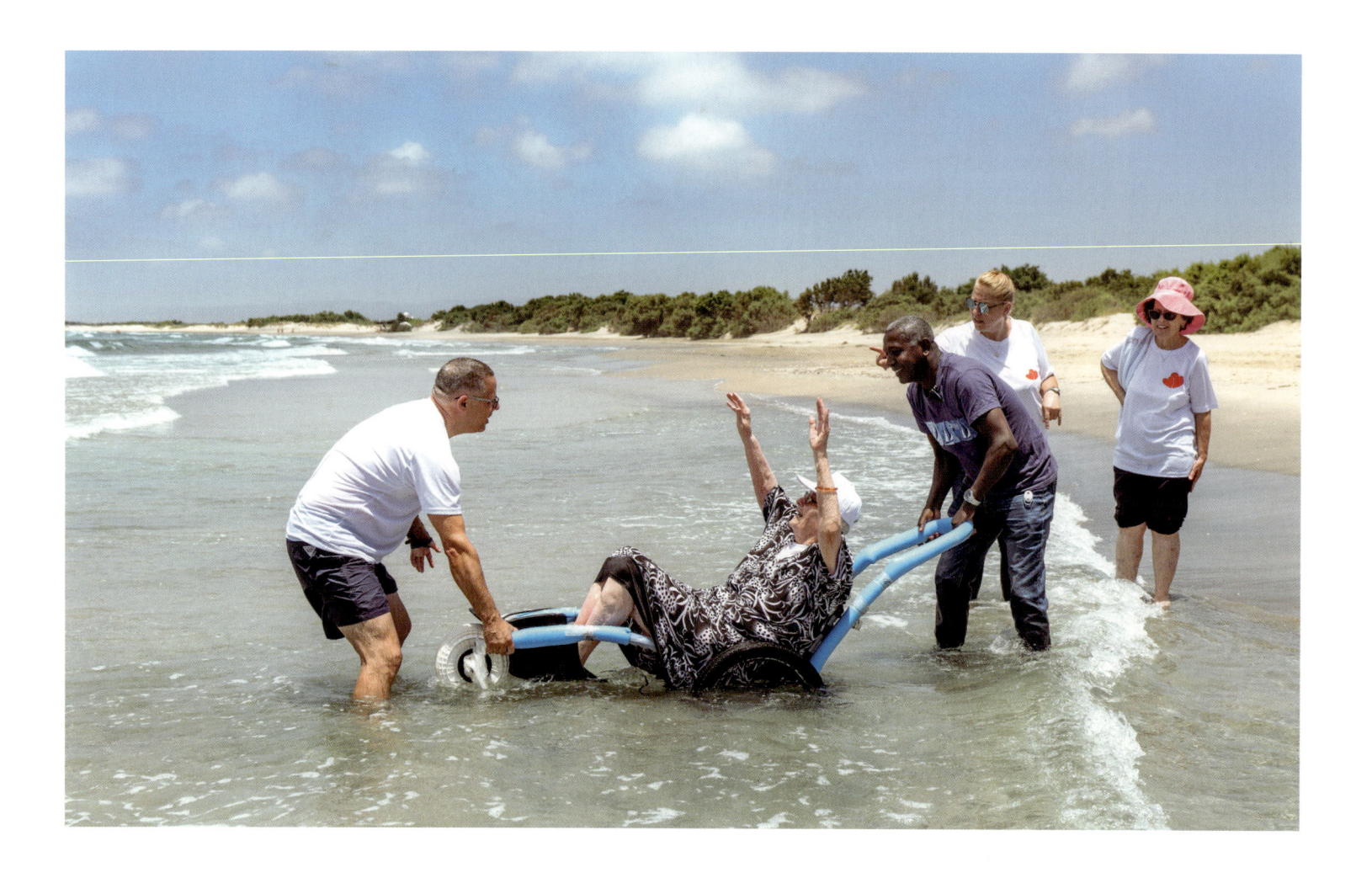

ELIRAN KEREN (L), the son of a Holocaust survivor and a volunteer assisting Holocaust survivors, along with SEGAL (R) another helper, assist JUDITH, a Holocaust survivor in her 80s, into the Mediterranean Sea at the beach at Kibbutz Ma'agan Michael, south of Haifa, Israel, June 27, 2019.

Survivor at the Med BY Jim Hollander USA
KIBBUTZ MA'AGEN MICHAEL, ISRAEL, 2019

RUTH OPPENHEIM was born in 1927 in Werne, a German town which had only 10 Jewish families. The harsh realities of Nazi rule shadow her memories of her childhood. During her first year in school, a decree prohibited Jewish students from participating in school activities. 'We had to sit in the back of the classroom. No one was allowed to speak to us, and I remember my embarrassment as I stood alone in the playground.' After the terror and trauma of Kristallnacht on November 9, 1938, Jews were no longer permitted to attend public schools. In May 1939, Ruth's oldest sister Julia, then 15, left for America. In August, their father Albert followed, intending to bring Ruth's mother Rosa, her older sister Hannelore, her younger brother Herbert, and Ruth herself, as soon as possible. After a period of great tension – hopes raised, hopes crushed, hopes raised again – on January 24, 1940, the four of them set sail on the SS *Veendam* from Rotterdam in the Netherlands, to New York City.

Ruth Oppenheim BY David H. Wells USA
PROVIDENCE, RHODE ISLAND, USA, 2019

Diamantina "Tina" Vivante Salonichio was born in 1928 in Trieste, Italy. In 1944, Diamantina was 16 when she was arrested along with her four sisters and mother in Trieste. After several weeks in the city's prison, the family was deported to the Ravensbrück concentration camp and later transferred to the Bergen-Belsen death camp, where her mother Sarina and four sisters perished. Diamantina was freed by British soldiers in 1945. She was the only survivor of the Holocaust from the Salonicchio-Vivante family. Tina lived in Trieste next to her son Sandro Salonichio, president of the Trieste Jewish Community. Diamantina "Tina" passed away on September 23, 2023. She was the last Holocaust survivor living in Trieste.

Diamantina "Tina" Vivante Salonichio BY Enrique Shore ARGENTINA
TRIESTE, ITALY, 2019

Yosef Ron was born in 1934 in Lodz, Poland. When he was five years old, Nazi Germany invaded Poland and his family moved to Ghetto Piotrkow. It was the first Jewish ghetto in Nazi-occupied Europe. Following the 1942 deportations to Majdanek and Treblinka death camps, some Jewish factory workers, like Yosef's father, still remained in the ghetto. Yosef was forced to separate from his mother Miriam who was transported with his brother Reuben to Ravensbrück while Yoseph and his father Moshe were transported to Buchenwald and later to Bergen-Belsen. Thanks to Count Folke Bernadotte – who, before the end of the war, led a rescue operation transporting interned western European inmates from German concentration camps to hospitals in Sweden – Yosef, after Bergen-Belsen was liberated, was sent to recover in Sweden, where the family was reunited. In 1949 they immigrated to Israel. Yosef never had a childhood and enjoyed time with his grandchildren Maya and Guy. Yosef Ron passed away in late August 2021.

Yosef Ron BY Alon Ron ISRAEL

HOLON, ISRAEL, 2019

GITTA RYLE was born in 1932, in Vienna. She was five when Adolf Hitler had risen to power in Germany and moved in to occupy Austria, where the Nazis began registering Jews and enlisting the men to work in labor camps. Gitta's father managed to sneak out into Belgium. The November 1938 pogrom and Kristallnacht forced the family into hiding. 'I had to hide in the closet if anybody came to the door.' Gitta's mother was assisted by the French organization called the OSE (Œuvre de Secours aux Enfants), which offered her daughters a safe way out of Austria. On March 22, 1939, Gitta and her sister Renee were put on a train to France. 'The Nazis took over Paris, and as soon as that happened, they trucked us to the center of France,' Gitta recalls. 'There, we went to Château du Masgelier. I remember the cold, the famine and we got sick a lot.' There the sisters were suddenly reunited with their father for a brief time. 'I don't know if he was trying to get us out of there, but all of a sudden he was gone. We know he died in Auschwitz.' The Nazis continued to take over more of France, thwarting any escapes the OSE tried to orchestrate for the children. Nazi pursuit forced the OSE to split Gitta and Renee up with separate families in a town called Romans-sur-Isère. That is when the war reached Gitta's doorstep. 'The planes were coming, and the bombs kept dropping, and they were shooting down. We were out in the fields with the goats and the sheep, and we had to rush undercover as the stuff was coming down. I was about 12, and I realized that this is what a war is.' Gitta and Renee survived and at the end of the war OSE brought the girls back to Paris and then on a boat across the English Channel to join their mother who had escaped to England after her own parents were captured. In 1946 Gitta, Renee and their mother boarded the RMS *Queen Elizabeth* headed for New York City. They arrived in America on Armistice Day, 1946, and settled first in Detroit and later in California where Gitta met and married her husband, Bob. Gitta raised a family and tried to put the past behind her. Telling her story of survival to school children has become Gitta Ryle's main purpose in life. 'I'm so full of joy now,' she says, 'and every morning I'm full of gratitude that I'm alive.'

Gitta Ryle BY Richard B. Ressman USA
SAN FRANCISCO, CALIFORNIA, USA, 2019

Mordechai and Yehudit Teichner were born in Budapest, Mordechai in 1930 and Yehudit in 1929. Both were rounded up with their families to the ghetto and from there to trains to concentration camps. 'When the war broke out, soon we were expelled from Hungary,' says Mordechai. 'All the Jews had to march towards the train and the Hungarians stood and rejoiced.' They met after the war. Both had been shipped by cattle trains to Auschwitz-Birkenau, and both were separated from their families upon arrival. Mordechai says, 'When Mengele asked my age I was warned ahead by my father to say I'm 17, and not 14, as I was. This saved my life.' Yehudit's mother, father and two younger brothers were sent to the gas chambers upon arrival. Mordechai and Yehudit both recall the freezing temperatures in the blocks and the starvation. Mordechai was 14 when he was moved to Dachau and from there to forced labor in Mildorf, where 'we worked till collapsing for seven months. About 2,700 people died where I was. My father was one of them.' In 1945 he was transferred to Germany. 'The Nazis opened the doors of the train and yelled to hurry out and that we were free. When I got off the train wagon, they were shooting at my direction. I was beaten while running back to the train and Jewish inmates presumed I was dead. The Americans attacked the train, which was surrounded by Nazi soldiers. The Jews climbed onto the roof and waved their prisoners' shirts and the planes left. We were liberated soon after by American soldiers.' Yehudit, in Auschwitz, hid from Mengele her true weight, 28 kg, and was sent to forced labor in a factory in Germany, where she was liberated by the Red Army. Mordechai located his surviving siblings on a list posted in a displaced persons camp where he also met his future wife Yehudit, who had lost her entire family in the Holocaust. Both immigrated to Israel in 1948 and joined Kibbutz Ein Hashofet.

Mordechai & Yehudit Teichner BY Yaaqov Shofar ISRAEL

KIBBUTZ EIN HASHOFET, ISRAEL, 2019

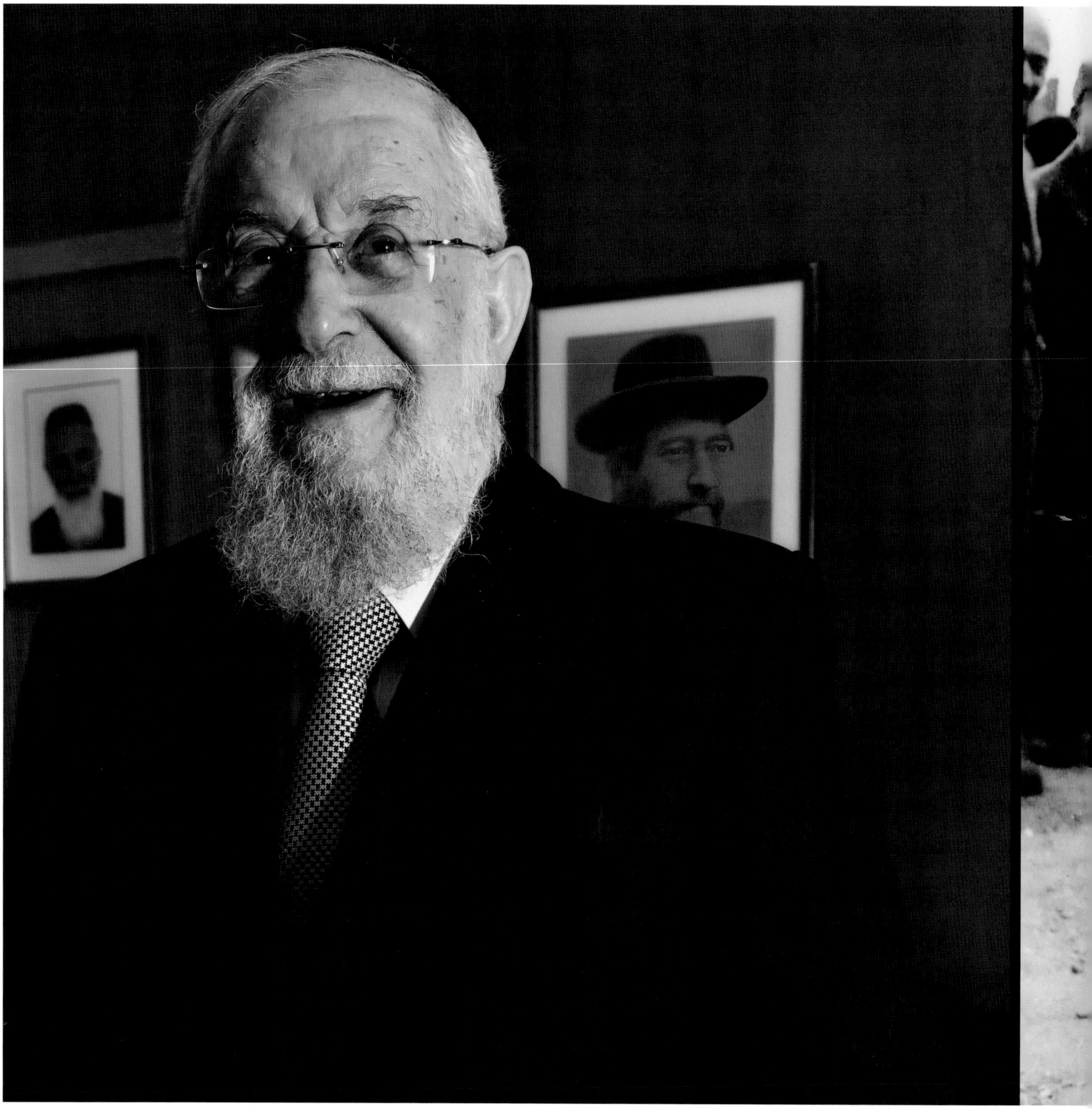

Born in June 1937 in the Polish town of Piotrków Tybunalski, at seven years old he was separated from his mother and imprisoned in a Nazi slave labor camp and then in the Buchenwald concentration camp. His older brother Naphtali Lau-Lavie concealed him. His father was murdered in the Treblinka concentration camp. **Meir Lau** survived and was freed from the Buchenwald camp in 1945. He became a poster child for miraculous survival, when a US Army chaplain, Rabbi Herschel Schacter, found him hiding in a heap of corpses when the camp was liberated. His entire family was murdered except his older brother and a half-brother and an uncle already living in Mandatory Palestine. Lau immigrated to Mandatory Palestine with his brother Naphtali in July 1945 and was raised by an aunt and uncle. He studied in yeshiva and was ordained as a rabbi in 1961. He was Chief Rabbi of Netanya (1978–1988), then elected Chief Rabbi of Israel in 1993. He served until 2003. He was also Chief Rabbi of Tel Aviv and was awarded the Israel Prize in 2005 for his stance on non-Orthodox denominations in Judaism. He was awarded the Legion of Honor by France's President Sarkozy in 2011. He served for many years as the Chairman of the Yad Vashem Holocaust Memorial in Jerusalem. Yisrael Meir Lau is the 38th generation in an unbroken family of rabbis. His son Moshe Lau currently serves as Israel's Ashkenazi Chief Rabbi. On April 11, 1945, **Yisrael Meir Lau** was eight years old when he was photographed leaving Buchenwald concentration camp after its liberation by the 6th Armored Division, United States Army. Seventy-five years later, Rabbi Lau was to observe the Passover Seder with social distancing and isolation from his many family members, like so many other Holocaust survivors. The rabbi says, 'This year the night of Passover will be different. This time I will not talk to people, but about history.'

Rabbi Yisrael Meir Lau BY Jim Hollander USA
TEL AVIV, ISRAEL, 2019

Towards the end of 1942, **Sonia Klein** (R) says, word began to spread that the people who had been deported from the ghetto, supposedly to labor camps, were in fact being killed. Her father and a few other men used their hands to dig a hiding spot for their families. Then the ghetto went up in flames. The houses were burning, and 'we said, "Well, either we go, or we burn right here." We went out.' Sonia and the dozens of people with whom she was hiding were taken to Majdanek death camp. For the act of not letting go of her young son's hand, Sonia's mother was killed. Her brother, too. Her father, who would die soon after, was separated from Sonia and her sister Sophie, who a few weeks later were transported to Auschwitz-Birkenau. Sonia and her sister were shipped from camp to camp and were on a months-long death march as the Allies closed in. All along, she said, she kept her spark of hope alive by promising herself that she would not be silent if she survived. Sophie passed away on December 1, 2019.

Sonia Klein & Sophie BY Yunghi Kim USA
BROOKLYN, NEW YORK, USA, 2019

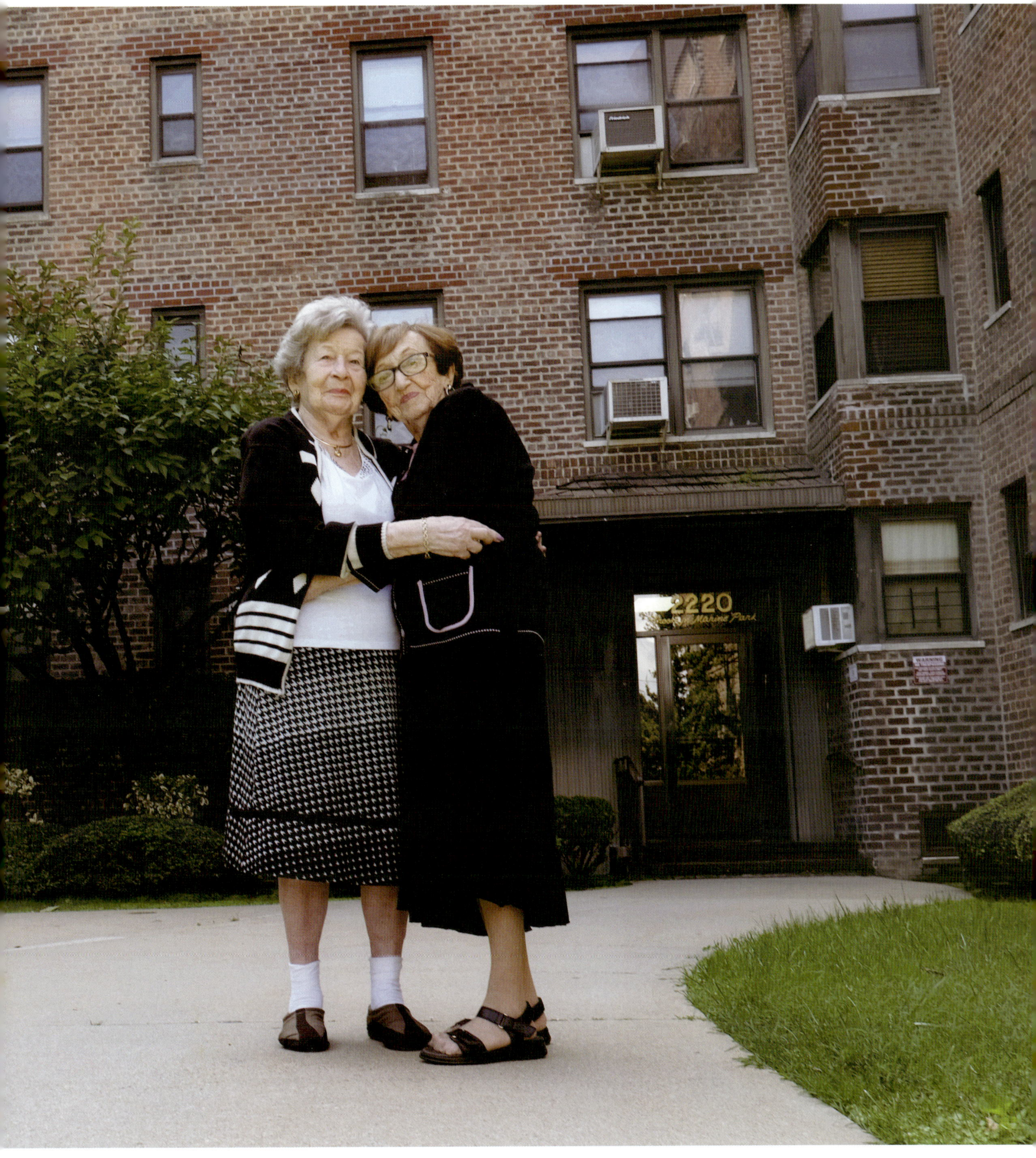
2220
Park

Professor **AL SILVERSTEIN** was born in Graz, Austria, in 1935. 'Overnight the Jews of Austria were like the Jews in Germany, subject to all the same restrictions.' His family was evicted from their apartment and banned from Graz, along with all Jews. His father began trying to find ways to get out through his older sister, who had lived in Queens, New York, since the early 1920s. She tried to sponsor them, but to no avail. The family tried to sneak into Switzerland, but were sent back, like many Jews trying to escape. The family went into hiding. When Kristallnacht struck, Al's father was arrested at a train station on another attempt to apply for a visa to a foreign country. Al's mother somehow obtained forged papers which indicated that her husband had an immigration visa to Shanghai. From his arrival on, he tried to get his wife and son out and to safety as well. The Kindertransport made that possible. The UK took in nearly 10,000 Jewish children from Nazi Germany and Nazi-occupied Austria. It took 'many bribes' but Al's father found a foster family to take in Al, then three and a half. Al does not have many memories of that time. His mother was able to join soon after as an adult chaperone on the last Kindertransport train. It took two and a half years for the family to unite when emigration to the United States was approved. They came to America in November 1940. Al obtained his master's at Yale and a doctorate at Berkeley, and has had a career as a professor of psychology.

Al Silverstein BY Stephanie Alvarez-Ewens USA
PAWTUCKET, RHODE ISLAND, USA, 2019

TRUDY ALBUM was born in 1929 in Samorin, Slovakia. In the spring of 1944, the German army occupied all of Slovakia. Earlier, Trudy's family was warned but refused to believe. 'By the time we received my grandmother's postcard, she and thousands of others from her town, Bratislava, were already taken to Terezin or Auschwitz and killed in a gas chamber.' Trudy remembers the humiliation of wearing the Jewish star, followed by orders to move to the ghetto, where her father was drafted to work. 'I never saw him again.' Then came deportation orders. 'We were marched and shoved into cattle cars where we could not breathe,' Trudy recounts, and when 'the doors opened, we are at the gates of Auschwitz,' where Trudy's mother and two younger sisters were separated from Trudy. The first sight of Auschwitz that Trudy recalls was 'huge chimneys with smoke and flames coming out of them. I asked people, "What is that odor?" and they responded, "They are burning your families."' Trudy's hair was shaved, she was tattooed with the number A17291, and sent to barrack C2 in Birkenau. 'The camp was primarily a killing station.' Trudy was transferred from Auschwitz to Plaszów camp near Krakow and later to forced labor in Augsburg, Bavaria. One day instead of being taken to work, Trudy and other prisoners were ordered off trucks and into the fields. 'Suddenly the German soldiers began firing machine guns' and while prisoners were killed near her, there was more shooting, and airplanes, and she refused to believe it was over. She saw soldiers in uniforms that were totally unfamiliar. They were American soldiers. Trudy spent months looking for surviving family members and found none. Her mother and sisters were killed upon arrival to Auschwitz, and her father was shot dead on a death march two days before the end of the war. Thanks to distant American relatives, she was able to immigrate to the United States in 1946.

Trudy Album BY Dana Goldstein USA
SUFFERN, NEW YORK, USA, 2019

ALICE EICHENBAUM was born in Vienna, Austria, in 1928. She was an only child who was used to commuting back and forth between Bulgaria and Austria. In March 1938, when Hitler's troops marched into Austria, Alice was in Bulgaria. The persecution of Bulgarian Jews began in 1939, intensified in 1941 and culminated in deportations of Jews living in Bulgarian-occupied territories to the Treblinka extermination camp, where they perished. 'We were the lucky ones, we had passports with a big J for Jew with a swastika on top. In November 1942, they issued to us the yellow star. We wore them on our jackets and we were dispersed into small ghettos. They shipped us on a train with all the people wearing the yellow star.' Alice and her family were herded into a building in the Karnobat Ghetto, where they stayed for two years, until the end of the war. The planned deportation of the Jews from within Bulgaria's prewar borders was never carried out. The Bulgarian public protested against the deportations and the survival rate of the Jews of Bulgaria was the highest in Axis Europe. On September 9, 1944, the Russians moved in through the Black Sea and Alice and her family were liberated. In 1958, Ruth immigrated to the United States, where she became a chemist.

Alice Eichenbaum BY Jonathan Sharlin USA
PROVIDENCE, RHODE ISLAND, USA, 2019

DR. MOSHE AVITAL was born in 1930 in Czechoslovakia, in an area which is now Ukraine. His father was a shochet (ritual slaughterer) and chazzan (cantor). Moshe was imprisoned in Ghetto Berehovo. In 1944, at the age of 14, he was deported with his entire family to Auschwitz, which he described as 'the largest slaughterhouse in all of Europe.' There Moshe was separated from his remaining family. He recalled the final moment he saw his mother, sisters and others. Moshe then worked in other concentration camps. He described working 12-hour shifts on little food and enduring harsh winters and the constant sight of soldiers with guns pointed at him. When liberated from a concentration camp by American soldiers in 1945, Moshe said he weighed a mere 70 pounds and had lost about 50 percent of his body weight. He went on a children's ship to Mandatory Palestine, enrolled in the Haganah paramilitary organization and fought during the 1948 war. He joined his only surviving brother in the US and continued his education to become a scholar. He said it was the duty of all survivors 'to tell the tragic truth in full.'

Dr. Moshe Avital BY Ed Kashi USA
NEW ROCHELLE, NEW YORK, USA, 2019

Regina Steinitz and her twin sister Ruth were born on October 24, 1930, in Berlin. Their mother, Martha, converted to Judaism when she married Jewish photographer Moritz Rajfeld. They had two children, Benno and Theo Rajfeld, in the 1920s. When the boys were six years old, their father, Moritz, died. Martha then married Moritz's assistant Simon Welner, and they had the twin girls in 1930. The sisters went to the Jewish girls' school in Berlin. After their father escaped to America in 1938 and their mother died in 1940, Regina and Ruth were taken into a Jewish orphanage. When it closed down they lived with a Jewish foster family. In March 1943, the SS and the Gestapo took the twin girls to a detention compound. 'I was a child, the same age as Anne Frank, 12 years old. We thought we were going to a ghetto. We were lucky. Ruth, my sister, smuggled a note to our uncle with someone about to be released and our uncle took us away from the Gestapo detention compound. He was the only reason we survived.' Regina's non-Jewish uncle Robert, her mother's brother, lied to the Gestapo and brought the twins to his home, saving both from deportation to death camps. 'I stood by the window on the fifth floor and watched the planes come in, Berlin lit up and the bombs fell. I was ready to give up my life, I didn't want to live anymore, I asked the good Lord to end the war, but my life was not important to me anymore,' recalled Regina. The twins lived with their uncle and aunt until the end of the war. In 1948, they immigrated to Israel. 'My brother Benno, who had survived Auschwitz, sent me to Kibbutz Netzer Sereni. That's where I met my husband.' Regina married and rebuilt her life with Zwi Steinitz, a survivor of death camps, in 1949 and created a family. The couple was married for 70 years; Zwi died in the summer of 2019. Regina Steinitz wrote her life story in the book *A Childhood and Youth Destroyed: My Life and Survival in Berlin*. The couple was the recipient on separate occasions of the Order of Merit of the Federal Republic of Germany awarded for their extensive contribution to Holocaust education.

Regina Steinitz BY Ami Steinitz ISRAEL
TEL AVIV, ISRAEL, 2019

Zwi Steinitz was born in 1927 in Poznań, Poland, to Herman and Salomea. He remembers his mother played the piano beautifully. He remembers the catastrophe as described in his book *As a Boy through the Hell of the Holocaust*, where he recounts the suffering in the Krakow Ghetto and the murder of his family in Belzec. 'It was my birthday, and it was the day I accompanied my parents and brother on their last journey. I was just fifteen on that day. I still see Mom, Dad and my brother as living people. I can't describe them as dead people. I recall Dad as he suddenly bursts like a volcano against the SS officers standing near the gate. I can see his eyes spit fire. I can hear his thunderous voice shout at the executioners, furiously screaming at the SS, "Killers! Criminals!"' Zwi survived Plaszów. He survived Auschwitz, Buchenwald, Gliwice, Sachsenhausen and death marches in the snow. 'I was walking with other prisoners, eleven days without food. I was hungry. I had no family, I had nobody and I should find my way in life.' He was liberated by the US Army in Schwerin and Zwi, alone, arrived in Mandatory Palestine in 1946. He was a founder of a kibbutz with other survivors, where he met his wife Regina. They called it Kibbutz Buchenwald, after the concentration camp from which its members had been liberated. Today it is called Netzer Sereni. Zwi passed away one month after being photographed for The Lonka Project.

Zwi Steinitz by Ami Steinitz ISRAEL
TEL AVIV, ISRAEL, 2019

BEN FERENCZ is not a Holocaust survivor. He is, however, directly responsible for hundreds of thousands of survivors. Ben Ferencz was born in Somcuta Mare, Romania (Transylvania), on March 11, 1920. He was an investigator of Nazi war crimes when World War II finished and was the Chief Prosecutor for the United States at the Einsatzgruppen trial, one of the twelve military trials held by the US at Nuremberg, Germany. Ben's parents immigrated to the United States when he was 10 months old to avoid persecution of Hungarian Jews at that time. He studied in City College in New York City and graduated law school at Harvard in 1943. He then joined the US Army and served in an anti-aircraft artillery unit, fighting across France and Germany. He was in General Patton's Third Army and was sent to the concentration camps as they were being liberated by the US Army to collect evidence of war crimes. He also landed in Normandy. He was discharged from the army with the rank of Sergeant and returned to New York but was recruited weeks later into the Nuremberg Trials in the legal team of General Telford Taylor, who appointed him chief prosecutor in the Einsatzgruppen Case, Ferencz's first court case, and what is called the biggest murder trial in history. All of the 22 men on trial were convicted: 14 of them received death sentences, of which four were carried out. Ben later worked for many years as a leading advocate for an international rule of law to hear instances of crimes against humanity and war crimes, and for the establishment of an International Criminal Court, which was established in the Hague in 2002. He remained in Europe after the trials and helped negotiate a reparations settlement for Germany to pay Jewish Holocaust survivors in Israel. He stated in 2013, about the Iraq War begun by US President George W. Bush, that the "use of armed force to obtain a political goal should be condemned as an international and a national crime." Ben Ferencz passed away on April 7, 2023, at age 103, as reported by the US Holocaust Museum.

Ben Ferencz BY Andy Anderson USA

DELRAY BEACH, FLORIDA, USA, 2019

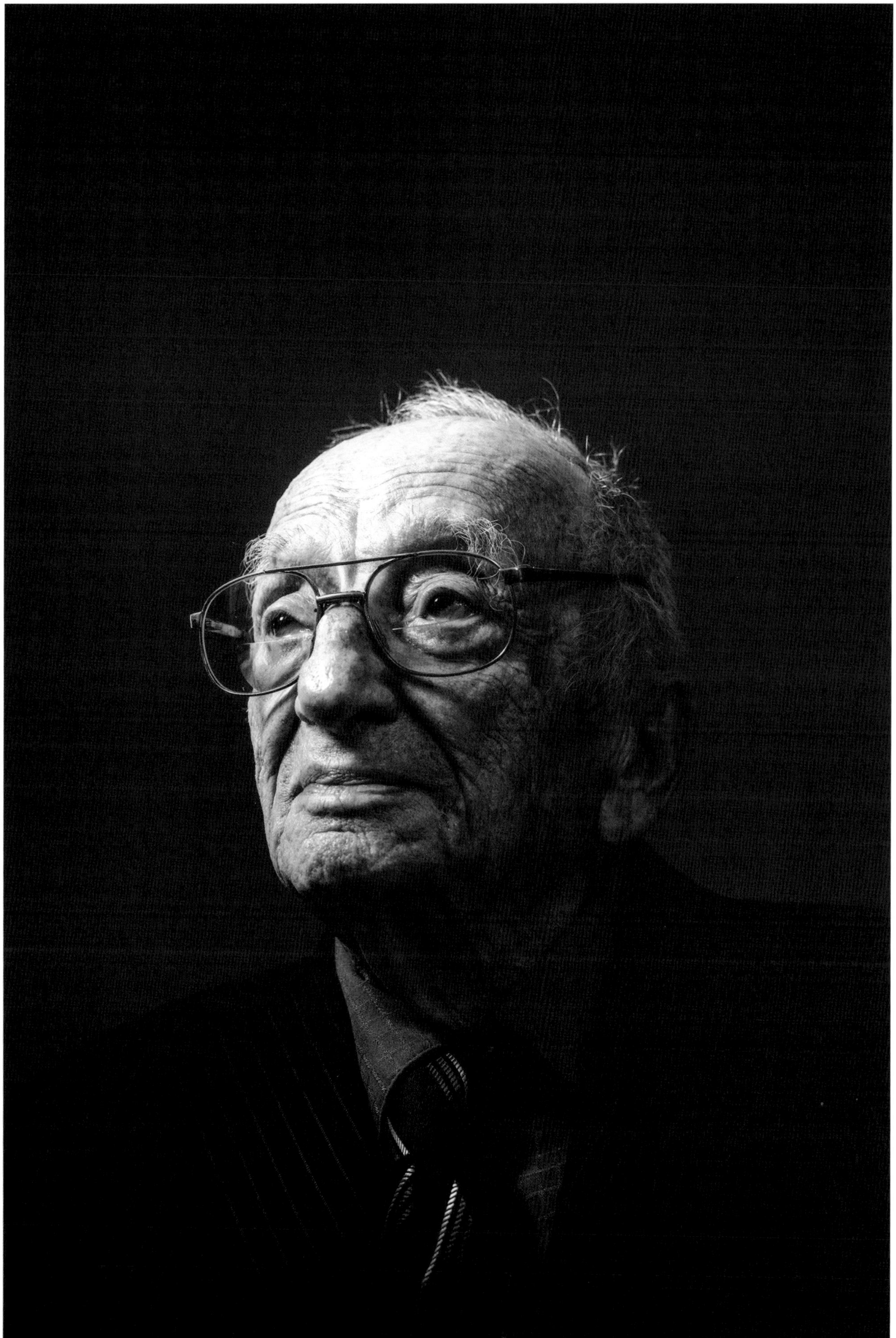

MOSHE ETZION, an 88-year-old Holocaust survivor, was one of the "Tehran Children." He was part of a group of Polish Jewish children, mainly orphans, who escaped the Nazi German occupation of Poland. This group of children found temporary refuge in orphanages and shelters in the Soviet Union, and was later evacuated with several hundred adults to Tehran, Iran, before finally reaching Mandatory Palestine in 1943. He lived in Israel at Kibbutz Nirim, along the border with the Gaza Strip and lost his son, Ze'ev, during Operation Protective Edge in 2014, when he was hit by a missile fired from Gaza. Moshe volunteered for The Road to Recovery, an organization that drives Palestinian children to hospitals in Israel. Moshe is pictured with a Gazan girl, Nur Haj, 11, who needed medical treatment and had just crossed the border from the Gaza Strip into Israel. 'After my son was killed, I've decided,' he says, 'a sick kid needs to get help whenever and wherever they can; being sick is not their fault. I think it's good that we help our enemies too, like the help we give the wounded Syrians. It is human.' Moshe was 88 years old when he took his own life at the grave of his son, Ze'ev, in Kibbutz Nirim. It was the anniversary of his son's death. "Moshe stood bravely not only in bereavement but all his life after the Holocaust," the kibbutz announced.

Moshe Etzion BY Miri Tzachi ISRAEL
EREZ CROSSING, ISRAEL, 2019

MOSHE NEUMANN was born in Belgium in 1930. German forces invaded neutral Belgium in 1940 and instituted anti-Jewish laws and ordinances. They restricted the civil rights of Jews, confiscated their property and businesses, banned them from certain professions, and in 1942 required Jews to wear a yellow Star of David. Belgian Jews were also rounded up for forced labor and in 1942 deportation of Jews began to concentration camps, mainly Auschwitz, where most perished. Moshe was gravely ill and was hospitalized when his parents Chaim and Roza were deported to death camps. One of the hospital nurses rescued his life by bravely bringing him to a monastery where he was raised as a Christian child. In a wartime convent, Moshe learned the secrecy, the deprivation and the kindness, within the backdrop of the terror of the Nazi occupation. Moshe was one of 3,000 children who found sanctuary in Roman Catholic convents and orphanages. The children had to face the loss of parents while struggling to adapt to the daily prayers and rituals until the liberation of Belgium in 1944 by the Allies. Some 48 Belgian nuns have been honored and recognized as Righteous Among the Nations. Among them are the Franciscan Sisters in Bruges, the Sisters of Don Bosco in Courtrai, the Sisters of Saint Mary near Brussels, the Dominican Sisters at Lubbeek, the Sisters of Charity and many others. After the war Moshe, who was left alone in the world, was located by the Jewish agency and arrived to Mandatory Palestine. He later married Zipora and the couple lives in Holon. In the photo, taken in Holon, Moshe and Zipora review a Torah scroll to be dedicated to the memory of his father Chaim who perished in the Holocaust.

Moshe & Zipora Neumann BY Yossi Gal Oliver ISRAEL
HOLON, ISRAEL, 2019

Dr. Ruth Westheimer was born in Germany in 1928, the only child of Orthodox Jews in the Nordend district of Frankfurt, where they lived. Ruth grew up in Germany until 1938 when the Nazis came to power. Her family thought the upheaval would be short-lived until the morning the Nazis walked into their apartment and led her father away to a forced labor camp a week after Kristallnacht in 1938. She remembers her father waving to her with a little smile. It was the last time she saw him. 'My mother and grandmother brought me to the railroad station in Frankfurt. That was the last I ever saw of them. Ruth's mother and grandmother decided that Germany was too dangerous and in January 1939 they brought her to the railroad station in Frankfurt and sent Ruth on the Kindertransport to Switzerland. 'That was the last I ever saw of them.' Ruth, age 11, arrived at a home of a Jewish charity in Heiden, and as the years passed, the home in Switzerland became an orphanage. Ruth took on the role of a caregiver and mother-like figure to the younger children. Ruth was not allowed to take classes at the local school, but a fellow orphan boy would sneak her his text books so she could learn and continue her education. Ruth corresponded with her mother and grandmother via letters. When the letters ceased in 1941, Ruth knew she would not hear from them again. Her father was killed in Auschwitz in 1942 and her mother and grandmother perished. Ruth says she is not a Holocaust survivor but a 'Holocaust orphan.' 'My parents gave me life a second time by sending me to safety in Switzerland, not knowing if they would ever see me again.' Ruth decided to emigrate to Mandatory Palestine. At 17, Ruth joined the Haganah defense in Jerusalem. Because of her diminutive height of 4 foot 7 inches she was trained as a scout and as a sniper. In 1948, Ruth was seriously wounded in action by an exploding shell during Israel's War of Independence, and it took months before she was able to walk again. In 1950, Ruth moved to France, where she studied and then taught psychology at the University of Paris. In 1956, she immigrated to the USA, settling in Manhattan and earning an M.A. degree in sociology and an Ed.D. degree from Teachers College, Columbia University, in 1970. Ruth is an American sex therapist, media personality, author, and radio and television talk show host.

Dr. Ruth Westheimer BY Rina Castelnuovo ISRAEL
JERUSALEM, 2019

ADA WINSTEN was born in 1934 in Poland. Ada was five when her family's lumber business and home in Baranowicze, Poland, was confiscated and the family of four was told to leave within 48 hours. Her father Michal Kuszner, who was a soldier in WWI, decided they would flee. Her parents begged extended family members to come with them. It was November 1939 and the family knew that they could not go West so decided to cross the border to Lithuania as illegal immigrants. The Kuszner family was among 15,000 Polish Jews who left Poland for Lithuania. They said goodbye to family members, many of whom would be killed. Ada remembers approaching the border in her father's arms, aware of the danger of getting caught. The Lithuanian soldiers came at the family with bayonets, and her aunt got down on her knees, and begged for their lives. The soldiers took Ada and her mother separately from her sister and her father, and they did not see each other for a few days. Ada does not remember how they reunited, but the family ended up spending a year and a half in Lithuania. At the border, Ada's memories stop and don't pick back up for another year, when the Kuszners fled again, this time on a train across Russia to Japan. Ada's family was saved by Chiune Sugihara, a Japanese diplomat who served as vice-consul for the Japanese Empire in Kaunas, Lithuania. During the Second World War, Sugihara helped some 6,000 Jews flee from Europe by issuing transit visas so that they could travel through to Japanese territory, risking his job and the lives of his family. From Japan, her family moved to Shanghai until 1948 and then on to the United States, eventually settling in the Bronx, in New York City. Ada became a successful clinical social worker specialist in Providence, Rhode Island.

Ada Winsten BY Steve Mason USA
PROVIDENCE, RHODE ISLAND, USA, 2019

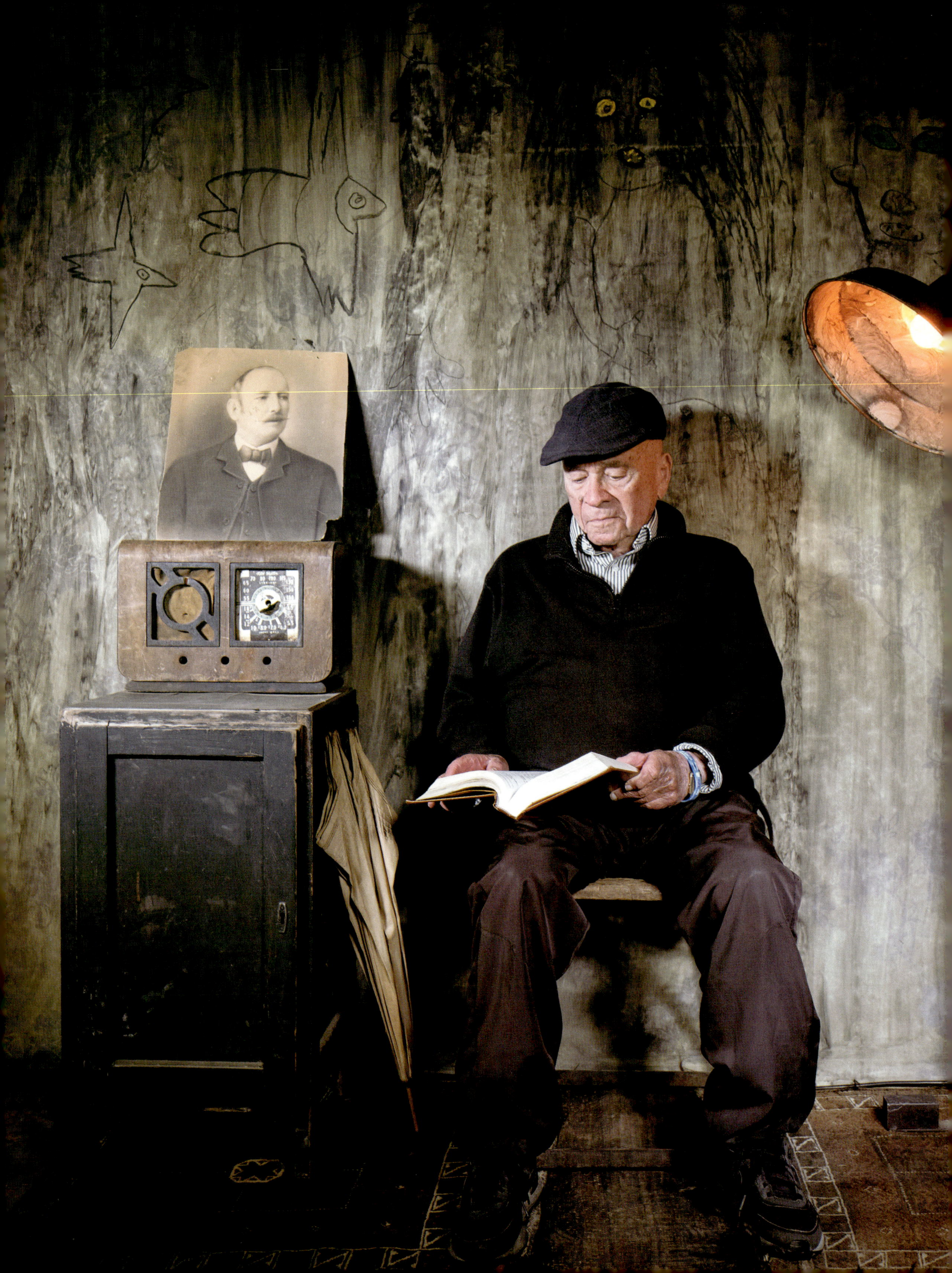

MORDECHAI PERLOV, photographed at 92 years old and living in Johannesburg, South Africa, was a Lithuanian-born Jew who was deported by the Red Army on June 14, 1941, from the shtetl of Rasein (Raseiniai) to the Gulag network of Soviet forced labor camps. Mordechai, his family and other Lithuanians were considered as enemies of the Soviet state and were taken as prisoners to chop trees in various labor camps. Mordechai recounted on his return from the forests to the family's barracks, 'I opened the door, and there both my parents are lying dead on the bed, and my sister Tova is lying in between them, sobbing.' Perlov's parents, like about a quarter of those sent to the Gulags, died of hunger and disease. Their family was among 5,000 Jews in the shtetl of Rasein expelled to the Gulag, crushed between Hitler's approaching troops and Stalin's suspicion of foreign residents who escaped from Poland to the former USSR during World War II. Mordechai miraculously escaped. He was 15 years old at the time and decided that he would rather 'escape this hell, than to die.' Mr. Perlov passed away at age 93 on January 20, 2020.

Mordechai Perlov BY **Roger Ballen** USA/SOUTH AFRICA
JOHANNESBURG, SOUTH AFRICA, 2019

IRÈNE (née Bibergal) and LÉON SAPIR were born in Paris in 1932. Irène escaped as a little child from the Vél d'Hiv Aktion (roundup) in Paris during the summer of 1942, when French police arrested 13,000 including 4,000 children, sending them all from Drancy to Auschwitz, including her mother and the rest of her family. In 1942, at ten years of age Léon Sapir joined the French underground and was assigned to cleaning weapons and as a young teenager became an expert in preparing explosives and fought against the Nazis. They have been married for 60 years.

Léon & Irène Sapir BY Thierry Soval FRANCE
LASCAUX, FRANCE, 2019

AHARON BARAK was born in Kaunas, Lithuania, the only son of Zvi Brick, an attorney, and his wife Leah, a teacher. After the Nazi occupation of the city in 1941, the family spent three years in the Kovno Ghetto. At the end of the war, after wandering through Hungary, Austria, and Italy, Aharon and his parents reached Rome, where they spent the next two years. In 1947, they received travel papers and immigrated to Mandatory Palestine. 'In July 1941, I was five when the Germans occupied the city of Kaunas in Lithuania, where I lived. We were 25,000 Jews in Kaunas and we were taken to a square where many were slaughtered. It was a pogrom. In 1943, the Germans carried out the Children's Aktion with the intention of eliminating all the remaining Jewish children. Miraculously I stayed alive finding refuge with my mother in a Lithuanian farm – Righteous Among the Nations – who saved our lives, until the Red Army came and liberated us from the Germans.' Barak played a key role in negotiating the 1978 Camp David peace talks with Egypt and was appointed to Israel's Supreme Court in 1978, a position he held for 28 years. In 1995 Barak wrote a decision helping to empower the court to strike down any laws it deemed unconstitutional. Barak was President of the Supreme Court for eleven years until retiring in 2006.

Aharon Barak BY Yossi Zamir ISRAEL
HERZLIYA, ISRAEL, 2019

Sisters **Goldie Szachter Kalib** (L) and **Rachell Szachter Eisenberg** (R) have their portrait taken at Goldie's home in Baltimore, Maryland, on July 21, 2019. They show the concentration camp number tattoos on their arms. A third sister with a consecutive number passed away recently. Just before the end of World War II, Dr. Josef Mengele made "the last Selektion." Goldie Szachter Kalib, then a 13-year old Jewish girl from Bodzentyn, Poland, was part of that Selektion, as well as her mother and sisters. The sisters' experiences included hiding with a Polish Christian family, and time spent in a slave labor camp. They were shipped to Auschwitz in 1944. The next year, the survivors of the extermination camp were forced on a death march to Bergen-Belsen.

Goldie Kalib & Rachell Eisenberg BY Carol Guzy USA
BALTIMORE, MARYLAND, USA, 2019

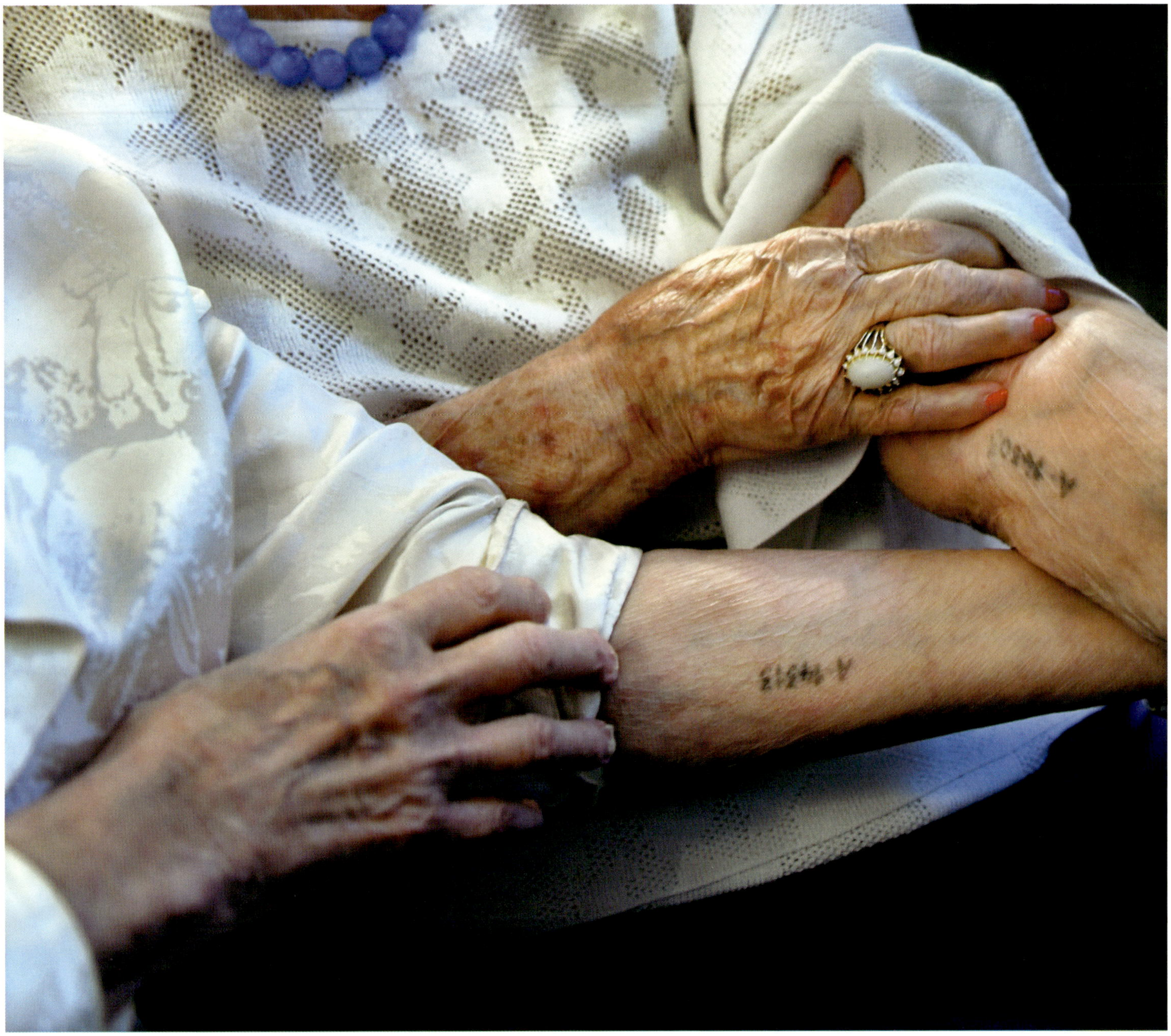

STELLA BICHLER was born in Zagreb, Croatia, in 1922. When the Germans invaded her family fled to Italy where they were caught in 1943. Stella, along with some of her family, was sent to Auschwitz-Birkenau extermination camp. 'We were not people in Auschwitz. We did not have a name. We were just a number. More than 75 years later I still repeat my number in German, 75692, even asleep. I didn't talk about the Holocaust with my kids. I just don't talk. The moment I do, I cry.' Her parents, two sisters and two brothers perished in the Holocaust. Stella immigrated to Israel in 1948, studied and then worked as a home economics teacher. Stella lives in Ramla.

Stella Bichler BY Yuval Chen ISRAEL
RAMLA, ISRAEL, 2019

Mordechay "Motke" Faer was born in Liège, Belgium, on 1934, the fifth child of parents who escaped from Mandatory Palestine following the 1929 Arab riots there. At the age of six, following the German invasion, his family escaped to France where they were captured and taken to the Agde concentration camp. After one year at the camp, the family managed to escape and lived in a village in Provence until the end of the war. Faer was raised as a Christian child, and only when the family arrived In Israel after the war he was told that he is Jewish. Faer lives today in Bitan Aharon. He has three children and five grandchildren.

Mordechay "Motke" Faer BY Gili Yaari ISRAEL
BITAN AHARON, ISRAEL, 2019

Eftychia Battinou Ezra was born in 1924 to Romaniote Jews, Behorakis and Stamoula Battinou, in Ioannina, Greece. Eftychia was the youngest of six brothers and sisters. On March 25, 1944, Greek Independence Day, she was arrested with her parents and three sisters, their husbands and two children. At the time, her brothers were in Athens and Egypt and succeeded in escaping arrest and expulsion. Eftychia was then transported to Larissa, one of the starting points for deportations to the Auschwitz-Birkenau death camp. In Auschwitz II-Birkenau she worked in the Kartoffelbunker (potato storage). She was also forced into Block 10, where women were subjected to Nazi medical experiments. In January 1945, as the Germans began to retreat, Eftychia was one of 60,000 prisoners who were forced on a death march. She was liberated from Bergen-Belsen by the British Army in April 1945. Eftychia returned to Greece, the only one of her family to survive the camps. Both her parents, and her three sisters with their husbands and two children, all perished. Eftychia passed away in August 2020.

Eftychia Battinou Ezra BY Artemis Alcalay GREECE
ATHENS, 2019

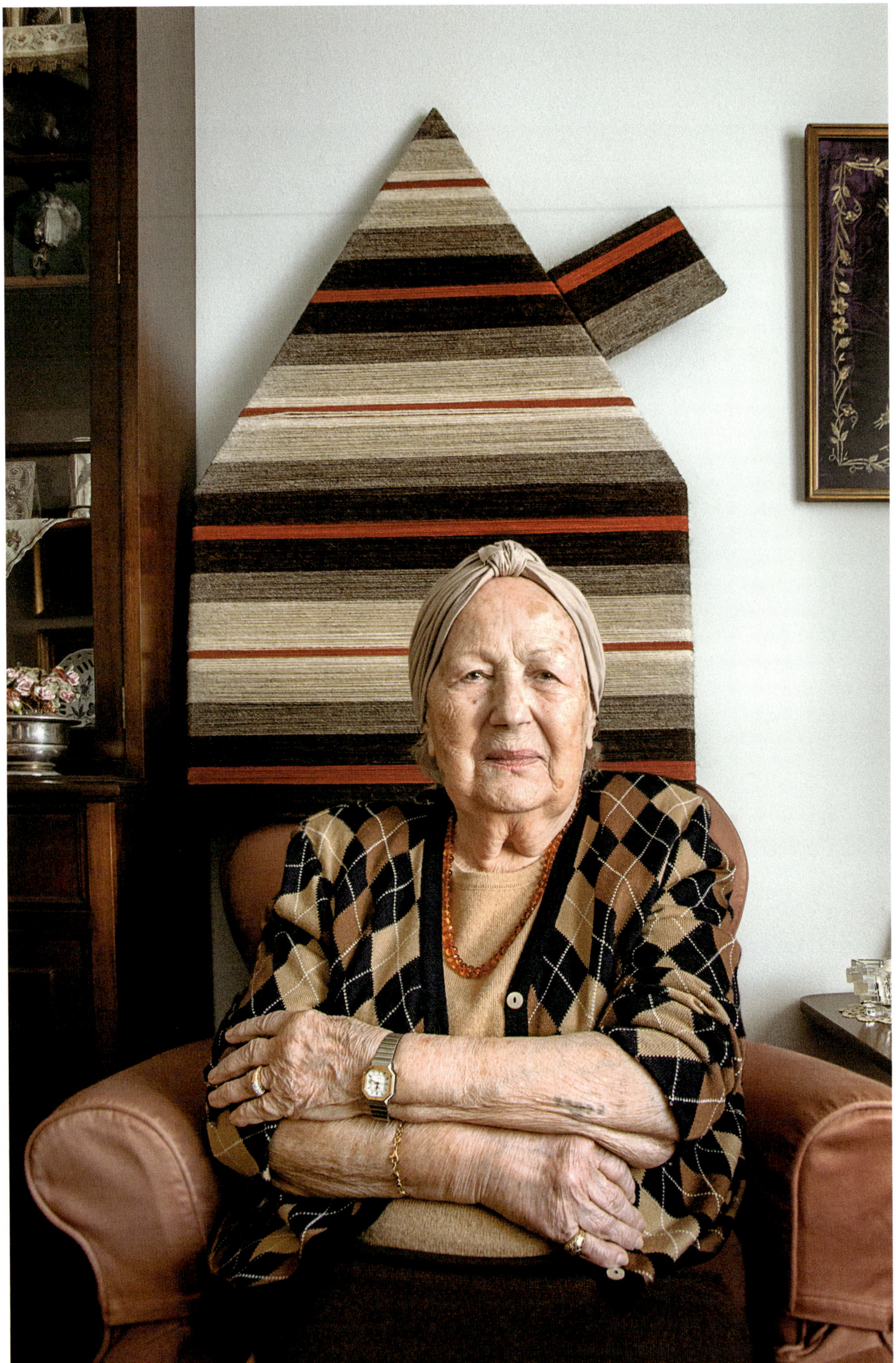

The fifth of 10 children, RALPH HAKMAN was born on March 11, 1925, in Radom, Poland. "You have to turn yourself in to the police," his mother Rose instructed her 17-year-old son after Ralph's oldest sister and her baby were caught in their hiding place and taken into custody. "Rivka and the baby will be released," Rose explained. Ralph was frightened and weeping, but he obeyed. "I knew I had to do it for my family," he said. In May 1942, after turning himself in, Ralph and other prisoners were marched through the ghetto to a waiting train. Ralph's mother and sister trailed him to the gate. 'That was the last time I saw them,' he said. Ralph was assigned to work in the Birkenau bathhouse, 75 feet from two crematoria. Ralph regularly observed his SS supervisor driving to the crematoria in a Red Cross van, donning a mask and emptying three canisters of Zyklon B crystal pellets into designated ports. Ralph heard the screams of the dying Jews, and then 15 minutes later, when the doors were opened, he saw the bodies tumble out. On January 18, 1945, as the Allies advanced, the prisoners were marched to Gleiwitz, divided into smaller groups and dispatched on death marches. Ralph trekked in the cold and snow with several hundred men for days and at gunpoint managed to flee the German guards, running until they spotted a Russian soldier on a bicycle, who told them the Allies had just liberated the area. It was May 7, 1945. Ralph Hakman passed away from COVID-19 complications in Los Angeles on March 22, 2020, just days after turning 95.

Ralph Hakman BY Barbara Davidson CANADA/USA
LOS ANGELES, CALIFORNIA, USA, 2019

Dov Landau was featured in the book *Exodus* by Leon Uris, and in the film. The only survivor of a large family, Dov was born in Brzesko, Poland, in 1928. On September 1, 1939, the Germans occupied his town and the synagogue was burned. Dov was apprehended at the age of 13 and sent to a labor camp. In 1942 the Germans transferred his mother and brother Naftali to a concentration camp. In August 1942, Dov escaped with his father and grandfather to the town of Bochnia. In 1943 he was recaptured by the Nazis with his father, two brothers and other family members. Dov and his father were sent to Auschwitz concentration camp, where he watched his family walk to the crematoria on November 5, 1943. On December 12, 1943, he was taken to work in the Jawisowiycz work camp. There Dov worked in the coal mines for a year and three months. On January 17, 1945, he was forced to walk on a death march to Buchenwald where, at the age of 16, he worked in a stone mine. On April 11, 1945, he was liberated by the US Army from the Buchenwald camp, the sole survivor of his large family. In June he was taken to France and boarded the boat Mataroa and on July 15, 1945, arrived at Haifa port in Mandatory Palestine. In 1948, while fighting in Israel's War of Independence, he was captured by the Jordanian army. A year later he was released in a prisoner exchange.

Dov Landau BY Nati Shohat ISRAEL
TEL AVIV, ISRAEL, 2019

ARIE AND BATYA SEGAL were born in Botosani, Romania, Arie in 1931 and Batya in 1941. When Romania entered World War II alongside Nazi Germany, the authorities expelled thousands of Jews living in the small towns and villages in historic Botosani County, forcing them into the city. Jews were subject to a wide range of harsh conditions, including forced labor, financial penalties, and discriminatory laws. Arie's father was taken to forced labor digging trenches in front lines. Batya's father was taken before her birth, which was so traumatic that it left Batya disabled. When the evacuation of Jews from villages and towns began, the clandestine Jewish Council learned of the details of the deportations to concentration camps and used personal contacts to gain the repeal of the agreement. Political conditions determined the destinies of the Romanian Jews, depending on the regions in which they were living, and their proximity to the frontline. The total number of deaths is not certain but estimated to be about 250,000 Jews and another 25,000 deported Romani. Most of the Jewish population living in Botosani survived the war. Arie and Batya both have memories of great hunger and hearing the shells and bombings by the advancing Red Army. They survived when Botoșani was captured on April 7, 1945, by Soviet troops. They immigrated to Israel after its establishment.

Arie & Batya Segal BY Corinna Kern GERMANY
BAT YAM, ISRAEL, 2019

RACHEL GERA was born in the Neve Tzedek area of Tel Aviv, then part of Mandatory Palestine. Known then as Rachel Steinberg, she sailed with her mother to visit family in Poland about half a year before the outbreak of World War II, while her father stayed in Tel Aviv. During visits with grandparents and aunts, her mother quickly realized an urgent need to find a way out of Poland, where Rachel saw the SS march Jewish men out of their homes. She and her mother packed valuables into corsets and took the family silverware as they fled to the Russian border. Soldiers at the border took their valuables, but in the confusion, someone bribed a boat owner to take them to Lvov on the USSR border. A few months later they were herded into trucks and sent to exile, to Siberia or the Urals. Rachel's mother was sent to forced labor cutting down trees. The children there were half-starved and freezing. In 1942, with the Stalin-Sikorski Agreement, Rachel and her mother were released, and they went to Tashkent. Her mother took her to a train station and hung a bag of cloth around her neck with a note on which she wrote Rachel's name and the address 19 Dizengoff Street, Tel Aviv, Palestine. Her mother, wearing a pink dress Rachel remembered, pushed her into a moving train that was meant for war orphans. The train went to Tehran where Rachel joined a small group of children bound for Palestine. Miraculously, Rachel's mother also arrived there some months later, and they were reunited. Rachel remembered she was wearing the same pink dress. Later still, after lengthy negotiations with British authorities, the Tehran Children sailed to Atlit on the Israeli coast, where Rachel again saw her father. Rachel's family announced on February 14, 2023, that Rachel had passed away.

Rachel Gera BY Heidi Levine USA

JAFFA, ISRAEL, 2019

JACOB (JACKIE) HANDELI was born in 1928 in Thessaloniki, Greece, to a family of six. The family's roots in Thessaloniki date to the 16th century. In 1941, the Germans entered Thessaloniki and applied anti-Jewish laws. The Baron Hirsch neighborhood of the city was turned into a ghetto for the city's Jews. Jackie's family was deported to Poland on a cramped freight train. After about a week, the passengers were left without water and food, and each time the train stopped, the Nazis would remove the bodies of those who had not survived the journey. There in the wagon, Jackie learned his first sentence in German: "You won't need it anymore." The train arrived at the Auschwitz death camp. Jackie was separated from his parents and sisters, and never saw them again. He and his brothers Judah and Samuel were separated among the sub-camps for forced labor. Jackie and his brothers, like the other Thessalonians, were unable to communicate with other Jews in the camp because they only spoke Greek. At Auschwitz (Bonn), Jackie's brothers were sent to death, and he was left alone. The Thessaloniki boxer Jacko Rezon managed to obtain food and shared it with Jackie, saving him from starvation. In January 1945, the prisoners were sent on a death march. Jackie remembers the snow-covered road that was stained with blood. Those who survived arrived at Bergen-Belsen, until the British liberated the camp. In 1947, Jackie sailed to Mandatory Palestine with other volunteers to take part in the 1948 war for Israel's independence. Jackie Handeli passed away just before Israel's Yom HaShoah in April 2021.

Jacob "Jackie" Handeli BY Simcha Barbiro ISRAEL

JERUSALEM, 2019

László Roth was born in 1920 in Romania. At the age of 21 he began studying composition and conducting in the Budapest music academy, but he was forced to quit in 1943 due to antisemitic proclamations. Roth and his parents were forced into the Budapest Ghetto. In 1944 the entire family was shipped to Auschwitz, with most being sent to their deaths upon arrival. In Auschwitz, Roth was forced for weeks to remove bodies from the crematorium. Later, he was sent with his father to the Mauthausen camp, where Roth was forced to serve in the camp's orchestra as an accordion player as prisoners marched to their deaths. Roth was later transferred to Ebensee camp, where he was released by US soldiers. Roth and his father were the sole survivors in his family. Roth had a rich musical career as both a composer and conductor before emigrating to Israel in 1960, where his career flourished.

László Roth BY Tzachi Ostrovsky ISRAEL

BAT YAM, ISRAEL, 2019

NINA DINAR from Kiryat Ono fulfilled a dream this week, a strange-sounding one to anyone not familiar with her amazing story. Dinar, who turns 94 next month, wished to hug a Great Dane, 'like the one that saved me during the Holocaust.' For two hours she stroked, hugged and patted the backs of two dogs that were brought especially to her house. The moving encounter was orchestrated by Tammy Bar-Joseph, who in recent years has been investigating an unusual branch of history: dogs in the Holocaust. Along with many testimonies of Nazis using dogs to attack Jews, she is documenting lesser-known stories having to do with Nazi-owned dogs saving Jews. This is how she reached Dinar, hearing her rescue story for the first time. Dinar was born in Warsaw in 1926. Ever since she was a child she loved and raised dogs. 'Even though it was said that Jews don't have dogs, I grew up with some,' says Dinar, speaking to *Ha'aretz* newspaper (August 2, 2019). 'Even my grandmother had dogs.'

Nina Dinar BY Ittai Bar-Joseph ISRAEL
KIRYAT ONO, ISRAEL, 2019

ARIE ESHEL "Leibale" was born in Romania in 1932. In 1941, Arie and his family were evicted from their home and began a period of hunger and wandering, looking for a shelter, only to be expelled from one place to another. Overnight, 'at age nine, I became a man.' His mother died first, and soon after, his father. Arie, his sister Chana and brother Shaul became beggars, knocking on doors for food and begging for shelter during the cold winters, suffering starvation and illness, wandering from one war zone to another for almost three years. Toward the end of the war, the children found temporary shelter in separate farms in exchange for labor. At war's end, Shaul left for Israel, and in June 1946 Arie and Chana joined other orphaned children for travel to Mandatory Palestine. British soldiers transferred Arie and Chana from the ship to the Atlit Detention Camp. For Arie, it felt like a 10-star hotel or something close to heaven. After a few weeks in detention, he was sent to a kibbutz where his life changed. 'Believe me, a huge miracle, I, Leibale, who survived the most terrible years of cold and hunger, I made it, I built a home with my Nira and a kibbutz, and brought to this world four beautiful boys, my pride, four Israeli Air Force pilots, they made me the proudest father in the world.' Arie Eshel passed away several weeks before Israel's Holocaust Remembrance Day, Yom HaShoah, in April 2023.

Arie Eshel BY Micha Bar-Am ISRAEL
TEL AVIV, ISRAEL, 2019

Ruby Sosnowicz was born in Warsaw, Poland, 81 years ago. He miraculously escaped the Warsaw Ghetto alone during the uprising and became a child in hiding. He hid in a barn for three years, thanks to a kind Polish farmer. Ruby is a retired musician and hairdresser, who survived and now lives in Delray Beach, Florida. Ruby has created many bands and orchestras including the original Holocaust Survivor Band, and has entertained thousands of people throughout the United States, Paris, Canada, Europe and Israel. He is a historian and archivist of Jewish music and performed at hundreds of venues including New York's Yiddish Theater, The Ed Sullivan Show, Jacob Javitz Convention Center, Kings Theater, Studio 54 and John F. Kennedy Center for the Performing Arts all with incredible reviews. In Florida he is part of the Holocaust Survivor Band, where they sing and play to remember and to forget.

Ruby Sosnowicz by Mauricio Candela USA
BOCA RATON, FLORIDA, USA, 2019

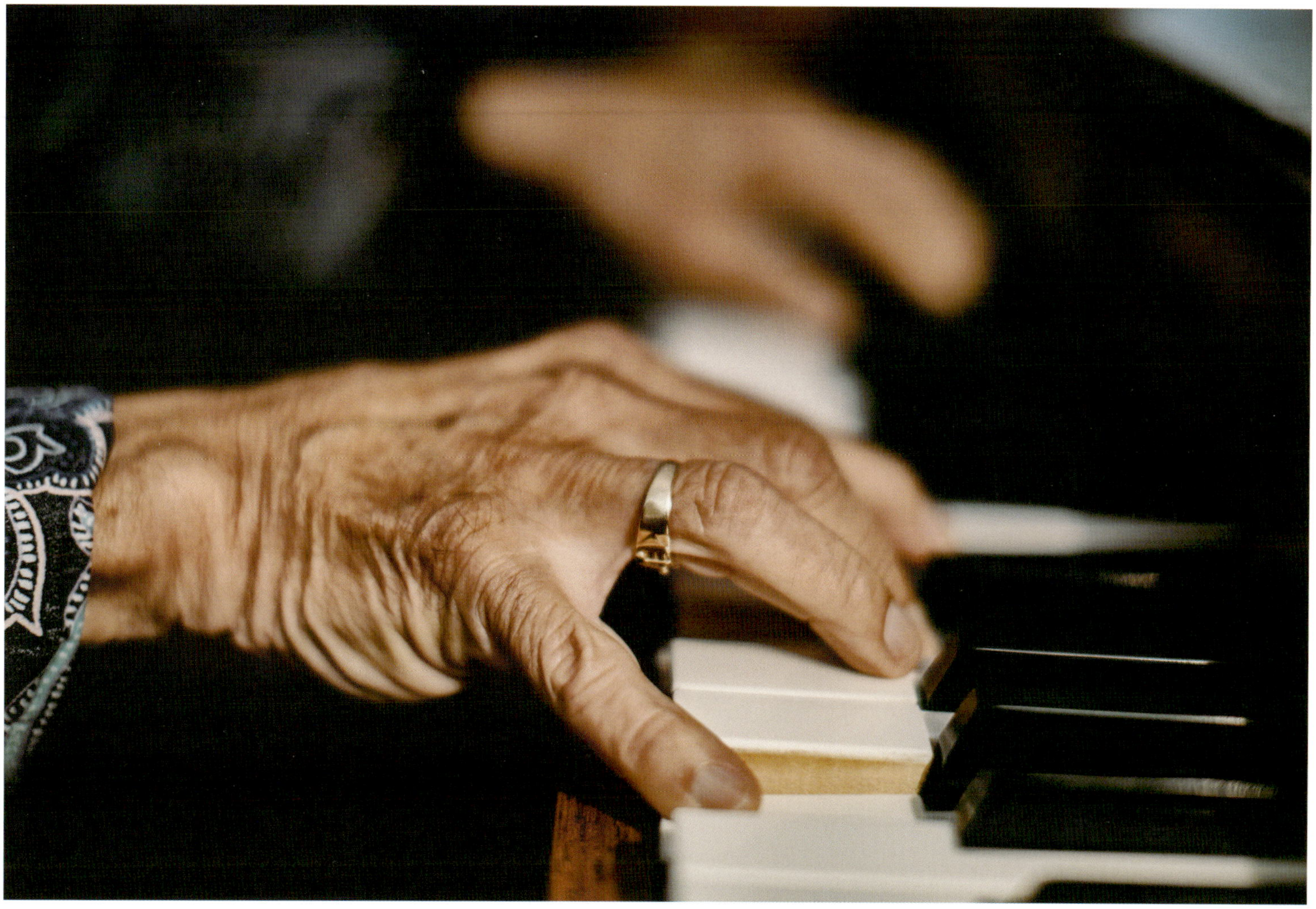

GERDA WEISSMANN KLEIN was born in 1924, in Bielsko, Poland. Gerda and her brother Arthur grew up relatively unaware of the spread of Nazism, until Poland was invaded in 1939. Gerda and her family watched in disbelief as people, ethnic Germans living in Poland, began flying the Nazi flag and using the Hitler salute. Soon after, Arthur was taken away on a transport and never seen again. In April 1942, Gerda and her parents were ordered into the Bielsko Ghetto. In 1942, Gerda was separated from her father, who was sent to a death camp, where he perished. Gerda was forced to separate from her mother, last seen when they boarded separate convoys to concentration camps. Gerda was sent to the Sosnowitz transit camp in Poland, and then moved from camp to camp. As Allied forces advanced in January 1945, Gerda was forced on a 350-mile death march along with 4,000 other women, including three close friends with whom she had been in the camps, Ilse Kleinzahler, Liesl Steppe, and Suse Kunz. During the death march, Ilse Kleinzahler died in her sleep after telling Gerda that she wouldn't be going further. The death march went through Dresden, Chemnitz, Zwickau, Reichenbach, Plauen, and on through Wallern (now Volary in the modern-day Czech Republic). Gerda was one of fewer than 120 women who survived the exposure to the winter, starvation and arbitrary executions. Gravely ill in May 1945, Gerda was liberated by forces of the United States Army. Among them was US Lieutenant Kurt Klein. Kurt was born and raised in Waldorf, Germany. When Hitler ascended to power, Klein's parents sent the 17-year-old Kurt and their other children to safety in the United States. In 1942, his parents were deported to Auschwitz, where they perished. Kurt was drafted that year and served in the US Army as an intelligence officer. In May 1945, he stumbled upon an abandoned factory in Volary, Czechoslovakia, where about 120 girls were near death. One of the girls guided Lt. Klein to her fellow prisoners, most of whom lay sick and dying on the ground. Gerda was white-haired, weighed 68 pounds, and was one day shy of her 21st birthday. A great love affair began. Gerda and Kurt married in 1946 in Paris before returning to Kurt's home in America. Settling in Scottsdale, Arizona, the couple had three children and eight grandchildren. Gerda was the subject of the Oscar-winning documentary *One Survivor Remembers*, based on her life. The story of Kurt's indefatigable but ultimately unsuccessful efforts to save his parents was chronicled in the award-winning PBS program *America and the Holocaust*. In 2001, Gerda and Kurt received joint doctorates from Chapman University for their collective work fighting racism and intolerance. In 2011, President Barack Obama awarded Gerda Weissman Klein the Presidential Medal of Freedom, the highest civilian award of the United States. On April 6, 2022, Yad Vashem in Jerusalem announced that Gerda Klein had passed away.

Gerda Weissmann Klein BY Patrick Zachmann MAGNUM PHOTOS FRANCE
PHOENIX, ARIZONA, USA, 2019

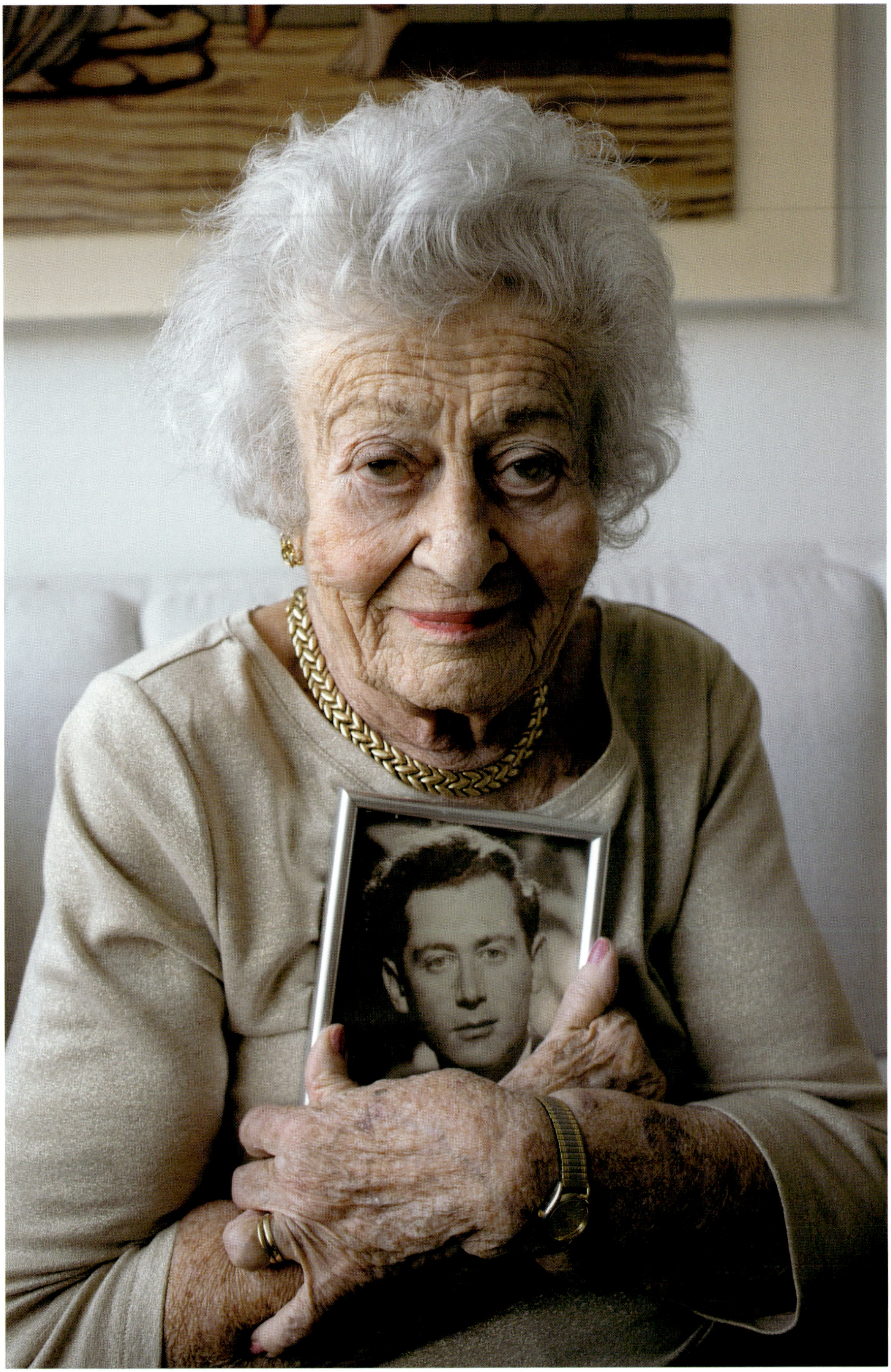

HANKA was born in Chmielnik, Poland. On September 5, 1939, the town was conquered by the Germans, who soon assembled Jewish dignitaries in the synagogue and burned them alive. In 1941, the Nazis established a ghetto, covering the whole city except streets adjacent to the fields, so Hanka lived at home until 1942. The liquidation of the ghetto began in 1942 and it was the last time Hanka saw her mother, when Nazis separated the men and women. About 12,000 Jews were deported to the Treblinka death camp. The majority of them were killed at once. A Polish friend of Hanka's father obtained Aryan papers for her, and she was smuggled out of the ghetto to a Polish family from October 1942 to January 1943, pretending to be Catholic. Frightened of being discovered by the Gestapo and of the risk to the Polish family should she be caught, she returned to Chmielnik. In January 1943, she was transported with her father to Kielce Hassag to work in a munitions factory. Hanka spoke fluent German and was sent to forced labor in an ammunition factory. In January 1945 she was transported to Bergen-Belsen concentration camp. In March 1945, the prisoners were told they were being transported to Bavaria to make ammunition there. The Allied bombing damaged the roads and trains. They never made it to Bavaria. An order came from Berlin to transfer all prisoners to Dachau. Hanka marched with other prisoners towards Dachau. When the Allies began bombing the roads, the Nazi guards scattered for cover, and Hanka and other prisoners ran away and went to a house on the outskirts of Turkheim on April 30. A German woman let them sleep at her home. Hanka was freed. Anne Weinbaum passed away on November 25, 2020.

Anne Hanke Weinbaum BY Debra Friedman CANADA
TORONTO, CANADA, 2019

INA REINART RAKAVY was born in Krakow, Poland, in 1935. Ina's teddy bear, Missio, was a gift from her grandfather Maurice. When Nazi Germany invaded Poland, Ina was four years old. Her family escaped and moved from one ghetto to another before reaching Warsaw where they went into hiding, assisted by Poles. After the Warsaw Uprising, in which Ina's father was murdered, the Gestapo rounded up thousands of Poles from the underground, including Jews who were sheltered by Poles. Entire neighborhoods were searched and exposed and evicted in house-to-house searches. Ina and her mother were among those captured and expelled to death camps. Just before their expulsion, Ina's mother sewed from a curtain a small backpack for Missio, tied it tight to Ina's backpack while boarding the train to Auschwitz and to their deaths. But the train stopped abruptly at the gates of the death camp. It was overcrowded, they were told, and as the train backed up towards the fields, its passengers fled. Ina wrote in her memoir that German soldiers took pity over her and her mother and took them, on their train, back to Krakow where the two went into hiding till the end of the war. When Ina immigrated to Israel in 1971, Missio came along.

Ina Reinart Rakavy & Missio BY Igal Slavin ISRAEL

JERUSALEM, 2019

ELLEN and her husband JERRY KAIDANOW are both Holocaust survivors. Jerry was born in 1933 in a small shtetl called Krivitchi in Poland. In April 1942, his parents were murdered by the Nazis. Jerry and his older brother Howard fled to Kurenets where they took refuge with their aunt's family. Later that year Jerry and his family escaped the liquidation of Kurenets by hiding in the Naroch Forest for the remainder of the war. Ellen Kaidanow was born Shifra Leviatin in Dubno, Poland, in June 1936. Her parents and two sisters were killed in the liquidation of the Dubno Ghetto. Ellen survived because of the bravery of her nanny Lena Dudzinsky. Lena took Ellen from the ghetto and presented Ellen to the world as her illegitimate daughter.

Jerry & Ellen Kaidanow BY Seth Harrison USA
WHITE PLAINS, NEW YORK, USA, 2019

YECHIEL ALEXANDER was born on March 19, 1927, in the city of Lodz, Poland, to a religious family. On May 1, 1940, he and his family were transferred to the ghetto. In 1941, his father was shot dead and his mother died of starvation. He stayed with his grandfather and his aunts. In July 1944, upon the liquidation of the ghetto, he was transferred to Auschwitz camp and received the number B7910. When the camp was liquidated on January 20, 1945, he was transferred to the Mauthausen camp for five days on a death march, and from there to other camps. On May 4, 1945, he was liberated by the US Army and transferred to Italy by Jewish Brigade personnel. From there he immigrated to Israel on the ship *Josiah Wedgwood* in June 1946. Upon his arrival in the country, he was transferred by the English to the Atlit Detention Camp and from there to Kibbutz Alonim. On Black Saturday, he was captured and transferred again to Atlit Detention Camp until October 1946. In November 1946 he was sworn into the Haganah paramilitary organization. Later, in March 1948, he enlisted in the Palmach, serving in Company C, in the 1st Battalion of the Yiftah Brigade.

Yechiel Alexander BY Avishag Shaar-Yashuv ISRAEL
KAKUR, ISRAEL, 2019

Four Holocaust survivors who do not know one another get together in Tel Aviv for a photo portrait, where they all display the tattooed numbers on their arms. Right to left, **Shmuel Blumenfeld** was born in Poland in 1926. He survived Poichov, Auschwitz and Theresienstadt. Shmuel was Adolf Eichmann's prison guard in Israel. **Yehuda Maimon** was born in Poland in 1924. He was a member of the "HaChalutz HaLochem" (The Fighting Pioneer) underground group in Krakow and is a survivor of Auschwitz. **Baruch Kasher** – 75 years later, he will not share his testimony. The tattooed number indicates he survived Auschwitz. **Tommy Schwartz Shacham** was born in Slovakia in 1933. In 1944, he was sent to the Auschwitz-Birkenau camp where the men, and the boys over 10, were separated from the women. He was left alone in the children's block. In 1945, the Germans took all the children still alive, on a death march from Birkenau to an unknown destination. The Red Army was approaching and during the march the Germans fled. The children continued alone until they arrived at Auschwitz, where they stayed until the liberation. Shmuel Blumenfeld passed away on the day before Passover, Thursday, April 14, 2022. He was 95. Yehuda Maimon, seen next to Shmuel, passed away in November 2020.

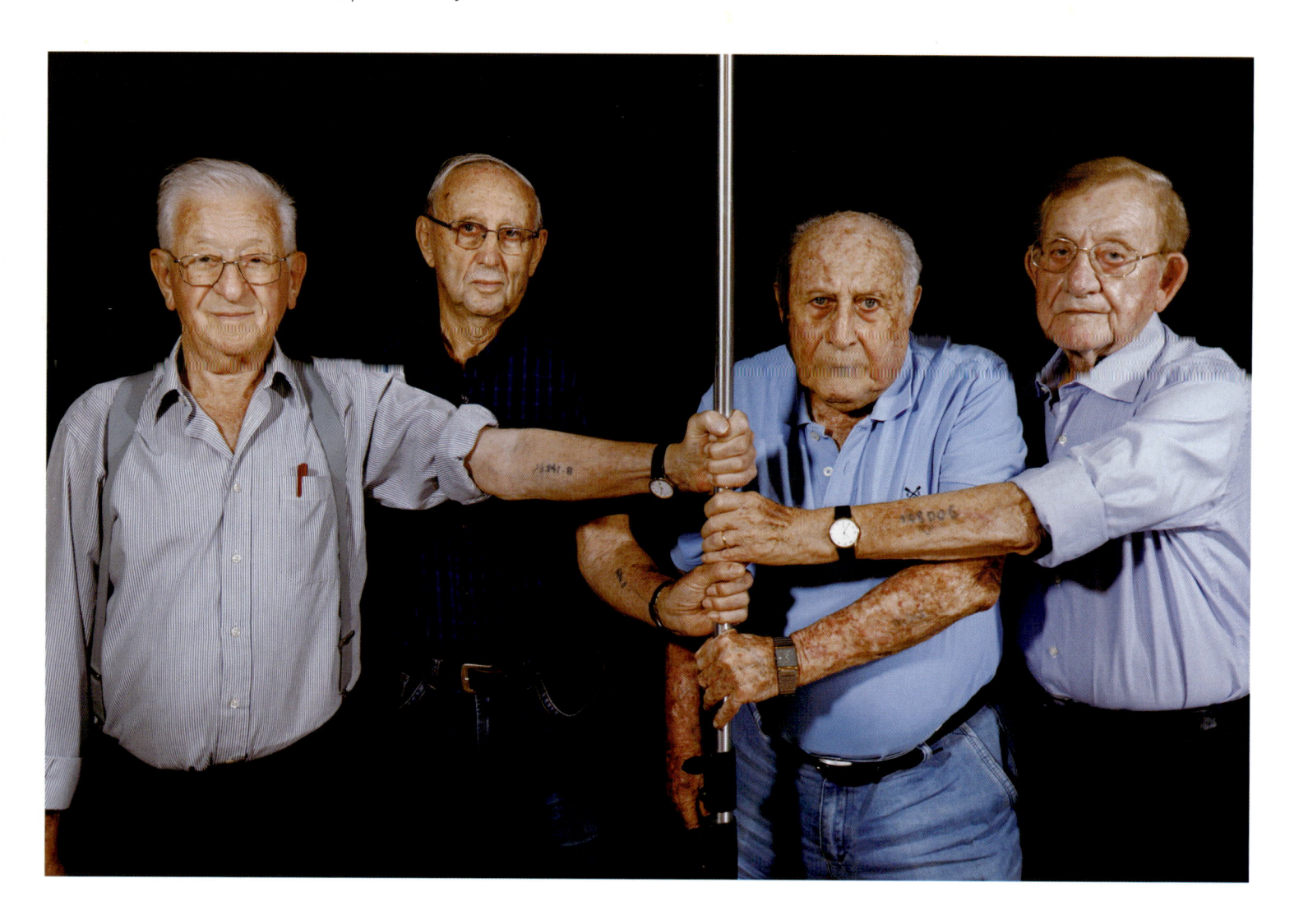

Four Auschwitz Survivors by Ziv Koren ISRAEL

TEL AVIV, ISRAEL, 2019

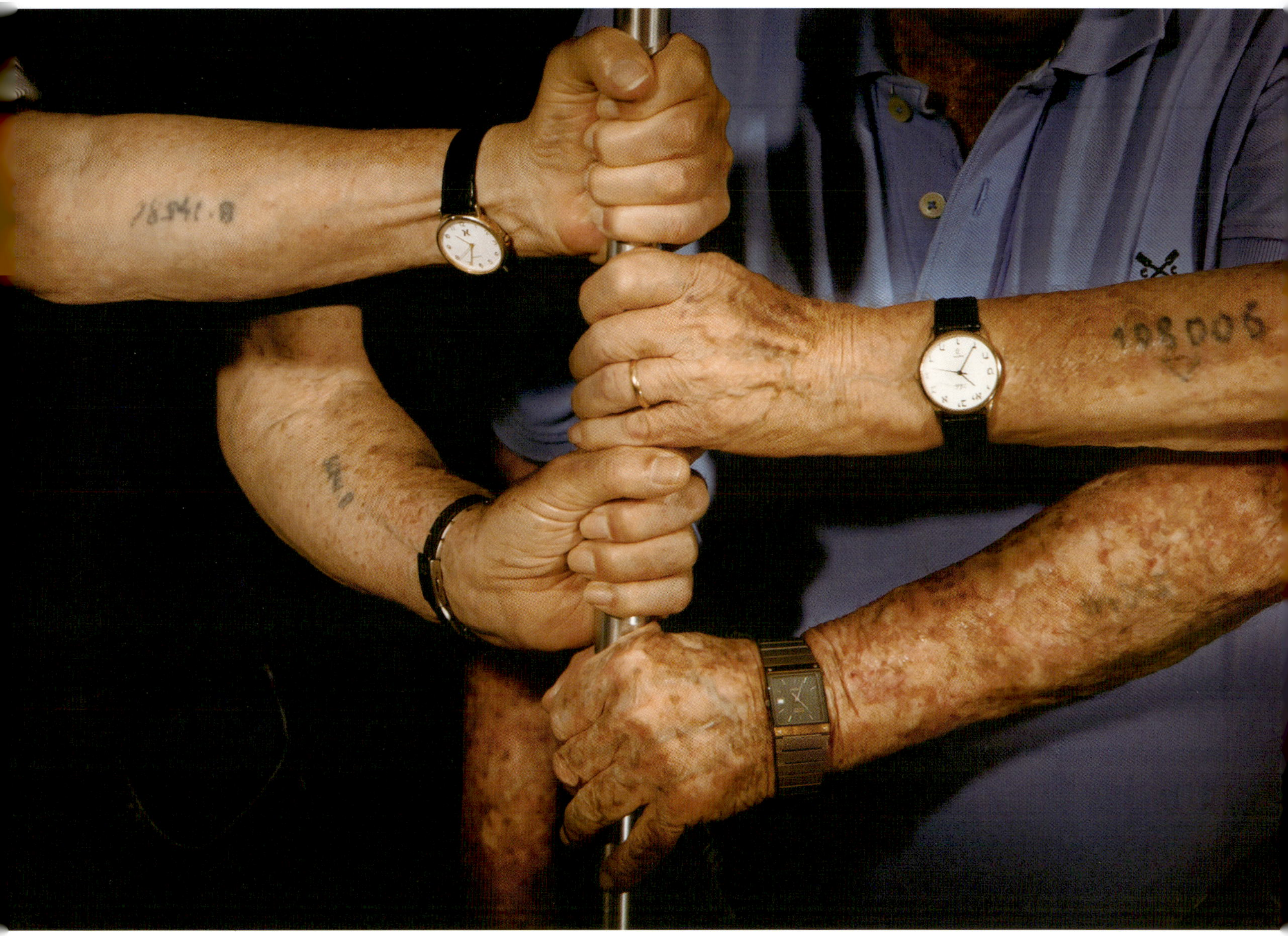

SARA (LILI) LEICHT was born in 1929 in Romania, and lived in Tileagd with her father Ignace (Yom-Tov), mother Ferenzi Hermina, and six siblings. In April 1944, weeks after the German occupation, Sara's family was deported to the Oradea Ghetto and from there to Auschwitz. In May 1944, upon arrival at the camp, Sara was separated from her family, who were all sent to their deaths. After being rescued from the gas chambers, she was sent to Fallersleben, where she worked in a weapons factory. With the advance of the Red Army, Sara was transferred to a labor camp in the city of Salzwedel, where she was liberated by the US Army. Sara immigrated to pre-state Israel on the illegal immigrant ship *Max Nordau*. With the outbreak of war in 1948, Sara joined the Palmach unit of the then-underground army and fought with the Harel Brigade for Israel's independence. Sara Leicht passed away just before Israel's Yom HaShoah in early April 2021.

Sara Leicht BY Raday Rubenstein ISRAEL
JERUSALEM, 2019

HENRY FRIEDMAN was born in 1928 in Brody, Poland. He recalls the discrimination he faced at the onset of the war when, at the age of 10, he was told by a classmate to 'wait until Hitler comes, he'll take care of you!' In 1939, when the Russians occupied Brody, his family lost their business and many of their private possessions. After the Nazis invaded in 1941, Henry recalls the police catching his mother without her Star of David armband and beating her so badly that she could not raise her arms for a month. One day in February 1942, a young Ukrainian woman named Julia Symchuck ran to the Friedmans' house and warned Henry's father that the Gestapo was coming for him, enabling Henry's father to flee in time. These roundups, called Aktions, sent 4,500 Jews to the Belzec death camp. In October 1942, the Friedmans were ordered to move into the ghetto, but were able to get help from two Ukrainian families who hid three of his family members in a barn. The space was about the size of a queen-size bed. Henry's father went to a separate hiding place nearby. They learned that most of the Jews in the Brody Ghetto were sent directly to their deaths in the Majdanek death camp. For 18 months, the Friedmans remained in hiding, freezing and slowly starving as food became scarcer. Finally, in March 1944, the Russians liberated the village of Suchowola, and the Friedmans. Later, Julia Symchuck was recognized as one of the Righteous Among the Nations by Yad Vashem, the World Holocaust Remembrance Center in Jerusalem, and was reunited with Henry Friedman in Seattle in 1989. Henry is a member of the Holocaust Center for Humanity's Speakers Bureau.

Henry Friedman BY Todd Weinstein USA
WEST BLOOMFIELD, MICHIGAN, USA, 2019

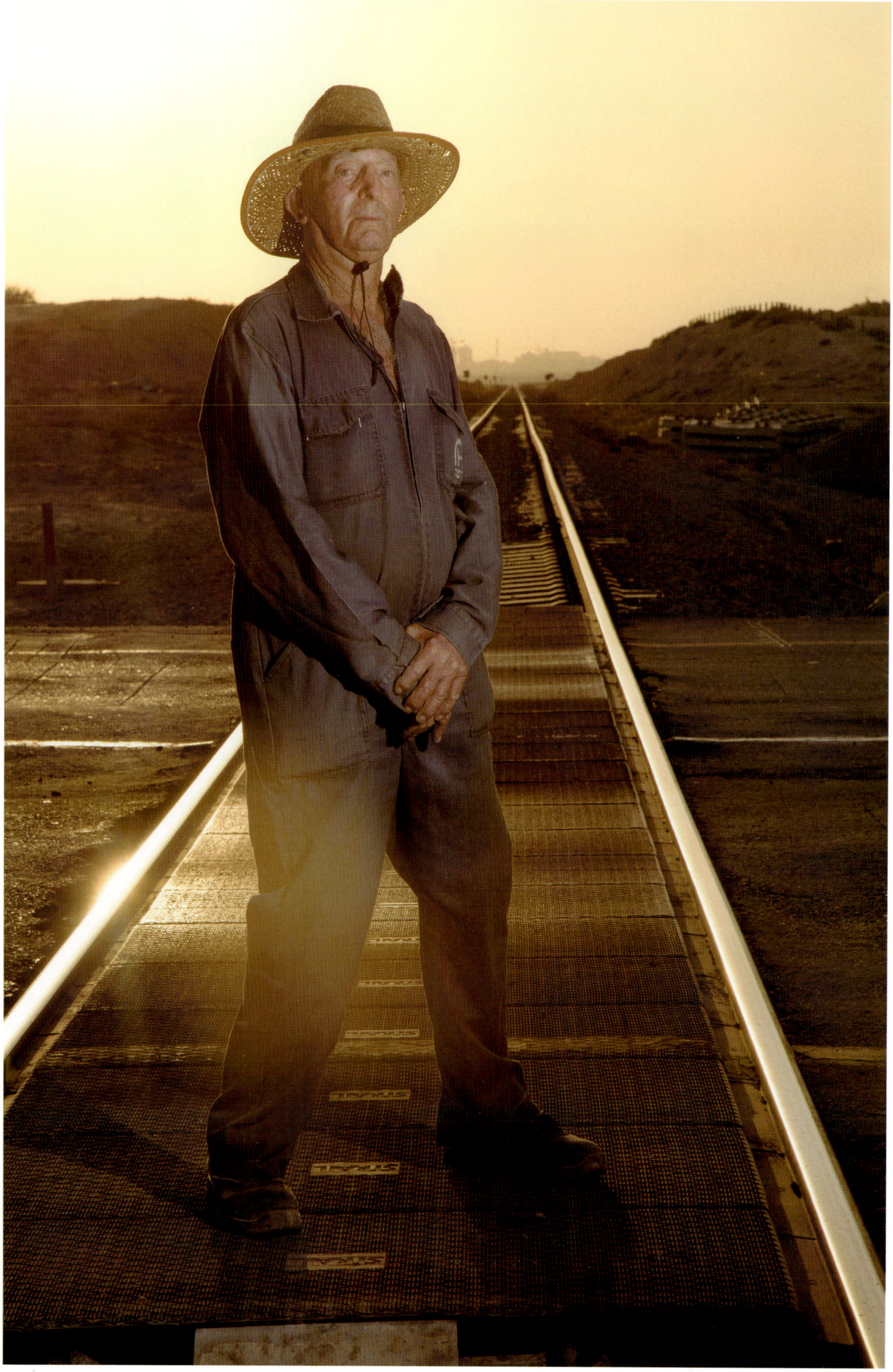

GERA GABRIEL was born in 1934 in Budapest, Hungary, as Gery Gorge. Gera was silent for 75 years, and only in 2019 shared his testimony for the first time. 'In 14 November 1944, the police were going from house to house, arresting all the Jews. My mom, my aunt with my cousin, we were all chased to a brick factory courtyard and pushed into an overcrowded train wagon. We traveled for [a] few hours and the train stopped, I remember it was hard to breathe. I believe we were at some border crossing when the train doors opened just a bit, I remember that fresh air. The Germans with the Hungarian police were guarding the train, my mom with my aunt pushed us through the people towards the exit door; there they bribed the Hungarian guard with their rings and jewelry, I [had] seen it when the guard turned his head away, I remember. My mother hugged me tight, kissed me and said, "be a good boy, make people love you." "Never ever say you are Jewish," she said and pushed me off the train. So was my cousin. We were sobbing, we knew, I tried hard not to, but we couldn't stop. My mom's last words were, "Go back to Budapest, I will return soon." We ran towards the fields and hid until it was dark, we started to walk, and we walked all night; it was cold, so cold and I don't remember but somehow, we reached Budapest. Juausz my cousin was crying all the time, I tried to make him stop and help him walk, even carried him a bit, but he couldn't. And then we saw the Danube, you can't be mistaken when you see the Danube, and we knew we have returned to the ghetto but our home was occupied by strangers. Some houses were bombed, we were hungry and cold most of the time but we had a place to sleep. Again, soon after our return the Germans rounded [up] all the Jews left in the ghetto and walk them to the river. I knew and I warned [my] cousin we should hide, we should stay in the back of the long line of people. When we reached the edge of the bridge, I pushed him over and jumped after him, we heard the shooting, the screams, the water became red and the ice floating on the river was red, I saw all the bodies of our people from the ghetto. No one survived. Me and my cousin, we did. We were hungry most of the time, hiding all the time, always close to death so many times. After the liberation we both were taken to an orphanage and from there to Israel – and I want to say – I win! I win! I win!'

Gera Gabriel BY Nadav Neuhaus ISRAEL
BE'ER SHEVA, ISRAEL, 2019

HELGA SCHMITZ was born in 1934 in Germany. Her large family had been the only Jewish family in town since the 1800s. When Hitler came to power, Helga's father was warned to get out of town. They fled to a relative in Luxembourg just as the Nazis were rounding up Jews there. The family was forced to separate. Helga and her mother were loaded on cattle trains to Gurs concentration camp in France. Her father was taken to Camp LeMille. Helga's mother played the piano and was a singer, and it saved her life; she played for the Nazi officer's club in the camp. Helga's mother trained her daughter to act as a non-Jew and taught her to dig bare-handed under the barbed wire, preparing her escape. Helga did escape into the woods. When French Jewish partisans found her, she had been eating mushrooms and flowers for days. Helga was smuggled into a convent where she was forced to convert to Catholicism. Her mother soon succeeded in escaping, and after locating Helga, the two escaped again, hiding with a French Catholic family who was paid by a clandestine Jewish organization. Fake documents were arranged and the two boarded an Italian freighter for Casablanca. Some time later they were reunited with Helga's father, who was gravely ill. They boarded a ship to New York, but they were denied entry. The Dominican Republic was the only country which allowed refugees to enter, and it became home for four years until they arrived In Florida. Later they settled in New York.

Helga Schmitz BY Nadav Neuhaus ISRAEL
NEW ROCHELLE, NEW YORK, USA, 2019

ABRAHAM MICHAEL GRINZAID was born in 1926 in Romania (now Moldova). Abraham was the only son. After the Nazi German invasion his parents decided to leave their home and their extended family and flee east. They were on the road for almost a year before succeeding to escape Nazi forces. After his father died, following an injury, and his mother was gravely ill, 'I understood what was happening to the Jews under Nazi occupation.' At age 17, Abraham located a safe place for his mother while he enlisted in the Red Army. 'I joined the Red Army to take revenge. My father died because of the Nazis, my relatives were in the ghettos and sent to their deaths. I was alone and my only desire was to avenge my family's deaths.' Abraham served in Unit 365 of the Red Army and after six months was sent to Estonia to the front lines. From there he was transferred to the Paratroopers Brigade and later served in an intelligence unit sent out to fight on Nazi German soil. 'We saw death in front of our eyes every day.' For his heroism in the war he received the Medal of Courage, and the Medal of Fame. After the war Abraham continued to serve in the Red Army until 1950. He completed his higher education and became a teacher and later a college principal in Kishinev. 'I appeal to the Jewish people, don't forget it! One million and a half Jews fought against the Nazis.' In 1990, he immigrated to Israel with his family and became the chairman of the National World War II Veterans Alliance. On the last visit of Russian President Vladimir Putin to Israel, they shook hands.

Abraham Michael Grinzaid BY **Kobi Wolf** ISRAEL

REHOVOT, ISRAEL, 2019

EDOUARD MENDELSOHN (LESSEL) was born in 1934 in Paris to immigrants from Poland. In June 1942, soon after Edouard was forced to wear the yellow star in school, his father hoped to find safety in the countryside but the family was arrested by the French police. Edouard's mother Perla was transferred to Drancy and deported to Auschwitz by convoy no. 10 on July 24, 1942. Soon after, Edouard's brother, Marcel, was also deported to Auschwitz and his father, Wolf, was denounced and transferred to Drancy and deported to Auschwitz by convoy no. 21 on August 19, 1942. Edouard was left alone. A French widow in the village, Lise Septier Fuga, gave the boy shelter and treated him like a son. After the war Moigny-sur-École was Edouard's home until he immigrated to Israel in 1958. On October 24, 2017, Yad Vashem in Jerusalem awarded the woman who sheltered Eddy, Lise Fuga, the title Righteous among the Nations. At 85 years of age, Eddy still works as a farmer in an agricultural village in Israel.

Edouard Mendelsohn Lessel BY Perry Trotter NEW ZEALAND

MOSHAV KOHAV MICHAEL, ISRAEL, 2019

ERNST VERDUIN was born in 1927 in Amsterdam to a non-religious Jewish family. In 1942, the family was forced to move to one of the ghettos in Amsterdam. The Verduin family went into hiding, but was arrested and brought to Camp Vught. Ernst was 15. In September 1943, he and his sister Wanda were deported with a group via Westerbork to Auschwitz. He was sent to the gas chamber. Ernst had been informed about the gas chambers by an SS man. He begged an SS man in Auschwitz-Birkenau for his life. The SS did not allow this, and sent him back to the gas chamber group. Ernst made a choice and walked over to the group of men who had to work. He ended up in Monowitz, the labor camp of Auschwitz. When the Russians arrived in Auschwitz in January 1945, Ernst was forced on a 40-to-60-kilometer-long march to Gleiwitz. Then he traveled by train to Buchenwald. In early April 1945, he was taken to Buchenwald concentration camp and claimed, as an uncircumcised person, not to be a Jew. He was sent to the Dutch barracks rather than to a certain death. Three days later, on April 11, 1945, Buchenwald was liberated by the US Army. In May 1945, Ernst Verduin returned to the Netherlands. He was miraculously reunited with his mother, receiving the news on his 18th birthday. She had survived concentration camps in Poland and Germany. They were reunited in August 1945. Ernst's sister and father both died in concentration camps in the East. How his father died is unknown. His sister Wanda was experimentally infected with typhus and died of it. Ernst regularly gave guest lectures at secondary schools, universities and other places to tell young people that the lessons of history should never be forgotten. Ernst passed away in mid-December 2021. He was 94.

Ernst Verduin BY Etienne Werner THE NETHERLANDS
OCHTEN, THE NETHERLANDS, 2019

"Yasya Lev, born in 1936 in Slavuta, Ukraine. Jew, school pupil. Executed by fascists 27.06.42. Buried in a mass grave in the town Slavuta, Khmelnytskyi district." So reads the death notice for Yasya Levit in the Book of Sorrow in Ukraine. That day in Slavuta a massacre took place and thousands of Jews were executed. The local Jews and those from nearby towns were rounded up in the square of the ghetto to be shot. 'All members of my family, including my eight-year-old brother, were shot and their bodies dumped in a ditch. According to the order of the fascist officer not to waste the ammunition, the Jewish children were dumped into a mass grave alive.' Yasya, age six, was dumped in a ditch as well, but by some miracle she managed to escape and survive. She was saved by guerrillas, transferred to Yaroslavl in Russia and placed in an orphanage. She has no memory of the tragic day. She learned of these facts many years later on a visit to her hometown Slavuta, searching for information about her roots. ASYA LEVIT (Rothenberg) moved to Germany with her husband a long time ago. He has since died, and she lives in Nuremberg, sings in the local synagogue choir and performs at concerts in various countries.

Asya Levit BY Natalya Reznik GERMANY
NUREMBURG, GERMANY, 2019

BERNARD OFFEN was born in Krakow, Poland. He survived the Krakow Ghetto and several concentration camps including Plaszów, Julag, Mauthausen, Auschwitz-Birkenau, and Dachau. His father was murdered in Auschwitz, but after the war he was able to reunite with his two brothers, Sam and Natan. In 1951, the Offen brothers immigrated to the United States. Bernard returned to Poland in 1981 and has continued to do so since 1991, taking people on tours of the former ghetto and of the concentration camps. He has made four movies of his experiences with the Holocaust and the "process of healing." In 1986, he refused to pay 25% of his taxes to the Internal Revenue Service, saying he would forward that money to an alternative fund because his experiences in the Nazi extermination camps made him unwilling to be an accomplice in the nuclear arms race, which, he said, 'could end life for 5,000,000,000 people, five billions, Jews.' Pictured, 90-year-old Holocaust survivor Bernard Offen (L) and JCC Krakow executive director Jonathan Ornstein passing a guard tower at Auschwitz I, on a tandem bicycle en route to JCC Krakow, during the 6th annual Ride for the Living, Oświęcim, Poland, June 28, 2019.

Bernard Offen BY Chuck Fishman USA
OŚWIĘCIM-AUSCHWITZ, POLAND, 2019

Holocaust survivors **Eugene and Margie Beko** in their apartment in Jerusalem, September 22, 2019. Both were liberated from concentration camps, married soon afterwards and went as displaced persons to the United States. They lived in New York City until three years ago when they made aliyah to Israel. Eugene passed away in September 2021.

Eugene & Margie Beko BY Ronen Zvulun ISRAEL
JERUSALEM, 2019

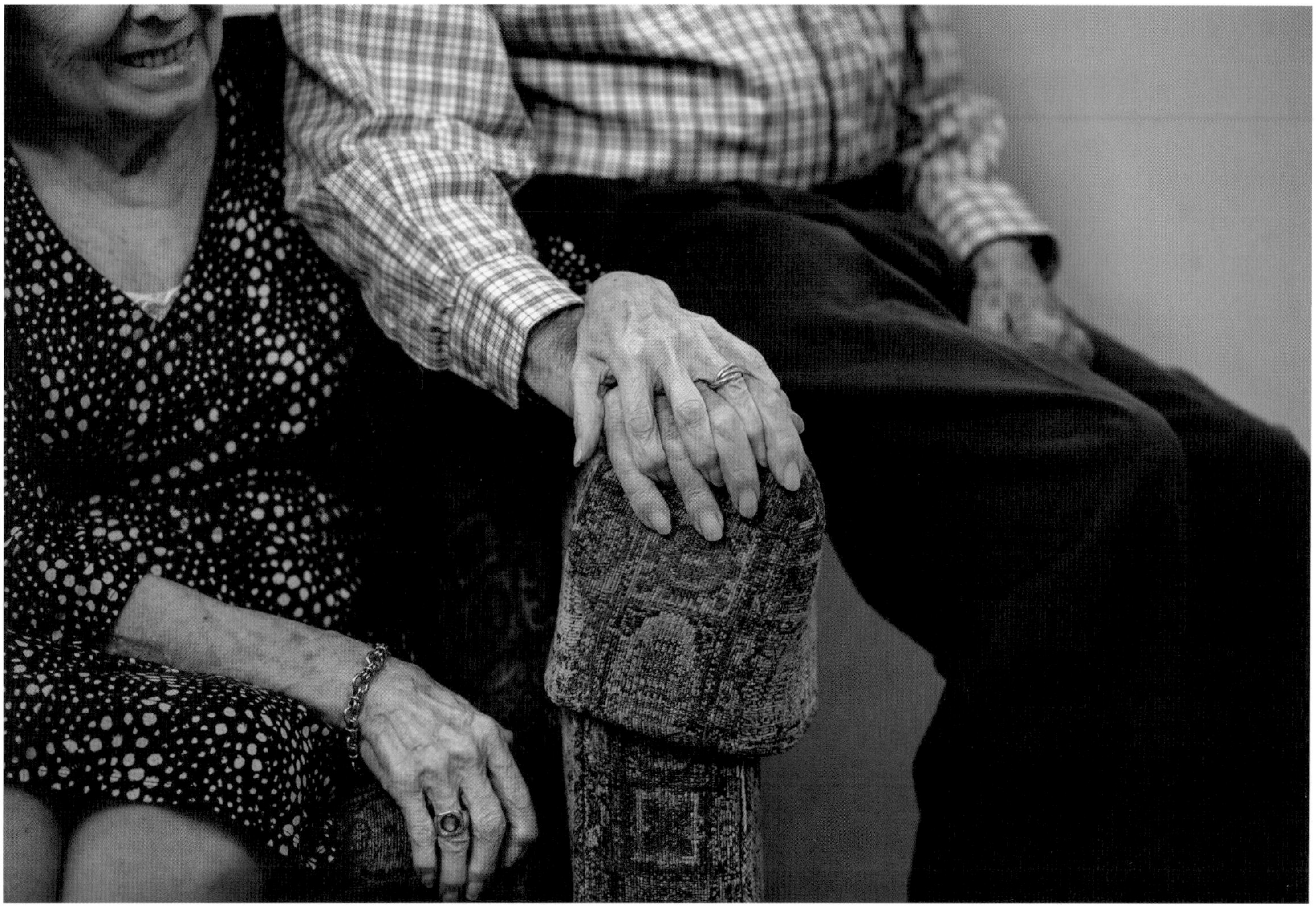

MENACHEM HABERMAN was born in 1927 in the city of Orlová, Czechoslovakia, but grew up in Munkács (today Ukraine). In 1944, Menachem and his seven siblings were forced into the Munkács Ghetto, and he was pressed into forced labor. In May 1944, all Jews from the Munkács Ghetto were deported to Auschwitz. During the Selektion, Menachem's mother and six of his siblings were sent to the gas chambers. His older sister later succumbed to illness, leaving Menachem as the last member of his family. He was put to work removing ashes from the crematoria and gathering excrement for fertilizer. Over time, he would carry equipment and horse feed around Auschwitz-Birkenau. An SS officer nearly executed him after catching him with food in his bag. He fell and nearly drowned in a pool of human ash from the crematoria. In January 1945, Menachem was sent with the rest of the prisoners of Auschwitz on a death march. The survivors were then put on train cars and sent west. Airplanes bombed the convoy during the trip. Menachem was wounded and pulled shrapnel out of his own shoulder. After a five-day journey, the train reached Buchenwald. Of the 150 prisoners who had been put in Menachem's car, 20 were still alive. Menachem stayed in the children's block in Buchenwald under dire conditions and hunger. When Buchenwald was evacuated in April 1945, he hid in a sewage pipe. He was caught and sent on a death march again, but escaped and returned to the camp. When the US Army liberated the camp the next day, Menachem weighed 34 kilograms (75 pounds). After recuperating he found out that his father, who had been drafted in 1940 into the Hungarian army's labor camps, had survived in the Soviet Union. He wrote his son, "If you go to Eretz Israel, there is a chance that we will meet." Menachem immigrated to Israel and settled in Jerusalem in 1950. He managed to get his father out of the USSR to Israel. Menachem married Rivka, a survivor from the Netherlands, and they created a family. He lit one of six torches at the State Opening Ceremony of Holocaust Remembrance Day at Yad Vashem in 2019.

Menachem Haberman by Jim Hollander USA
JERUSALEM, 2019

Born in Vienna, Austria, in 1930, **Rabbi Arthur Schneier** survived the Holocaust, and even as a child has vivid memories of synagogues burning, men being led away, and Kristallnacht in Vienna. On September 1, 1939, he fled to his grandparents in Hungary on a tourist visa. He lost his father at a young age before the war began. His grandfather was a rabbi in the Carpathian Mountains, and in 1944 his grandfather and grandmother were deported to Auschwitz. He and his mother survived in Budapest in a safe house established with the help of Raoul Wallenberg and the Swiss Consul Carl Lutz. In three months in 1944, some 430,000 Jews were deported from Hungary to Auschwitz. In October 1944, Rabbi Schneier was selected for a death march from Budapest to Hegyeshalom at the Austrian border. He had a US affidavit with the colors pink, blue, yellow and white. Rabbi Schneier says those colors saved his life. He showed the paper to the young person who arrested him, and with that the future rabbi said he was an American. He was let go. After the war he returned to Vienna and graduated from high school and, In 1947, immigrated to the United States. Rabbi Arthur Schneier is recognized internationally for his leadership on behalf of religious freedom, human rights and tolerance, and his activities have spanned the globe for more than four decades. He has played a major role in addressing issues in the former Soviet Union and Russia, China, Central Europe, Latin America and the Balkans. For over 50 years Rabbi Schneier has been the Senior Rabbi of the 125-year-old Park East Synagogue, one of New York City's historic landmark houses of worship and home to one of the leading modern Orthodox congregations in the US. Rabbi Arthur Schneier poses in the sanctuary of the Park East Synagogue in Manhattan's Upper East Side.

Rabbi Arthur Schneier BY Allan Tannenbaum USA
NEW YORK CITY, NEW YORK, USA, 2019

WALTER SPITZER was born in Cieszyn, Poland, in 1927. When the ghetto was liquidated in June 1943, Spitzer's mother was shot, and the sixteen-year-old Walter was deported to Blechhammer, a sub-camp of Auschwitz. There he made his first drawing, with a burnt stick on an empty cement bag. Spitzer describes the moment when his life was, quite literally, saved by drawing. During the final months of World War II, Spitzer was an inmate in the Buchenwald concentration camp and was summoned to appear before the German political prisoner who was in charge of his barracks. Spitzer's name was on a list of inmates to be sent off the next day to a work camp, a move which would mean certain death for him. His anti-Nazi block master told the artist he would delete him from the transport list on one condition. Spitzer had to promise, if he survived, "to tell with his pencils all you have seen here." Spitzer lived to honor his vow, providing generations with an artistic record of the Holocaust and crimes against humanity. Walter Spitzer has lived and worked since World War II in France, where he studied at the École des Beaux Arts in Paris, becoming a renowned painter and print maker. Walter Spitzer passed away from complications due to the COVID-19 pandemic in mid-April 2021, at the age of 93.

Walter Spitzer BY Alfred Yaghobzadeh IRAN/FRANCE
PARIS, 2019

Samuel Bak is an American artist who survived the Holocaust, immigrated to Israel in 1948, and in 1993, to the United States. He was born in Wilno, Poland, and at an early age was recognized as having artistic talent. Samuel was six years old when the war began, and he was transferred to Lithuania. When the Germans occupied it, he and his family were forced to live in the ghetto, where he had his first exhibition at the age of nine. He and his mother were deported to a forced labor camp but took refuge in a Benedictine convent, where they remained in hiding until the end of the war. He and his mother were the only members of his extensive family to survive the Nazis. His father Jonas was shot by Nazis in July 1944, a few days before Samuel was liberated by the Russians. He says there were only some 300 Jews remaining of the 70,000–80,000 Jews who had lived in Vilna. Samuel lived with his mother in a displaced persons camp in Germany and studied painting and art in Munich. In 1948, he and his mother immigrated to Israel, where he studied at the Bezalel Academy of Arts and Design in Jerusalem. He served in the Israel Defense Forces and then continued his art studies in Paris, spending time in Rome, Paris and Switzerland before settling in the United States.

Samuel Bak BY Nati Harnik USA/ISRAEL
OMAHA, NEBRASKA, USA, 2019

Agnes Keleti BY **Tamas Revesz** HUNGARY
BUDAPEST, 2019

The artistic gymnast **Agnes Keleti**, a Hungarian Olympic champion, was born in Budapest in 1921. Although already a leading athlete, in 1941 she was expelled from her gymnastics club for being Jewish. Agnes was forced to go into hiding. She bought and used false identity papers and worked as a maid. The Swedish diplomat Raoul Wallenberg saved her mother and sister. Her father and most of her family did not survive. They were gassed in the Auschwitz concentration camp. In the winter of 1944, during the Siege of Budapest, Agnes would collect bodies and place them in a mass grave. After the war ended, Agnes returned to gymnastics and was selected to represent Hungary at the 1952 Olympics in Helsinki, and again at the 1956 games in Melbourne. She won 10 medals in the two summer Olympics, five of them gold.

Agnes Keleti by Bea Bar Kallos ISRAEL/HUNGARY
BUDAPEST, 2019

FRANCO SCHÖNHEIT, born in 1927 in Italy, was captured along with his parents by Italian police in Ferrara in February 1944. Only in recent years has Franco shared his testimony. He was deported to the Fossoli "sorting" camp in Modena province in 1943. He was imprisoned with his father. Both were deported to Buchenwald, while his mother was transferred elsewhere. Assuming the identity of *ebrei misti* (mixed Jews) saved the two from death in Auschwitz.

Franco Schönheit BY Mario Tedeschi ITALY

MILAN, ITALY, 2019

BEN ZION IZIDOR FISCHLER was born on May 24, 1925, in Romania. During the summer of 1941, the Jews of the town, Izidor among them, were forced to wear the yellow star. By autumn, he was detained in a huge courtyard and sent to forced labor. In November 1941 he was loaded on a cattle train and taken to the river banks of Danislav and Mogilev. 'We were taken off the wagons and told to walk, and we walked for days in terrible cold until we reached Ghetto Shargorod' where 'inhuman brutal conditions, terrible hunger, cold and fear of the Romanian guards was our daily routine.' In March 1942, his father, already broken and exhausted, fell ill with typhoid and died. 'For many, many years I was not capable to bring myself to speak or think of that period of darkness and horror. That is why I have not testified in Yad Vashem, and I will never watch a film or read a book about the Holocaust. Neither did I ever apply to receive financial compensation.' He was liberated by the Red Army in the spring of 1944. Soon after, Izidor boarded the ship *Geula* on his way to Mandatory Palestine. 'The British soldiers were about to seize the ship and we had to throw all our documents to the sea. We were taken to Cyprus detention camp and my name was changed to an Israeli-sounding name, Ben Zion.' Ben Zion ז״ל passed away in December 2019, one month after he was photographed for the Lonka Project.

Ben Zion Fischler BY Quique Kierszenbaum ISRAEL

JERUSALEM, 2019

IRENE is a Holocaust survivor who is 97 years old. She is Polish and was in a concentration camp, and was liberated by the Russians. Her parents and a brother were killed when she was 16 or 17. She is lucid and remembers many moments but, often feeling tired, she forgets many things.

Irene BY Leo Barizzoni URUGUAY
MONTEVIDEO, 2019

RAPHAËL ESRAIL was born in Turkey in 1925, to a Jewish family who emigrated to France when he was nine months old. They settled in Lyon. The first antisemitic laws came into effect in 1940. It spurred him to join the Resistance, the underground network of fighters against the Nazis. He was tasked with making forged work permits and travel documents for Jews until he was arrested by the Vichy French authorities on January 8, 1944. For several days he was tortured before being placed on the dank train car that would haul him to Auschwitz death camp in convoy 67 on February 3, 1944. He survived 11 months. On January 18, 1945, he was forced by the SS on a death march from which he tried in vain to escape. Evacuating the camps just days before liberation, the Nazis pushed tens of thousands of weakened prisoners into long treks toward distant trains bound for other facilities from the approaching Allied forces. On hard ice the prisoners marched, many of them barefoot. 'Their feet would freeze, and they would fall to their knees,' Raphaël said. 'When they fell, a Nazi soldier would stick a gun to their heads and pull the trigger. I could only think of my mother, think that I would never see her again, that I would die before reaching the age of 20.' Raphaël survived the march and arrived to Dachau concentration camp, and then transferred to a sub-camp, Ampfing Waldlager. On April 25, 1945, the camp was evacuated. Raphaël was liberated by American soldiers near the village of Tutzing on May 1, 1945. He returned to Lyon and learned that all his family perished. Raphaël became a successful engineer at Gas France. He did not share his wartime memories with his family until the 1980s when he decided to devote his life to Holocaust commemoration and education in France. Raphaël was President of the Auschwitz Survivors Union in France from 2008 and was the recipient of the French Légion d'honneur and German Order of Merit awards. In 2017, he published his testimony. He passed away just before International Holocaust Remembrance Day in late January 2022.

Raphaël Esrail BY Daniella Zalcman USA
PARIS, 2019

ROBERT WAJCMAN was born in Paris in 1930. In 1942, his family tried to conceal their identity by moving to Masseret, but soon thereafter, the local authorities told them to leave. They moved to Lyon in March 1944. On May 24, Robert was arrested on the street with his father. His mother was deported from their home, and his little brother escaped arrest. Robert and his father were held at Fort Montluc. His father Maurice tried to escape and was executed on June 3, 1944. Robert was transferred to Drancy detention camp, where Jews were held before being sent to the extermination camps. In Drancy, Robert was reunited briefly with his mother before they were separated. He was taken to Auschwitz by convoy no. 76 from the Bobigny freight station in the suburbs of Paris, on June 30, 1944. He was 14 years old. There were 1,156 deportees in that convoy, 167 of them children. Upon arrival in Auschwitz, 479 were gassed immediately. A total of 398 women and 223 men were selected for forced labor including Robert, who concealed his young age. Only 167 survived the convoy. Robert was sent to Buchenwald. After some weeks there, he was transferred again, to Theresienstadt. On January 18, 1945, he was forced on a death march and survived. Robert was liberated on his birthday on May 8, 1945, and returned to France, where he found his mother had survived.

Robert Wajcman BY Alain Keler FRANCE
PARIS, 2019

RENATA REISFELD was born in Poland. Her mother died shortly after giving birth. Her family was able to escape and made its way to Siberia. She arrived in Israel in 1950 and was very good at languages but had little formal education. She attended Hebrew University in Jerusalem and became a professor of chemistry and a leading expert on solar energy. She is the author of some 532 scientific papers and four books and has been cited more than 30,000 times. On July 4, 1976, she was taken hostage aboard Air France 139 traveling from Tel Aviv to Athens on its way to Paris. Palestinians and German gunmen hijacked the plane to Entebbe, Uganda, where she was among 102 passengers held hostage for a week. 'You know the traditional Chinese curse, "May you live in interesting times"? I have had a very interesting life,' she was quoted as telling an Israeli interviewer. She invented a pink energy-generating windowpane, called a luminescent solar concentrator, and greenhouses made of a nanomaterial that enhances plant growth and generates solar electricity. Professor Renata Reisfeld holds a sample of her invention, the pink pane, called a luminescent solar concentrator, in her apartment in Jerusalem, October 7, 2019.

Renata Reisfeld BY Debbie Hill USA

JERUSALEM, 2019

Dorothy Bohm BY Marissa Roth USA
LONDON, 2019

Dorothy Bohm (née Israelit) was born on June 22, 1924, in Königsberg, East Prussia, to a German-speaking family of Jewish-Lithuanian origins. She lived under Nazi rule until age 14, when her family sent her to England. Her father, Tobias Israelit, an industrialist and also an enthusiastic photographer, gave Dorothy his Leica camera at the station as a parting gift saying, "This might come in useful." She attended boarding school and hoped to become a doctor. She later moved to London where she met Louis Bohm. They married in 1945. Her husband's work called for travel, and they lived in Paris and then in New York and San Francisco. She traveled to Israel and Mexico, where in 1956 she began shooting in color for the first time. Most of her work is in black and white, but on the urging of André Kertész, she began experimenting in color photography. From 1984 on, she worked exclusively in color. Her work has been called "humanist street photography," and she has been friends with such photographers as Bill Brandt, Henri Cartier-Bresson, Brassaï, and André Kertész. In 1969, Bohm had a major exhibition alongside Don McCullin. She co-founded The Photographers' Gallery in London with Sue Davies in 1971, becoming known as one of the doyennes of British photography. She has published some 14 books. In 2009, she was appointed an Honorary Fellow of the Royal Photographic Society. Dorothy has said about her photography, 'The photograph fulfills my deep need to stop things from disappearing,' and also, 'I've seen a lot,' she says, 'but I don't show the ugliness of life, I try to show the good.' Dorothy passed away on March 15, 2023, a few months shy of her 99th birthday.

RENE SLOTKIN was born to Ita and Herbert Guttmann, who fled the Nazi regime from Dresden, Germany, into Czechoslovakia, where their twins Rene and Renate were born in 1937. Herbert was sent to Auschwitz and executed in 1941. Their mother Ita and the twins were sent to Theresienstadt and, soon after, the three were deported to Auschwitz. Rene arrived in Auschwitz in December 1943. In March 1944, their mother was killed. Only twins, doctors and nurses were saved, and Rene and his sister Renate were part of Josef Mengele's monstrous experiments on twins. Rene remembers Mengele well: his Mercedes, his boots and the torture the twins underwent. As it became clear that the Nazis were losing the war, Mengele left Auschwitz and the prisoners were forced on a death march. Rene was saved by the Russian army, but the child's ordeal continued for another year until the Slotkin family located and adopted him and brought him to the United States, where he was reunited with his surviving twin.

Rene Slotkin BY Ron Haviv USA
NEW YORK CITY, NEW YORK, USA, 2019

DAN HADANI was born Donk Złotowski in Lodz, Poland, in 1924. In 1939, with the outbreak of war, all Jews were rounded up and confined to the Lodz Ghetto. In 1942, living conditions deteriorated. His father died, and his body was thrown at the doorstep of the flat that Dani shared with his mother and sister. In 1944, Dani was 18 when all the ghetto Jews were sent to the Auschwitz concentration camp. In Auschwitz, he was separated from his mother and sister, who were sent to their deaths. After some months in Auschwitz, he was selected for forced labor at an ammunition factory in Germany, and his life was saved. In 1945, as the war ended, Dani returned to Lodz to look for surviving relatives. He was the only one to survive. Dani decided to leave Europe for Israel and joined the convoys that made their way to European ports. Upon his arrival in 1948, he enlisted in the Israeli army, becoming an officer and later an army spokesman.

Dan Hadani BY Shabtai Tal ISRAEL
TEL AVIV, ISRAEL, 2019

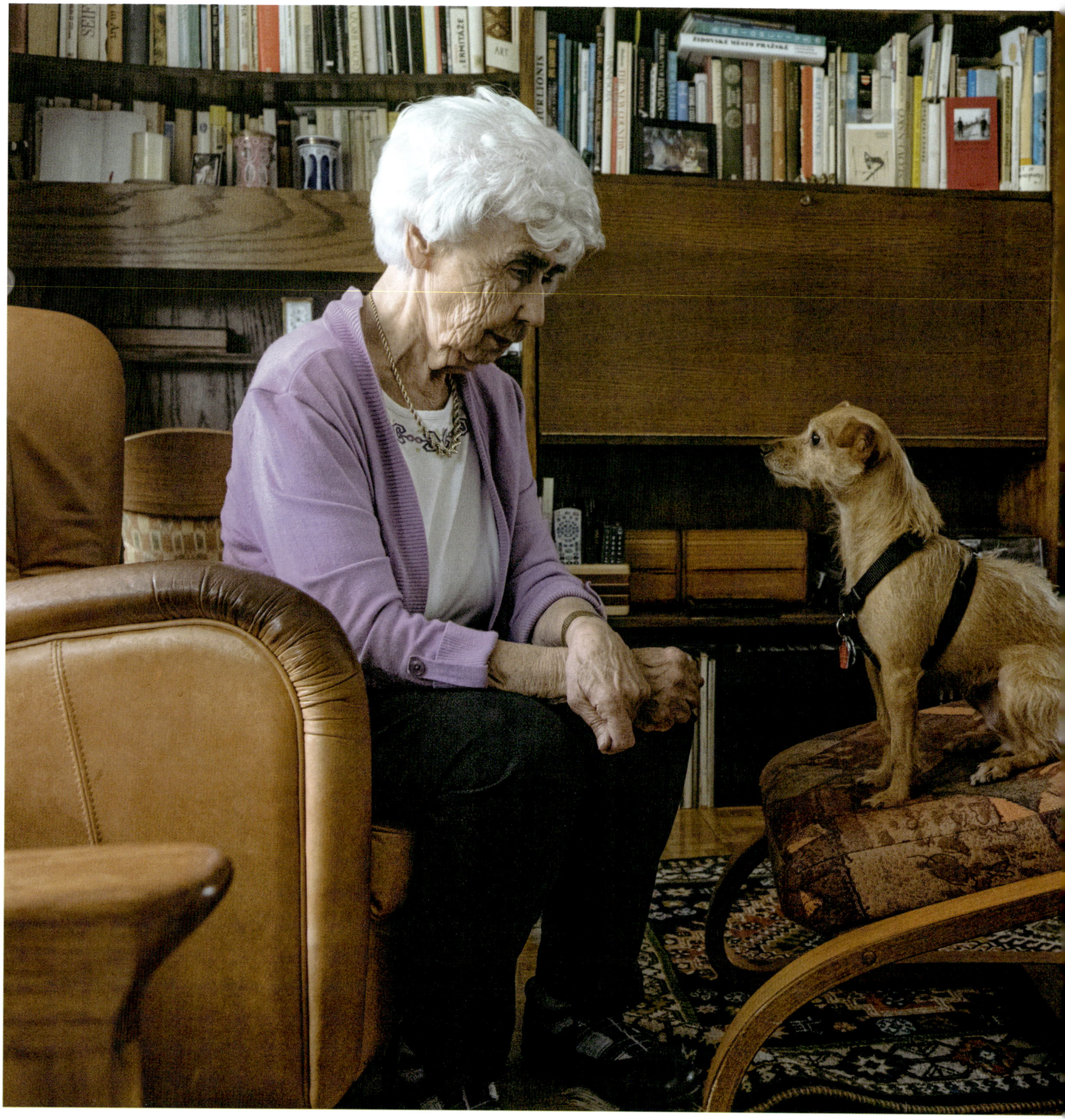
ŽIDOVSKÉ MĚSTO PRAŽSKÉ
ERMITÁŽE

Renata Polgar Laxova was born in Brno, Czechoslovakia in 1931. In 1939, at the age of eight, she was sent by her parents to England on the Kindertransport. The Kindertransport from Prague to London transported 669 Jewish children to safety as Nazis were rounding up Jews to be sent to concentration and labor camps. Renata left Prague on July 31,1939, on the last of eight Kindertransport trains traveling through Germany to Holland, and then by ship to England. The ninth Kindertransport train, a month later and the largest one, with 250 children on board, was loaded and ready to pull out of the Prague train station on September 1, 1939, when it was stopped. All the country's borders had been closed by the occupying Nazis as Hitler's troops invaded neighboring Poland. None of the 250 children were ever heard from again, and it is believed they were all killed by the SS. Both her parents survived the war by changing their identities and living covertly. Renata was reunited with her parents and moved back to Brno in 1946. She relearned the Czech language, attended university and started a career as a pediatric physician and geneticist. Renata and her daughter, on the advice of a friend, took a bus convoy to Vienna, barely missing the Soviet invasion of Czechoslovakia amid the Prague Spring of 1968. The family eventually immigrated to the United States. Renata was Emeritus Professor of Genetics at the University of Wisconsin. She discovered the New-Laxova syndrome which is a rare congenital abnormality. She lived with her terrier, Breenie, named after her hometown in the former Czechoslovakia. Renata passed away on November 30, 2020, at age 89 after a brief illness.

Dr. Renata Laxova BY Michael Nelson USA
MADISON, WISCONSIN, USA, 2019

Four Holocaust survivors who joined the Israeli Air Force after the founding of the state in 1948. From right to left: Lieutenant Colonel **Itzchak Biran** was born in Romania in 1935. He was staying with his uncle when villagers murdered all the Jews in the village. Itzchak hid in the cornfields near their house and saw his uncle captured and murdered. He fell ill with typhoid fever and his mother died in January 1942. Itzchak then joined a group of Jews hiding in the forests and survived by stealing food and goods from the villagers. He was adopted later by a Soviet artillery battalion. He tried to immigrate to Israel in 1947 on the ship *Exodus* but was sent to the detention camp on Cyprus, finally arriving in Israel in April 1948. Lieutenant Colonel **Moshe Eshel** was born in Poland in 1936. His family fled the Warsaw Ghetto, surviving in the city with false papers. He remembers Sundays, as good Poles, going to church. He witnessed executions and watched the Warsaw Ghetto Uprising from a hideout, the heavy smoke and fires rising from buildings. He was taught to keep a secret, never mentioning the word Jew. Most of his extended family perished. Lieutenant Colonel **Aryeh Oz** was born in 1936. After Kristallnacht he fled to the Netherlands with his mother and sister, receiving refugee status. In 1942, at the age of six, Aryeh was left on a farm and hid in an attic until the end of the war. He would look out from the window at the warplanes. Thus began his love of flying. Lieutenant **Nachmann Magen** was born in Romania in 1940. In 1942 the family was expelled to the local ghetto where they were able to bribe an official, enabling the family to flee and to sail to Mandatory Palestine. It took years to reach the shores. These pilots took part in many of Israel's wars up to and including the Yom Kippur War in 1973.

Four Pilots BY Rina Castelnuovo ISRAEL

HOD HASHARON, ISRAEL, 2019

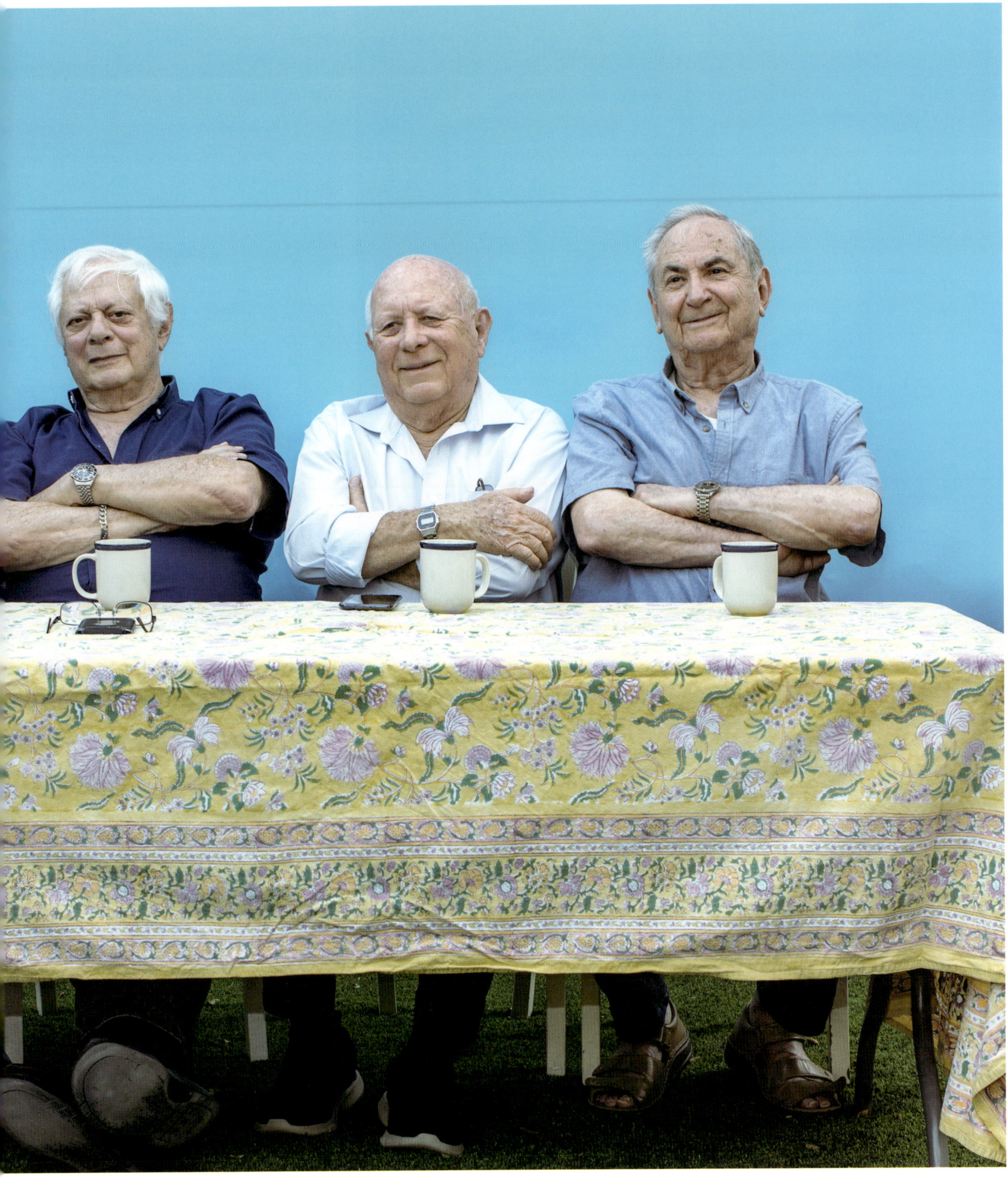

Stephen Jacobs BY Max Hirshfeld USA
NEW YORK CITY, NEW YORK, USA, 2019

Stephen B. Jacobs was born in Lodz, Poland, on June 12, 1939. The family moved to Piotrków and in 1944 was separated – the men taken to Buchenwald and the women to Ravensbrück camps. Stephen has memories of life in the Buchenwald concentration camp. 'In my case, you didn't eat in Buchenwald unless you worked. So, I was given an identity card that said I was 16 years old,' he told *Newsweek* magazine in 2018. 'I was five.' He worked in a shoe factory. Those not able to work were sent to their deaths. Stephen credits the camp's underground resistance for staying alive. The Buchenwald camp was started before the war to hold prisoners such as communists. He believes the prisoners organized and protected one another by arranging counterfeit paperwork and hiding the children. He was hidden several times in the camp, once in a tuberculosis ward where his father worked as an orderly, and where German soldiers did not like to patrol. He remembers being liberated by the US Third Army amid an uprising within the camp. The family reunited after the war and fled to Switzerland and then to the US in 1948. Stephen pursued his interest in art but turned to architecture after admitting he 'was a lousy painter.' He enrolled in Pratt Institute and completed a master's in architecture in 1965. He became renowned for "sensitive renovation" projects and adaptive reuse of old industrial and manufacturing properties and designed some of New York City's earliest boutique hotels. He designed the Holocaust memorial at Buchenwald, for which he received no payment for his work. It was announced Stephen B. Jacobs passed away on December 14, 2021, age 82.

TIBOR SPITZ tells his story through his art. He was born in 1929 in Dolny Kubin, Czechoslovakia. Of some 100 Jewish families who lived there, 93 were taken to Auschwitz as Slovakia enacted the Jewish Codex, consisting of 270 laws denying Jews their rights as citizens. Jewish businesses were seized. Soon after the murder of their extended family, the Spitz family began planning their hideout. The family ran from their town and hid from the Nazis in a forest in an underground hideaway. The hideaway had been built ahead of time by Tibor's older brother Ernest, on a steep incline near a stream, a place where horses wouldn't go. They would crawl out at night to a creek fed by melting snow. There they would catch trout as they huddled between the rocks. They were buried in snow for 200 days, often keeping silent for days. 'There were foot patrols in the forest; we could have been discovered at any time.' They were caught by local residents and lined up to be executed, but were left to freeze. They survived. By the time the Red Army arrived in April, the Spitz family had been in hiding for over a year. Broken and sick, Tibor had tuberculosis, and the family had to be convinced the war was over before emerging from their hideout, only to discover that all the Jews in their town were gone. 'Painting is a way of getting rid of those memories, nightmares. When I paint, I am liberated of them.'

Tibor Spitz BY Lori Grinker USA
KINGSTON, NEW YORK, USA, 2019

A happy childhood in an assimilated Jewish family in Warsaw came to an end on Alina's sixth birthday, when the city was bombed by the invading Nazi army. The family fled to Russia, where her father was recruited into the Red Army. Alina, her mother and 11-year-old old brother Emil were sent to Siberia. This was the start of a long and painful journey, marked by hunger and cold. In 1941, they moved to Samarkand, where they were joined by her father, who succumbed to typhus shortly afterwards. At a loss, her mother placed her children in a Christian orphanage. They would never see her again. It was there that they were found by the emissaries of the Youth Aliyah organization, who took them to Tehran, and from there to Mandatory Palestine in 1943, part of a group of mainly orphans, known as the Tehran Children. Alina, now Ilana, and Emil, now Emmanuel, were sent to Kibbutz Ginegar, which became their new home. In March of 1948, Emmanuel – a Palmach fighter – was killed in an operation to stop an Arab convoy loaded with ammunition on its way to Haifa. Ilana was 14 years old. A year later Emmanuel was awarded the "Hero of Israel" medal by the IDF, one of 12. Ilana, at 15, went on stage to receive her brother's decoration, awarded by President Weizmann and Prime Minister Ben Gurion. Following her military service, Ilana studied social work in Jerusalem, graduating in 1956. She worked as a juvenile probation officer. In 1960, she married Hanania Karniel, a graduate of the Bezalel Academy of Arts, and they had three children. 'If I had a mission in life, then it was twofold: perhaps the more important one was to start a family as an answer to the family I lost, and the other was to develop professionally and help people,' says Ilana in her recorded memories. She lives in Jerusalem.

Ilana Karniel BY Yigal Gawze ISRAEL
JERUSALEM, 2019

SARA SHAPIRA (née Zeidner) was born in 1933 in the city of Rădăuți in Romanian Bukovina, the youngest of five children in a Vizhnitzer Hasidic family. In late 1941, the Romanians deported the Jews of Rădăuți. The deportees were crammed into freight trains, and during the long journey, many died from the overcrowding, hunger and thirst. They were then put on rafts on the banks of the Dniester. Some of them, including Sara's grandmother Malka, fell into the river and drowned. The rest were transferred to Mogilev, and then marched to Kuzmintsy, a village further north. There they were concentrated in a stable without food or water, and in poor sanitary conditions. Her sister Bina and uncle Itzik died from a typhus epidemic, and her mother Taube died soon after. 'At night I slept next to my mother, embracing her,' recalls Sara. 'I didn't know in the night that she was already gone. I was alone. A nine-year-old girl.' Sara was transferred to a Jewish orphanage in Mogilev, where she lived in constant hunger and neglect for two years. In 1944 she was one of 4,000 Jewish children (including the Transnistria orphans) in Romania waiting to go to Mandatory Palestine. In 1947, she boarded the Haganah ship the *Jewish State*. But it was blocked from entering, and Sara spent four months in British internment camps in Cyprus before arriving In Israel. In 2002, Sara's son, Rabbi Elimelech Shapira, was killed by Palestinians in a shooting attack in Bnei Brak, a suburb of Tel Aviv.

Sara Shapira BY Gil Cohen-Magen ISRAEL
JERUSALEM, 2019

Fortouni Politi Gani, 92, holds a photo of herself and her sisters Chrysoula and Anna, and their brother Moyses, taken before World War II in Ioannina, Greece. Fortouni Politi Gani and her family were arrested in Ioannina in northwest Greece, by German soldiers on March 25, 1944, and were taken to the Auschwitz-Birkenau death camp. Fortouni Politi Gani and her sister Chrysoula were released from the death camp of Mauthausen on May 5, 1945. All other members of their family were murdered in the camps. Fortuni and Chrysoula live in Athens. Asked if the tattoo with the number 77180 bothers her, she replied, 'No, I want to remember.'

Fortouni Politi Gani BY Orestis Panagiotou GREECE
ATHENS, 2019

JOSEPH ALEXANDER was born in 1922 in Kowal, Poland. He enjoyed a stable life in Blonie until Nazi Germany invaded Poland in 1939. In late 1940, the German military transported Blonie's Jews to the Warsaw Ghetto. Joseph's father bribed some guards to let Joseph and two of his siblings escape back to Kowal. It was the last time he saw the rest of his family. From Kowal, the Nazis sent him to 12 different concentration camps, including Dachau and Auschwitz-Birkenau. After the 1943 Warsaw Ghetto Uprising, he was sent from Auschwitz back to the Warsaw Ghetto to clean up the destruction's aftermath. As the Polish Home Army advanced towards Warsaw, the Nazis sent Joseph to camps in Germany and then on a death march. While a captive, he endured forced labor under threat of death and conditions of starvation. He experienced severe illness while huddling for days behind brick piles in the destroyed Warsaw Ghetto, suffering from typhus. American troops liberated him in 1945 at Dachau. He immigrated to the United States in 1949, continued his work as a tailor in Los Angeles, and is a leading voice on Holocaust remembrance.

Joseph Alexander BY Davis Factor USA
LOS ANGELES, CALIFORNIA, USA, 2019

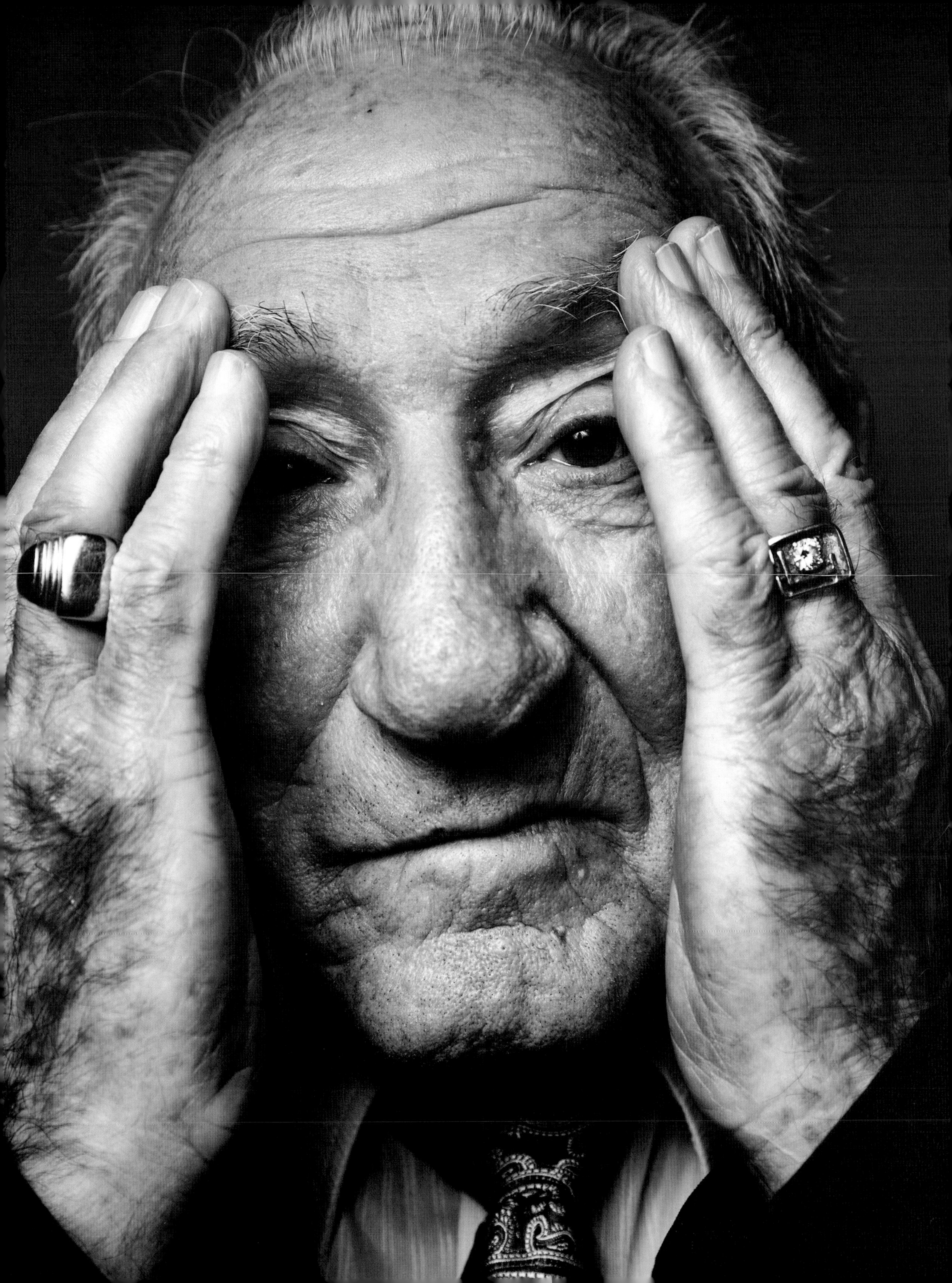

Krystyna Linden was born on September 9, 1942, in the Warsaw Ghetto. On September 6, 1942, Rutka Labenska Lindenbaum was nine months pregnant and stood between her sister-in-law Renia Landau (later Rebeka Ilutovich) and Renia's husband Michal Landau. They covered her bulging belly with a raincoat, and due to a complete miracle, passed the German Selektions as the "great deportation" from the Warsaw Ghetto took place. Only 32,000 Jews had "life numbers," which meant that they were employed by German workshops in the ghetto. Krystyna's father had a workshop in the ghetto. After the birth, the two German guards in the workshop wanted to throw the baby girl out. But the Jews working there bribed them not to. Two weeks later the baby was wrapped in newspapers, and a friend of the family, a Polish Catholic woman named Mary Gasinska smuggled the baby to the Aryan side of Warsaw. The baby was brought to a village outside Warsaw and a childless woman, Michalina Janiszewska, agreed to take her in and care for her. She received money for the baby's upkeep and kept her for almost five years. A cousin came to take Krystyna immediately after the war ended. They adopted Krystia, as she was called then, but they never told her about her adoption. She remained in Warsaw, and discovered she was adopted by researching family papers. She studied at law school in Warsaw, and after one year there, came to Israel in 1962. She met her parents, who managed to flee the Warsaw Ghetto just before the uprising in April 1943.

Krystyna Linden BY Miriam Alster ISRAEL
TEL AVIV, ISRAEL, 2019

MELLPOMENI DINA, 92, from Greece was reunited in Jerusalem with the two surviving members and 40 descendants of the Jewish family she and her sisters saved during the Holocaust by helping them escape Nazi occupied Greece during World War II. Sarah Yanai and her brother Yossi Mor of the Mordechai family lived near Thessaloniki, where nearly the entire Jewish community was annihilated within a few months, in one of the most brutal executions by the Nazis. Dina, then a teenager, and her two sisters took in the family of seven around 1944, hiding them in their own single-room home on the outskirts of the city. Someone ratted Dina and her sisters out. Still, they helped the Mordechai family flee in different directions, providing them with clothing for the journey, though they were orphans and impoverished themselves. Sarah Yanai headed for the woods, another sibling ran to the mountains and their mother headed out on foot with Yossi Mor and his brother. After the liberation, the family reunited and moved to Israel.

Mellpomeni Dina BY Emmanuel Dunand FRANCE
JERUSALEM, 2019

Motek Mordechai Szymonowicz was born on April 26, 1927, in Lodz, Poland. He was 12 when the Nazis invaded Poland. His family was confined to the Lodz Ghetto. His father and older sister managed to escape, leaving him with his mother and younger brother. Motek worked in forced labor in a metal factory for three years. At age 15 he was captured on the street and loaded onto a truck and then into a packed cattle wagon to Auschwitz. At one of the stations he fled into the forest. Two Doberman dogs gave chase and spotted him in a tree. Motek jumped and grabbed the dogs by the leash and hugged them as a German SS officer took in the scene.

Motek Mordechai Szymonowicz by Gideon Markowicz ISRAEL
PETAH TIKVA, ISRAEL, 2019

The officer said Motek could work with the dogs of the SS troops at Auschwitz. Motek considered himself lucky since he could eat some of the dogs' food, as they were well fed. Later he moved to the Mauererschule, bricklaying school for adolescents, in Auschwitz I and was tattooed with the number B-8088. From Auschwitz, Motek was transferred to the Sachsenhausen concentration camp, where he worked in the weapons factory. In winter, Motek and other prisoners were sent on a death march and, starving, he collapsed on the snow. Days later he woke up in a Red Cross hospital. He was free. With thousands of orphans from all over Europe, Motek immigrated to Israel on the ship *Estate* that arrived at Haifa port on his birthday, April 26, 1946. Motek knows nothing of his entire family's survival or death. He supposes all his relatives were killed, as he could locate no one. In the Lodz Ghetto, he was told of two relatives living in Mandatory Palestine. He remembered when he arrived in Israel, but never told his family until they were all gathered to hear his story in 2019, more than 70 years after the establishment of Israel.

Eugen Yanek Yakobovitz was born in 1928 in Slovakia in the city of Mikhailovce. By 1942, when German forces were approaching their home in Slovakia, his father decided to move the family to Bratislava, where they hid with a false identity of Proslavs, using fake certificates. In 1944, caught by the Gestapo, they were separated from each other (parents, Yanek and his brother). Their money was taken from them, they were tortured, and they were forced on a terrible journey to the Oranienburg camp, not far from Berlin. In the concentration camp, he stayed with his father, who was rescued by his knowledge of the German language, until April 1945, when the Germans were cornered by American and Red Army forces. Those who remained in the camp were forced on a long death march, which continued to an unknown destination. One day at dawn, after they had lain awake on the snowy ground, trying to fall asleep huddled together, Yanek, his father, and the rest of the camp heard the sound of Russian and American tanks growling. Yanek survived with his father and sister. His mother and brother were murdered. In 1948, Yanek immigrated to Israel. Yanek passed away in May 2022.

Yanek Yakobovitz BY Shabtai Tal ISRAEL
TEL AVIV, ISRAEL, 2019

MIMI REINHARD was born in Vienna in 1915. After marrying, she arrived in Krakow in 1936. Her son Sasha was three months old when the war broke out. The German army occupied Krakow within days, and Mimi and her husband managed to smuggle their son with his grandmother to Hungary using Aryan documents, a journey they made on foot. Mimi was arrested, and her husband was shot and killed at the gate to the ghetto while trying to escape. Like most Jews of Krakow, Mimi was sent to the Plaszów concentration camp in Poland, en route to death camps. Because of her knowledge of German and her typing skills, she was assigned to work in the Plaszów camp administrative offices. In 1944, she typed an important version of the manifest of prisoners bound for Oskar Schindler's munitions factory. By adding her name and the names of two friends to the 1,200 listed Jews, she almost certainly saved her own life and theirs. Schindler was making efforts on behalf of "his Jews" at the factory and, by means of deception and bribery, he saw to better conditions for them. However, when the train left Plaszów for the Brinnlitz factory in the autumn of 1944, the Germans routed it to Auschwitz. 'We were certain that we were done for,' said Mimi, but Schindler managed to have them released. He saved more than 1,000 Jews, his typist Mimi among them. Mimi passed away on April 27, 2022, at age 107.

Mimi Reinhard BY Gideon Markowicz ISRAEL
TEL AVIV, ISRAEL, 2019

Franz Michalski was born 1934 in Görlitz, Germany. His mother, Lilli, converted to Catholicism when she married Herbert, a Christian, but the Nuremberg Laws classified Lilli as a Jew and Herbert as Aryan. Herbert refused to divorce Lilli and was kicked out of the German army. In the 1940s, fearing for his family's deportation by the Nazis, Herbert created a strong circle of friends and relatives who would help his wife and children to survive. The family was hiding in Berlin and with the Gestapo in their street, they escaped again to occupied Austria with the help of a German, Gerda Mez. Lilli left Franz and his baby brother on a farm of their former caregiver, Anna, to be raised as her own boys but it was too dangerous and Herbert arranged their crossing to Czechoslovakia. Herbert gave Franz a loaded gun and instructed him to shoot his brother, mother and then himself if the Gestapo came to their door again. Herbert was delayed and 10-year-old Franz stopped Lilli from pulling the trigger but that night Lilli tried again to jump into the Elbe River with her baby son. Franz wrestled with Lilli and succeeded in grabbing his baby brother from her arms. The next day, his father joined his wife and children. Herbert brought his family back to Berlin. They survived the Nazis but not without enduring trauma. Franz resumed his education and experienced antisemitism in school, which led the boy to attempt suicide. Franz Michalski and his wife Petra are dedicated to share with young people the story of Franz's escape through Europe during the Holocaust.

Franz Michalski by Maurice Weiss GERMANY
BERLIN, 2019

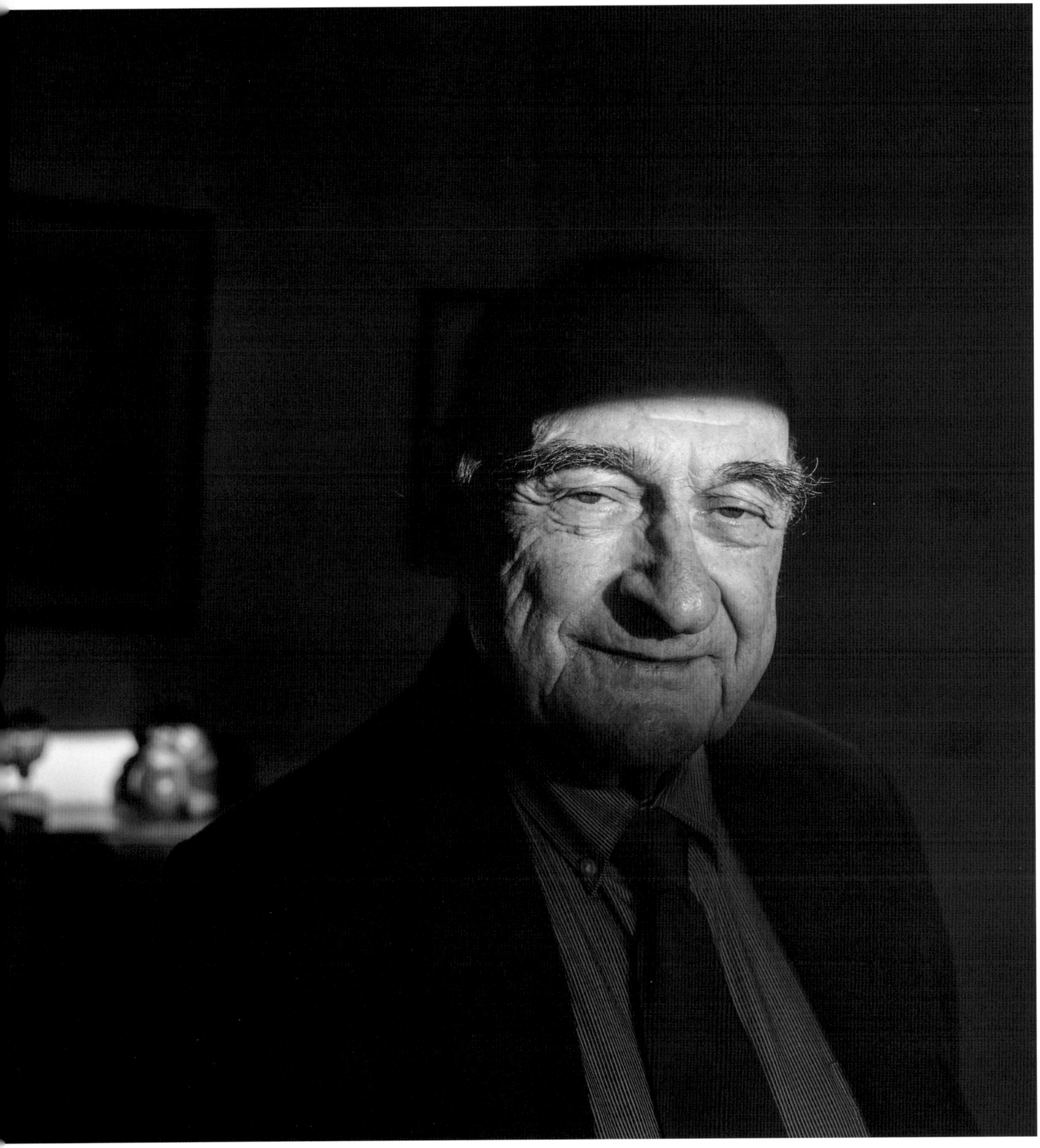

ALEX GROSS was born in 1928 in Czechoslovakia, the youngest of six boys and one younger sister. When Alex was 11, his town was annexed by Hungary. Alex's friends became Hitler Youth and tormented him endlessly. In 1944, Alex and his family were forced to the Munkács Ghetto, where they stayed for a few weeks before being sent in a cattle car to Auschwitz. There the Jews were sorted into groups. Alex's mother and father were sent to their deaths. As the Nazis began to lose the war, Alex and the remaining prisoners were forced on a death march from one concentration camp in Poland to another until they reached the Buchenwald concentration camp in Germany. Most prisoners froze to death on this journey. In Buchenwald on April 11, 1945, Gross was freed by United States forces. After the war, Alex was reunited with all of his siblings, the only family in which all eight children survived the Holocaust.

Alex Gross BY Lauren Koplowitz USA
MIAMI, FLORIDA, USA, 2019

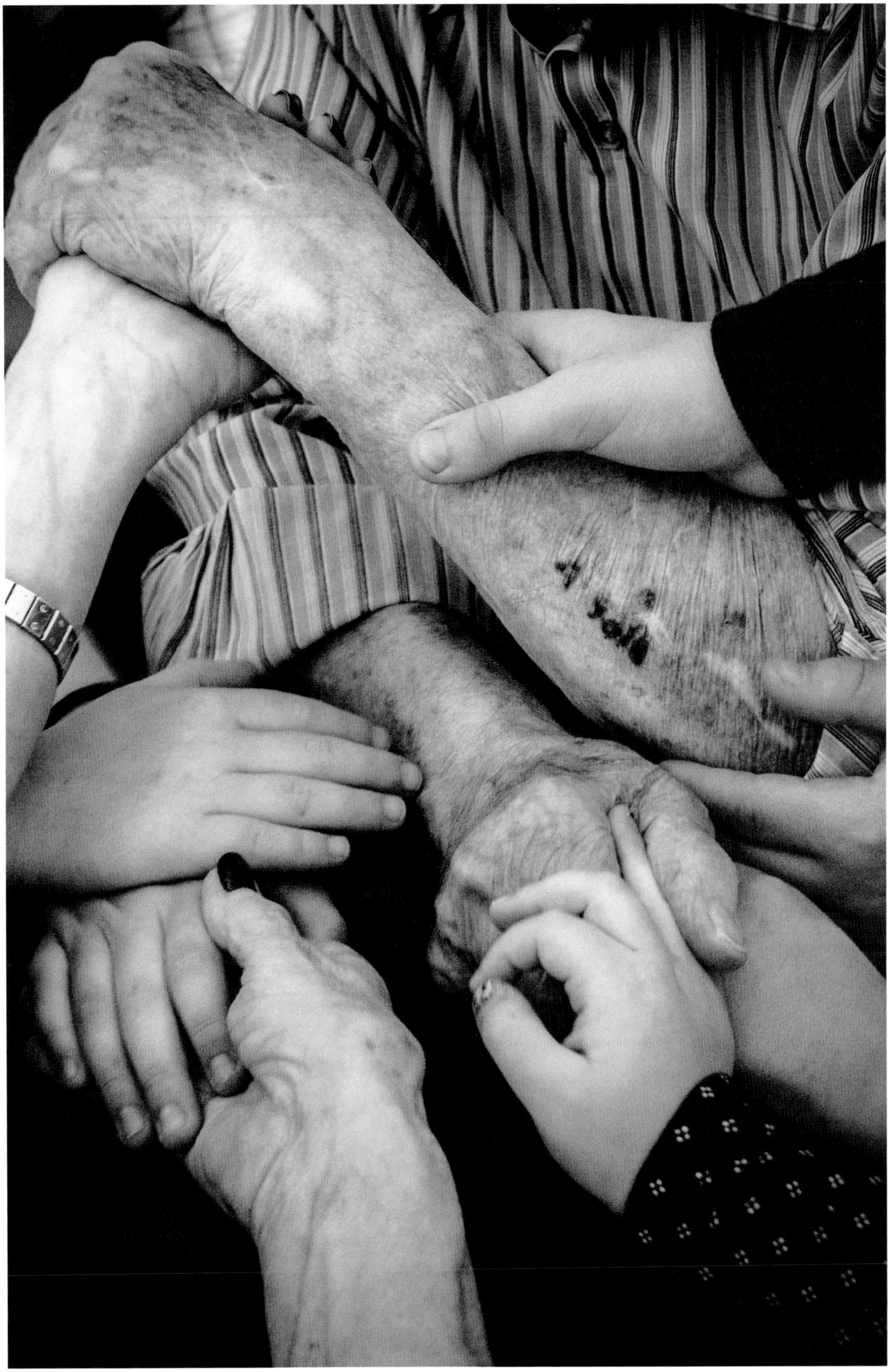

Helmut Wolff was born in Hamburg in 1933. 'My parents gave me away when I was five years old. When they knew they were to be deported, they took sleeping pills, lay down at the Elbstrand, and the water took them both. Suicide was their answer. They were Jews and they knew their life was ending. I was a child but felt their fear. At school, kids hit me, threw insults and dirt at me. Those fears and images still haunt me 75 years later. My parents saved my life. I spent years with strangers who sheltered me, putting their own lives in danger. From Potsdam to Hamburg, I lived in some six different households. I vaguely remember any details. I do remember the farmlands where I was sheltered during the long journeys, destinations unknown. My parents' fate I did not know, and I did not know I was a Jew. I learned I was a Jew long after the war. I also learned I was the only survivor of my family. I keep an escape backpack in my apartment and a small suitcase ready in case I'm forced to leave again. The suitcase is my childhood inheritance, containing the fears of a child left alone.'

Helmut Wolff by Armin Smailovic BOSNIA/GERMANY
HAMBURG, GERMANY, 2019

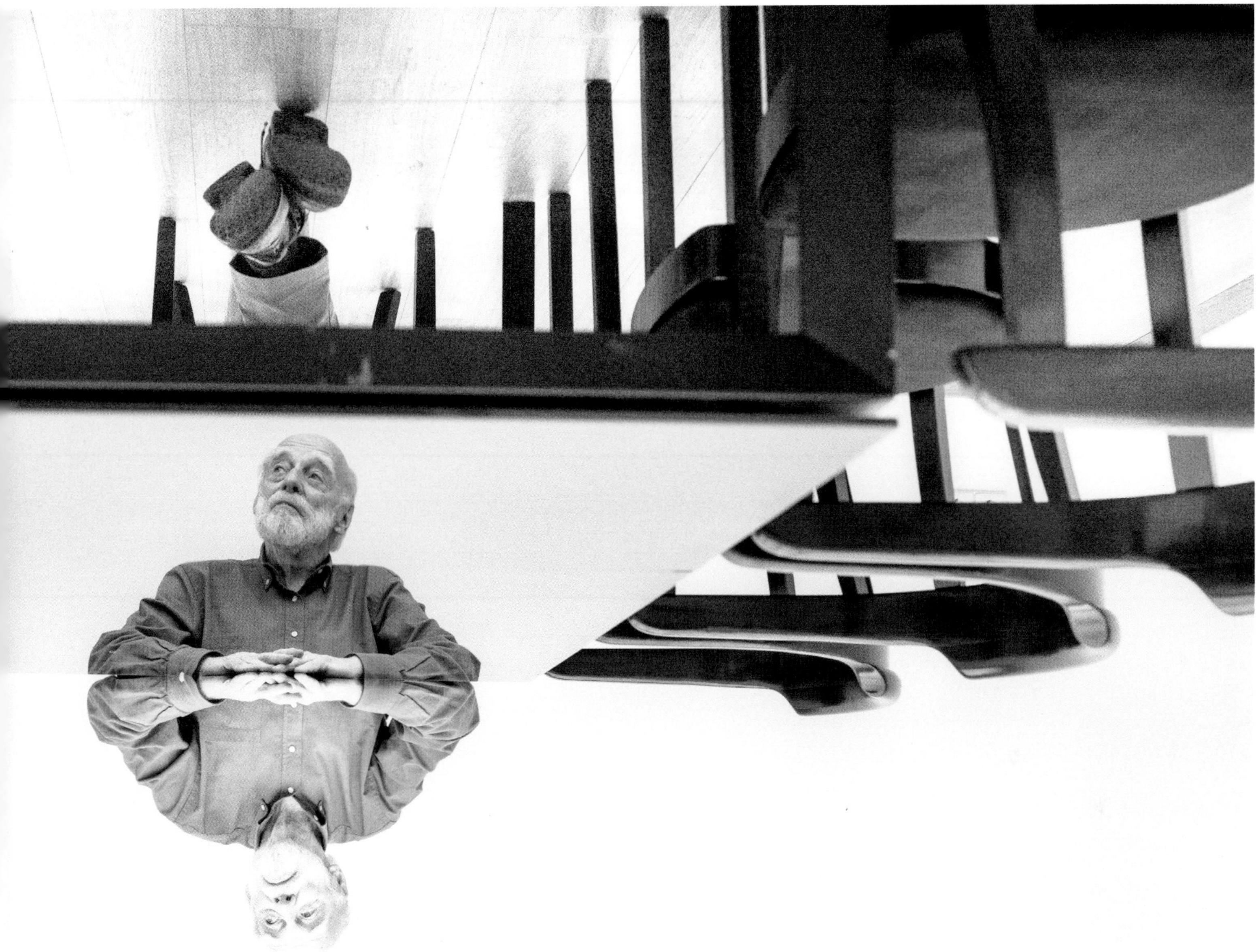

Itzhak Arad was born in Święciany, Poland (now Lithuania), in November 1926. During the war he joined the ghetto underground for two years. Then, in 1943, he joined the Soviet partisans of the Markov Brigade, where he encountered antisemitism in the non-Jewish unit. Yitzhak remained in that unit until the end of the war, taking part in attacks on Nazi railroads, bridges and trains in the forests of Belarus and in eastern Lithuania. In 1945, Yitzhak arrived illegally in Mandatory Palestine. He joined the Israeli army, rising to the rank of Brigadier General. Later he became the director of the Yad Vashem Holocaust facility in Jerusalem for 21 years from 1972 until 1993. Itzhak Arad passed away in May 2021.

Itzhak Arad BY Yoav Alon ISRAEL
RAMAT HASHARON, ISRAEL, 2019

Moshe Schleifstein was born in Krakow, Poland, in 1919. At the outbreak of the war, the family lived in Lancut, Poland. After the German occupation of the town, his father, Berl, took Moshe and Rojzale and they fled eastward into Soviet-occupied territory. His mother Chana was left with five children. In June 1940, Moshe with his father and his sister Ruizela were sent to Siberia where they worked in forced labor under extremely harsh conditions. In September 1941 they fled to Uzbekistan. In the summer of 1942, Chana and her children were murdered. In early August 1944, just four months after their killing, Lancut was liberated by the Red Army. In Uzbekistan, Moshe married Esther and their son was born. Moshe returned to Poland in early 1946 and located his mother's grave with three of her children. Moshe later immigrated with his family to Israel in 1949 and lived in Safed. In 2019, Moshe, at 100 years old, presented an ancient scroll of the Book of Esther he claims was written by Rabbi Zusha of Hanipol some two hundred years ago. Moshe passed away in 2020.

Moshe Schleifstein by David Cohen ISRAEL

SAFED, ISRAEL, 2019

ARON BIELSKY is the youngest of four brothers, after Asael, Tuvia and Alexander ("Zus"). He was born on July 21, 1927. The family were farmers in Stankiewicze, Poland, in present-day Belarus. When the Nazis invaded in 1941, his older siblings refused to go into the ghetto and fled into the forest. Two of his other siblings were not so lucky and were murdered. His parents were killed in a mass murder in their village in December 1941. The brothers formed a partisan group that became known as the Bielsky Brothers, the Bielsky partisans, or the Bielsky Brigade, with Aron playing a large part in guiding Jews from the ghetto out into the forest encampment. The Bielski brothers brigade was one of the most significant Jewish partisan resistance efforts against Nazi Germany during World War II. They fought the Nazis while providing a safe haven for Jewish women, children, and the elderly who were helped fleeing into the forests. The Bielski Brigade, with Aron's help, grew to some 1,200 Jews by the end of the war. After staying in Poland for some time after the war, Bielsky immigrated to Mandatory Palestine and in 1954 settled in the United States, joining his surviving family members. He changed his family name to Bell, owned and drove trucks in New York City, and is now living in Florida.

Aron Bielski BY Harry Benson USA
PALM BEACH, FLORIDA, USA, 2019

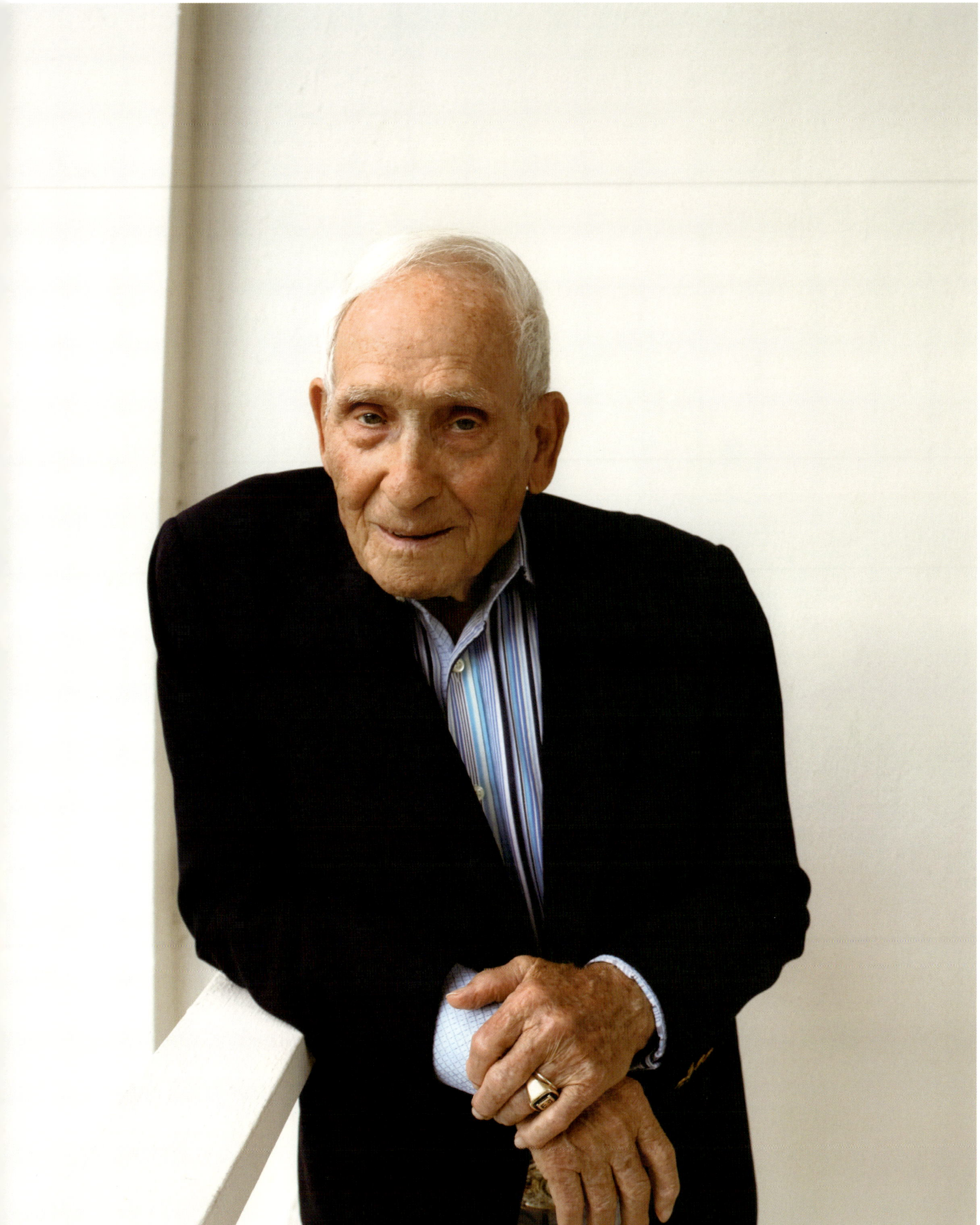

Esther "Stenia" Mannheim was born in Krakow in 1924. When the Nazis captured Krakow, she was no longer allowed to attend school, and had to wear the yellow star while cleaning the streets of Krakow. Then came the ghetto in Krakow, but the family felt lucky for being able to stay together – Esther (Stenia), her parents, sister and grandparents. During her life in the ghetto, Esther had to work in a factory, and one day, 'I waited for my mother to come and pick me up from work, but she didn't arrive. I never said goodbye to my mother and I never saw her again.' Esther learned her mother was deported to a death camp. Then the grandparents passed away and Esther's father was sent to the Mauthausen concentration camp. Esther and her sister were sent to four different camps before Auschwitz, where she remembers the smell and the smoke from the bodies that were burned. 'They tattooed us with a number and soon after they put us on a death train. A German asked if there were any sick people. We said no. They took all the sick people on the wagon and killed them on the way.' In 1944, when the Nazis wanted to eradicate the camp, Esther and her sister were forced on a death march to Malkov. They were starving and thirsty, but Esther and her sister survived. American soldiers arrived and liberated them. Esther and her sister returned to Krakow looking for surviving relatives and there in the synagogue Esther received news that her father was alive and in Mandatory Palestine. Soon after, Esther and her sister reunited with their father in Israel. Esther passed away on May 17, 2020.

Esther "Stenia" Mannheim BY Oded Balilty ISRAEL

TEL AVIV, ISRAEL, 2019

MARIAN TURSKI was born on June 26, 1926, in Druskienniki, in today's Lithuania. His birth name was Moshe Turbowicz. In 1942, he was confined to Ghetto Lodz. He was deported to the Auschwitz concentration camp in 1944. In the spring of 1945, he lived through the death march from Auschwitz to Buchenwald. In 1945, Marian Turski became an active member of the youth branch of the Polish Workers' Party (PPR), and later worked in the Press Department of the Polish United Workers' Party (PZPR). Since 1958, he has headed the history section for *Polityka* newsweekly. He married Halina, a survivor of the Warsaw Ghetto. He is chairman of the Jewish Historical Institute Association in Warsaw, and a member of the International Auschwitz Council, the Association Board that oversees the Wannsee Conference Center, and the Council of the Museum of the History of the Polish Jews.

Marian Turski BY Witold Krassowski POLAND
WARSAW, 2019

FIRST ROW: FANIA ITSKOVICH, MICHAEL BIEDER, ADELA MANHEIMER, BARBARA DROTOW.
SECOND ROW: MIRIAM REITZENSTEIN, PAULA GOLDSTEIN, REGINA LEWIN, MARIA ROSS.
THIRD ROW: KATHY SCHENK, ERNEST LORANT, TOBY TAMBOR, INGE BOOS.
FOURTH ROW: ARTHUR AND ROCHELLE ZICHERMAN (both survivors).

CAFÉ EUROPA STORIES

Holocaust survivors, photographed by Ethan Pines at the weekly "Café Europa" meeting of Holocaust survivors in the National Council of Jewish Women building, Los Angeles, CA, 11/5/2019.

TOP ROW, L TO R:

FANIA ISTOVICH Born in Mukatchevo, in the present-day Czech Republic. She spent the war years in the Auschwitz-Birkenau camp. She lost her parents and five siblings in the war. One uncle and one aunt survived the war. She immigrated to the United States in 1973.

MICHAEL BIEDER Born in 1923 in Ivanhorod, present-day Ukraine. He lost a younger and an older brother and an older sister. He took a train to Budapest, then to Austria, then after the war back to Ivanhorod. One sister survived the war. In 1975, he immigrated to the United States. Michael passed away at the end of May 2021.

ADELA MANHEIMER Born in 1921 in Poland. Her parents were killed in the war. She was in Auschwitz camp and on the death march to Prague. Nobody survived in her family. Immigrated to the USA in 1951.

BARBARA DROTOW Born June 1, 1933, in Lodz, Poland. Her parents were killed, but an older sister survived. Barbara was smuggled out from the Lodz Ghetto, and grew up in an orphanage in Uzbekistan. After the war she was evacuated back to Lodz. She immigrated to Israel in 1948. She met her husband on a blind date in Israel in 1960.

SECOND ROW, L TO R:

MIRIAM REITZENSTEIN Born in Poland. Her parents and four sisters were killed. One brother survived. She ran away to Ukraine and spent two years in Siberia, then Uzbekistan, and at war's end was transported back to Poland with other children. She then traveled to Haifa, but was sent to Cyprus before continuing to Israel. She immigrated to the United States in 1955.

PAULA GOLDSTEIN Born in Kalish, Poland, on January 9, 1922. Her parents, twin sisters and two brothers were killed in the war. She spent the war years in Czestochowa, Poland. She and two other brothers survived. After liberation, she went to France and then to Israel in 1948, then immigrated to the United States. Asked if she wanted to add a note she said, 'Keep Israel strong!'

REGINA LEWIN Born in Cenzin, Poland. She was in a ghetto, then in southern Germany in the mountains in a forced labor factory for three years. She was evacuated by the Red Cross back to Poland at war's end. Only some distant cousins survived. She moved to Brussels, Belgium, where she obtained legal identification, then moved to Melbourne, Australia, and from there to the United States.

MARIA ROSS Born on November 7, 1930, in Kishniev, Moldova (present day Romania). During the war, she moved to a little village in Russia, then to Siberia, then to Turkmenistan. Her parents and one aunt survived the war. She returned to Romania after the war, then immigrated to the United States in 1973.

THIRD ROW, L TO R:

KATHY SCHENK Born in Poland. She spent the war years in Germany, moving from concentration camp to concentration camp. After liberation she went to Austria. No one in her family survived. She immigrated to Michigan in 1999.

ERNEST LORANT Born in 1923 in Budapest. He spent the war years in the Auschwitz concentration camp. None of his family survived. He immigrated after the war to Israel, and in 1947 went to the United States.

TOBY TAMBOR She guesses she was born in 1932 in Belarus. During the war she was in a ghetto and then in the forests. After liberation she went to Belarus / Russia, was in a displaced persons camp in Austria, and then traveled to Israel. Her mother survived the war. She immigrated to New York in 1967.

INGRID "INGE" BOOS Born September 10, 1934, in Frankfurt, Germany. Most of her family went to Minsk and died. She was in the Theresienstadt camp with her mother. They were both liberated there by Russian soldiers. They returned to Frankfurt after the war. Both Inge and her mother immigrated to the United States in 1950.

BOTTOM ROW:

ARTHUR AND ROCHELLE ZICHERMAN (both survivors) Arthur was born in 1927 in Czechoslovakia. One sister and one brother survived the war. Three brothers and his parents were killed. He lived in a ghetto during the war years. His wife Rochelle was also born in 1927 in Czechoslovakia. Of 11 siblings in her family, only one brother and two sisters survived the war. She was in the Auschwitz and Buchenwald concentration camps. She married Arthur in 1970 in Los Angeles.

Café Europa BY Ethan Pines USA
LOS ANGELES, CALIFORNIA, USA, 2019

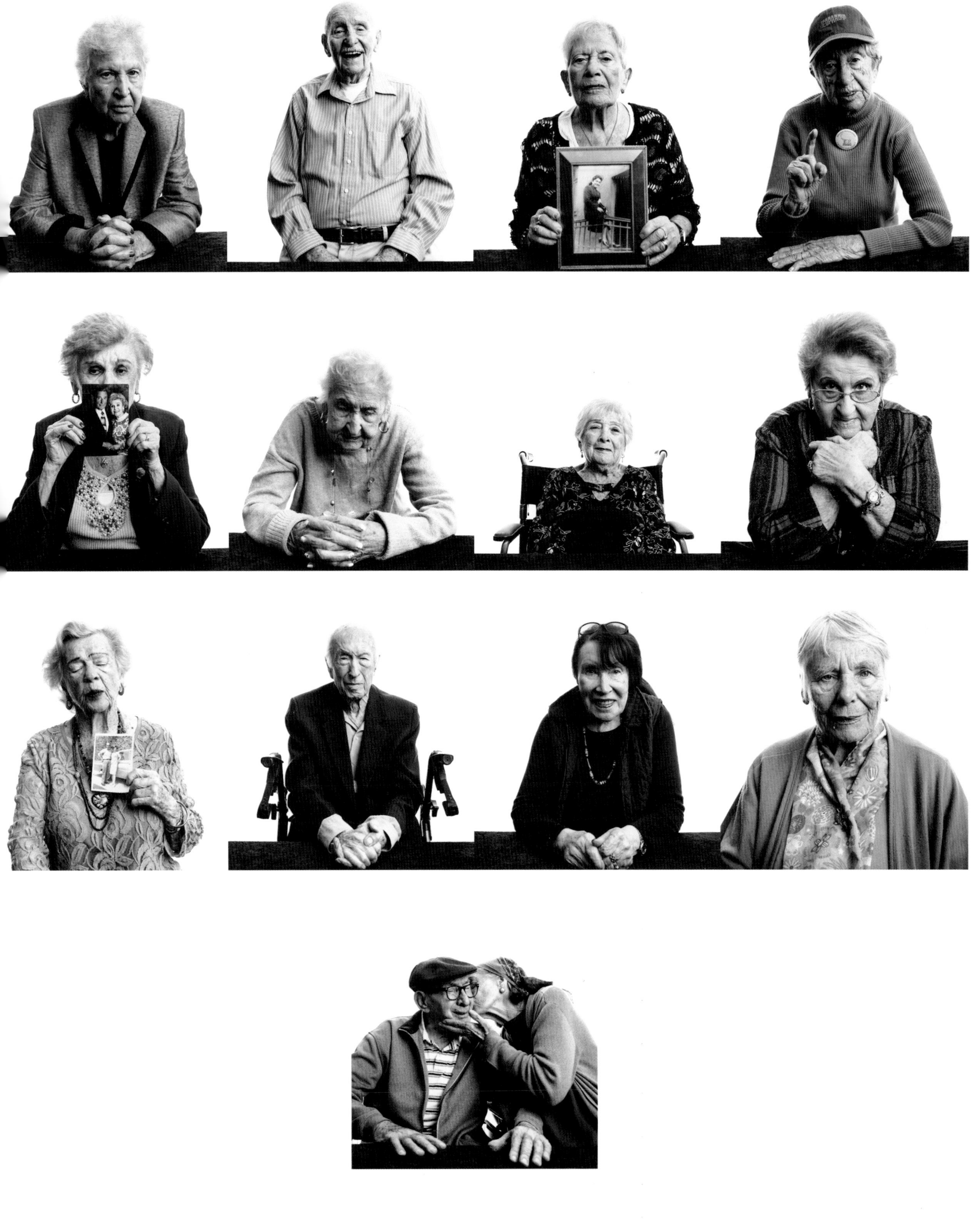

Shaul Paul Ladany BY Tsafrir Abayov ISRAEL
OMER, NEGEV DESERT, ISRAEL, 2019

Professor Shaul Paul Ladany was born in Belgrade, Yugoslavia, in 1936. He is a two-time Olympian race walker. In 1944, when he was eight years old, Shaul survived the Bergen-Belsen concentration camp and in 1972, as an Israeli Olympic athlete, survived the Munich massacre. In 1941, the Germans attacked Belgrade and Shaul's family fled to Hungary where his parents briefly hid him in a monastery, warning him not to tell he is Jewish. In 1944 his family was captured by the Nazis and shipped to the Bergen-Belsen concentration camp. Shaul recalls, 'I went into the gas chamber and was reprieved. God knows why.' In December 1944, he was saved by American Jews who had paid a ransom in an attempt to save Jews from extermination. Shaul and his parents were on the Kastner train from Bergen-Belsen to Switzerland and survived the Holocaust. In December 1948, when he was 12 years old, the family emigrated to Israel. In 1972 while taking part in Olympic Games in Munich, Shaul was one of five Israeli team members to escape death at the hands of the Palestinian terrorist group Black September. Shaul broke the world record for the 50-mile speed walk in 1972 in New Jersey, USA, and continues to hold the record today.

ADA WILLENBERG was born in Warsaw in 1929. When Nazi Germany invaded Poland, her father volunteered for the Russian army and died there, and her mother was captured during the "Grossaktion," the Nazi code name for the deportation and mass murder of Jews from the Warsaw Ghetto beginning in July 1942. She was sent to the Treblinka death camp. Ada Willenberg was 14 and decided to jump over the walls of the ghetto and run for her life. 'I was alone, I did not have anybody to lose.' She jumped into the hands of a Polish smuggler who helped her into hiding with a Polish couple, the Majersky family (later recognized as Righteous Among the Nations by Yad Vashem). They did not know she was Jewish. When the war ended, she married Samuel Willenberg, considered the last Holocaust survivor of the Treblinka revolt. He fled to Warsaw, where he joined the Polish resistance. Some 200 prisoners escaped from the burning Treblinka camp and were later killed by the guards' gunfire. Ada and Samuel immigrated to Israel in 1950. Samuel passed away in Israel in 2016, leaving behind his sculpted bronze statues to tell the horrors of Treblinka. Ada quotes her late husband, 'The sculptures will continue talking for me.'

Ada Willenberg BY Karen Gillerman ISRAEL
TEL AVIV, ISRAEL, 2019

TOMI REICHENTAL was born in Slovakia in 1935. He was nine when he was captured by the Nazis in November 1944 along with his mother, his brother Miki, and members of his extended family. They were soon herded into a cattle car. 'We were the first transport from Slovakia of children and elderly that was diverted en route to Auschwitz-Birkenau, the gas chambers were blown up by the Germans, fearing the Russian troops' advance towards the camp.' When the doors were flung open, they were at the Bergen-Belsen concentration camp. 'What I have seen upon arrival were SS armed men with barking dogs and skeletons walking around very slowly, falling, never to get up again.' Tomi was sent to block 207 'In front of our barrack, we would find corpses in the mornings,' Tomi recounts. 'Prisoners threw themselves on the barbed wire at night to be shot in order to put an end to their misery.' Tomi, his mother and older brother Miki survived. Thirty-five members of his family perished. Bergen-Belsen camp was liberated by the British in 1945. Tomi came to Ireland in 1959 and lives in Dublin.

Tomi Reichental BY Amelia Stein IRELAND
DUBLIN, 2019

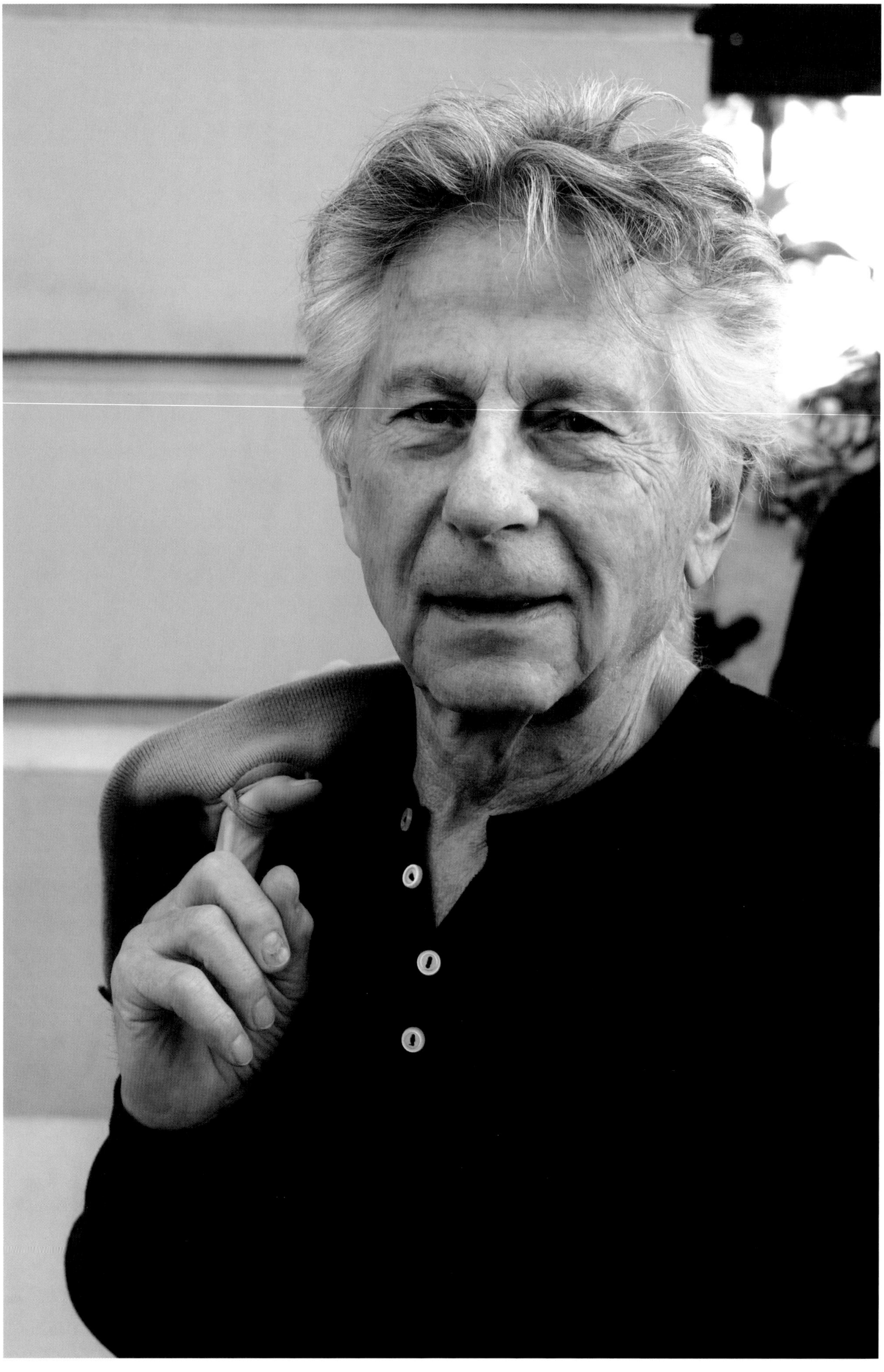

Roman Polanski, among the world's greatest film directors, was born Raymond Liebling in 1933 in Paris, to a Jewish Polish family. In 1936 the family returned home to Poland and when Roman was six years old they were caught up in the horrors of the war. Roman watched the construction of the ghetto walls in Krakow, where he lost his childhood, witnessing atrocities, executions in the ghetto where Nazi guards separated "able workers" from those who were sent to be executed. Roman's mother, Bula, expecting a child, was taken from her family and sent to death in the gas chambers of Auschwitz. Roman's life was saved when his father Ryszard succeeded in smuggling him out from the Krakow Ghetto on the verge of its liquidation in 1943, with many of its inhabitants dead. Roman's father was taken to the Mauthausen camp for forced labor. At age nine, Roman, alone, was hidden by a Polish family and passed the next two years of the war as a Catholic boy with the name Roman Wilk, being transferred from one hiding place to another. Roman was reunited with his father in 1945. In an interview to *Hollywood Reporter* Roman Polanski was quoted saying that for years he was hopeful that 'Mother will come back.'

Roman Polanski BY **Franck Leclerc** FRANCE
NICE, FRANCE, 2019

MARGOT PINS was born in 1931 in Breslau (today Wrocław), Germany. Following anti-Jewish legislation in prewar Nazi Germany, Margot, then seven, remembers signs announcing that Jews were no longer welcome to use the city park benches. Her father, Salo Cassel, was fired in 1935 from his managerial post, and he and Erna, her mother, understood the danger they were facing. They decided to leave Germany. At the time, no country was offering entry visas to Jews, except the Philippines. The Cassel family left Germany in early November 1938, missing the devastation of Kristallnacht by a few days. They settled in Manila. In 1942, the Japanese overran the US defenses in the Philippines. Manila itself became a battleground. Margot recounts, 'I did not feel abandoned in any way, and I was not given to panic. I felt protected.' Together with the rest of the city's population they were caught in a struggle to survive and forced to flee, as the Japanese set homes ablaze. They began walking, often crawling, to avoid being shot, as they made their way to what they hoped were the American lines. When the battle for Manila ended on March 3,1945, 'You would walk in the streets. You got used to seeing a body being covered with newspapers. People had starved to death, people had been stabbed to death,' she recounts. The civilian casualties in Manila surpassed 100,000. Margot and her parents were among some 1,300 German Jews who did survive after being taken in by the Philippines. Their extended large family in Breslau perished. In Manila, Margot met a young American GI named "Arnie" Pins, and the two married a few years later in New York. In 1974 Margot and Ernie immigrated to Israel. Margot has been returning to Manila yearly, and is active on behalf of supporting the Philippines community in Israel.

Margot Pins Kestenbaum BY Rustam Bayramov ISRAEL
RIMONIM, 2019

'My name is **Hela Blumenthal** and I am a survivor. I survived the horrors of the Warsaw Ghetto, the gas chambers of Majdanek, the depravity of Auschwitz and the utter hopelessness of Bergen-Belsen. I lost 23 members of my immediate family, my parents, my brothers, my sisters, their spouses and eight nieces and nephews – the only other survivor being my eldest niece, Roma. But for me, while abnormal, this is not extraordinary. That I went on to love, to talk, to write, to have toast and tea and to live my life – that is what is extraordinary. Although I have spoken many times about the war years – the struggles and heartbreak that followed the liberation remain untold. The fight back from the brink of death was, in many ways, more difficult than the battle to survive. I will never forget the morning of the 15th of April 1945. It was the morning that the rumbling of British military tanks was heard on the Lager Strasse of Bergen-Belsen. We saw our erstwhile lord and master, Lager Commandant SS officer Josef Kramer seated next to a British officer looking defeated and pathetic. The loudspeakers were blaring, "You are free. The British Army has liberated you. Food, water and medicine are on their way." Our long nightmare had ended. Before the liberation, conditions in Bergen-Belsen had declined. Bread rations were reduced to less than a slice and then stopped completely. There was no more drinking water. Nazi officers were pushing wheelbarrows packed with documents, and some of the watchtowers were empty. Krammer's original plan was to seek a 24-hour truce with the British, claiming a typhus epidemic as an excuse to keep the Allies out of Bergen-Belsen. The British refused the request, and what they saw on entering the camp was thousands of near-naked, starved skeletons moving about mountains of decomposing bodies. Although we were actually too weak to celebrate, those of us who were still alive cried tears of joy and relief. We were dusted with DDT and deloused. Water was restored. The British soldiers offered us their own food rations, cans of meat and beans. I warned Roma not to touch it as our shrunken stomachs could not digest the rich foods. Some could not resist the temptation and paid with their lives.'

Hela Blumenthal BY Rodger Bosch SOUTH AFRICA
CAPE TOWN, 2019

NAT SHAFFIR was born in Iasi, Romania, in 1936. The Fascist Iron Guard identified the family as Jews in 1942, and armed guards took the family to a nearby ghetto that day. Nat and his sisters, Sara and Lili, were no longer allowed to attend school. 'Never give up,' his father said before he was taken for slave labor in early 1944. Those words have kept Nat going for his entire life. Nat, then seven, was the one in charge of bringing food rations for his sisters until the war ended. In 1945, after days of heavy bombing, Russian soldiers liberated the ghetto and months later his father returned from the labor camp. Nat learned that 32 of their relatives perished in the Auschwitz-Birkenau and Buchenwald concentration camps. In 1961, a surviving uncle sponsored Shaffir to immigrate to the United States. Nat became a marathon runner at age 65, and on August 24, 2019, Nat Shaffir was on top of the world; he had reached the summit of Mount Kilimanjaro.

Nat Shaffir BY Dave Burnett USA
WASHINGTON, DC, 2019

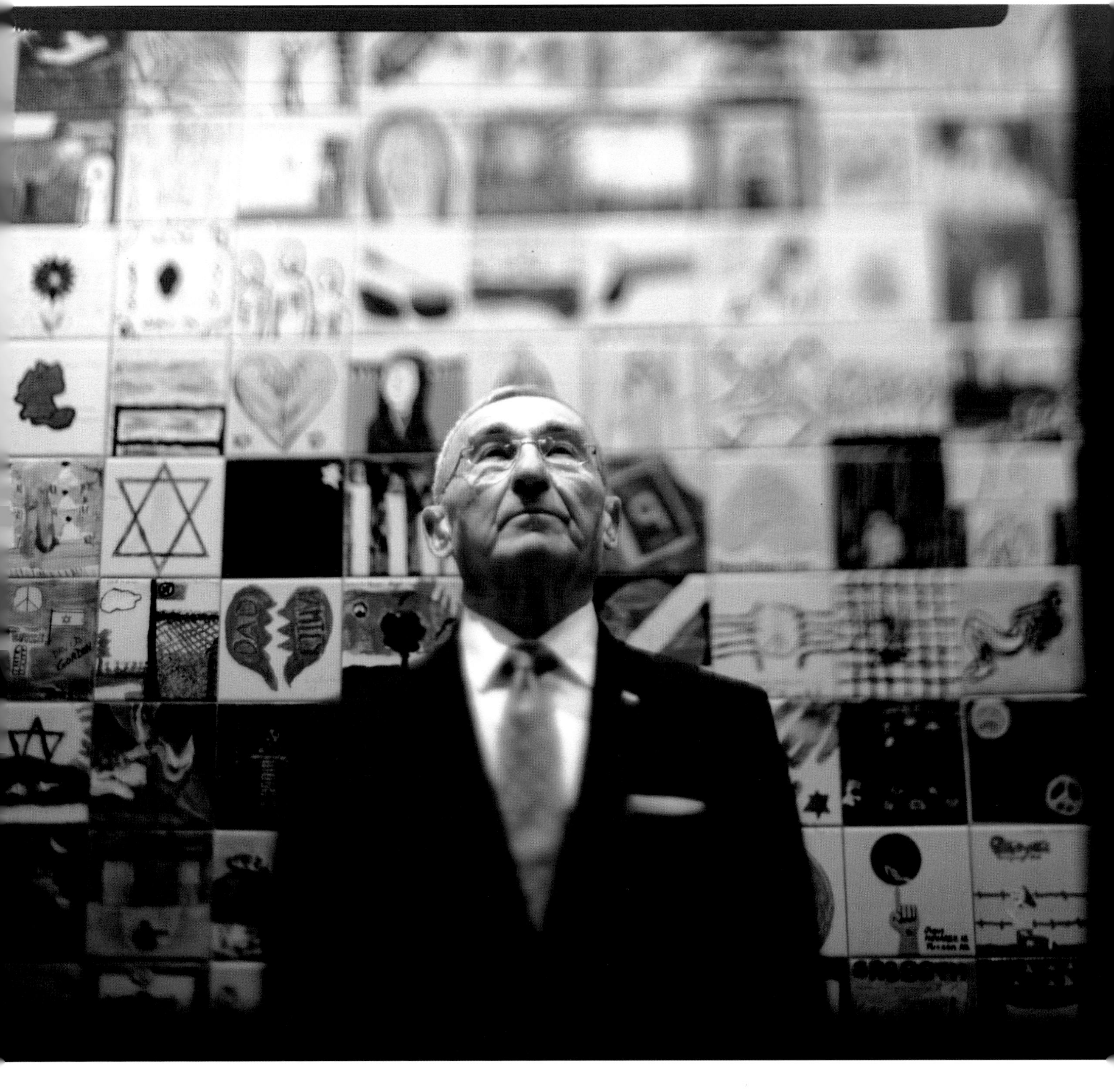

JUDITH KENIGSBERG was born in 1929 in Nitra, Slovakia. When World War II began, she was expelled from school, and also expelled with her family into the city's ghetto. In 1944, and on her sister's birthday, all the Jews were rounded up and taken to the railroad tracks, loaded into freight cars and shipped to the Auschwitz death camp. Upon arrival, Judith, 14, with her 10-year-old sister and their mother, were separated from Judith's father, whom they would not see again. They were in Auschwitz until its liberation by the Red Army. Judith was malnourished. After wandering through various displaced persons camps throughout Europe, in 1947 Judith boarded the ship *Theodor Herzl* to Mandatory Palestine. The ship was captured by British soldiers and all passengers were transported to a detention camp in Cyprus where she spent two years before arriving In Israel in 1949.

Yehudith Kenigsberg BY Emanuel Ilan ISRAEL
KIBBUTZ HAHOTRIM, ISRAEL, 2019

BERNIE GROSS was born in Czechoslovakia in 1922, the third of six brothers and a sister. In 1939, his father had to report to the Hungarian authorities, and at age 17, Bernie worked to support his family. In 1941, Nazi-allied Hungarians conscripted Bernie into the Munkatabor, a forced labor camp. Later he was marched to the front lines, where the detainees were subjected to atrocities like marching into mine fields to clear the area for advancing German troops, killing many of the detainees. In late 1944, Bernie and three other inmates ran away from the guards, members of the fascist Arrow Cross Party, after learning that the railroad cattle cars they had been forced into were headed to Nazi extermination camps. Bernie hid in the snow for three days until the trains left. They hid from the Nazis for months. Bernie was liberated by the Russians and was reunited with all of his siblings, who also survived the war. In 1949, Bernie immigrated to the United States.

Bernard Gross BY George Pirkle USA

ATLANTA, GEORGIA, USA, 2019

URI ORLEV was born in Warsaw in 1931. When Poland was invaded, Orlev's father was a physician in the Polish Army and was captured on the Russian front. Uri, his mother and young brother were taken to the Warsaw Ghetto. After their mother was killed by the Nazis, the two boys were smuggled out of the ghetto and hidden by Polish families. They were identified as Jews in 1943 and shipped to the Bergen-Belsen concentration camp. During his two years in the camp he wrote his first poems in Polish about what he witnessed, the suffering, hunger and death day after day. 'God, where is justice, where is morality, when some are dying while others live.' He described Jews crammed into trains transported to their deaths. Uri and his brother were liberated by American soldiers. In 1946 Uri arrived in Mandatory Palestine and eight years later he was able to be reunited with his father. In Israel, Uri is a celebrated author of childrens' books on the Holocaust. Uri Orlev passed away on July 26, 2022.

Uri Orlev BY Dusan Vranic SERBIA
JERUSALEM, 2019

LYDIA ABRAMSON was born in 1931 in Globuck, White Russia, then a part of Poland. They were a family of two brothers and two sisters. After the outbreak of the war the family was deported from their home into the overcrowded Globuck Ghetto. 'In 1941, after heavy bombardment, the Germans invaded, and we were ordered to wear the yellow badge identifying us as Jews. After a few months, the Nazis started the executions of the elderly and the sick; the firing took place at the pits dug by prisoners in the nearby forest. One day the Nazis ordered all the Jews to the market area for another Selektion. My uncle's family was sent to the right while we were sent to the left. Those on the right were murdered and thrown into a common grave in the woods. I was told to sort the left-behind clothing. I saw my aunt's scarf, but then I didn't understand its meaning.' In August 1943, Lydia heard shots and shelling. 'We hid in the attic, but the wooden log houses were set on fire and forced us out. My brothers and my mother were a bit ahead of me when shooting resumed. My mother ordered me and my brother to lie flat down; she lifted her head and was shot dead. My brother and I pretended to be dead, and later quietly got up, but soon after my brother was caught and killed. I fled the ghetto and went on an arduous 200km journey through the forests. I ate berries until I found the Russian partisans. They used to move from one place to another and sometimes forgot and left me behind, and I would find myself alone in the woods until the Bielski brothers, Jewish partisans, found me.' In May 1945, the war ended and Lydia returned to Globuck. 'I lost my parents, two brothers and a sister, and the entire families of my parents. I was transferred to an orphanage near Lodz, and in 1946 to displaced persons camps and to France, where I boarded an illegal immigration ship of mostly orphans of war bound for Mandatory Palestine.' Lydia served in the army and rebuilt her life in the farming community of Tzofit.

Lydia Abramson BY Sivan Farag ISRAEL

TZOFIT, ISRAEL, 2019

JOSEPH PELL was born Yosel Epelbaum on May 5, 1924, in the small town of Biala Podlaska, Poland. In September 1939, shortly after Nazi Germany's tanks rolled into Poland, Joseph's parents decided to abandon their home and escape east with hundreds of other Jewish families. Nearly all of the Jews who remained in Biala Podlaska would be murdered by the Nazis. The family found refuge in the town of Manievich, near the border of Ukraine and Belarus. There was no escape when Nazi Germany invaded the area in June 1941. Many of the Jews were shot by Nazi soldiers going door to door, rounding them up into ghettos. During the sweep, Yosel's father, Hershel, and two of his brothers, Simcha and Moishe, were denounced, captured and taken to killing fields out of town where they were stripped and executed along with hundreds of others, into a massive open grave. Yosel, his mother Rivka, sister Sima and brother Sol did not have time to grieve when they were forced to relocate into a ghetto. One day, his sister Sima didn't return home and Yosel never saw her again. Yosel and brother Sol had a plan to hide in the nearby hayloft should they hear the dreaded "*Juden, raus*" (Jews, outside) on the bullhorn, which meant death. That day arrived in 1942, when Nazis and Ukrainian thugs entered their house. Yosel raced towards the barn as he planned with Sol. He hid in the barn's loft beneath the hay. An armed Ukrainian entered, searched the barn and left. 'Sol must have been caught, inside or in front of the house, and now along with our mother, was on his way to a terrible death.' Yosel made it to the forests where he spent months hiding in barns throughout the winter's cold, dazed, hungry, and his spirit shattered. Yosel joined a band of escaped Jews, Poles, Ukrainians, Soviets and others who were hiding in the woods, and who wanted to fight the Nazis. At age 18, Yosel embarked on dozens of missions to disrupt the Nazi war machine by blowing up train tracks, bombing bridges, cutting telephone lines and damaging highways. Partisan life was fraught with danger, but it did offer comradeship and a measure of protection. Yosel subsisted in the woods with his partisan group throughout the war. At war's end, the sole surviving member of his family, he was footloose, traveling and trading to make some living before immigrating to America in 1947 where he would begin his life as Joseph Pell. After passing through Ellis Island, with no English, a few dollars, and a Leica camera, a poster featuring the Golden Gate Bridge caught his attention. Joseph boarded a bus for San Francisco where he met EDA, who was smuggled out of Nazi Germany as a child and arrived in the US as a war orphan. They married in 1953. Joe never stopped missing the family he lost, but he was proud of the family he raised with Eda, that grew to include four children and nine grandchildren. Joseph became a successful businessman and a philanthropist. In 2005 Joseph decided to write his memoir *Taking Risks*, co-authored by historian Fred Rosenbaum. It was his way to confront the past. 'I wanted to be a witness to the past, present and future deniers of the Holocaust.' Joseph Pell passed away in December 2020.

Joseph & Eda Pell BY Lori Adamski-Peek USA
SAN RAFAEL, CALIFORNIA, USA, 2019

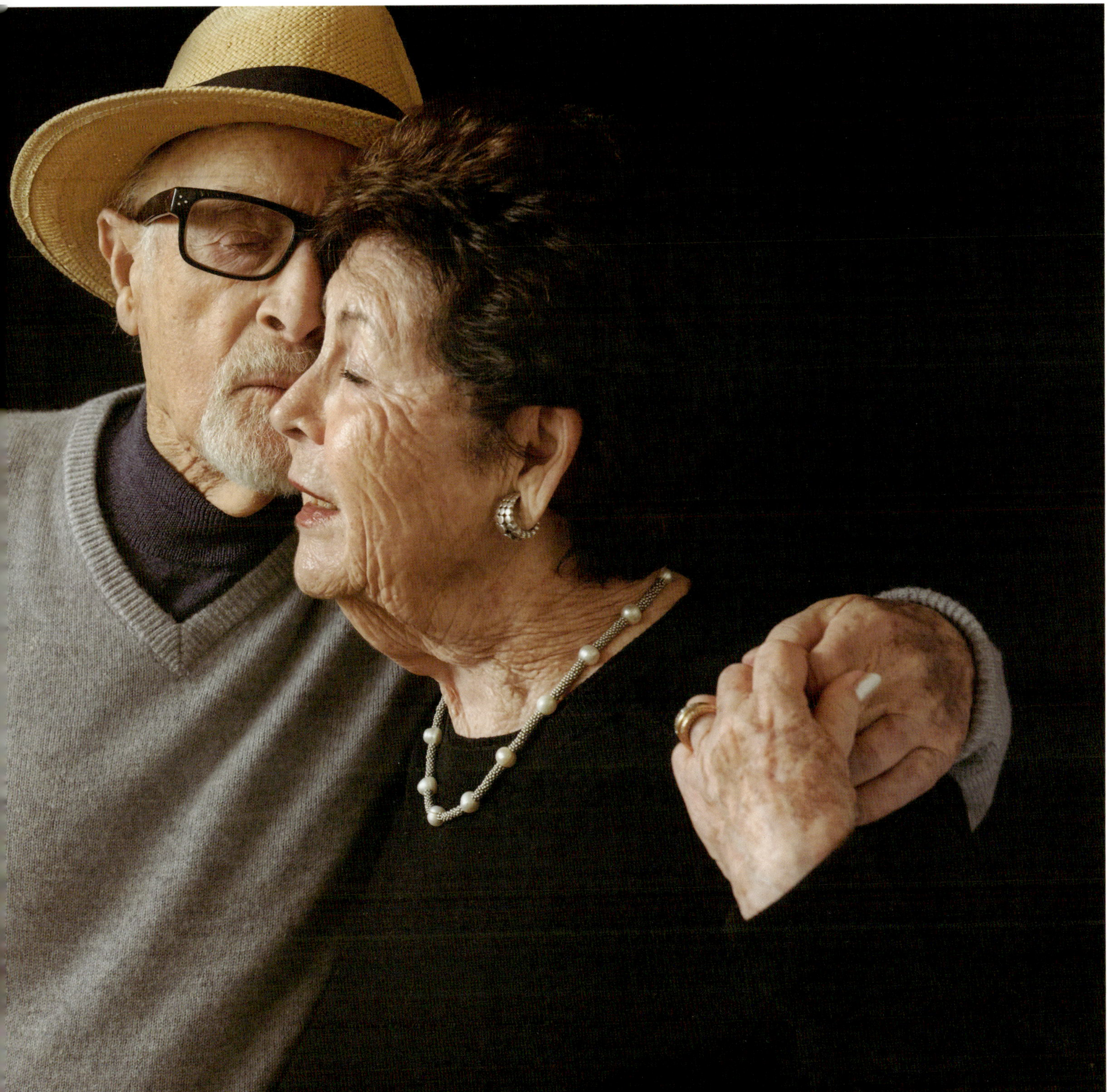

YEHUDIT ASHRIEL was born in Hungary in 1926. In 1944 she was deported from the ghetto to the Auschwitz-Birkenau extermination camp with her family when she was 18. 'We arrived at the train station at night. The doors opened and the place was lit with large lanterns as if it was the middle of the day. SS soldiers everywhere with dogs. As soon as the doors of the wagon opened we were shouted at to get out faster. I asked what about the suitcase and they said they would bring it to me later. I did not know people were lying, I believed everything. The first Selektion was by Dr. Mengele – a Satan who separated men and women. I have not seen my father since. I stayed with women on the ramp and Dr. Mengele sitting on a high chair wearing polished, shiny uniforms, white gloves; he would gesture, right and left: life or death. SS soldiers forced us to undress and fold neatly our clothes; we were left naked like animals. It was very cold. We were marched to a hut – and set on the ground – about 200 women. We clung on the ground to each other to keep warm. I fell asleep from exhaustion and I woke up to screaming. A Polish Jew who was held in the camp pointed to us the smoke coming out of a chimney and said that this was where all are being exterminated. She wanted us to know what awaited us, what would be the end. None of us said a word – this was the first time we heard the truth.' Judith managed to survive in the death camp and after a period she was sent to forced labor in an AEG industrial plant with a group of Jews. Judith's resourcefulness and knowledge of German gained the trust of the engineer in charge of her, and led to her rescue and the rescue of the group that was with her. In May 1945 she was liberated by the Red Army. She returned to her home to look for members of her family. Only her sister survived. The family's candlesticks, hidden by neighbors from looters, were all that was left from her family home. Judith immigrated to Israel in 1949 and dedicated her life to help new immigrants and commemorations of the Holocaust. She passed away in Oct. 2020.

Judith Ashriel BY Maya Maymoni ISRAEL
BE'ER SHEVA, ISRAEL, 2019

RACHEL GREENFELD was born in Lodz, Poland, in 1926. She was 13 when the Nazis invaded Poland. In the Lodz Ghetto, Jews were rounded up. 'Then they got us in the train cars to Auschwitz. We were sorted into men and women and since then I have never seen my father and brother again. Mum and I stood together, and I was holding her so tight but the Nazi separated us, and I haven't seen her since. I had nothing to live for.' In Auschwitz one night, Rachel ran away from her block to another. 'The next day they sent all my block to death. A few days later, the gas ran out and we were sent to a labor camp in Germany. I will never forget the day when the French came into the camp and shouted, "The war is over, you are free."' Rachel returned to Lodz to look for relatives. 'I was left alone.' ELIEZER GREENFELD was born in 1925 in Lodz. His father was among the first victims to be executed on the city's main street. Eliezer and his mother were taken into the ghetto. Nazis declared a curfew and began the deportation of all Jews to the extermination camps. Men and women were separated. 'I thought I will never see my mother again.' Eliezer was taken to a forced labor camp. 'I weighed 40 pounds then, and when I put sacks on my back I fell. I fled with a few prisoners to the forest.' They hid until the roaring Russian tanks approached. War was over. Eliezer returned to Lodz. 'On the steps of the house, my mother was waiting for me; we both survived.' Eliezer and Rachel met in Lodz and were among the first couple of survivors to marry. They immigrated to Israel in 1956. Eliezer passed away on April 19, 2020.

Eliezer & Rachel Greenfeld BY Moti Milrod ISRAEL
HOLON, ISRAEL, 2019

SOLOMON SOLLY (SHLOMO) PEREL was born on April 21, 1925, in the town of Peine, Germany. That is what he told the German soldier who asked the 16-year-old Solomon if he was Jewish. In a split-second life-or-death decision, the Jewish youth choose survival. Solomon and his brother Isaac left their parents in the Lodz Ghetto and fled to the eastern Soviet Union. His father told Solomon, "Always remain a Jew," while his mother Rivka implored, "You have to live." He was placed in an orphanage and on June 22, 1941, the 16-year-old Solomon was captured by invading German troops in an open field around Minsk. Solomon buried his papers just before being captured by German soldiers. A Nazi asked him, "Are you a Jew?" and he replied he was a "Volksdeutscher" (an ethnic German living abroad). He took the name Josef Perjell, donned a Nazi uniform, and became an interpreter in a German army unit. He translated the interrogation of Joseph Stalin's son, Yakov Dzhugashvili, for his German army unit. On another occasion, Solomon even photographed Hitler when the führer visited Perel's unit on the front. As a circumcised Jew, Solomon was constantly in danger. He repeatedly attempted to flee. Being a minor, he could not remain with the army, and he was sent to a Hitler Youth boarding school in Braunschweig, where he was forced to study Nazi Aryan racial doctrine. He became convinced of the superiority of the Aryan race. He later said that the 'Solomon inside me completely disappeared. I began hating myself for being Jewish.' Solomon Perel was sent to the Western Front and assigned to a German unit guarding bridges. In 1945, close to the end of the war, Perel was captured by a US Army unit and was released a few days later. He learned that his father had died of starvation in the ghetto, his mother was murdered in a gas execution truck in 1944, and his sister was shot while on a death march. Perel moved to Munich where he was a translator for the Soviet Army during interrogations of Nazi war criminals. He emigrated to Mandatory Palestine and fought in the War of Independence as a member of the Palmach strike force in the Jerusalem Brigade. He was also reunited with his brother. Solly wrote an autobiography in German in 1990, which was translated into English as *Europa Europa*. The book was made into a movie, winning a Golden Globe award, and was nominated for an Oscar. Shlomo Solly Perel traveled the world lecturing of his experiences always stressing people should "accept the other," and reject racism in all its forms. Shlomo Perel passed away in early February 2023, at age 97.

Shlomo Perel BY Odd Andersen NORWAY
LEIPZIG, GERMANY, 2019

LEA GOLDBERG was born in Singapore in 1937. In 1942, the Japanese occupation of Singapore began, and Jews were mandated to wear armbands and medallions with the word "Jews" inscribed on them. During the occupation, Lea with her family were taken to prisoner of war camps located at Changi Prison, and to the Sime Road concentration camp. In the camp, the prisoners suffered from malaria and typhus. Many died of malnutrition and disease. Lea's sister, Alida, was among the dead. The Jews were allowed to keep a kosher kitchen and were able to build a makeshift synagogue. On May 1, 1944, due to overcrowding, civilian prisoners, including Lea's family, were transferred to the Sime Road Camp. In 1945, after the Japanese surrendered to the British on September 2nd, they were freed. Lea eventually immigrated to Israel.

Lea Goldberg BY Kobi Kalmanovitz ISRAEL

JERUSALEM, 2019

MADELEINE KAHN was born in 1933 in Paris. In June 1939, her parents sent her to her grandmother, who lived in Stanesti de Jos Bukowina (present-day Ukraine) for the summer holidays. In August 1939, the borders were closed, and the six-year-old girl couldn't return to France. After the 1941 pogrom in Stanesti de Jos, the women and children were sent to the concentration camp in Transnistria in November 1941, first by cattle train, then on foot. Madeleine remained in the camp for the next two years with her grandmother, her aunt and her one-year-old cousin. She was rescued by the French consul in Romania, who took the child from the camp, separating her from her aunt and cousin, and brought her to the consulate in Galatz. Because she was gravely ill, she was sent to the hospital of the sisters of Saint Vincent de Paul. The religious community kept the small girl in hiding until April 1946, when she was repatriated to France at age 13 and was reunited with her parents. Madeleine Kahn became a medical doctor, a historian and a writer. She moved with her husband to Israel in 2014, and lives in Tel Aviv.

Madeleine Kahn BY Tomasz Lazar POLAND
SAINT-PAUL DE VENCE, FRANCE, 2019

WOLF GALPERIN was born in Kovno, Lithuania, in 1928. When the Kovno Ghetto was liquidated in 1941, Wolf and his brother Shlomo were among the group who had survived the Kinder Aktion, where many were executed. Later, the surviving women and children were taken off the train at the station in the vicinity of Stutthof concentration camp, where the children parted from their mothers. Wolf was the oldest of the group of children, later known as "131 Kovno children," and when they were shipped to Dachau and later to Auschwitz-Birkenau, Wolf was tattooed with the number B 2819. He took on the role as leader of the remaining children, instructing them how to obey the Nazi rules. 'I taught them to walk, to stand in the ranks and to salute. I was the father of 130 children,' which saved the lives of some 39 children from being immediately sent to extermination. Wolf later was forced on a death march and fled into the woods in 1945. After the war, he returned to Lithuania, served in the Russian army and immigrated to Israel in 1990. Wolf lives in Sderot.

Wolf Galperin BY Avi Roccah ISRAEL
SDEROT, ISRAEL, 2019

Yitzhak Wollach was born in Sarajevo in 1940. Nazi Germany invaded the city in 1941 and his parents sent him and his younger brother into hiding at a Christian family's farm. In 1944, 'Nazis also came there, and sent us to the Bergen-Belsen concentration camp.' Yitzhak was five at the time and remembers his grandfather, a devout religious man, praying during the long journey on the freight trains. 'We were hungry and thirsty. One day the train's door opened, and my mother handed a bottle to a soldier to fill it with water. She was pushed back by him and then hit him with the bottle while screaming that she had small children to look after.' Upon arrival to the death camp his grandfather was executed. Yitzhak also remembers a moment of rare kindness when, days later in Bergen-Belsen, the soldier who had refused his mother water recognized her in the camp and brought water for them. 'We were locked in barracks with many beds and no mattresses and toilets…lots of illnesses, and cures – there are none.' Yitzhak and his parents and younger brother survived; the extended family perished. In 1945 they were freed and the family returned to Yugoslavia. In 1948, Yitzhak immigrated to Israel.

Yitzhak Wollach BY Gali Tibbon ISRAEL
JERUSALEM, 2019

Charlotte Knobloch was born in 1932 in Munich, Germany, the only child of Fritz Neuland and Margarethe who converted to Judaism upon marrying Neuland. After the passing of the Nuremberg laws, Margarethe left the family in 1936 and Charlotte was raised by her grandmother Albertine Neuland. As a child, she witnessed Kristallnacht after her father, fearing arrest, felt it would be too dangerous to stay home and safer to be in the streets. She was six years old, holding her father's hand on a Munich sidewalk and looking up at the fire-blackened synagogue. In 1942, Fritz brought Charlotte to Kreszentia "Zenzi" Hummel, a Catholic woman they knew. Her father was arrested by the Nazis and her grandmother was deported to death camps where she perished. Charlotte's life was saved by Zenzi Hummel who brought her into her family of farmers in Franconia. From 1942, for three years, she lived with the Hummels who introduced Charlotte as their own daughter. In May 1945 Charlotte was reunited with her father, who had managed to survive forced labor. Charlotte remained in Munich and is a leader in the German Jewish community.

Charlotte Knobloch BY Thomas Dworzak MAGNUM PHOTOS GERMANY
MUNICH, GERMANY, 2019

Danilo Nikolić was born in 1938 in Sarajevo, Bosnia and Herzegovina. When Sarajevo came under Nazi German shelling in 1941, the Nikolić family escaped from Bosnia and Herzegovina to Montenegro, where they stayed until 1943. His father joined the partisans who were fighting the Nazis, and went missing in action in Slovenia in 1945. Danilo and his mother spent the first years of the war in hiding, and later with the partisan fighters in Montenegro. In 1945, right after the liberation of Bosnia and Herzegovina, they returned to Sarajevo. Of the 47 members of Danino's family, only two of his uncles survived the war. Danilo lived in Sarajevo, as well, during the 1992–1995 siege on the city, which lasted 1,425 days.

Danilo Nikolić by Armin Smailovic BOSNIA/GERMANY
SARAJEVO, 2019

SAMI MODIANO was born in 1930 on the Greek island of Rhodes, at the time an Italian province. On the island, Jews, Christians and Muslims coexisted peacefully until the enforcement of racial laws in 1938. Sami, identified as a Jew, was expelled from school. 'That day I lost my innocence. That morning I woke up like a baby. At night I fell asleep like a Jew.' His father lost his work and his mother died of an illness. Nazi Germany invaded Rhodes on July 23, 1944, and Rhodes' Jews were rounded up and deported by ship to Piraeus. There they were loaded into sealed cattle train wagons and shipped to the Birkenau camp. Upon arrival, men and women were separated and Sami, 14, was selected by Dr. Mengele for death in the gas chambers. He was saved by his father Jacob who pulled him away from the death line. Sami was registered with the number B7456. After a few months in the camp, his sister Lucia and his father Jacob perished. Sami, left alone, befriended an Italian boy, Piero Terracina. 'It was a true, deep, fraternal friendship.' At the next Selektion Sami, malnourished and weak, was sent again to the gas chambers and was saved by a transport of potatoes when the SS needed a worker to urgently unload the trucks. In 1945, the Soviets were approaching, and the SS forced Birkenau prisoners to march to Auschwitz. During the march Sami collapsed and was saved by two unknown men who camouflaged him with piles of corpses. When he regained some strength, he began walking and found his friend Piero Terracina together with Primo Levi. The next day, January 27, 1945, they were liberated by the Soviet army. 'I was now a free man, but there was no joy. I felt guilty.' Only 31 men and 120 women remained from the Rhodes Jewish community. After liberation, Sami arrived briefly to Italy and later emigrated to the Belgian Congo where he married and tried to rebuild his life, disrupted again with the outbreak of a civil war. Sami returned to Italy to be close to his friend Piero Terracina and in 2005 they visited Auschwitz. During the visit, Piero convinced Sami to dedicate his life to Holocaust education. Sami spends the summer in Rhodes where he takes care of the ancient synagogue and the small Jewish community on the island. In 2013 he published a memoir, *For This I Lived.* In 2020 he was honored with the Knight Grand Cross of the Order of Merit of the Italian Republic. Russia's Chief Rabbi Berel Lazar places tefillin on Holocaust survivor Sami Modiano in Rome in a photo from August 5, 2019.

Sami Modiano BY Stefano Montesi ITALY

ROME, 2019

Ben Stern was born in Poland in 1921 to a large religious family, and was a teenager during the Nazi Germany invasion. After being herded into the Warsaw Ghetto where he lived with his parents and eight siblings in squalor and hunger for two years, Ben was forced to separate from his family on August 15, 1942, and was deported to the Majdanek concentration camp. He was later transferred to Auschwitz, where he survived by falsifying his tattooed number 129592, constantly worrying about the crematorium and death Selektions. Ben endured forced labor in nine concentration camps and survived two death marches. In 1945 he had to march from Buchenwald to the Tyrolean mountains near the Austrian border. 'Seven thousand young men left Buchenwald; we were 156 who survived.' Ben was liberated by American troops in 1945. He was 24 and weighed 78 pounds. His family perished in the Holocaust. Ben never gave up hope that he would find his family. When he visited the Treblinka death camp in 1988, he left a note in the visitors' book that said: 'I'm looking for my mother.'

Ben Stern BY Yuval Rakavy ISRAEL
SAN FRANCISCO, CALIFORNIA, USA, 2019

GAD PARTUK was born in Tunisia in 1931, the fourth in a family of six sons. Beginning in 1940, Tunisian Jewry suffered from Nazi rule. Nazi Germany's racial laws were applied to them, and when the local government began harassing Jewish families, Gad's father, who was head of the Nabel city Jewish community, was briefly arrested. The family moved to the capital Tunis after Gad's mother died. After the Germans invaded Tunisia, one of their headquarters was established near the home of the Partuk family. One day Gad's father disappeared, and then one by one the three eldest brothers. 'I was 11 years old and only saw German patrols around our house. My father and brothers disappeared and I did not ask any questions.' Gad was left with his father's second wife Miriam and two younger brothers, and had to take on the role of an adult and provide for the family. 'Dressed in a jalabiya and speaking only Arabic, I would go daily to bring any food I could find. Even bread crumbs. The Germans would come to us daily, looking for my father and brothers, and took the money and valuables of Miriam. She gave them all, just so they would not touch us. Then one morning Dad showed up at the house and after a while my brothers came back too. My father told me that he found refuge from the Germans near us, disguised as an Arab cloth merchant. When he realized that my older brothers were in danger of arrest, he took them one by one and hid them.' After the war Gad joined a Zionist youth movement. His father gave his permission, and in less than a week in late 1947, Gad boarded a ship to Marseille, changed his name from Hamees to Gad, and immigrated to Mandatory Palestine aboard a small fishing boat, on a 16-day voyage. At the end of an arduous journey, he arrived at Kibbutz Beit Zera in the Jordan Valley, where he met Mona, who later became his wife and the mother of his children. In 1950, Gad was sent to establish Kibbutz Karmia, near Ashkelon. His passion for photography increased and after ten years of living on the kibbutz, Gad requested to be allowed to join a photography course, which required a vote by the members. 'The request was denied. I was in shock. I got up and said four words: "Goodbye, friends, I'm leaving." The very next day he moved to nearby Ashkelon as a photographer, and his works flowed non-stop. In 1961, Gad and Mona opened the legendary "Photo Gad" studio. Every year, Gad participates in a Holocaust remembrance project. 'I tell about the Tunisian Jews' ordeal during the Holocaust, the many who were sent to forced labor camps and those who never returned.' Gad has continued to pursue photography until the present day.

Gad Partuk BY Moran Ahdut Nissim ISRAEL
ASHKELON, ISRAEL, 2019

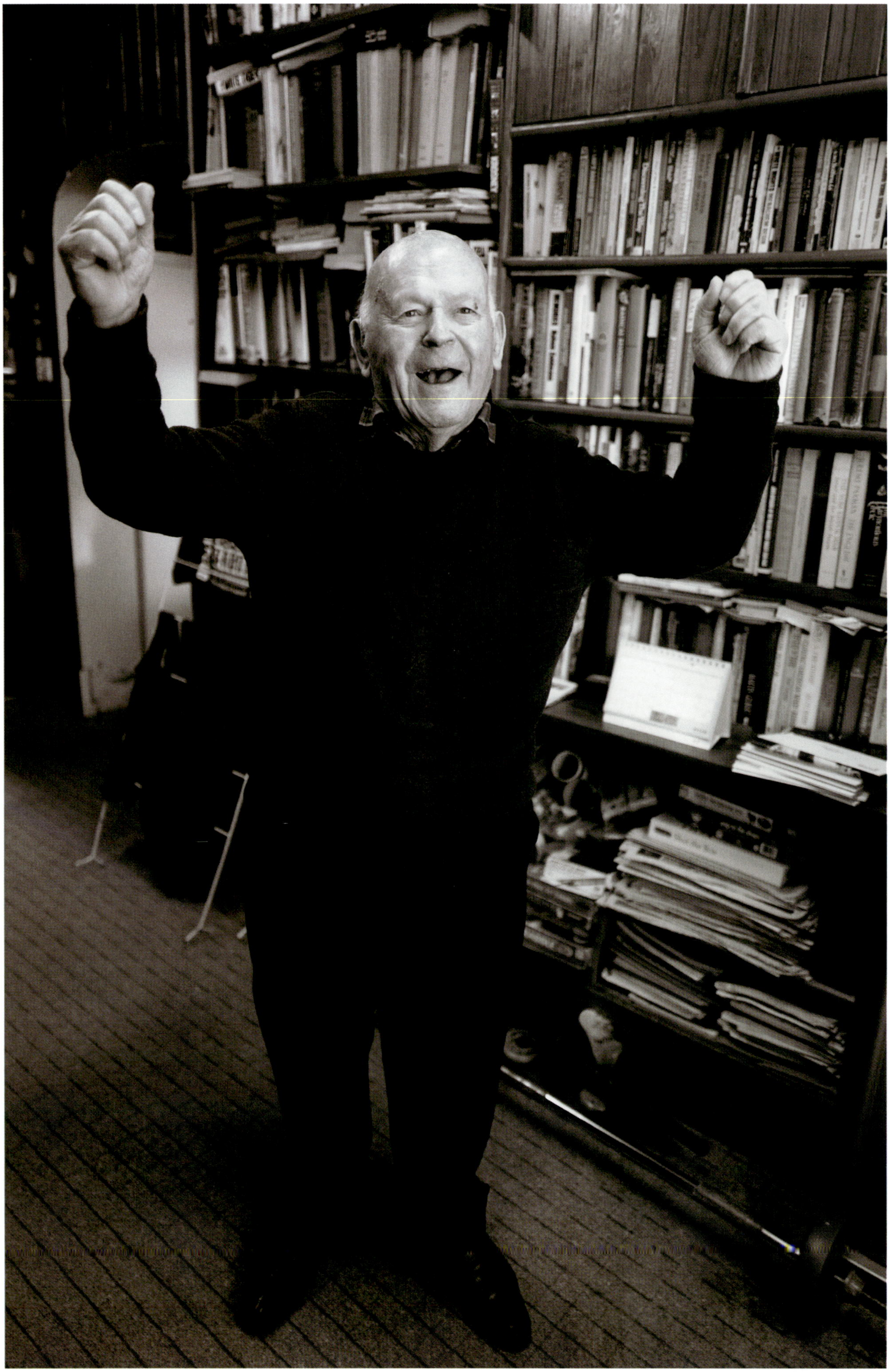

Sir Ben Helfgott was born in Piotrkow, Poland, in 1929. He was ten when Germany invaded Poland. In 1942, the Nazis herded the Jews into the Piotrkow Ghetto. Ben, then 12, registered to work at a glass factory, having heard rumors that if one had a job assisting the war effort of the Third Reich, one would not be taken away. 'We did not know where Jews were taken – we heard stories of gas chambers, but who could believe it?' The factory's manager, Mr. Janota, treated him brutally. But when SS guards marched into the glass factory and rounded up workers for transport to Treblinka – Ben among them – Janota came to Ben's rescue. Janota lied to the SS men, risking his own life and saving Ben by saying that Ben was a non-Jewish Pole. Later, Ben was caught and sent to Buchenwald. 'It was a terrible place. All we had to eat was soup that smelled like urine and a crust of bread.' Later he was shipped to Theresienstadt, where he was eventually liberated, weak, emaciated and starving. Ben's mother Sara and sister Lusia had been rounded up and murdered in a forest. His father was shot trying to escape from a death march from Buchenwald, just days before the war ended. Ben was sent to England after the war at age 15 with 700 other orphans. A mere 11 years later, Ben was part of the 1956 Olympic Games in weight-lifting, a feat he repeated in 1960. He is one of two Jewish athletes to have competed in the Olympics after surviving the Holocaust. Ben was appointed a Knight Commander of the Order of the British Empire in 2018 for service to Holocaust remembrance and education, and in October 2020 Sir Ben was awarded the Pride of Britain award, also for his outstanding contributions to Holocaust education. Sir Ben passed away, age 93, on June 16, 2023.

Sir Ben Helfgott BY Greg Williams GREAT BRITAIN
LONDON, 2019

Ester Erna Kaveson Debevec was born September 18, 1933, in Sarajevo, Bosnia and Herzegovina. When the first bombs fell on Sarajevo in April 1941, Ester, her sister and mother escaped to Mostar in Bosnia and Herzegovina. Ester's father joined them just a few weeks later. In 1942 they had to move to Split in Croatia. After that they were deported to the island of Brać, just opposite Split, then further to their final destination, a prisoner camp of the Italian army on the island of Rab in Croatia. At the end of 1943, partisans freed them, and after two years in Croatia they returned back to Sarajevo in August 1945, just after the liberation of Bosnia and Herzegovina in April 1945. Ester Erna Kaveson Debevec also lived in Sarajevo during the 1992–1995 siege of the city, which lasted exactly 1,425 days.

Ester Erna Kaveson Debevec BY Armin Smailovic BOSNIA/GERMANY
SARAJEVO, 2019

ABRAHAM HAR SHALOM was born in 1925 in Pruzhany, Poland. In June 1941, Nazi Germany invaded Pruzhany and in 1943 began the deportation of Jews from the ghetto to the Auschwitz death camp. Abraham's parents were immediately taken off the train ramp and sent to the gas chambers. Abraham and his brother Sioma were together in Auschwitz, but after a few weeks Sioma was sent to the gas chambers. In 1944, Abraham fled Auschwitz with two other prisoners. For a few days they hid in a pit covered with dirt, but were caught and were badly beaten. Abraham was marked with a red badge of a criminal. In October 1944, about 10,000 detainees including Abraham were evacuated from Auschwitz and sent on a death march to Buchenwald. 'Whoever stumbled was shot dead.' From Buchenwald, Abraham was on a "transport" of detainees to other labor camps. When the train stopped, Abraham fled and jumped on a coal train with two other prisoners. They hid among piles of coal all the way to Prague where, 'we stood in prisoners' garbs, covered by coal, and we didn't know what to do.' A passing boy came to their rescue and brought them to his mother's house. Janina Sobotkova sheltered them in a flower shop. She was later honored with the Righteous Among the Nations award by Yad Vashem. In 1945, Abraham was recruited by the underground. He was trained to use weapons and fought the retreating Germans. When the Red Army liberated Prague from the Nazis, Abraham, whose entire family perished, chose to remain in Prague, where he was awarded Czechoslovakian citizenship and honors. In 1947, Abraham was recruited by Israeli envoys for a pilots course in order to fight for Israel's independence. In March 1949, Abraham immigrated to Israel and served in the Israeli Air Force.

Abraham Har Shalom BY Nir Elias ISRAEL
RAMAT GAN, ISRAEL, 2019

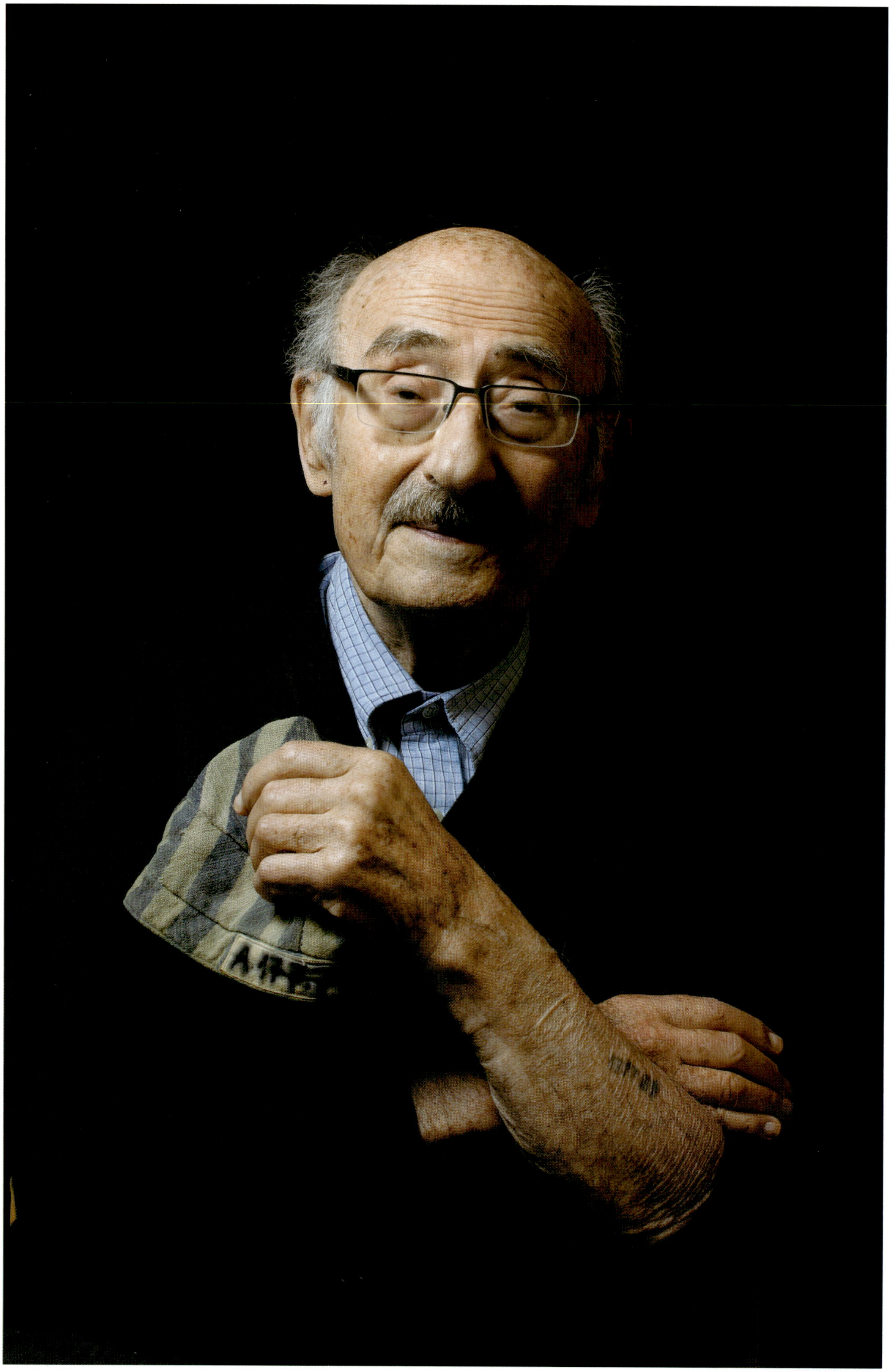

HENRI KICHKA was born in 1926 in Brussels, Belgium. His parents came from Poland. In May 1940, the family was stunned by the Nazi invasion of Belgium but Josek, Henri's father, had no illusions about the fate awaiting the Jews. In the first week of September 1942, they were taken from their Brussels home as the Nazi soldiers sealed off the street in the middle of the night and went from building to building forcing all Jews from their homes. The family was herded into cattle wagons in a railway transport heading east first to Germany and then to Nazi-occupied Poland. Henri and his father Josek were taken off the train with the other men in the small town of Kosel. They were to work in slave labor for the Third Reich. Henri's mother, Chana, his sisters Bertha and Nicha and his Aunt Esther were shipped to Auschwitz and upon arrival they were gassed. Henri ended up imprisoned in ten concentration camps: Camp d'Agde, Camp de Rivesaltes, Sakrau, Klein Mangersdorf, Tarnowitz-Nord, Sankt Annaberg, Kattowitz-Schoppinitz, Blechhammer, Gross-Rosen, and Buchenwald. On January 21, 1945, with the advance of the Red Army, they were forced on a death march with some 5,000 prisoners – only 750 survived. Henri's father died a few weeks after surviving the death march. Henri was liberated on April 11, 1945. Three days later Henri turned 19. Henri returned alone to Brussels and succeeded to rebuild his life. On April 25, 2020, Michel Kichka announced his father's death, "A small microscopic coronavirus has succeeded where the whole Nazi army had failed."

Henri Kichka BY Pascaline Lefin SWITZERLAND/BELGIUM
BRUSSELS, 2019

PEGGY PARNASS was born in Hamburg in 1927. In 1939 her mother took the decision to separate from her children and send them to safety. Peggy remembers her mother walking her and her little brother Gady to the train where the children boarded the Kindertransport – an organized rescue effort of children, mostly Jewish, during the nine months prior to the outbreak of WWII. 'Mummy took us to the train and said she will join us soon. Although she knew she would never see us again, she stood there and laughed…waving as long as we could see her…' Only after the war Peggy learned from her aunt Berti that her mother stayed on the train's platform long after the train left and mourned their separation for days. In Stockholm, Peggy's brother Gady was sent to an orphanage and Peggy lived with 12 foster families in six years. She did receive letters from her parents. They were sent from the Warsaw Ghetto, until the day when the letters stopped. Peggy's parents were deported to Treblinka extermination camp where they were murdered in 1942. In the 1950s Peggy returned to Hamburg and her brother Gady joined a kibbutz in Israel. In Hamburg, Peggy's circle of friends included influential figures in post war Germany and Peggy became an acclaimed journalist, author and film maker. She wrote hundreds of articles about Nazi mass murders, the Baader–Meinhof Group (RAF) trials, and is considered as an outspoken icon for the gay movement and the oppressed. Her books, such as *Prozesse* (Trials), published in 1978, won her the Joseph Drexel Prize in 1979 in journalism. Other awards include an Order of Merit of the Federal Republic of Germany.

Peggy Parnass BY Axel Martens GERMANY
HAMBURG, GERMANY, 2019

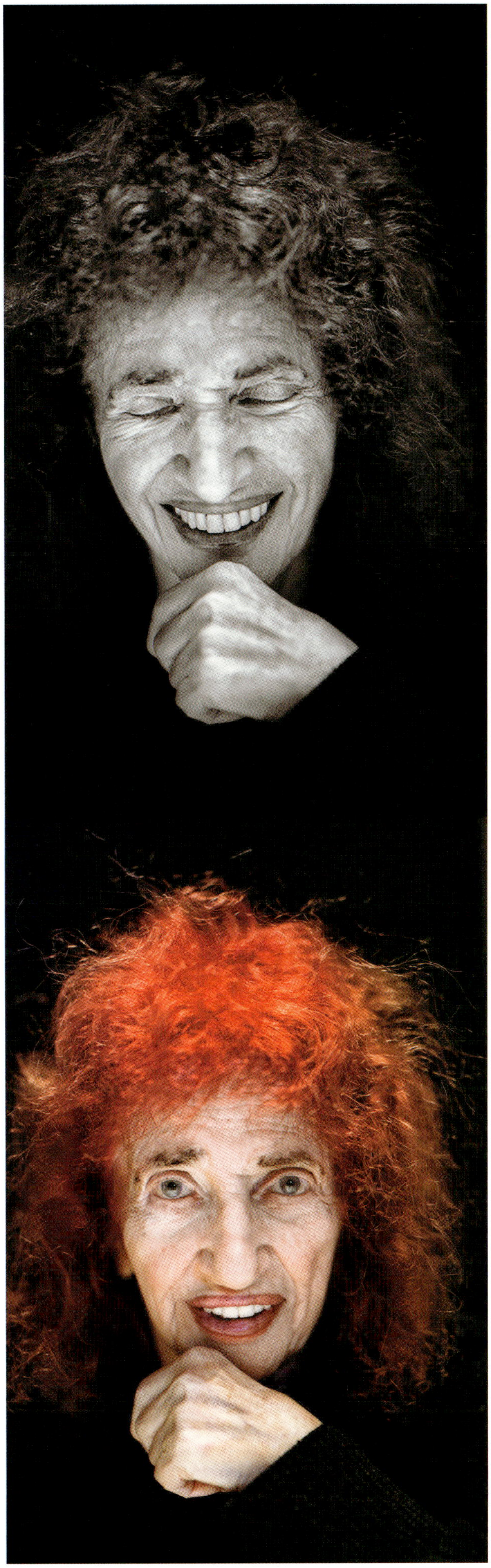

Vitzek Avi Shtembuj BY Jorge Novominsky ARGENTINA / ISRAEL
MODI'IN, ISRAEL, 2019

VITZEK AVI SHTEMBUJ was born in Lodz, Poland, in 1944. The Lodz Ghetto had been sealed off by the Nazis since 1940, and the murder of the Jews in the ghetto and the surrounding areas continued intermittently until January 1945. Chana and Israel Shtembuj managed to hand over their newborn baby to a Catholic priest, and Vitzek was saved. When the war ended, it was Vitzek's uncle who returned to Lodz to search for his dead brother's child. Vitzek was adopted by his uncle and together they immigrated to Israel in 1950. Vitzek grew up unaware of his past. Only in 1969, when Vitzek was a fighter in the Israeli army, was he prepared to find out what happened to his parents, who had perished in the Holocaust. Visiting the Yad Vashem Holocaust memorial and research center in Jerusalem, a man caught Vitzek's attention. It was Simon Wiesenthal, who had dedicated his life to hunting down Nazi war criminals. Vitzek decided to act. 'I handed him a note with my phone number, and the phrase "God avenge their blood."' Six months later, Vitzek was recruited into Wiesenthal's secret team. To Vitzek's surprise, Wiesenthal's team was well aware of his military service as a paratrooper. Vitzek was an expert in sabotage and martial arts, and a talented sniper. 'They asked me if I was capable of killing, and made it clear I would receive no support should the operation fail.' He was given the operational file and prepared for his first mission. The target was SS officer Hans Krieger, responsible for the murder of thousands of Jews. 'I arrived in Vienna and, after days of fieldwork, I shot two bullets into Krueger's head.' A few days later, he was assigned to kill the Nazi war criminal Carl Schmidt. Vitzek traveled by train to Stresa, Italy, where Schmidt lived. 'The mission there was complex,' he recalls. He was accompanied by two team members. 'We made our way to the villa where Schmidt lived.' Long, tense hours went by until Vitzek found himself facing Schmidt in his bedroom. 'Schmidt saw the gun in my hand,' and told Vitzek, "I know you came to take my soul, but my soul belongs only to Hitler." Vitzek recounts the dramatic moments. 'Schmidt walked towards the balcony and jumped to his death. Not a single shot was fired. They were murderers who were responsible for terrible atrocities. Today I can cope with that.' Vitzek, a family man, found comfort. 'For my parents, for me. I closed a circle.'

RACHEL GIDALI was born in Romania in 1934. Romania became an overtly antisemitic state in 1937. When Rachel was five years old, her father was taken to a Romanian forced labor camp. 'Because we were Jews,' Rachel recounts, their landlord threw her mother along with Rachel and her two siblings into the street. Her family later found refuge in the home of a Romanian Christian family around the time of the Iasi pogrom in 1941, one of the worst massacres of Jews during World War II. Rachel's only memory is learning how to sew a "yellow star" on her coat. 'We were always scared. I was not allowed to speak to anybody except my family. We are hiding in a cellar, and we were isolated from the world.' Rachel has a vivid memory of the day in 1944 when Russian troops liberated the town of Vaslui. For the first time, Rachel was allowed to leave their hiding place. She joined the dancing in the streets as Red Army tanks roared through. Rachel's father survived, and the family continued to live in Romania until 1959, when they immigrated to Israel. Through matchmaking, Rachel married a survivor of the death camps who was living in the United States. There the couple would build their home and family.

Rachel Gidali BY Andrew Bordwin USA

NEW YORK CITY, NEW YORK, USA, 2019

Dr. Moshe Meron was born in Budapest in 1935. Holocaust horrors were at their peak in Hungary in the spring of 1944, when the Nazis' severe restrictions were imposed. Schools were closed and the Jewish community was concentrated in the city's ghetto. Moshe's father was sent to the Mauthausen concentration camp, 'We didn't see him again.' Moshe, his little brother, and his mother lived with some fifty other people in one of the ghetto houses. 'One day we were all forced to the town square. My mother slowly pulled us back to the edge. The Hungarian police officers, they had no special interest with us, but they followed the Nazi German orders. My mother pulled off her last precious necklace and placed it in one of the Hungarian policeman's hands. He accompanied us back home to the ghetto. Only when I grew up, I understood what she did, on her tombstone I wrote, "She saved her children during the Holocaust."' Moshe, his brother and mother immigrated to Israel in 1949.

Dr. Moshe Meron BY **Effi Sharir** ISRAEL
BUDAPEST, 2023

A doorbell panel features the names of Jewish residents who used to live in the building at 35 Kaethe-Niederkirchner Strasse in Berlin. The plaque was unveiled on May 12, 2019, next to the building's entrance, in memory of some 80 Jewish residents and landlords who became victims of the Shoah, murdered in Auschwitz, Theresienstadt, Kulmhof, Lodz, Minsk, Piaski, Raasiku, Riga, Sachsenhausen, Treblinka, and Warsaw.

Stolpersteine by John MacDougall CANADA
BERLIN, 2019–20

View of eight Stolpersteine ("stumbling blocks") created by German artist Gunter Demnig, commemorating Holocaust victims (from top left) Jacob and Selma Kaufmann, Samuel, Resi and Regina Heim, Gitel Brzezinski, and Alexander and Moritz Eugen Simon in Berlin's Prenzlauer Berg district on January 20, 2020. The stumbling stones, topped with small brass plaques, are installed in front of houses where Jews who were deported to death camps during Germany's Nazi regime once lived. German artist Gunter Demnig, who started the project in 1993, has already installed thousands of Stolpersteine in cities where Jews lived in Germany and abroad.

CLAUDE LELOUCH is a French film director who was born in Paris. He and his mother moved through Europe during World War II to evade the Nazis, but were captured toward the end of the war and spent three months in the Dachau concentration camp. During the war, the Lelouch family had left Paris for the south of France, just one week before the Nazi invasion. 'My father was a shopkeeper, but he was very sharp. He suspected that the Jews would be exterminated,' Claude Lelouch said. 'Every time someone knocked at the door, I hid in a cupboard. I had a list of phone numbers stuffed under my belt in case of emergency. Still today, I'm psychologically scarred by this. I never really let go, except when I'm in love.' In order to hide him from the Nazis, his mother entrusted him to an usherette in a local cinema. 'I spent my time in the cinema and I developed a passion. Cinema is the best vehicle to go from barbarity to civilization,' he said. 'Cinema made me aware of the world. It made me love life. It is my mother and my father in one.' The war period strongly influenced his films. 'It is important for me to explore this theme that dominated my childhood,' he said.

In his films *Les Uns et les Autres* and *Les Misérables*, the children escape Nazi persecution just as he did. 'During the war, a German officer asked me to drop my trousers. I told him I was circumcised because I peed sideways. I recited a Catholic prayer, which saved my life.'

Claude Lelouch BY Shaul Dishi ISRAEL
HAIFA, ISRAEL, 2019

ITZCHAK BELFER was born in 1923 in Warsaw. He was four when his father died, and his mother was left to care for six children. Educator Janusz Korczak briefly interviewed Itzchak, and accepted him into his orphanage home. Itzchak recalls seven most meaningful years, in which he studied in a local school and lived in the orphanage home with 104 children. Korczak's assistant Stepha Vilichenska encouraged Itzchak to take up drawing. In 1939, the Nazis conquered Poland. Itzchak decided, at 17, to run away from Poland and join the Russian armed forces, in order to fight against the Nazis. Itzchak and his friend approached Korczak to get his blessing, which he gave and even equipped them with an allowance. In 1940, Itzchak came to the Malkini refugee camp. He started working in odd jobs before he was drafted into the Red Army and was stationed in one of the cavalry regiments. After the war, Itzchak returned to Warsaw and found it in ruins. Neither his family nor the orphanage had survived. All were murdered by the Nazis in the Treblinka concentration camp. Itzchak began a period of wandering in Europe until he reached Genoa, where he joined a group of refugees who were set to reach Mandatory Palestine. In 1947, the ship he boarded was stopped by British soldiers and all passengers were sent to detention camps in Cyprus. In 1949, he was able to reach the newly established State of Israel. Itzchak dedicates his life to art of commemoration, which combines art, education and the heritage from the orphanage home in the manner of Janusz Korczak, drawing themes of the Holocaust.

Itzchak Belfer BY Ariel Shalit ISRAEL
TEL AVIV, ISRAEL, 2020

RYSZARD HOROWITZ was born in Krakow, Poland, in 1939. Four months later, following the German invasion of Poland, Ryszard's entire family was forced into concentration camps. From September 1944, he was imprisoned at Auschwitz. He later became known as among the youngest people to survive the Auschwitz concentration camp and to be listed on Schindler's list. He was the youngest survivor of Auschwitz when it was liberated in January 1945. At the war's end, five-year-old Ryszard was reunited with his family, when his mother found him in an orphanage. Fourteen members of his family survived the Holocaust thanks to Oskar Schindler, and they were amongst the few Jewish families to re-establish themselves in Krakow. Ryszard began taking pictures at the age of fourteen. For a brief period of time during his childhood he grew up alongside Roman Polanski, with whom he created his first photographic enlarger from cardboard. Ryszard immigrated to the United States in 1959.

Ryszard Horowitz BY Gilles Peress FRANCE
NEW YORK CITY, NEW YORK, USA, 2020

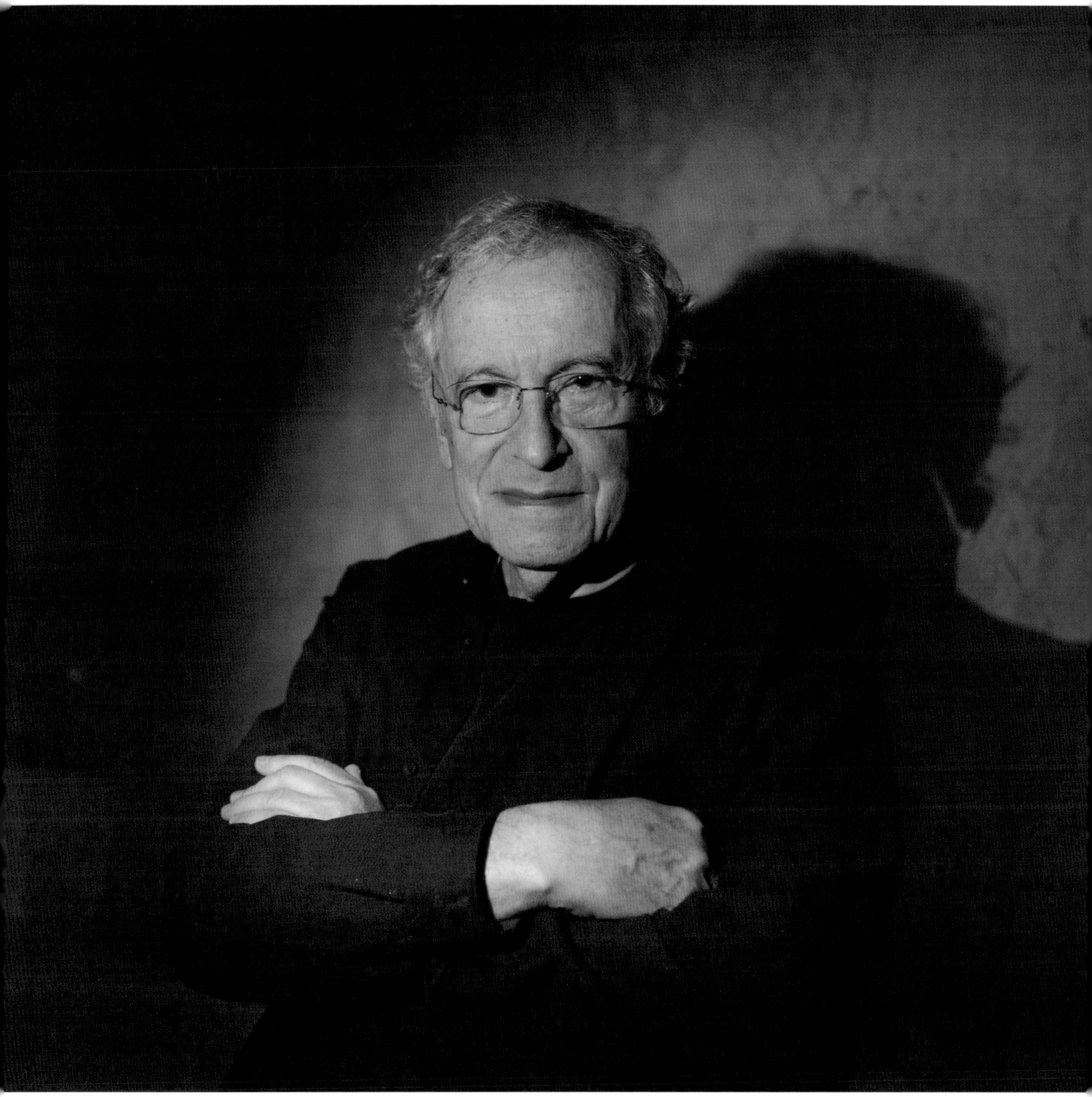

Holocaust survivor **Dov Landau** is the guest of honor at the Siyum HaShas celebration in the ultra-Orthodox neighborhood of Bnei Brak in Tel Aviv. Siyum HaShas is a celebration of the completion of the Daf Yomi program, a roughly seven-and-a-half-year cycle of learning the Oral Torah and its commentaries, in which each of the 2,711 pages of the Babylonian Talmud are covered in sequence – one page per day. Dov Landau was featured in the book *Exodus* by Leon Uris and in the film. The only survivor of a large family, Dov was born in Brzesko, Poland, in 1928. On September 1, 1939, the Germans occupied his town and the synagogue was burned. Dov was apprehended at the age of 13 and sent to a labor camp. In 1942 the Germans transferred his mother and brother Naftali to a concentration camp. In August 1942, Dov escaped with his father and grandfather to the town of Bochnia. In 1943, he was recaptured by the Nazis with his father and two brothers and other family members. Dov and his father were sent to Auschwitz concentration camp where he watched his family walk to the crematoria on November 5, 1943. On December 12, 1943, he was taken to work in the Jawisowiycz work camp where Dov worked in the coal mines for one year and three months. On January 17, 1945, he was forced to walk on a death march to Buchenwald where, at the age of 16, he worked in a stone mine. On April 11, 1945, he was liberated by the US Army from Buchenwald camp, the sole survivor of his large family. In June he was taken to France and boarded the boat *Mataroa* and in July 15, 1945, arrived at Haifa port in Mandatory Palestine. In 1948, while fighting in Israel's War of Independence, he was captured by the Jordanian army. A year later he was released in a prisoner exchange.

Dov Landau BY Yechiel Hakoen ISRAEL
BNEI BRAK, ISRAEL, 2020

ASSIA RABERMAN was born in 1928 in Mizoch, Poland, now Ukraine. She was 13 years old in 1942 when the Nazis occupied her town. When it became apparent to parents Meir and Rosa Berez that they could not escape, Maria, a Christian friend, offered to shelter Assia. Her parents refused. Then the killing started, and in a short time the Nazis with their accomplices executed 1,700 Jews. Her parents made Assia flee that night to save her life. She was hidden at the neighbors' home inside a cabinet. She could hear the screams outside – "Don't kill me, I want to live." She recognized one friend's voice. The victims were led to the killing place in groups and forced to lie down among the prior victims, to be shot in the head. Fearing for their own safety, the neighbors forced Assia to leave their house at dark. She walked all night to the home of Maria, the Polish Christian friend who initially offered to hide her. Her parents, who survived the mass killing in Mizoch, succeeded in seeing her for one last time. They were murdered soon after. Assia spent the rest of the war posing as Maria's Christian relative. On February 2, 1944, the Russian army liberated Rovno. During the fighting, Maria, who had been like a mother to Assia and her family, was killed. When the war ended, Assia believed that she was the only Jew alive. One hundred fifty of her relatives perished. Assia's older brother Isaac, who survived the war in Russia, found her, and in 1947 the two reached British Mandatory Palestine. Assia took part in the fighting for Israel's independence in 1948.

Assia Raberman BY Ancho Gosh ISRAEL

HAIFA, ISRAEL, 2020

ARIE GOLDBERG was born in 1926 in the town of Chelm, Poland. When World War II broke out and the Nazis captured Chelm, Arie and his family were transferred to the Sobibor concentration camp. His father, who was a rabbi, was murdered at the age of 52. 'My sister was killed by the bombings. When the Germans came, they took 2,000 Jews and killed them. Every child at the age of 13 had to sign up. They let me carry bricks and cut straw for the horses.' After a period in Majdaneck death camp, Arie was transferred to Auschwitz in 1943. 'I was beaten badly by Nazis. I don't know how I stayed alive,' he said. He survived but lost his entire family except his mother. In 1948, at age 22, he immigrated to Israel.

Arie Goldberg BY Marlen Noy ISRAEL
AFULA, ISRAEL, 2020

JAY (JACOB) IPSON was born in 1935 in Kovno, Lithuania. Jay was forced into the Kovno Ghetto with his family at age six. During a failed attempt to escape the ghetto, his baby sister died. In November 1943, another 28,000 Lithuanian Jews were rounded up for execution. Among them: Jay, his mother and father. A family friend, a police officer, pulled them from the line. They were the only ones to survive. They escaped into the countryside, where they spent much of the next nine months beneath a potato field, in a crawl space hand-dug by Ipson's father. They were liberated by the Red Army, and briefly returned to Kovno. In 1945, they escaped from the Russians, into the American zone of Germany. In 1947, the family immigrated via Munich to the United States, settling in Richmond, Virginia. In 1954, Jay joined the Army Reserve and served as an instructor attached to the 2079th JAGC (Judge Advocate General Corps), receiving an honorable discharge as a sergeant in 1963. 'I was grateful, and I wanted to pay back this nation.' Jay is a co-founder of the Virginia Holocaust museum. Jay's life mission is to educate, 'We must embrace all cultures to avoid the horrors of the past.'

Jay Ipson BY Scott Elmquist USA
RICHMOND, VIRGINIA, USA, 2019

HENRI MASS COLEMAN was born in Antwerp, Belgium, in 1936. The Mass family was from Lvov, Poland, and immigrated to Antwerp where their three children were born. After the Nazi Germany invasion in May 1940, the family fled to the south of France. When France fell in June 1940 the Mass family found themselves under the rule of the Vichy regime and they were deported to Rivesaltes concentration camp in southern France. Henri's mother through a resistance member, appealed to save her children to the AFSC, an American Quaker aid organization, who were rescuing children from Europe. Henri, age six, and his sister Mimi, eight, were placed on a convoy of refugees that left Marseille bound for Portugal, where the ship *SS Serpa Pinto* was docked. Their youngest sister Helene was given to a French Catholic family. The *Serpa Pinto* left Portugal, docking in Casablanca and Bermuda and reached Staten Island on June 24, 1942. When Charlotte and Marvin Coleman learned about the plight of the 50 lone Jewish children onboard, they volunteered to foster Henri and Mimi in their Chicago home. When the war ended the Colemans learned that Henri's parents perished in the Holocaust and the couple adopted both children. Back in France, thanks to Marvin Coleman's efforts, younger sister Hélène, then 16, discovered her Jewish identity and the three siblings were reunited in the US in 1953. The circumstances of their escape and the tragic fate of their birth parents were never discussed. Henri became a father to three children and retired to Arizona where he passed away in 2020.

Henri Coleman by John Pregulman USA
TUCSON, ARIZONA, USA, 2020

Rena Quint was born in Poland in 1935. Nazi Germany invaded Poland in 1939 and Rena's family had to relocate to the Jewish ghetto in Piotrków. In 1942, Rena's family was ordered to the town's synagogue. Piotrków Ghetto was liquidated on October 14, 1942, in four days of deportations to Treblinka and Majdanek. 'I don't know if my mother pushed me, if God pushed me...but I ran out of that door.' It was the last time she saw her mother and brothers, who were murdered in Treblinka death camp. Rena, age seven, was deported with her father to a labor camp, where she pretended to be a boy in order to survive. Rena's father perished and Rena was shipped to the Bergen-Belsen concentration camp. As the war drew to a close, conditions in Bergen-Belsen were desperate. 'The smells never leave you. The soup in Bergen-Belsen, the smell of dead bodies...' In those final days Rena was deathly ill with diphtheria and typhus. As women cleared their bunker, she was laid next to those who were nearly dead. On April 15, 1945, the British liberators of Bergen-Belsen evacuated her to hospitalization and later for recovery in Sweden where she was adopted. Rena was almost ten when her adoptive mother died on a trip to the USA. Rena was adopted again by a childless couple in Brooklyn in 1946, and emigrated to Israel in 1984. 'I had a very good life, it just started 10 years after it should have.' Rena earned her bachelor's and master's degrees in education and has been volunteering for more than 30 years in lectures about the Holocaust.

Rena Quint BY John Pregulman USA

JERUSALEM, 2020

FRANK LOWY was born in Czechoslovakia in 1930. In 1942, the family fled from Czechoslovakia to Budapest and were forced into the Budapest Ghetto. When the extermination of Hungarian Jews began, Frank's father, Hugo, left home one day and never returned. When the 13-year-old Frank wasn't scratching around for food on the streets of Budapest or trying to dodge the Nazis, the boy sat by the window waiting for his father to walk through the door and save the family. Frank's father was murdered in Auschwitz, his older brother survived forced labor camps and he and his mother survived in the Budapest Ghetto. After the war, in 1946, Lowy tried to reach Mandatory Palestine and was interned by the British in Cyprus before finally arriving and fighting in Israel's War of Independence. He immigrated to Australia in 1952 and returned to Israel in 2019.

Frank Lowy BY **Yossi Zeliger** ISRAEL
TEL AVIV, ISRAEL, 2020

Rabbi Yechezkel Roth, known as the Karlsburger Rabbi, was born in Arad, Romania, in 1930 to a Hungarian ultra-Orthodox Jewish family. In August 1941 all Jewish males 18–55 years old were drafted into labor battalions. The Jews from the Arad district, together with those of the district of Timişoara, were slated to be deported to the Belzec extermination camp in 1942, at the very beginning of a massive joint Romanian-German operation which targeted all the Jews from Regat and southern Transylvania. On October 11, 1942, the order to deport the Jews of Arad was rescinded. In August-September 1944 most of the Jews in Arad fled to Timişoara. Together with the majority of the Jews of Regat and southern Transylvania, the Jews of Arad survived the war. The Rabbi like most of the ultra-Orthodox community does not talk about his teen years during the Holocaust. The Rabbi of Karlsburger shared his time between New York and Mt. Meron in Israel, and was known to be one of the greatest authorities on Jewish law. Rabbi Roth passed away in the United States on March 6, 2021, and was buried in Israel.

Rabbi Yechezkel Roth BY David Cohen ISRAEL
MOUNT MERON, ISRAEL, 2020

Gaby Koren was born in Przemyśl, Poland, in 1941, during the Nazi German occupation. Gaby was born in an underground basement to a young Jewish couple who married just when the war broke out. Gaby would learn about his past only after the war. For a year and a half, baby Gaby grew up underground in darkness and silence. Food was supplied occasionally by local Polish farmers, and he grew malnourished, unable to make a sound or walk. Outside, Jews were being executed. The family knew their days were numbered, according to the Polish woman who rescued him. Wrapped in a sack with his birth certificate and a will written by his parents, Gaby was smuggled out of the basement to a monastery in town, where 12 Jewish children were already in hiding. The Nazis pulled his parents and his entire family out from their hiding place, and sent them to the gas chambers in Auschwitz. The baby was raised by the nuns in the monastery until the end of the war, then handed over to a Jewish orphanage. There he was adopted by a Jewish couple who lost their child in Auschwitz, and with his adoptive family he immigrated to Israel in 1948. In 1949, his only surviving relative found out that her sister's only child was alive. Israeli courts ruled that the boy should be handed over to his only surviving family member, in Kibbutz Yad Mordechai. From an early age he had decided to live his life to its fullest, believing that no one would ever come looking for him. Gaby grew up in the kibbutz of Holocaust survivors, who enveloped him with love. When he joined the IDF, he became an elite unit fighter, but found it difficult to adapt to family life. Change came after the first Lebanon war in 1982, when he fathered a child for the first time and was able to spell out the words "mother" and "father" for his daughter. 'I live that dark past every moment of my life, but I also learned to be a happy man, because my parents' memory lives on, in my children and the large family I have today.' Only in 2014 were children placed in monasteries recognized as Holocaust survivors. Gaby's monastery was recognized as among the Righteous Among the Nations. Gaby Koren passed away in 2023.

Gaby Koren BY **Ronen Akerman** ISRAEL
KIBBUTZ YAD MORDECHAI, ISRAEL, 2020

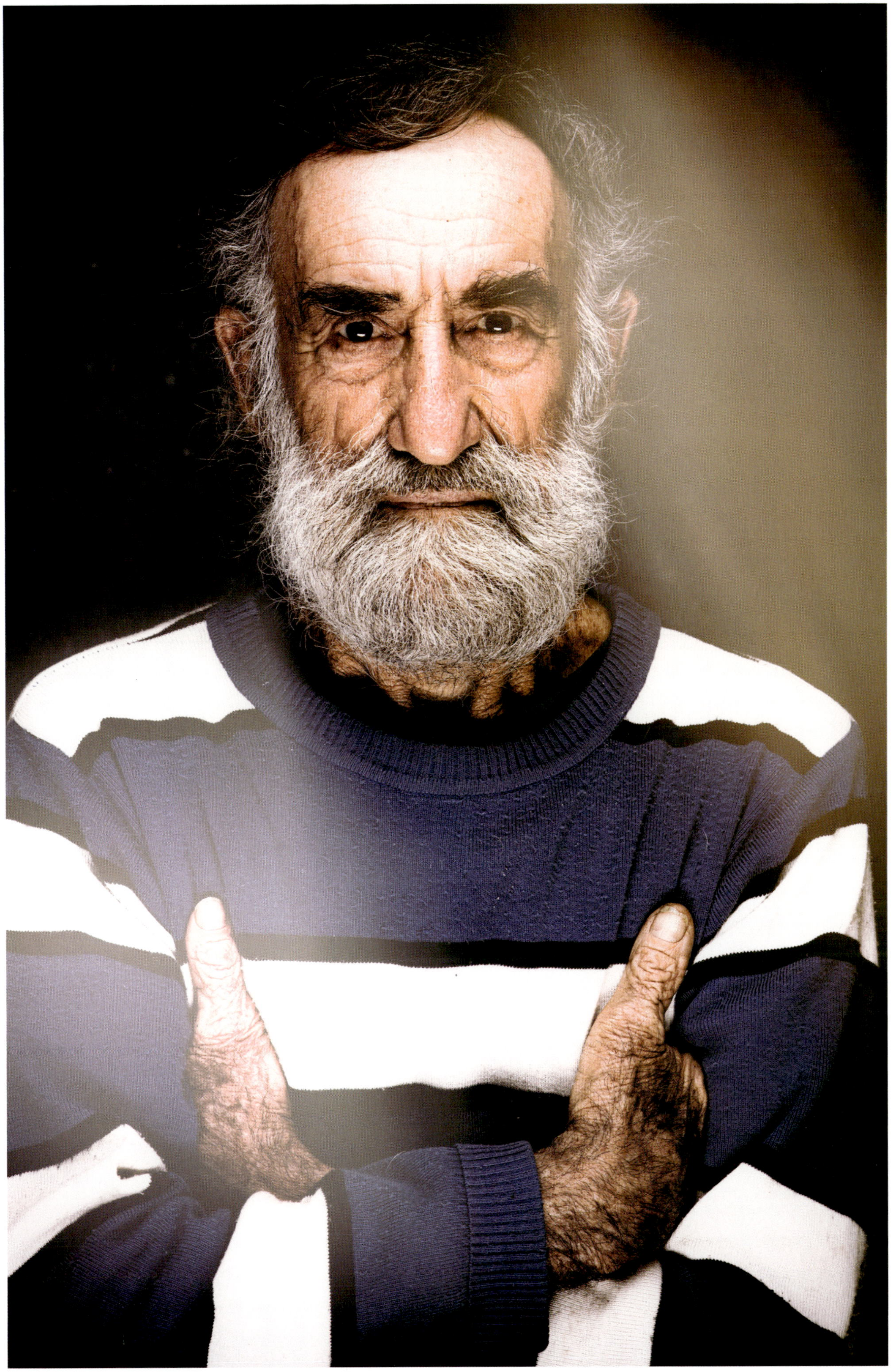

FISHEL RABINOWICZ was born in 1924 in Poland. His talent for painting was discovered at an early age and encouraged by his father. His town, Sosnowiec, was occupied four days after German troops invaded Poland on September 1, 1939. In 1941, Fishel was apprehended by the Gestapo in a street raid. He was transported to a Nazi labor camp and later to nine different concentration camps, where Fishel was given the number 19037. 'From that moment on, I was no longer a human being, only a number.' He was assigned to forced labor. Few survived from his group. In 1943 his mother Sara and his six siblings were killed in Auschwitz. His older brother perished at the Faulbrück concentration camp, and Fishel's father was shot dead in Flossenbürg. In 1945, he was one of 1,220 prisoners forced on a 325-kilometer-long death march to the Buchenwald concentration camp. Fishel marched for 55 days. Those who collapsed from exhaustion, cold or hunger were killed by the SS. When they reached Buchenwald, Fishel was close to death when, in April 1945, the Buchenwald concentration camp was liberated by the US Third Army. Fishel rebuilt his life in Switzerland and became a world-renowned artist. Through his art, Fishel reappraises his traumatic experiences. Fishel here is photographed next to his artwork *Survivor, 1994*. The frame with the falling letters represents the chaos of the Holocaust, and part of the letter remains within the frame, since the artist survivor is forever marked by what he has experienced.

Fishel Rabinowicz BY **Stefano Spinelli** SWITZERLAND
LOCARNO, SWITZERLAND, 2020

PETER GARDOSCH was born in 1930 in Romania. He was 13 years old when he was deported to the Auschwitz death camp, on June 7, 1944. 'The wagon doors were thrown wide open on a ramp. We saw endlessly long wire fences, and barracks that stretched to the horizon, and huge, square brick chimneys with smoke and fire coming out in the middle.' The Gardosch family did not know their whereabouts. They had been told that they would be deported to Germany to work. After the first Selektion, they knew death was everywhere. Peter's mother, little sister, and grandmother were sent to the gas chambers. Peter's life was saved when he pretended to be 17 and capable of hard work. Father and son were transported to Kaufering in Bavaria to build underground aircraft factories for the Nazis. Many of the prisoners there perished. Peter was lucky again. The camp's officer made him his personal servant. 'In this role I survived to the end [of the war].' When the American shelling began, chaos ensued, and Peter and his father managed to escape. After the war, father and son first returned to Romania and later to Israel. In the early 1960s, Peter returned to Germany, where he has lived ever since. 'I grew up with German culture. That was the country I wanted to go,' he said, 'I'm German and I really feel at home here.'

Peter Gardosch BY José Giribás Marambio CHILE
OŚWIĘCIM-AUSCHWITZ, POLAND, 2020

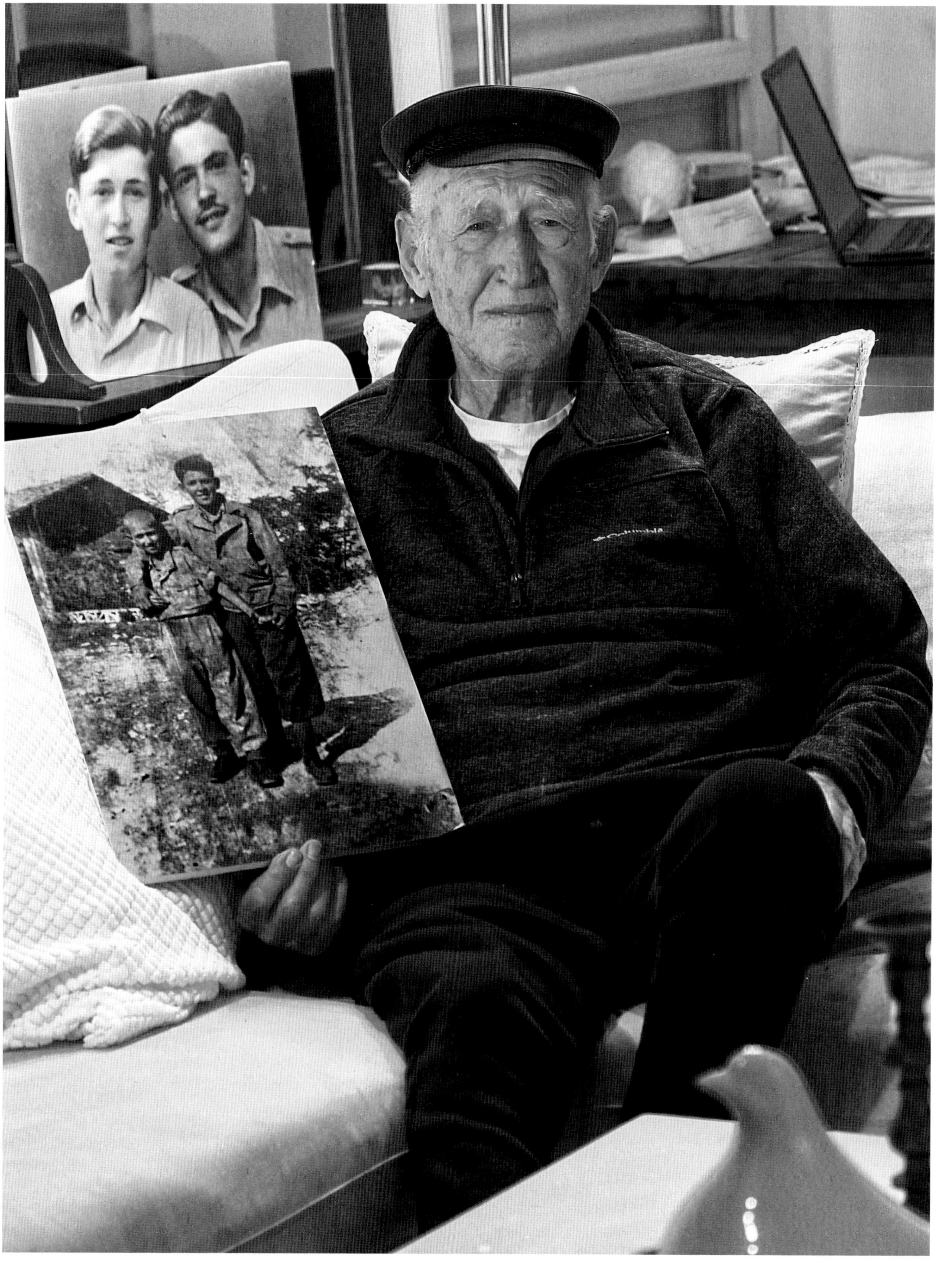

Daniel Chanoch was born in 1932 in Lithuania. His family was herded into the Slobodka Ghetto. Chanoch scavenged for food and saw elderly people crawl the streets with yellow stars pinned to their shoulders. He stayed with his parents until they told him, "We cannot protect you anymore. You must hide yourself." He dodged the Nazis until the SS deported the family in 1944. Chanoch boarded the train with his father and brother. He never saw his mother and sister again. Chanoch was 11 when he arrived at Dachau and was put to work in the SS kitchen. After several months, he and 130 other children were sent to Auschwitz-Birkenau. A teenager named Volpke, who led the children's group, taught them the left-right marching drills in German. When the children reached the ramp in Birkenau, they entered carrying out the marching drills they'd learned. This caused Mengele to choose not to send them to the gas chambers. Thus, thanks to their young leader Volpke, their lives were saved. As the Russians closed in on Auschwitz, Chanoch joined the death march out of the camp. But he made his escape in Austria as the war was coming to an end. One day a truck arrived at the postwar displaced persons camp, and his brother Uri got off the truck. Coincidentally, there was a photographer who commemorated the moment the two brothers reunited. Soon after, they were taken by the Jewish Brigade and, in 1946, arrived in British Mandatory Palestine. Chanoch fought for the just-declared State of Israel in 1948.

Daniel Chanoch BY Ilana Shapira ISRAEL
KARMEI YOSEF, ISRAEL, 2020

ANAT HARPAZ was born in Poland in 1934. In 1941 Anat and her family were forced to live in the city ghetto. 'Here I was first exposed to hunger, overcrowding, and the dreaded fear of the Nazi executions. The hunger in the ghetto was terrible and people were shot dead on streets.' In the course of a Nazi Aktion, her grandmother was caught and did not return. 'I remember how we walked during a Nazi Selektion. Some Jews were turned to the right and some to the left, those to life and those to death. Dad, carrying my sick sister in his arms, passed her to my mother. I ran over to him and clung to him; my father had a work permit, so our group were left alive. We were marched back from the forest to the ghetto. As we reached the outskirts of the forest, shots rang out and we realized the Nazis had murdered all the remaining people in the forest. Our group all burst into tears and cries – at that moment I realized that my mother and sister were no longer alive.' One day Haim and Marishka Weinreich, friends of her father, showed up at the ghetto gates. Anat's father knew that these were the last days of the ghetto, and convinced them to smuggle Anat out with them to Warsaw. Her father promised to come after her – he was murdered in the ghetto. Along the way, Anat was taught how to cross herself and recite Christian prayers. The war ended when the Red Army reached Warsaw. Anat and a group of orphaned children from Lodz were sent to board the ship *Theodor Herzl*. British soldiers stopped the ship off the coast of Haifa. 'Then we were all put on British destroyers and sent to the Cyprus detention camp, behind barbed wire. When the mandate ended, we arrived in Israel.'

Anat Harpaz BY Eli Hershkowitz ISRAEL
KIBBUTZ GAN SHMUEL, ISRAEL, 2020

LILY GUMBUSH was born in 1930 in Croatia. At the outbreak of World War II, Lily and her family fled to Bacarz, a fishing village on the Italian border, where an Italian family sheltered them for a while from the Italian fascist police. But they were caught and were all forced to move into an Italian ghetto. From there they were transferred to several concentration camps and then shipped to Auschwitz. Lily was forced to work in construction and later in a weapons factory. Lily was sent to her death to the gas chambers, but was rescued miraculously, and later she survived the death march. After the war she returned to Yugoslavia. In 1948 she immigrated to Israel. Lily is known for her many years of being a top supporter of the Hapoel Jerusalem basketball team who surprised her with a basketball signed by all players during a recent game. Lily passed away in the beginning of April 2021.

Lily Gumbush BY Oren Ben-Hakoon ISRAEL

JERUSALEM, 2020

Sonia Kam (R) was born in Germany in 1931. Her parents were living in Belgium, often visiting Germany, where her grandparents lived. 'My mother tried to persuade my grandparents to come with us, but they refused. "We are Germans!" they said, When Kam's family returned to Brussels, a large sign from the Gestapo hung on the door, "No entry, property of the Gestapo." Sonia and her sister went back to school, but they now had to wear the yellow star. The head of a summer camp agreed to take care of Kam and her sister **Hannie** (L) with false identities. 'One day the Gestapo stood at the door and said they knew that two Jewish children were hidden on the premises and that they should get rid of us. She contacted my father and he had to pick us up.' The two sisters then lived with their parents in hiding for a few months and, 'one morning my father said goodbye to my mother and drove off to work. It was the last time we saw him.' The family was separated. Sonia was taken to a monastery and her sister to another hiding place. The mother was hiding elsewhere. After the US Army liberated Brussels, the girls were reunited with their mother. Their father Shaul was murdered in Auschwitz and the rest of their entire family perished in Nazi concentration camps. In 1949 they immigrated to the US.

Sonia Kam & Hannie Dauman BY Steve McCurry USA
RIVERDALE, BRONX, NEW YORK, USA, 2020

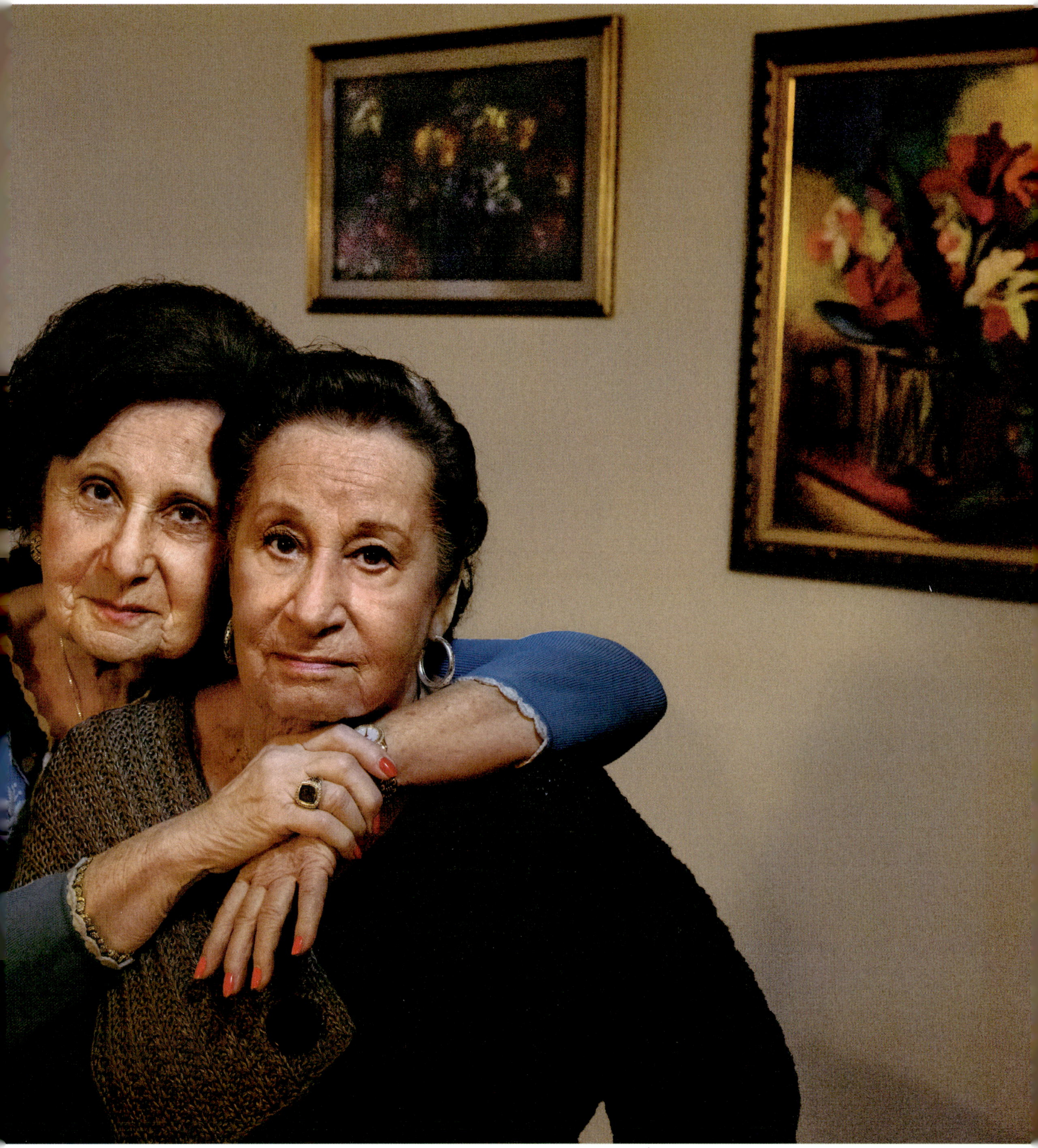

RAY KANER was born in Lodz, Poland, in 1933. Trapped in the Lodz Ghetto until the 1944 liquidation, and after their parents had died in the ghetto, Ray and her sister were forced to board a freight train to the Auschwitz death camp. In Auschwitz, prisoners were beaten, stripped naked and their heads shaved bald. The nightmares of her time at the death camp never go away. 'The cries, I can hear them, the cries and the pleading.' As a teenager, Kaner watched young children pulled from their parents and sent to gas chambers to death. 'The smell of burning flesh and bones haunts you the rest of your life.' She was also imprisoned in Bergen-Belsen, and in the Hambierten labor camp in Germany. In the Hambieren camp, Ray had been assigned by an elder German officer, Willy Minke, to do indoor work cleaning the SS officers' barracks. She was 17 but was so small and thin she barely looked 13. Menke took pity on Ray's physical condition and gave her some of his food, which she shared with other prisoners. Ray was marched to Bergen-Belsen camp in January 1945, and Minke accompanied the prisoners. There he was credited with saving prisoners when their train was bombed. Following her liberation by British forces, Ray wrote a personal diary of her years in the Holocaust. Ray was able to meet Willy Menke after her liberation. He had been arrested by the Allies, but was released due to testimony of one of the Jewish prisoners whom he rescued from the bombed train. She and Minke remained friends until his death in the late 1950s. She and her husband Leon, also a survivor, arrived in New York City in 1946.

Ray Kaner BY Jean-Andre Antoine HAITI/USA
NEW YORK CITY, NEW YORK, USA, 2020

Zvi Eichenwald was born in Poland in 1926. Zvi was 13 years old when Nazi Germany invaded Poland and Zvi and his family were deported to the Będzin Ghetto. 'We were ten children in the family.' In the summer of 1942, the children of the Eichenwald family were separated from their parents, never to see them again. In the summer of 1943, after four years of suffering and worsening conditions in the Będzin Ghetto, all the Jews were deported to the Auschwitz-Birkenau extermination camp. Zvi arrived at the gates of the camp and received the number 134105, which is burnt on his arm to this day. Zvi was sent to forced labor at the Fünfteichen camp. Later he was taken to work at the German Krupp factory, where he made guns and ammunition for the German army. As the Russians approached Germany, the camp's prisoners were transferred to the Gross-Rosen concentration camp, and from there to the Herzebrock camp. In April 1945, Zvi was led along with hundreds of other prisoners on the last death march across Germany. In May 1945, Zvi was liberated by the US Army. His parents and nine brothers and sisters were all killed during the war, leaving him the sole survivor of his family. In March 1949 he boarded a ship to Israel. He was immediately recruited for military service and fought in the last stages of Israel's War of Independence. Zvi passed away on September 24, 2022.

Zvi Eichenwald BY James Andrew Rosen CANADA
BNEI BRAK, ISRAEL, 2020

LEON KANER, 95, has not been able to talk about the past. Leon survived Bergen-Belsen concentration camp, where he lost his entire family. And it is in Bergen-Belsen that he met his future wife Ray. The two immigrated to the US in 1946.

Leon Kaner BY Oliver Halsman Rosenberg USA

NEW YORK CITY, NEW YORK, USA, 2020

IGOR MALICKIJ was born in 1927 in Ukraine. He was arrested in Kharkov (Ukraine) in the spring of 1942 and was supposed to be transferred to a labor camp in Germany, but he was able to flee. He was captured and shipped from Theresienstadt to the Auschwitz-Birkenau concentration camp. Igor Malickij was very young at that time and with the help of older prisoners he survived all the camps. Igor, prisoner number 188005, wept as he recalled the horrors he saw as a 17-year-old. 'I was assigned to take the bodies out of the gas chamber,' he said. 'In addition to a dead naked woman I saw a child crawling around who had apparently not been killed by the gas. I said, "Mr. SS man, the child is not yet dead." So the henchman hit the child's head against the ground and threw it on the pile.' He was liberated from the Mauthausen concentration camp, and later became a professor of engineering.

Igor Malickij BY José Giribás Marambio CHILE
OŚWIĘCIM–AUSCHWITZ, POLAND, 2020

MIRIAM ZIEGLER was born in Radom, Poland, in 1935. She was an only child. In 1939, as Nazi forces invaded Poland, her mother escaped with her in a buggy from Radom to Ostrowiec, but they were thrown off the buggy after the driver heard German soldiers shooting. Miriam and her mother hid in bushes on the side of the road. They watched the soldiers kill their driver. At night, they walked to the Ostrowiec Ghetto, to her grandparents' home. Miriam's parents were forced to work at nearby factories and kept Miriam hidden inside the Ostrowiec Ghetto, where she saw her own cousins executed by hanging. Her parents smuggled her into the Ostrowiec working camp to be with them, since no children were allowed in the forced labor camp. In 1944, when Miriam was nine, all the prisoners were put on cattle cars and deported to Auschwitz, where Miriam was separated from her parents. Her father was killed in the gas chambers. Miriam was tattooed with the number A16891. She was shaved and kept in the barracks where experiments were performed on the children. Miriam managed to survive until Auschwitz was liberated on January 27, 1945. Miriam didn't know that she appeared in one of the haunting photos from the end of the war. In the photograph, she stands among a group of children behind the wire at Auschwitz. Auschwitz child survivors were taken to an orphanage in Krakow, where Miriam was reunited with her mother and aunt, who had survived the death camps. In February 1948, Miriam was able to immigrate to Toronto, Canada. She lived with relatives until her mother and aunt were able to join her two years later.

Miriam Ziegler BY Moe Doiron CANADA
TORONTO, CANADA, 2020

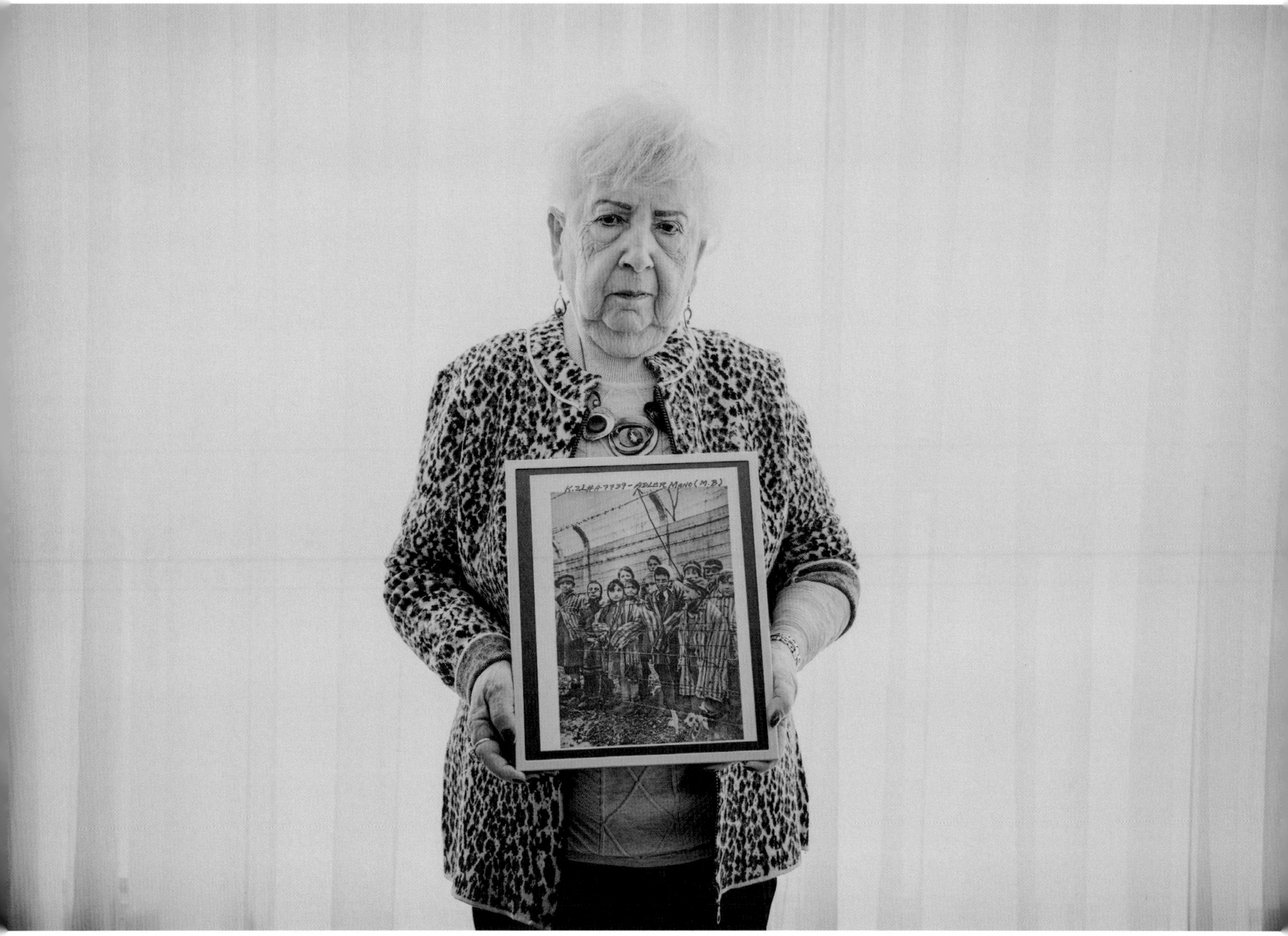

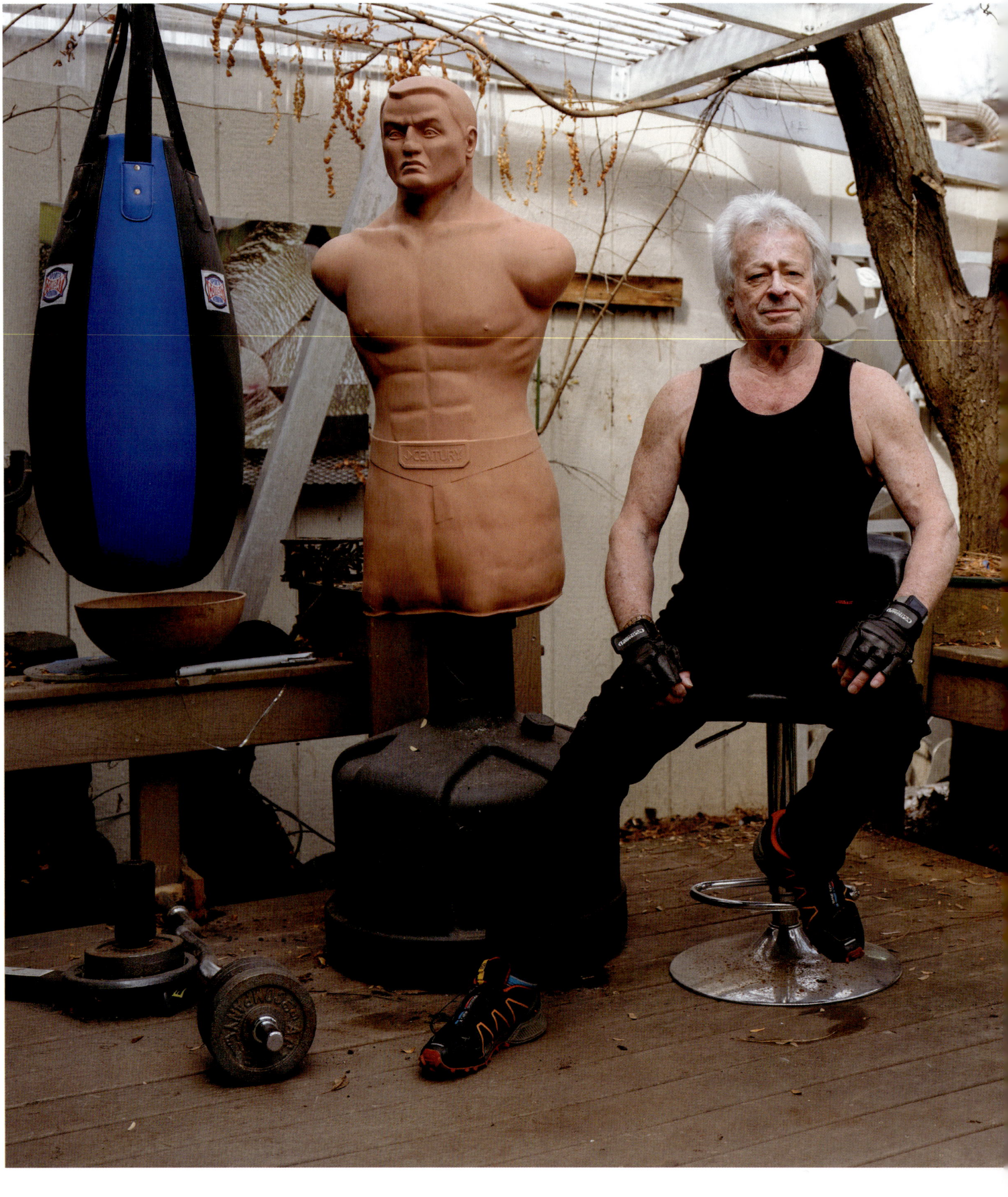
CENTURY

Adam Han-Górski was born in 1940 in Lvov, son of Szymon Han and Helena Pliz, a renowned pianist. In September 1939, the family fled from their hometown Jaworów (in today's Ukraine) to Lvov, where Helena was employed by a dance company. Soon after Adam's birth, she left on a tour of the Soviet Union, while Adam was looked after by a Christian caretaker, Katarzyna Chytra. In 1941, Nazi Germany occupied Lvov, and Adam's mother Helena was cut off from her husband and baby son. Szymon took Adam back to his parents in Jaworów and into hiding, but after Szymon's father and two brothers were murdered in Jaworow, Adam was saved by his caretaker Katarzyna Chytra, who, when Adam's father was sent to forced labor camps in the Gulag, was instructed to take the child to his grandparents in the Krakow Ghetto. In 1943, after hearing that Adam's grandparents had been transported to their deaths at Bełżec concentration camp and that he had been left with neighbors, Katarzyna Chytra rushed to rescue the two-year-old Adam from the Krakow Ghetto, just before its liquidation. Katarzyna, risking her life, brought Adam back to Lvov, where she baptized him and changed his name. During the Nazi occupation, she married Jan Witz, a railway worker, and both, despite the death threat for hiding a Jewish child, looked after Adam as their own child until the arrival of Soviet troops in Lvov in July 1944. Adam was reunited with his parents at age five, when Helena returned from the Soviet Union and, in 1946, her husband Szymon was released from a labor camp. Adam learned to play the violin in Katowice. At seven years old, Adam made his debut as a violinist. In 1957, the Han-Górski family emigrated to Israel. Some years later, the legendary violinist Jascha Heifetz, having heard Han-Górski in Paris, invited him to take part in his master class, and shortly afterwards, Adam moved to the United States. In 2012, Katarzyna Chytra and Jan Witz received the title of Righteous Among the Nations.

Adam Han-Górski by Alec Soth USA
PLYMOUTH, MINNESOTA, USA, 2020

HEDVA KATZ was born in Budapest, Hungary, in 1930. During the war, Hedva was taken to Auschwitz with her twin sister, Leah Feuerstein, and into Mengele's experimental clinic. In January 1945, Hedva and her sister were put on a death march. On their way they passed through Ravensbrück and Malachow, arriving by train to Rikenwald, where they were liberated. Hedva traveled to Israel with forged certificates on a tourist ship and disembarked at Haifa's port during the war for Israel's independence in 1948.

MIRIAM WOLBERG was born in Czechoslovakia in 1930. In 1941 she was sent to Ukraine and stayed there until 1944, when she was sent to the Auschwitz-Birkenau camp. On January 18, Miriam survived the death march to Ravensbrück. She was liberated by the Red Army. After recovery in a Prague monastery, she joined a Jewish youth movement and immigrated to Mandatory Palestine onboard the ship *Cairo*.

MAGADI UNGER was born in Hungary in 1928. 'June 1944, we reached Auschwitz camp. I was 16, accompanying my little sister and my mother. SS guards were screaming to us to hurry, my mother was worried about my grandfather and father in another freight wagon, and asked me to try to find them. I couldn't and returned, but my mom and sister were gone. An SS soldier sent them directly to where nobody was able to return from, they were directed to the gas chambers. I never said goodbye, not a last smile or hug, my mom and sister just vanished. I was all by myself in concentration camps, dreaming that maybe my father survived and one day we will meet again.' At the end of the war Magadi learned that none of her family survived. In 1948, Magadi immigrated to Israel.

LEA LANDSMAN was born in Hungary in 1931. In 1944 her father and mother were taken by the SS and did not return. At age 14, alone, she was rounded up with other Jews in the ghetto and shipped in freight train to Auschwitz. 'On the very first Selektion Mengele sent me to live. On the next Selektion we already understood – one line to work and life, and one line to the gas chambers. I was skinny and small, and this time Mengele sent me to the gas chambers. But each group was composed of five and one was of four. Mengele asked how old I was and I lied, saying 16. He pointed to join the group of four and I was spared again.' Lea immigrated to Mandatory Palestine in 1947.

SARA SHEFER was born in Hungary in 1936. In 1944, her father was taken for forced labor and never seen again. Sara and her twin sister Leah were shipped to Auschwitz along with their mother. On the first Selektion, the twins were taken by Mengele for medical experiments and their mother was sent to the gas chambers. All their family perished. In 1947, the orphaned twins arrived in Mandatory Palestine.

DAVID DUGO LEITNER was born in Hungary in 1930. After Nazi Germany invaded Hungary, local Nazi gendarmes rounded up all Jews, putting them into the ghetto. After six weeks, most were transported by freight wagons to Auschwitz-Birkenau. He was separated from his mother and two sisters, who were sent to extermination. His father and brother were sent to Buchenwald and from there to Bergen-Belsen. In one of the Selektions, David was destined for extermination, and he marched with hundreds of children to the crematorium. 'The children shouted all the way, "Shema Yisrael." They were stripped of their clothes, but all of a sudden it stopped.' Fifty-one children including David were chosen to unload potatoes from trucks, and his life was saved. In January 1945, David was sent by transport to Mauthausen. In April, David and many thousands were on a death march to Gunskirchen. After liberation, David found his brother, the only other member of his family to survive. In 1949, David and his brother arrived in Mandatory Palestine. He was drafted while still on the ship and went straight into his service in the IDF. David Dugo Leitner passed away in July 2023.

ELIEZER SHIMONI was born in Feldebro, Hungary, in 1928. In 1944, after some time in the ghetto, he was deported to Auschwitz-Birkenau. Three days later he moved to Auschwitz and thence to Beaver-Monowitz (Auschwitz III). He was sent on a death march to Gleiwitz. In January 1945, he arrived in Buchenwald, where he was liberated after several months. He immigrated to Israel in 1947, after spending ten months in a detention camp on Cyprus. His parents and five siblings all perished.

Seven Survivors BY Gadi Kabalo ISRAEL
NIR GALIM, ISRAEL, 2020

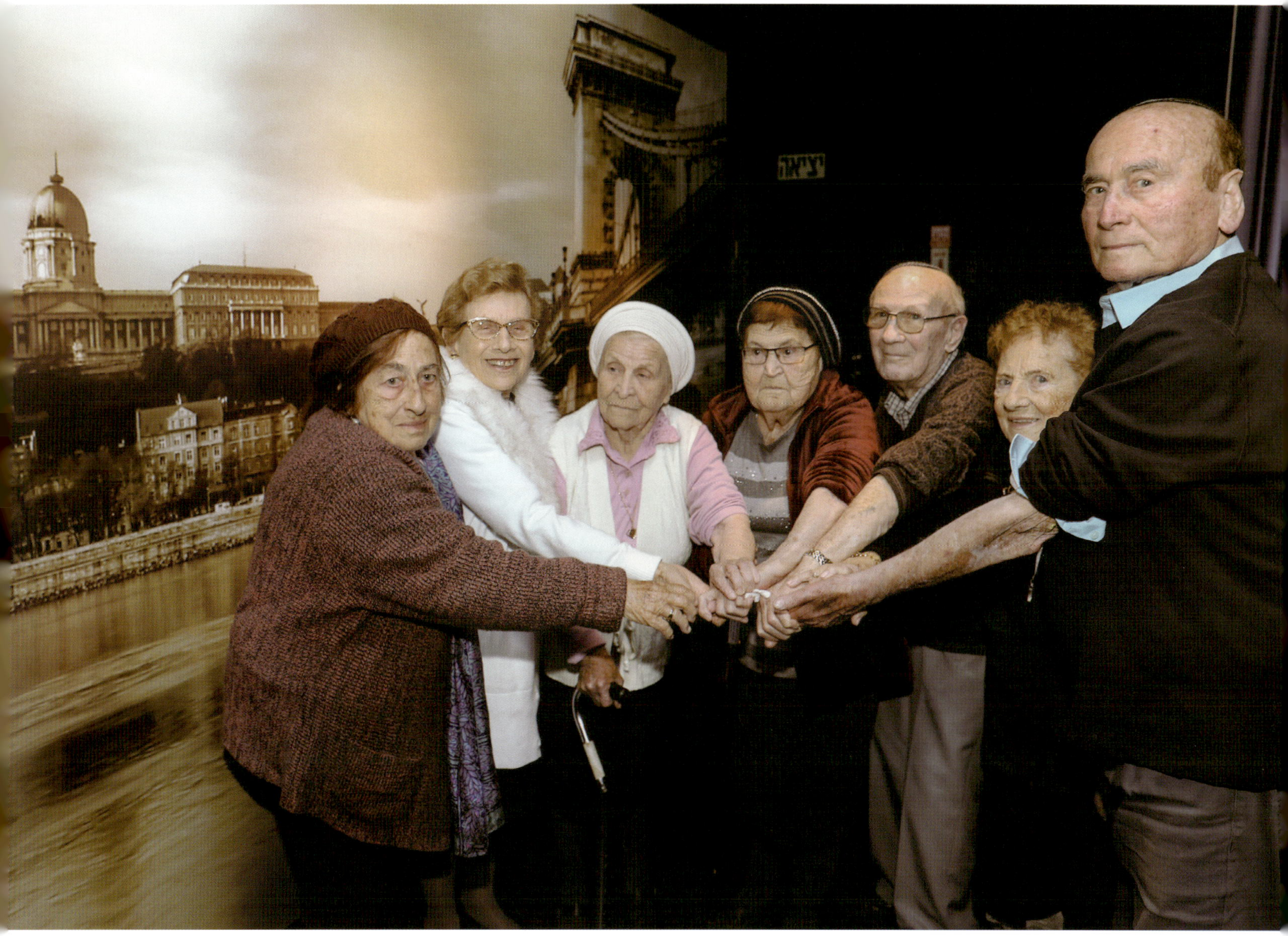
יציאה

MONIKA SEARS was born in Poland in 1939. That year, her father Pawel Rozenfeld, a young factory owner, was taken from his hometown in Lodz, and shot by an Einsatzgruppe (death squad) in the Lagiewniki woods outside the town along with 14 others. When he didn't return home, her mother Edyta took the infant Monika to Warsaw to look for him, and both ended up in the Warsaw Ghetto. Monika's earliest memories are of her mother's newly bleached hair – colored so that she could pass as an Aryan – fake identity cards, and gold coins sewn into the lining of coats to buy another few hours of life during the war. Monika, with her dark hair and dark eyes, was kept in hiding, moving between her mother who escaped the ghetto and her nanny Pola, who risked her life to help save the child. When she could, Pola took Monika out of Warsaw to the country. 'I didn't cry. I never said I was hungry.' She remembers being a stowaway in a countess's flat in Warsaw, sitting quietly under a table with her toy doll. On the single occasion she disobeyed by peeking through a window, a bullet whistled past her, and killed Monika's closest friend, Bolek, a seven-year-old boy. She saw him fall to the ground beside her. She remembers bending down to try 'to stuff his guts back into his broken body' when her mother pulled her away. In 1991, years after the war, when she was already living in Chile, she wrote a letter to her first grandchild, Edoardo, after her very first return to Poland since the war, with her son Oliver, 'From my War, to your Peace, Love Nonna.'

Monika Sears BY Alvaro Hoppe CHILE
PIRQUE, CHILE, 2020

AVRAHAM AVIEL (LIPKONSKY) was born in 1929 in Poland, in the Jewish village of Dugalishok. He studied at a small yeshiva in Radon. In June 1941, Nazi Germany invaded and forced all Radon Jews into the ghetto, and a year later the ghetto was surrounded for its liquidation. The Nazis forced Jews to dig burial pits for the Jews of the town. During the digging, some managed to escape, including Avraham's father and his brother Pinchas. Avraham and his mother and younger brother were marched to the town square, where many Jews were shot, and then to the death pits, where he heard his mother last words, "Children, say Shema Yisrael, we will die as Jews." Avraham watched rows of people shot and fall into the pits. His mother and younger brother Yekutiel-Kushke were murdered together with all the Jews of the ghetto. Avraham and Pinchas managed to escape. They looked for their father, and with the help of an acquaintance were able to find him. They were able to move together for several days before they separated. Avraham and Pinchas lived in hiding in the woods, where a hole had been dug in the ground, but their identity was revealed by a local farmer and they had to flee again. When Avraham and Pinchas tried to join partisans in the area, they encountered an ambush of collaborating Germans and police, and Avraham lost his brother Pinchas who was shot and killed before his eyes. Avraham managed to join a camp of Jews living in the forests. Alka Ariowitz, who headed the camp, saved about 100 Jewish women and children who had been taken into the encampment. The young men of fighting ability an *otriad* (detachment) of warrior partisans, Avraham among them. He later learned that his father had been murdered by an antisemitic unit of the Armia Krajowa, or home army of the Polish underground. In 1943, the Germans bombed the woods and Avraham, along with a number of surviving members of the group, joined the partisan fighters until July 12, 1944, when the area was liberated by the Red Army. He was among the illegal immigrants on the ship *SS Henrietta Katriel Yaffe*. He was captured by the British and exiled to a detention camp on Cyprus. He arrived at Kibbutz Mishmar Hasharon at the end of 1946. In early 1948, Avraham enlisted in the Sixth Battalion of the Palmach and fought his way to Jerusalem. At the Eichmann trial in 1961, he appeared as a witness for the prosecution, and testified on the massacre of Radom Jews.

Avraham Aviel (Lipkonsky) BY Lior Mizrahi ISRAEL
TEL AVIV, ISRAEL, 2020

SALO MULLER was born in 1936 in Amsterdam, his parents' only son. In the winter of 1942, his mother, Lena, held her six-year-old son Salo by the hand as the two were standing outside his kindergarten in Amsterdam. 'She told me, "I'll see you tonight, promise to be a good boy," and gave me a big hug,' but it was the last time he received a mother's embrace. Salo's mother and father were detained by the Nazis at the Hollandsche Schouwburg, a theater in Amsterdam, where they were gathered along with many other Jews. Salo was taken from the kindergarten by friends of the family and that night there was banging on the door of their home. 'The Nazis, reinforced by Dutch police, were at the door.' Salo was taken by the police to the detention area '…and suddenly I saw my parents there! I ran with my hands outstretched to my mother and called out, "Mama, I'm so happy to see you." A hand grabbed me before I was able to reach her, and a soldier and a nurse took me away. It was the last time I saw them.' Salo was once again picked up by friends of the family, beginning an incredible journey that stretched over four years and eight houses.

Salo Muller BY Friso Keuris THE NETHERLANDS
AMSTERDAM, 2020

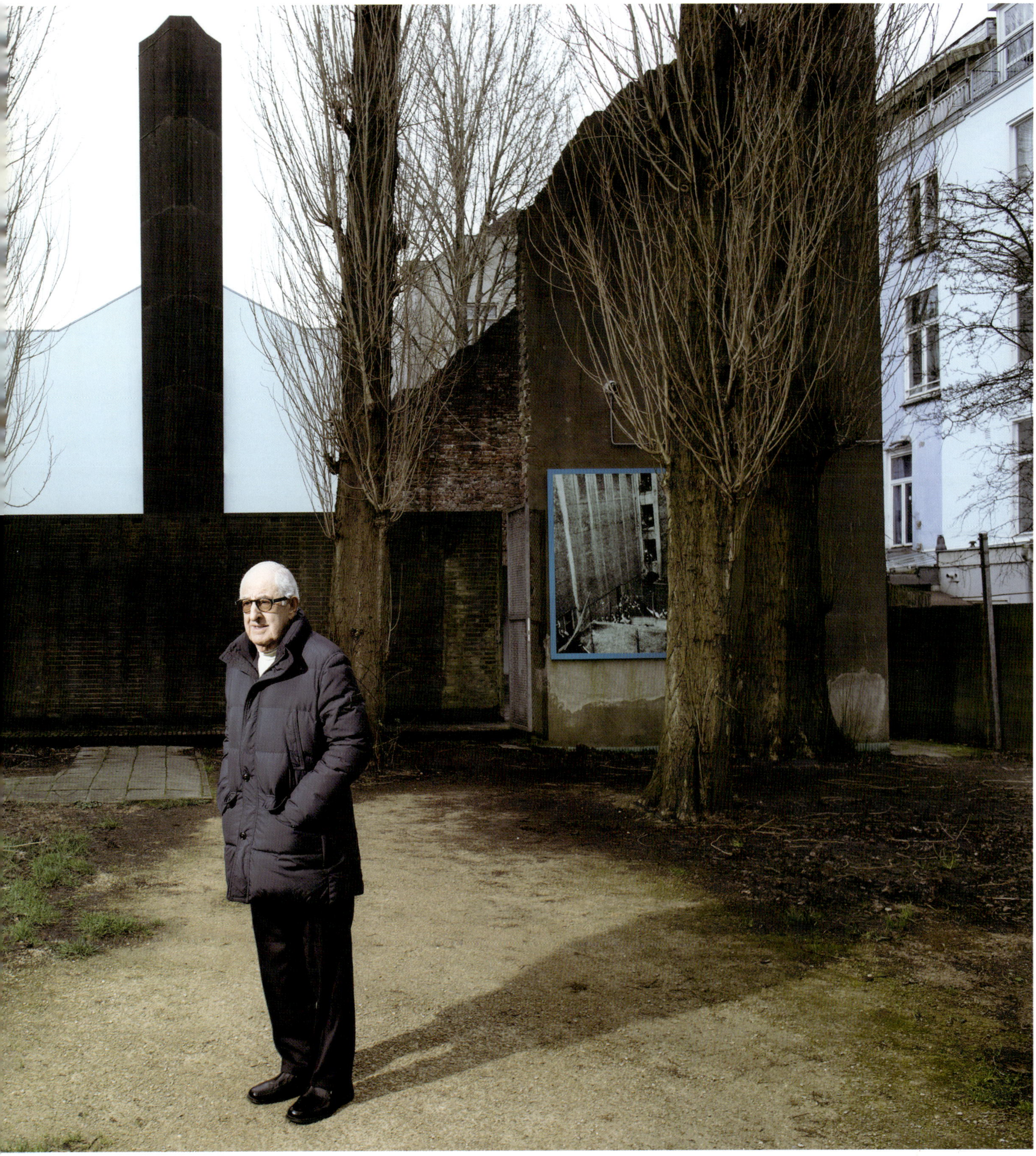

Hermann "Mano" Höllenreiner was born in 1933 in Hagen, Germany, to a German Sinti family. In March 1943, when Mano was nine years old, he and his family were deported from Munich to Auschwitz, to the Roma section of the camp. There he was tattooed with prisoner number Z-3526 (Z for Sinti and Roma prisoners). The "Gypsy Camp" at Auschwitz-Birkenau was eliminated the night of August 2, 1944, when thousands were killed in the gas chambers. Shortly before, Mano had been transferred with his parents and his sister Lilly to the Ravensbrück concentration camp, and later that year to the Sachsenhausen concentration camp. Towards the end of the war he was able to flee a death march. After the war, he was sent to France along with other French prisoners of war, where he said he was a French Jew (his mother had Jewish ancestors). He concealed his German origins. The Höllenreiner family lost 36 members to Nazi persecution. He was taken in by a family in Paris, and was treated for severe trauma. It was only then that his prisoner's tattoo was discovered and, in 1946, the surviving members of his family were able to locate him. Only years later was Mano able to tell of his experiences during the Holocaust.

Hermann "Mano" Höllenreiner BY José Giribás Marambio CHILE
OŚWIĘCIM–AUSCHWITZ, POLAND, 2020

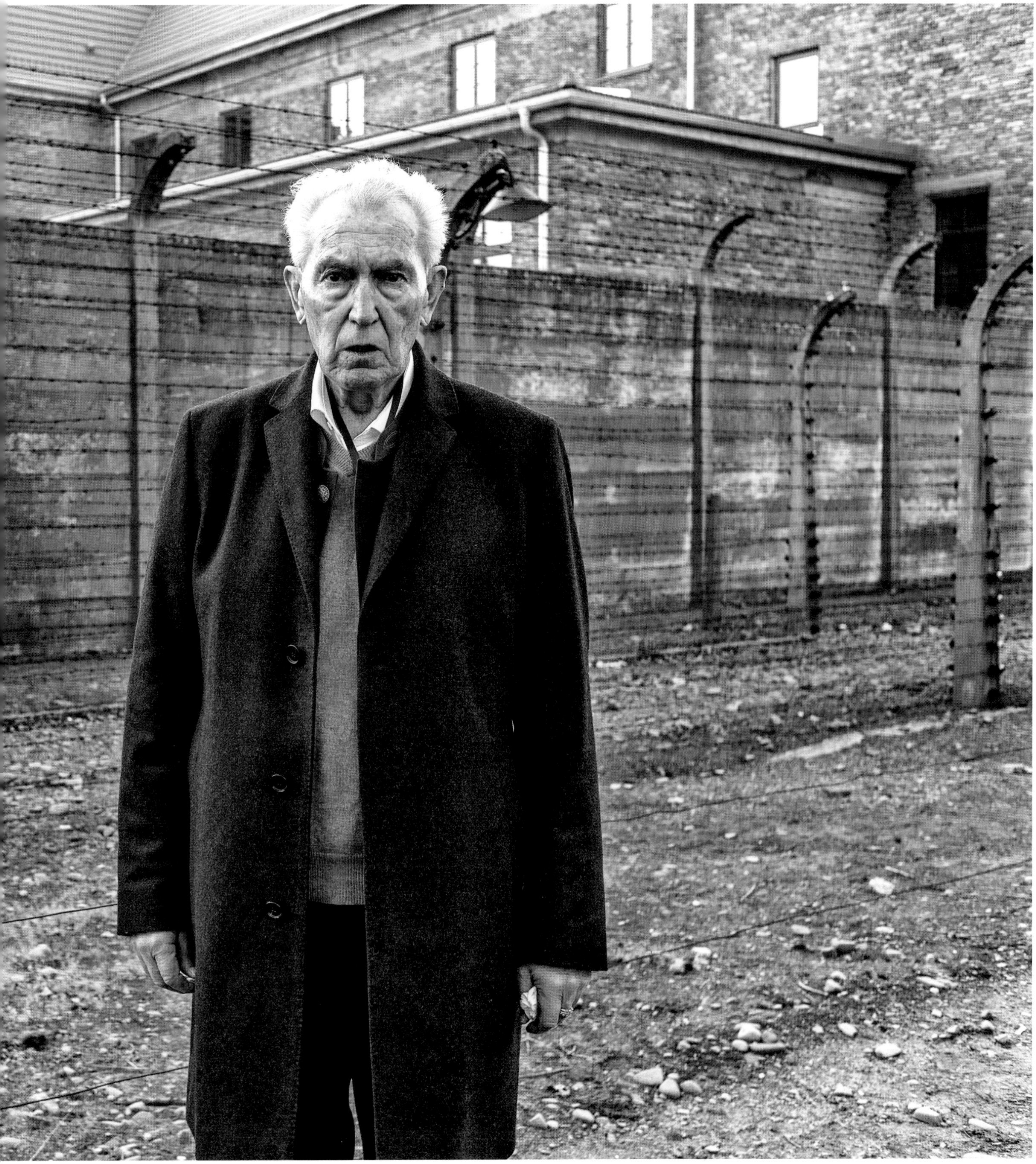

BELLA, right, celebrates her 97th birthday together with RIVA, GENIA and LEON, at a volunteer emergency aid center for Holocaust survivors in Ramat Gan, Israel. Here they can receive physical and social assistance for impoverished Holocaust survivors in Israel. There are many survivors who are lonely or living below the poverty line. Volunteer emergency aid centers give them the chance to live their lives with dignity, and provide emotional support and care.

Birthday BY Rina Castelnuovo ISRAEL
RAMAT GAN, ISRAEL, 2020

ISABELLE CHOKO was born in Lodz, Poland, in 1928. She was sent to a ghetto when she was 11 and lost her father, who died of starvation in 1942. The Nazis later shipped her to the Auschwitz-Birkenau death camp with her mother who was put into forced labor and then transferred to Bergen-Belsen, where her mother died. In 1945, Isabelle was ill with typhoid and weighed just 25 kilos. Her life was saved by an American doctor who was part of the US troops who liberated Bergen-Belsen. Later she was sent to Sweden with other youth to recover. She returned to Paris in 1946 and was raised by a surviving relative. No other member of her immediate family escaped the camps. Isabelle was photographed with a French girl, Constance Dicale, age 16, the same age Isabelle was when deported to the death camps. The photographer Karine Sicard Bouvatier is working on a project on generational encounters between teenagers and Holocaust survivors, remarking that the young generation now will be the last one to be in contact with the last survivors and will be the ones to tell their children, "I met a man or a woman who was deported to an extermination camp and survived the Holocaust."

Isabelle Choko BY Karine Sicard Bouvatier FRANCE
PARIS, 2020

NAHUM AND GENIA's love story began at the Oskar Schindler factory in Krakow. **NAHUM MANOR (MONDERER)** was born in Krakow, Poland, in 1923. In his infancy, his family immigrated to Mandatory Palestine, but a few years later returned to Poland. During his high school studies, Nahum underwent pre-military training and when the war broke out he was drafted into the Polish army. A few days after the German invasion, Nahum fled eastward, toward the Soviet Union, as did many Krakow residents, but the advancing German army rounded up the escapees and returned them to Krakow. Nahum and his family were forced into the Krakow Ghetto. 'Early one morning, the ghetto is already surrounded. No one comes in or out. Every few steps, an SS soldier stands with an aimed rifle, shouting at tens of thousands in one huge yard. My family, we hugged, kissed and it was the last time I saw my parents and sister and twin brothers. It was the hardest day of my life.' In early 1944 Nahum was transferred to Oskar Schindler's factory. **GENIA WOHLFEILER** was born in Krakow in 1926. During the liquidation of the ghetto, Genia's family hid and from the attic she watched the deportation of Krakow's Jews to extermination. Soon after, Genia's brother was caught and about to be executed when Oskar Schindler suddenly arrived on the scene, saving his life. Genia's father was murdered in Plaszów hospital. "Schindler's list" was created. Genia and her mother were sent to Auschwitz along with 300 other women, but Schindler managed to save them a month later on the grounds that he needed them as skilled personnel, to establish his new factory in Brinnlitz in the Czech Republic. 'In May 1945, the war ended, and our camp was liberated by the Red Army. Suddenly, in a dream, Russian soldiers came to our camp. A Russian officer speaks Yiddish on a white horse. We kissed his hands crying, kissed the horse, it was like a miracle.' After their liberation in May 1945, the two returned to their hometown of Krakow, but their ways separated. Nahum was the only survivor in his family. From displaced persons camps, he embarked on a journey which led him to enlist in the "Gideonim" group of the Palyam, the "navy" of the pre-state Palmach underground, serving on illegal immigration ships to Mandatory Palestine. In 1950, Genia, whose mother and brother survived, immigrated to Israel, where the two were married.

Nahum & Genia Manor BY Noga Friedman ISRAEL
BE'ER SHEVA, ISRAEL, 2020

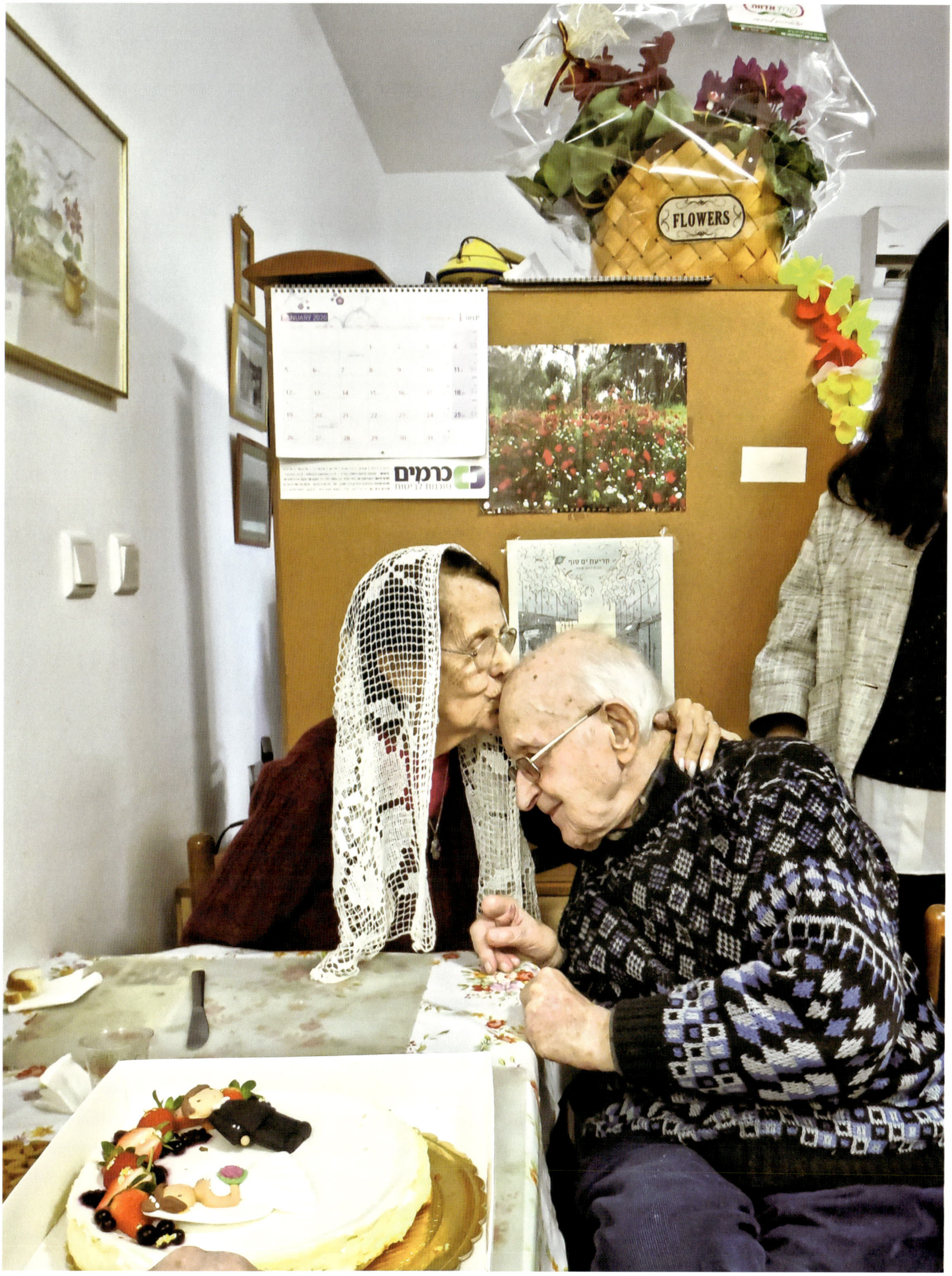
FLOWERS
כרמים

Aliza Vitis-Shomron was born in Warsaw in 1928. As a teenager she joined the Hashomer Hatzair youth movement. She was 13 years old when the family was forced to move into the Warsaw Ghetto. Inside the walled ghetto she became a member of the Jewish underground. She was active in distributing leaflets and also, 'I was smuggling weapons. I had to go through Nazi guards and each time there was a search, I feared death.' Aliza acted as a liaison during the Warsaw Ghetto Uprising, between the uprising's commander Mordechai Anilevich, and uprising headquarters on Mila Street 61-63. Two days before her comrades embarked on a final act of resistance, Aliza was ordered by the commanders to "leave and tell the world how we died fighting the Nazis." She has been doing that ever since. The end was near. Nazi troops had encircled the ghetto, and the remaining members of the Jewish resistance inside were prepared to die fighting. Nearly all her friends perished. Aliza and her mother and sister went into hiding on the Aryan side of the ghetto. They were captured and shipped to Bergen-Belsen death camp. Her father was killed in Majdanek. She was 17 when the Bergen-Belsen camp was liberated. She was transferred to Belgium, where she joined the illegal immigration as part of the Aliyah Bet operations, and in 1945 arrived to Mandatory Palestine.

Aliza Vitis-Shomron by Tsafrir Abayov ISRAEL
KIBBUTZ YAD MORDECHAI, ISRAEL, 2020

NICOLE KAHN was born in France in 1933. 'On February 3, 1944, when I was 10 years old, French militia and Nazi Germans came to our home in Marseille. My father and my brothers Francis and Georges, who were active in the Réseau Gallia French resistance, my mother Edith, Micheline, a cousin, and myself – our entire family of Alsatian Jews, who thought they found a refuge in Marseilles – were arrested. My mother and I and our cousin were brought to the Baumettes jail in Marseilles, and so was my father and my brothers. I stayed with my mother in a tiny cell with a very strict incarceration regime. On March 9, 1944, we were shipped by train and truck to the Drancy camp, outside of Paris, where I "celebrated" my 11th birthday. In order to avoid deportation (Drancy was the French concentration camp from which Jews were deported to the extermination camps), my mother pretended she was not Jewish, which made my father a spouse of an Aryan woman; that situation was irregular for the Nazis. Before deportation, each family had to appear before Brunner, chief of the Drancy camp, and his deputy, an evil man known as the "Butcher." My mother never lost her courage. She spoke good German and saved us until the Liberation of Paris. There are no words to describe the pressure she had to endure, nor our life at Drancy; I, a young girl, had to witness daily the assassinations, the suicides and the tortures. As soon as Paris was liberated, Françis Weill, my older brother, who was already a hero of the French Resistance in Marseilles, joined the army. He was Sous-Lieutenant under the orders of General Patton. He died in glory on September 26, 1944, commanding a battle to recapture the city of Metz. With great difficulty, my remaining family returned to Strasbourg, which was finally liberated. I have had the joy of marrying Jean Kahn, a human rights activist of the French community. We have two sons, Daniel and François, and our family continues our tradition to honor France and Judaism.'

Nicole Kahn BY Regina Recht GERMANY
STRASBOURG, FRANCE, 2020

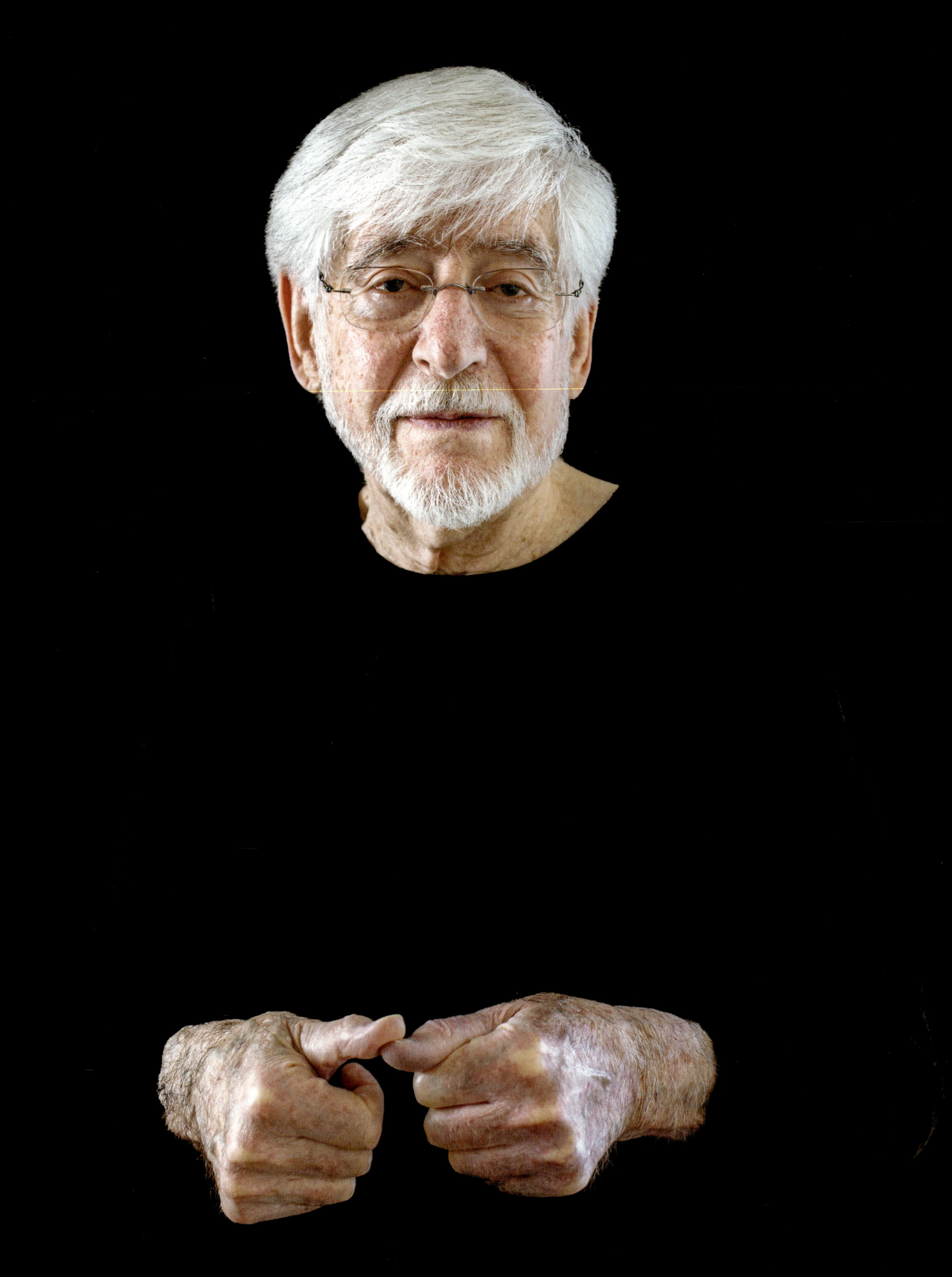

Harry Markowicz was born in Berlin in 1932. In 1938 the family escaped the rise of the Nazis by moving to Belgium, shortly before Kristallnacht. When Nazi Germany invaded Belgium in 1940, the family tried to escape again. Harry's first memory at age three was of hiding in a ditch on the side of the road. German planes bombed the road on which refugees were attempting to escape. Harry's family huddled in the ditch to wait out the bombings. When they reached the French border, they were turned away, and forced to remain in Belgium. In 1941, the Nazi authorities detained Jewish men for forced labor in factories or farms in Germany to replace their soldiers and were relocating Jews to the East. In 1942, the Markowicz family went into hiding. The parents rarely left their hiding place for years at a time, while their children were separated and hidden with various families. Harry was hidden with several different families and in children's homes in Brussels until he was taken in by the Vanderlindens, a Belgian family with a teenage daughter. He became their "son" until the liberation of Brussels in September 1944. Despite his young age, Harry was aware throughout the war of the anxiety of the adults around him and behaved in ways that did not attract attention. The Markowicz family survived the war. Most of their extended family perished. Harry Markowicz passed away on September 15, 2020, in Silver Spring, MD, USA.

Harry Markowicz BY Jono David UK/USA
WASHINGTON, DC, 2020

GERSHON KLEIN was born in 1932 in Poland. After the Nazi German invasion of Poland and the decrees against Jews, Gershon and his parents were given shelter by a Polish farmer in a barn outside their city Piotrków Trybunalski. 'The Polish farmer, for no financial gain, looked after us and fed us at nights,' but Gershon's family had to return to the Piotrków Trybunalski Ghetto, the first Jewish ghetto established by the Nazis before it was closed to the outside world in October 1939. Jews were sent as slave labor to factories taken over by the Germans, and Gershon was sent to work at the Hortensja Glassworks. The ghetto liquidation action began on the night of October 13, 1942. Some 22,000 Jews were herded onto the synagogue square and underwent a Selektion. Men and women were separated and were marched in columns to the railway station, where they were loaded onto freight trains to their deaths. Gershon remembers the most painful moment in his life, when he watched his mother lined up with other women along the opposite train tracks. 'I heard my mother calling me, and I cannot remember what happened next, how we separated from each other, I can't remember, or I chose to erase this pain from my memory.' His mother was taken to Ravensbrück camp, never to return. By the end of 1944, Gershon, 12, was shipped with his father to Czestochowa labor camp, where the majority of Jewish forced laborers either died of starvation or were sent to death when they fell ill or weak from work. Gershon and his father were shipped to Buchenwald camp, where prisoners only had the choice between slave labor or inevitable execution. 'They took from me my father, I was left with my cousin Ben (Helfgott) and sent to the children's block.' When they began to hear the cannons of the Allied forces, Gershon and Ben were loaded with others onto open cattle trains to Theresienstadt. 'For one month we ate potato peels and grass.' In Theresienstadt Gershon, then 13, was looked after by his cousin Ben Helfgott, age 15, until they were liberated by the Soviet army in 1945. In 1952, Gershon immigrated to Israel. He was not able to tell his story of survival until he turned 65 years old.

Gershon Klein BY Jonny Baker ISRAEL
KIRYAT MOTZKIN, ISRAEL, 2020

Jacobus Mozes "James" Van Ameringen was born in 1921 in Amsterdam, The Netherlands. In May 1940, the Dutch army was defeated by the Nazis in five days, and by the end of 1940, all Jews were forced to wear a yellow badge bearing the Star of David. Jacobus was supplied by the Dutch resistance fighters with false identity cards, but in 1941 it became more difficult to attend school during sudden roundups by Nazi troops of young men bound for forced labor in Nazi Germany. Dutch Nazis were spying on Jewish homes. Jacobus went into hiding outside Amsterdam, but had to return home to Amsterdam. 'In early 1943, Nazi Germans broke into our home, seized my mother and sister and shipped them to Westerbork.' In early 1943, he was smuggled into Belgium and spent the rest of the war with a false identity. His life was saved for his knowledge of French and German. After the war he found his sister Helen who had survived. His parents and his extended family were deported by cattle trucks to the Sobibor death camp and perished there. In 1952, he sailed with his finance Alice (Aaltje) Ekkelenkamp from Amsterdam to New Zealand on a troop carrier converted into a "liberty ship" named *Southern Cross*. On 22 January 2022, Jacobus died peacefully at his home, with his family, aged 100 years.

Jacobus Mozes Van Ameringen BY **Perry Trotter** NEW ZEALAND

TAURANGA, NEW ZEALAND, 2020

LEON SCHWARZBAUM was born in Hamburg, Germany, in 1921. His parents were Polish Jews who had moved to Hamburg shortly before World War I, returning to their hometown, Bedzin, Poland, prior to World War II. Soon after Nazi Germany invaded Poland in 1939, the synagogue in Bedzin was set on fire and dozens of people were murdered. Leon and his family were forced into the Kamionka Ghetto and Leon was taken to forced labor. In the summer of 1943, all the Jews in the ghetto were deported to the Auschwitz extermination camp, 60 kilometers away. Most were gassed upon arrival. Leon survived two years in Auschwitz, working as a forced laborer for Siemens until January 1945, together with 250 other men and 30 women. In 1945, the Russian army came closer. The death march from Auschwitz began and Leon was taken away by fleeing Nazis as the Allies advanced. Leon was marched to Gliwice, and from there, in open wagons, to Buchenwald. Siemens engineers reappeared there and ordered 88 forced laborers to Berlin. Allied bombing raids began, and Leon was sent on a second death march towards Schwerin. Thousands died of weakness or were murdered. In May 1945 Leon was liberated by the American army. Soon after, Leon learned that his parents were murdered in the gas chambers upon arrival in Auschwitz in 1943. An image of prisoners driven to the gas chambers has haunted him his whole life: 'Naked people in a truck – their arms in the air praying, crying.' Thirty-five members of his family were killed. Left alone, Leon joined a group of Auschwitz survivors who stayed in Berlin.

Leon Schwarzbaum BY Eric Schütt GERMANY
BERLIN, 2020

Moshe Barth was born in 1926 in Rimanov, Poland, the youngest of four sons. In September 1939, Nazi Germany captured Rimanov. Moshe was ordered to forced labor. The family lived in the Rimanov Ghetto from 1941. In 1942, SS Germans and Ukrainians rounded up all the Jews in the town square. Moshe's family was deported to the Belzec extermination camp. At the end of 1942, Moshe was transferred to the Rzeszow Ghetto. Most of the ghetto's Jews by then were murdered. Moshe was shot and wounded by Nazis while searching for food, but managed to return to the ghetto. In the spring of 1943, Moshe was transferred to a camp in the city of Postkov. In July 1944, Moshe and his campmates were forced into cattle cars and, after a three-day trip, arrived at Auschwitz. Moshe was tattooed on his arm with the number 17967A, and he was held at Birkenau. From there he was sent to work on weapons production. In mid-January 1945, Moshe survived another human shipment in cattle cars, where many of the prisoners died. He was transported to Mauthausen and Güzen camps and imprisoned in the Millendorf camp. In the spring of 1945, Moses was forced on a death march north where those who survived arrived at the Bergen-Belsen camp. In the distance they saw large piles. 'We thought these were cabbage stacks. As we approached, we saw that these were piles of bodies. I was frozen and starved. I knew it was my end. We didn't get any food.' Moshe was ordered to drag bodies from the pile and throw them into a huge pit. On April 15, 1945, on the verge of death from exhaustion and starvation, Moshe was released by the British Army. 'I got a slice of bread. So, I realized I would live and get to tell my story.' Moshe lived in the Bergen-Belsen displaced persons camp and later returned to Poland to find that from all his family, only one brother had survived. In 1949, Moshe arrived in the United States. In the early 1950s, during the Korean War, Moses was drafted into the US Army and came to Germany with the American forces. In 1997, Moshe immigrated to Israel.

Moshe Barth by Yonatan Sindel ISRAEL
JERUSALEM, 2020

Miriam Kato Galai & Edith BY "Koko" Meir Ben-Ari ISRAEL
KFAR WARBURG, ISRAEL, 2020

MIRIAM KATO GALAI was born in Czechoslovakia in 1926. Her parents were Hungarian, and Miriam was one of their four children, all of whom loved to bathe in the Danube River next to their home. 'I was 18 when we felt the antisemitism towards us from the townspeople. When the Nazi Germans arrived, we were taken to Donhasherhai, to the ghetto, and my dad was taken away for forced labor in a camp. My mother and us children were herded to a freight train to Auschwitz in Poland. When we got off the train we were in the line of Mengele's Selektion. He sat on a horse and decided who goes right and who goes left, who will live and who will die. He sent the adults and babies to the gas chambers to die and the young to work. We were separated from our mother. She was sent to the gas chambers. That was the last time we saw our mother. People explained to us that whoever is marked with tattoo, goes to work and lives. Then I got the number 17511A. My three sisters had consecutive numbers together with our neighbor Edith, born in 1925' – pictured on the right, who became Miriam's sister-in-law after the war. 'Later we were taken from Auschwitz for forced labor in Plaszów camp near Krakow, where we carried heavy stones from one place to another. We were always together, during Selektions. My sister was sick and we all held her up straight between us, so the Nazis didn't notice her weakness.' From Plaszów they were transferred to an aircraft factory in Germany and then by train again, when the train suddenly stopped in the woods. 'The Nazis dropped us off the trains preparing to shoot at us, when we heard shouts that the orders were changed.' Again, they were placed on a train. They heard shooting and screams and ducked under the wagons when they realized that they were being liberated. Soon after, they decided to immigrate to Mandatory Palestine. Miriam and her sister-in-law EDITH live in Kfar Warburg, Israel.

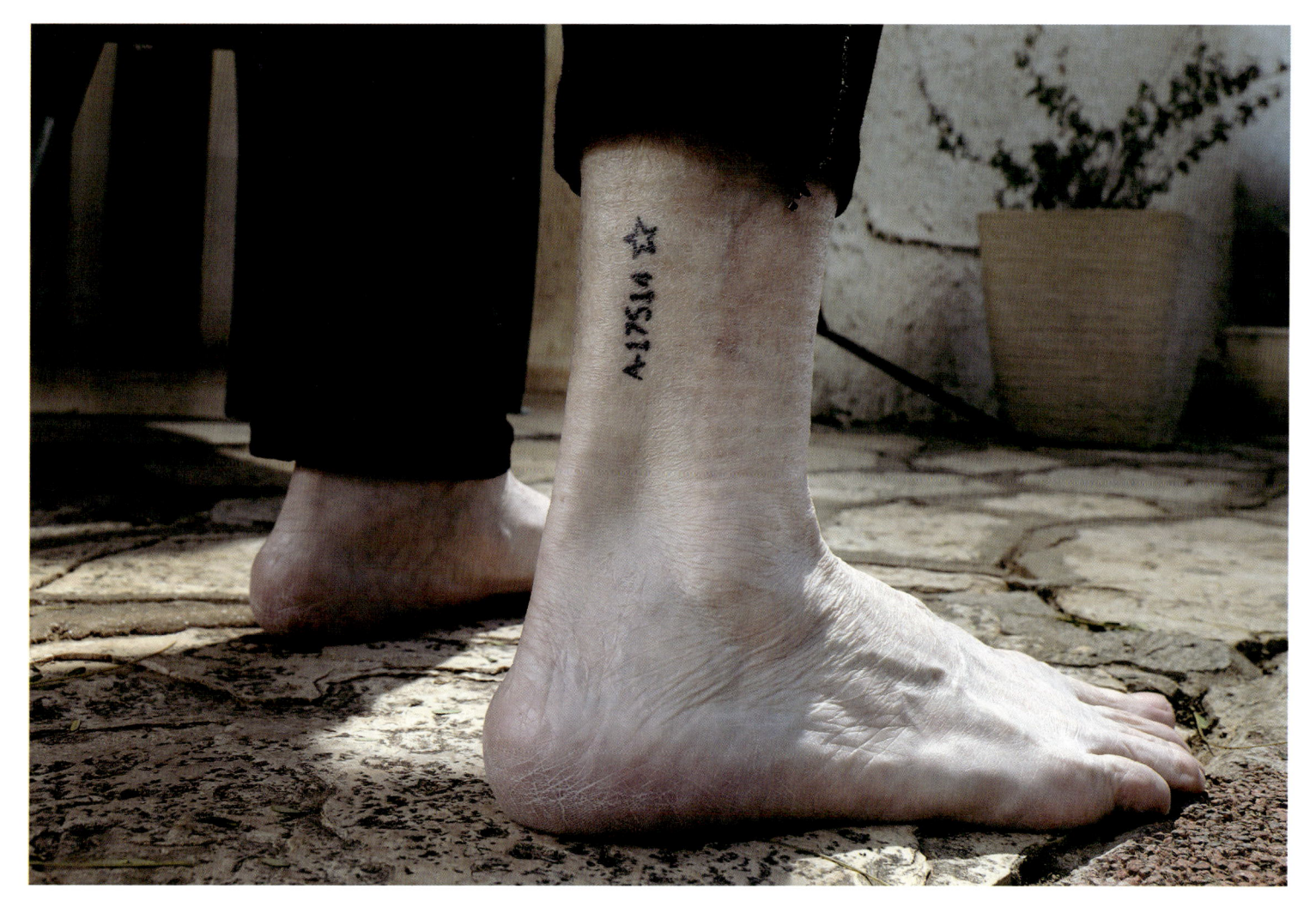

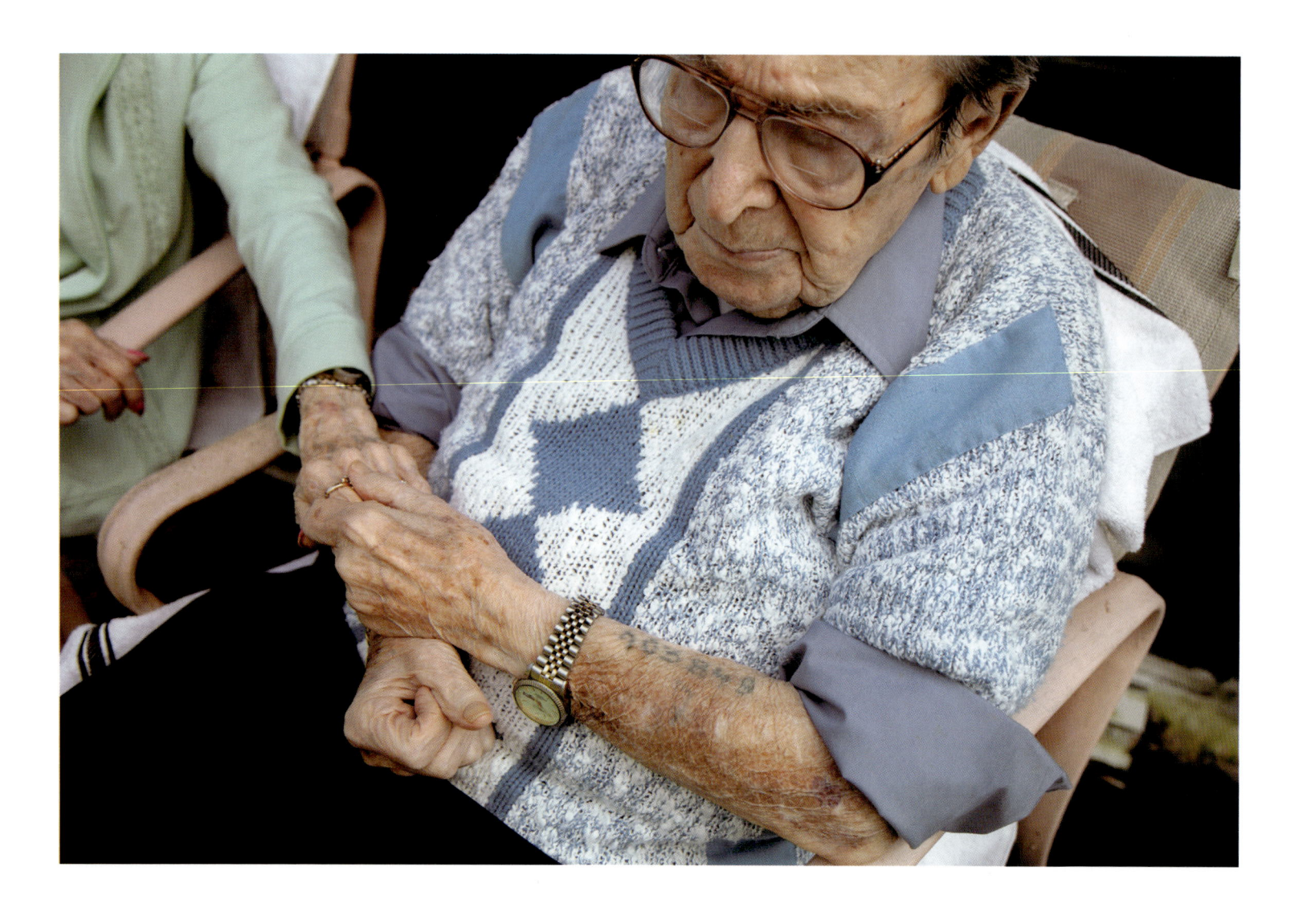

Horace Hecht was born in 1922 in Berlin. In 1940, Horace, who married at age 19, was forced into slave labor in Berlin's railways. In 1943, the Nazis shipped him and his family off to Auschwitz, where his wife, his parents, three sisters and a four-year-old nephew were murdered. "It is impossible to encapsulate all he witnessed and all he endured, but I will mention just one act of barbarity: his appendix was removed without anesthesia," writes Steve North, who interviewed Horace in 2020. After Auschwitz, Horace was moved to other camps and forced on a death march where he escaped execution by the Nazi guards, but witnessed his closest friend killed next to him. Horace was liberated by Allied troops in 1945. He immigrated to the USA, remarried and rebuilt his life. Horace passed away in March 2020, two weeks after being photographed for The Lonka Project. His wife Mildred is also a Holocaust survivor.

Horace Hecht BY Cindy Karp USA
MIAMI BEACH, FLORIDA, USA, 2020

ELLA ROSENBLATT KRZETOWSKI was born in Lodz, Poland, in 1925, one of four siblings. Ella was 14 years old when Nazi Germany invaded Poland in 1939, and the antisemitic decree was issued that all Jews had to wear the yellow badges. Jews were sent to the Lodz Ghetto, where Ella stayed until 1941. During that time, she worked in a tailor's shop, sewing German uniforms for German soldiers. The ghetto was fenced off in April 1941. Right before the closure, her brothers managed to escape to Russia. She remembers the Selektions and the food rationing. The liquidation of the ghetto took place in 1944, and Ella was forced on a cattle car to Auschwitz where she was selected for work by Mengele and sent to the Bergen-Belsen concentration camp (1944–1945), and from there to the Magdeburg concentration camp and forced labor in a German ammunitions factory. Ella was liberated in 1945 by the Russian army while on a forced death march near the German-Polish border. Ella returned to Lodz to look for her family and she learned her parents Benjamin and Fajga, her sister Esther, and older brother Aaron had all perished in the Holocaust. She met Leon, her future husband, while back in Lodz. They had known each other in the Lodz Ghetto in 1941 where he repaired her shoes. They were married in July 1946. In 1952 after a long period in DP camps where two of their daughters were born, they immigrated to the US. One of the daughters, Flo Golden, born in a DP camp, is pictured with her mother.

Ella Rosenblatt Krzetowski & Flo Golden BY Rick Katz USA
MORTON GROVE, ILLINOIS, USA, 2020

Dr. Helga Feldner was born in 1929 in Vienna. Helga's mother was considered by the Nazis "Mischling," the legal term used in Nazi Germany to denote persons deemed to have both Aryan and Jewish ancestry, according to the Nuremberg Race Laws. Local Nazi authorities repeatedly put pressure on Aryans to leave their Jewish spouses and get a divorce. Helga and her sister Elizabeth lived in Vienna until 1943, and had to wear the Judenstern, the Jewish star. The family was separated and Helga's father was deported to Buchenwald and Auschwitz concentration camps. In 1943 Helga, her mother and her sister Elisabeth were deported to Theresienstadt concentration camp. Helga remembers their life being dominated by hunger. She was rounded up and taken to a death camp, but thanks to her mother she managed to escape death before that camp was liberated in 1945. Her father survived the camps and the family was reunited. Dr Helga Feldner-Busztin became a respected doctor in postwar Austria and till today works as an internist.

Dr. Helga Feldner-Busztin by Chien-Chi Chang MAGNUM PHOTOS TAIWAN
VIENNA, 2020

EVA KEPES was born in 1936 in Hungary. In 1944, following Nazi Germany's occupation of Hungary, Eva, eight, and her sister Sosa, 10, along with their mother Miriam were deported to Bergen-Belsen concentration camp. Eva's father had already been sent to forced labor, in 1939. Miriam volunteered to do extra work in the camp's kitchen and was able to smuggle food to her daughters and keep them alive. Just before the camp was liberated, Eva, Sosa and mother Miriam were loaded onto a train whose intended destination was unknown. The train and its inhabitants were found by American servicemen at Magdeburg. Several months after being liberated, the Red Cross informed Miriam that her husband had survived. Miraculously the family was reunited. Eva met her husband Andrew Kepes, a Holocaust survivor, and the couple immigrated to New Zealand in 1956. They married soon after arriving.

Eva Kepes BY Jared Buckley NEW ZEALAND
MAHAKIPAWA, PELORUS SOUNDS, MARLBOROUGH, NEW ZEALAND, 2020

Yitzchak Turner was born in Poland in 1920. 'In 1939, German soldiers broke into homes situated near the synagogue. Nazi soldiers threw in hand grenades, shooting in all directions, and ordered everybody out. Many Jews that ran to the synagogue and entrenched themselves in it met their deaths in the burning down of the synagogue. Many others were taken by the Nazi German soldiers and were ordered to stand by the church wall, and most were shot and killed. Commotion ensued and cries and screams for help and Shema Yisrael were heard. I ran into the church up the hill. The German soldiers shot at us, and my friend Wik Strier, who ran next to me, was killed. I was injured in my left hand while running. I ran to the church door. As we approached, Priest Mieczysław Zawadzki opened the gate and instructed people to come in quickly. Priest Zawadzki then instructed the nuns to treat the wounded. After receiving first aid, he saved my life and others'. At first light, I got up from my hiding place and went to the hospital for medical assistance and was helped by a local doctor.' Yitzchak was captured later by the Nazis and sent to Birkenau. He was shipped to other concentration camps for forced labor and was liberated in Reichenbach by the Russian army. 'They opened the camp's gates for us and told us, "you are free now," but most of us like me had nowhere to go, no family left or home.' In 1946 Yitzchak immigrated to Mandatory Palestine.

Yitzchak Turner by Reuven Kastro ISRAEL
RAMAT GAN, ISRAEL, 2020

LEILA JABARIN was born Helen Brashatsky in 1942, inside the Nazi death camp of Auschwitz. Her mother and father were living in Yugoslavia when they were deported to Auschwitz with their two young sons in 1941. 'My mother was pregnant with me when they were sent to Auschwitz, and when she gave birth, a Christian doctor in the camp saved our lives. He hid me, wrapped in towels, and sheltered us for three years in the basement of his house inside Auschwitz.' Her mother was the doctor's maid and her father was his gardener. Leila was rarely allowed outdoors until the camp was liberated in 1945. The family all survived, and after three years in a displaced persons camp, they left for Mandatory Palestine. When she was 17, Helen Brashatsky met Muhammed Jabarin and converted to Islam, her name was changed to Leila, and after they married they moved to Umm al-Fahm, an Arab town in Israel, causing a split with her family, which they later reconciled. 'I hid my pain from my family for 52 years. I hid the fact that I was born in Auschwitz and what that past means.' Only after she registered with Israel's Holocaust survivor program did she tell her eight children and over 30 grandchildren of her past.

Leila Jabarin BY Debbie Hill USA
UMM AL-FAHM, ISRAEL, 2020

INGE GINSBERG was born in 1922 in Austria. In 1938, following the annexation of Austria by the Nazis, anti-Jewish laws were implemented, and thousands of Jewish families were evicted from their homes. Inge's father was sent for forced labor at Dachau, but was released and then deported on the *St. Louis*, the infamous ship that set sail from Germany on May 13, 1939, carrying more than 900 Jews fleeing Nazi persecution. The ship was denied permission to dock in Cuba, Canada, and the U.S., and was forced to turn back to Europe. Inge's father disembarked in the UK. Inge, her mother, and brother were left in Vienna and went into hiding with fake documents. Inge worked in forced labor at night in a spinning mill. In return for Inge's mother's jewels, an influential count involved in smuggling helped the family to cross into Switzerland. After a short time in a refugee camp, Inge was tapped to manage a villa set up by the American OSS to spy on Nazis and coordinate operations by partisan groups fighting the Germans. After the war ended, Inge moved to Hollywood and became a journalist and composer for pop stars, sharing time between Israel and US. When she turned 96, she performed as a singer in the death metal band, Inge & the TritoneKings. When she was well over ninety, she took part in the Swiss qualification for the Eurovision Song Contest. To hard rhythms she delivered messages like: 'If you want to live long, laugh at death!' In March 2020 Inge contracted COVID-19 at the age of 98. She survived, she tells a Swiss newspaper, 'I neither know how I got Corona, nor how I survived it. The six weeks are like obliterated. My memory was impaired, my head wasn't working properly, I was between reality and nightmare. I can say so much, otherwise I'll have a total blackout.' Inge Ginsberg passed away on July 20, 2021, at age 99. She was living in a Zurich care facility and one of her band members said due to the isolation, she died of boredom, loneliness, and depression created by the COVID-19 pandemic.

Inge Ginsberg BY **Ursula Markus** SWITZERLAND
ZURICH, SWITZERLAND, 2020

YOSEF DEKEL was born in Czechoslovakia in 1915, the eldest son of a family with eight children. Yosef served in the Czech Army and later joined the Bnei Akiva movement, where he met his future wife Attara, in preparation for immigrating to Mandatory Palestine. The couple married a few hours before the Nazi German invasion. In November 1940, they attempted to reach the shores of Mandatory Palestine, with Attara giving birth on the high seas. Their entry was denied by the British, and they were ordered deported to a detention camp in Cyprus aboard a ship called the *Patria*. The Haganah, a paramilitary group of Jews, tried to block the deportation by sabotaging the *Patria* with small explosives, which caused the dilapidated ship to sink within minutes. Yosef held his baby Zipora and jumped into the water with his wife, who could not swim. Zipora held onto Yosef's leg while he swam to the shore. They survived. A total of 267 men, women and children, fleeing Nazi Europe, drowned in the *Patria* disaster. After eight months in the Atlit Detention Camp, they settled in Netanya where Yosef fought as a soldier during the 1948 war of independence. RIFKA HELFAND, a younger sister of Yosef, was born in 1925. After the Nazi invasion Rifka, their parents and six children were sent to Auschwitz. Rifka was 18 and remembers Mengele separating her from her parents and sister. She worked in the camp's kitchen and risked her life in smuggling potatoes to her sick sister and other prisoners dying of starvation. Rifka survived Auschwitz but her parents and sister perished. Six of her siblings succeeded in immigrating to Israel, settling in Netanya where they were reunited with their brother Yosef. Yosef Dekel passed away in late June 2021, age 106.

Yosef Dekel & Rifka Helfand BY Amir Levy ISRAEL
HADERA, ISRAEL, 2020

MORDECHAI CHECHANOVER was born in Poland in 1924. In 1939, days after German forces occupied his town, Maków, he was sent to forced labor. In late 1940, the Jews of the town were forced into a ghetto. On November 18, 1942, the ghetto was liquidated, and Mordechai was sent to Auschwitz with his family. 'I cried when I said goodbye to my mother and sister. I took one last look at them and we entered the camp.' His mother Rachel, and his sisters Rebecca and Hannah, were murdered in the gas chambers upon arrival to Auschwitz-Birkenau. 'On the first night in the barracks in Auschwitz, I was told that the chimney's smoke are our families. Those who are weak will be eliminated, and those who are strong will work until they die.' Soon after, he was separated from his father and moved from camp to camp. The last was Bergen-Belsen, where he was liberated on April 15, 1945. After liberation, Mordechai was reunited with his father at a DP camp, and the two immigrated to Mandatory Palestine in 1945. He fought in Israel's War of Independence, in the Alexandroni Brigade.

Mordechai Chechanover BY Amit Shabi ISRAEL

RAMAT GAN, ISRAEL, 2020

Dr. Viola Torok was born in 1916 in Czechoslovakia. Viola was expelled from medical studies for being Jewish. She married Dr. Aladar Neuwirth, a physician. In 1944, the couple was deported to Auschwitz. Viola was later sent to Lichtewerden women's camp, where she worked in a clinic. She was liberated from the camp on May 8, 1945. After the war, she returned to her hometown, looking for her family. She discovered that her husband and most of her family had perished. Viola went on to complete her studies and became a doctor. For a while she worked assisting Holocaust survivors. She immigrated to Israel in 1949, remarried, and became the driving force in developing medical care in southern Israel, especially in the Bedouin community. Dr. Torok passed away in August 2022 at age 106.

Dr. Viola Torok BY **Amnon Gutman** ISRAEL
BE'ER SHEVA, ISRAEL, 2020

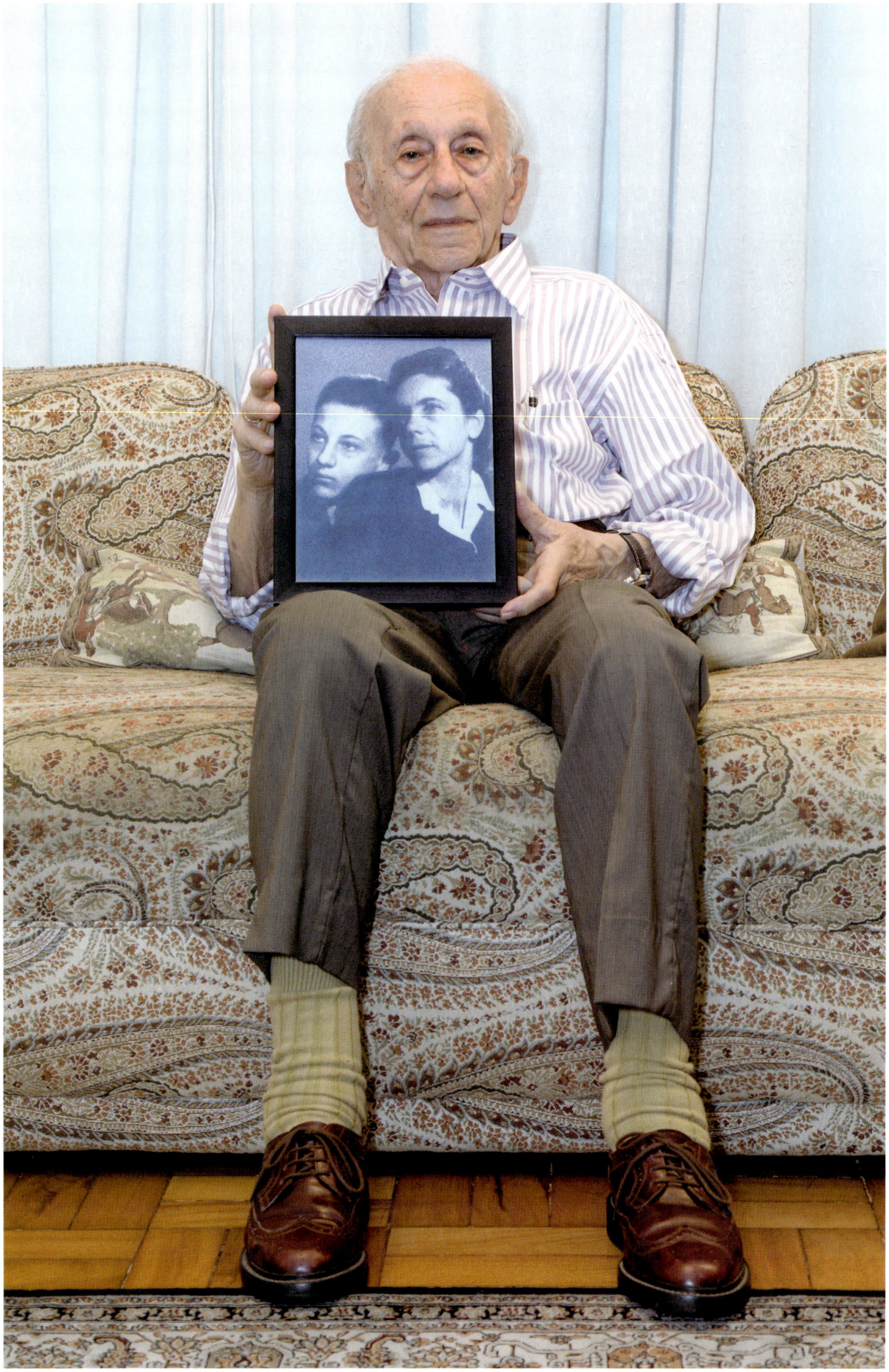

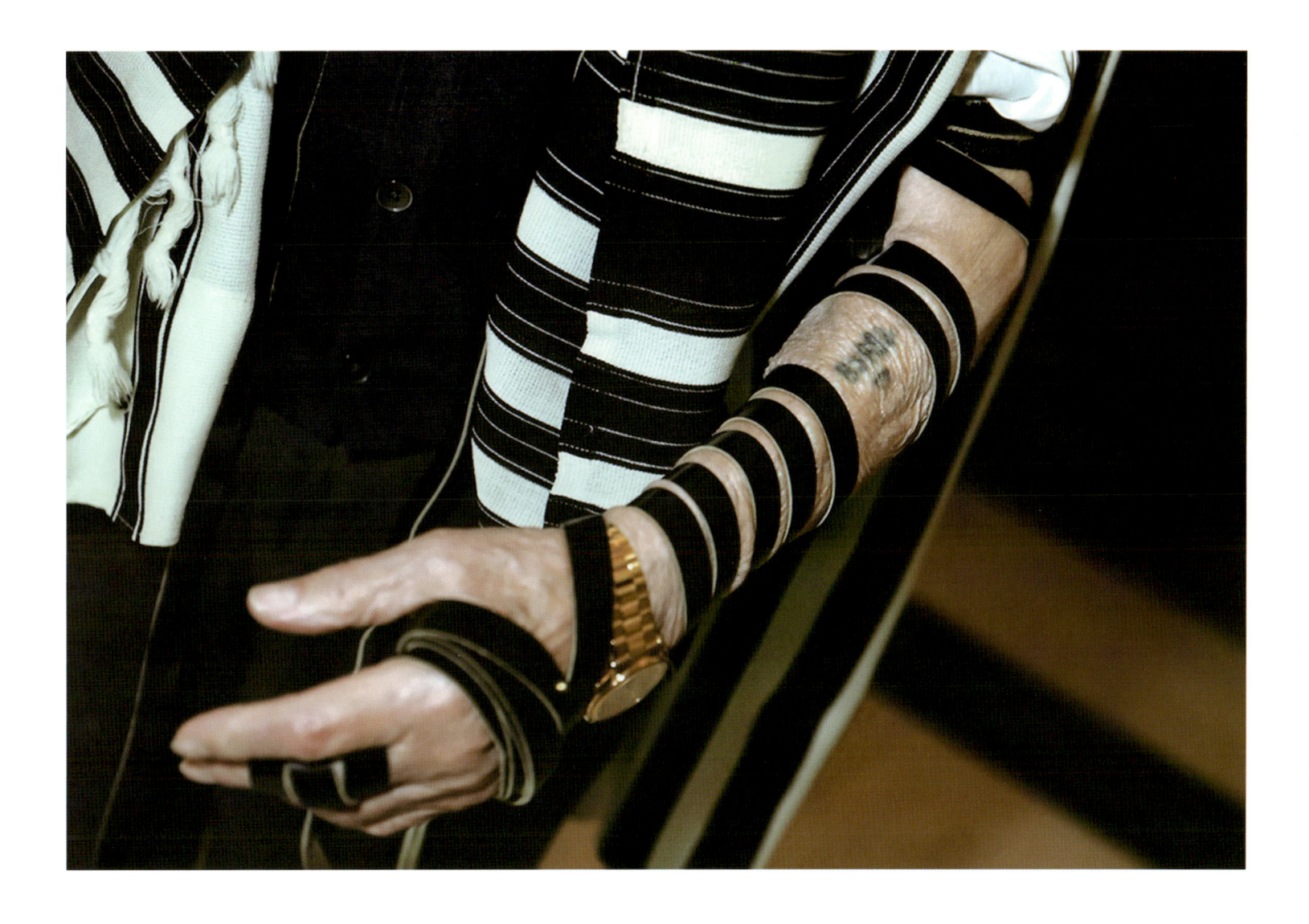

ANDOR STERN was born in 1928 in São Paolo, Brazil. In 1931, when he was three years old, the Stern family moved from Brazil to India, where Stern's father worked for a mining company. Six years later, they moved to Hungary, where his grandparents lived. The family went into hiding in Budapest. When Brazil entered World War II and sent troops to fight for the Allies in Italy, Andor, considered a Brazilian Jew, was classified as an enemy and sent immediately to forced labor camps. He managed to escape and return to his family. In April 1944, the entire family was placed on a freight train to Auschwitz, where his mother and grandparents were sent to the gas chambers. 'I saw my mother coming out of the chimney on Oct. 6, 1944.' Andor was later shipped to numerous forced labor camps. He was liberated in Seeshaupt, Germany, where he and 3,000 other slave laborers riding a freight train to oblivion were freed by the advancing soldiers of Patton's 3rd Army. 'I was 17 and weighed 28 kg,' Andor recalls. He returned to Brazil in 1948 and was the only Brazilian-born survivor of the Holocaust. Andor Stern passed away in Brazil in April 2022.

Andor Stern BY Milton Gevertz BRAZIL
SÃO PAULO, BRAZIL, 2020

SAMUEL BELLER was born in 1927 in Oświęcim (Auschwitz) Poland. In 1939, the day the war broke out, Nazi Germany took over the town. Soon Jews were ordered to leave their homes and move to the Bedzin Ghetto. Samuel's father was taken away, and Samuel was taken for forced labor in the ghetto. In 1943, he went into hiding, witnessing his mother and his younger two brothers being taken from home and shipped to the Auschwitz death camp. Samuel was deported to several slave labor camps and was forced into crowded cattle cars for days on end. 'In cattle trains, hundred people or more, no light, no sanitation. We were all bunched up.' The Germans established a sub-camp of Auschwitz in1944 when they placed the Jewish forced labor camp near Blechhammer under the command of the Auschwitz III-Monowitz concentration camp. From there, Samuel was one of 60,000 prisoners who were forced onto the death march from Auschwitz in January 1945, part of the Nazis' attempt to hide their crimes and escape Allied forces. Samuel was shipped to Buchenwald. 'Finally, they open up the cattle train one day. Two American soldiers came, and they told us, "You're free, you're free." We didn't know what "free" is.' Samuel immigrated to the USA and kept silent about what he saw in Auschwitz for forty years.

Samuel Beller BY **Marty Umans** USA

BROOKLYN, NEW YORK, USA, 2020

Rabbi Moshe Stern was born in Hungary in 1922. He is known for having saved hundreds of lives during Nazi Germany's invasion of Hungary in 1944, when he derailed one of the last trains en route to Auschwitz death camp. Rabbi Stern, pretending to be a railway worker, stopped the train from continuing to its final destination, and with other underground members was able to derail the wagons. The train came to a stop, and most of those on board managed to escape. The 97-year-old resident of the Mea Shearim neighborhood of Jerusalem, a devotee of Toldot Aharon, was involved in clandestine operations on behalf of the Jewish Agency during the Holocaust of Hungarian Jewry. He passed away on July 18, 2020.

Rabbi Moshe Stern BY Chaim Goldberg ISRAEL

JERUSALEM, 2020

ELAZAR (GUSTY) and **ZEHAVA BLAU** were born in small towns in Hungary, Gusty in 1925, and Zehava in 1927. When Nazi Germany invaded Hungary in 1944, Gusty and his family were detained and shipped in cattle trains to Auschwitz. Gusty was separated from his parents as they arrived in the death camp, and his mother and father were sent to the gas chambers. Gusty was taken for forced labor from one camp to another until the end of the war. Zehava, her mother and six siblings were also sent to Auschwitz death camp from the Debrecen Ghetto, where they had been forced to live since 1939. 'We were so lucky; the Russians were approaching and the train to Auschwitz stopped and changed its route. We were saved.' Gusty and Zehava survived. After spending time in DP camp, Zehava with her mother boarded a ship en route to Mandatory Palestine. The ship was intercepted by British soldiers and she was sent first to a detention camp in Cyprus before being allowed into Mandatory Palestine months later. Gusty arrived to Israel during the 1948 War of Independence. They married in Israel in 1955.

Elazar (Gusty) & Zahava Blau BY Eyal Landesman ISRAEL
RAMAT GAN, ISRAEL, 2020

YITZHAK COHEN was born in Thessaloniki, Greece, in 1922. He is the only one of a large family to have survived the Holocaust. He was a prisoner in the Auschwitz-Birkenau extermination camp. 'After my two brothers were sent to death in Mengele's Selektion on Yom Kippur 1943, I was left alone in the world, I saw no more sense to go on living. I decided to throw myself on the electrified fence that surrounded the camp, when suddenly I heard "Maoz Tzur" being sung by Jewish prisoners from a nearby block. I changed my mind. I decided to survive.' Yitzhak was taken later to forced labor in camps in Germany. He was liberated in the Buchenwald concentration camp in April 1945. Yitzhak immigrated to Israel in 1946 on the illegal immigration ship *Rafah* as an activist in the Palyam team. He enlisted in the army and served in the IDF for seven years.

Yitzhak Cohen BY Dor Pazuelo ISRAEL

JERUSALEM, 2020

ZENI ROSENSTEIN was born in Romania in 1935. In 1941, some 15,000 Jews were sent to the ghettos and camps of Moghilev-Podolski. 'I was with my family in a closed ghetto. A Nazi who thought [at] first I was a Christian – I was blonde with blue eyes – realizing I was a Jew, he brutally assaulted me. My face was burned by cigarettes and I was raped. His dog bit my face.' According to Jenny, the rape of Jewish girls by Nazi soldiers was not uncommon. 'There were girls who after being raped ran away and committed suicide.' Zeni witnessed the brutal murder of her baby sister, aunt and grandmother. Zeni was shot in the leg. The bullet was only removed after the war. 'I became an object, a thing, after my family was massacred in front of my eyes. I can barely remember the years that followed in the camps.' Zeni was liberated by the Russians in 1945. In 1946, 'the Russians took all the children and sent them to hospitals for treatment. I was sent back to Romania.' In 1950, Zeni immigrated to Israel.

Zeni Rosenstein BY Oded Wagenstein ISRAEL
TEL AVIV, ISRAEL, 2020

FRIDA KOH WASSERMAN and TOVA KUPEL WASSERMAN (R), twin sisters, were born in Uzhgorod, Czechoslovakia, in 1929. They were 13 years old when they arrived at Auschwitz in June 1944, following days of being crammed in a cattle car, where many aboard died. Upon arrival at Auschwitz, their mother was immediately sent to her death in the gas chambers. Dr. Mengele separated the twins from their father and older brother and they were placed in the infamous Block 10. Their father was sent to forced labor, witnessing the murder of their brother. 'We became numbers.' Tova A-7405 and Frida A-7406. Each day, the two girls underwent experimental tests such as blood transfusions and eye injections. Tova remembers how painful it was when a spoon was used to turn their eyeballs, which blinded them for days, which they spent hiding in the block, crying, until the pain went away. Each early morning they witnessed naked women forced to stand in the snow for Selektion. Some froze to death. The survivors were later put to work to the loud sounds of a prisoners' marching band. Those who did not keep pace were shot at the scene. 'We were lucky to have each other.' When the Nazi Germans realized that Russians troops were approaching, they began massacring prisoners in their barracks. The nights were filled with screams of the dying. The remaining Jews in the camp, including the twins of Block 10, were led on a death march in the snow and torrential rain. Those who did not keep up in lines were beaten and murdered. Few survived. In 1945 the camp was liberated by the Russians. 'We were three twin couples who had nowhere to go.' One of the older set of twins took care of them and they returned to their hometown. The girls learned that the father survived. Frida, who was stronger, set out to search for him, crossing into the USSR. Soon after, the borders were closed and the sisters' fates were unknown to each other. In 1948, Tova succeeded in immigrating to Israel. Only in 1967 did Tova hear that Frida and their father were alive in the Soviet Union. In 1972, the family was finally reunited in Israel. Their father died a year later. Every Thursday morning, Tova takes a bus from Haifa to Nazareth to visit Frida, and she returns in the evening.

Frida Koh Wasserman & Tova Kupel Wasserman BY Shay Aloni ISRAEL

NAZARETH, ISRAEL, 2020

MOSHE KRAVITZ was born in Kovno (Kaunas), Lithuania, in 1931. Ten years later his family tried to escape on bicycles across the border into Russia but were forced to return and live in the Kovno Ghetto subjected to Selektions in which Moshe witnessed many Jews who froze to death. In 1944 Moshe was deported by a transport to the Landsberg camp. A week later he was transferred to Dachau and from there to Auschwitz-Birkenau. 'What happened from Auschwitz onwards was unsurprising. We knew they were burning people. We saw it and we smelled it. I don't know if today anybody can explain that cruelty, the brutality, beating, shouting… Auschwitz, it was a place where screams of agony prevailed or silence, for fear.' He was in another labor camp and a death march and while approaching Buchenwald, they were liberated by Allies. From his group of 131 Kaunas children, he was the only survivor. His mother survived, but his father and siblings perished. He found his mother after the war and they immigrated to Mandatory Palestine in 1946. In 1948 he was a soldier fighting for Israel's independence.

Moshe Kravitz BY Eldad Gershgoren ISRAEL
HAIFA, ISRAEL, 2020

GEORGE SOROS was born in Budapest, Hungary, in 1930. During the interwar period, anti-Jewish policies grew increasingly repressive and in 1936, his father, Tivadar, a noted lawyer, changed the family surname as a defense, from Schwartz to Soros. In March 1944, Nazi Germany invaded Hungary. George had to be identified as a Jew by wearing a Star of David on his clothes. Movement for Jews was restricted, and Jewish property was seized. George, like all Jewish children, was forced to leave his school. At age 14, he found work as a courier, delivering messages from the local Jewish authority to community members. Alarmed by the content of those messages, his father, Tivadar, instructed him to warn the recipients that they must go into hiding as they were about to face deportation. The persecution of the Jews turned murderous and George's father managed to obtain falsified documents which identified the family as Christians, while arranging similar fake ID for other Hungarian Jewish families, which saved their lives. To avoid the apprehension of his sons by the Nazis, a Hungarian official was paid to pose as George's family. The Jews of Hungary were soon deported to extermination camps in the east. George's family went into hiding. George survived the siege of Budapest, when Red Army and Romanian soldiers encircled on the city on December 26, 1944. During the siege, about 38,000 civilians died of starvation and bombardments. Budapest lay in ruins. Years later, George recalled, 'instead of submitting to our fate, we resisted an evil force that was much stronger than we were – yet we prevailed.' After the war, at age 17, through his uncle in London, George was able to leave Hungary under Soviet occupation. In 1947, he became a student at the London School of Economics, graduating with a Ph.D. In 1956, George became an American financier, an author of books, and one of the world's leading philanthropists.

George Soros BY Official Photographer

USA, 2020

Zvi Gil (né Glazer) was born in Zdunska-Wola, Poland, in 1928. After the 1939 Nazi German invasion of Poland, Zvi lost his boyhood when, in 1940, he was deported with his family to the town's ghetto until its liquidation in the summer of 1942. His father, grandfather and two brothers were deported to the Chełmno extermination camp where they perished. Zvi and his mother were deported to the Lodz Ghetto, where the two survived until its liquidation. Between 1944 and March 1945, Zvi endured forced labor and starvation in concentration and death camps, Auschwitz, Dachau and Ridlaw. At age 14, Zvi was forced to remove frozen corpses of victims, and contracted typhoid. Barely alive, he was forced to carry wooden beams, and Zvi says his life was saved by an elderly German soldier. He was placed on a death train, from which he escaped during strikes by Allied planes. Posing as a Polish man, Zvi managed to work for nearly two months in a cowshed of a German village until he was liberated by the Second Armored Division of French General Keller. Later in 1945, Zvi arrived in Mandatory Palestine, and in 1948 he was a fighter in Israel's War of Independence. 'We did everything possible to bury the past as deep as possible, in our consciousness… Our childhood experiences, our bereavement…the Nazi hell. And if I ran away from myself, I'm the one who got so caught up too late.' Zvi became a leading journalist and one of the founders of Israeli broadcasting. In 2002, Zvi was chosen to read the survivors' names of the Holocaust declaration, "Our Living Legacy," the moral compass for humanity, in Yad Vashem's Valley of the Communities.

Zvi Gil by "Koko" Meir Ben-Ari ISRAEL
TEL AVIV, ISRAEL, 2020

SHEINDI MILLER was born in Galanta, Hungary, in 1930. At 14, when the Nazis invaded Galanta, she began to write her diary. In the spring of 1944, on the day of her deportation she wrote, 'June 1944: We are packing. Everyone has something in their hands. Hurry, hurry. Everything has to get out of the apartment…I hear the keys in the lock… A piece of my heart has broken.' Sheindi and her family were crammed into the freight car of a cattle wagon. It was a journey to death. Upon arrival at Auschwitz-Birkenau, through the Nazi Selektion process, Sheindi's grandparents, parents and some of her siblings were sent to the gas chambers. Sheindi and her sister Yetti were sent to forced labor in an arms factory in Lower Silesia. Throughout the whole ordeal, she kept the pages of her diary, crumpled pieces of paper and collected discarded index cards, using them to pursue her diary. She managed to keep her notes hidden until her liberation in May 1945. Sheindi, her sister Yetti and her brother Yezeziel were the only survivors of their family. In 1949 Sheindi immigrated to Israel. In 1973, her son, a paratrooper in the IDF, died during his military service. Her diary was first revealed 75 years after the liberation of Auschwitz.

Sheindi Miller BY Oren Ben-Hakoon ISRAEL
JERUSALEM, 2020

Mona Levin was born in Oslo, Norway, in 1939. Mona was three when 763 Jews were rounded up into the German transportation ship *Donau* anchored in Oslo harbor, and deported to concentration camps in Germany. It was November 26, 1942. A lack of communication in the Norwegian police saved her family from the Nazis. 'When the State Police came to our Oslo apartment to deport us, we were already in hiding since our apartment was confiscated.' The resistance was contacted and a plan to flee to Sweden was set. After a train ride, during which they were in hiding in the bathrooms, 11 people, mostly Jews, were on the run towards a lake and the Swedish border. At night, the group boarded two rowboats to cross the waters towards the border. 'I was screaming non-stop and others, I was told, were panicked when floodlights swept the water.' They succeeded in evading the Germans, and were met on the other side of the lake by Iver Skogstad, a farmer, and his family, who helped the group and would guide them across the border to safety. It was an icy November night. 'I was given a sleeping pill to stop me from crying. I cried and cried and endangered the entire group, who considered to get rid of me. More sleeping pills were crushed and given to me, and I slid into a coma while my mother Solveig carried me in a backpack for hours in minus 18 degrees Celsius across the border.' Upon arrival, Mona was unconscious and briefly presumed dead. Mona's father, Robert, a renowned composer, went into hiding in Norway separately and managed to escape to Sweden, where the family was eventually reunited. They are among the 24 Norwegian Jews who survived from the 763 who had been rounded up.

Mona Levin BY Anne Helene Gjelstad NORWAY

SANDEFJORD, NORWAY, 2020

BINA AND JOSEPH GANZ were born in Transylvania. Yosef was born in 1920 and Bina in 1925. Nazi Germany occupied Hungary in March 1944, and quickly began readying the Jews for the "Final Solution." Bina was deported to a ghetto briefly before being sent on cattle trains directly to Auschwitz. Upon arrival, her mother was sent to death in the gas chambers. Bina and her sister Frida were selected for forced labor and sent to Mauthausen. From there the sisters were forced on a death march of 60 kilometers. On the verge of death, Bina and Frida reached the camp of Gunskirchen, where they were liberated by the US Army. Captain Fletcher of the US forces described entering Gunskirchen camp, "As we entered the camp…almost every inmate was insane with hunger. Just the sight of an American brought cheers, groans and shrieks. People crowded around to touch an American, to touch the jeep, to kiss our arms – perhaps just to make sure that it was true. The people who couldn't walk crawled out toward our jeep. Those who couldn't even crawl propped themselves up on an elbow, and somehow, through all their pain and suffering, revealed through their eyes the gratitude, the joy they felt at the arrival of Americans."

In 1944 Joseph was sent to forced labor camp. He escaped with another prisoner and his life was spared along with a few thousand other Jews who worked for Hungarian Colonel Imre Reviczky. The Colonel, who was awarded the Righteous Among the Nations award, refused Nazi orders to send his prisoners to the Auschwitz death camp. Joseph was liberated by the Red Army. Joseph and Bina were married in 1946. Both lost their families in the Holocaust. The couple immigrated to Mandatory Palestine in 1947. Their ship, *Pan Crescent*, was stopped by British soldiers at sea. All onboard threw their documents into the sea, and eventually were detained in a Cyprus camp before finally reaching Israel in 1949. Joseph and Bina became farmers. Joseph passed away on June 12, 2020, in his sleep.

Joseph & Bina Ganz BY Sara Gold ISRAEL

MOSHAV KFAR PINES, ISRAEL, 2020

EDITH GLUCK was born in 1928 in Transylvania, Romania. They were three sisters and two brothers. Edith's father died in 1937. In April 1944, the family was taken from their home to the Borsa synagogue and kept there for one month. In May 1944 they walked to the Vişeu Sus Ghetto, where they remained for a month. In June 1944, they were taken on cattle trains to the Nazi Auschwitz extermination camp. On arrival, they were stripped and inspected by Dr. Mengele. Edith was sent one way, and their mother and younger sisters and brother another. Auschwitz, Edith recalls, was 'Hell on earth, hopelessness and destruction of my family.' Edith never saw her mother and siblings again. In November 1944, she was taken to Mährisch Weisswasser labor camp in Czechoslovakia, where she remained until Liberation. Edith returned to Borsa, but no one else returned. Edith joined a group of orphans taken to Ireland. She stayed there for nine months before immigrating to Israel in 1948. After marrying, she emigrated to Melbourne, Australia, in 1958. She traveled to Auschwitz in January 2020 to attend the 75th anniversary of its liberation.

Edith Gluck BY Christopher Hopkins AUSTRALIA
MELBOURNE, AUSTRALIA, 2020

MOSHE TIROSH was born in Warsaw in 1937. In October 1940, the family was forced by the Gestapo into the Warsaw Ghetto. His mother Regina searched for food outside the ghetto until her Jewish identity was revealed, but she was saved by a young Polish man, Zygmunt Pietack, who helped her back to the ghetto unharmed and became the savior of the family. After the mass deportation to the Treblinka death camp in the summer of 1942, Warsaw Ghetto Jews, led by Mordechai Anielewicz, began to fortify themselves. At that time, Moshe's father connected with the underground and Regina gave birth to Samuel in the ghetto. Samuel's cries endangered those hiding in the bunkers. Regina, with Pietack's help, had to leave the baby on a Warsaw street sidewalk. Pietack watched as Samuel was taken by a policeman to an orphanage. Pietack helped again by smuggling the family out of the ghetto, hiding the children in potato sacks. He contacted Dr. Jabinsky, director of the Warsaw zoo, who sheltered Jews in underground pathways and cages, and also used the zoo to store arms for the resistance. Dr. Jan and Antonina Jabinsky hid Moshe's parents in the zoo cages and the children in their basement. In April 1943, during a German Aktion, the Warsaw Ghetto Uprising broke out. Thousands of Jews were murdered daily. The hiding place at the zoo was no longer safe and Moshe's parents paid a Polish woman to hide Moshe in her home. His siblings were smuggled to monasteries. The Warsaw city uprising was nearly over in October 1944 when Moshe's hideout was bombed. "Panny Vala" with her daughter, escaped, abandoning seven-year-old Moshe in the rubble. 'I was taught that if I was alone, I should shout: "Oh, Jesus, where's my aunt?" I shouted and men took me to a bunker packed with injured people. I still remember the smell of blood.' Moshe was taken to a Warsaw orphanage that soon after was ordered by the Gestapo to relocate to Staniatki Monastery near Krakow. Moshe was liberated by the Red Army in the winter of 1944–45. For two years his parents searched for their children and located them in orphanages and monasteries. In 1957, Moshe immigrated to Israel, where he became a high-ranking army official. Pietack and the Jabinski family were recognized as Righteous Among the Nations.

Moshe & Samuel Tirosh BY Tomasz Solinski POLAND
CARMIEL, ISRAEL, 2020

ALIZA BUNZEL was born in 1932 in Czechoslovakia. In 1944 her older brothers were in labor camps when Nazi Germany invaded her town. On Passover night her family was deported to a ghetto and, a few weeks later, transported by freight cars on a journey that lasted for a week, to Auschwitz-Birkenau extermination camp. Upon arrival in Auschwitz, Aliza and her mother and grandmother were separated from her sister Eva. Her mother pushed her at the very last moment to stand with Eva 'so that she would not be alone.' Her mother saved her life. Moments later she watched her mother and grandmother marched to the gas chambers. Aliza and Eva had their hair shaven off and were sent to Birkenau camp block C24 with another 900 women. After several months in Birkenau, during one of the Selektions, Mengele sent her to be marked with an X mark on her chest, signaling she was destined for the gas chambers. When guards were busy removing a woman who had fainted during the Selektion, her sister quickly erased the sign on Aliza's chest, saving Aliza's life. Both sisters were sent to a labor camp in Germany to work in an armaments factory. In May 1945 they woke up hearing shelling and did not see the usual German guards. They watched the Red Army break through the gate aboard their tanks, and Aliza and Eva were freed. After a long journey they made it back to Czechoslovakia. Aliza was 13 years old and weighed less than 30 pounds. Two of their brothers survived as well. Aliza's 13th birthday was already celebrated in London, as part of a group of orphans. After four years in England, Aliza immigrated to Israel and rebuilt her life. 'As I look around – my children, grandchildren and great-grandchildren, my heart is filled with pride, it's my victory over the horrors of the Holocaust.'

Aliza Bunzel Family BY Yanai Rubaja ISRAEL

HOLON, ISRAEL, 2020

Holocaust survivor **Max Kirschberg** was born in Germany in 1925. On the night of Kristallnacht in 1938, Max's family was living in Berlin. His father was taken away, never to be seen again. The next year, the family was deported to Poland and eventually forced into the Płońsk Ghetto. The ghetto was liquidated in 1942, and all the Jews were sent to Auschwitz-Birkenau. Upon arrival, Max's mother and little sister were immediately sent to their deaths in the gas chambers. He spent over two years there as a slave laborer and witnessed unspeakable cruelties. After being liberated from Buchenwald in 1945, Max desperately tried to locate family. He knew he had an uncle in Colombia, but no idea where. So, with little to lose, Max wrote a letter to the President of Colombia! The letter was delivered to the Jewish community, and a month later Max received a letter from his uncle, Juan Hanfling. Max left Germany and arrived in Bogotá, Colombia, at the end of 1946. Like many survivors, he wanted to go somewhere where someone knew his name – where he wasn't just the number 77362 – he was Max Kirschberg. Max passed away on January 26, 2021.

Max Kirschberg by Marcial Guillén SPAIN
CABO DE PALOS, MURCIA, SPAIN, 2020

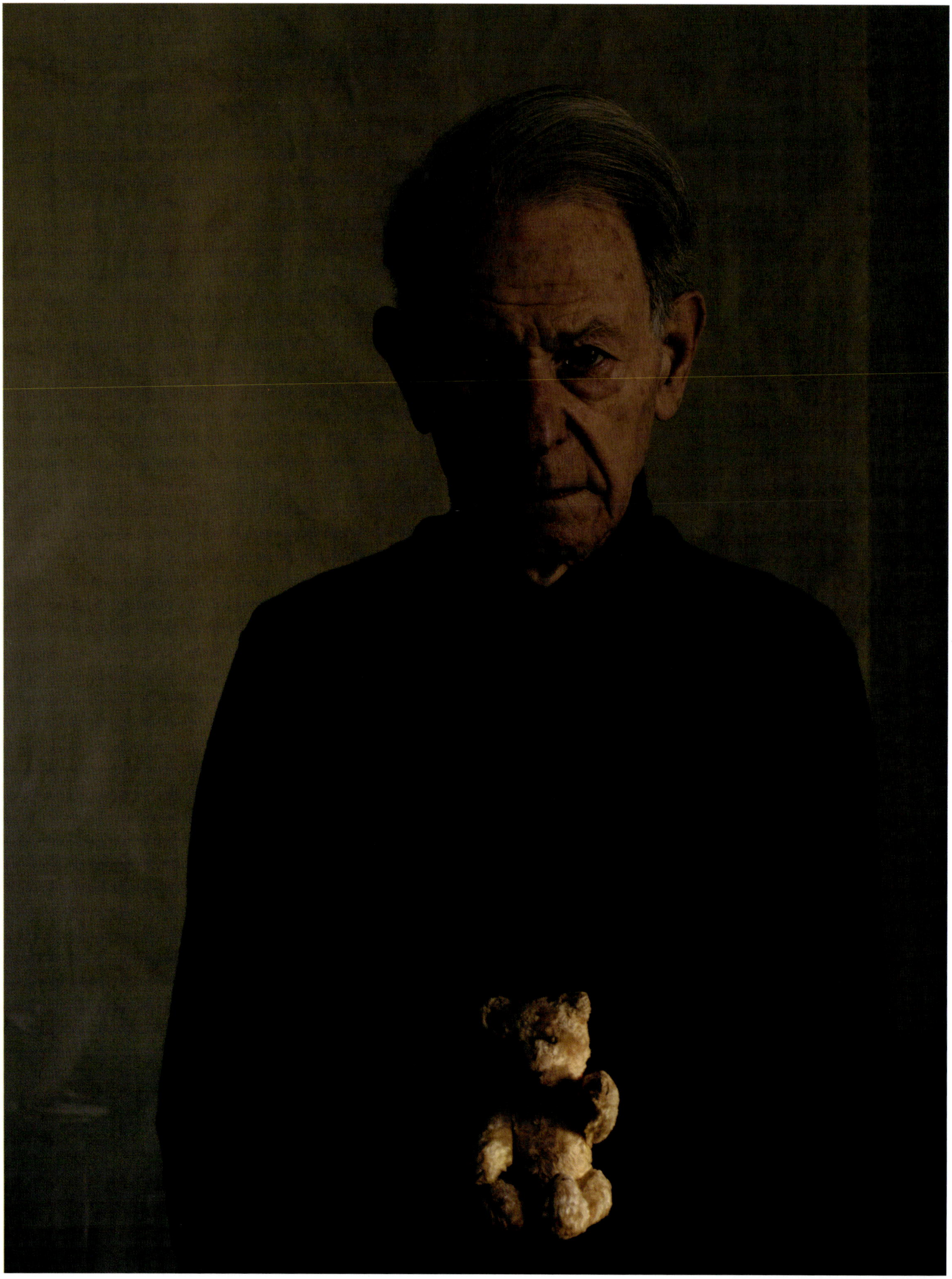

JOHN HAJDU was born in Budapest in 1937. In 1941, Hungary allied with Nazi Germany and more restrictions were imposed on the Jewish community. John's mother raised him alone after his father was taken to a forced labor camp. On April 5, 1944, all Jews were ordered to wear a yellow star. John and his mother were confined to a building, and one family member was allowed outdoors two hours daily to buy food. From the start of the German occupation of Hungary in 1944, Jews and Roma were deported to the Auschwitz concentration camp, where hundreds of thousands of Jews and Roma perished. John was separated from his mother who was taken away to concentration camps. His life was saved by his aunt Iby, who rushed him into hiding in a non-Jewish neighbor's flat to escape the deportation. Soon after, John and his aunt had to move into the Budapest Ghetto. The Budapest Ghetto was cut off from the outside world, like all ghettos across Nazi-occupied Europe. No food was allowed in. The dead lay on the streets and piled up in front of bombed-out stores and buildings, leading to the spread of typhoid. As the Red Army troops advanced, John and Iby were freed on January 17, 1945, just minutes before the Nazis were going to blow up the ghetto. John's mother survived the Mauthausen concentration camp and was freed by the US Army. John's father survived forced labor camps, but his parents went their separate ways. After the war, John and his mother returned to Budapest. But after the 1956 Hungarian Revolution, they chose to flee rather than live under Soviet occupation. After walking over 20 miles through the night, avoiding searchlights and mines, they crossed the border into Austria, where they obtained permission to enter England, ending up in London. Besides a successful business career, John held several grassroots roles, including that of magistrate, and has been helping his local community. In 2020, he was awarded an MBE by the Queen for services to Holocaust education and commemoration.

John Hajdu BY Jillian Edelstein GREAT BRITAIN
LONDON, 2020

ESTHER BÉJARANO (née Löwy) was born on December 15, 1924, the daughter of Jewish cantor Rudolf Loewy, in French-occupied Saarlouis. The family later moved to Saarbrücken, which was controlled by France and known as Saarland following the World War I Treaty of Versailles. Esther enjoyed a musical and sheltered upbringing until the Nazis came to power and the city was returned to Germany in 1935. Her parents and sister Ruth were deported and killed, while Esther had to perform forced labor before being sent to Auschwitz-Birkenau in 1943. There she became a member of the girls' orchestra, playing the accordion every time trains full of Jews from across Europe arrived. Esther said that music helped keep her alive. 'We played with tears in our eyes, the new arrivals came in waving and applauding us, but we knew they would be taken directly to the gas chambers.' Because her grandmother was a Christian, Esther was later transferred to the Ravensbrück concentration camp and survived a death march at the end of the war. She recalled her rescue by US troops who gave her an accordion, which she played the day American soldiers and concentration camp survivors danced around a burning portrait of Adolf Hitler to celebrate the Allied victory over the Nazis. She emigrated to Mandatory Palestine in September 1945 and married Nissim Béjarano. The couple had two children before returning to Germany in 1960. Encountering again open antisemitism, Esther used the power of music to fight antisemitism and racism in postwar Germany and became politically active, co-founding the Auschwitz Committee in 1986 to give survivors a platform for their stories. She received several important German medals, including the Order of Merit first class, for her "relentless activity for peace and against antisemitism, racism and fascism." Esther died at age 96 in Hamburg on July 10, 2021.

Esther Béjarano BY Eric Schütt GERMANY
HAMBURG, GERMANY, 2020

SIMCHA APPLEBAUM was born in 1927 in Pruzhany (today Belarus), to a traditional Jewish family. In November 1941, Simcha and his parents, Yaakov and Rachel, and his sister Ella (Elka), were deported to Bereza Kartuska. After the murder of local Jews, they fled to the Pruzhany Ghetto. In May 1942, Simcha joined the Jewish partisans and Soviet soldiers in the nearby forests. He returned to the ghetto with a group of friends to get some provisions. The Germans fired at them, and several were injured. With the liquidation of the ghetto at the beginning of 1943, Simcha and his family were sent to Birkenau. His relatives were all murdered, but Simcha pretended to be older than he was, and was sent for forced labor. He worked in the construction of crematoria IV and V and the Gypsy camp, laying the train tracks in Auschwitz I, and at various factories nearby. On January 18, 1945, Simcha was sent on a death march to Gleiwitz, near Auschwitz, and from there west in an open train. He jumped from the train and hid with the help of local farmers, but was caught by the Gestapo, tortured, and sent to Buchenwald, and then Sachsenhausen. On April 22, he was sent on another death march in the direction of the Baltic Sea. After liberation, Simcha joined "Kibbutz Buchenwald" in Germany, and in March 1946 came to Mandatory Palestine and fought in the war for Israel's independence. On June 20, 1948, during the first ceasefire, he went with 16 Kibbutz Buchenwald members and laid the foundation for the kibbutz, which is today called Netzer Sereni. Simcha fought in all of Israel's wars including the Yom Kippur War in 1973. The colonel with his tattooed Auschwitz number became a symbol to Israel when he led his battered armored corps soldiers back into battle. Simcha dedicated his life to teaching about the Holocaust.

Simcha & Naomi Applebaum BY Roy Mizrachi ISRAEL

KIBBUTZ NETZER SERENI, ISRAEL, 2020

ANDREA ANATI was born in 1931 in Florence, Italy. In 1942, shortly before the deportations of Florentine Jews to the Auschwitz death camp, Andrea, his parents and two brothers escaped the city. They fled from village to village, but it became increasingly dangerous and they found refuge in a forest near Villa a Sesta, a town some 50 miles from Florence. With the help of locals, Andrea's father dug a cave, and the family lived underground from 1944 until the end of the war. They survived and immigrated to Mandatory Palestine in 1945. Andrea is a Doctor of Physics, and an avid rock climber who took up the sport at age 40.

Andrea Anati BY Roni Sofer ISRAEL
EIN PRAT NATURE RESERVE, 2020

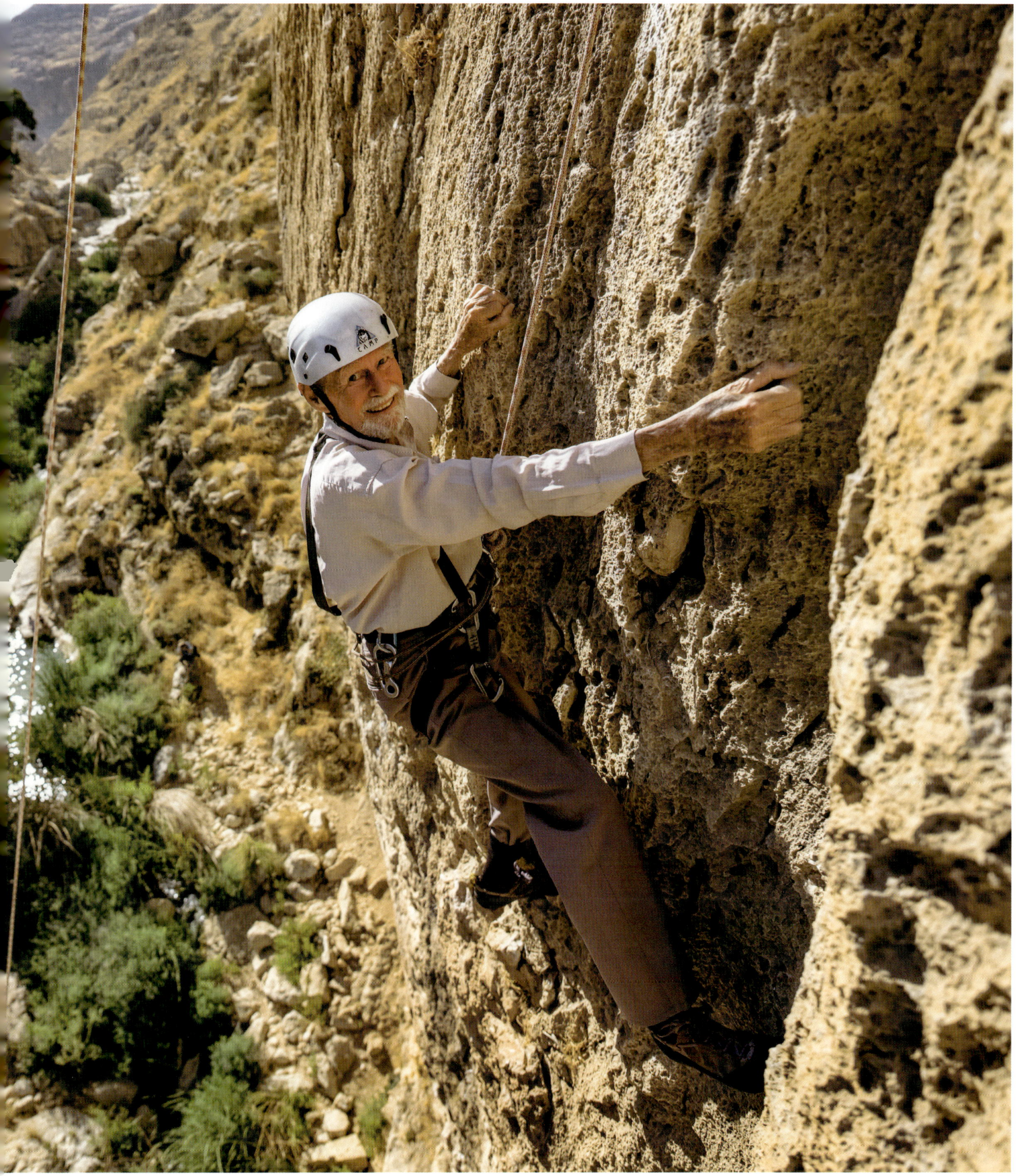
CAMP

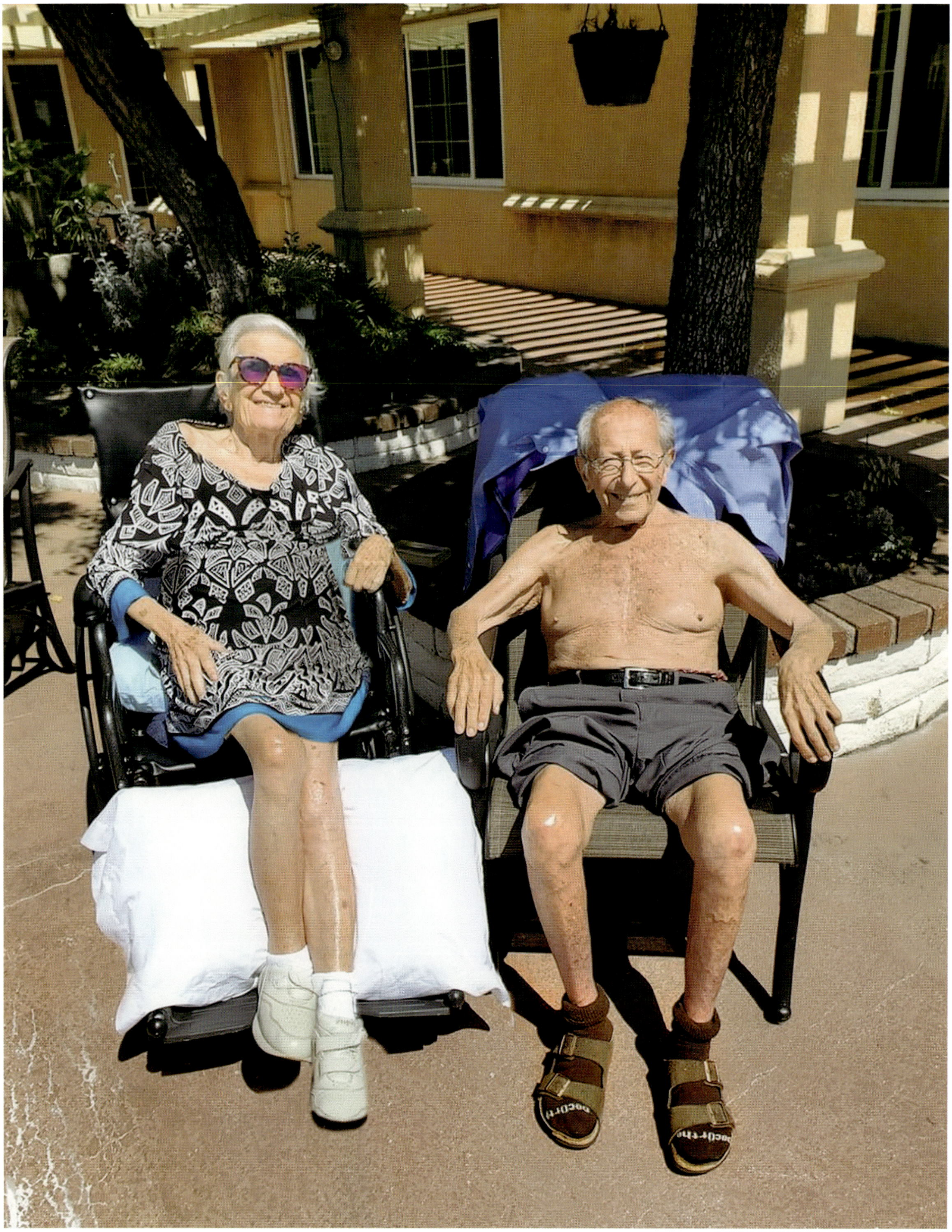

Dr. William Ze'ev Good was born in Stolpce, Poland (now part of Lithuania), in 1924. As soon as the SS Einsatzkommando arrived in Vilna in 1941, the massacres of the Jews began. William, 17, was rounded up and taken to the notorious Ponary killing ground with hundreds of Jews who were stripped before being shot. 'I understood, but I didn't believe this was the last moment of my life.' The bullet meant for William missed, he recounts, 'I tripped, I fell and the shot rang out, several people fell on top of me.' William felt the convulsions of dying people while he remained buried under corpses for many hours. He succeeded in escaping, digging with his bare hands under a barbed-wire fence and then was assisted by Polish residents nearby. In September 1941 William's mother and his brother Motl were captured and murdered by Lithuanian Nazi collaborators along with 750 Jews. For three years William and his father hid in the forests, avoiding capture. With the partisans they sabotaged Nazi rail lines, aided by a few neighbors who risked their lives helping them survive. It was while hiding in the woods that William decided to become a doctor. After Vilna was liberated by the Red Army, William made a perilous journey out of the Soviet-controlled zone into Italy, where he studied medicine at the University of Torino. There were other Holocaust survivors and the students formed a community of lifelong friends. William met **Pearl**, a survivor from Vilna, who came to Torino to earn her doctorate in chemistry. During the war, Pearl and her parents lived in a forced labor camp called HKP 562. This was run by Major Karl Plagge, a Nazi officer and the commandant of the slave labor camp, where 14-year-old Pearl was interned and to whom she and her family owe their lives. On July 1, 1944, Major Plagge assembled the Jews in the camp, under the watchful eye of SS representatives, and told them that the Jews would be "evacuated" by the SS who would shortly arrive. It was a hidden warning to the Jews to save their lives. Over half the camp's prisoners heeded that warning before the SS death squads arrived on July 3. A few dozen young men jumped out the window and escaped. Hundreds rushed to conceal themselves in bunkers and underground sewers without food, water or clean air. At least 500 people were caught when the SS death squads arrived and swept through the camp. The prisoners were herded to the Ponary killing fields. Vilna was liberated by the Red Army on July 13. Pearl and some 200 Jews shakily emerged from their hiding. Pearl and William completed their studies in Torino and came to America in 1952, beneficiaries of the Displaced Persons bill. They married in New York in 1952 and later built a house and raised their family in the hills of Los Angeles, California. Will could speak 11 languages, which was helpful to the largely immigrant population as there was nothing that Dr. William Good enjoyed more than helping people in distress. William and Pearl raised a family of medical doctors who continue their father's legacy. Major Plagge died in Germany in 1957. He was awarded the Righteous Among the Nations title by Yad Vashem 2005, in a ceremony that Pearl Good attended in Jerusalem. Dr. William retired from medical practice at the age of 89, and was living in an assisted living community before succumbing to complications of COVID-19 in July 2020.

Dr. William Ze'ev & Pearl Good by Tiffany Luna USA
AZUSA, CALIFORNIA, USA, 2020

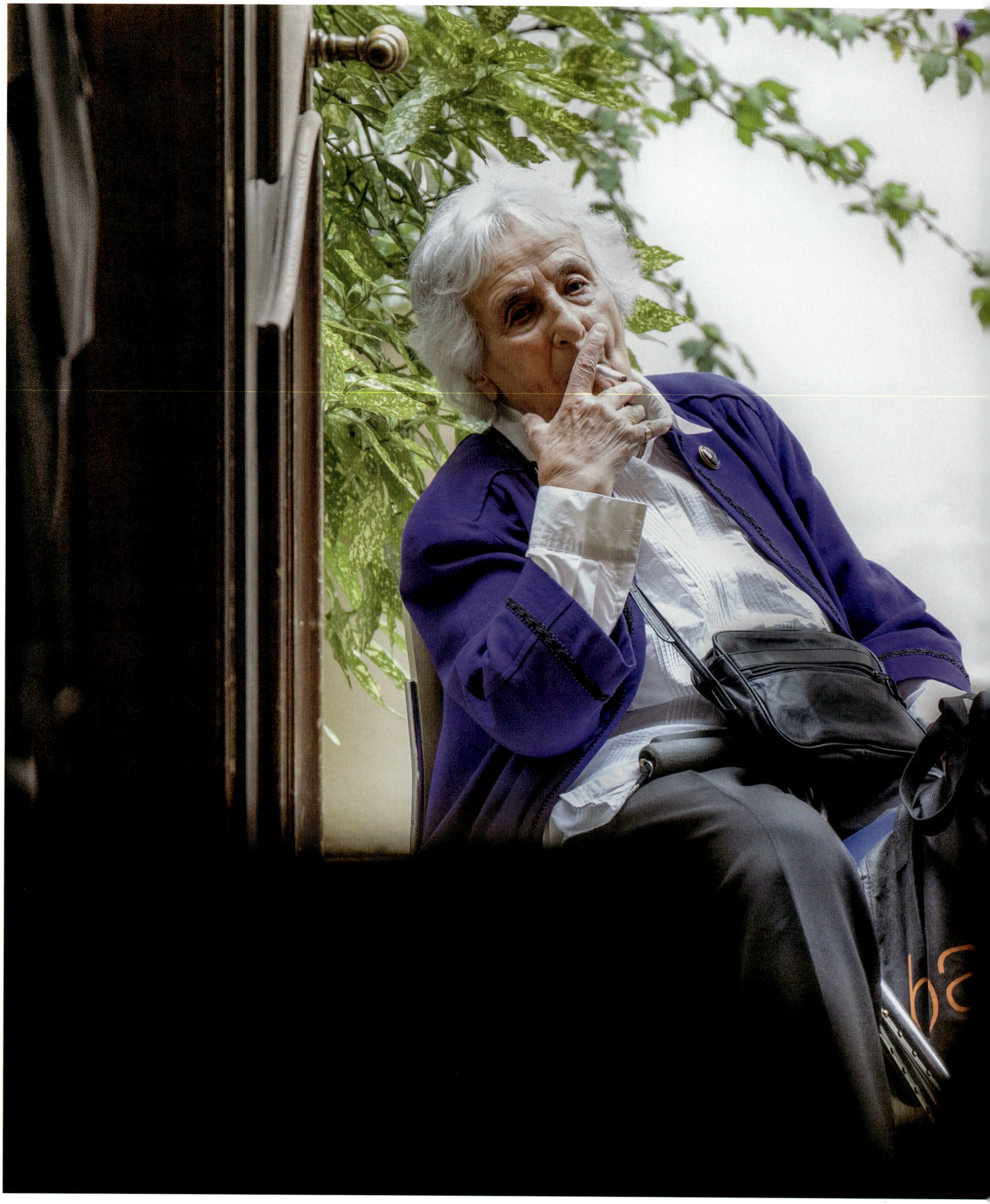

Cellist **Anita Lasker-Wallfisch** was born in Breslau in 1925. The youngest of three sisters, Anita grew up in a home filled with chamber music. She studied cello with Leo Rostal in Berlin, returning to her family in Breslau after Kristallnacht in 1938. Anita's family tried to emigrate from Nazi Germany, but to no avail. Their home was sealed by the Gestapo, and the family was separated. 'The war broke out and we were finally trapped. My parents were deported and sent on a transport to the East, to Isbiza near Lublin… I never saw them again. I was 16 years old. I involved myself in clandestine activities – forged papers for French prisoners of war to escape with. I tried to escape myself with forged papers.' Anita was caught, imprisoned and sent to Auschwitz-Birkenau in 1943. As a convict, she was saved from Selektion, where SS guards chose who should live and who should die in the gas chamber. Anita joined the camp orchestra as the cellist. 'I survived nearly one year in Auschwitz… our task consisted of playing morning and evening at the gate of the camp so that the outgoing and incoming work commandos would march neatly in step to the marches we played. We also had to be available at all times to play to individual SS staff, who would come into our Block and wanted to hear some music after sending thousands of people to their deaths. Although we were somewhat privileged, we had no illusions, that we would end up in the gas chamber.' In 1944 she was transferred to the Bergen-Belsen camp. 'There are no words to describe this inferno. The dead bodies piling up, no food, no water – nothing. It was clear that we had come to the end of the line. It was about 5 p.m. on April 15, 1945…the first British tank rolled into the camp. We were liberated! No one who was in Belsen will ever forget that day.' Anita and her sister Renate survived. Their parents were killed by the Nazis in 1942. In 1946 Anita was finally allowed into England. She studied at the Guildhall School of Music, married the pianist Peter Wallfisch and had two children. She co-founded the English Chamber Orchestra. In 1996, Anita broke her silence and published her memoirs, *Inherit the Truth*. Anita is a Member of the Order of the British Empire. In 2019 Anita was awarded the German National Prize for her campaigning against antisemitism.

Anita Lasker-Wallfisch by Omer Messinger ISRAEL
BERLIN, 2020

Mina Heilig was born in Poland in 1924. When her town, Borislaw, came under Soviet administration in 1939, the Jewish institutions were disbanded. Soon after, the war with Germany broke out and the town fell to the Nazi Germans on July 1, 1941. The following day the Ukrainians staged a pogrom against the Jewish community, killing hundreds of Jews. Mina and Zvi, who had been together since Mina turned 15, went into an underground hiding place, in what they called the "bunker," where Zvi promised to look after her for the rest of his life. In the first SS Aktion in November 1941, thousands of Jews were murdered in the forests of two neighboring villages. The following winter, Jews who survived hunger and disease were sent to the labor camps and the Belzec death camp. The extermination of the Jews continued with executions at the city slaughterhouse, on February 16–17, 1943 – women, children, and elderly people. Jews who tried to hide in the forests and in the city itself were mostly caught and killed by the Nazis, aided by the cooperation of local Ukrainians. Mina and Zvi emerged from their underground hiding place in August 1944, the day the Red Army entered Borislaw. The liberation day was also a day of mourning, when Mina learned that her parents' hiding place had been discovered and that all were murdered – her mother on a death march in Auschwitz, and her father and brothers in the Mathausen death camp and the killing pits. The fate of her older sister, Roja, was unknown. Zvi and Mina immigrated to Israel in 1949. They raised a family, and after 80 years together, Zvi passed away. In her living room, Mina keeps a replica of the painting *Yom Kippur* by Mauricio Gottlieb, a painting much admired by her family in Borislaw. 'When I was a child, I would look at the picture and tell myself a family story…it's my father, it's my mother…' Mina passed away in early October 2020.

Mina Heilig BY Maya Maymoni ISRAEL
SAVYON, ISRAEL, 2020

Zvi Unger was born in Poland in 1929. When the war broke out, his father helped raise funds to buy aircraft for the Polish army. In 1941, Zvi and two of his brothers were sent to relatives in the Świerzawa Ghetto. When the ghetto was liquidated, they tried to hide, but were captured, and Zvi was sent to Auschwitz-Birkenau. Upon arrival to the concentration camp, an inmate whispered to him that he must pretend to be 18, and Zvi survived the first Selektion and later others by hiding under benches in the workshop of the camp. Zvi also met members of the "Sonderkommando," composed of mostly Jewish prisoners who were forced to aid with the disposal of gas chamber victims during the Holocaust. He witnessed their revolt – the Sonderkommandos rebelled at Crematorium IV in Auschwitz II. For months, young Jewish women workers had been smuggling small packets of gunpowder out of a munitions factory in an industrial area between the Auschwitz I main camp and Auschwitz II. The plan was to destroy the gas chambers and crematoria before launching an uprising. But, on the morning of October 7, 1944, the camp resistance gave advanced warning to the Sonderkommando in Crematorium IV that they were due to be killed. The Sonderkommando attacked the SS guards and 451 Sonderkommandos were killed on that day. In January 1945, Zvi was sent on a death march and after ten days was loaded on a train to the Buchenwald camp. On April 11, 1945, he was liberated from Buchenwald by American soldiers. Zvi was the only survivor of his family. He was sent to an orphanage in Paris and a year later, in 1947, he immigrated to Mandatory Palestine. He joined the youth group at Kibbutz Ramat Hakovesh, and fought together with them in the War of Independence. In 1949, he was among the founders of Kibbutz Malkiyah on the Lebanese border. The kibbutz has been his home ever since.

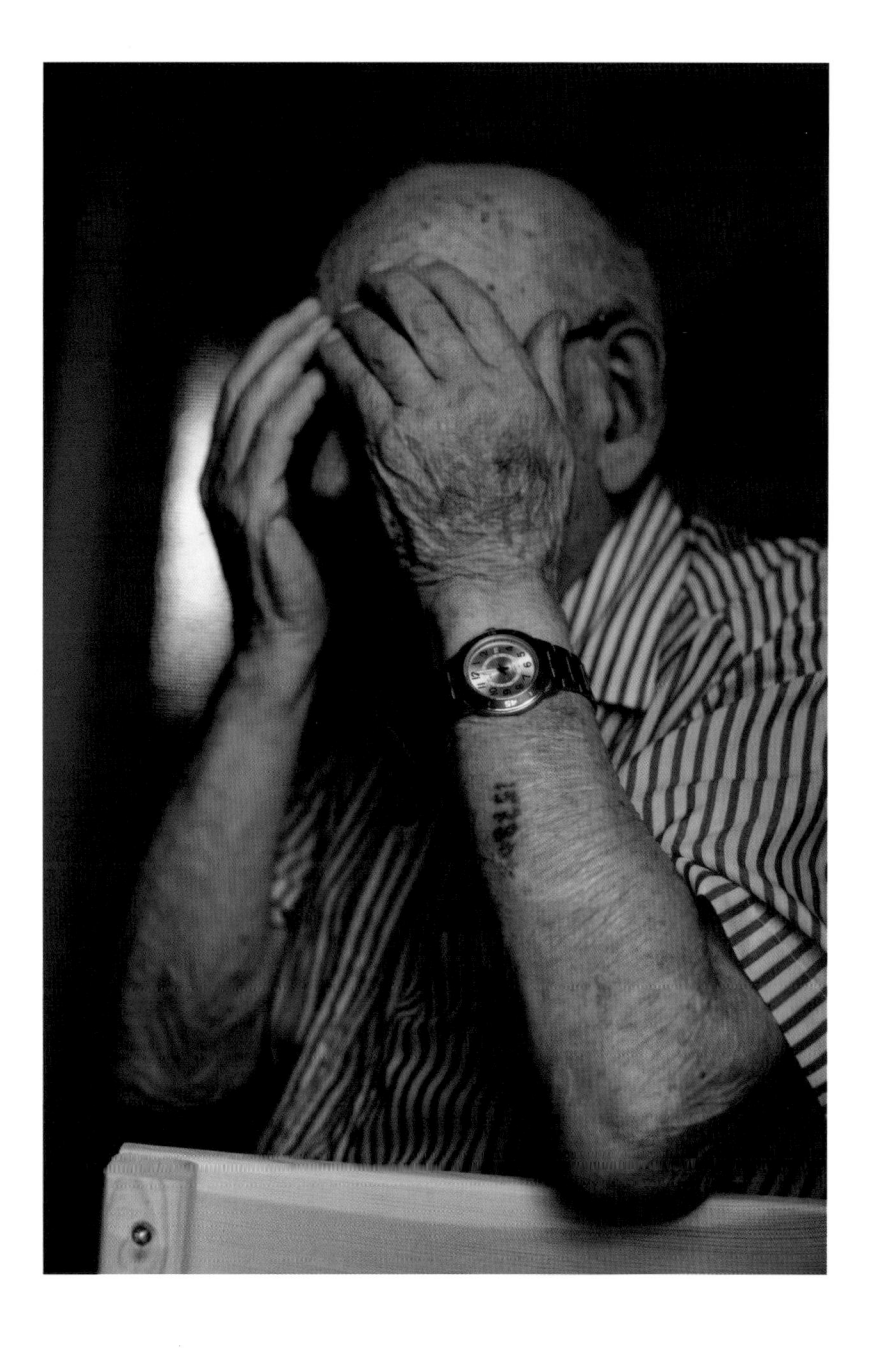

Zvi Unger BY Avichai Nitzan ISRAEL
KIBBUTZ MALKIYAH, ISRAEL, 2020

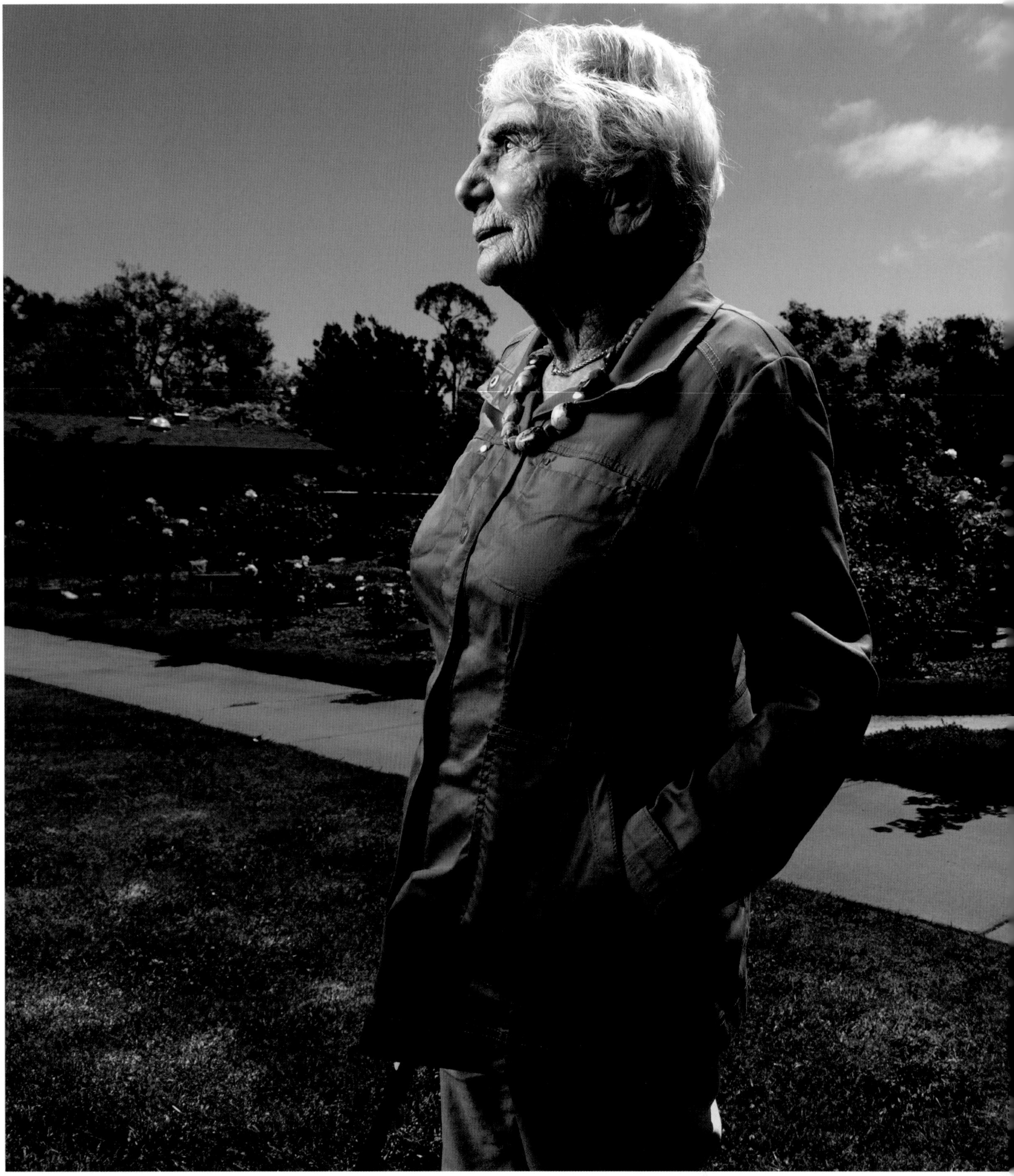

JULIANE HEYMAN was born in the Free City of Danzig (now Gdansk, Poland) in 1925. When the Nazis came into power in 1933 and amid rising antisemitism her parents, after being imprisoned, took her in 1938 in the middle of the night and crossed the border to Gdynia, Poland, and later to Brussels, Belgium. In May 1940, the Germans invaded Belgium and Juliane's family fled again. 'We crossed the French border on foot, but the German troops arrived. A French baker sheltered us and I learned to bake bread. One day my brother, Lothar, and I were stopped by German soldiers who asked if we were Jewish. One soldier pointed his gun at us and threatened to kill us. We fended them off by pretending not to understand German.' The family fled Belgium to Paris and after several months there obtained false papers allowing them to escape into the unoccupied zone where they lived on a winery. They then continued their escape and were smuggled on foot at night through the Pyrenees from France into Spain, 'in total silence throughout the crossing.' They made their way by train through Spain into Portugal without getting caught. Juliane and her family arrived in late 1941 to New York by freighter from Lisbon. Juliane became the first woman training officer for the Peace Corps in 1961. She worked as a an international development consultant in educational and social projects in Africa, Asia, and Latin America, the Caribbean and Central America. Juliane is an avid skier and hiker; she divides her time between Aspen and Santa Barbara. 'My challenging life experiences have given me depth and understanding of different peoples, and I hope I have touched the lives of some.'

Juliane Heyman BY Brent Stirton SOUTH AFRICA
SANTA BARBARA, CALIFORNIA, USA, 2020

DR. ROBERT KRELL was born in The Hague in 1940. He grew up silent and Christian in Nazi-occupied Holland. Robert was two years old when his parents Leo and Emmy were ordered to report for deportation. The Krells knew that no one deported by the Nazis had ever returned. They left their only child with a neighbor and Robert ended up in the home of Albert and Violette Munnik and their daughter Nora, all of whom risked their lives to protect him. His father went into hiding in the attic of his business partner, while his mother lived alone with false papers. Robert Krell became Robbie Munnik. He did not leave the apartment throughout the Nazi occupation. 'I did not cry – ever. I was a very dark, curly-haired kid in a family of blonds so I could not have been spotted by anyone.' About 90 percent of Jewish children in Nazi-occupied countries did not survive; many of them were betrayed to the Germans. The Hague was liberated by Canadian soldiers in May 1945. Five-year-old Krell had forgotten his own family. 'I was given into hiding by my Jewish parents and now I had to leave my Christian parents for my Jewish parents.' For decades, Robert, like other child survivors, did not talk about his fragmentary Holocaust memories. Robert emigrated to Canada in 1951, and has had a psychiatric practice in Vancouver treating traumatized Holocaust survivors. He co-founded a child survivors' group and helped launch the First International Gathering of Child Survivors in New York City in 1991. Many child survivors, like himself, were struggling to come to terms with lost childhoods, death, grief and trauma. 'Silence was the language of the child survivor.' Robert is a Professor Emeritus of Psychiatry at the University of British Columbia and also the founder of the Vancouver Holocaust Education Centre where youth is taught of the consequences of racism and intolerance. Dr. Krell was awarded the Elie Wiesel Remembrance Award, and is an author of several books on child survivors.

Dr. Robert Krell BY Andy Clark CANADA
VANCOUVER, BRITISH COLUMBIA, CANADA, 2020

HAIM ARBIV was born in Benghazi, Libya, in 1934. The family of nine lived in a mixed neighborhood of Arabs, Jews and Italians. At the end of 1940, the British launched an attack on Cyrenaica, and held it for several months, until the Germans pushed them out and reinstated the Italians. During the battles, Haim and his mother fled the city to seek shelter from the bombings. After the Italians regained power, the treatment of Jews worsened. Jews in Benghazi were arrested. Most Jewish property was confiscated. In 1942, Haim's family was deported to the Giado Nazi concentration camp, 1,200 kilometers away from Benghazi. Before the horrific journey, his parents managed to hide gold coins inside loaves of bread, suitcases and belts, hoping it would help them survive. In Giado, every family received a small amount of living space inside a shack, with only bedsheets separating them. The food in the camp consisted mostly of meager, moldy bread. Hundreds of Jews died of hunger, fatigue and disease in Giado, among them Haim's newborn niece. Haim's immediate family avoided starvation in exchange for the gold coins given to Bedouins for bread. Guards would shoot anyone who approached the camp fences. In late 1942, Haim learned that the Jewish men in the camp were to be rounded up for execution. As Haim ran to alert his family, the executions were called off. After their liberation by the British Army in 1943, the family returned to Benghazi. They rebuilt their destroyed home, and Haim attended a Hebrew-language school set up by soldiers from the Jewish Brigade. In 1947, as the fighting between Jews and Arabs in Mandatory Palestine intensified, Jews were suffering harassment in Libya. Haim's grandfather was murdered by rioters. The family's home was attacked, but an Arab neighbor fired a pistol to disperse the rioters, and took Haim's family into his home until tempers cooled. In 1949, Haim and his family went to Tripoli and boarded a ship bound for Israel. Due to his command of Arabic, Haim served in the Intelligence Corps for 40 years in various capacities. He traveled to Cairo with the entourage of Prime Minister Menachem Begin during the peace talks with Egypt, and is the author of *Dark Star in the Desert*. Haim is a volunteer chess teacher in schools and senior citizens clubs.

Haim Arbiv BY Liat Schnitman ISRAEL
HOD HASHARON, ISRAEL, 2020

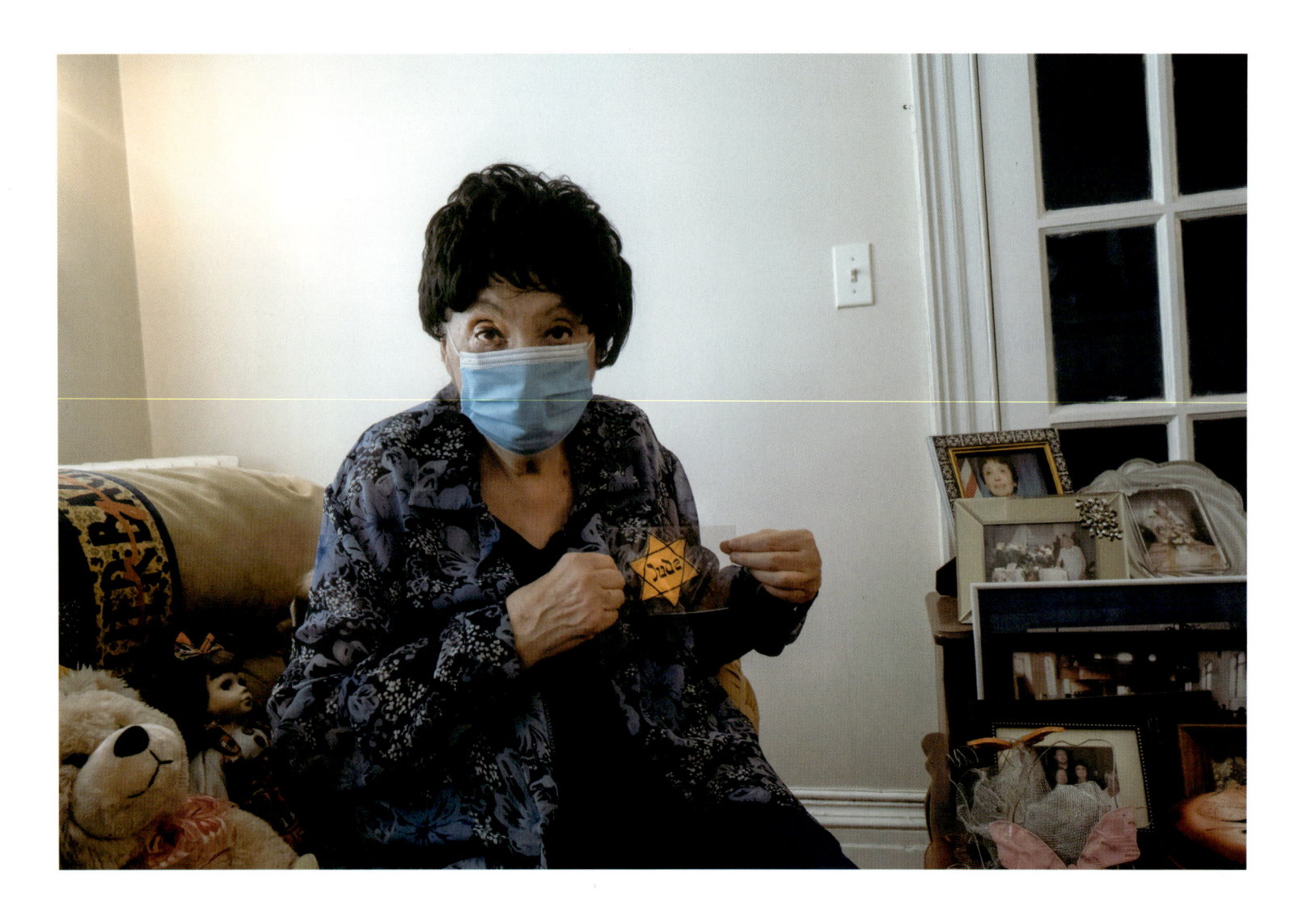

Inge Auerbacher was born in Germany in 1934. She was the only child of Berthold and Regina Auerbacher, whose family had lived in Germany for many generations. Inge's father was a soldier in the German army during World War I. He was wounded badly and consequently awarded the Iron Cross for service to his country. In 1938, her father and grandfather were arrested and taken away during the chaos of Kristallnacht. They were sent to the Dachau concentration camp. Inge, her mother and grandmother were able to hide in a shed during Kristallnacht and were not harmed. Inge's father returned home with her grandfather, who died shortly after in 1939. Harsh restrictions were imposed, and a former housekeeper provided them with food. Inge could no longer attend the local public school. In 1941, she was forced to wear the yellow star, and was taunted by other children. In late 1941, Inge, her parents and her grandmother were told to report for "resettlement." Her father, being a disabled World War I veteran, obtained a postponement, but her grandmother was sent to Latvia, where she was murdered. On August 22, 1942, Inge and her parents were arrested and deported to the Theresienstadt Ghetto in Czechoslovakia, to the ghetto's disabled war veterans' section, where they were allowed to stay together. Inge was hungry, scared and sick most of the time. In the spring of 1945, the Germans began building gas chambers in Theresienstadt, but on May 8, 1945, Soviet troops liberated the remaining Jews in the camp. Inge and her parents were among the 1 percent who survived. In 1946, Inge and her parents immigrated to the US. Inge became a chemist, and is an author of books on the lives of children during the Holocaust.

Inge Auerbacher by **Stephen Ferry** USA
JAMAICA, QUEENS, NEW YORK, USA, 2020

Roza Fatter Winter was born in Romania in 1923. Roza was the youngest of eight children. In 1937, Rosa was expelled from school, along with all of the other Jewish children. After the Nazi invasion, the family was separated when her father, Mordechai, and four of her seven brothers were taken to forced labor camps. Three of her siblings disappeared. Roza and her mother Bracha were left on their own, and afterwards their home was confiscated. In 1941, the two were deported to concentration camps. 'From all the towns in the area, Jews were sent off on foot to Transnistria.' Roza and her mother were forced on death marches to Transnistria, to the Shargrod camp and to the Mogilov camp. On the long journey, which took three months, Bracha fell ill and was barely alive when the two were ordered with 3,000 others into an abandoned structure. Roza stole a mattress for her ill mother, who begged her to leave her and run away. Roza promised they would survive or, 'You remain with me till death.' They escaped but were caught and brought back to the encampment. They were punished with severe beatings, which Rosa would never forget. They tried three more times, and on the fourth attempt they sneaked into one of the villages and hid, helped by a local farmer. Roza realized that they were close to the location where they were initially deported. Through the local farmer, she notified a family acquaintance, the Winter family, who were of German origin and concealed their Jewish identity from the locals and the Nazis, and were living as farmers in that area. When the Winters heard about Roza's escape, they sent their son Levy, a horse rider, to locate their hiding place and bring the mother and daughter to safety. The Winter family hid Roza and her mother in their farm until the war ended. Levy Winter fell in love with Roza, and the two married when the war ended. In 1946, they arrived in Bucharest to reunite with Roza's only surviving brother, Marcel. In 1948, Roza kept her promise to her mother that should they survive, they would immigrate to Israel. She settled with Levy and their newborn baby in Even Yehuda in Israel. Roza's mother stayed behind, waiting for her boys to return. When she learned they all perished, she joined Roza and her growing family in Israel three years later.

Roza Fatter Winter BY Daniel Bar-On ISRAEL
PARDESIYA, ISRAEL, 2020

Dr. Herman van Norden was born in 1920 in Amsterdam. Herman was living with his mother when Nazi Germany invaded the Netherlands in 1940. He was forced out of medical school and was enlisted as a medical assistant, stationed inside a holding area for Jews who were rounded up for deportation to Nazi concentration camps. 'I saw thousands of people…brought in and soon after loaded on trains to death camps, including my cousins.' One night, Herman saw guards carrying a woman. 'I was suddenly face-to-face with my mother who was among the deportees. I picked her up as if she was sick and carried her to the medical department, and later I smuggled her out and back home.' Herman's mother survived in hiding for another year and a half before she was caught again by the Nazis and sent to the gas chambers in Auschwitz. In 1944, conditions in the Netherlands under Nazi occupation deteriorated, leading to starvation. Herman was in hiding, assisted by the Dutch resistance, and moving from one place to another. In 1945, Canadian forces liberated the Netherlands. Herman then learned that most of his family perished along with three quarters of Dutch Jewry. When he returned home from hiding, he found the house stripped bare, except for a barometer, a gift that Herman's father received for his wedding. The barometer was saved by the neighbors and returned to Herman. Herman resumed medical school. He immigrated to Canada with his wife, Julia, who survived the Holocaust by joining the underground resistance movement, fighting the Nazis. The couple rebuilt their lives in Vancouver, where both were known as compassionate physicians who helped many in need, new immigrants and the poor. Julia van Norden was honored with a Knighthood by Queen Beatrix of Holland for her distinguished work in different fields. Julia passed away in 2008. Dr. Herman van Norden passed away in his sleep in August 2021, several weeks after turning 101.

Dr. Herman van Norden by Leonardo DeGorter CANADA
VANCOUVER, BRITISH COLUMBIA, CANADA, 2020

Ibolya "Iby" Knill was born in Czechoslovakia in 1923. Her parents smuggled her over the border to Hungary immediately after being warned that Jewish girls were being rounded up to be taken to work as prostitutes for the Nazi German soldiers on the Eastern Front. In 1944, Nazi Germany invaded Hungary and quickly began deporting Jews. Iby was preparing for her wedding with her fiancé Gaspar the following week when the police raided the flat and arrested everyone. Iby was deported to Auschwitz-Birkenau in cattle wagons and arrived on what was supposed to be her wedding day. 'The whole place smelt of burning flesh.' Her language skills helped her to communicate with the guards, which resulted in better food rations. She pretended to be a nurse and on July 26, 1944, Dr. Mengele asked for volunteers and Iby "volunteered" to accompany a slave labor transport of 530 Hungarian women to Lippstadt. In the final days of the war, the camp was evacuated by the Nazis and the prisoners were forced on a death march. Anyone who couldn't keep up was shot. Iby was struggling to walk and her friends supported her. She was liberated by the American army on Easter Sunday, 1945. After the war Iby learned that Gaspar, her fiancé, died as a Nazi slave working in a Serbian salt mine. Her father died in Auschwitz and her mother and brother were alive. While working as a translator for the British military, Iby met Bert, a British Army officer, and the couple came to England in 1947. In 2019 Iby received the British Empire Medal (BEM). Iby spoke regularly about her story to young people. 'I think that unless we can teach people to understand each other, to tolerate and respect the differences, there is really no future for mankind.' Iby passed away in April 2022.

Ibolya "Iby" Knill BY Veronika Merkova GREECE/CZECH REPUBLIC
BRISTOL, ENGLAND, GREAT BRITAIN, 2020

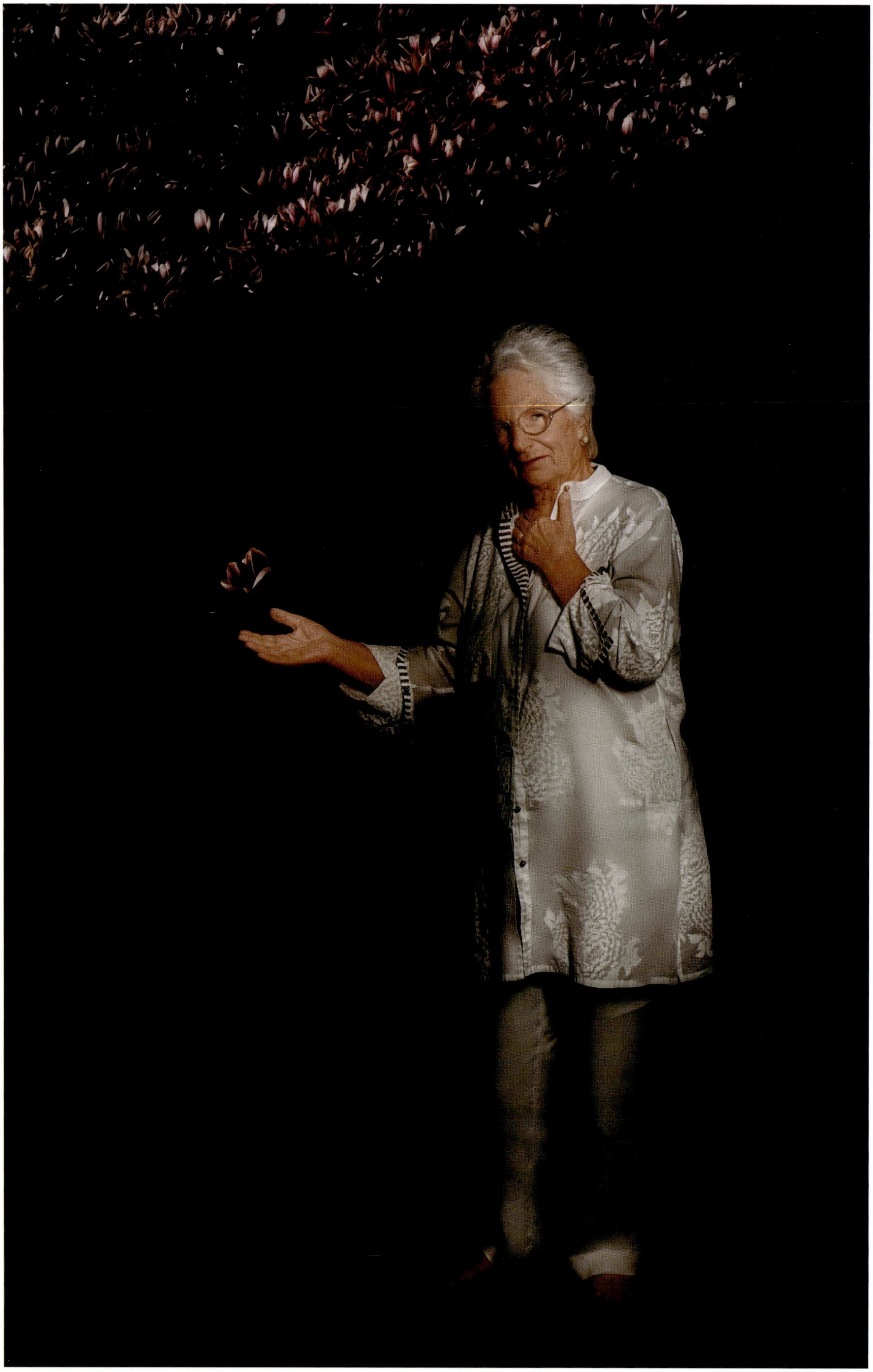

Senator Liliana Segre was born in Milan in 1930. Liliana was raised by her father Alberto and her paternal grandparents. Her mother died when she was an infant. The awareness of being Jewish came to Liliana only after she was expelled from school, following the Italian Racial Laws of 1938. When the persecution of Italian Jewry intensified, her father hid her at a friend's home with fake documents. Liliana was 13 when she and her father tried to flee to Switzerland in December 1943. Both were turned back by the Swiss authorities and were arrested by fascists in Varese. After one week in Varese prison, she was transferred to Como and back to Milan where she was detained for 40 days. In January 1944, Liliana was deported from platform 21 of the Milano Centrale railway station to the Auschwitz concentration camp. Upon arrival, Liliana was separated from her father, whom she never saw again. At the Selektion, Liliana was tattooed with the serial number 75190. In May 1944 her paternal grandparents were arrested near Como and deported to Auschwitz, where they were killed. She was sent to forced labor in an ammunition factory which belonged to Siemens. She underwent three more Selektions and in January 1945, after the evacuation of the camp, she was forced on a death march towards Ravensbrück concentration camp in Germany. After weeks of this ordeal, she was marched on to its satellite, Malchow concentration camp, where she was liberated by the Red Army on May 1, 1945. Liliana was one of 776 Italian children under the age of 14 who were sent to Auschwitz – 25 of those children survived. After liberation, Liliana located her maternal grandparents, the only surviving members of her family. In 1948 she met Alfredo Belli Paci, a Catholic survivor of Nazi concentration camps, where he was imprisoned for refusing to join the Italian Fascist Party. The two married in 1951 and had three children. For a long time, like many children who survived the Holocaust, Liliana kept silent about her experience. In the 1990s she started to speak in public about the Holocaust to young people, and against indifference towards migrants and victims of people-traffickers in Europe. In 2018 Liliana was appointed a senator for life. Liliana's goal, she says, is to pass on the memory and 'to bring to life the voices of the thousands of Italian Jews who suffered the humiliation of the Racial Laws in 1938 and after the Nazis occupied the country, Jews were deported, mainly to Auschwitz, where they perished.'

Senator Liliana Segre BY **Tom Vack** USA

MILAN, ITALY, 2020

JOSHUA KAUFMAN (R) was born in Hungary in 1928 to a large family of ultra-Orthodox Satmar Hasidim. Joshua was 14 when he was separated from his family and sent to forced labor in Auschwitz-Birkenau. Days after his arrival, he learned that his mother and siblings died in the gas chambers. Joshua wound up with the task of having to break apart fused body remains, caused by the lethal gas used by the Nazis. Joshua strove to give the remains a dignified rest, as if they were among the 94 of his family members who died in the camps. Some of the inmates working with him broke down and committed suicide by electrocuting themselves on the wire fence surrounding the camp. Joshua, who was the first to check through their pockets, often found a piece of bread that gave him strength to survive. After he endured Auschwitz, he was transferred to Kaufering, the largest and worst of the 11 sub-camps of Dachau in Bavaria, where prisoners died from hunger, disease, executions and death marches. Joshua was saved by American soldiers. After liberation, Joshua was reunited with his father in Hungary and left for Israel in 1949. He joined the IDF, fighting in several wars. While visiting Los Angeles, Joshua met and married his wife, Margaret, and the couple stayed in the US. Joshua became a licensed plumber. In 2019 Joshua was given Presidential recognition by President Trump and honored in the State of the Union address. Paratrooper and liberator VINCENT J. SPERANZA, 95 (L) and Holocaust survivor Joshua Kaufman, 93. Speranza was among the troops who liberated Kaufman from the Kaufering concentration camp, a sub-camp of Dachau, 75 years ago. The two men met for the first time on September 2, 2020, as part of a Victory Over Japan Day celebration that kicked off at Long Beach Airport in California. 'I'm speechless,' Kaufman said, 'I cannot express my happiness. I don't believe it's true, but it's true.'

Joshua Kaufman & Vincent J. Speranza BY Brandon Richardson USA

LONG BEACH, CALIFORNIA, USA, 2020

David Gur was born in 1926 in Hungary. In 1938, the Hungarian regime began to implement anti-Jewish laws and the family's situation worsened. David went to Budapest to learn a useful trade and while working for a Jewish contractor, he began to take part in the underground activities of the Jewish youth movement, and helping refugees who were fleeing into Hungary from neighboring countries. In March 1944, Germany invaded Hungary, and the underground created a united defense committee of rescue activities that resulted in the saving of thousands of Jewish and non-Jewish lives. David joined a cell in charge of forging documents. One day he and his friends were caught by Hungarian detectives. They swallowed the forged documents, but the equipment in their suitcases gave them away. They were then tortured, and one of them died during the torture. The rest of the group was taken to the military prison in Budapest. David was sentenced to execution, but was freed thanks to the bribing of a senior prison warden by the underground. After the war, David discovered that his father had perished in Auschwitz, but his mother and sister had survived. In 1949, when the Zionist movement was prohibited by the Communist regime, David commanded the last escape operation, helping smuggle surviving Jewish youths out to Israel. In 1949, he himself immigrated to Israel. He graduated from the Technion in Haifa, and became a construction engineer.

David Gur BY Tal Shahar ISRAEL

RAMAT GAN, ISRAEL, 2020

DOV LIVNE was born in 1927 in Poland. Dov was orphaned of his father at a young age, and grew up in a poverty-stricken home with his mother and four brothers in the Jewish ghetto of Święciany. Following the Nazi occupation, most of the Jews were executed. Zvi and his brothers fled, but had to split up. Zvi managed to hide in a Polish hospital, carrying water and chopping wood until he had to flee from the SS. In 1943, Zvi was deported to Ponary by train. Upon arrival, he saw Jews being taken off the train, which was surrounded by SS guards, and then ordered to march to the killing pits, where they were forced to lie on top of each other with their faces down. A riot broke out in his train car, when one Jew screamed, "Escape!" Zvi ran into the forest and his life was saved. He began wandering in the forests and between villages, searching for his mother until he found her near Vilna. With nowhere else to hide, they entered Vilna's ghetto. During the approximately two years of the existence of the Vilna Ghetto, starvation, disease, street executions, maltreatment, and deportations to concentration and extermination camps reduced the ghetto's population from an estimated 40,000, to several hundred. Those who managed to survive did so by hiding in the forests surrounding the city and by joining Soviet partisans. Zvi's mother was killed in the Vilna Ghetto. Zvi was left alone in an orphanage, where he worked as a forced laborer. He escaped, but was caught and deported to a forced labor camp in Estonia, where he worked paving roads and laying railway tracks until all the laborers were transported to Germany. He was sent to Stutthof camp and two other camps and on a death march. In the end he was stranded in Poznan. Zvi was liberated by the Red Army in 1945, but his entire family perished. In 1946, Zvi tried to reach Mandatory Palestine, boarding the *Tel Chai* ship, which was captured by British forces offshore. Zvi was sent to Atlit Detention Camp until he was allowed to stay. Zvi was drafted into the Haganah underground in Mandatory Palestine, and fought for Israel's independence. Later he joined Kibbutz Ma'apil, where he met his wife Esther. In June 1948, Kibbutz Reshafim was established and Dov at last had a home. He worked in every possible odd job on the kibbutz – as an ambulance driver, a plumber, a farmer and a teacher. He devoted his senior years to crafts and his large family. Noam passed away on October 8, 2020, some seven weeks after his portrait was made sitting outside his home.

Dov Livne BY Noam Warshavsky ISRAEL

KIBBUTZ RESHAFIM, ISRAEL, 2020

LIA LESSER was born in Czechoslovakia in 1931. During the months before her escape, Lia had already moved three times because of hatred towards Jews. Her mother Ida took the decision to send her only child away from the Nazi grasp. With the help of Sir Nicholas Winton who persuaded the UK Home Office to issue visas to Jewish Czech children, unaccompanied children escaped on eight trains to London, a rescue operation known as the Kindertransport. A ninth train carrying 250 children was due to leave on September 3, 1939 – the day Britain declared war on Nazi Germany – but never left the station, and the children were never seen again. 'I remember being seen off at the station in Prague, with my mother… I thought she was coming on the train… It took courage to watch us leave. Our parents did not know if they would ever see us again.' Lia's parents were killed by the Nazis along with the remaining 15,000 Jewish Czech children. Her mother died in the Terezin Ghetto and her father Pavel in the Auschwitz extermination and concentration camp. Lia was eight when she was met at the London train station in 1939 by her future guardian, Florence Hall from Anglesey, where Lia was the only refugee on the island. Lia spent her professional life as a nurse in Britain, working as a ward sister and in midwifery, trauma, family planning, surgery and casualty.

Lia Lesser BY Liz Gregg GREAT BRITAIN
BIRMINGHAM, ENGLAND, UNITED KINGDOM, 2020

Reverend John Fieldsend was born as Hans Heinrich Feige in 1931 in Czechoslovakia, but moved to Dresden, Germany, as a baby. It was his father's hometown. The family fled back to Czechoslovakia in 1937 to escape growing persecution against Jews after Hitler came to power in 1933, only to find themselves again under threat. In 1939 John was seven years old when he was forced to escape from Czechoslovakia to England as part of a rescue mission by Sir Nicholas Winton to save hundreds of Jewish children in the lead up to the war. John and his 10-year-old brother Gert left behind their mother Trude and father Kurt and traveled to England in what is known as the Kindertransport, via train and boat. Upon arrival they were separated to be fostered by different families. In 1946 he received a package through the Red Cross of photographs and albums of his family and the last letters from his parents who died in the Auschwitz concentration and extermination camp. In the letter his mother details all his family members who were killed by the Nazis and adds, "Thank those who have kept you from a similar fate. You took a piece of your poor parents' hearts with you, when we decided to give you away. Give our thanks and gratitude to all who are good to you." She added, "in December it will be our turn." John is a retired Anglican vicar in the Church of England, who converted from Judaism as a young man. In 1988 he met the man who saved his life and his brothers. The retired British stockbroker Nicholas Winton was on a BBC television show and Fieldsend attended along with an audience made up of people Winton had saved via the Kindertransport. Fieldsend was one of 669 mostly Jewish children whom Winton rescued from Czechoslovakia just prior to World War II. For his heroic efforts, Winton became Sir Nicolas Winton and is known as "Britain's Schindler." He died at age 106. He and the Reverend John Fieldsend became good friends and often lunched together in a local pub. Reverend John Fieldsend in 2019 was awarded a British Empire Medal (BEM) for his services to Holocaust education.

Rev. John Fieldsend BY **Harry Borden** GREAT BRITAIN
THAMES, ENGLAND, GREAT BRITAIN, 2020

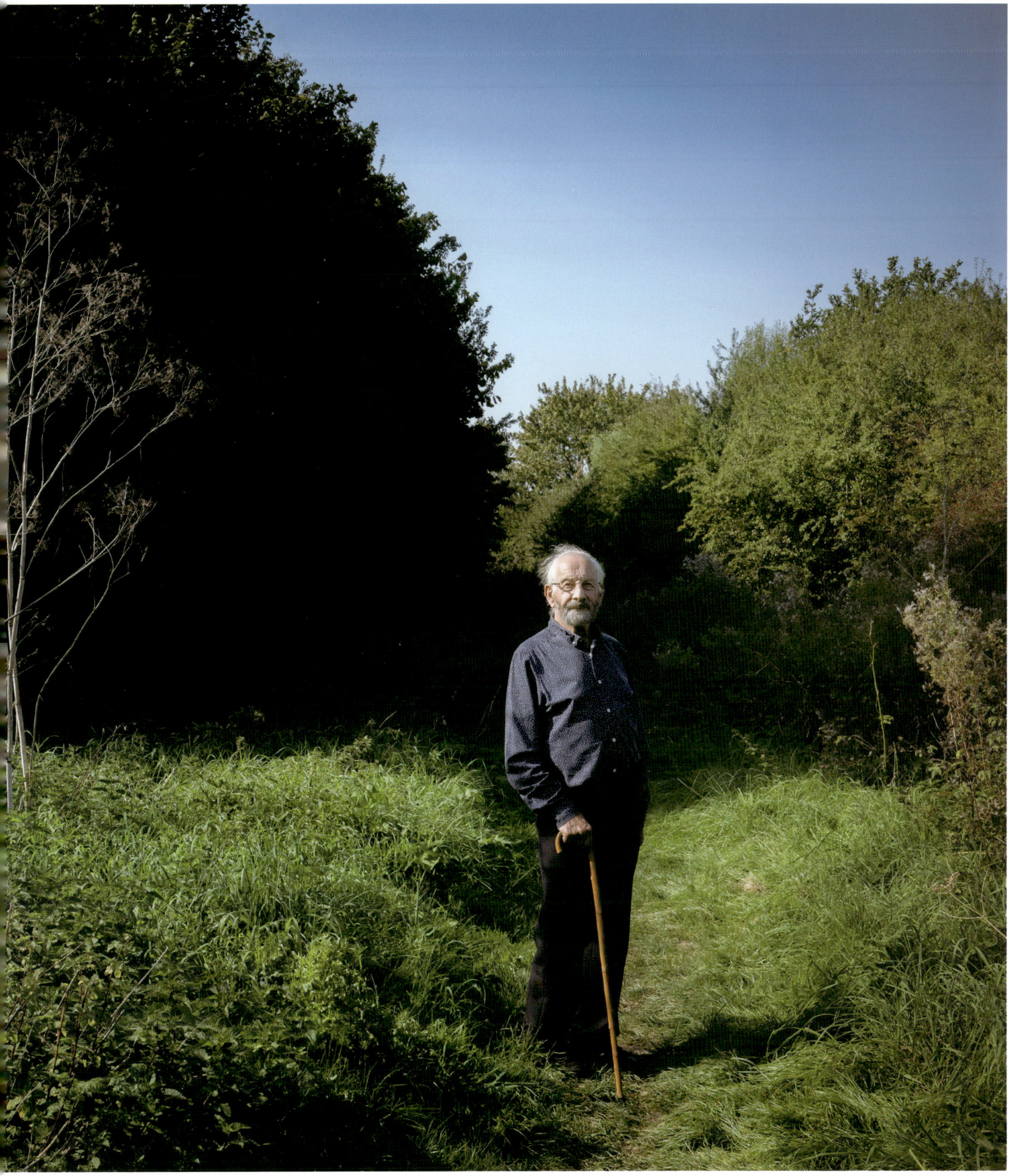

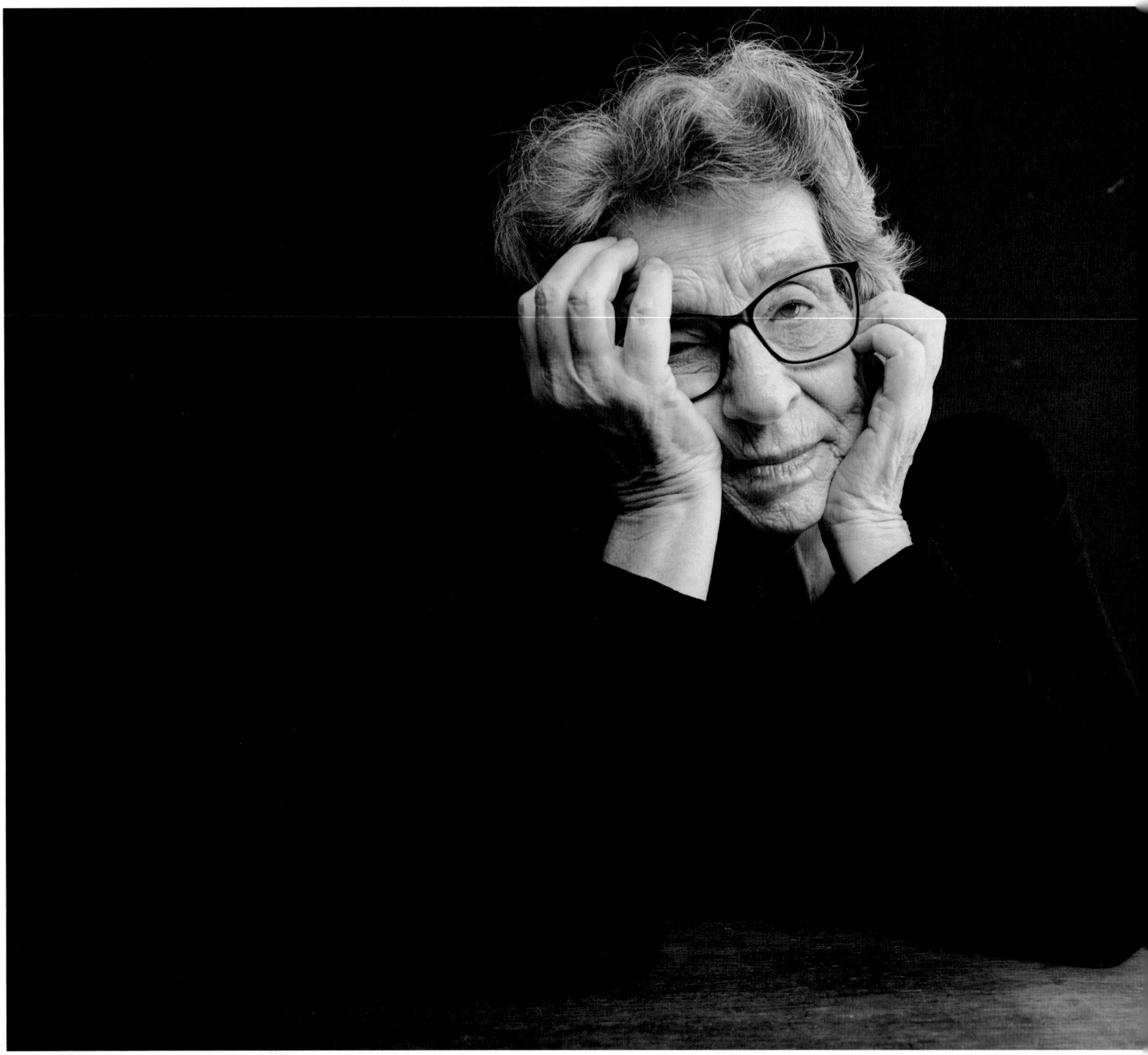

SALOMEA GENIN was born in Berlin in 1932. Her Jewish-Polish parents divorced and she was raised in what she calls 'a dysfunctional family' in an increasingly antisemitic Nazi Germany. As a young girl she recalls enduring abuse in the streets, even from little girls who would hurl insults of her Jewish identity. After Kristallnacht, when synagogues and Jewish property were burnt down in Nazi Germany, her father fled and Salomea would never see him again. Pushed out by the violence of Nazism, her mother took her two daughters and the three sailed to Australia where Salomea remained until 1954. Salomea's experiences pushed her to the other end of the political spectrum at the time and in 1949 she joined the Australian Communist party. 'The Communist Party became my substitute family.' She returned to Berlin in 1954 and was recruited and worked as an informant for the Stasi and in 1963, she was allowed to move to East Germany. In 1982 she realized that she was living in a 'police state' and became suicidal. Salomea confessed her activities to those she had spied on including a church group she had infiltrated. Touched by both the Holocaust and East German totalitarianism in the postwar period, Salomea Genin is living the weight of the past in Berlin today. She joined a group known as Child Survivors Deutschland, an organization that is committed to helping child survivors of the Holocaust work to overcome trauma, and is an author of the book *Shayndl and Salomea* in which she describes the effects of a family's struggles for their very survival against the shadow of the Nazis' rise to power.

Salomea Genin BY **Kristian Schuller** GERMANY
BERLIN, 2020

SOLOMON KOFINAS was born in Athens, Greece, in 1936. Three years into the Nazi occupation of Greece, Solomon remembers a terrible hunger. In 1944 the Nazis had issued an edict urging Jews to register at the main synagogue of Athens for food rations of flour and sugar. Solomon's father, Haim, added his name and, accompanied by his teenage daughter, they went to the synagogue and never returned. His father and sister are believed to be among hundreds of Jews inside the synagogue on March 23 who were trapped by the Gestapo when they sealed its doors. Most were sent to the Auschwitz-Birkenau extermination camp in Poland. Back at home, Solomon's mother, Rachel, realized her husband and daughter were captured and ran with her newborn baby and the two boys to seek shelter in a nearby shop. When Rachel briefly returned home to collect supplies, she was arrested by the Gestapo. 'A youth from the neighborhood heard the commotion and her screaming and came and told my brother, "Your mother is screaming for your baby brother." So my brother gave him the baby, grabbed me and we ran away, far from our home.' Rachel and the baby were 'gone,' he said. 'They disappeared.' Solomon and his brother fled into the countryside, hiding in non-Jewish homes, pretending to be Christians. They slept in backyards and sold cigarettes on the streets of Athens. The two brothers survived the war. In 1955, Solomon immigrated to the US, settling in New York City. He found New York a place of adventure with a future and created a new life, a family with a strong community of friends, all Shoah survivors.

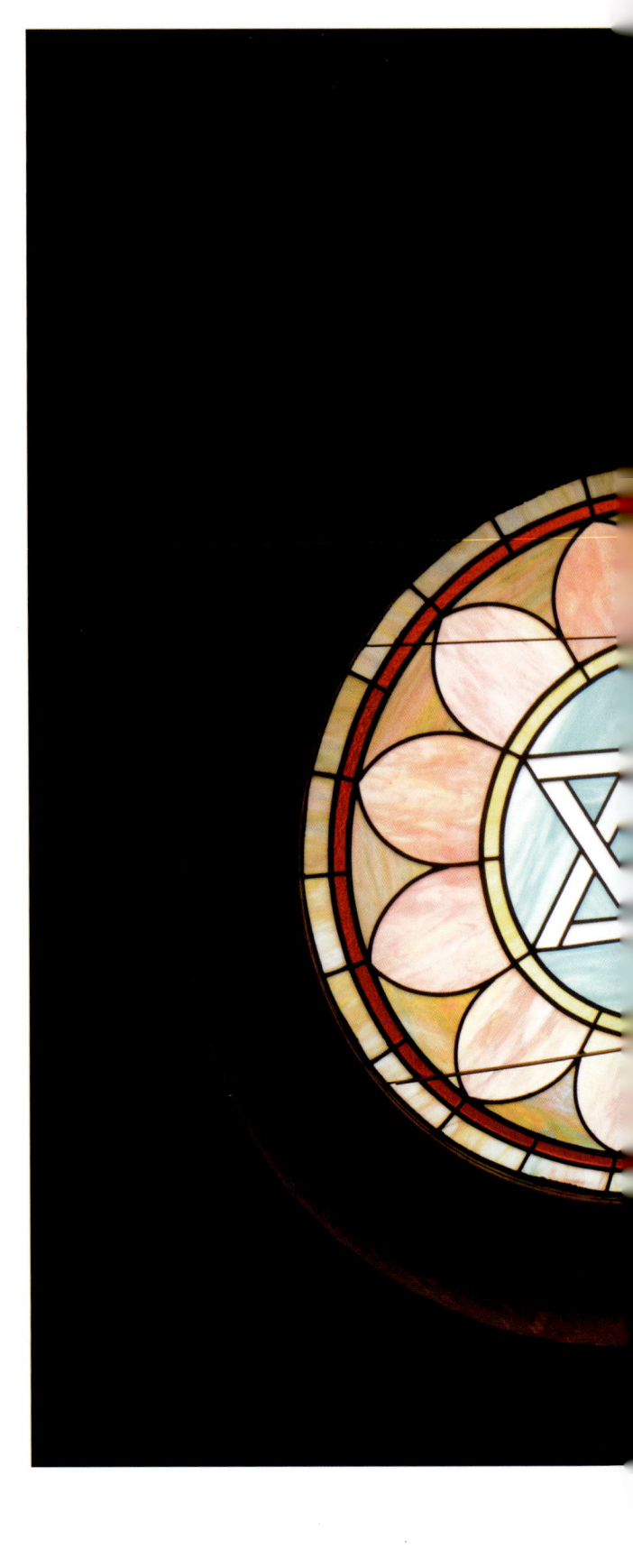

Solomon Kofinas BY B.A. Van Sise USA/ITALY
NEW YORK CITY, NEW YORK, USA, 2020

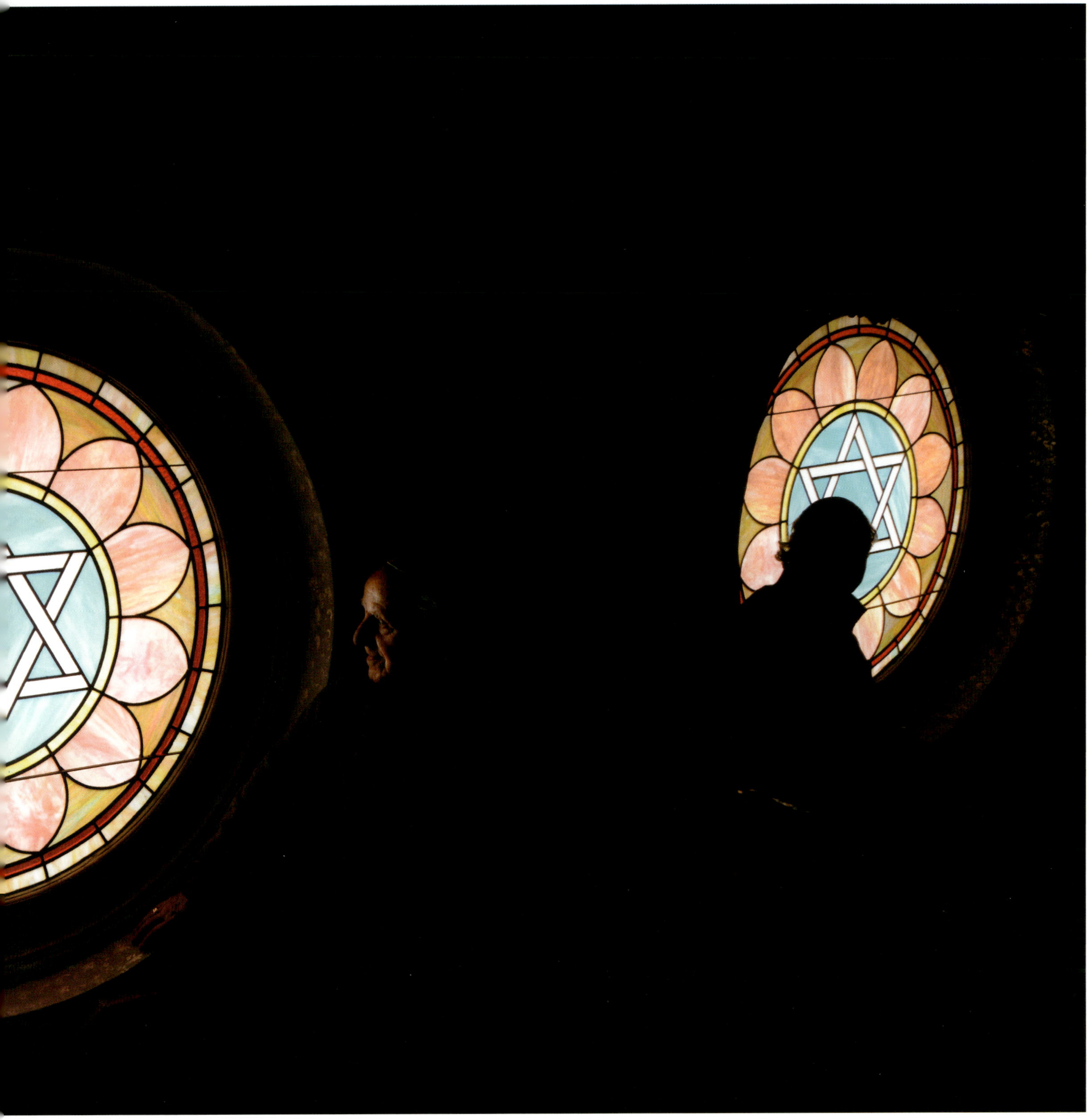

FISHEL GOLDIG was born in 1933 in Mielnica, Ukraine. In 1942, Fishel and his family were forced into the Borszczow Ghetto. When it became evident that Nazis were to round up Jews for executions, his family tried to escape through a hole cut in the barbed wire separating the ghetto from the rest of the city. Fishel's father succeeded before the Nazis opened fire. They killed Fishel's cousins. Fishel and his mother fled into the forest. There they found many Jews in hiding, and the family was reunited, spending several months in the woods. Late in 1942, Fishel, his parents and relatives were sheltered by a Ukrainian farmer. He hid them in his potato cellar, where they remained until liberation in the spring of 1944. In 1946, they were smuggled into Germany and spent two years in a displaced persons camp. They immigrated to Canada two years later, settling in Montreal. Fishel studied literature, philosophy and music. He performs in a Yiddish theater and sings in synagogue as a cantor, as well as contributing to Holocaust education at the Montreal Holocaust museum.

Fishel Goldig BY James Andrew Rosen CANADA
MONTREAL, CANADA, 2020

TED BOLGAR was born in Hungary in 1924. Nazi Germany occupied the country in March 1944. In April, the Jews of Ted's town, Sarospatak, were forced into the ghetto. When the ghetto was liquidated in June, all the Jews, including Ted and his family, were deported to Auschwitz. Upon arrival, Ted and his father were selected for work. His mother and 13-year-old sister were immediately sent to death in the gas chambers. 'My father and I were lucky; we were selected for slave labor.' A few weeks later, Ted and other prisoners were sent to clear the rubble in the demolished Warsaw Ghetto, after the uprising. As the Soviet army approached Warsaw, the prisoners were forced on a death march to Dachau. Ted was in two of Dachau's satellite camps (Muhldorf and Mittelgars), where he worked on the construction of an underground factory. When the Germans liquidated the camp in May 1945, the prisoners were sent by train to an unknown destination. The camp guards abandoned the train a few days later and the prisoners fled. Ted was taken to the Feldafing displaced persons camp. When he heard that his father had survived, he returned to his hometown, Sarospatak. Ted lived with his father for one year. After his father remarried, Ted applied for an emigration visa to Canada, and arrived in Montreal in June 1948. Ted rebuilt his life and raised a family. Ted is a volunteer speaker at the Montreal Holocaust Museum, where he shares his story with students.

Ted Bolgar BY James Andrew Rosen CANADA
MONTREAL, CANADA, 2020

Naphtali Bilu was born in Romania in 1932. He was seven when Nazi troops were approaching his small Jewish town near Moldova. His parents escaped, but his grandparents were unable to make the journey and were murdered by the Nazis. They were part of a large group of Jews on the run from the German forces. When they reached the Dnieper River bridge, they were caught in a Nazi bombardment of the bridge where Naphtali's father, Shaul, was killed. In 1941, after escaping mostly on foot, Naphtali and his mother reached Uzbekistan, where his mother found work in a textile factory. Near the factory there was a deep-water reservoir into which Naphtali, identified as a Jew, was thrown by local assailants. He taught himself to swim in that assault. In 1945, Naphtali and his mother returned to Romania, only to learn that all the residents of his Jewish town had been killed. Naphtali and his mother boarded a ship packed with survivors trying to reach Mandatory Palestine illegally. They were intercepted by British police at sea and were sent into detention in Cyprus. After his release, he was sent to a kibbutz, which was attacked during the 1948 War of Independence. At 17, he enlisted in the IDF. After his army service he worked in Israel's ports, including Ashdod, where he lives, and where he became, and remains today, an avid surfer.

Naphtali Bilu BY Rafi Amar ISRAEL
ASHDOD, ISRAEL, 2020

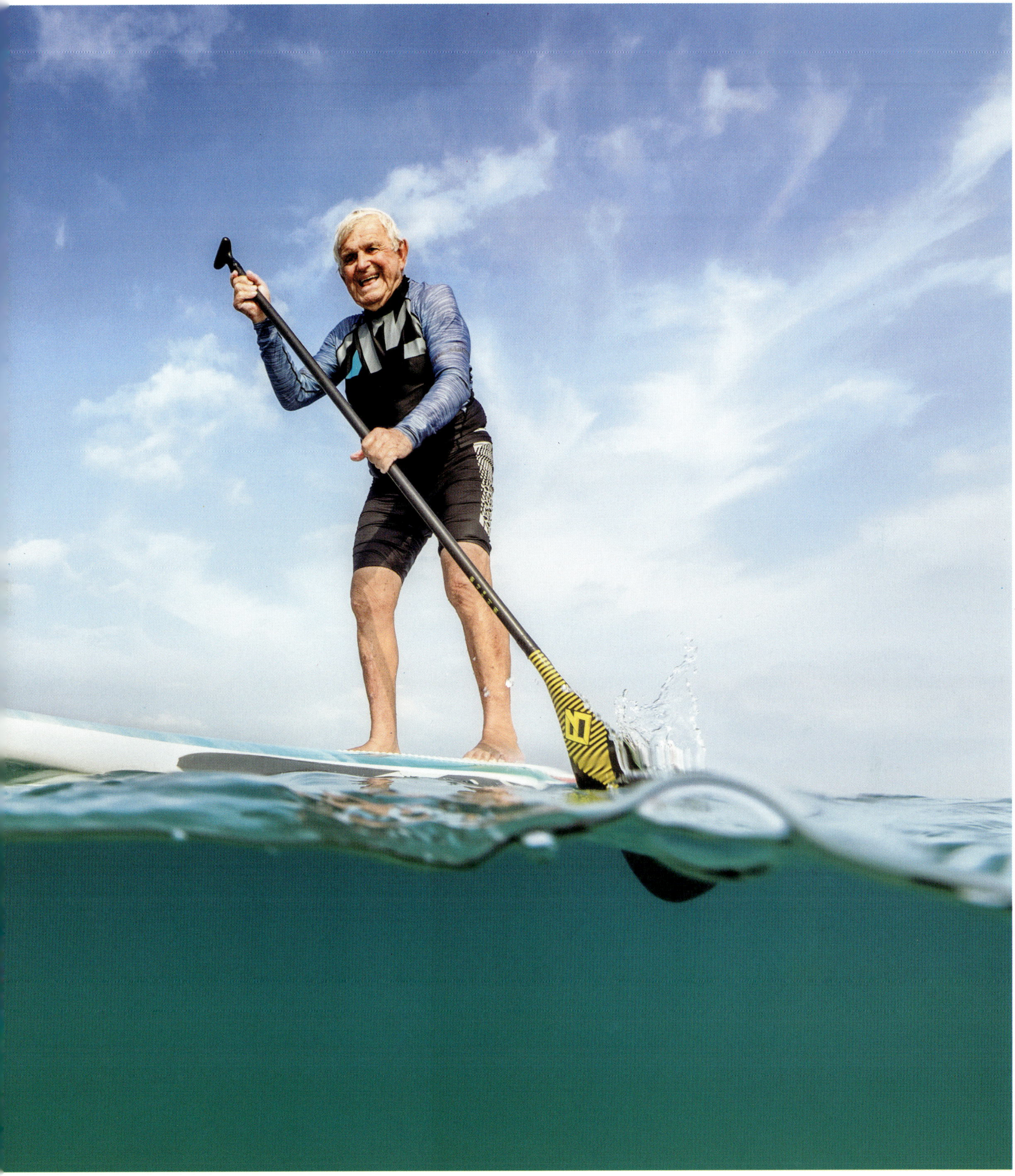

JAKUB WEKSLER, who bore the name Romuald Waszkinel for most of his life, was born in the ghetto of the town of Stare-Swieciany in Poland, now Lithuania, in 1943. The son of Polish Catholics Piotr and Emilia Waszkinel, at age 17 he told his parents of his desire to become a priest. In 1966, when he was about to be ordained, the rector disclosed to him that there were suspicions that he had not been baptized. The church objections were withdrawn, and he became a priest and a teacher at Lublin's Catholic University, later receiving a Doctorate in Philosophy at the Sorbonne, France. Over the years, however, he sensed a family secret. In 1978, when his mother Emilia was hospitalized, 'I kissed her hands, I told her that the time had come to reveal to me the secret in our family.' For the first time he learned that, like thousands of Jewish children hidden by Catholic families and convents during the war, he was born a Jew. In 1943, Emilia had received a newborn, wrapped in a blanket, who became her beloved son. She told the priest that she could not recall his given name, but remembered that his father was a Jewish tailor, trapped in the ghetto with his wife Batia, and an older child named Samuel. It was Batia who had made the contact, begging Emilia to save her baby. The priest decided to tell no one except Pope John Paul II. A supportive letter came back from the Polish pontiff, and the priest carried on for years with his church duties. The remaining details of his identity emerged when a nun, Sister Klara Jaroszynksa, helped to research his past through her connections in Israel. Sister Klara met survivors who recognized his father, Jakub Weksler, nicknamed "Jankel the tailor," and his mother Batia. 'In 1989, my Polish mother passed away in my arms and in the spring of 1992, I traveled to Israel.' At the airport, he was met by Zvi Weksler, his father's brother, who had survived the Holocaust. The priest learned that his parents perished in Ghetto Vilna or Sobibor, and that the fate of his brother Samuel was unknown. It took years for the tormented priest to disconnect from his church duties, adopt his father's name, Jakub, and immigrate to Israel in 2009. Jakub lives today in Jerusalem. He works full-time in the archives of Yad Vashem. His adoptive parents, Piotr and Emilia Waszkinel, have been recognized as Righteous Among the Nations. 'I carry within me the love of my parents, Jewish and Polish.'

Jakub Weksler BY Jim Hollander USA
JERUSALEM, 2020

YOSEF KLEINMAN was born in Hungary in 1930 and is the last living survivor who testified against Adolf Eichmann at his trial in Jerusalem. 'I was one of about 3,000 teenage boys who wound up together in Auschwitz in the summer of 1944. We were considered too young to work and so we spent the entire summer in our barracks waiting for the end and hoping to survive. It was March 19, 1944,' he recalls, 'the Satmar Rabbi was visiting our village and he announced: "Everyone is to go home; it is dangerous to remain here." Chaos ensued, and then we learned the Germans had taken control of Hungary.' The Jews were herded into the ghetto, and the deportations to death camps began. 'We were 80 people crammed into a cargo train without food or water, like animals.' When they arrived in Auschwitz, 'Suddenly the doors were flung open and the Nazis howled: "Everyone out! Leave your things outside!" My mother disappeared. I never saw her again. When I reached the Selektion platform, I saw the officer deliberating which side to send me to. I clutched my father's hand – he was barely standing up – the officer separated us, sending me to work - which meant life. I never saw my father again.' Over the next seven weeks, 438,000 Jews arrived in Auschwitz in 150 trains. The boys in his group were too young to work. The 3,000 young boys were shut into barracks, from which they could see the Sonderkommando, the lifeless men who transferred the bodies from the gas chambers to the crematoria. Dr. Mengele and his deputy Dr. Thilo arrived. 'They made us line up and ordered us to disrobe. All the skinny boys were sent out, including me. But I left the line and made a dash for my brother's barracks, and from there, back to my own bunk. The boys who had been selected were loaded onto trucks. They knew exactly where they were going to. Cries of Shema Yisrael pierced the air.' Five months later the Kleinman brothers succeeded in smuggling themselves into a group that left Auschwitz for Kaufering slave labor camp, a subsidiary of Dachau concentration camp in Germany. 'Work was the ticket to life.' While they were incarcerated in Kaufering, Europe was liberated from the Nazis and the war came to an end. Yosef finally arrived in Mandatory Palestine after a perilous sea voyage on an illegal ship, capture by the British, and incarceration in Cyprus and in Atlit. Kleinman passed away at age 91 in early May 2021.

Yosef Kleinman BY Yonatan Sindel ISRAEL

JERUSALEM, 2020

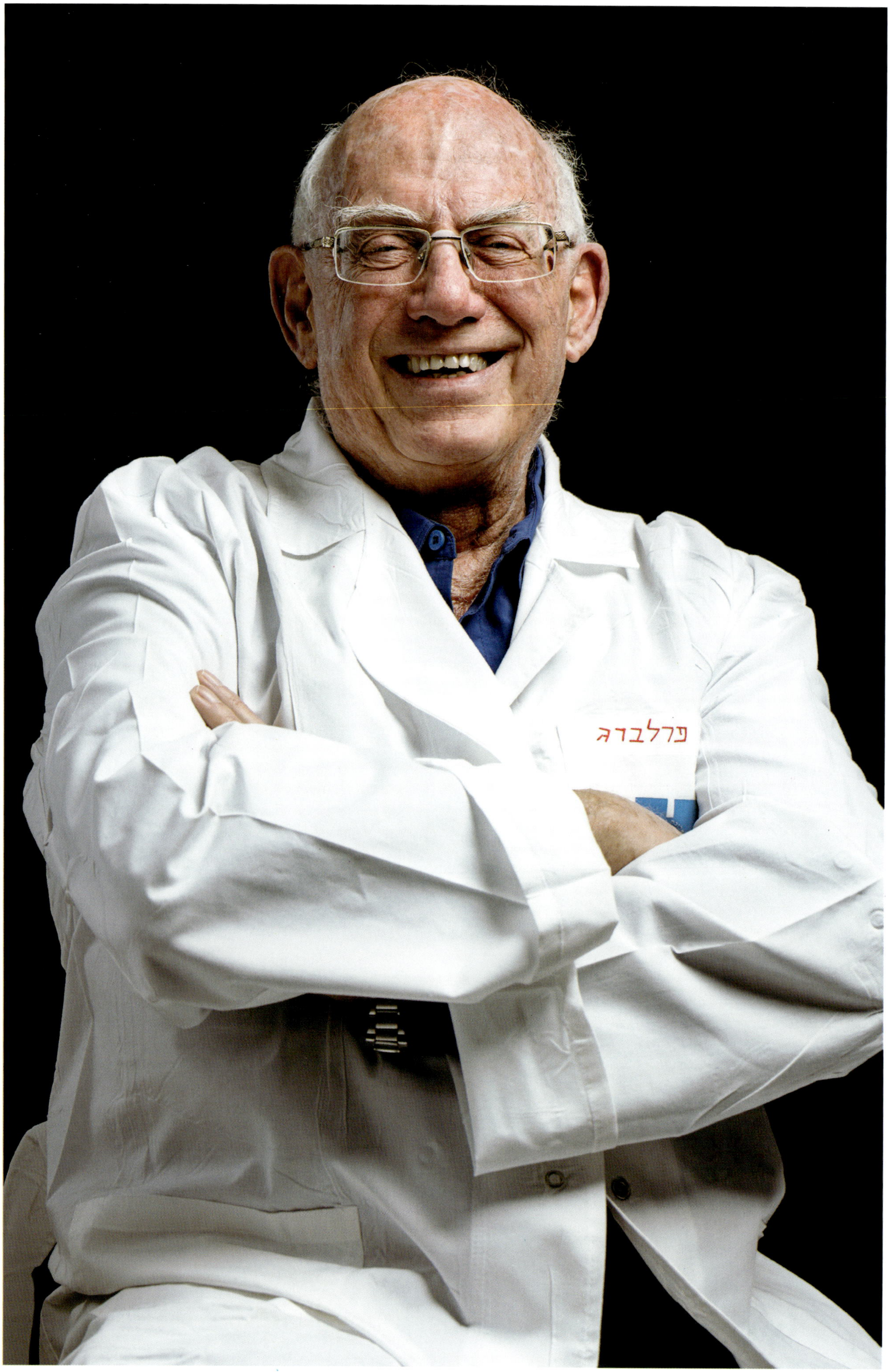
פרלברג

Dr. Shaul Perlberg was born in a Brussels apartment in 1940, when German troops had overrun Belgium. 'Our next-door neighbor was the elderly Madame Pirotte. My parents connected both apartments, and I became Madame Pirotte's grandchild, renamed Popol.' In April 1943 an informant alerted the Nazis that Jews were hiding in an attic with their baby. Shaul's parents were captured by the Nazis and deported to Auschwitz. Partisans ambushed the train, but his parents were not among those able to flee. In Brussels, the Gestapo repeatedly sought the baby boy listed in their records. On one raid, Shaul was caught and told to pull down his trousers to prove he was not a Jew. He was saved by Madame Pirotte's dog, who scared off the Gestapo men. In 1944, Shaul, then four, was caught and taken to an institution from which Jewish children separated from their parents were shipped to concentration camps. The Nazis planned to deport all 500 children there to their deaths in Auschwitz. The night before the planned deportation, the Belgian resistance smuggled the children to safety in monasteries and farms. The Nazis, now in retreat from Allied forces, abandoned their search. At war's end, 'My mother, who survived Auschwitz and death march, was searching for me. She did not know how will she ever recognize her two-year-old baby, now five,' Shaul says. From the entrance hall of the orphanage, 'she heard sounds of children playing. Suddenly the door above the staircase opened wide and a small child appeared, he looked at her for one split second and came running down the stairs screaming Mom, Mom! I recognized her immediately! She did not.' In 1949, Shaul and his mother sailed with other survivors to Israel. Shaul studied medicine and established the urology department at Hadassah Hospital on Mt. Scopus. For 60 years, he kept silent. Then a book about the 500 was published in French. Only then did Shaul gather his family and tell them, 'I'm one of the 500 children.' Dr. Perlberg passed away on August 22, 2022.

Dr. Shaul Perlberg BY Eyal Granit ISRAEL
JERUSALEM, 2020

LIESE SCHEIDERBAUER was born in Vienna in 1936. When Nazi racial laws were implemented in Austria, Liese's mother converted to Judaism so she could remain with her children and her Jewish husband. Liese's father was deported in 1938 to Buchenwald, and later to Auschwitz. Liese, her mother and her sister were deported to the Theresienstadt concentration camp. 'My mother…she did not have to go with us. I had scarlet fever. My mother, my sister Helga and I were picked up. I was lying in the luggage storage wagon… I was quite sure that they were going to kill us…' Liese's worst fear was to be separated from her mother. At age seven, Liese arrived at Theresienstadt. Of the camp, she recalls always to have been dancing, which helped her to overcome her fears. Liese, Helga and their mother were liberated by the Red Army in April 1945. 'We could not leave. The camp was closed because of typhus.' Liese's father survived Auschwitz, and they were able to return to Vienna, where the family was reunited. After Liese completed her studies at the Academy of Music and Performing Arts, she became a dancer in the Ballet at the Volksoper. 'I had a very good life afterwards, I must say – with interruptions, like everyone else,' adding, 'I live my life like a gift.'

Liese Scheiderbauer BY Lois Lammerhuber AUSTRIA
VIENNA, 2020

SHLOMO ARAD was born in 1935 in Poland. Shlomo and his brother were infants when they were hidden from the Nazis in a monastery and their lives were saved. At the end of WWII the boys were taken away from the nuns to a Jewish institution and in 1947, with other orphans of the Holocaust, shipped separately to Mandatory Palestine, only to be reunited a year later. The search for surviving relatives never stopped for Shlomo, a renowned photojournalist who keeps silent about his childhood during the Holocaust. He created this self-portrait with his late cousin Gusti. **GUSTI SHOVAL** was born in 1923 in Ocwiecim (Auschwitz). After Nazi Germany invaded Poland, her parents with their five children were forced to relocate to the Chrzanow Ghetto. In the 1942 roundup of the ghetto Jews, Gusti was sent to forced labor in the Trzebinia salt mine, in the Gross-Rosen sub-camp and Neusalz slave labor camp. With the Red Army approaching, Gusti was among 12,000 women forced on a death march to Flossenburg camp, where only 300 survived. In 1945 Gusti was shipped by cattle train to Bergen-Belsen camp where she endured typhoid and starvation. British soldiers rescued Gusti from a room full of dead bodies. After liberation and brief recovery in Sweden, Gusti learned that her brother and only family survivor was alive in Israel. In 1949, Gusti immigrated to Israel where she rebuilt her life with Zvi, a survivor from Poland. In 1955, Shlomo located Gusti, from whom he learned about his mother and a family lost.

Shlomo Arad BY **Shlomo Arad** ISRAEL
TEL AVIV, ISRAEL, 2020

Eddie Jaku was born in Leipzig, Germany, in 1920. Eddie's life had changed on Kristallnacht, when Eddie returned home from boarding school to an empty house. At dawn Nazi soldiers burst in, Eddie was beaten and taken to Buchenwald concentration camp. Eddie was later released and escaped with his father to Belgium and France, but again he was captured and en route, Eddie managed to escape and make his way back to Belgium where he lived in hiding with his parents and sister. In October 1943 Eddie's family were arrested and deported to Auschwitz death camp where his parents were murdered. In 1945, Eddie was sent on a death march but once again escaped and hid in a forest until June 1945 when he was rescued by Allied soldiers. In 1950 he moved to Australia where he rebuilt his life, and was one of the founders of the Sydney Jewish Museum. In 2020 Eddie celebrated his 100th birthday self-proclaimed to be 'the happiest man on earth' who made a vow to himself to smile every day. His best-selling memoir *The Happiest Man on Earth* was published in 2020. Using past trauma to spread a hopeful message, Eddie devoted himself to Holocaust education, 'I teach children and adults not to hate.' Eddie Jaku passed away in Sydney in October 2021, age 101.

Eddie Jaku BY Louise Kennerley AUSTRALIA
SYDNEY, AUSTRALIA, 2020

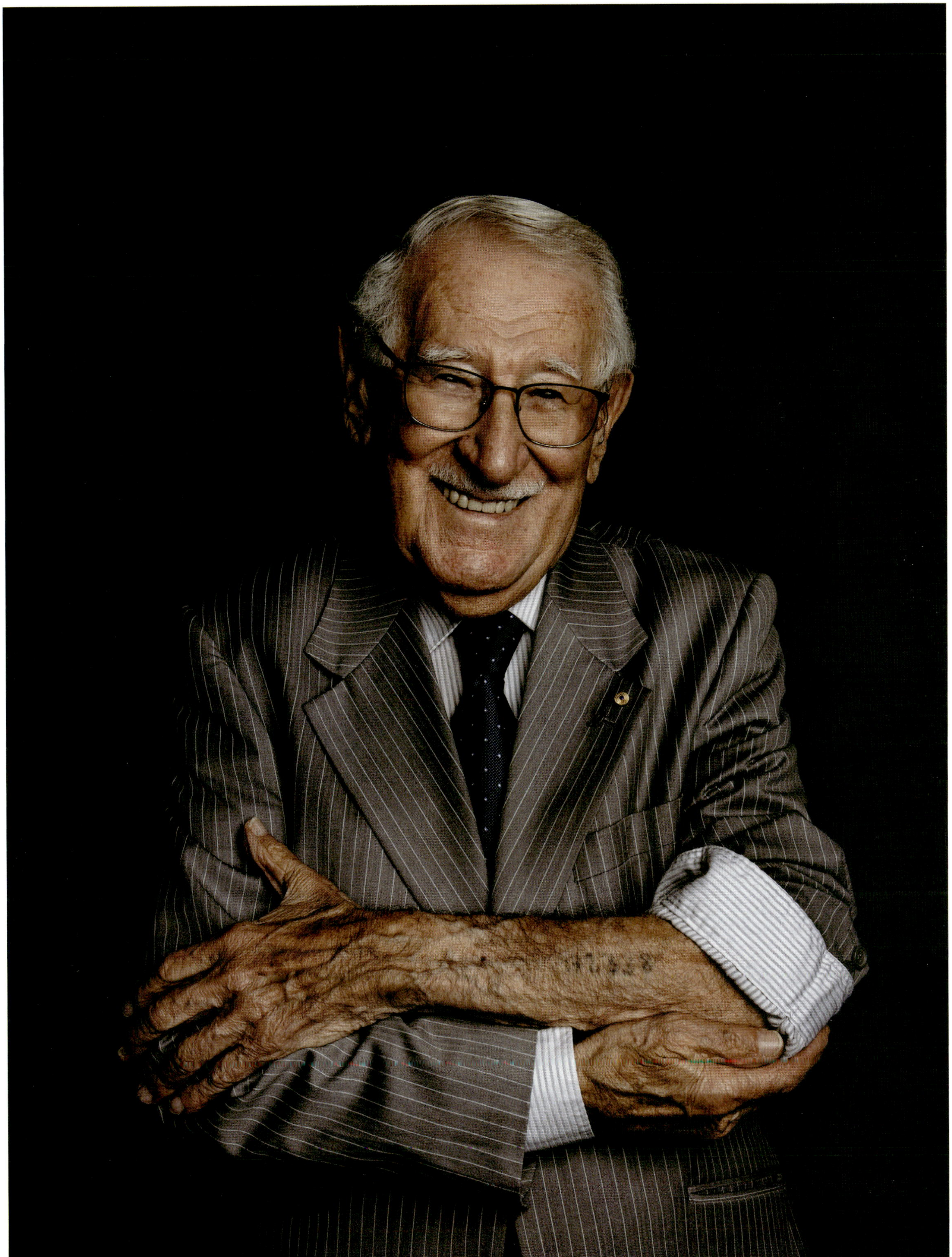

GEORGETTE BLAJCHMAN was born in 1932 in France, an only daughter of Polish immigrants. When WWII broke out the family lived in Paris and her father volunteered for the French army frontline, serving in a foreign regiment. Georgette, then seven, was sent to safety in the countryside in Normandy. When her father was dismissed from his army unit he remained in the south of France, not yet occupied by the Nazis, and smuggled his wife and child to be with him. It was the beginning of a journey of hiding and moving from village to village. Georgette fell ill and was taken to a children's convalescence home where she remained in hiding as a Catholic child. 'My parents warned me I should never disclose I'm a Jew.' Her father was denounced by the mayor of the French village where the parents were hiding and Vichy militia arrested her father, never to be seen again. Georgette and her mother were eventually smuggled through the border into Switzerland and returned to Paris after the war where Georgette lives today.

Georgette Blajchmann BY Richard Kalvar FRANCE

PARIS, 2020

HERTA CASPI was born in the Netherlands in 1931. After the Nazi Germany invasion of Holland, Herta's father, her older sister Dusi, and her husband Leo were all deported to Westerbork concentration camp in Drenthe. Herta's mother fled with her two girls and their grandmother Eva to Zeist, where a member of the Dutch resistance led them to shelter at the Christian family named Versluis. For two years Herta was hidden in an attic, and was only allowed outdoors after nightfall. The elderly Versluis couple and their young daughter Mien provided for Herta until it became too dangerous. Herta was then moved for another year in hiding with the Verheul family. Ferdinand Boschrart was the man who saved Herta and other Jews by locating Christian families willing to provide shelter. He also provided fake identity papers. In May 1945 Herta, now 14, was reunited with her mother and sister and they returned to their village. Herta's father, her older sister Dusi, her husband Leo and thirty-three other family members were all murdered in Auschwitz, Bergen-Belsen and Sobibor death camps. In 1948 Herta emigrated to Israel. She married Hezi Caspi, a Palmach soldier, and the couple had three daughters. Reli Avrahami, the artist of this photograph, is their youngest daughter. In 1986 Herta and her sister Selma appealed to award the Righteous Among the Nations title to the Versluis, Verheul and Boschaart families, who had saved their lives. Herta is seen during the COVID-19 pandemic as she moves apartments in Tel Aviv.

Herta Caspi BY Reli Avrahami ISRAEL

TEL AVIV, ISRAEL, 2020

GABOR HIRSCH was born on December 9, 1929, in Békéscsaba, Hungary. In June 1944, at age 14, he was transported with his mother and more than 3,000 other Jews in cattle cars to the Auschwitz extermination camp. He was then separated from his mother, who was murdered at the Stutthof concentration camp. That October, the Nazis sent Gabor to the gas chambers along with 600 other Jews. His life was spared at the last minute when, during a physical examination, officers deemed him fit enough to work. After the Soviet Army liberated the camp on January 27, 1945, Gabor was able to reunite with his father, whom the Nazis had sent to a forced labor camp in Budapest. During the 1956 Hungarian revolution, Gabor immigrated to Switzerland. In 1994, along with Otto Klein, who had endured the medical experimentation of Auschwitz doctor Josef Mengele, Gabor co-founded the Swiss Contact Point for Holocaust Survivors self-help group. The objective of the association was to raise awareness of racism, antisemitism and Holocaust denial, and to reappraise the role of Switzerland during World War II. The association was eventually dissolved in 2011. Gabor died in August 2020, at 90 years of age. His message to future generations was, 'Be aware of and fight any indoctrination and any kind of discrimination, racism, antisemitism or other kind of exclusions.'

Gabor Hirsch BY Vera Markus SWITZERLAND

ZURICH, SWITZERLAND, 2020

ABRAHAM MICHAEL GRINZAID was born in 1926 in Romania (now Moldova). Abraham was the only son. After the Nazi German invasion his parents decided to leave their home and their extended family and flee east. They were on the road for almost a year before succeeding to escape Nazi forces. After his father died, following an injury, and his mother was gravely ill, 'I understood what was happening to the Jews under Nazi occupation.' At age 17, Abraham located a safe place for his mother while he enlisted in the Red Army. 'I joined the Red Army to take revenge. My father died because of the Nazis, my relatives were in the ghettos and sent to their deaths. I was alone and my only desire was to avenge my family's deaths.' Abraham served in Unit 365 of the Red Army and after six months was sent to Estonia to the front lines. From there he was transferred to the Paratroopers Brigade and later served in an intelligence unit set out to fight on Nazi German soil. 'We saw death in front of our eyes every day.' For his heroism in the war he received the Medal of Courage, and the Medal of Fame. After the war Abraham continued to serve in the Red Army until 1950. He completed his higher education and became a teacher and later a college principal in Kishinev. 'I appeal to the Jewish people, don't forget it! One million and a half Jews fought against the Nazis.' In 1990, he immigrated to Israel with his family and became the chairman of the National World War II Veterans Alliance. On the last visit of Russian President Vladimir Putin to Israel, they shook hands.

Abraham Grinzaid BY Oded Wagenstein ISRAEL
REHOVOT, ISRAEL, 2020

Chaya Gantz was born in 1924 in the Czech-controlled town of Bedevlya, today a part of Ukraine. During the early war years, Chaya was sent to live with an aunt in Romania, returning in early 1944 to be briefly reunited with her family, only to fall victim to the Nazi occupation. In April 1944, local police forced them from their home, deporting them to Mateszalka concentration camp in Hungary. The family endured hunger and torture for days. Then Chaya and her family were loaded onto closed train cars, about 80 people in each. They were taken to Auschwitz-Birkenau. Upon arrival, during the first Selektion, Chaya and a younger sister, Dora, were separated from their parents and siblings. After some months in the death camp, Chaya and Dora were sent to Reichenbach, a forced labor camp, where the two sisters endured an agonizing separation from each other. Chaya was then transferred to the Breslau camp and later to the Gross-Rosen camp. She survived a death march to Mauthausen, and later to Bergen-Belsen, where she was liberated by British troops. Barely alive, Chaya received assistance from the Red Cross and the Joint Distribution Committee. As soon as she was able to walk again, she returned to her hometown in search of surviving family members. Chaya learned that Dora and two brothers were the only survivors of their large family. Chaya's parents, grandfather, and her youngest sister, Sarah, aged 12, all perished in Auschwitz. After a brief sojourn in Prague and later Budapest, Chaya married Mendel Gantz and, after the birth of two sons, they immigrated to Israel in 1950. Chaya often asks, 'Who could have imagined I would reach this remarkable age?' Chaya Gantz holds a rare photo of her father, Shmuel Zalman Bistrizer, given to her after the Holocaust.

Chaya Gantz BY Rafi Koren ISRAEL
HOLON, ISRAEL, 2020

DAVID SARID was born in Czechoslovakia (Hungary) in 1928. On his Bar Mitzvah in 1941, David, one of 10 siblings in a *haredi* family, was sent by his father to a yeshiva for religious Jewish studies. It was the last time he would see his family. When the Nazi occupation began, his family was deported to camps. Jewish schools were ordered closed, and David found himself alone and homeless, begging for food and surviving on handouts until he was caught in 1944 and sent to Auschwitz in a "transport" of Jews, Roma and Sinti. He survived Auschwitz camp doctor Mengele's Selektion of entering prisoners to be murdered, and was sent to forced labor at the Mauthausen concentration camp, where he was imprisoned until December 1944. The area was bombed by the Allies. David and most of the Jewish prisoners were forced on a death march to the Gunskirchen camp. On May 4, 1945, the Nazi guards in the camp vanished, and David was liberated by the 71st Infantry Division of the US Army. David returned to Czechoslovakia after liberation and learned from his only surviving brother that their family had perished. He was taken to an orphanage and later to a displaced persons camp in Germany, where he completed his studies and became a teacher for the American Jewish Joint Distribution Committee in Norway, preparing survivors for immigration to Israel. In 1950, he immigrated to Israel with his wife. David served in the IDF and completed his M.A. in Jewish history. David became a beloved headmaster to generations of high school students in Tiberias. David Sarid passed away in late December 2021, age 93.

David Sarid BY Gil Eliayahu ISRAEL
TIBERIAS, ISRAEL, 2020

YOCHEVED HALPERIN was born in 1930 in Korets, Poland (today Ukraine). In 1941, Nazi forces invaded Korets. Yocheved's father was abducted and never returned. Yocheved's mother was sent to forced labor to sweep the town streets. 'When she got tired, I replaced her.' On May 21, 1942, Yocheved, her mother and brother Noah were saved from a massacre in which 2,200 of the Jews of Korets were murdered. 'We fled to my grandmother's village of Vodnik and returned to Korets the next day. All the survivors of the great massacre were ordered to the ghetto.' In September 1942, on the eve of Rosh Hashanah, the ghetto was liquidated. Yocheved and her family escaped from the ghetto with the help of a Polish acquaintance named Antek Tselinsky. The Nazis were conducting searches throughout the forests and farms for the Jews still in hiding. Again, Antek Tselinsky came to their rescue and sheltered them in his farm under bales of straw until the day they were told that partisans were arriving. 'We left our hiding place to greet them, but only my brother Noah was allowed to join them.' As soon as they left, Yocheved and her mother heard Noah's screams. 'Those were not partisans, and they murdered Noah with their bayonets.' After Yocheved and her mother buried Noah, they fled deeper into the forest and joined other Jews who dug a bunker in the depths of the forest. They stayed there until liberation. Yocheved decided to immigrate to Mandatory Palestine. 'On October 19, 1946, I boarded the illegal immigrant ship *Latrun* with 1,252 illegal immigrants onboard. We were captured by the British and deported first to Cyprus, and in 1947, we were sent to Atlit Detention Camp and at last, after a few months to Kibbutz Ginosar.' Yocheved rebuilt her life and family, in which she takes great pride. She spent her working life in banks and in the prime minister's office. But she adds, 'All my dreams are dreams about the Holocaust. The sound of my brother's cries come back to me again and again. And I ask, why was the world silent?'

Yocheved Halperin BY Meital Dor ISRAEL
TEL AVIV, ISRAEL, 2020

KAMA GINKAS was born on May 7, 1941, in Kaunas, Lithuania. When Kama was barely three months old, the Nazi authorities announced that the Jews of Kaunas would be forcefully relocated into the ghetto, which was formed in the outskirts of the city. Kama has no memories of his time in the ghetto, where his relatives died, but he heard the stories from his parents. His family survived on potato peels, which they used to scrounge beside the German canteens. After a year and a half in the ghetto, his parents managed to escape with their son. A friendly Lithuanian family took them in until the Red Army liberated the city on August 1, 1944. Kama Ginkas graduated from the Vilnius Conservatory and the Leningrad State Institute of Theatre, Music and Cinema, where he trained under Georgy Tovstonogov. He became a prominent theater director, with his plays performed around the world. In 1988, he started an ongoing collaboration with the Moscow Young Generation Theatre. Ginkas was awarded the title of People's Artist of the Russian Federation, as well as the State Prize of the Russian Federation, and numerous other prestigious awards.

Kama Ginkas BY Anna Shmitko RUSSIA
MOSCOW, 2020

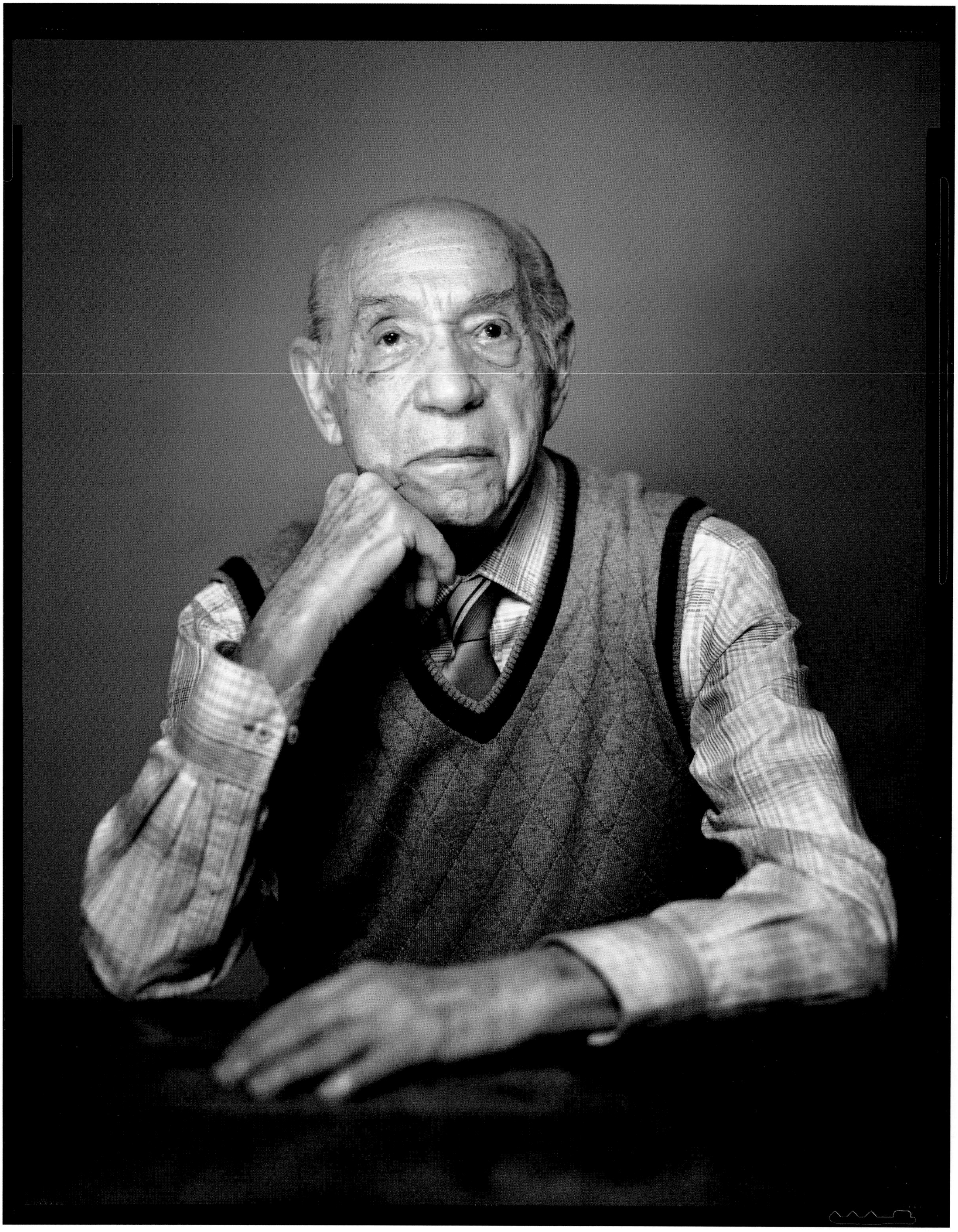

DAVID LENGA was born in Poland in 1927. On September 8, 1939, David watched Nazi soldiers marching into Lodz, accompanied by tanks and flying swastika flags. The family was separated. His father was sent to a labor camp, and the rest were transported into the Lodz Ghetto. In a large Aktion, David, 15, his brother Nathan and their grandmother were selected for deportation. David escaped to look for his mother, but she was already in the hands of the Gestapo. In August 1944, as the Lodz Ghetto was being liquidated, David, now alone, went into hiding and emerged after a week pretending to belong to a cleanup crew that remained in the ghetto. But the group, including David, were loaded on trucks and shipped to Auschwitz. During the first Selektion of prisoners, to determine which would be sent to the gas chambers and which to forced labor, camp doctor Mengele rejected David from labor for being too young. David understood that this meant death. He sneaked into the workers' line twice and three days later he was on a train headed for the forced labor camps in Kaufering, Bavaria. In late April 1945 as US troops approached, the prisoners were evacuated and marched for hours to open cattle cars. The convoy proceeded slowly, and David and two others jumped off, escaping into the forest. They reached a farmhouse where the farmer allowed them to stay in the barn. 'We were given the opportunity to be human beings,' David recalled. On May 5, 1945, they heard the thunderous roar of tanks and yelled, 'We're liberated.' An American officer approached and asked them in Yiddish, "You boys are Jews? We're taking you with us." Later, in a displaced persons camp, David learned that his mother and brother were murdered in Chelmno. There was no word of the fate of his father. David then traveled to Sweden where he met and married Charlotte, a survivor, and learned that his father was alive and living in Israel. 'That was a meeting I will not forget for my entire life.' In 1954, the family immigrated to the United States where they raised their children. David, who began telling his story only in 2013, says of the risky escapes during the Holocaust, 'The fact is, I dared it, and I made it. I'm very proud of it.'

David Lenga BY Douglas Kirkland CANADA/USA
HOLLYWOOD, CALIFORNIA, USA, 2020

Simon Gronowski was born in Brussels in 1931. In 1943, the Gestapo arrested 11-year-old Simon, his mother and 18-year-old sister Ita in their Brussels hiding place. All three were transferred to the Nazi transit camp in Mechelen. His father had escaped the roundup. Simon's sister was deported alone to Auschwitz. Simon, his mother Chana and 1,630 others were packed in a train known as "Convoy 20." As soon as the train left Mechelen's station, Belgian resistance fighters attempted to free imprisoned colleagues aboard the train. Chana pushed her son towards the door and lowered him so that Simon could jump off the accelerating train bound for Auschwitz. His mother did not follow. Simon waited, then ran like dozens of others who escaped to the surrounding trees and farmland. He walked and ran all night, reaching the house of Jan Aerts, a policeman who sheltered Simon and arranged his safe return to his father in Brussels. Simon's mother Chana was sent to the gas chambers on arrival at Auschwitz. His sister also perished there. Simon and his father spent the remaining war years hidden separately. His father died within months of the end of the war, and Simon grew up in foster families. Later he became a Doctor of Law. While struggling to rebuild his life, he taught himself to play the piano in memory of his sister Ita, who had been a pianist. Simon plays jazz. Fifty years would pass before he shared his past, writing his book, *L'Enfant du 20e convoi*. The Aerts family, who had sheltered him the night of the escape, were awarded the honor of Righteous Among the Nations. During the COVID-19 pandemic lockdown, Simon has been playing his jazz piano regularly at his window for his neighbors to enjoy. After British composer Howard Moody heard Simon say, "Ma vie n'est que miraclesl" he wrote a community opera, *PUSH*, that told of Simon's escape from the 20th Convoy on April 19, 1943.

Simon Gronowski BY Sébastien Van Malleghem BELGIUM
BRUSSELS, 2021

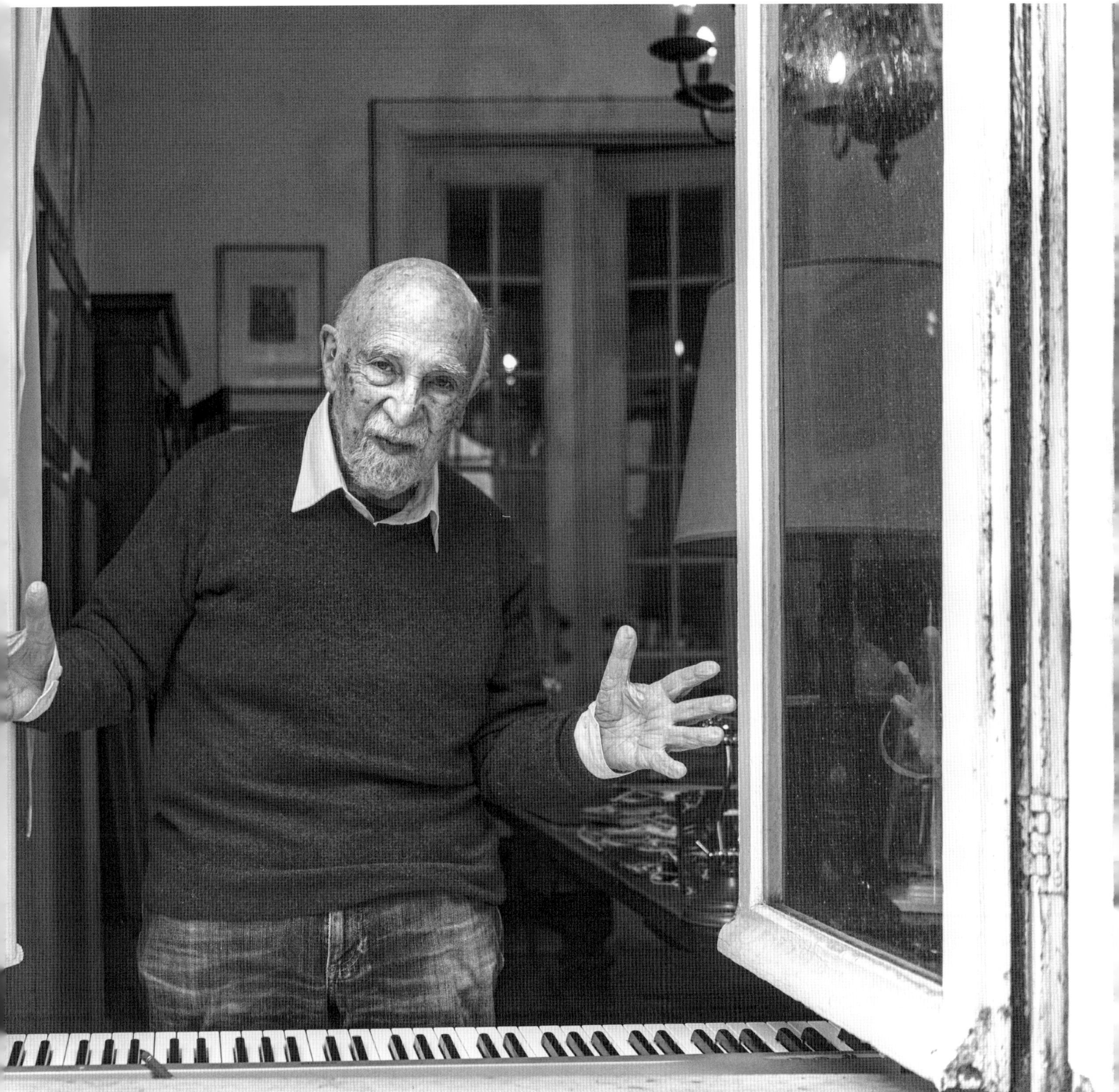

Esther Senot was born in Poland in 1928. In 1930, her family immigrated to France. Soon after Paris fell to Nazi Germany in 1940, the persecution and deportation of Jews and Roma began. One day in July 1942, her parents sent Esther to find out if their scattered family members in hiding had escaped the latest Nazi roundup. Discovering that the relatives were all gone, she returned home, only to learn that her parents and younger siblings had been arrested and deported to the Drancy camp. Esther was left alone. A month later, her parents and two of her six siblings were shipped to Auschwitz-Birkenau and murdered on arrival. For the next year, Esther lived in orphanages in Paris. In July 1943, Esther was sent on an errand, but was not wearing the yellow badge that Jews were ordered to wear. She was arrested and, in September, sent to the women's camp in Auschwitz-Birkenau, where she found her sister Fanny and her aunt. Esther was put to forced labor until the camp was evacuated in January 1945. Fanny was killed by a guard's dog. 'Fanny made me promise just before she died that if I survived, I would tell everyone what we went through.' Esther survived a death march, and the Bergen-Belsen and Mauthausen concentration camps. In May 1945, Mauthausen was liberated by the US Army. Her brother Maurice, who participated as a soldier in the liberation of France, survived. Her brother Israel remained in the USSR. Esther lives in Paris and is dedicated to Holocaust commemoration. 'I defeated Hitler,' Esther says. 'I do not know how we survived, but with my three children, six grandchildren and six great-grandchildren, I look to the future, while educating others about the past.'

Esther Senot BY Roberta Valerio ITALY/FRANCE
PARIS, 2020

Shoshana Sivron Davidman was born in 1929 in Poland. After the Nazi invasion, her family was forced into the ghetto of Stryi, where her father was put to forced labor. In 1943, the family was detained and moved to a prison, and from there by trucks to Holobotow Forest, where death pits were dug for mass executions. The trucks were surrounded by Nazi guards when Shoshana jumped off and ran away to her former caretaker, who was working in a convalescent home for German soldiers. Her nanny, Nusia Klimczak, sheltered her till the end of the war, by telling her neighbors the girl was a Polish orphan whose home was destroyed in a bombing. After liberation, Shoshana learned she had surviving family members in Mandatory Palestine. In July 1947, Shoshana, with a group of orphans, arrived in France and boarded the ship *Exodus*. The ship, bound for Mandatory Palestine, carried 4,500 Jewish Holocaust survivors who had no legal immigration certificates. In July 1947, British soldiers boarded the ship and all its passengers were returned to refugee camps in German territory. The treatment of the survivors at the camps caused an international outcry, as they were likened to conditions in the German concentration camps. Six month later, Shoshana was freed and arrived to Mandatory Palestine. She rebuilt her life in Israel and became a Hebrew teacher.

Shoshana Sivron Davidman BY Oren Ziv ISRAEL
HAIFA, ISRAEL, 2020

MIRIAM TOBOL was born in Algeria in 1938. Her father was a shoe manufacturer for the Algerian military who later moved his workshop to the city of Oujda in Morocco. During World War II, the situation of the Jews in Morocco deteriorated, as in the other areas under the French Vichy regime. Under Vichy rule, the Jews of Morocco were subjected to persecution. The Moroccan borders were closed to the Jews and the only way out was via the port of Algiers. Oujda served as a transit place. The echoes of war and antisemitism did not skip Oujda and national movements affiliated with Nazi-racist ideology penetrated the local population's turn against the Jews. The first anti-Jewish laws were enacted in Morocco in 1940. The Sultan of Morocco had to implement the new racial laws against the Jews in his kingdom and, although he saw them as harming legal citizens and the Moroccan economy, he complied. 'Nazi propaganda led to riots…burned our house and my father's shoe store. My mother and eight brothers, we were hiding in a secret basement under the house with several other families for many weeks. My father disguised himself as a policeman and helped smuggle Jewish families out of Oujda to Algeria and from there to France. The ambition was to immigrate to Israel.' Miriam says she was smuggled across the border into Algeria on trucks. In 1949 they immigrated to Israel and settled in a transit camp in Pardes Hanna and from there moved to Jerusalem. Miriam became chief housekeeper in the Prime Minister's residence in Jerusalem and served Levy Eshkol, Golda Meir and several other Israeli Prime Ministers. Since retiring, Miriam has been volunteering for the elderly for many years and sees it as a mission that gives her strength and 'adds meaning to my life.'

Miriam Tobol BY **Tom Bickles** ISRAEL

ADAM, 2021

SAM RON was born in Poland in 1924 in a small village outside Krakow. Sam's family, assisted by local Poles, found shelter in the Krakow Ghetto while Nazi forces were executing most of its Jewish inhabitants. After the Nazis liquidated the ghetto in March 1943, Sam's family had to split up. Sam, then 17, was taken to the Plaszów concentration camp. Many of the prisoners were executed or died from slave labor. 'Let me tell you, suffering, that's something, we Polish Jews got used to it,' Sam says. 'I would wake up in the morning and somebody next to me is dead.' Sam recalls how he witnessed Jews being hanged. He was then sent to the Sachsenhausen concentration camp. Of the roughly 200,000 prisoners who passed through Sachsenhausen, some 100,000 died there. Sam has described how he and thousands of other prisoners were taken out of the camp toward the war's end. 'We went on a death march for two and a half weeks, and when we reached a forest, the Nazi guards disappeared; in the morning we were free.' Sachsenhausen was liberated on April 27, 1945, by advance troops of the Soviet army. 'By some miracle,' says Sam, he survived the Nazi camps and so did his parents. After being liberated, he participated in an organized operation to smuggle 600 orphaned children out of the Eastern Bloc to other European countries and later to Mandatory Palestine. In 1947, his parents immigrated to the US. Sam came to Mandatory Palestine and joined Kibbutz Nevatim in the Negev Desert. He was wounded during an attack on the kibbutz in December 1947. In the 1948 war, he became a truck driver in convoys bringing supplies to remote kibbutzim and outposts under siege. In 1956, he and his wife and two children joined his parents living in the US. Sam became a successful contractor in Ohio and retired to Florida where he often lectures in schools about the Holocaust.

Sam Ron BY **Marko Dashev** USA
BOCA RATON, FLORIDA, USA, 2021

OLEG YEFIMOVICH MORTKOVICH was born in 1939 in the shtetl of Dashev in the Vinnytsia region of Ukraine. When Dashev was occupied in July 1941, the Germans executed over 800 local Jews. Oleg's father, Yefim Meerovich, joined a partisan unit as a medic. Oleg's mother also took part in the partisan movement. Both of them were killed by the Nazis. Oleg's mother had put Oleg under the care of a woman who later abandoned him. A teenaged shepherd, Volodya Babenko, found the two-year-old boy in the fields by the shtetl. The little Jewish orphan was then taken in by Natalya Fedorovna Bondar, a single woman living in the nearby village of Huncha. Little Oleg had to hide in the cellar until March 13, 1944, when Dashev was liberated. After the war, his grandmother managed to locate the boy. Oleg Mortkovich became a famous nephrologist. He assisted with developing the USSR prototype for an artificial kidney device, and performed hemodialysis. The wondrous story of his rescue was revealed to him only in 2020, when Oleg came across a document indicating that the son of an executed partisan medic was being raised by Natalya Bondar. Oleg traveled to the Vinnytsia region in search of those who had saved him. Bondar had passed away in 1957. In 2012 she was posthumously recognized as a Righteous Among the Nations. Vladimir Babenko passed away in August 2020. Oleg Yefimovich Mortkovich is the head of the Moscow organization of former ghetto and concentration camp prisoners.

Oleg Mortkovich BY **Jegor Zaika** RUSSIA
MOSCOW, 2020

ALEXANDER ISAAKOVICH GELMAN was born in 1933 in Bessarabia, then part of Romania. His hometown of Donduşeni is currently the administrative and cultural center of a district of Moldova. From childhood, he was able to speak Romanian, Russian and Yiddish. In June 1941, all the Donduşeni Jews, including the Gelman family, were deported to the ghetto which was formed in Bershad – a town in the Vinnytsia region of present-day Ukraine. It took them several days to reach their destination on foot. Alexander's brother Velvele (Volodya) died during the journey. He was an infant, born just before the war, and his mother could not breastfeed him, having lost her milk supply. Tsyupa, his grandmother on his mother's side, also perished during the journey. During the cold winter of 1941–1942, almost all of Alexander's relatives died in the ghetto: his mother and her brother along with his wife and son, his mother's sister with her husband and son, and his mother's cousin with their children. His father's relatives died in a different ghetto. Of the 14 family members, only two survived – Alexander and his father, Isaak Davydovich. The Bershad Ghetto was liberated by the Red Army on March 14, 1944. Gelman recalls how a tank drove inside the ghetto. A young soldier popped out of the hatch and asked: "Hey, *zhidy* [a plural of *zhid*, a Russian-language slur for Jews, akin to the English term kike], are you alive?" Alexander recalls his reaction: 'As soon as we heard the word *zhid*, we took it for a precious, delightful word! He said it in such a heartfelt, sympathetic manner! I will never forget that we were liberated by a Soviet, a Russian soldier.' After the war, Alexander returned to his home in Donduşeni. He finished school and graduated from a military college, joining the army as a Senior Lieutenant. In 1966, he began making his way into journalism, working with newspapers in Leningrad. Alexander Gelman became a famous playwright and screenwriter, awarded the USSR State Prize, and the "Golden Mask" Russian National Theatre Award.

Alexander Gelman BY Olga Izakson RUSSIA
MOSCOW, 2020

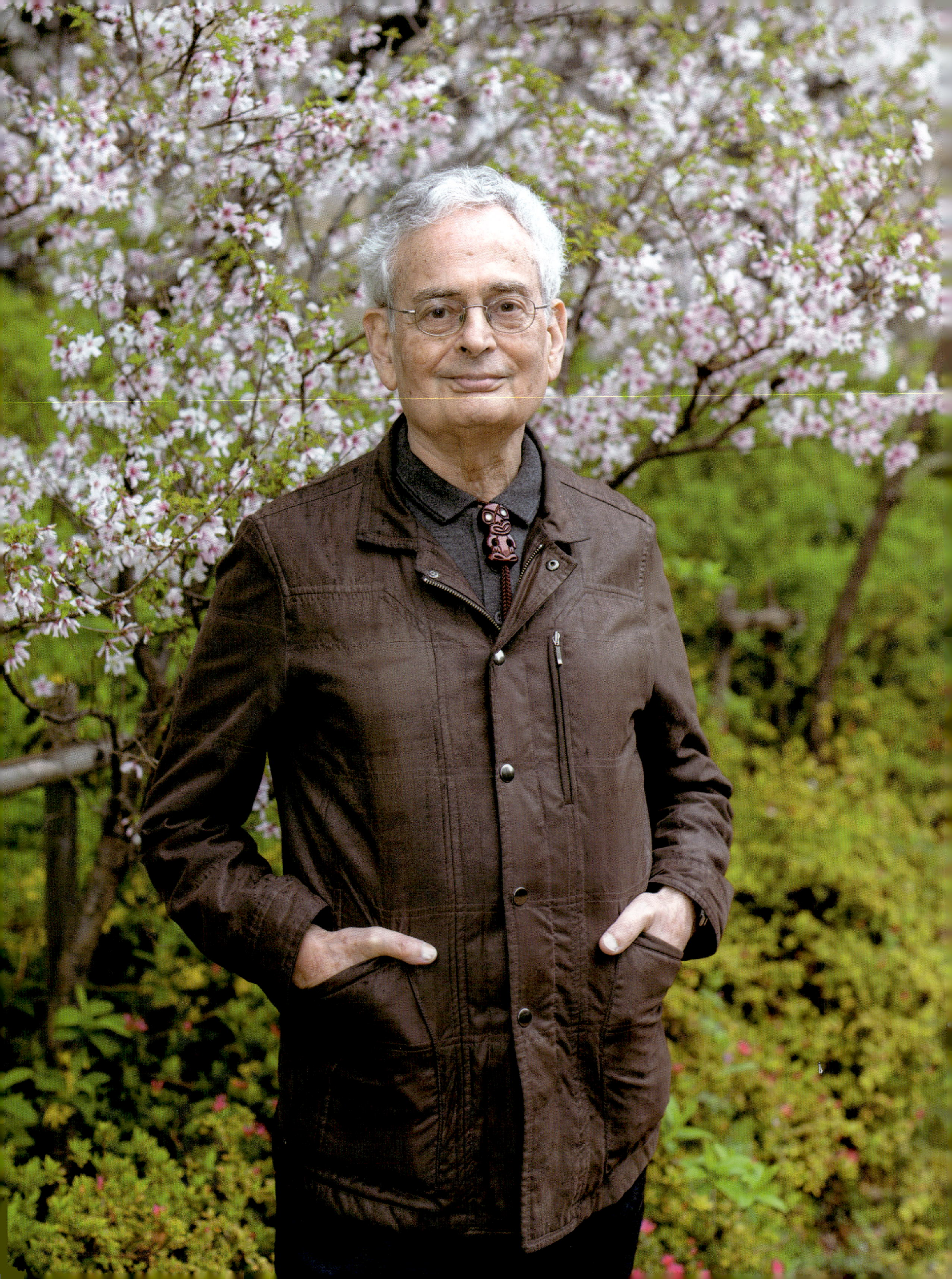

Janos Cegledy was born in Budapest, Hungary, in 1937. Janos was seven and his brother Steven nine when Nazi Germany occupied Hungary. Janos remembers how his mother cut the yellow star out and sewed it on his coat. Janos tells of June 1944 how Jews were forced to move into designated apartments for Jews only – "Yellow Star homes" – where the houses and their residents were obliged to display the yellow star by Budapest mayoral decree. Janos and Steven spent their days in the courtyard. 'Aunt Olga arrived at the railway station from Slovakia, but she was arrested and never seen again, and Great Aunt Paula's husband was beaten to death by Nazis in Vienna; she tried to flee, was arrested and never seen again.' Janos's father was sent to forced labor on the front lines. Hungarian Nazi allies, the Arrow Cross militias took over Hungary in October 1944, and in no time the "Yellow Star building" where Janos lived was raided. They lined up all the Jewish men against a wall in the courtyard, including Janos's grandfather. Janos, Steven and their mother were hiding in the basement while the militia conducted a search of the building. They lay concealed under rugs that blended with the stored firewood; it was the building's caretaker who bravely intervened to force the armed men to leave and he was murdered soon after. Their lives were saved. Janos's mother was ordered to report for forced labor. Before leaving, she told her boys, "If your father does not return, go to your uncle in New Zealand." She made the boys memorize their uncle's address. In Budapest, Swedish diplomat Raoul Wallenberg and Swiss diplomat Carl Lutz tried rescuing Jews by issuing them a protection document and by providing safe homes. Janos, Steven and their grandparents moved to a building under Swiss protection. In October 1944, Soviet troops launched their offensive on Budapest to oust the Nazis. The Jews were marched out of their safe house, among them Janos and Steven, who had to move out from the Swiss safe home into the Jewish ghetto where they hid in an air raid shelter with many others. Janos remembers the hunger. On January 17, Janos and Steven left the shelter. There were Russian soldiers amid the destruction and carts with frozen dead bodies piled high. They were liberated. A few month later on April 2, 1945, their mother was freed from Lichtenworth camp, one of 400 to survive of some 2,000 women who were incarcerated. Janos's father was liberated from concentration camps (Mauthausen and Gunzkirchen). After the war they moved to New Zealand. Janos pursued a career as a concert pianist. In 1967, he came to perform in Japan and has lived there ever since. Janos played in many concerts around the world. Until 2018 he refused to talk about his childhood experience during the war.

Janos Cegledy BY Jono David UK/USA
TOKYO, 2021

GISELLE CYCOWICZ was born in 1927 in Khust, Czechoslovakia, briefly Hungary and today in Ukraine. In 1939, Hungary took over the region, and all the Jewish children in the town were expelled from school. Giselle was 12 years old at the time, the youngest of three daughters. In March 1944, the Nazis marched into Hungary. Within three months, all Jews were sent to the ghettos. Five weeks later, Giselle's entire family was sent to Auschwitz by train. She remembers her father, Wolf Friedman, telling them, "Be sure to make yourself useful. That's how you will survive." 'My father worked for five months in coal mines on 200 grams of bread a day. He was a skeleton without any flesh on his bones and was brought back to Auschwitz and sent to the gas chambers.' Lager C in Auschwitz housed 30,000 women at the time, with two bathrooms, a slice of bread in the morning and muddy soup at noon. In the daily Selektions, no one knew who would be next to be sent to the gas chambers. Giselle was in Auschwitz for half a year with one of her sisters and her mother, Hanna, who was frail. Keeping their mother alive became their mission, but they were separated. Giselle, mother and sister were sent to different forced labor camps where they remained until their liberation. Giselle recalls how the SS lined them up one morning and told them, "You can leave now, the Russians are coming." After liberation Giselle's family moved to the US where she became a psychologist. After her husband passed away she followed her children and immigrated to Israel in 1992. Dr. Giselle has since been providing psychological support for Holocaust survivors through the AMCHA organization and broke her own 50 years of silence regarding her past during the Holocaust.

Dr. Giselle Cycowicz BY Ariane Littman ISRAEL
JERUSALEM, 2021

SARA ATZMON was born in 1933 in Hungary to a a family with sixteen children. At the age of seven, her father and four of her brothers were taken to forced labor. In 1944, the family was deported on the first transport from the Debrecen Ghetto to Auschwitz, about a hundred people to each train wagon. At the Polish border the train stopped for about ten days, with passengers dying of thirst as the wagon's doors remained locked. Those who survived were sent to Austria to a forced labor camp. In 1944 her father died of starvation. By the end of November 1944 Sara was shipped with surviving family members to the Bergen-Belsen concentration camp. For six months during the daily Nazi inspections, Sara stood for long hours in the snow wearing on one foot a girl's red shoe and on the other a high-heeled women's shoe. In April 1945 prisoners were loaded on trains, destination unknown, with Allied bombing underway. They were released by the American army, near the city of Magdenburg. Sara, 12, weighed about 17 kilograms. Sara's father and three of her brothers perished in the camps. Sixty members of her extended family were also murdered. In 1945, Sara's mother and her surviving siblings boarded a ship and sailed to Mandatory Palestine. They were housed in the Atlit transit camp as the first group of postwar immigrants. Sara lives with her husband Uri in Kfar Sirkin, surrounded by their large family. She has turned her war memories into art, commemorating the Holocaust in her paintings, which are exhibited worldwide.

Sara Atzmon BY **Shay Aloni** ISRAEL
KFAR SIRKIN, ISRAEL, 2021

Paulette Angel was born in France in 1927. After Nazi German troops seized her hometown, Metz, in 1940, Paulette and her family were forced to flee from their home. They went into hiding, moving from town to town but in 1942, within days, thousands of French Jews were rounded up and deported to Drancy, an assembly and detention camp for confining Jews who were later deported to the extermination camps. Paulette's family realized they must separate and attempt individually to cross into the Zone Libre, a partition of the French metropolitan territory that they hoped would keep them from the death camps. In September 1942, Paulette and her sister Sophie were arrested by the Nazis. The two teenage girls were imprisoned in Allemans near Limoges, then in the Château de La Rochefoucauld, then in Angoulême prison, in the French internment camp in Poitiers (Camp de la route de Limoges). From there, the girls were transported and interned in the Drancy camp, last stop before Auschwitz. The sisters received help from the French resistance and were released later that same year ,1942, but remained detained, this time in a home for children under the age of 17. Paulette was 15. They were released and managed with help from the French resistance to join their parents in the Zone Libre. On July 21, 1944, Paulette's father, Moïse Rozenberg, was denounced, arrested, tortured and executed by the Nazis in Isère. He refused to give out names of resistance fighters and Paulette says, 'He died for France,' just three weeks before the area was liberated. Paulette and her sister returned to Metz with their mother, who survived. In 1953, Paulette moved to Switzerland, where she dedicates her life to the education and commemoration of the Holocaust.

Paulette Angel by Paolo Pellegrin ITALY
GENEVA, SWITZERLAND, 2021

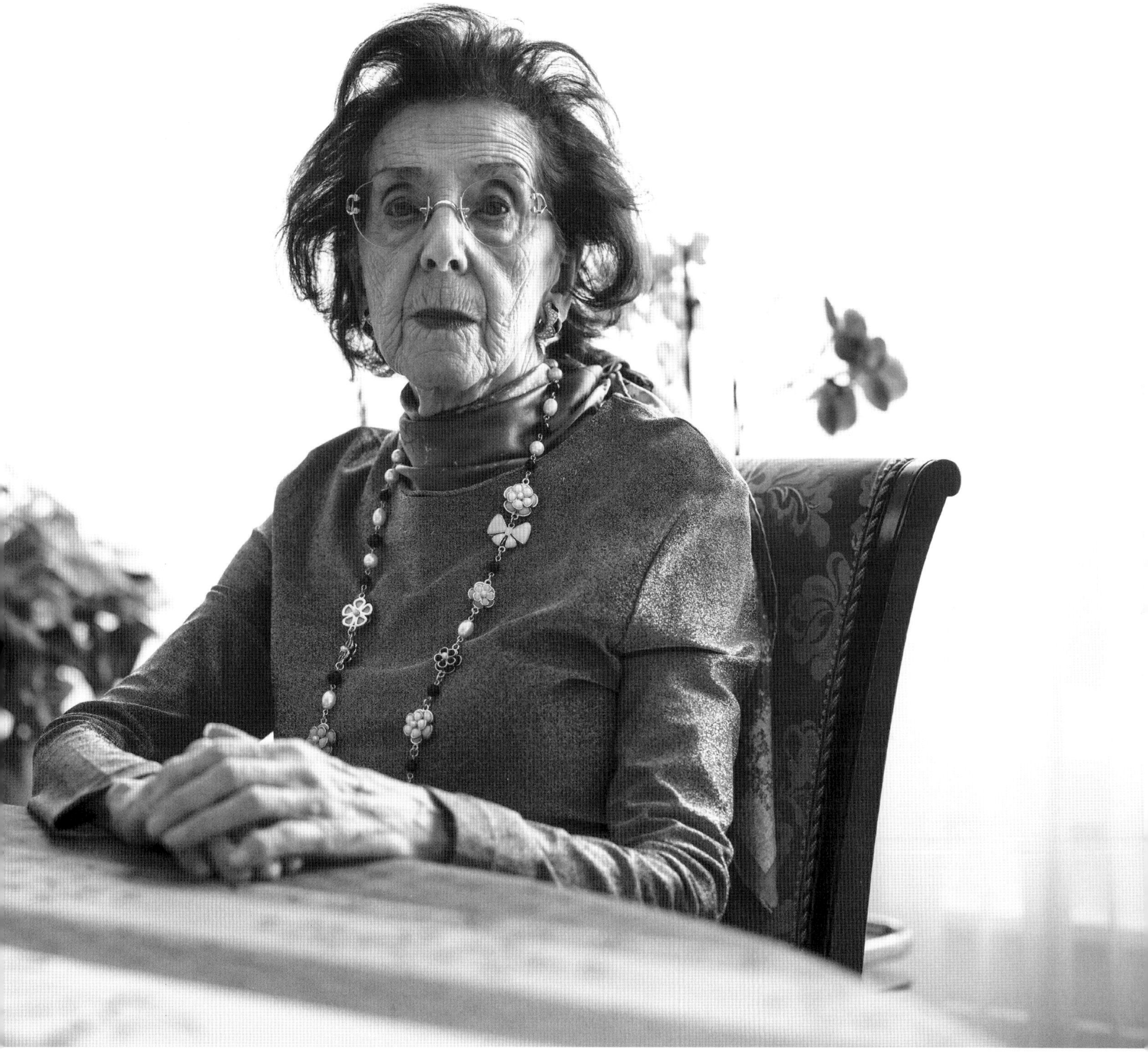

EMIL FARKAS was born in 1929 in Slovakia, then part of Czechoslovakia. In April 1942, Emil's two older brothers, who were skiers on the Czechoslovak ski team, were forced into slave labor and never heard from again. In June, his sister and her daughter were arrested and sent to die in the Auschwitz gas chambers. Emil and his brother David with their parents were sent to the Novaki concentration camp, where Emil worked repairing sewing machines. In August 1944, the camp was attacked by Slovak partisans. His father and brother fled with the partisans. Emil and his mother found refuge in a peasant house, pretending to be Christians. The Germans captured Emil and his mother and later David, and transferred them to the Sered camp. From the Sered camp the mother was transferred to the Ravensbrück camp and the sons were transferred to KZ Sachsenburg. After one night, David was taken to Germany and Emil no longer knew the fate of his family until the end of the war. In the Nazi camp KZ Sachsenburg, Emil and other inmates were selected to test special shoes intended for SS officers. Emil was required to walk all day to try out the footwear and in return received an extra slice of bread per day. Later, Emil went through medical experiments; he was injected with various substances and tortured, in order to test prisoners' resistance to torture. The frequent beatings damaged his hearing and he was transferred to Dachau, where he was assigned to slave labor again. As the American forces approached, Emil and other prisoners were taken to a remote village, where Emil was liberated by an American Jewish officer. After the liberation he found his father and in Prague he found his mother and later also his brother, David. Two brothers, Emil's sister and his niece perished. Emil became a member of the Czechoslovak national gymnastics team. He immigrated to Israel in 1949. After his service in the IDF, Emil became a champion in gymnastics and joined the Israeli national team and went on to win numerous competitions and medals.

Emil Farkas BY Oz Moalem ISRAEL
KARMIEL, ISRAEL, 2021

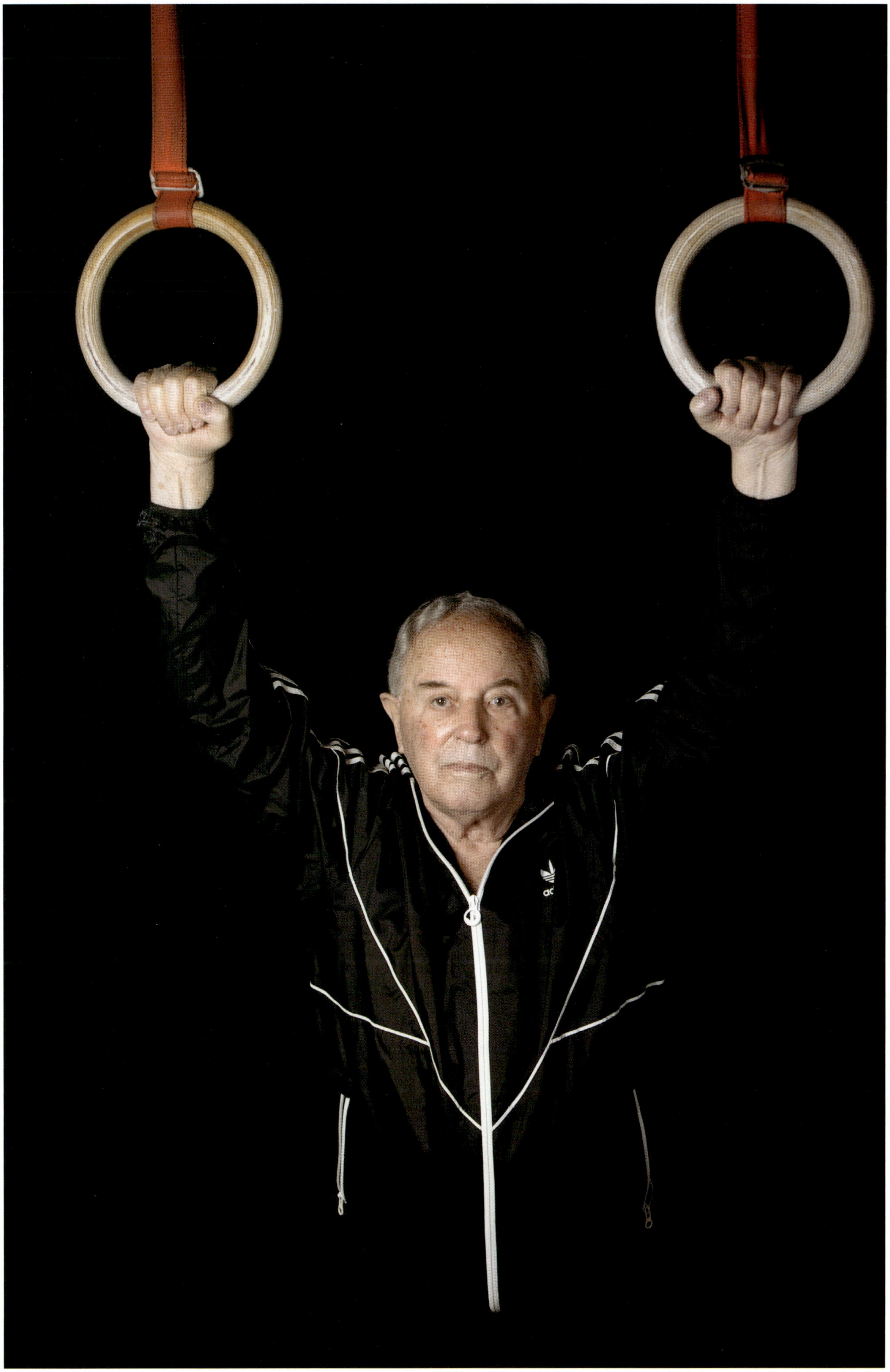

URI ESHED was born Leo Wesreich in Berlin in 1923. Leo attended the Jewish school in Berlin, where he was drawn to Zionism and studied Hebrew. With the rise of the Nazi Party in Germany in the 1930s, the sense of security which Leo and his classmates had enjoyed began to falter, and they were subjected to violent antisemitic attacks by teenagers. The Jews of Germany were denied their rights, and freedom of movement and ownership. Many were exiled to Poland. In November 1938, the pogrom known as Kristallnacht took place. Leo witnessed the riots that broke out in the city. 'Jewish business windows shattered, Jews attacked. I will never forget the mob pulling Jews by their beards, dragging them through the streets.' A few days later Nazi German police broke into the family's apartment. Leo, then 15, and his father Alexander were taken to detention and were imprisoned along with dozens of other Jews. In the police cells, with little water and food, Leo realized that they had to leave Germany at once. After several weeks of imprisonment, they were unexpectedly released and destined for deportation to Poland. Leo had no doubt, as he told his parents, that, 'I am immigrating to Mandatory Palestine with the Aliyat Hanoar movement.' His father, however, believed that Germany would recover, thus sealing the bitter fate of his family. After a six-week training period, after the Passover of 1939, Leo said goodbye to his family for the last time on the train station platform, along with other teenagers, none of whom would ever see their families again. In Mandatory Palestine, Uri became a farmer and served in the Palmach, the Haganah and the British Army, to which he enlisted when he learned of his father's murder in Dachau in April 1941. "Be brave and healthy," his mother wrote in her last letter. "You are our only hope." His mother Berta and sister Fanny perished in Riga in January 1942. In the midst of Israel's 1948 War of Independence, Leo, by now renamed Uri, married Esther. At her death, they had been married for 67 years. Uri worked in the Department of International Cooperation at the Ministry of Agriculture, and contributed greatly to strengthening ties with developing countries in Africa and Latin America. At the same time, he established a thriving farm. Uri has two children, six grandchildren, and eighteen great-grandchildren.

Uri Eshed BY Or Perevoznik ISRAEL
MOSHAV BEER TUVIA, ISRAEL, 2021

YAACOV HOLZMAN was born in Poltusk, Poland, in 1937. On the eve of the war, his father was drafted into the Polish army and did not return. Poltusk was occupied by Nazi Germany on September 7, 1939, and racial and antisemitic decrees were imposed on the town's Jewish population including a ban on walking on sidewalks, foreclosure of bank accounts and an obligation to pay ransom. Many were rounded up for forced labor. On September 11, the Nazis murdered dozen of Jews and deported about 300 families to the east, including two-year-old Yaacov, his mother and two siblings. Under shelling, hunger and in terrible cold, the mother and her children crossed the border into Russia where they were detained and exiled by train to a forced labor camp in Siberia. In June 1941 they were released from the concentration camp and the mother decided they would start walking to Uzbekistan. After wandering for weeks, they came to Samarkand where they remained until the end of the war. In 1945, after several attempts, they managed to return to Poland, but refrained from returning to their town Poltusk after being warned of pogroms against returning Jews. Their mother met up with Israeli emissaries who were assigned to bring war orphans to Mandatory Palestine. Due to the restrictions, the children were separated and 10-year-old Yaacov boarded alone the ship *Alexandria* and arrived to Haifa port. He later learned that his father had been murdered in Treblinka. Yaacov rebuilt his life in Israel. He was the recipient of the prestigious "Kaplan" award for his contribution to the development of military equipment and for his contribution to Israel's defense. Yaacov Holzman passed away in mid-January 2022.

Yaacov Holzman BY Chen Shuval ISRAEL

HOLON, ISRAEL, 2021

HILDA SIMCHE was born in Berlin in 1923, the only daughter of David and Susanna Grinbaum. Hilda was 15 when her father was deported to Poland and her mother was jailed after trying to obtain fake travel permits to Belgium for herself and Hilda. Despite her mother's pleas, Hilda refused to leave Nazi Germany on the Kindertransport while her mother was imprisoned. ELI HEINEMAN was born in Breslau in 1926. In 1940, Hilda and Eli were part of a Zionist youth movement that prepared and trained them for life in Eretz Israel. In 1942, they were deported by the Gestapo to the Neudorf forced labor camp. By orders of the Third Reich, on April 19, 1943, the Neudorf youth were sent to extermination in Auschwitz death camp. A train carrying 117 boys and girls arrived at the platform of Birkenau, and only 45 survived. With the establishment of the "Women's Orchestra" in Auschwitz-Birkenau, musicians were sought among the inmates. Hilda, who played the violin, was chosen to join the orchestra, whose members were given larger food rations than other prisoners, enabling Hilda to deliver some extra food to starving inmates. The Women's Orchestra was conducted by Alma Rosé, daughter of Austrian Arnold Rosé, leader of the Vienna Philharmonic Orchestra for 50 years. Her mother, Justine, was Gustav Mahler's sister. Alma saw the orchestra as a means of survival for women and was able to achieve better conditions for the

Hilda Simche & Eli Heineman BY **Yoav Gad** ISRAEL

KIBBUTZ NETZER SERENI, ISRAEL, 2021

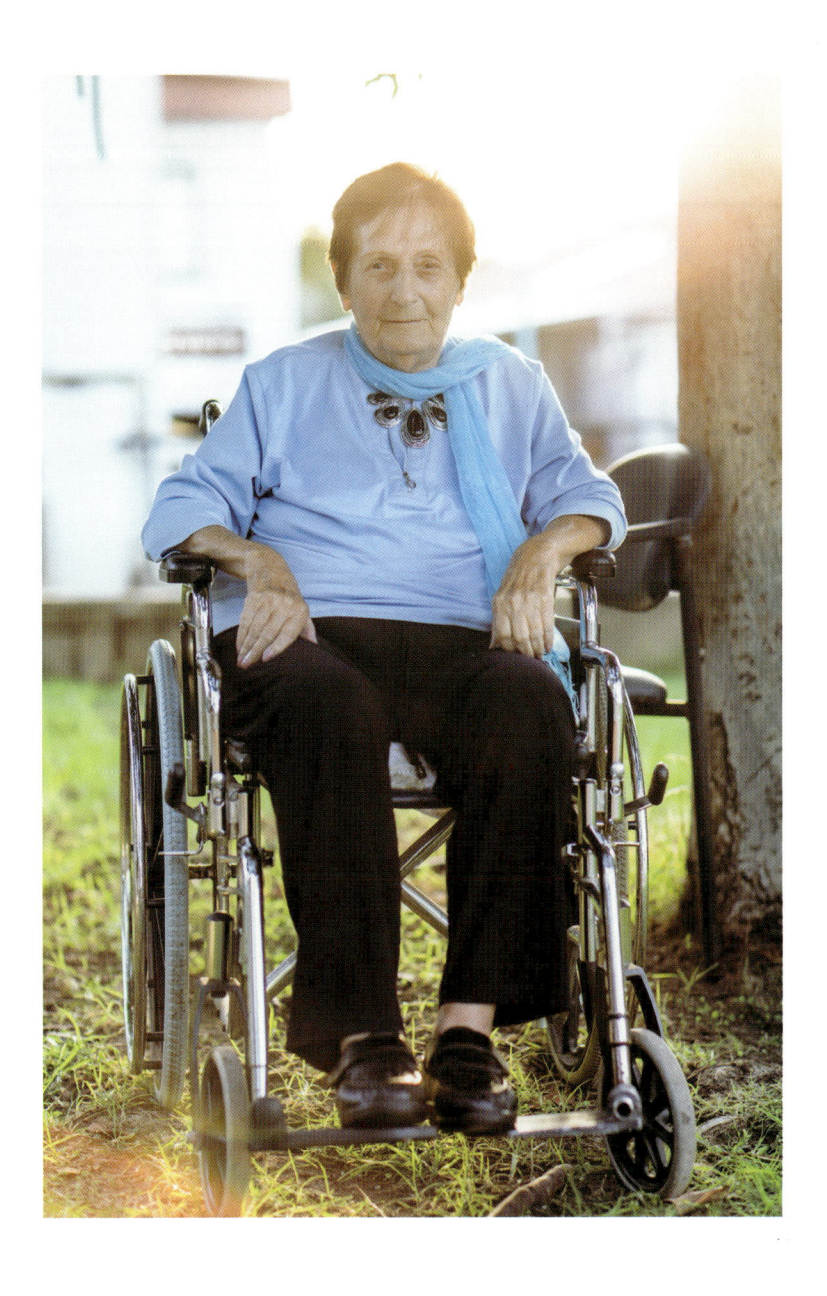

orchestra members in the camp. Hilda initially played the violin but fell ill, which prevented her from playing. She became Alma Rosé's personal assistant and responsible for the musical compositions, which she kept hidden in a pillowcase. Alma Rosé perished in Auschwitz but saved the lives of most of the orchestra members. Hilda survived and saved Alma's musical portfolio. In November 1944, the women from Auschwitz were sent to the Bergen-Belsen camp, and on April 19, 1945, Hilda was liberated by the US Army. In the DP camp, Hilda met Pisa (Azriel) Simche, who later became her husband, and both immigrated to Mandatory Palestine. Eli Heineman also succeeded in reaching Mandatory Palestine. They established a kibbutz in 1948 named "Kibbutz Buchenwald" after the concentration camp in which many of its founders had been imprisoned. The kibbutz was later renamed Netzer Sereni after Enzo Sereni, a Jewish Italian intellectual and Jewish Brigade officer who was parachuted into Nazi-occupied Italy in World War II, was captured by the Nazis and executed in Dachau concentration camp. Hilda and Eli are photographed with the backdrop of the first kibbutz building. Hilda's fourth-generation family are Netzer Sereni kibbutz members; she has two sons, six grandchildren and twelve great-grandchildren.

Hilda Simche BY Eyal Pe'er ISRAEL
KIBBUTZ NETZER SERENI, ISRAEL, 2021

IDA FRIEDMANN was born in Romania in 1922. Her father died before the war, and her mother raised her four children alone. They were all shipped to Auschwitz. There the children were separated from their mother, who was sent to the gas chambers. Ida was sent to Stutthof, Riga, Tourne and Magdeburg. Two of her brothers survived. In 1964, Ida immigrated to Israel and opened a restaurant in Tivon. Ida refuses to talk about her experiences during the Holocaust.

Ida Friedmann BY Limor Friedmann ISRAEL
KIRYAT MOTZKIN, ISRAEL, 2021

SHEINE DEYZH was born in Satmar, Hungary, in 1938. After Nazi Germany invaded Hungary in 1944, Sheine, her sister Chaya, and their mother were deported from the ghetto to the Auschwitz death camp. 'When we entered Auschwitz, [the infamous Nazi doctor Josef] Mengele took me and my sister for twins – we were not. We were told to join the line on the right without Mother…our lives were saved.' Sheine was six years old and her sister was seven. The girls underwent painful medical experiments, and eventually Mengele discovered they were not twins. The Russian army was advancing from the east. The three were then sent to the gas chambers. 'We were inside, women screaming around us…we were so afraid…there was a huge disorder and there were benches, from outside it looked like a dressing hall where you hang your clothes, and inside a huge hall with shower heads… and the SS guard opened a door – they ran out of gas…' Soon after, Russian and Allied forces started bombing attacks in the area. The Germans disappeared and 'we were freed, my sister Chaya and my mother.' Sheine belongs to the Satmar Hasidic dynasty, one of the largest in the world, founded in 1905 and re-established after World War II. It is characterized by strict religious adherence and rejection of modern culture.

Sheine Deyzh BY **Baruch Yaari** ISRAEL

JERUSALEM, 2021

LIDIA MAKSYMOWICZ is believed to have been born in Belarus, possibly in 1939. Lidia was about four years old in December 1943, when Nazi German forces deported her and her family from the Minsk area to the Auschwitz-Birkenau concentration camp. Upon arrival at the death camp, Lidia was separated from her mother and sent to the children's barracks. There the children suffered from hunger and cold, and feared visits by the notorious Dr. Josef Mengele. 'I can't remember his face, just his polished boots,' Lidia said. 'Hearing his footsteps, I crawled, ducked, and closed my eyes. I thought he would not find me.' Lidia did not manage to hide from Mengele. He tested vaccines on the girl. After countless injections, she was more dead than alive. One day Lidia's mother sneaked into the children's barracks to bring her daughter food and found her lying unconscious with a high fever. Lidia saw Auschwitz liberated by the Red Army on January 27, 1945. After the war, she was raised by a Catholic Polish family. Born Ludmila Boczarowa, she did not know that her birth mother had survived. They were briefly reunited shortly before her mother's death in the early 1960s. Lidia became a chemist, married, and ran a company. Her family life suffered from the trauma of her imprisonment at Auschwitz. In 2021, at age 81, Lidia met Pope Francis. When she rolled up her left sleeve to show him the number 70072, he kissed it and she hugged him. Lidia lives in Krakow.

Lidia Maksymowicz BY Vatican Media VATICAN CITY
VATICAN CITY, 2021

EVELYN LIPPMAN was born, presumably, in Vienna in 1924, the only child of Fritz and Lily Guttmann. With the adoption of the Nuremberg Laws, which banned Jewish children from attending school, she did what she could to carry on learning. She was denounced by another pupil who asked the teacher why he was teaching a Jew. The elderly teacher felt compelled to declare that henceforth no 15-year-old would attend life classes in the art school. Evelyn was determined not to give up on art and on Sundays when there were guides giving talks, at immense risk to her safety, she would remove her yellow star and quietly enter the Albertina Print Gallery to gaze at the pictures unnoticed. By the early 1940s, Jews were ordered to move to a specific area in Vienna and she and her mother were made to sew German army caps for 10 hours a day. When the deportations began, the family was sent first to Terezín in Czechoslovakia in 1943, and later transported to Auschwitz where prisoner number A25466 was tattooed on her arm. Both Evelyn and her mother survived 18 months in camps. They were liberated by US forces in 1945. After the war they discovered that Fritz did not survive, nor did they ever find out how or when he died. In 1947 the mother and daughter moved to England and within a year Evelyn met and married her husband Eric and settled in Walton-on-Thames where they created a family. Evelyn, who had no education certificates, was enrolled in a foundation course in 1972 and went on to study for her degree over six years. In her 50s she achieved an OU degree. Her children say it is only then they began to understand what she had endured. "She locked up her memories and threw away the key," said her son Anthony who graduated from Oxford nearly the the same time as his mother. "I know whose was the greater achievement," concluded Anthony.

Evelyn Lippman BY Emma Cattell GREAT BRITAIN
WALTON-ON-THAMES, ENGLAND, GREAT BRITAIN, 2021

Miriam Seidel Volk was born in Kalisz, Poland, in 1922. In 1939, Kalisz was invaded by Nazi forces. 'Right away we knew they were going to go after the Jewish population.' Her family was evicted from their apartment. 'All the Jews in the area were forced to live in a cordoned-off market area.' Through a family connection, she and her parents worked in a hospital caring for the elderly for several years. In 1942, 'the Nazis decided to get rid of all the old and sick people – to eliminate them. We all assumed they were gassing and killing them.' Her family was then forced into the Warsaw Ghetto. 'A starvation place. The hunger was unbelievable.' Miriam was trapped in the ghetto for two years, until 1944, 'then they started to liquidate the ghetto.' She was transported to Auschwitz in a cattle car with no food, no toilet, no air. 'Like animals they put us together.' Upon arrival at the death camp, all were stripped, their clothes searched for valuables. Miriam's head was shaved, and she was ushered into a shower. A "doctor" selected people one by one. Those deemed skinny or sick were lined up to the side. It was the last time Miriam ever saw her parents. Her mother was murdered that day. Her father later perished in the camp as well. After six weeks in Auschwitz and with Soviet troops approaching, SS units began the final evacuation of prisoners from the camp complex, marching them on foot toward the interior of the German Reich. Miriam was marched toward Bergen-Belsen. A farmer she came upon then sheltered her on his farm until the war ended in 1945, believing that the blonde and blue-eyed Miriam was not Jewish. At war's end, she returned to Kalisz looking for family members. 'I did not find anybody. All my relatives did not make it. I was the only one.' While in a displaced persons camp, she remembered an uncle in the United States, and she applied for a visa. At the DP camp, she met a survivor from Kalisz, and the two married and immigrated to the US in 1947. They arrived penniless, Miriam says, and they worked hard to have a family and a home. She lives in Salt Lake City, Utah. Miriam says self-preservation got her through. 'Everybody, no matter what and how, they want to live.'

Miriam Seidel Volk by Natalie Behring USA
SALT LAKE CITY, UTAH, USA, 2021

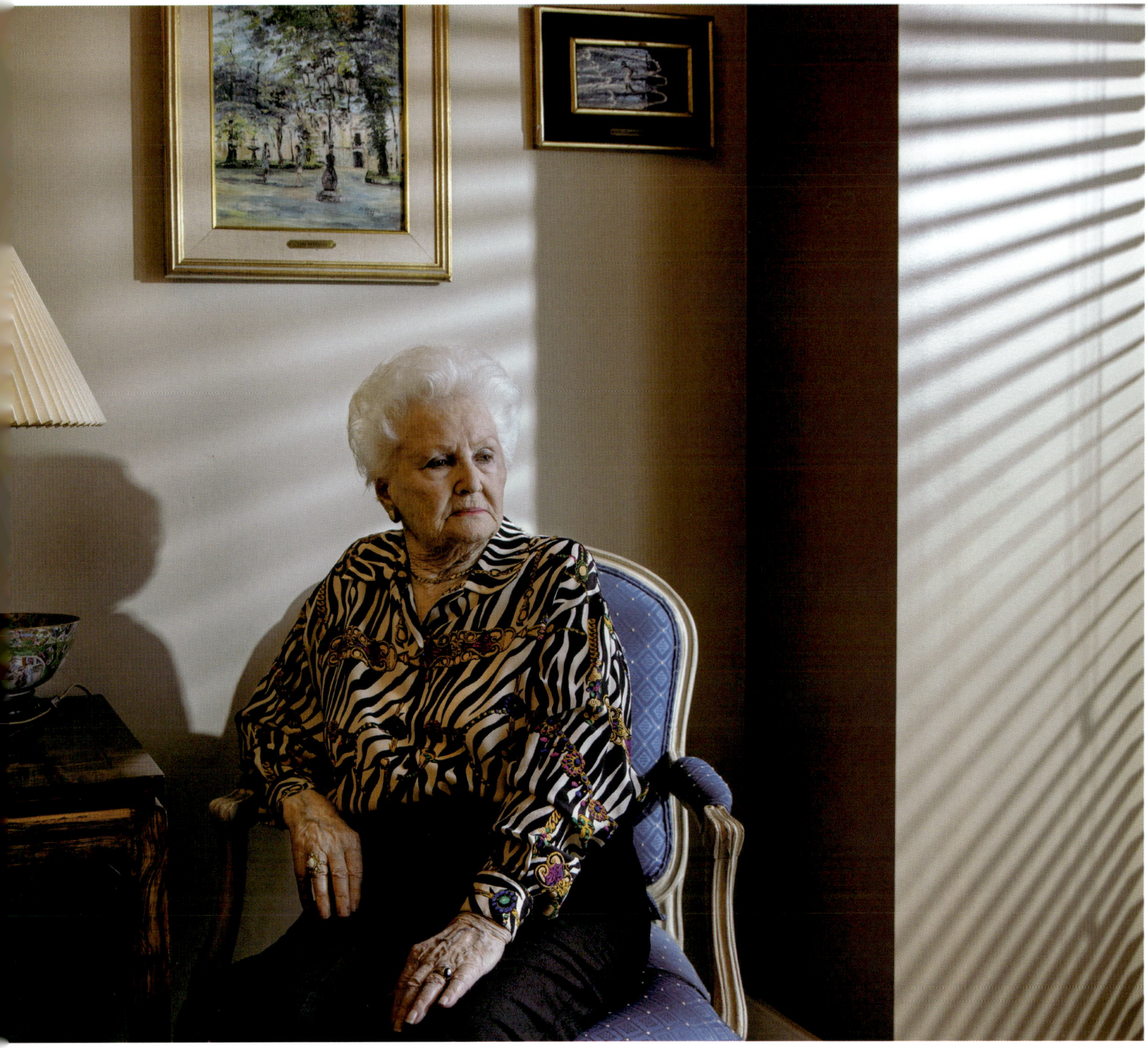

SHELOMO SELINGER was born in Poland in 1928, in a small town near Oświęcim (Auschwitz), where he received both a traditional Jewish upbringing and a Polish education. In 1943, he and his father were deported from the Chrzanów Ghetto to the Faulbrück concentration camp in Germany. Three months later his father was murdered. Shelomo remained alone in the camp. His mother and one of his sisters also perished during the Holocaust. Selinger survived nine German death camps: Faulbrück, Gröditz, Markstadt, Fünfteichen, Gross-Rosen, Flossenburg, Dresden, Leitmeritz and finally Theresienstadt, as well as two death marches. He was discovered still breathing on a stack of dead bodies when the Red Army liberated the Terezin camp in 1945. The Jewish military doctor who pulled him out of the pile of corpses transferred him to a military field hospital, where he recovered but suffered from amnesia for seven years. In 1946 he boarded the *Tel Haï*, headed for British Mandatory Palestine, along with a group of young death camp survivors who, with the help of the Jewish Brigade of the British Army, had crossed illegally through Germany, Belgium and France. The ship was seized outside the territorial waters of Haifa by the British Royal Navy. The passengers were interned in the Atlit detainee camp. After his liberation from the camp, Shelomo joined a kibbutz near the Dead Sea. He participated in the fighting during the 1948 war. His kibbutz, Bet Haarava, was destroyed. He was then one of the founders of Kibbutz Kabri in the Galilee where, in 1951, he met his future wife, Ruth. They were married in 1954. At that time, he began to sculpt. In 1955, Shelomo was awarded the Norman Prize. A year later he enrolled in Paris at the École Nationale des Beaux-Arts. Granite became his favourite stone and he also carved wood, mostly using available firewood. The first acknowledgement of his talent in Paris earned him the Neumann Prize of the city of Geneva. His art is now part of the permanent collection of the Musée d'Art Moderne de la Ville de Paris. Shelomo became a renowned sculptor of birth, rebirth and life itself. He continues to exhibit and was awarded numerous prizes. In 1973, he was named Chevalier to the prestigious French Legion of Honor by President François Mitterrand. Since 2006, he has held the title of Officier de la Légion d'honneur. Shelomo and his wife have been living in Paris since 1956. He continues to work in marble, granite, stone and wood.

Shelomo Selinger BY Nissim Sellam FRANCE
PARIS, 2021

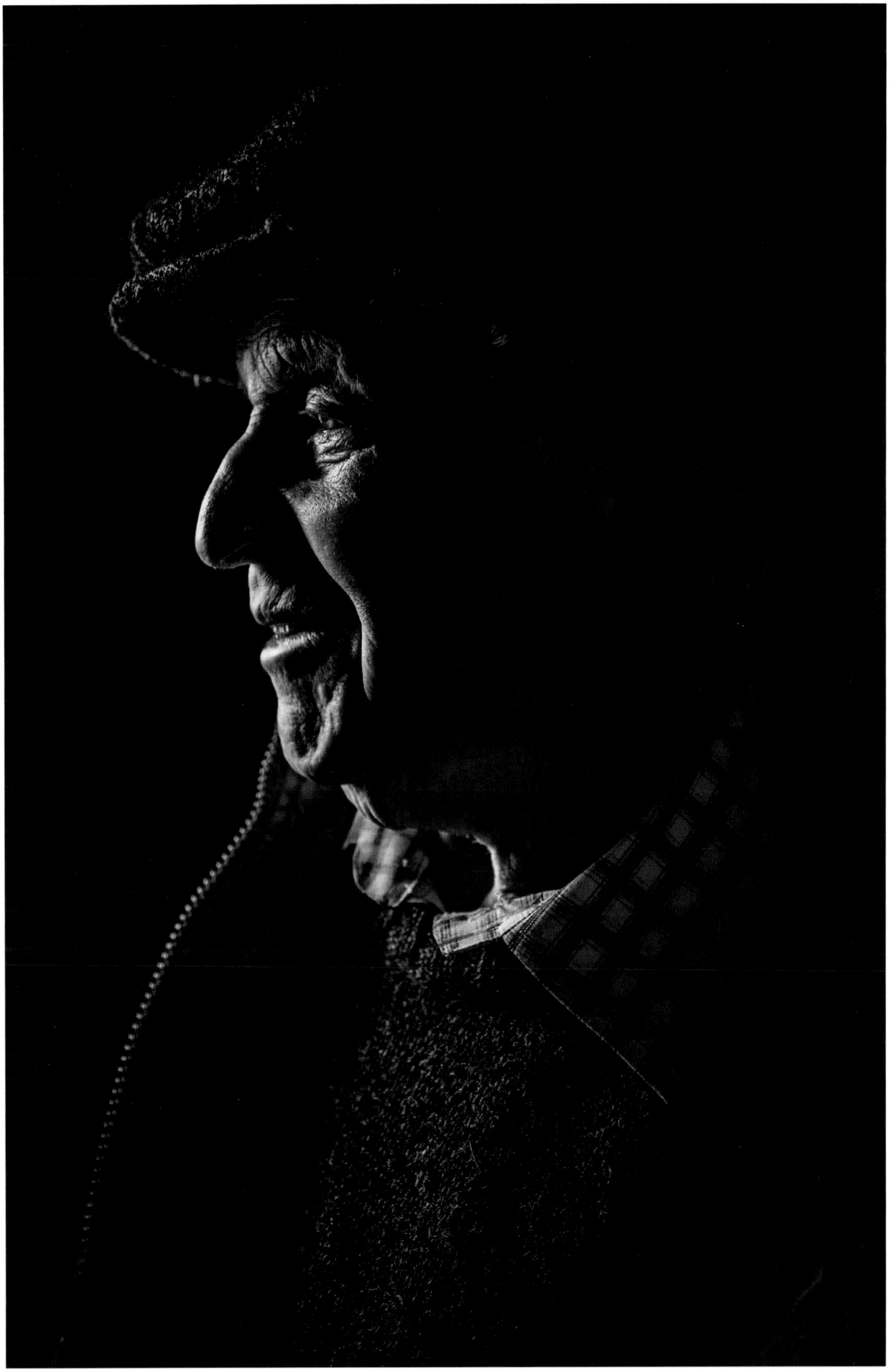

Moshe Fish (Dagan) was born in Piotrków, Poland, to parents Zelda and Ruven on April 15, 1924. The family lived at 41 Jeruzalemska Str., the last house on the border of the ghetto. His parents and sister were sent to their deaths in Treblinka. Moshe worked in the ghetto in forced labor assignments in jobs such as flattening river banks, clearing stables and hanging curtains. Then he worked at the Bugai Plywood factory and, until his brother Abraham's death in 1943, as a messenger boy in "Shop 24." Then Moshe and his brother David were transported to Bliżyn. In October 1944, Moshe was sent to Auschwitz-Birkenau. He stayed at what had been the "Gypsy camp" for two weeks, then was taken to the forced labor Camp B, where he worked at dismantling planes which had been shot down during the war. Moshe was taken on a death march in January 1945 through the Czech Republic to Austria, and in an open train to Mauthausen, where he stayed for two days until being taken to Melek to build bunkers for a German secret weapon. Two months later, he was taken to KZ Ebensee, where they neither worked nor ate for an entire month, until the Americans arrived. Moshe and his sister Sarah were the sole survivors of their family. Moshe entered Mandatory Palestine with the illegal immigrant ship *Shabtai Luzinski* on March 13, 1947. His group was part of the Palmach, the elite fighting force of the Haganah, the underground army of the Yishuv Jewish community during the period of the British Mandate for Palestine. They were trained in Brindisi, Italy. Moshe Dagan recounts, 'I've lived in Israel as an Israeli for fifty years. I did neither want to know nor delve into the past. When I retired, in 1989, I was suddenly taken by deep longing for Poland and went there a number of times with my wife, Aviva. I've returned to Poland 14 times since then as a Holocaust witness, escorting youth and General Security Service delegations.'

Moshe Dagan BY Nissim Sellam FRANCE
GIBTON, ISRAEL, 2021

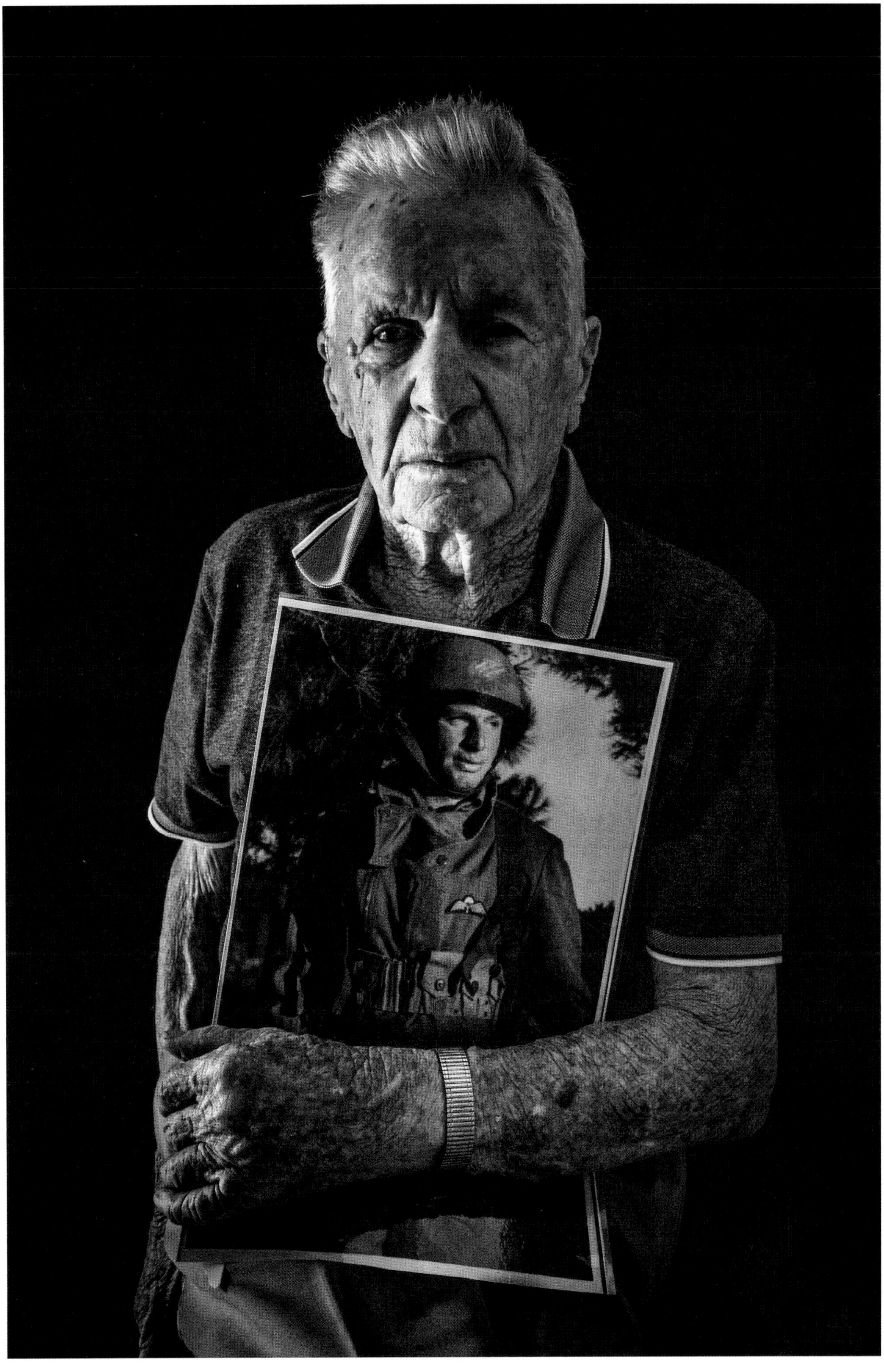

JACOB BLANKITNY (R) was born in 1926 in Maków Mazowiecki, Poland. 'Two days into [the] Nazi invasion to Poland, the Nazis were in my hometown, using the synagogue as a stable, destroying Jewish symbols and demanding that Jews be identified by a Star of David with the inscription "Jew." After two weeks, we started moving via peasant cart to the Mlawa Ghetto, finding the place empty when we arrived because the previous inhabitants had all been transferred to Auschwitz. There was a train station in which we stayed for 10 days and worked on construction projects until transfer. First, the elderly and women with small children were transported to Treblinka. Our transfer to Auschwitz began and I will never forget when my mother gave the German Nazi soldiers her favors in exchange for half a glass of water. When we arrived at our tragic fate, I was only 16 years old. Even today, my ears echo the painful cries of people there. We were separated by women and men. Women were sent directly to the gas chambers, later to the crematoria – my mother and sister were among them. My father and I stayed united. Amid a whirlwind of Nazi police with packs of dogs, we crossed to my uncle in another line that took us to Auschwitz-Birkenau. The crematoria smoke could be seen for kilometers around, there were approximately 6,000 people in our transport, 200 people were left to enter Auschwitz. We were tattooed with numbers on our arms, it was winter and the cold burned us; all the camp was flooded and muddy. Dressed in striped pajamas, we were placed in different barracks, with three-story bunks, twelve humans per bunk. We worked outside the camp until seven o'clock at night. Each evening we returned with four or five cadavers of our friends, who were taken directly to the crematoria. I was forced to say goodbye to my father and he said these last words to me: "I will not see you anymore. It may be that you are able to save yourself. Though I am abandoning you, you have an obligation to go and save yourself." I never saw him again. I was moved about five kilometers away, to Auschwitz I, where there was a woodworking shop. I was diverted to work on the railroad. I saw my feet freeze and chunks of flesh and skin fall from my fingers. I was left to recover for three days when [Nazi doctor] Josef Mengele arrived for an inspection, dividing some of the sick to the left and some to the right. I was lucky, as most were sent to death. Since I worked the saw well enough, I could stay working there until 1945; this was my salvation. On January 18, 1945, the Russians began to close in on Auschwitz, and the Germans made us walk about 90 km to the Leslau Station. Many were killed on the road. Upon reaching the station, we were forced into open wagons bound for Mauthausen. Half the people traveling in these railcars died freezing. We were transported to Melk, where we worked in mines for the munitions factories until March 1945 when we were clandestinely informed that the Americans were closing in on us. For this reason, the Germans decided to move us to Upper Austria, into a camp called Ebensee. We were taken to the camp and lined up to be shot. At that time, a German commander approached and said, "It's not worth killing these people; they are not even worth the bullet. No matter – they will die in the camp." We ate one meal a day and it consisted of a soup with potato peels – scraps of food from the SS. Every day we watched as between 400 to 500 prisoners died in the camp. On May 4, 1945, the Americans were very close. There were about 10,000 people left in the camp. People rose up and decided not to comply, so the SS, rushed for time and trying to escape, decided to lock the camp with the prisoners inside and they, themselves, left. Finally, the next morning, American soldiers and tanks arrived and liberated us. Of all the people in my city, Maków Mazowiecki, where 4,000 Jews originally lived before the start of World War II, only 42 survived. Of all my family in Poland, I was the only survivor.' Jacob Blankitny passed away on his birthday February 14, at the age of 96.

SHLOMO REICHIK (L) was born in 1924 in Maków Mazowiecki, Poland. 'When Nazi Germany occupied the town, a Polish neighbor warned Dad and he immediately fled to Russia. His traces have not been known since. We moved to the town ghetto. At the end of 1942 we were sent by transport to Birkenau. During the Selektion, my mother pushed me into another line so I was saved, and my mother, my brother and sister were taken to extermination on the same day. Since that day I have lost the ability to cry. I became prisoner 81736. In Birkenau I worked in collecting garbage. In January 1943, I was transferred to Auschwitz to Block 7a. At the end of 1943 during the Selektion by Mengele I was disqualified and transferred to a block destined for extermination. There in the block I was saved by a hometown fellow. In November 1944, following the Sonderkommando uprising in Birkenau, I was transferred to the Stutthof camp. There I worked in the forests before a transfer to Heiflingen to the airport where I worked in building bunkers for aircraft. From there to Dotmergan and later to Elek [near Dachau] and from there to extermination by train. The train traveled back and forth because the US Army shelled the track, and on May 1, 1945, the Americans grabbed the train and released the prisoners from the Nazi trains. This is my day of liberation from the war. We were given battle rations and warned not to eat because we might die [due to the prisoners' weakened condition]. From there we moved to the Feldafing DP camp in Germany, where the Jewish Brigade took care of me. I received documents from a British soldier and a uniform and in 1946, I immigrated to Mandatory Palestine with a Biriya ship from Marseille. The ship was captured by the British and I was transferred to Atlit camp. I was released and reunited with distant relatives, the Abramitsky family in Jerusalem, who took care of all my needs. In March 1948, I was drafted into the Palmach for the War of Independence, and I took part in the battle on the siege of Jerusalem. The armor on which I was overturned injured my head and I was taken to a hospital by Rehovot. I participated in the conquest of Eilat and the conquest of Be'er Sheva. Upon my release from the army in January 1950, I married Tirza and we created a family home and careers. Tirza died. We were married happily for 70 years.' Shlomo worked for the Israel Electric Corporation until his retirement. Both survivors had children, who married each other, and now their joint great-granddaughter Noga plays alongside them during their photo portrait session.

Shlomo Reichik & Jacob Blankitny BY **Yehoshua Yosef** ISRAEL

NETANYA, ISRAEL, 2021

'When Nazi Germany occupied Mikulince, Ukraine, in June of 1941, all the Jews had to wear a blue Star of David, and from the very beginning of the occupation, the Nazis, with the help of the Ukrainian People's Militsiya, rounded up all of the Jewish males, including myself, for hard labor without food or water, while [we were beaten] all the time. In November of 1941, I was taken together with a lot of young men to a labor camp, called Borki Wielkie, in the province of Tarnopol. We worked from dusk til nightfall, again under inhumane conditions. Given only a piece of hard bread and a little water, we worked on the railroad, fixing roads, digging and hauling stones on our backs. Many died. In September 1942 I took a chance and ran away during the night, returning to Mikulince. A few days later, I was taken again with my brothers and many other young Jews to work on a big farm that was about 25 kilometers from Tarnopol. At night they put us into the stables like cattle and we slept on dirt floors. We were constantly beaten by the Ukrainian Guards. I worked on that farm until September 1943, when the German SS came to liquidate all of us. At that time, the German SS with the help of the Ukrainian militiamen, rounded up a lot of people and started to shoot. Four of my brothers were shot plus many others. Those still alive were forced to dig graves for the dead as well as themselves, since they too were shot. One of my brothers and myself started to run. We figured we were dead anyway, and we had nothing to lose. My brother and I ran all night, till we found a place in a village where we hid for a couple of days. We were eight brothers; only two of us survived. From September 1943 until the end of the war I was hiding but I was fortunate and survived. In April 1944, I was liberated by the Russian Army. The nightmares and the horrible dreams still haunt me.'

Harry Zipper BY Clifford Lester USA
LAGUNA NIGUEL, CALIFORNIA, USA, 2021

LIKE CATTLE AND WE SLEPT ON DIRT FLOORS
NO BLANKETS OR STRAW WORST THEN THE ANIMALS.

EDGAR MORAN was born in Romania in 1928. After Romania aligned itself with Nazi Germany, half of the 780,000 Romanian Jews were murdered, many in Romanian-controlled areas. At the age of 15, Edgar joined the Underground Resistance movement of the Zionist Youth. His role was to transport documents and medications for American pilots, and communications with other Resistance cells for acts of sabotage. Edgar barely escaped death when he was in an area surrounded by the police. He panicked and started to run. When he was stopped, a police officer who happened to know his father let him go, and Edgar's life was saved. Edgar studied and practiced medicine and after six and a half years of perseverance, he received his permit to leave Romania for Israel. He served as a doctor in the Israeli Navy, and then studied anatomic pathology at the Hebrew University Medical Center in Jerusalem. He specialized in medical oncology at the University of Chicago, where he taught until 1976. He then came to California and established the first medical oncology service at the City of Hope Medical Center in Duarte, California. As a professor of medicine at the University of California, Irvine, he dedicated his professional life to the care of United States veterans, to cancer research, and to teaching medical students and young doctors.

Edgar Moran BY Clifford Lester USA
LONG BEACH, CALIFORNIA, USA, 2021

An American hero, **Lieutenant Colonel Sam Sachs** was born on April 26, 1915, in Grand Forks, North Dakota, USA. He enlisted in the North Dakota National Guard at the age of 17. In 1941, he was called to active duty in the Army, and three years later was company commander of logistics for the 325th glider infantry of the 82nd Airborne in France, which made one of the first troop glider landings beyond the beaches of Normandy, on D-Day. Sam took part in the D-Day landing, and later liberated a death camp in Germany. He liberated prisoners and witnessed piles of bodies over eight feet (about 2.3 meters) high, and many teenage kids barely alive in their bunks. He recalled feeling extreme horror upon walking into the camp, asking why any nation would do such a thing to humanity. As a Jewish soldier who was determined never to be taken prisoner by the Nazis, he had taken on fire from German forces while landing behind the lines at Utah Beach in France during the D-Day invasion. Sam prayed for a gift of 24 hours to live after he landed his glider, called the "Flying Coffin." He examined his plane after landing and was astounded that he could find only one bullet hole. Sam took off his helmet, placed it over his heart, and looked up at the sky as he thanked G-d. Sam received the French Legion of Honor from French President Macron and was appointed a Chevalier. When the COVID-19 pandemic forced the cancellation of his 105th birthday party, a parade of well-wishers in cars, military vehicles and a Los Angeles County sheriff's helicopter was held in his honor. Sam Sachs died of natural causes one month before turning 107.

Lieutenant Colonel Sam Sachs BY Clifford Lester USA
LAKEWOOD, CALIFORNIA, USA, 2021

IRENE PERBAL was born in the Netherlands in 1933. Irene was seven years old when, on May 10, 1940, Nazi Germany invaded her country. She lived in a part of Amsterdam not far from where Anne Frank and her family had lived before they went into hiding. She and Anne had frequented the same Montessori School. In March 1941, the Nazis began issuing identification cards. Jews received cards marked with a "J," and were forced to wear the Star of David. Soon began the mass deportation of Jewish residents to concentration camps. 'The Nazis raided all of the houses in our neighborhood in search of Jews, they shut off the street on both sides, and went into one house after the other, taking away whole families – separating women, children, men. There was a lot of screaming and crying.' Irene's grandfather, father and uncles became active in the resistance to the occupation, and her parents took Jews into hiding, ignoring the Nazis' threat that whoever helped a Jew would be treated like one. Irene said, 'When injustice becomes law, resistance becomes your duty.' Days after Irene's 10th birthday in 1943, the Gestapo raided her home. They arrested two Jewish men in hiding as well as Irene's father. All three were taken away to the Gestapo headquarters. Irene never saw her father again. She later learned that he perished in a concentration camp. The winter of 1944–45 in Amsterdam became known as the "Hunger Winter" and Irene, her mother, little sister, and two little brothers barely survived. On May 6, 1945, the Canadians entered Amsterdam, followed soon by the Americans. Allied bomber crews began to make food drops over the Netherlands. 'We saw the planes swooping over Amsterdam and dropping packages of food,' Irene said. 'We all went to the roof – Thank you, Allies!' Irene lives in the US and shares her experiences with students. She became the first female president of a local Rotary Club. 'My father had no intention of being a hero,' Irene says, 'but he left us a legacy of great courage and humanity…and told us always to stand up for our principles.'

Irene Perbal BY Clifford Lester USA
MOKELUMNE HILL, CALIFORNIA, USA, 2021

EVA SCHNEIDER was born in 1933, in Nitra, Czechoslovakia, today Slovakia. Eva was an only child. After years of hiding with her family throughout Slovakia and Hungary, dodging the wrath of the Gestapo, Eva endured the arrest of her father and, shortly after, Eva and and her mother were rounded up and loaded on a cattle train to Auschwitz. In the concentration camp their hair was shaved and arms tattooed. Eva became number A27078. They had to remove their clothes and were marched straight to the gas chambers. Their lives were saved when a bombing caused a malfunction of the crematoria. Eva was left alone in Auschwitz after her mother was taken to Bergen-Belsen, a concentration camp referred to as Hell on Earth. Eva was sent on a death march with thousands of other prisoners. They were forced to walk for many days towards the Mauthausen death camp, as the Nazis tried to evade the nearing Soviet Army troops and to continue to use the prisoners as slave labor. Eva cannot forget having witnessed piles of dead bodies at Mauthausen six to eight feet high. She was taken into a barracks where ladies were kept for the soldiers' "pleasure," she recalls. After pleading with a doctor that she was 11 years old, she was released and taken to the Lenzing camp, where she would ultimately be liberated by US armed forces on May 5, 1945. 'US soldiers came running and told us…you are free, the war is over!' Six weeks after liberation, upon returning to Bratislava, she contracted typhoid fever and was hospitalized for a month. Shortly after recovering, Eva was reunited with both her mother and father. They found out they had lost 30 members of their family. In 1950, Eva and her parents immigrated to the US, where they rebuilt their life.

Eva Schneider BY Clifford Lester USA
FULLERTON, CALIFORNIA, USA, 2021

COLETTE AVITAL was born in Bucharest, Romania, in 1940. As a small child, she and her mother were forced to hide continuously from the Nazis, as one after another of her family members were being murdered. She immigrated to Israel with her family in 1950. Colette Avital first rose to prominence as a senior diplomat, serving as Israeli ambassador to Portugal, as Consul General in New York, and as deputy Foreign Ministry director in charge of Western Europe, the third most important position in the Ministry. She then turned to politics. A long-standing member of Labor, she served as a member of Knesset, and as the party's International Secretary. In 2007, she became the first-ever woman candidate for the Israeli presidency. As chair of the Center of Organizations of Holocaust Survivors in Israel, representing some 50 organizations which assist survivors, Colette Avital has said her own trauma hiding from the Germans as her family members were killed inspired her to promote Holocaust commemoration, a task she said grows in urgency every year as survivors advance in age.

Colette Avital BY Daniel Tchetchik ISRAEL
TEL AVIV, ISRAEL, 2021

Juergen Kliger was born in Lodz, Poland, in 1924. Juergen, who lives today in Berlin, has been silent for years. As a young teenager in the Lodz ghetto, Juergen was forced each morning to walk with a cart and collect bodies of Jews who had died the previous night. The more than 200,000 residents of the ghetto lived under unspeakable conditions of hard labor, overcrowding, starvation, and, for most, neither running water nor a sewer system. The overwhelming majority of ghetto residents worked in Nazi German factories and received only meager food rations. More than 20 percent of the ghetto's population died as a direct result of the harsh living conditions. The Nazis deported nearly all of the surviving ghetto residents to the Auschwitz-Birkenau extermination center in August 1944. Juergen was among them. In Auschwitz, he was tasked with removing the Nazis' victims from the gas chambers and disposing of the bodies. At the peak of Auschwitz's operations, up to 6,000 Jews a day were gassed by the Nazis.

Juergen Kliger BY John MacDougall FRANCE
BERLIN, 2021

DAVID APTOWITZER was born in 1923 in Tarnopol, Poland. He was the youngest of the seven children of Chaya and Yitzhak, a boot maker. In September 1939, David visited his sister Bronia and her husband Shmuel, who worked for the Russian railroad and arrived just before Nazi Germany invaded Poland. He found Bronia packing a suitcase and she told him, "If you want, you can join us." This is how David's life was saved: what was meant to be a trip of a few days became a five-year journey. David escaped with his sister and her family into the Soviet Union. During these five years, David worked as a laborer, then was drafted into the Russian Army and later into the Polish Army. As the Soviets began to push the Nazi Germany forces back in 1944, David stumbled upon the concentration camp at Majdanek, a place which he recalled as being 'beyond human comprehension.' Once the war ended he learned that nearly his entire family – his parents, four siblings and their families – had been killed. The only survivors were a sister, one brother and himself. He spent two years in a displaced persons camp in Germany and in 1947, he and 1,500 other war orphans sailed for Halifax, Nova Scotia, aboard a Canadian navy ship. During the voyage he met Gitta Adler, a survivor of Auschwitz. In 1951 the couple married. David was approached by Agudath Israel Congregation to audition to be its first chazzan and teacher, a position he would hold for 42 years. Cantor David Aptowitzer retired in 1994. He made aliyah to Israel with Gitta in 2013. He has 14 grandchildren and 17 great-grandchildren.

David Aptowitzer BY Tali Nachshon-Dag ISRAEL

SHORESH, ISRAEL, 2021

RABBI NISSAN MANGEL was born in 1933 in the town of Kosice, now in Slovakia. On March 16, 1944, Nazi soldiers invaded his hometown. 'We escaped to the capital of Slovakia. We crossed the border, despite the SS seeing us, and hid. There were a few thousand Jews still there and eventually, the SS found us and took us to Auschwitz. When we arrived, Dr. Josef Mengele (who performed horrible experiments on child inmates) made the Selektion of who went to the gas chamber and who went to work. They sent any child who couldn't work to die. I was 10 and obviously not capable of working. I said I was 17 since I had no chance. But 17 doesn't look like 10. I wasn't tall. Mengele burst up laughing, saying, "You don't look older than 11." Nevertheless, he sent me to work with my father. I can't explain why. He sent over a million children to the gas chambers. Why did he spare me? I cannot say. Everybody was thinking of how they could survive.' Rabbi Nissan was sent on a death march from one concentration camp to another. Those who could not keep up were shot. Nissan recalls that one shoe was too big for his foot and every single step he took caused him terrible pain until his leg was almost paralyzed. He decided that he would step out of line so that the SS would shoot him and put him out of his misery. Rabbi Nissan experienced rare acts of kindness from a guard that he believes saved his life. The guard helped him walk and gave him water. Rabbi Nissan yet again survived this march at just 10 years old. After liberation, as the sole survivor of his family, Rabbi Nissan Mangel immigrated to America and chose to live a life dedicated to the Jewish community as a scholar, author, speaker and philosopher of Judaism. Holding up his arm with his identification number, he said, 'I consider this tattoo a badge of honor.'

Rabbi Nissan Mangel BY **Marko Dashev** USA
BROOKLYN, NEW YORK, USA, 2021

Leon Weintraub was born in Poland in 1926, the fifth child of an impoverished Jewish family from Lodz. His father died the next year, and Leon was raised by his mother and four sisters. At the age of 13, Leon witnessed the Nazi invasion and occupation of Poland. His family was forced into the Lodz Ghetto, the second-largest ghetto in occupied Europe. Lack of running water, hard labor, and starvation were the dominant features of life. In 1942, when Nazis began deportations to death camps, Leon's family went into hiding. They were rounded up in 1944 and deported to Auschwitz. Upon arrival, at the first Selektion, Leon was separated from his mother and sisters. To escape death, he managed to strip off his prisoners' clothes and blend in with a group of naked prisoners who had just received their tattoos. Several weeks later, he escaped Auschwitz by joining a group of inmates assigned to the Gross-Rosen concentration camp. He later learned that all the other boys from his block in Auschwitz had been killed in the gas chambers. In February 1944, he was transferred to Flossenbürg, and the next month, to Natzweiler-Struthof. When the French army came closer, the SS guards forced the prisoners on a death march. Leon and other inmates escaped the SS guards, and after walking all night, the group reached Donaueschingen on April 23, 1945, two days after the French had occupied the city. His weight was down to 35 kilos and he suffered from typhus. He was hospitalized in a French military hospital, where he learned that his mother and one sister had been killed in Auschwitz, but three sisters had survived the Bergen-Belsen camp. Leon went on to study medicine and became a physician, earning his degree in 1966. In 1969, he emigrated to Sweden, wanting to live in a neutral country in order to avoid more wars. Leon serves in Sweden as a witness and oral historian of the Holocaust, giving lectures in Germany and Poland to scholars and students. He is the recipient of the Order of Merit of the Federal Republic of Germany.

Dr. Leon Weintraub by Jonathan Nackstrand SWEDEN/ISRAEL
STOCKHOLM, 2021

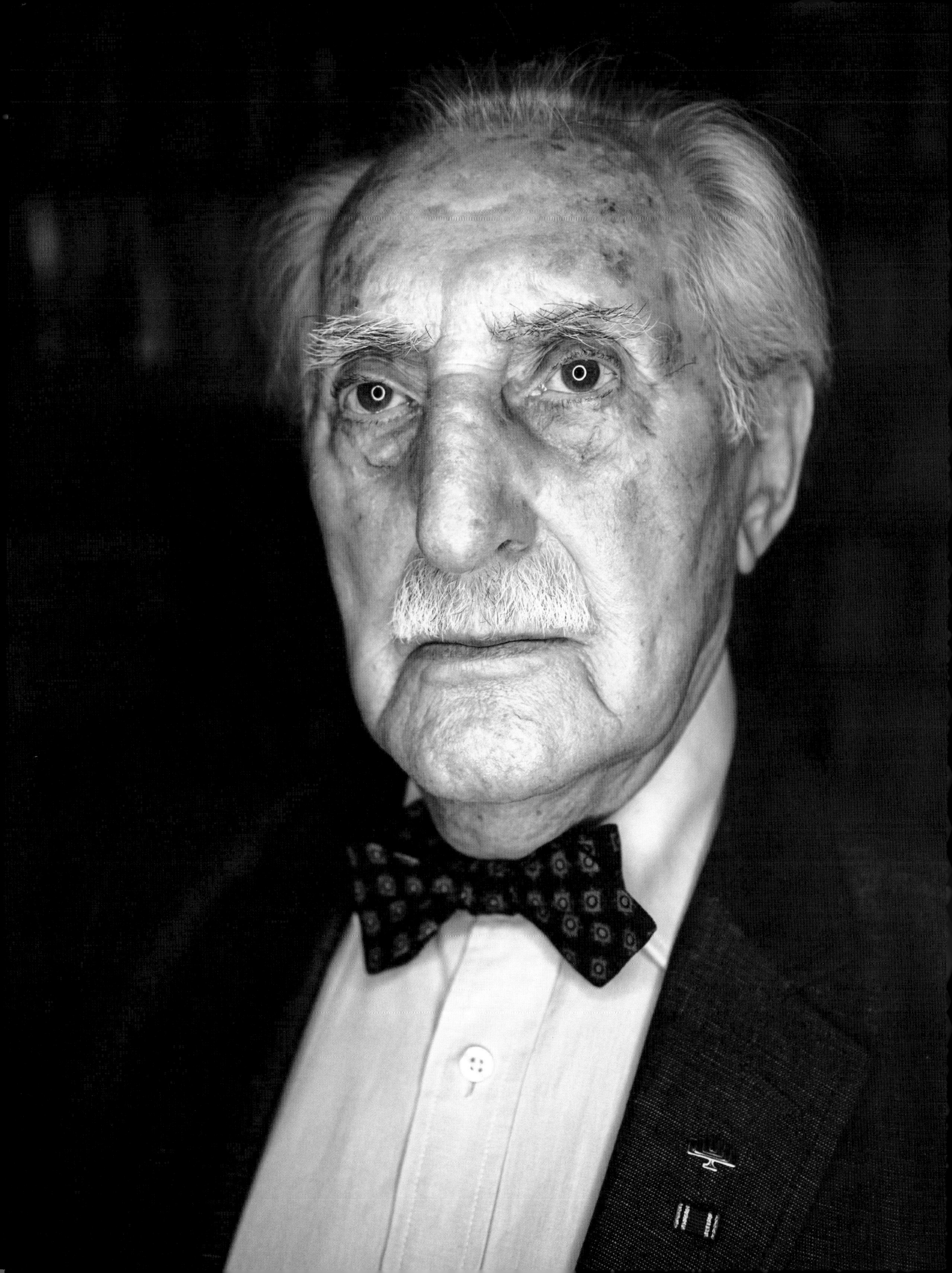

Ida Spektor BY James Hill GREAT BRITAIN
MOSCOW, 2019

IDA SPEKTOR was born in 1932 in Tulchyn, in today's Ukraine. In 1941, after Nazi Germany invaded the USSR, Ida's father was drafted into the Red Army and killed at the front. In 1941, Romanian authorities who sided with Nazi Germany forced all of Tulchyn's Jews into a ghetto where the malnourished inhabitants suffered from severe overcrowding and typhus. Three thousand Jews were herded into the Pechora concentration camp, and Ida remembers the horrors there. She was eight years old at the time. She can still hear the victims' screams and mostly the cane that a certain Smetanovsky, a member of the camp's auxiliary police, used to beat her till she would faint. The worst came in 1943 with the mass executions. Ida's mother was shot alongside hundreds of others. Ida recalls the carts loaded with the corpses. The Soviets arrived at Pechora in March 1944, but the camp's survivors did not believe they were liberated and a Jewish Red Army soldier had to address the camp's survivors in Yiddish that their ordeal was over. After the war Ida ended up at an orphanage. Her immediate family perished, except one uncle who took her to Moscow, but in 1947 he was arrested as "an enemy of the people." Ida,15 and on her own, worked at a factory and studied to become a psychiatrist. Ida worked as a hospital nurse for 40 years. Ida started her own family and says she 'loves life no matter what.' Ida takes part in commemorations for Vinnitsa Jews in Moscow, where survivors celebrate life with music and dancing and share their stories.

Ida Spektor BY Maria Gruzdeva RUSSIA
MOSCOW, 2021

ABRAHAM FOXMAN was born on May 1, 1940, in Baranovichi, Belarus. 'My parents decided to move east, hoping that they could outrun advancing Nazi Germany troops.' As his parents fled, 'The Germans caught up with us in Vilnius, the capital of Lithuania.' When his parents were ordered into a ghetto, his nanny, Bronislawa Kurpi, a Catholic woman, agreed to take the one-year-old Abraham into her home. His parents thought it would be for a few months. 'They could never explain to me how they made that decision, for parents to be separated from their own child. It was a horrendous decision that saved my life, and it saved their lives because, separately, they were able to fend for themselves.' Months stretched into years and Abraham was raised as a Catholic in the city of Vilna. Abraham was given a non-Jewish name, Henryk Stanislaw Kurpi, and was baptized a Catholic. In early childhood, he learned the rites and rituals of the Roman Catholic faith. He wore a crucifix and was taught to make the sign of the cross at church and to hold priests and Catholic clergy in high esteem. At war's end, Abraham's parents, who both survived the Holocaust, came looking for their son, then six years old. But by then, the nanny loved him as her own child and was unwilling to give him up. 'My nanny said I belonged to her and to the Catholic Church.' Eventually, his parents won a bitter custody battle and Abraham was returned to them. 'My parents asked my nanny to become part of our family since we lost all the rest of it, to be my grandmother. But she just couldn't take that. It was a tragedy of love.' For a period of time, Abraham was attending the Jewish synagogue with his father on Saturdays and the Catholic Church on Sundays. 'I know my parents remained in contact with her, supporting her as much as they could, but I never saw my nanny again. She died in the 1950s.' Abraham says he owes his life to the courage of his nanny, Bronislawa Kurpi. He and his parents lived four years in a displaced persons camp in Austria before immigrating to the US. Abraham was 10 years old when they arrived in New York City. He went on to receive a law degree and later joined and led the Anti-Defamation League, fighting antisemitism for 50 years. For his service, Abraham was awarded numerous honors and awards, among them, France's highest civilian honor as Knight of the Legion of Honor, the Raoul Wallenberg Humanitarian Leadership Award, and the Interfaith Committee of Remembrance Lifetime Achievement Award. In 2016, he became vice chairman of the board of trustees at the Museum of Jewish Heritage in New York City.

Abraham Foxman BY Harvey Stein USA
NEW YORK CITY, NEW YORK, USA, 2021

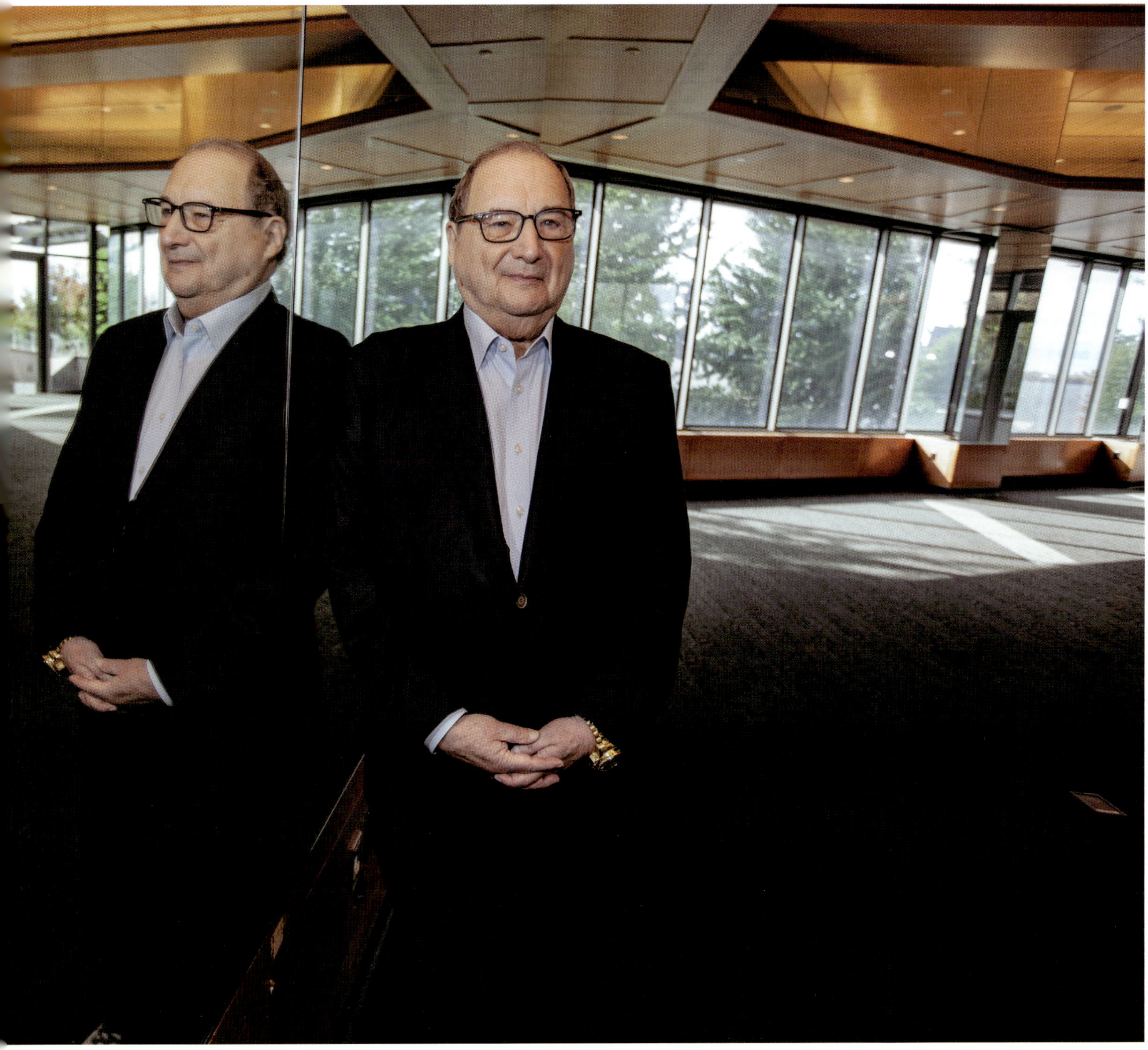

YESHAYAHU FOYER was born in Galicia to a Polish family in 1933. During the early years of World War II, Jews fell victim to violence from all the sides then fighting in Galicia. The peak of the massacres took place in July and August 1943. Most of the victims were women and children. The members of Yeshayahu's family parted ways when they went into hiding. Yeshayahu would never learn their fate. At age eight or nine he hid in the woods, all alone. Each time the Nazis approached, he would move from one hiding place to another. After not eating for a few days, he went to see Poles who knew him. They gave him a whole loaf of bread and sent him out, on his way. To this day he always makes sure he has a whole loaf of bread at home. Later, he joined partisans in the forest. He was a child on his own, and he was sent on missions to the enemy's rear. On one of the missions, he was spotted and eventually captured and questioned about Jewish partisans in the forest. He lied and said he knew nothing. 'At first they treated me rather nicely,' he recalls, 'then they started torturing me.' In a moment of resourcefulness he escaped. 'I wanted to return to the bunker and realized I was lost. All the trees looked the same. I was afraid.' A partisan in the bunker rescued the boy. Toward the end of the war, some of his comrades were killed in exchanges of shelling. At war's end, he was taken to a Jewish orphanage. He arrived in Israel alone in 1948. 'I never told anything; in the early years they also did not want to hear. Here they wanted us to be heroes with a boob hat and shorts,' says Yeshayahu. He studied at the Hebron Yeshiva, but left to enlist in the Golani Brigade. When his partisan colleagues arrived in Israel, they asked him to join them in Ashkelon. 'I had nowhere to go, we were together in the forest, we would continue to be together in Ashkelon.' Ever since, Yeshayahu has lived in Ashkelon, a city frequently targeted by rockets fired from Gaza. A widower and the head of a large family he created with his late wife Dina, whom he met on an Ashkelon beach, Yeshayahu has been active in sharing his story with city youth. For the past six years, students from the ORT Ronson School in the city have been visiting his home.

Yeshayahu Foyer BY Eli Basri ISRAEL
ASHKELON, ISRAEL, 2021

JACQUES WEIMANN was born in Antwerp, Belgium, in 1939. 'I was born in my parents' home at Provinciestraat 199, where they also owned a shoe store.' In 1940–41, the Belgian political and administrative elite accepted Nazi Germany's laws in a political climate tinged with xenophobia and antisemitism, and the first anti-Jewish ordinances were decreed. Ninety percent of the Jewish community in Belgium was made up of foreigners, and the Belgian system "sacrificed" that community. From December 1940 to June 1942 in then-occupied Belgium, anti-Jewish persecutions were carried out. Jews were rounded up and sent to forced labor, organized by the National Labor Office and by Belgium's municipal administrations, who provided the data to the Nazis from their registrations of Jews and foreigners. The Antwerp police accompanied the detained Jews until their departure in convoys to northern France. Jacques's father, Herman, was forced into hard labor at the Judenlager in Les Mazures, a small village near Charleville Mézières. 'Of the 288 Jews who were deported from Antwerp to forced labor, 237 of them, including my father, died in the Nazi extermination camps. My sister Dina and I were hidden with Belgian farmers, thanks to a Jewish-Christian resistance network. At first, I was placed in Liege, in a foster family that my mother paid to look after me. She quickly noticed that I had become stunted and could no longer stand on my own two feet because they didn't feed me properly. She took me away and I was placed with another family, where she had to take me away again just as quickly, because their 18-year-old nephew had gone to denounce me to the Germans to obtain a bonus of 500 Belgian francs. Malnourished children from the cities were sent to farmers' homes and the Judeo-Christian resistance network managed to include Jewish children. I was one of them. The resistance network intervened once again and I was hidden with the Flemish family of farmers named Meersters in Bilzen. I have remained in contact with this family of Righteous Among the Nations to this day.'

Jacques Weimann BY Olivier Fitoussi ISRAEL

JERUSALEM, 2021

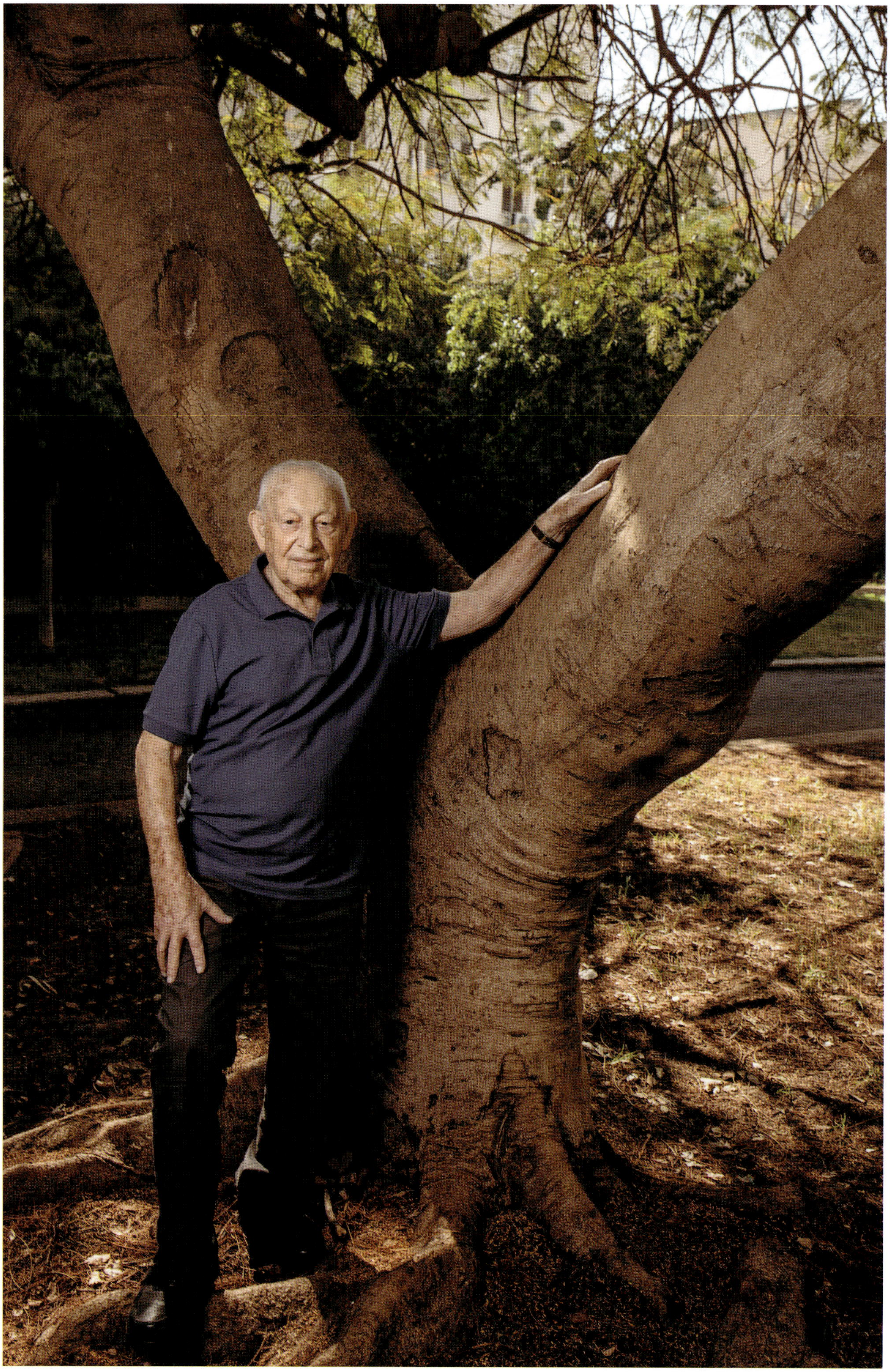

AVRAHAM AVIEL (LIPKONSKY) was born in 1929 in Dowgalishok, Poland. The Radom Ghetto was set up by Nazis in March 1941, and in 1942, the ghetto was surrounded by Nazi troops for liquidation. Jews were rounded up to dig death pits in a nearby forest. Avraham's father managed to escape, but his brother Pinchas was forced to dig mass graves. Avraham, his mother Mina and his younger brother Yekutiel were marched to the town square, and from there, with the Jews of the Radom Ghetto, to the pits of death. Avraham remembers his mother's last words, 'Children, say "Shema Yisrael" – we die as Jews.' Avraham, 14, witnessed families lined up and led to the open pits. He witnessed their executions, and their bodies falling into the open pits. Amid the horror, screams and shooting, Avraham jumped over the heads of the people, running with all his might towards his brother Pinchas, at the end of the line, and the two boys escaped into the forest. Their mother and younger brother Yekutiel-Kushke were murdered along with the Jews of the ghetto. Later, the brothers joined the partisans in the area. They were ambushed by Nazis, and Avraham watched as Pinchas was shot and killed. Again, Avraham ran and hid with a small group of partisans. When the snow melted, they were able to join some 100 people, including children, hiding in the forest. Avraham learned that his father had been murdered. He also learned to shoot, and fought the Nazis. In 1943, the Nazis surrounded the forest and shot dead most of the families living there in hiding. Avraham and the partisans fought until July 12, 1944, the day the area was liberated by the Red Army. At the end of the war in May 1945, Avraham, together with other Jewish orphans, boarded the ship *Katriel Yaffe* headed for Mandatory Palestine. The ship was captured by British soldiers, and all passengers were exiled to a detention camp in Cyprus. When Avraham was released, he joined the Sixth Battalion of the Palmach and fought for Jerusalem, then under siege. At the Eichmann trial in 1961, he appeared as a witness for the prosecution and recounted the massacre of the Radom Jews. Avraham is an author of numerous books about the Holocaust.

Avraham Aviel (Lipkonsky) BY Tomer Appelbaum ISRAEL
TEL AVIV, ISRAEL, 2020

Niusia Horowitz-Karakulska was born in Krakow, Poland, in 1932. Following the Nazi invasion, Niusia was nine when she and her parents Regina and Dolek and her toddler brother Ryszard were taken into the walled Krakow Ghetto and later to the Płaszów concentration camp. 'I was 11 years old when I saw the first execution – we were entering the camp, and the Nazis were hanging a man. It turned out later that it was my relative.' In Płaszów, she was employed in the enamel factory run by Oskar Schindler, a German industrialist and a member of the Nazi Party, who saved the lives of 1,200 Jews by employing them in his enamelware and ammunitions factories. Niusia was his youngest girl worker. When the Red Army approached Poland in 1944, Schindler transferred his factory and his Jewish workers to Brněnec, now in the Czech Republic. On the way to Brněnec, Niusia was trapped and imprisoned in the Auschwitz death camp. She was twice hand-picked for the gas chamber, and both times cheated death at the last minute. 'It was a place without God. If God had existed, he would not have allowed Auschwitz to happen. People went insane out of fear and hunger. There was no empathy; no one felt sorry for anyone. Everyone just tried to survive.' It was Schindler himself who saved her next. He appeared at the camp after seven weeks to demand back the women whose lives he had bought as workers. Thanks to Schindler, both her parents and her brother also survived the war. After the war, Niusia became a beautician. In the 1990s, she was a consultant on the Oscar-awarded Steven Spielberg film *Schindler's List*. She lives in Krakow to this day, and keeps in close contact with her brother, Ryszard Horowitz (page 246), in New York City.

Niusia Horowitz-Karakulska BY Grzegorz Litynski POLAND
KRAKÓW, POLAND, 2021

IRENA DANKA LUSTIGER was born in the Warsaw Ghetto in 1940, the only child of Stanislaw and Romana Rubinski. In 1942, two-year-old Danka was smuggled out of the ghetto, and until 1943 she was hidden by a Polish caregiver. Her father managed to leave the ghetto and lived under a false identity. In 1944, Danka was returned to her mother, and her parents were deported from Warsaw to Krakow, later fleeing to the village of Oitzow. In May 1945, the area was liberated by the Soviet army and the family survived. At the end of the war they moved to Lodz. In 1957, they sailed to Israel on the ship *Theodor Herzl*. In 1961, she married Iz'o Lustiger, a cousin of the Cardinal Jean-Marie Lustier, who served for 24 years as Archbishop of Paris. Danka, a widow, has a son, Danny, and four grandchildren.

Irena Danka Lustiger BY Mika Gurovich ISRAEL
TEL AVIV, ISRAEL, 2021

GIZELLA SCHÖNER MAN was born in 1929 in the small town of Csenger in Hungary, the fifth of seven children of a shoemaker. In 1944, under occupation by Nazi Germany, all 600 of Csenger's Jews were forced to the ghetto of Mátészalka. Six weeks later, after Hungarian Gendarmes performed humiliating gynecological examinations on each woman – including Gizella at age 14 – searching for internally hidden valuables, all the 600 were deported to the Auschwitz death camp. From Auschwitz, Gizella was transported to forced labor in Horneburg, Germany, where she worked in a factory. In the spring of 1945, the Nazis loaded all the female workers onto trains, and transported them from one location to another for hard physical work. In April 1945, a Wehrmacht soldier told them, "Hitler kaput," but they only believed the war was over when the Red Cross delivered a bowl of soup to each of them. The Red Cross sent Gizella to Sweden to recover. She sent a letter to her former neighbor in Csenger, and received a response from her sister, Rózsi, that five of their seven siblings had survived the war. Her parents and grandparents, her older sister's baby and Gizella's two youngest siblings had perished. In the spring of 1948, Gizella moved to Budapest, where she met her future husband, Joel Man. In 1948, they arrived in Israel, which had just declared statehood. The couple immigrated to the United States with their two sons in 1964. Her husband passed away at a young age, and years later Gizella married David Horovitz. After being widowed for the second time, Gizella established her permanent home in Israel. Gizella began leading organized tours to Auschwitz, and she often speaks to young Israelis about the Holocaust.

Gizella Schöner Man BY Bea Bar Kallos ISRAEL/HUNGARY
MEVASERET ZION, ISRAEL, 2021

HANA KANTOR was born in Strzemieszyce, Poland, in 1926, but the exact date is unknown. One of eleven siblings, Hana was a teenager when Nazi Germany invaded Strzemieszyce on September 3, 1939. In 1940, an "open" ghetto was established in the town, and Jews were sent each day to forced labor in the area. Beginning in December 1940, the Jews were required to be identified by wearing a badge. In 1942, 1,800 Jews lived in the ghetto. Several hundred were deported to the Auschwitz extermination camp. On June 15, 1943, the SS executed 43 elderly Jews, some of them ailing, in addition to scores of children who were unable to report for deportation. Hana recalls her baby nephew and niece, whom she last saw when they were hidden in a chicken coop. They are believed to have been among the babies executed that day. Hana saved her sister by convincing the SS that they both were fit for hard labor. Hana survived a string of forced labor camps. Most of her family perished. She was liberated by Russian forces. Years later she learned the terrible fate of three of her brothers, who died in a barn set on fire by Nazis. When the war ended, she met and married Anschel Kantor. After time spent in displaced persons camps, the couple arrived in New York City in 1949. They created a family, four children, 12 grandchildren, 12 great-grandchildren – and still counting.

Hana Kantor BY Joyce Ravid USA
FOREST HILLS, NEW YORK, USA, 2021

ANDRZEJ (ANDREW) STEFANSKI was born in Poland in 1926. He was a teenager when Nazi Germany invaded Poland on September 1, 1939, and the Soviet invasion began on September 17. He remembers bombings around the city, and his school class growing smaller each day. Nazi Germany suppressed the Poles by murdering thousands of civilians, establishing massive forced labor roundups, and relocating hundreds of thousands. Teachers, priests, and other intellectuals were executed in mass killings. At the same time, Poles suffered from Soviet suppressors as well. The Nazis sent thousands to the Auschwitz extermination camp, to Stutthof, and to other concentration camps in Germany, where non-Jewish Poles constituted the majority of inmates until March 1942. Nazi officials imposed on Poles a labor obligation, which came to include children as young as 12. Police grabbed Poles off streets and trains, and from marketplaces and churches, as raids were set in motion to fill labor quotas. A year after the spring 1943 uprising by the Jews of the Warsaw Ghetto, Andrzej, then 19, took part in an uprising by Poles in Warsaw against the Nazis. Andrzej guided soldiers through the trenches. After the uprising was crushed on October 2, 1944, Nazis captured Andrzej, and he was deported as a slave laborer to Magdeburg, Germany. The Nazis left Andrzej and other prisoners, including a group of Russian soldiers, on a frigid train covered in ice. 'I was completely frozen,' he said, but 'somehow I survived.' Andrzej recalls Russian soldiers being thrown off the train by the Nazis. They had frozen to death. Andrzej was forced to work long days, mainly digging. The Nazis murdered over two million non-Jewish Polish civilians and at least three million Jewish citizens of Poland. The number of Poles who died as a result of Soviet repression in the period 1939–1941 is estimated in the tens of thousands. In April 1945, American troops liberated Magdeburg. After World War II, Andrzej worked as an engineer. In 1958, he arrived in the United States, where he rebuilt his life, created a family, and became a real estate agent. Only in 1961 could Andrzej, now known as Andrew, return home and see his mother, from whom he had been separated for 15 years, due to Soviet control over Poland.

Andrew Stefanski BY Madeleine "Maddie" Hordinski USA
LOS ANGELES, CALIFORNIA, USA, 2021

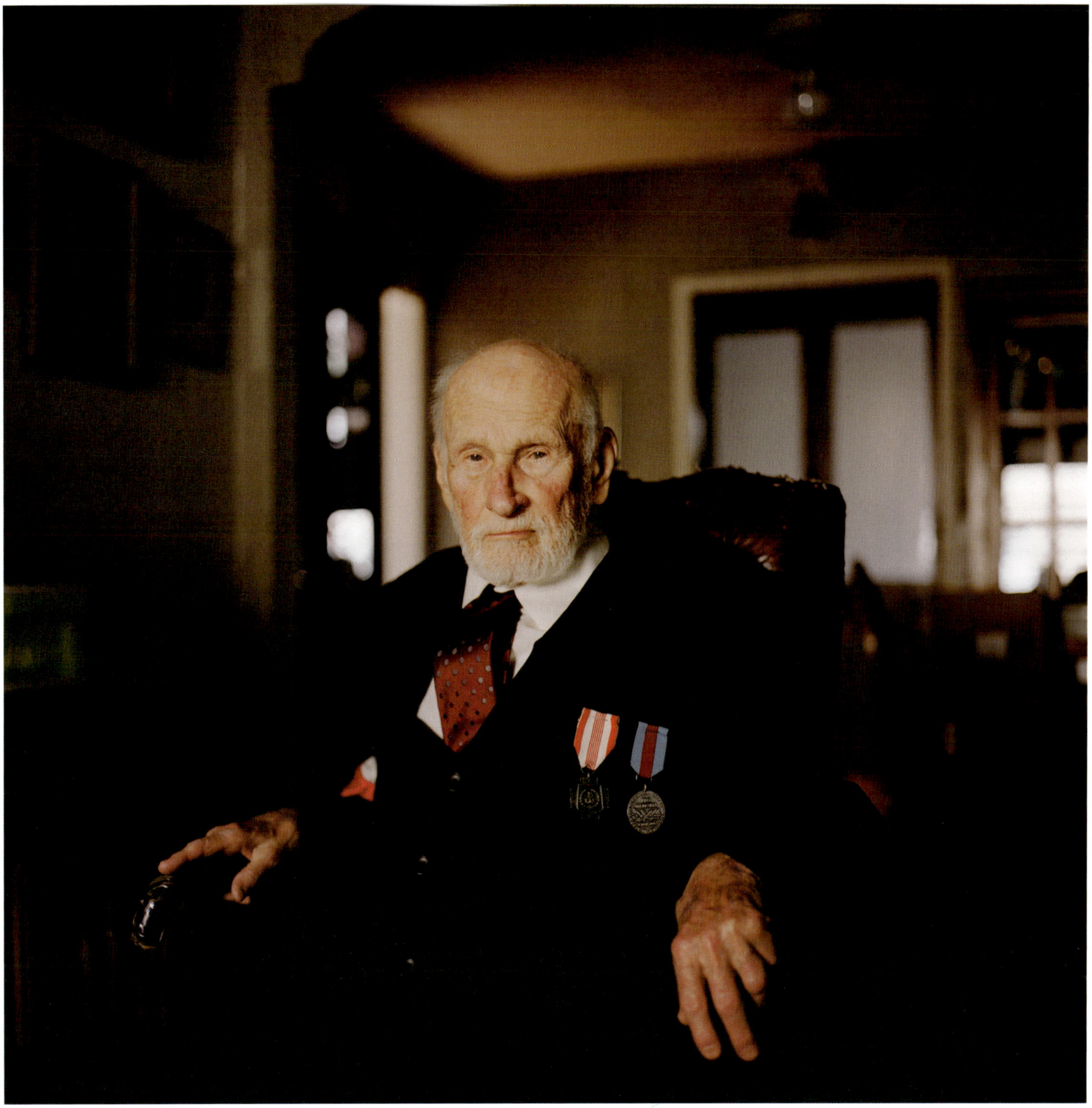

PETER BACHRACH was born in Bielsko, Poland, in 1927, and ESTHER LAVON in Mikulas, Slovakia, in 1926. The two fell in love as teenagers in Mikulas, where Peter and his older brother Hans found a temporary refuge after their father was killed by the Nazis. To save her sons, their mother sent them away, across the snowy mountainous border to Slovakia on December 24, 1939, to join Gordonia, a Zionist youth movement. Their mother believed that with the help of Gordonia, her sons would immigrate to Mandatory Palestine. On March 1, 1942, Hans was arrested and shipped on a transport to a death camp. Peter and Esther's teenagers' love came to an abrupt end when Peter was forced to flee from Mikulas. He was caught and was crammed in the last car of a train to an extermination camp in Poland, along with hundreds of elderly people. Peter threw himself off the car, to the cries of the elderly. Bruised, he fled to the mountains and later joined the partisans. Revenge became his motive to live. Twice wounded, he became one of the youngest guerrilla fighters to fight against Nazi Germany in Slovakia. Esther believed Peter would never return. When the war ended, Peter weighed 28 kilos. After recovering, he went to look for his loved ones. His entire family had perished. He went on to search for Esther, but discovered she was in a relationship with another man. She had survived the war with partisans, elsewhere in the Slovakian mountains. Peter was drafted into the Palmach pre-state underground, boarded an illegal ship to Mandatory Palestine, and was sent directly to fight in the Harel Brigade, where a third of the fighters were Holocaust survivors and battle orders were given in Yiddish. Esther immigrated to Israel in 1950 with her husband, and the couple had two sons. Peter and Esther would not meet again for years. Peter went on to become a Lieutenant Colonel in the reserves, married the women he loved, and fathered three sons. He divorced three times. His last active duty was in the First Lebanon War in the summer of 1982, into which he was drafted with two of his sons. Peter's son Doron, a paratrooper, was killed in Lebanon. Years went by, Esther was widowed, as was Peter from his fourth wife. At age 93, 'a miracle happened to us,' say Peter and Esther. The two, who had lived a parallel life for 80 years, found each other and renewed their love that had 'never stopped.' Peter is determined not to let the love of his life slip away from him this time, saying 'at my age, there is no time to waste.'

Peter Bachrach & Esther Lavon BY Rina Castelnuovo ISRAEL
KFAR SABA, ISRAEL, 2021

SELMA VAN DE PERRE was born in 1922 in Amsterdam, the Netherlands. Selma had two older brothers, David and Louis, and a younger sister, Clara. Her eldest brother sailed with the Dutch Steamboat Company during the war, while her youngest brother lived in England. In 1942, her father was arrested and taken to Westerbork concentration camp. Selma helped her mother and sister go into hiding in Eindhoven. She took on an assumed identity, dyed her hair blond, and joined the Dutch Resistance movement, using the pseudonym Marga van der Kuit. For two years "Marga" risked it all. Using a fake ID, she passed as a non-Jew, traveling around the country and even to the Nazi headquarters in Paris, sharing information and delivering papers. 'Although many people worked in the resistance, and many non-Jews lost their lives because they were hiding Jews, many other Christians betrayed Jews or resistance fighters in hiding just for money. They got seven guilders for every Jewish person they betrayed,' Selma explained.

In June 1944, she was betrayed. Selma was arrested as a political prisoner but her Jewish identity remained unknown, and she was sent to Ravensbrück. On April 23, 1945, Selma was liberated in Ravensbrück and, via the Swedish Red Cross, was taken to Gothenburg. Once there, she revealed that her name was not Marga, but Selma. Upon her return to the Netherlands, Selma learned that her father, mother and sister had been murdered in Auschwitz and Sobibor. Selma moved to the UK in 1945, at the behest of the Dutch Ministry of War. She met her husband, the journalist Hugo van de Perre, while working at the BBC. She later became a teacher. In 1983, Selma was awarded the Resistance Memorial Cross in the Netherlands, and the Order of Orange-Nassau by the Dutch government. Her book was published in the Netherlands in 2020 under the title *Mijn naam is Selma*, or *My Name Is Selma*. Selma turned 100 on June 7, 2022.

Selma van de Perre BY Roger Cremers THE NETHERLANDS
AMSTERDAM, 2021

SEATED FROM L TO R: ELIEZER SHIMONI, MEIR KEIZER, PNINA BERKOWITCH, MAGADI UNGAR.
STANDING FROM L TO R: YESHAYAHU DEUTSCH, ISRAEL GOLDBERGER, DAVID (DUGO) LEITNER, ELIEZER & SARA SHEFER.

SEATED FROM L TO R:

ELIEZER SHIMONI was born in Feldebro, Hungary, in 1928. In 1944, after having lived in the ghetto, he was deported to the Auschwitz-Birkenau extermination camp. Three days later he was moved to the main Auschwitz camp, and from there to the Beaver-Monowitz forced labor compound, also known as Auschwitz III. He was later sent on a death march to Gleiwitz. In January 1945, he arrived in Buchenwald, where after several months he was liberated. He immigrated to Mandatory Palestine in 1947, after spending ten months in a detention camp on Cyprus. His parents and five siblings all perished.

MEIR KAISER was born in Netherlands in 1929. In 1935, the family moved to the city of Utrecht. When Germany attacked the Netherlands in 1940, Meir's father was taken to a labor camp, and later was murdered in Auschwitz. In order to evade the searches being carried out, the family wandered between different hiding places for years, until their liberation at the end of 1944. Meir immigrated to Israel at age 20.

PNINA BERKOWITCH was born in Romania in 1930. After the conquest of Romania by the Russians, Pnina was given a fictitious name, so as not to be taken back to Ukraine. Pnina arrived in Israel on the ship *Transylvania*. She enlisted in the army and served as a kosher supervisor for in the 13th Battalion of the Golani Brigade.

MAGADI UNGER was born in Hungary in 1928. 'June 1944, we reached Auschwitz camp. I was 16, accompanying my little sister and my mother. SS guards were screaming to us to hurry, my mother was worried about my grandfather and father in another freight wagon and asked me to try to find them. I couldn't and returned, but my mom and sister were gone. An SS soldier sent them directly to where nobody was able to return from, they were directed to the gas chambers. I never said goodbye, not a last smile or hug, my mom and sister just vanished. I was all by myself in concentration camps, dreaming that maybe my father survived and one day we will meet again.' At the end of the war Magadi learned that none of her family survived. In 1948, Magadi immigrated to Israel.

STANDING FROM L TO R:

YESHAYAHU DEUTSCH was born in 1927 in Hungary. After the Nazi German invasion, Yeshayahu was separated from his family and transferred to Warsaw, forced to work clearing the ruins of the ghetto after the uprising. He was ordered on a death march from Warsaw to Dachau, and later to a labor camp set up in Kaufering. He was sent yet again on a death march, this time to Allach, near Dachau, where he was released by American troops. He sailed from Marseilles on the ship *Theodor Herzl* headed for Mandatory Palestine, but the ship was diverted by British authorities to Cyprus. In Cyprus, Yeshayahu was in detention camp number 65 before arriving in Israel.

ISRAEL GOLDBERGER (Story opposite)

DAVID DUGO LEITNER was born in Hungary in 1930. After Nazi Germany invaded Hungary, local Nazi gendarmes rounded up the Jews, forcing them into the ghetto. After six weeks, most were transported by freight cars to Auschwitz-Birkenau. David was separated from his mother and two sisters, who were sent to extermination. His father and brother were sent to Buchenwald and from there to Bergen-Belsen. During one of the Selektions, David was chosen for extermination, and he marched with hundreds of children to the crematorium. 'The children shouted all the way, "Shema Yisrael." They were stripped of their clothes, but suddenly it stopped.' Fifty-one children including David were chosen to unload potatoes from trucks, and his life was saved. In January 1945, David was sent by transport to Mauthausen. In April, David and many thousands were on a death march to Gunskirchen. After liberation, David found his brother, the only other member of his family to survive. In 1949, David and his brother arrived in Israel. He was drafted while still on the ship and went straight into his service in the IDF. David Dugo Leitner passed away in July 2023.

ELIEZER SHEFER was born in Hungary in 1924. In May 1944, Eliezer was deported to the Sachin Ghetto. Eliezer managed to escape but found no place to hide. He turned himself in to the police and was sent into a labor camp. He was forced on a death march to the Mauthausen camp. On the way, Eliezer's leg was wounded in bombings. He was hospitalized, managing to hide his identity until the end of the war. In November 1945, five months after the end of the war, Eliezer decided to flee the hospital. He discovered that his father and sister had survived the war. Eliezer arrived in Cyprus and was held in British detention camps number 55, 60 and 61. After an 11-month stay in Cyprus, he arrived in Israel.

SARA SHEFER was born in Hungary in 1936. In 1944, her father was taken for forced labor and never seen again. Sara and her twin sister Leah were shipped to Auschwitz along with their mother. On the first Selektion, the twins were taken by Dr. Mengele for medical experiments and their mother was sent to the gas chambers. All their family perished. In 1947, the orphaned twins arrived in Mandatory Palestine.

Israel Goldberger was born in 1922 in the Romanian town of Satu Mara – in Yiddish, Satmar. Israel was five when his mother died, the seventh of eight children. Israel's family belonged to the Satmar Hasidic group in the town, where 17,000 Jews were living on the eve of World War II. As a child, Israel, called Srulik, became a singer. As he grew older, his voice now a tenor-baritone, he was sent to study with the chief cantor of Satmar. But his studies were cut short, he recalls, as 'a little later the war broke out.' In 1940, the Nazi regime transferred Satmar, part of Transylvania, to Hungarian rule. In March 1944, the Nazis entered Hungary, and the Nazi efforts to murder the Jews of Satmar were rapid. In April 1944, the Jews were concentrated in the ghetto, and within two weeks, beginning on May 20, they were sent to Auschwitz in six transports. 'Dad and his second wife were on the first shipment. Dad kissed me and we said goodbye. We did not think it was the last time, but it was, and I never saw him again. My aunt, my second mother, was the first to go to the gas chambers in Auschwitz, hand in hand with my little sister.' Srulik was drafted into forced labor and sent to Ukraine, and from there to Budapest, Hungary, where he was captured and taken on a train to the Bergen-Belsen concentration camp in Germany. 'The task of the survivors was to get the dead out of the barracks, to lay them by the door until they were taken in a cart and burned in pits. The cart turned back and forth all day long, and you see hands here, feet there… I also worked in burial. I got the little bread of the dead that I threw in the pit. We did everything we could to put something in our mouths.' Srulik continued to walk around the camp and sing. 'Thanks to the cantorship, I survived, ate grass and sang.' With neglect, starvation, disease, and exhaustion rampant, Bergen-Belsen became a death camp. The prisoners were given one slice of bread a day, until even that scant ration stopped. Srulik does not remember a moment when his voice fell silent, even in the face of the most difficult of sights. After seven months in Bergen-Belsen, he was taken by train to the Theresienstadt concentration camp in the Czech Republic. 'Americans bombed the carriages, and many people were killed. My miracle was that I jumped into a pit in the woods. When I got up, everyone around me was dead.' After a month in Theresienstadt, he was freed but ill with typhus, and was brought to a hospital established by the Russians. 'After I recovered, I discovered only one brother and sister survived besides two brothers who lived in Israel before the war. We immigrated to Mandatory Palestine.' In young Israel, he enlisted in the IDF's Carmeli Battalion, married and created a family. In 1953, they joined Moshav Nir Galim, where he has been the cantor ever since.

Israel Goldberger by Seffi Magriso ISRAEL
MOSHAV NIR GALIM, ISRAEL, 2021

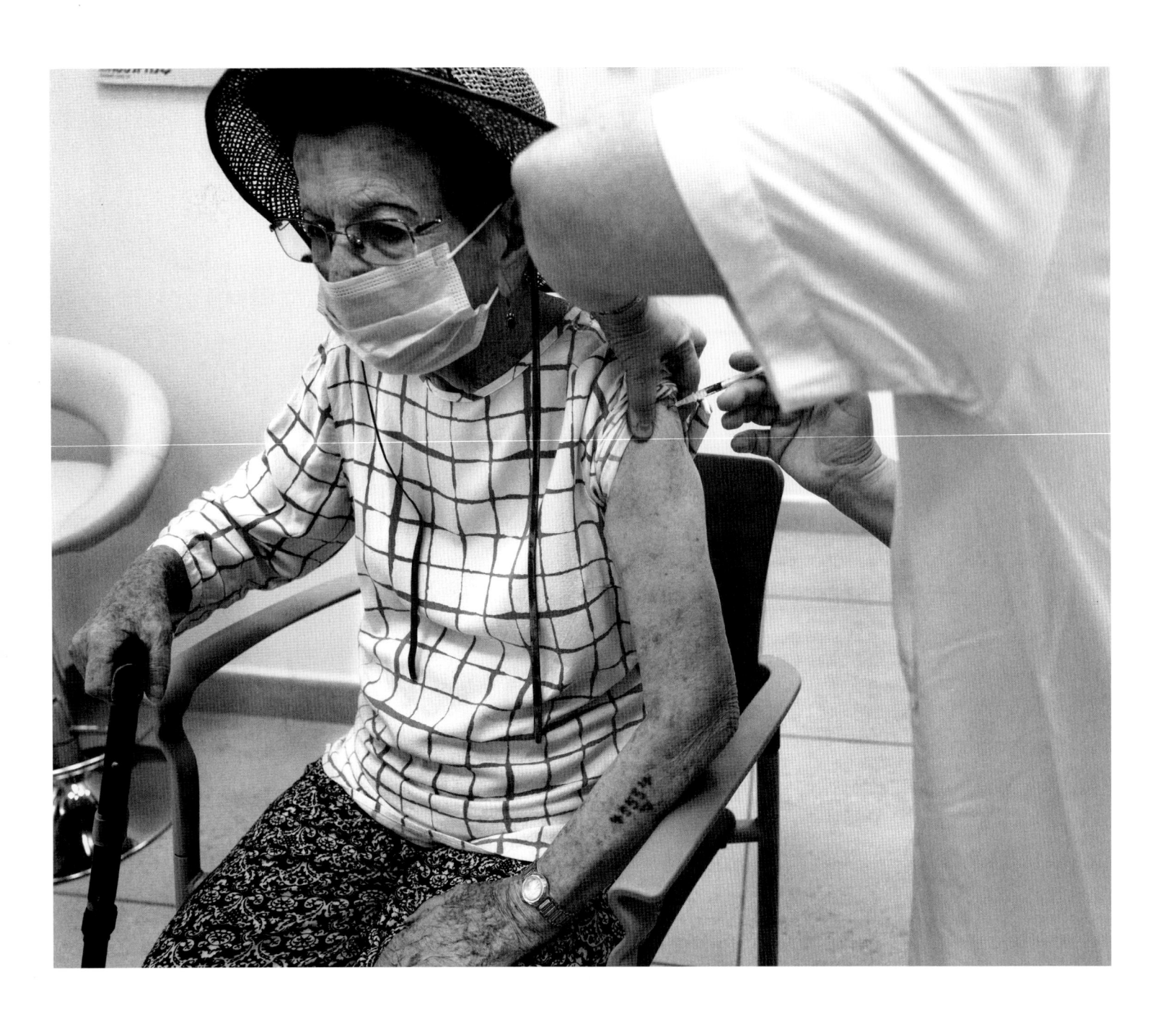

Bat-Sheva Dagan BY **Jim Hollander** USA
HOLON, ISRAEL, 2021

The lockdown and social distancing during the COVID-19 pandemic prompted isolation for many of the elderly, and for Holocaust survivors, has been a throwback to traumas of the past. Bat-Sheva Iza Dagan, 95, who initially did not wish to postpone her scheduled portrait session, asked the photographer to return another day. Batsheva was born in Poland in 1925. She was deported to Auschwitz and is the sole survivor of a large family.

BAT-SHEVA IZA DAGAN was born in Lodz, Poland, in 1925. In 1940, two ghettos were set up in the city of Radom, and she and her family were held in the "large ghetto," where Bat-Sheva became a member of the clandestine Hashomer Hatzair Jewish youth group. She was sent with Aryan papers to the Warsaw Ghetto to obtain a copy of the movement's underground newspaper *Pod Prąd* (*Against the Current*) from Mordechai Anielewicz, and bring it back to Radom. During the liquidation of the "large ghetto" in August 1942, Bat-Sheva's parents and older sister were deported and murdered in the Treblinka extermination camp. She and her younger sister, Sabina, were sent to the Radom "small ghetto." The sisters decided to try to escape. Sabina was shot and killed in the attempt. Bat-Sheva made it to Schwerin, Germany, where she used false papers to get a job as a maid in a Nazi household. After a few months she was discovered, arrested, and imprisoned. In May 1943, she was deported to the Auschwitz concentration camp and tattooed with the number 45554. In the camp she became a nurse in the prison infirmary, and herself survived typhus. Bat-Sheva later worked in the "Kanada" commando, sorting the belongings taken from camp victims on their way to the gas chambers. As the Red Army approached Auschwitz in January 1945, she was forced on a death march to the Ravensbrück and Malchow concentration camps. She survived another death march to Lübz, where she was liberated by British troops on May 2, 1945. She immigrated to Mandatory Palestine in September 1945, the only one of her siblings to survive the war. She became an author of books and poems for children and young adults on Holocaust themes.

Bat-Sheva Dagan BY Rina Castelnuovo ISRAEL
HOLON, ISRAEL, 2021

Wiktor Bodnar was born in Stanisławów, Poland, in 1937. In 1941, 42 members of his family were shot. Only his parents and his maternal grandmother survived. They were baptized and, with the help of a priest and false Aryan papers, survived the Holocaust. They moved to Krakow in 1947. Wiktor studied neurology and psychiatry at the Medical University of Krakow. He continued his professional career as a medical doctor both in Poland and Canada. He met his current wife Hana at the Jewish Community Center in Krakow. He meets regularly with a group of friends for bridge matches and Shabbat dinner. Wiktor Bodnar passed away on November 3, 2023.

Dr. Wiktor Bodnar BY Grzegorz Litynski POLAND

KRAKÓW, POLAND, 2021

ANNA JANOWSKA was born Hanna Kleinberg to a Polish Jewish family in Krakow, Poland, on May 5, 1936. She had a sister named Ewa, four years older than her. Her father Roman was a dentist and had his own practice in Rabka, a health resort about 50 kilometers south of Krakow. At the outbreak of World War II, Hanna's father was drafted into the Polish army and was later taken prisoner by the Soviets. He died of typhus in Uzbekistan in January 1942. Hanna, her mother Alicja and her sister Ewa were hiding with their grandparents until January 1940, when Hanna was evicted from her apartment with her mother and sister, and her father's dental practice was confiscated. They moved from one hiding place to another until they ended up in a ghetto. In May 1942, the two grandmothers were shot in a mass shooting in the forest. Anna's grandfather Wilhelm Kleinberg was a famous Krakow photographer. He was killed by the Nazis in 1942. Hanna, her mother and sister were on a list of Jews to be liquidated. With the help of her brother-in-law, the mother managed to entrust Hanna and Ewa to a Pole who hid them in a rural village. The mother obtained a forged identity card in the name of Maria Janowska and they lived in hiding for three years, in constant fear of being betrayed. After the war Anna Janowska, as Hanna Kleinberg was now called, studied at the Technical University in Krakow, and became the general planner of transport in Krakow. Anna Janowska-Ciońćka is widowed, has two children and five grandchildren. She lives in Krakow and is a member of the "Holocaust Children" association. Anna is photographed with a photograph of herself taken as she came out of hiding at the close of the war.

Anna Janowska BY Grzegorz Litynski POLAND

KRAKÓW, POLAND, 2021

MICHAEL SIDKO was born in 1935 in Kiev, Ukraine. He was six years old when he witnessed Nazi German troops and their Ukrainian collaborators murdering his infant bother Volodya, his baby sister Clara, and his mother. He remembers her screams while the Nazi troops kept firing. The massacre at Babi Yar lasted two days, September 29 and 30, 1941. A total of 33,771 Jews were murdered in the massacre. For 60 years, Michael kept his Jewish identity and Babi Yar a secret. 'I remember even the small details, it hurts too much,' says Michael. 'They took our documents, the jewelry. The healthy men were sent to one side, the women and children to another, the old and the young, all were sent to the pit.' The entire Jewish community of Kiev was wiped out in the massive death pit on the outskirts of the city. Michael and his older brother Grisha miraculously survived. 'When we witnessed the murder, I screamed and my brother covered me, so I wouldn't see anything, and that's how we stood until nightfall,' he says. Michael and his brother were taken by the Nazis and held in a basement. 'They took us after some time up to the second floor, and there we saw a German officer with his dog and a translator, Ivan Ivanovic, who was our neighbor. He said, "These are the children of my friend." He took us and thanks to him we survived.' The two brothers escaped death several times. Their Ukrainian neighbor Sofia Kondratieva pretended that they were her sons. 'We stayed with Sofia and her daughter as her sons, and that's how we survived until the war was over.' Sofia was later awarded the honor of Righteous Among the Nations. Michael is now the last living survivor of the massacre in the Babi Yar ravine in Kiev (Kyiv), Ukraine. Following the rise of antisemitic incidents in Ukraine, he immigrated to Israel where he broke his silence. Knesset Speaker Mickey Levy and Natan Sharansky awarded him the Knesset State Medal, commemorating the 80th anniversary of the horrific massacre.

Michael Sidko BY Nimrod Gluckman ISRAEL
BET SHEMESH, ISRAEL, 2021

BATYA SCHON was born in 1943 in Kazakhstan. Years before, as soon as Nazi Germany invaded Poland on September 1, 1939, her parents, Haim and Hana Feldheim, along with Hana's two brothers, had escaped eastward from Warsaw. They were detained by the Soviets, and together were sent in 1942 to camps in Siberia, where Hana delivered a baby boy. Eventually released, they boarded the Trans-Siberian railroad, bound for Iran. But the baby boy fell gravely ill, and they had to leave the train in an isolated area in Kazakhstan in order to rush the boy to a clinic, where the infant died. They suffered from hunger, and with nowhere to go, they paid a farmer the little money they had left, to sleep in his barn. Haim was caught stealing a loaf of bread from a passing truck. From then on, until the end of the war, his whereabouts were unknown. Hana, then pregnant, was left with her two young sons. Weak and hungry, she walked to the nearest hospital, where she delivered Batya. She was told that the baby was under two kilos, and was not going to survive. Hana breastfed Batya, who was wrapped and kept in a shoebox, looked after by her uncle. They managed to survive the ordeals, and in 1945 they returned to Warsaw. They found Haim, near death, in a Red Cross hospital. They all suffered from illness and malnutrition, and were sent to the displaced persons camp which had been set up in the former Nazi death camp of Bergen-Belsen. In 1947, they immigrated to Mandatory Palestine. Batya became a teacher, and in 1965 married Paul Schon, also a Holocaust survivor. She wrote two books dealing with her family's ordeals and survival, and about their difficult absorption in Israel. Batya dedicated herself to children with learning disabilities.

Batya Schon BY Yuval Rakavy ISRAEL
HOLON, ISRAEL, 2021

Walter Bingham was born as Wolfgang Billig in Karlsruhe, Germany, in 1924. His family was religious, and he remembers seeing his local synagogue burning on Kristallnacht, in November 1938. After Kristallnacht, he seized the opportunity to leave for England with other members of his religious Zionist youth movement on the Kindertransport, which brought thousands of Jewish children and teenagers out of Nazi-occupied countries, without their parents. He changed his name from Wolfgang to Walter after joining the British Army during the latter part of World War II. 'Being a soldier about to go into battle, it occurred to me that there's a chance of being taken prisoner; I decided to conceal my identity of a German Jew.' Walter took part in the Normandy landings of 1944 as an ambulance driver, receiving an award for bravery from King George VI. He was also awarded France's highest honor, the Légion d'honneur, for his participation in the Normandy invasion. Walter became an intelligence officer in the British Army. He interrogated Nazi commanders, including Joachim von Ribbentrop, Hitler's Foreign Minister. 'Ribbentrop looked me in the eye and told me he didn't know anything about the Final Solution: "It was all the Führer," recalls Walter, 'I could have choked him, but as a British intelligence officer, I could only react with another question,' adding, 'he was the first to be hanged.' Walter returned to England and had a career as an actor and broadcaster. He also played the wizard in two of the Harry Potter films. At age 80, Walter immigrated to Israel, settling in Jerusalem in 2004. There he resumed his career in journalism. On his 95th birthday, Walter became the oldest Israeli to skydive. As anchor of *The Walter Bingham File*, he is a certified Guinness Book of World Records holder, as the oldest living radio-talk show host.

Walter Bingham BY Nir Keidar ISRAEL
JERUSALEM, 2021

Ruth Pardess was born in 1940 in the ghetto of Ostrowiec Świętokrzyski, Poland. The ghetto later became a forced labor camp. Her parents, Guta and Henryk Schwarz, had to hide in different places during the war. Guta and Ruth were among the thousands of refugees who fled to Sambir, then Poland, in an attempt to escape the Nazi German occupation of western Poland. They were imprisoned and later sent to the Sambir Ghetto, established by the SS in March 1942. Guta worked outside the ghetto as a cook in a pub, serving senior SS officers. Ruth would play in the pub's backyard. One day, her mother was watching through the window as her daughter danced in the center of the pub's dance floor, surrounded by cheering SS officers. Guta then knew how to save her child. Just before the ghetto was sealed from the outside world on January 12, 1942, Guta sent a message to Alojzy Plewa, Ruth's father's friend from the interwar period, asking him to rescue her two-year-old child and take her with him. The young single man took Ruth from the ghetto, and after a short stay, Alojzy brought the little child to his parents, Antoni and Anna Plewa, who were farmers. They lived in Kliny, near the town of Kępno. The Kliny villagers were informed that this was Alojzy's illegitimate child, and that her name was Antośka. Ruth was baptized, and throughout the war years, attended church with her caretakers. Guta survived the war and came to Kliny in 1945. Antośka did not recognize her mother. Of Antoni and Anna Plewa, her wartime family, Ruth recalls, 'They were good people, for me, they were my true grandparents.' Ruth's adoptive family returned Ruth to her mother, who continued to take her to church as a way of preserving the life she had known. In 1946, Ruth and her mother immigrated to Mandatory Palestine. Ruth's father, Henryk Schwarz, remained in Poland. In 1978, Alojzy Plewa visited Ruth in Israel, where he was awarded the Righteous Among the Nations medal. In 2011, Ruth visited her birthplace and her wartime hiding place. She also met with the next generation of the Plewa family, and took part in a cultural event in her honor. Ruth lives in the Galilee and dances as a way of therapy, for herself and others.

Ruth Pardess BY Itzik Yogev ISRAEL
HARARIT, THE GALILEE, ISRAEL, 2021

LEILA ROMANO was born in 1925 in Yugoslavia. 'Dad was from Hungary, Mom from Croatia, and I had an older brother. We lived in the town of Chakovich, a home to some 70 Jewish families. When World War II broke out, my parents tried to hide my brother in Budapest. He was caught, taken to a labor camp and disappeared forever. In April 1944, we were taken to Auschwitz. Dad, who was 52, was killed upon arrival. Mother managed to survive for four months. She fell ill with typhus, and when I came to her block, she was gone. I started screaming. A Czech woman approached me and this is when I heard for the first time about the gas chambers extermination. I was so attached to Mom, and I was left alone. A woman whose fifteen-year-old daughter also died took care of me. We worked in weaving fabrics and rubber used for bombs. We had to keep up, otherwise they would have exterminated us. All the women lost their menstrual cycle, both from the stress and the bromine that was added to tea. I walked around in a torn cotton dress. My childhood friend risked her life to pass me a dress. We ate radish cooked in water and one slice of bread per day. In September 1944, we were transferred to the Czech Republic. I was advised of my luck, "Whatever you are asked, say you know how." We worked in a factory for spare parts. We were called by name and not by number. I was lucky again when I was sent to work in an office. I slept in one bed with Clara and Anushka, who worked in the kitchen and helped me survive. In April 1945, the Russians entered the Czech Republic and liberated us. We rode on train's roofs and on foot until Budapest. I was a skeleton with no strength to walk. In Budapest, the JDC picked us up and helped us. Dad had a gentile friend named Kronos who worked in a bank. Dad left with Kronos money and valuables and Kronos kept all and returned it to me. With that money I managed to renovate our family's destroyed house. On a visit to Zagreb I was introduced to Albert who was a barber. It was love at first sight. He also was a sole survivor of his family. In 1946, we were married. Our daughter Aviva was born in 1947. Albert wanted to immigrate to Israel, I hesitated. We gave up all our property to be allowed to leave and boarded the ship *Radnik*. We arrived in Israel in December 1948. We were housed in an immigrant camp near Gedera. Albert's uncle, Aaron Romano, lived in Moshav Beit Zayit and persuaded us to move in next to him. It was hard life, no electricity, outdoor toilet, outdoor water faucet…but it was our permanent home. Albert fell ill and I had to work cleaning and cooking. We barely survived. In 1985 Albert died. I'm among the only survivors from my city. Our generation is disappearing.' Leila passed away in November 2021.

Leila Romano BY Rina Castelnuovo ISRAEL

MOSHAV BEIT ZAYIT, ISRAEL, 2021

Sheila Kuper was born in 1925 in Maków Mazowiecki, Poland. At the outbreak of World War II, there were about 3,500 Jews in Maków Mazowiecki. When the Nazis established the Maków Mazoweiki Ghetto, Sheila was a young teenager, the third-youngest of seven children. Sheila recalls how the Nazis rounded up the Jews in the town's square. She witnessed the hanging of young men and the Selektion of Jews for transport to death camps. After two years of forced labor and enduring the Maków Ghetto, Sheila's father, a tailor, took the decision to escape. Sheila's mother insisted that her husband try with the older children first, and that she would stay behind with the little kids. 'The Germans won't hurt a woman with two small children,' Sheila remembers her mother saying. Sheila and her father crawled through the ghetto fence. A farmer, a Polish client of her father, risked his life sheltering them in the root cellar of a horse barn in the Polish countryside, bringing food and water when he could. Sheila remembers not being able to stand up in the cellar throughout her years in hiding, until the end of the war. After liberation, Sheila and her father were reunited with two of her older sisters and the surviving brother. Sheila's mother, her five-year-old sister, and the youngest brother were all murdered in Auschwitz. Most of their extended family and the majority of the Jews of Maków Mazowiecki perished in death camps. The surviving family decided to escape from the pogroms which Sheila witnessed in postwar Poland. They went to a displaced persons camp in Germany, eventually immigrating to the United States. They lived in Brooklyn, later moving to Queens, where Sheila married a Holocaust survivor from Poland. Sheila rebuilt her life and created a family. Two of Sheila's sisters and her brother, who had also gone into hiding and survived the war, lived nearby for their entire adult lives. The three sisters survived their husbands, and all took apartments in the same complex in Bayside, Queens, New York. Anna died at age 100 a few years ago. Helen, turning 101, lives on the first floor, and Sheila on the third floor, where she remains till this day. Sheila's niece, the photographer, says Sheila prepares the best handmade gefilte fish on the planet.

Sheila Kuper BY Ruth Fremson USA
BAYSIDE, QUEENS, NEW YORK, USA, 2021

Naomi Perlman BY Rina Castelnuovo ISRAEL
ASHKELON, ISRAEL, 2021

Naomi Perlman was born in Sosnowiec, Poland, in 1932. On September 4, 1939, Nazi Germany occupied Sosnowiec. Its Great Synagogue was burned, and soon after, Jews were rounded up for forced labor. Street executions began. When Naomi's family were evicted from their home, they took their only child on a horse-drawn cart and fled eastward from Nazi troops then sweeping across the Polish landscape. The family crossed rivers on makeshift wooden rafts, and Naomi helplessly watched their beloved horse slipping from a rickety raft into the river, drowning in front of her eyes. They continued fleeing on foot, traversing combat zones amid shelling, starvation and freezing weather. Naomi fell ill with typhoid, and her father was detained by the Soviets in a camp near Chernobyl. Eventually released, the family reached Uzbekistan, where they found refuge. Naomi became a peddler on the streets of Tashkent. She didn't mind. For her, this was paradise. After the war, they returned to Sosnowiec. They learned that most of their family had perished. Encountering hostility, their home occupied by strangers, they immigrated to Israel in 1951. Upon arrival, they were sent to the southern coastal town of Majdal. The Palestinian residents of Majdal had been forced to abandon the town in the 1948 war and had fled to the Gaza Strip. Naomi married Yankale, a Polish Jew who had escaped the Nazis, and lost family in death camps. They built their home and created a family in the town, now renamed Ashkelon. For the past twenty years, Ashkelon has been a frequent target for Gaza rocket fire. Yankale passed away, but Naomi remained in her home. On March 11, 2021, a rocket fired from Gaza crashed through Naomi's roof. A neighbor, Avi Franco, ran inside and pulled Naomi out from the rubble. Both her legs were torn from her body by the force of the explosion, and she was covered in shrapnel. Her caregiver, Soumya Santosh, was killed by the devastating impact. Naomi's injuries were healing, but the trauma transported her back to her childhood home. A spark of hope appeared for her family when Naomi murmured in Yiddish to a nurse, 'I have no legs; a bomb fell on me.' Naomi Perlman died in February 2022 at age 91.

EVA ARBAN was born in October 1930 in Prague. Eva remembers how already in 1938, warning signs were posted across the city, reading "Jews and dogs are forbidden." Eva's family was forcibly evicted from their home, and in December 1941, the family was deported to the Terezin Ghetto. Life there was initially 'tolerable.' She lived in one room along with her parents. In October 1944, her father was taken to Auschwitz. Eva and her mother were next and, she recalls, 'happy to join my father.' They boarded a train from Terezin to Auschwitz, and soon after, they were transferred to Gross-Rosen. Toward the end of January, Eva was forced on a death march. Her mother died at night during the march. Eva woke up alone. She wandered off next to the railroad tracks until she collapsed in a field. She later came to in the home of Jan and Ludmila, farmers who found her unconscious in the field. Risking their lives, they sheltered Eva in their house until the end of the war. Eva was reunited with a surviving aunt, but her aunt's inability to believe the horror stories Eva had lived through caused Eva, then 14, to escape by train to an orphanage in Prague. Later she attended nursing school. In 1948, during a party honoring Israel's proclamation as a state, she met Peter. They married in Paris in October of that year. They arrived in Israel in April 1949. First, they lived in a rented room in Haifa. Then, in 1951, they moved to Ashkelon. In 1956, they moved to a house which Peter had built for them. Peter passed away in 2017. Eva still lives in their home. Eva dedicates her time to sharing her story with young people, and to commemoration of the Shoah.

Eva Arban BY Moran Ahdut Nissim ISRAEL

ASHKELON, ISRAEL, 2021

LEONID (LEIZER) KRET was born in 1938 in the village of Peschanka, in today's Ukraine. Before the outbreak of the war his father was drafted into the Red Army. His mother was left with small children and was unable to leave Peschanka in the early days of the war. The Jews were ordered to leave, marching on foot for miles on an endless journey. Leonid's grandmother Khova died of exhaustion. When they reached the village of Kodym, Leonid's mother was forced by the uncertainty of their circumstances to save her baby Roza (Raya) by giving her to a willing local woman. When they reached Bogdanovka, shootings began. Their guards, who had been recruited from among local villagers, gave them a chance to escape. They showed them a safe route out. In November 1941, they finally made it to Bershad, and found that their mother's family were all alive. In 1944, Bershad was liberated by the Soviets. Leonid's father, who had been injured in Stalingrad, had located his family by the end of 1945. The Krets returned to Peschanka and tracked down Roza, but it took a court to order her adoptive family to return Roza to her biological parents. Roza decided to stay with her adoptive family. Leonid's parents had another baby girl, Eva, and in the 1990s, Eva emigrated to the US with her parents. Leonid moved to Moscow and worked as a neurologist for more than 50 years. His huge extended family spans different continents and cities. They all continue to keep in touch.

Leonid Kret BY Maria Gruzdeva RUSSIA
MOSCOW, 2021

HANNAH PICK-GOSLAR was born in Berlin in 1928. Her father, Hans Goslar, was deputy minister for domestic affairs in Germany until 1933. After the election of the Nazi Party to the Reichstag and Hitler's appointment as Chancellor, Hans Goslar was forced to resign and the family moved to Amsterdam. Her mother died giving birth. Known as Hanneli, she attended the Sixth Public Montessori school where she became best friends with Anne Frank. Later the two enrolled in the Jewish Lyceum. The two girls appear in a photograph at Anne's 10th birthday party with another girl whose parents later became known Nazis. In June 1943, Hanneli with her entire family were arrested and sent to the Westerbork camp, and in February 1944, to Bergen-Belsen. The Goslar family had Palestine passports and were detained in an improved section of the camp. In January to mid-February 1945, Hanneli and Anne were able to meet briefly through a hay-filled barbed wire fence dividing two sections of the camp. 'The fence was high, it was night and there were many women,' Hanneli recalls. 'Another woman caught the package for Anne and ran away.' Anne cried, and Hanneli consoled her. They would try again. The second time, Hanneli threw the package of bread and socks over the fence and Anne caught it. It was the last time the two girls met. Anne Frank is thought to have died from typhus in Bergen-Belsen camp in late February or early March 1945. On April 15, 1945, British troops liberated Bergen-Belsen. Hanneli and her sister Gabi survived 14 months at Bergen-Belsen. Her father and grandparents died before liberation. Hanneli was rescued on what is known as the Lost Train, intended to transport prisoners from Bergen-Belsen to Theresienstadt during the last hours of World War II. Allied troops approached the camp, and the prisoners were freed by the Red Army. Hanneli and her sister Gabi, the only surviving family members, immigrated in 1947 to Mandatory Palestine, settling in Jerusalem where Hanneli became a pediatric nurse. She married Dr. Walter Pinchas Pick. They had three children and created a family that includes 31 great-grandchildren. Over the years, Hanneli appeared in numerous documentaries and books related to her friend Anne Frank and has traveled the world in order to educate about the Holocaust. Hannah passed away with family by her side on October 29, 2022, just two weeks away from her 94th birthday.

Hannah Pick-Goslar BY Eric Sultan ISRAEL
JERUSALEM, 2021

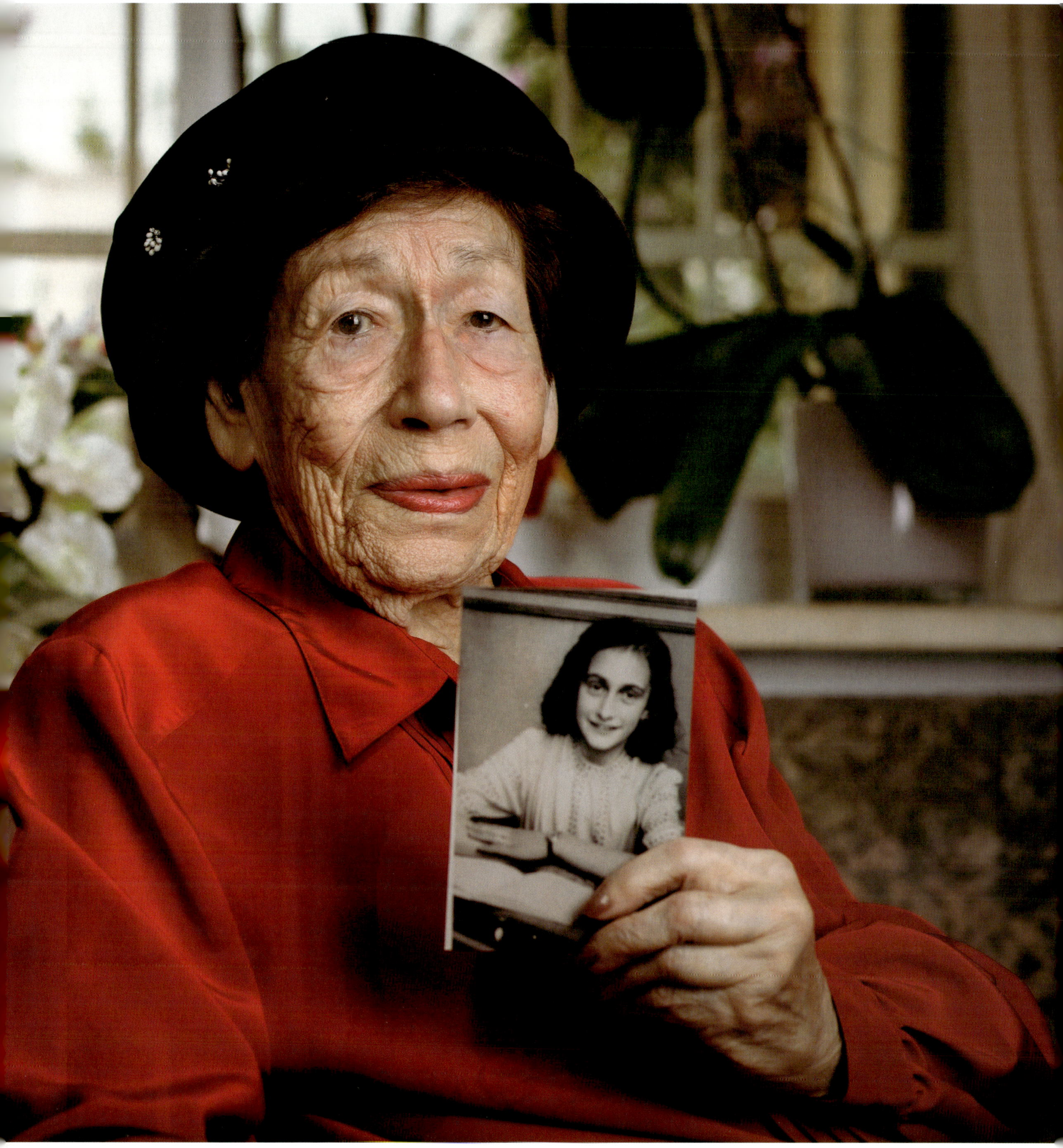

GODEL KLEINMAN was born in 1934 in Ukraine. In 1941, Nazi Germany, with their Romanian allies, invaded his village, Novoselitsa. After several months of repeated pogroms and murders of Jews, the Nazis and their allies decided to expel about 900 Jews to the Transylvania Ghetto, 600 kilometers away. Before the expulsion they set Godel's family home on fire. Godel and his family were sent on the long death march in the freezing weather of Eastern Europe. 'When we crossed the Dniester River's bridge, we saw bodies floating in the river, of Jews and Soviet soldiers – the Germans were riding motorcycles with a side cart where a mounted machine gun would shoot at those who were unable to continue walking. They were shot on the spot.' Each night they stopped to sleep on the freezing ground, and in the morning they would discover those who did not wake up because they had frozen to death. One of the victims was his mother, and on another night, his older brother. Godel had to continue walking, unable to bury their bodies. Most of the Jews on the march died. Godel arrived at the Transylvania Ghetto with about 80 others. What kept Godel alive was the support and love of his devoted grandfather. After one year, the Germans left, handing over the ghetto to their Romanian allies. The Romanian officers took pity on the Jews and their dire condition, providing them with food, water and work. This allowed them to survive until the Red Army liberated the area in spring of 1944. Godel returned to his village, finding that all the Jewish homes had burned to the ground. His father and sisters survived. His father remarried soon after, but it was his grandfather who sheltered Godel and raised him and sent him to school to learn how to read and write. In 1958, Godel married Sima and they rebuilt their life in Ukraine. In 1970, Godel and his family were allowed by the Soviet government to immigrate to Israel. Godel describes himself today as 'a family man with an endless joy of life.'

Godel Kleinman BY Amir Levy ISRAEL
PARDES HANNA, ISRAEL, 2021

GABRIELLA KARIN was born in 1930 in Bratislava, then Czechoslovakia. When anti-Jewish measures were enacted at the outbreak of World War II, she was removed from school. Her parents obtained false identification papers for her and sent her to the Ursuline convent in Bratislava. She remained in hiding there for almost three years. In 1942, Gabriella's mother brought her home after Slovakia's President Tiso halted the mass deportations of Jews, but by August 1944, Nazi German forces had entered Slovakia and reinstituted the deportations to death camps. Gabriella's family went into hiding in the home of attorney Karol Blanar, her aunt's boyfriend. His family saved Jews by letting them hide in a one-bedroom apartment in the center of town, just across the street from the Nazi-Slovak Gestapo. During her nine months in hiding, Gabriella rarely dared peer out through a tear in the cardboard of the covered windows. She remembers watching Nazis pulling two of her Jewish girlfriends from the convent and into their headquarters. By late March 1945, the Russian Army was heavily bombing the city. Gabriella and her family miraculously survived. After the war, Gabriella settled first in Israel and later in the United States, dedicating her life to Holocaust education. She is an accomplished artist, turning her pain into works of art. Karol Blanar, her family's savior, was posthumously granted the status of Righteous Among the Nations by Yad Vashem in Jerusalem.

Gabriella Karin BY James Marcus Haney USA
LOS ANGELES, CALIFORNIA, USA, 2021

YEHUDA BACON was born July 28, 1929, in Ostrava, in today's Czech Republic. In the fall of 1942, at the age of 13, Yehuda was deported with his family to the Theresienstadt Ghetto. Ever since his childhood, Yehuda had wanted to draw. In Terezin, he studied under the imprisoned artists Leo Haas, Otto Ungar and Karl Fleischmann. Otto and Karl were later murdered. In December 1943, Yehuda was transported to the Auschwitz-Birkenau extermination camp, where he was one of the children in the so-called "family camp" – used by the Nazis in an effort to hide from the outside world their genocide of the Jews. Yehuda was part of a group of some 20 children whose job was to pull wagons laden with the bodies of the dead, which he depicted in his drawings. He drew on wrapping paper, hiding his drawings in various places around the camp. 'I drew what we saw: the camp near us, how the dead were carried… I was very curious. The first time I looked, I noticed there were no holes in the showerheads. I walked there with the Sonderkommando' (inmates forced, under threat of death, to help dispose of corpses). In June 1944, Yehuda's father was murdered in the gas chambers. His mother and his sister Hanna died in Stutthof concentration camp a few weeks before its liberation. On January 18, 1945, Yehuda was forced on a death march, which led him through the Mauthausen-Gusen concentration camp to its sub-camp Gunskirchen. In March, he was sent on another death march to a sub-camp of Mauthausen, where Nazi SS guards poisoned food before leaving the camp. On May 5, 1945, Yehuda was liberated by the US Army. Many of his liberated colleagues and inmates died from having suddenly eaten amounts of food their bodies could no longer handle. After his recovery in a hospital, Yehuda returned to Prague and lived in an orphanage. In 1946, he immigrated to Mandatory Palestine, studying at the Bezalel Academy of Arts, where he became a professor of graphic art and drawing. Yehuda's drawings show what he witnessed in the concentration camps. His drawings served as evidence in prosecutions of Nazi criminals in the Eichmann trial in Jerusalem and the Frankfurt Auschwitz Trials. In the 1950s, Yehuda took part in interfaith dialogues and Israeli-Palestinian dialogue. His art is shown in museums and collections including the Israel Museum Jerusalem, Yad Vashem in Jerusalem, the United States Congress in Washington, DC, and in the collections of Theodore Roosevelt, John D. Rockefeller, Martin Buber and Chaim Weizmann. Yehuda lives with his wife Lea in Jerusalem.

Yehuda Bacon BY Jim Hollander USA
JERUSALEM, 2022

SAADIA BAHAT was born in Alytus, Lithuania, in 1928. After the outbreak of World War II and the June 1941 Nazi invasion of Lithuania, Saadia's family moved to Vilna. In September of that year, the family was forced into the Vilna Ghetto. During one of the deportations from the ghetto, Saadia's father was murdered. His mother managed to save Saadia and his sister. In a ghetto workshop, Saadia learned to work as a carpenter, locksmith, and blacksmith. In late 1943, he was taken to forced labor camps in Estonia, where he felled trees in forests. After the evacuation of the Estonian camps, Saadia was transferred to Stutthof concentration camp and then to the Gotentof camp. The camp was liberated in March 1945, by the Soviet Red Army. In 1946, Saadia immigrated to pre-state Israel, enlisting in the Haganah and the Palmach militias. He later studied machine engineering, serving in research and development roles, and then as a senior engineer in Israel's security establishment. At the same time, Saadia engaged in artwork, which he had pursued before the Holocaust. Dozens of his statues have been displayed in Israel and internationally. One of them was the bronze sculpture *Beacon of Resurrection*.

Saadia Bahat BY Itzak Yogev ISRAEL
KIRYAT BIALIK, ISRAEL, 2022

YAACOV GUTERMAN was born in Poland in 1935. He lived in Plock, where a third of the inhabitants were Jews. Yaacov was four at the outbreak of World War II. He and his parents endured imprisonment in the ghetto, then deportation to the Soldau concentration camp. Simcha, his father, risked his life to document the reality of the time. He wrote his account in Yiddish on long pieces of paper, which he hid in bottles, and later in basements. Dozens of years later, one of the bottles was found and its contents made public. In order to survive, the family obtained fake IDs. Yaacov was taught to recite Christian prayers in Polish. In 1942, the Nazis began exterminating Jews in the gas chambers. 'Now began the torturous wandering and the threats of our Polish neighbors, who found us in our hiding places to give us over to the Germans.' Toward the end of the war, Yaacov was separated from his parents. 'I worked as a cow-herder for a family of farmers in the village of Zabady, outside Lowicz. I was nine at the time, and my parents remained in terror-stricken Warsaw.' Yaacov's father, a fighter in the Polish A.K. underground movement, was killed on the first day of the 1944 Warsaw Uprising. After the war, Yaacov spent time in the Zakopane orphanage, headed by Lena Kichler. She had gathered some 100 Jewish orphans, who had been hidden in monasteries and villages in Poland. Yaacov's mother survived and remarried. Together with Yaacov, the three immigrated to Israel, where they lived in transit camps. 'Seven years after our arrival, my mother died of cancer. I married Ruti, whom I fell in love with during my military service. Ruti and I had two wonderful boys, Raz and Tal. At 29, Ruti died of cancer.' One year after Ruti's death, Yaacov moved with his two toddlers to Kibbutz HaOgen. On the kibbutz, Yaacov became an artist and an author. His son Raz served in one of the elite combat units. On the first night of the First Lebanon War, during the battle of the Beaufort, Raz and five of his fellow soldiers were killed. After the death of his son, Yaacov became one of the leaders of the protest against the war. He was among the first to join the forum of Israeli-Palestinian Bereaved Families for Peace. The author of dozens of books, Yaacov provides students testimonies of his memories of the war. He also participates in tours of Poland with Israeli youth.

Yaacov Guterman BY Galia Gur Zeev ISRAEL
KIBBUTZ HAOGEN, ISRAEL, 2022

SVETLANA SAMILOVA was born in 1938 in Romny, Ukraine. Romny was occupied by Nazi Germany on September 10, 1941, and Jews were ordered to register and to wear yellow Stars of David on their sleeves. Jews were then forced into hard labor. At the end of October 1941, the Jews of Romny were evicted from their homes and sent to two remote streets of the town. The area was fenced in with barbed wire, creating a ghetto. Svetlana and her family were sent to the ghetto, where her mother gave birth to her younger sister. Her parents were able to bribe a Ukrainian ghetto guard to smuggle Svetlana out to distant relatives nearby. The same policeman notified her parents that they were due to be murdered, and he urged them to throw the newborn baby onto a garbage heap. From there the baby was taken to Svetlana. The two sisters, in hiding, were the only family members to survive. On November 9, 1941, Ukrainian police forced all the Jews of Romny and the village of Zasul'e into a two-story military barracks on Mayakovskigi Street. In the days that followed, all the Jews were escorted two kilometers from the city to Peski, where they were executed in three ravines by members of the 1st Motorized Infantry SS Brigade. A total of 1,233 Jews were murdered there. Members of mixed families were not killed at the time, but a year later, in February 1942, they were arrested. Four months thereafter, on June 6, 1942, they were murdered in a gypsum quarry near Zasul'e. Executions were performed by members of the SD "Plath" command. Only a few Jews managed to escape. After the war, Svetlana lived in the Kyiv suburb of Bucha, where she built a family. Some of her children immigrated to Israel. When Russia invaded Ukraine, Svetlana believed that no harm would be caused her, and she stayed in Bucha. But missiles struck homes around her, and friends were murdered. Svetlana says she witnessed how the soldiers were burning corpses in their courtyards. She managed to escape, renting a house briefly in Western Ukraine until she ran out of money and was forced to return to Bucha. She received medications and first aid through the photographer, who brought over a friend from the Jewish Agency. The friend explained the process of immigrating to Israel. Svetlana said she is now ready to leave Ukraine.

Svetlana Samilova BY Jonny Daniels UKRAINE
BUCHA, UKRAINE, 2022

HANNAH DAVIDOVICH was born in 1929 in the village of Kolacheva in Carpathian Russia (then part of Czechoslovakia, now Ukraine). Hannah was one of six siblings. In 1944, the Jewish community was rounded up, sent to a ghetto, and deported by train to the Auschwitz death camp. Hannah's life was saved three times. First, during a Selektion in which the Nazi camp officials chose who were destined for extermination, and who would be sent to forced labor. A Jewish prisoner separated Hannah from her mother and pushed her to the line of those who would live. She managed to dodge the executioners during another Selektion, when a death line was sent to the crematoria, and another line put to work outside Auschwitz in excavation and building trenches for the Nazis. A third time, in the Stutthof camp, when transports arrived from all over Europe, the older prisoners managed to mingle with the new arrivals and were sent on a death march to Hinuv (Chinow) near the city of Danzig, where they were liberated by the Red Army. After liberation, Hannah learned that her five siblings, her parents and grandparents had all perished in the Holocaust. Weakened and in poor health, she was hospitalized. Later she joined Jewish youth in Warsaw preparing for immigration to Palestine. They reached an "Italian survivors" camp, from which they boarded an illegal immigrant ship, the *Shabtai Lodzensky*. Hannah arrived in British Mandatory Palestine in March 1947. The ship was discovered by the British Army near Nitzanim beach and all onboard jumped into the sea. They were saved from drowning by members of the pre-state Haganah underground, who brought them to shore in their boats. But all were then arrested by British police, who detained them in the Atlit prisoners' camp. After her release from Atlit, Hannah eventually settled in Kibbutz Mizra. In 1948, Hannah was recruited to the Palmach underground militia, serving in the Negev Brigade. In 1956, Hanna married Professor Chaim Gevaryahu, a widower, who had three children from his marriage to Hannah's late aunt. Hannah is a mother to two daughters. Her stepson Captain Reuven Gevaryahu was killed during the Yom Kippur War.

Hannah Davidovich BY Alex Levac ISRAEL
TEL AVIV, ISRAEL, 2019

FEIGA BELOSTOTSKY was born in Ukraine in 1914. After the Nazis occupied her hometown, she took her four children and fled eastward. Her husband, then serving in the Red Army, was killed fighting Nazi Germany. At the end of the war, she remarried and had another child. In 1991, Feiga decided to immigrate to Israel with her family. She says it was always a dream of hers. Since then, Feiga, who just celebrated her 108th birthday, lives in Ashkelon, a coastal southern Israeli city frequently targeted by rockets fired from Gaza.

Feiga Belostotsky BY **Tsafrir Abayov** ISRAEL
ASHKELON, ISRAEL, 2022

ZEHAVA (GENIA) was born in 1930 in Lodz, Poland. On September 8, 1939, Nazi Germany occupied Lodz and the persecution of Lodz's Jews began immediately, with arrests, forced labor, abuse and humiliation. Zehava witnessed her grandfather Chaim Fuchs being beaten, and his beard set on fire. The grandparents and one of her brothers fled, and were never again heard from. Zehava and her parents survived, only to reach the Warsaw Ghetto. Zehava's mother, Fela, placed her in Janusz Korczak's orphanage for a short period, after which her parents arranged for a paid hiding place outside the ghetto for Zehava and two other girls. They escaped via the sewage tunnels, but were abused by the people concealing them, and made their way back to the ghetto. Zehava's mother Fela was murdered in the ghetto while waiting in line for food. Zehava and her father, Hirsch, ended up in the Piotrkow forced labor camp, where Zehava was sent to work. During one of the Selektions, in which Nazi officials decided who would work and who would be sent to their deaths, Hirsch managed to pull Zehava over to the men's group from the deathline of mothers and children. Hirsch hid her in the men's barracks while the men went out to work. Later, Hirsch was transferred. Zehava, left alone, was sent to the Ravensbrück concentration camp in Germany. From there she was taken with a group of women to the Bergen-Belsen camp, where she arrived in a poor physical state. Dr. Ada Bimko (later Hadassa Rosensaft), a Jewish doctor imprisoned in the camp, managed to transfer her to the orphanage in Bergen-Belsen, populated mainly by Dutch children. On April 15, 1945, British troops liberated Bergen-Belsen. Among the Jews liberated were some 300 children, including Zehava. After liberation, a children's home and school were established in the Bergen-Belsen Displaced Persons Camp, where Zehava's father found her. 'He told me he wanted us to travel to America. I told him I was staying with my friends… I was going to Eretz Israel.' In 1946, Zehava immigrated to Mandatory Palestine on the boat *Champollion* with a group of children. She arrived in Kibbutz Kiryat Anavim, where she joined the Palmach. 'I was given an Italian rifle bigger than I was. We would do guard duty in shifts at the kibbutz and attend to cows. On one of the skirmishes, my friend was killed and another was badly wounded,' Zehava says, recalling her kibbutz days. About a year later, her father immigrated as well. Her brother Nachum and her grandparents had been murdered in the Holocaust. Zehava studied nursing, married Shaul Shamir, and they live with their family in Israel.

Zehava Shamir BY Ofra Moran Kurnick ISRAEL
HERZLIYA, ISRAEL, 2022

Rachel Barda was born in Benghazi, Libya, in 1935. Libya was then a colony of Mussolini's Italy. All Jews, more than 3,000, were ordered evacuated, and were forced to go to concentration camps. Rachel was seven years old when she was imprisoned with her family along with the Jews of Benghazi in the Giado concentration camp, built by fascist Italy, the harshest labor camp in Libya during World War II. There were no German administrators at Giado, only Italian officers, and the guards were Arab and Italian policemen. Rachel recalls how they enjoyed embarrassing and harassing the prisoners. The camp was overcrowded, and cold water was rarely supplied. Contagious diseases spread throughout the camp, among them a typhus epidemic during December 1942. 'My sister Masuda, only 18, and my aunt perished from starvation. Hunger was unbearable.' After they had been in Giado for two years, British forces liberated the camp in January 1942. In all, suffering from disease and terrible living conditions, 562 Jews died at Giado, the highest number of Jewish victims in Islamic countries during the Second World War. Survivors returned to their homes for a while, but eventually all of them left Libya. 'We returned home, but the Arab local population harassed us. The choice was to immigrate to Israel. We arrived to Haifa in 1949 and from there to absorption camps. At 12 years old I had to help support my family, who were weak and sick from the years of incarceration and the journey. Lack of education accompanied me for a long time. My mother did not allow me to go to the army, nor to move to a kibbutz, where I would probably study. I married Nissim, who was of Turkish descent. We lived in a two-room makeshift hut until the birth of my first daughter. I worked for 23 years as a caregiver for children.' Rachel, who has ten grandchildren and eleven great-grandchildren, holds a photograph with her elder sister Buba.

Rachel Barda BY Ofra Moran Kurnick ISRAEL
OR YEHUDA, ISRAEL, 2022

Arkady Frechenco was born in 1930 in Ukraine. When World War II broke out, his father enlisted in the army. His mother decided to escape eastward with their four children. While they were crossing a bridge, it came under attack and was bombed. In the chaos, Arkady was separated from his mother and was lost. Arkady survived with the help of strangers, then joined the partisans in the forests. He remained with them till the end of the war. He was to learn that his father had been killed in combat against the Nazis, but that his mother and siblings had survived. Arkady became a steel worker. He married and started a family. One of his two daughters lives in Israel, and the other in Germany. He and his wife lived in Zaporizhzhia, Ukraine, where he remained after he was widowed. When Russian troops invaded Ukraine in February 2022, Zaporizhzhia was the scene of some of the most intense fighting. Under heavy shelling, Arkady escaped, as he had 81 years ago. This time, though, he boarded a bus, leaving as fast as he could. Wearing just his sleeping clothes and slippers, he carried a small but heavy bag filled with his documents and lots of tinned food. 'Even in my nightmares I never imagined such horror could happen again,' Arkady said. Now he hopes the war in Ukraine will also be the last he will ever experience. Arkady was taken into a refugee facility operated by the Jewish Agency in a town near Lvov, and from there was transferred to the Aliya Center in Poland. Later, Arkady took off on a Jewish Agency rescue flight from Warsaw, and was able to embrace his daughter Ina and her family when they were reunited in the southern Israeli city of Ashkelon.

Arkady Frechenco BY Jonny Daniels POLAND
WARSAW, 2022

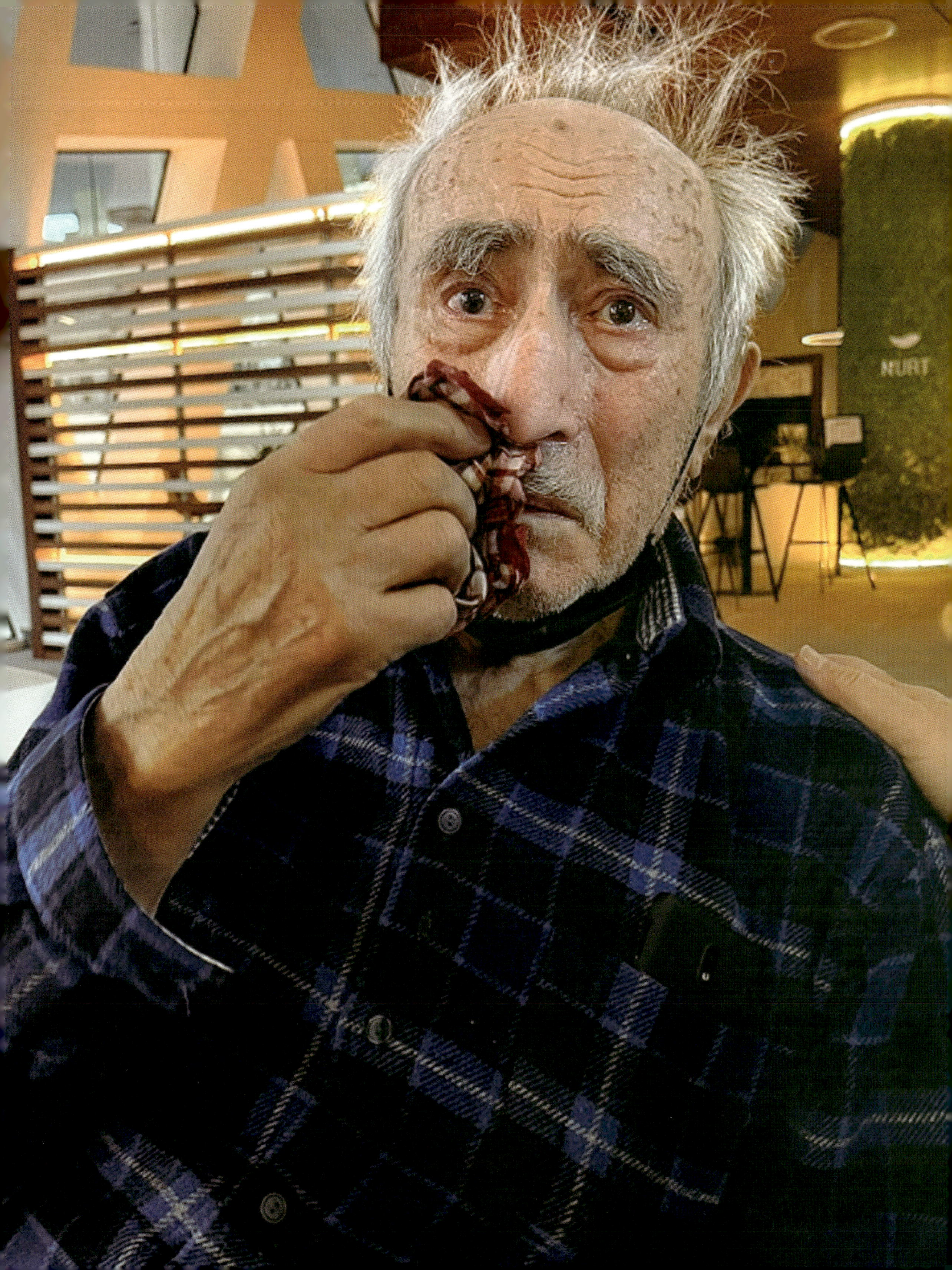
NURT

GRETE GLOTMAN was born in 1925 in Czernowitz, Romania (today Chernivtsi, Ukraine). The persecution of the Jews began at the hands of the Romanian fascist regime, but following the Ribbentrop-Molotov Pact, Czernowitz was briefly ruled by the Red Army. After Nazi Germany invaded the Soviet Union, the Red Army withdrew from the city, then home to 50,000 Jews. Romanian soldiers returned to Czernowitz along with Nazi troops, imposing Nazi racial laws and taking part in the execution of thousands of Jews. On October 11, 1941, the Nazis concentrated the Jews of Czernowitz into a ghetto. They confiscated their property and began deporting them to Transnistria, in southern Ukraine. Grete and her family were sent to forced labor and were abused by the Ukrainian Nazi collaborators. Grete fell severely ill with typhus. She miraculously survived. The Jews were transferred from camp to camp and sent on death marches, where most of the Czernowitz deportees perished. At war's end, Grete returned to Czernowitz, where her home was occupied by strangers. Grete and her sister Thea boarded the ship The Independence with hundreds of young Holocaust survivors on their way to Mandatory Palestine. Greta met her future husband aboard the vessel. The ship was captured by the British navy, and the passengers deported to a detention camp in Cyprus. After their release, the couple were married on a rooftop in Tel Aviv, where she lived and created a family. In the late 1990s, Shuka, Grete's son, met Rula Halawani, a Palestinian who was photographing Palestinian refugees in London with objects they kept from their old world. Shuka writes, 'I remembered that my parents did not have any artifacts left from their prewar home. In fact, my mother was left with one single silver tablespoon and one single fork. Rula was stunned, since she was unaware most Israelis were refugees. I told my mother about Rula's reaction and she insisted that I take the two utensils. "You know what to do with it!" she said, referring to my artistic practice. My mother passed away and this is what is left.' On the photo it says in Hebrew, "Grete, my mother, what is left…"

Grete Glotman BY Shuka Glotman ISRAEL
ABIRIM, ISRAEL, 2022

MARION KUNSTENAAR was born in March 1937, in The Hague, the Netherlands. She experienced the war as a young child on the run, hiding from the Germans. In 1943, following the construction of the Atlantic Wall of Nazi German coastal fortifications, she and her parents were ordered to move to Amsterdam, where they were rounded up with their entire family and transported to Westerbork concentration camp. Marion and her parents were the only survivors. The rest of her family were murdered in the Sobibor concentration camp. The three spent the remainder of the war in hiding, first in a commercial laundry in Voorschoten. They later fled to the west of Holland, where they suffered the "hunger winters," severe food shortages, which were especially hard on those being hidden. Marion had multiple close escapes from the Germans. Of the immediate postwar period, she recalls the trauma of the Red Cross letters, which desperate families relied upon to find news of their relatives, so often only to learn of their deaths in concentration camps. Marion has lived in Jerusalem since 1995. She is a painter whose art expresses her struggles with memory, alienation, and reconciliation. Marion is active in Jewish and interfaith activities, and started a local Israeli NGO, Yad Elie, which has supplied several million lunches to needy Jewish, Muslim, and Christian children in East and West Jerusalem over the last quarter-century.

Marion Kunstenaar BY Reza Green ISRAEL
JERUSALEM, 2022

Dov Sacajiu was born in 1936, in Romania. When he was six, World War II broke out. The Romanians collaborated with the Nazis, and Dov, his parents and two grandmothers were expelled from their home and fled on a horse cart with only their clothing. Dov recalls fleeing while Romanians threw stones at them. Dov survived thanks to a bucket that his mother placed over his head. Dov and his family fled to the town of Solica, and from there were taken to Botosani, where his father and older brothers were taken into forced labor. Dov was separated from his parents and joined other children who were concentrated in a large synagogue without supervision. Terrible conditions prevailed there: overcrowding, severe hunger, freezing cold, and disease. Dov and the other children roamed the town at night in search of food scraps. To keep warm, they would sneak into barns and sleep in hay stacks. Dov recalls the Red Army bombing the town, and its eventual liberation from the Nazi Germans. The streets were littered with dead bodies, which he as a young boy had to place on carts. His family miraculously survived the war, but continued to live in great deprivation. In 1951, they were granted a permit to leave Romania and immigrate to Israel. Difficulties continued to plague them in Israel as well. They were sent to a makeshift camp in Ashkelon and lived in a tent for a period of time. He recalls how food was scarce, and at the age of 14 he was working in a bakery and delivering bread to support his family. The change came when Dov was drafted into the army, where learned to read and write. Dov, who fought in Israel wars, later established his own trucking business. He built a large family in Ashkelon – 'My pride and my victory.'

Dov Sacajiu by Edi Israel ISRAEL
ASHKELON, ISRAEL, 2022

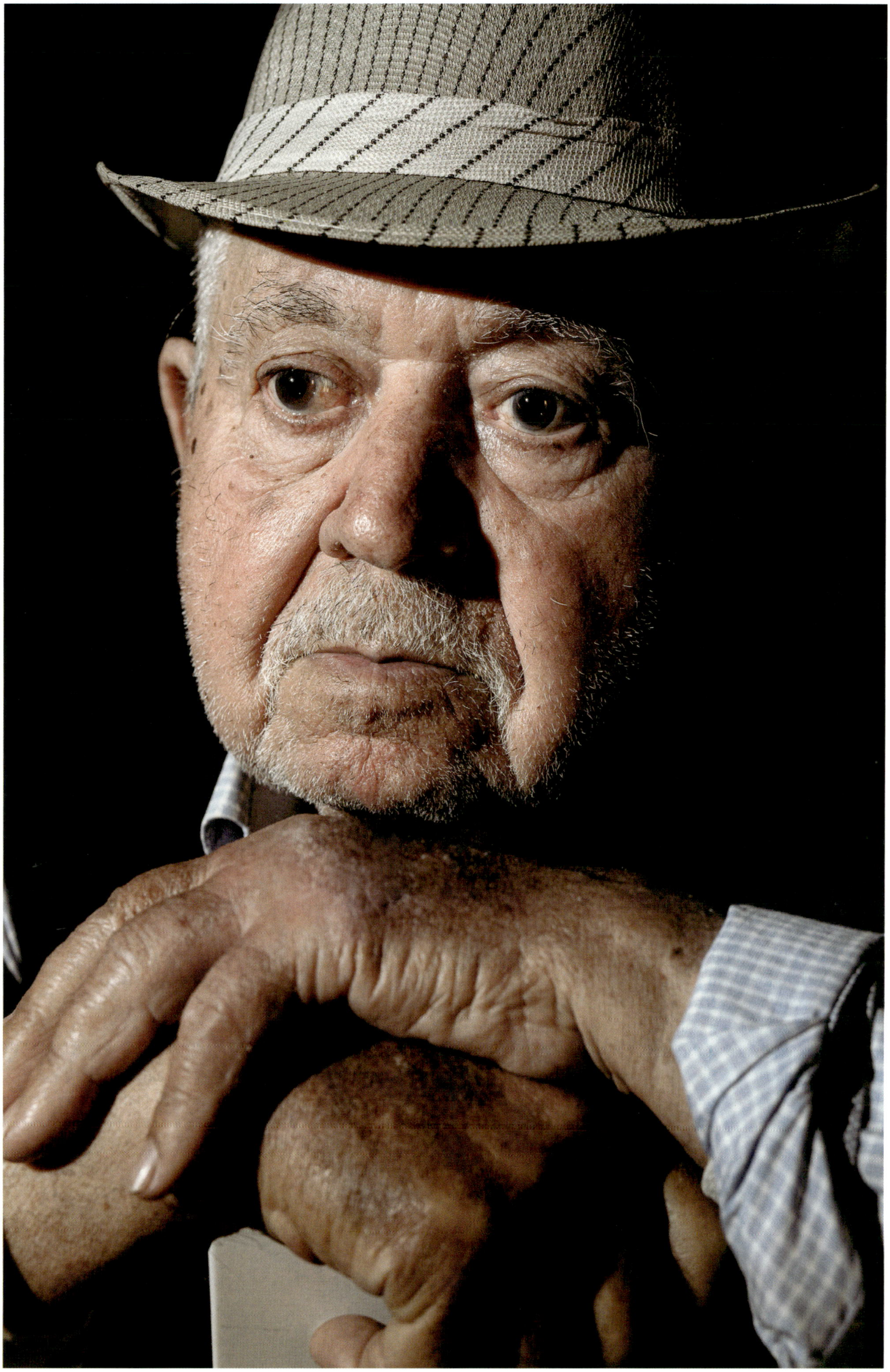

NAFTALI FÜRST was born Juraj Fürst in 1933 in Petržalka, then Czechoslovakia. After the signing of the Munich Agreement in September 1938, Petržalka became part of the Third Reich. Juraj and his family were deported to the Sered labor camp. At the end of 1944, Juraj, his older brother Shmuel and their parents were shipped to Auschwitz. He recalls the train cars opening and the barking of dogs. The brothers were separated from their parents and put in Block 29, the children's block. 'Whole families entered Birkenau and were placed in the barracks. Smoke and fire were coming out of the chimneys.' They were tattooed. 'Dad was 14024, my brother 14025, and I was 14026,' recalls Naftali. He remembers the horrible starvation. After some time, the children were ordered on a march. 'It was like passing through the gates of hell. Those images cannot be described. Blood, crying, dead bodies.' They arrived at Buchenwald on January 23, 1945. 'In Auschwitz they murdered with gas chambers and slave labor,' he says, 'and in Buchenwald with starvation and filth.' It was in Buchenwald, five days after its liberation by the US Army, that the skeletal 12-year-old Juraj was caught on camera by an American lieutenant, Harry Miller. Juraj found an aunt who had survived. One day, he heard his mother's name in a list of survivors read out on the radio. Later he learned his brother and father were alive. His family was reunited. In 1949, Juraj became Naftali and immigrated to Israel, rebuilding his life in Haifa, where he lives today. 'After 60 years of silence, I gave the Germans a kind of pardon. It's not the same generation. I began to tell my story,' he says, adding, 'We are the coals that were not burned in the great fire. It is the last time that we will be able to tell our story and pass it on to future generations.' On October 7, 2023, Naftali woke up to the news that Hamas terrorists had invaded dozens of Israeli communities along the Gaza border. Naftali's granddaughter Mika, her husband Sefi Peleg and their young daughter Neta were hiding without food or water in their safe room in Kibbutz Kfar Azza. "The baby did not cry and the dog did not bark," Mika told Naftali. 'They understood they must be quiet to survive,' says Naftali. At 2 a.m., after 20 hours, the three were rescued by Israeli soldiers, and Naftali could breathe again. 'In the Holocaust, a little bit of luck was not enough to survive. I must have survived because I had a lot of luck. What happened to my family on October 7 is another huge luck, that my granddaughter, her husband, and my sweet great-grandchild were saved from the inferno.'

Naftali Fürst BY Rabia Basha ISRAEL
HAIFA, ISRAEL, 2021

Nikolaus Grünerwas was born in Hungary in 1929. In April of 1944, his entire family was deported to Auschwitz-Birkenau. On arrival, the German SS took the infants from the arms of their mothers. In the first Selektion they went through, as Nazi officials chose who would live and who would be sent to be executed, Nikolaus was separated from his mother and little brother. Nikolaus, his father and older brother were deemed fit to work. The number A11104 is the prisoner's tattoo on his arm. His father and brother were numbered 102 and 103. They were rounded up with hundreds of other men, when an SS officer appeared. "If you work, you'll do fine," he said, and then he pointed to a window; a big fire was blazing. Nikolaus discovered that his mother and little brother had been sent to the gas chambers. On April 16, 1945, five days after the Buchenwald death camp was liberated, US Army Private Harry Miller took the famous photograph of starving prisoners who had been freed and left behind in the barracks. The boy in the bottom left, with his ribs showing, looking frightened at the camera, is Nikolaus. It was several days after his 16th birthday. His lungs were ruined, filled with the coal he had been breathing while doing forced labor. Mentally, however, he was in worse condition. It took him three years to understand that he was not going to be taken away and led to the gas chambers. Nikolaus has been living in Sweden since the 1960s and is keeping the truth about the Holocaust alive. In 2022, while on a visit to Israel, he was reunited with **Naftali Fürst** (opposite page) from his barrack in Buchenwald (seen in the circled image they hold).

Nikolaus Grünerwas & Naftali Fürst BY Ancho Gosh ISRAEL
TEL AVIV, ISRAEL, 2022

ROMAN SHVARTSMAN was born in 1936 in Ukraine to a family of nine children. In 2022, at the age of 86, he is one of the last remaining Holocaust survivors in Odesa. At the outbreak of war, the Red Army drafted Roman's father and older brother, sending them to the front lines. In 1941, the whole of Ukraine was occupied by Nazi Germany and Romanian Axis troops. Roman's mother and her eight siblings tried to escape on a horse-drawn cart, but failed. Soon, two ghettos were established in the city, and Roman's family moved into the Bershad Ghetto. Jews were deported to the ghetto from Bessarabia and nearby areas of the Vinnytsia region. From June 1941 until March 1944, German and Romanian fascists killed a total of 13,871 Jews. In 1942, one of Roman's brothers was killed. The family's intolerable living conditions in the ghetto would mark Roman for life. On March 29, 1944, the city of Bershad was liberated by the Red Army. In 1946, after the end of the war, Roman's father returned home. But Roman's older brother never returned, and only in 1953 was the family notified that he had died heroically while defending Leningrad. At the end of the 19th century, Odesa had the third largest Jewish population in the world, after New York and Warsaw. Even today, in war-torn Ukraine, Odesa is still home to thousands of Jews living in the city. Roman himself is deputy chief rabbi of Odesa. He also leads the association of Jews and of the former ghetto and concentration camp prisoners in the region.

Rabbi Roman Shvartsman BY Daniel Pilar UKRAINE
ODESA, UKRAINE, 2022

HARRY J. FRANSMAN was born in Rotterdam, the Netherlands, in 1922. Harry's family moved to The Hague after the Dutch capitulation to the Germans in 1940. Harry was first sent to a labor camp and then to Westerbork. Then he was taken to Blechhammer, a sub-camp of Auschwitz, where he was held for three years. He was forced on a death march to Gross-Rosen in 1945 and put on a train to Buchenwald but managed to jump from the train into the snow. He returned to the Netherlands after the war, only to find most of his family had perished at the hands of the Nazis. Harry moved to Australia, but the Holocaust still haunts him. He is an accomplished artist and has written several books on his Holocaust experiences. The photo was made on the occasion of Harry's 100th birthday. Harry J. Fransman passed away in Sydney on September 11, 2023.

Harry J. Fransman BY D-MO AUSTRALIA
SYDNEY, AUSTRALIA, 2022

ABBA NAOR was born in 1928 in Kovno (Kaunas), Lithuania. In August 1941, a ghetto was established in Kovno in which the city's Jews were imprisoned, including Abba's family. His eldest brother, Haim, was caught while searching for food, and murdered. The remaining family members were deported to the Stutthof concentration camp, where they were separated. Abba and his father were sent to a Dachau sub-camp to perform forced labor, and sometime later they too separated. Abba's brother Beraleh, and mother Hannah, were sent to Auschwitz. 'The moment I saw my mother and brother heading towards the train, I realized that was it,' recalled Abba. In the Dachau sub-camp Abba was forced to work at construction, digging and driving a diesel train. Later he was transferred to the Kaufering camp. In April the inmates were forced on a death march. They walked without food and water, in rain and snow, eating grass along the way. On May 2, 1945, the Nazi guards disappeared; American soldiers arrived and informed them, "You are free." The war was over. Abba reached a displaced persons camp near Munich where he met his father, and the two moved to Lodz, Poland. In Lodz, Abba joined a Kibbutz Lohamei Haghetaot nucleus, and in 1946 he boarded an illegal immigration ship to Mandatory Palestine. In 1950 he married Leah, and they had two children. Over the years, Abba has worked for Israel's General Security Forces, the Weizmann Institute, and the Mossad. After the end of his state service, he began activities to preserve the memory of the Dachau concentration camp.

Abba Naor BY Michael Shubitz ISRAEL/LITHUANIA

MIKVEH ISRAEL, ISRAEL, 2021

AVRAHAM CARMI was born in Poland in 1928. During the Nazi German invasion, his parents fled to Warsaw, where his uncle, Moshe Posner, was the manager of the Jewish cemetery. Moshe's home was destroyed in the bombings, and Avraham, his parents and other relatives, lived in the cemetery, where he celebrated his Bar Mitzvah. In order to meet the quota for a food ration card, Avraham assisted in building the walls of the Warsaw Ghetto. Amid deportations from the Warsaw Ghetto to the extermination camps in the summer of 1942, the Nazis raided the Jewish cemetery and caught or shot dead those who tried to run and hide. The cemetery watchman, Moshe Gelbkrin, was ordered to leave the Umschlagplatz (deportation area) to take care of the burials. He pretended that Avraham's mother was his wife, and the two smuggled Avraham out in a backpack. Avraham's father was deported to Treblinka, where he perished. Avraham, his mother and his uncle assisted in the burial of the victims of the cemetery killings. During the Warsaw Ghetto Uprising in the spring of 1943, the bunker where they were hiding was discovered. Avraham, his mother and his uncle Moshe were shipped to Majdanek, where his mother, Lea, was murdered. Avraham and his uncle Moshe were taken to a labor camp in Budzyn, where they worked in an aircraft factory. Later they were sent to a forced labor camp in Radom, and on a death march towards Tomaszów Mazowiecki, Birkenau and other labor camps. Moshe, who watched over Avraham, died of exhaustion just two days before liberation. In September 1945, Avraham immigrated to Mandatory Palestine. In the 1948 War of Independence, Avraham fought in the Etzion Bloc and was taken prisoner by the Jordanians. After his release from captivity, Avraham worked in the Mikveh Israel Agricultural School and was an inspector in the Education Ministry. He married Rivka, a survivor of Bergen-Belsen, and they created a family. Avraham lit one of the six torches on Holocaust Remembrance Day at Yad Vashem in 2020.

Avraham Carmi BY Eric Sultan ISRAEL
JERUSALEM, 2022

DALIA HOFMEKLER GINZBURG was born in 1938 in Kovno, Lithuania. 'My father was a well-known musician in Lithuania, Michael Hofmekler, a violinist and conductor. My grandfather played the cello and contrabass. My father and grandfather formed an orchestra together with other musicians and played for the Germans. This was during the "quiet" period of the ghetto. After the Aktions, the killing of academics and intellectuals, a short period of calm followed. When they decided to liquidate the ghetto, they killed little children who could not work and old people who could not contribute. When it became known that there was to be an Aktion against children and the elderly, my mother obtained the address of Mania, our cousins' housekeeper. I remember the separation to this day. A five-year-old girl's separation from her mother leaves a lifelong trauma. This was not the last parting. She dressed me up and prepared me to go with Aunt Mania who would take me to her village. A German officer named Berter, who rescued some children from the ghetto, hid me in a small kitchen cupboard with top drawers that he opened so I could have some air, and loaded the cupboard on a cart pulled by a mare. The ghetto was liquidated. My grandfather was sent to Auschwitz, my grandmother was killed in the ghetto, my father was sent to Dachau, and my mother was sent with the rest of the women to a camp on the Polish-German border. Father again survived because of his music. Mom endured because she knew she had to survive to get back to me. She became ill with typhus and fell during the death march on a pile of dead in the snow. She was rescued by a Russian soldier passing by. Father was rescued by the Americans, and he arrived to Israel in '48. I stayed with my rescuers until Kovno was freed and sent to a new orphanage for children who had survived the killings. Of 1,500 children, less than 200 survived. My mother found me, but she was sent to the Urals as a political prisoner. I was thirteen in 1952 when we were reunited at last, and we had four good years together. In '56 my father succeeded in obtaining permission for us to immigrate to Israel. My parents did not reunite and did not live together because he already had someone else.'

Dalia Hofmekler Ginzburg BY Michael Shubitz ISRAEL/LITHUANIA
ASHDOD, ISRAEL, 2022

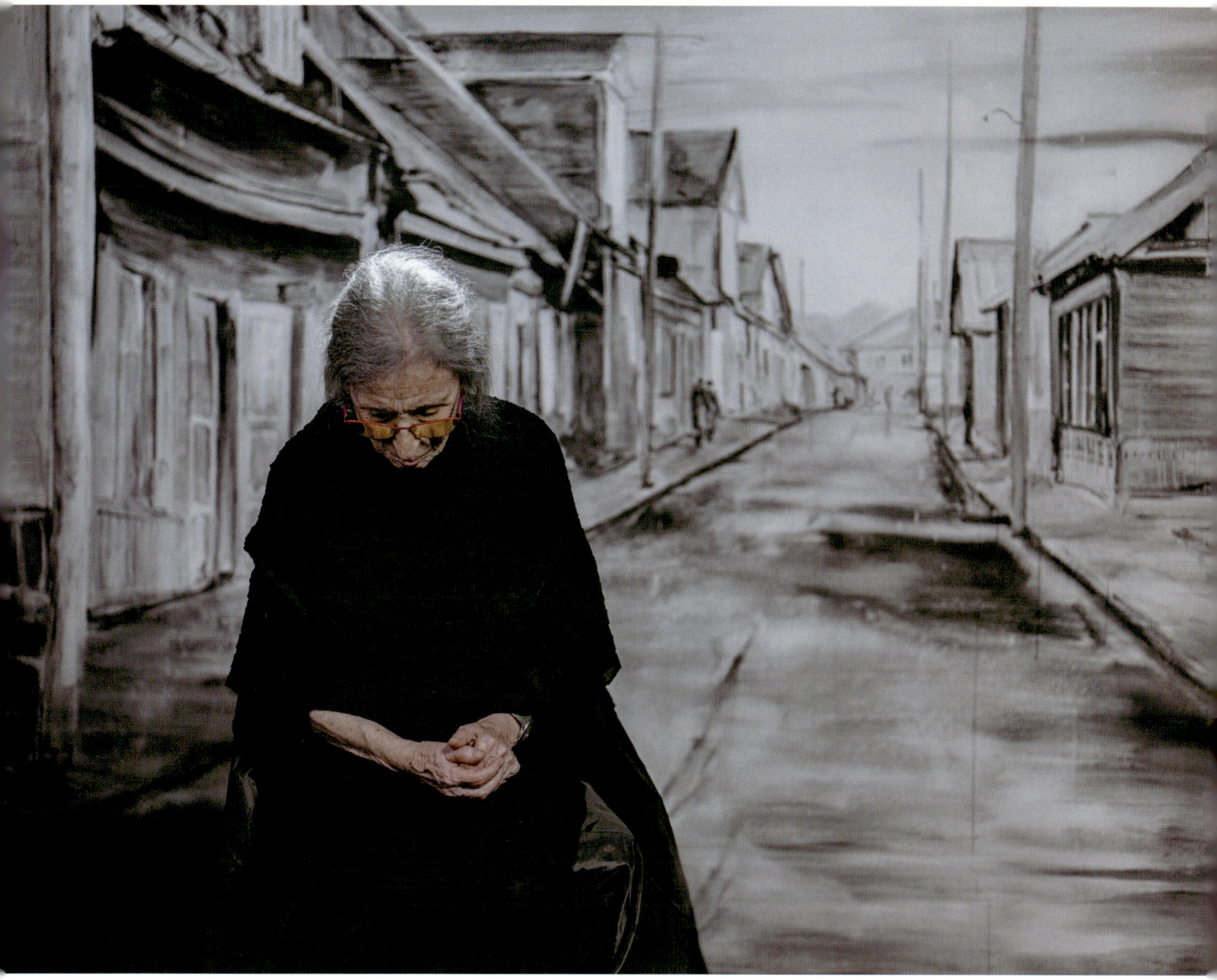

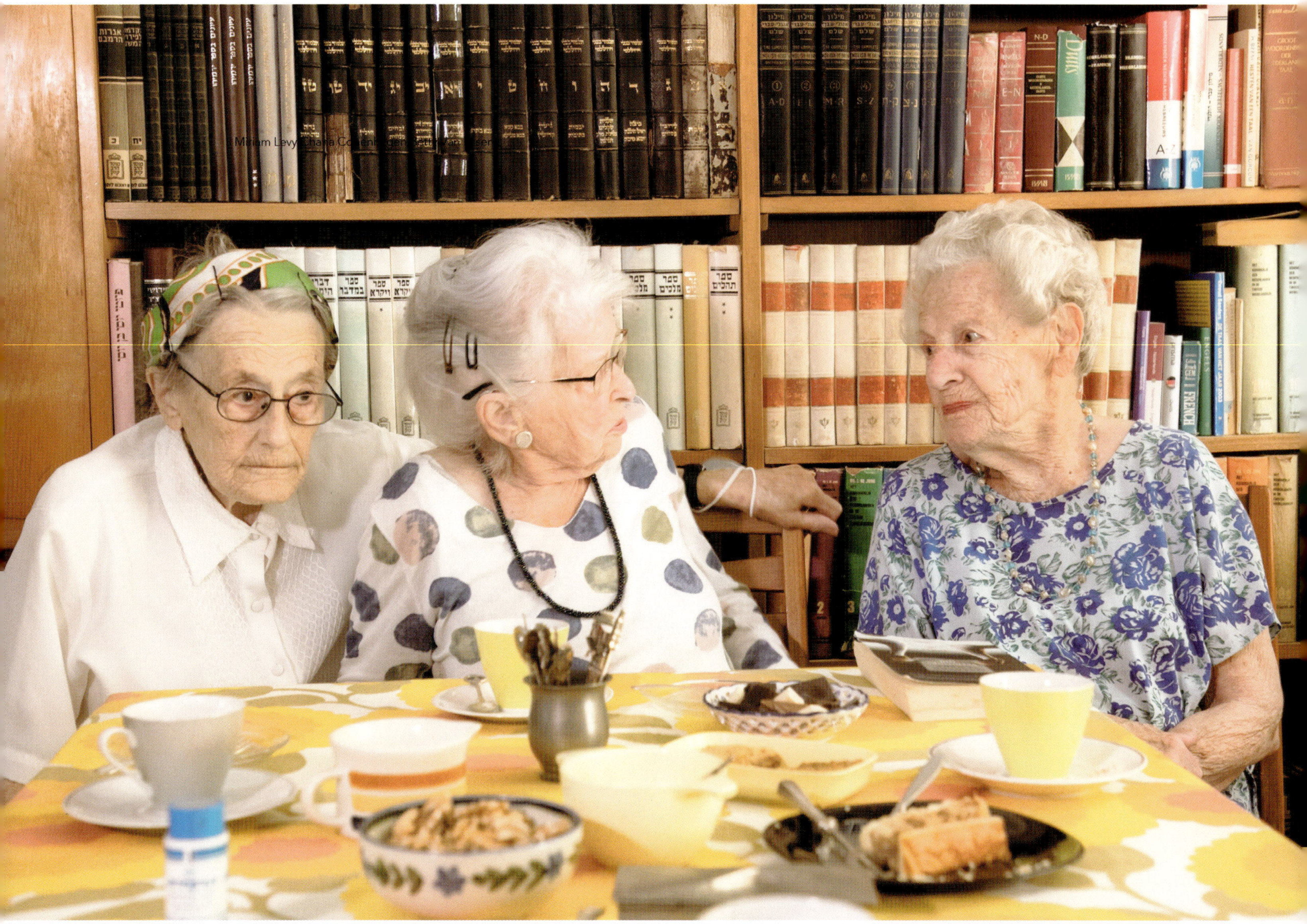

CHANA ANNA COPENHAGEN (L) was born in Amsterdam in 1924. 'I grew up in a religious family. Father was a Jewish community official in Amsterdam. I had an older sister who was a nurse in a Jewish hospital. When Nazi Germany occupied the Netherlands my parents and my sister received a permit to leave but I did not, and they never left. A relative, who was Christian, arranged for separate hiding places for my sister and myself but my parents were caught and sent to their deaths in Sobibor camp. In 1951, I left the Netherlands to marry in Israel. I worked as a nurse for the first president of the State of Israel, President Chaim Weizmann.'

BETTY VAN ESSEN (C) was born in Amsterdam in 1924. 'My family was forced to move into a Jewish ghetto established during WWII in the city center. My younger and older brothers were captured at the start of the Nazi occupation and were murdered in Mauthausen concentration camp. My parents died in the gas chambers.' Betty was taken to a hiding place in 1942 by her cousin's husband, a member of the Dutch underground, who was caught by the Nazis and murdered. She was given a fake identity and her life was saved by Piet and Griet Heymans who sheltered her throughout the war. When war ended Betty returned to Amsterdam, but there was no family left and no home. About 100 of her family members perished during the Holocaust and their names are inscribed on Monument Schaduwkade in Amsterdam.

MIRJAM BOLLE LEVY (R) was born in Amsterdam in 1917. 'My father was a "crazy" Zionist, but it saved our lives. He was the chairman of the Jewish National Fund (KKL) in Holland and he was also registered in Mandatory Palestine. Nazi Germany held five prisoner exchanges during the Shoah in which German Templars living in Mandatory Palestine were swapped for Jews who had residency in Palestine. We were part of the fourth exchange. We were held in Bergen-Belsen concentration camp and my sister and I with our parents were saved. Our extended family all perished in death camps. We arrived in Mandatory Palestine on July 11, 1944. I lived in Jerusalem and worked at the Dutch council and later the embassy till 1991.' All during the Nazi occupation of Amsterdam and through two prison camps Mirjam Bolle wrote, and was able to keep, letters she wrote to her fiancée, Leo Bolle. These letters written over 18 months shed light on the "Judenrat" or Jewish Councils who were responsible for implementing Nazi orders in the Netherlands. Mirjam Bolle miraculously was able to save the letters by throwing them over a prison fence and then, after arriving in Mandatory Palestine in 1944, stashed the letters away for decades until coming upon them in the year 2000. She decided to publish them under the title *Letters Never Sent*, which has been translated into many languages. In the book she writes, "I am vain enough to believe that this diary may be found hundreds of years from now and serve as an important source of information." Mirjam, well past 100, continues to travel and speak out on the Holocaust.

Chana Copenhagen, Betty Van Essen, Mirjam Bolle Levy
BY Sasson Tiram ISRAEL
JERUSALEM, 2022

ANNA ORNSTEIN was born in 1927 in Hungary. Her hometown, Szendrő, had only 40 Jewish families, and Anna felt the presence of antisemitism while growing up. In 1944, Nazi Germany invaded Hungary. The Jews of Szendrő were identified, forced to wear yellow stars, and designated for extermination. Anna and her family were sent to the Auschwitz death camp. The Nazis killed her father and grandmother and her extended family on their arrival in Auschwitz in June 1944. Her two brothers were sent to forced labor, and perished. Anna was 17 when she was imprisoned in Auschwitz along with her mother, whose vision was impaired. Her glasses were taken away and Anna became her mother's eyes and hands. The powerful bond between the two was an important factor in their survival. Anna recalls her initial denial of the crematoria, and of Nazi soldiers who would snuff out a human life. Anna and her mother were transferred to Plaszów, but were returned to Auschwitz. Later they were transferred to the Parschnitz forced labor camp. They were liberated from Parschnitz on May 8, 1945, by the Soviet Army. Anna was reunited with her boyfriend Paul Ornstein after the war. They married in 1946. The couple attended medical school in Europe before immigrating to the United States in 1951. There, in Cincinnati, they rebuilt their lives. Anna is a professor of child psychiatry at Harvard University, and professor emeritus of child psychology at the University of Cincinnati. In 2004, she published her memoir, *My Mother's Eyes: Holocaust Memories of a Young Girl*, a collection of short stories of her life during the war. Anna's husband, Paul, passed away in 2017. Anna continues her mission as an educator on the Holocaust and talks to students at universities and groups around the world.

Anna Ornstein BY **Kristen Joy Emack** USA
BOSTON, MASSACHUSETTS, USA, 2022

OTTO DOV PRESSBURGER was born in 1923 in Czechoslovakia. He had four siblings. In April 1942, Otto, his father and his older brother Yulios were among the first deported to Auschwitz. His brother Latzi was murdered at Majdanek. His mother and grandmother were also killed. Otto's prisoner number, 29045, was tattooed onto his chest. His father was murdered three weeks later. Otto and Yulios witnessed the Germans' first gassing experiments. Otto had to dig a pit into which the victims of the experiments were thrown, dead or alive. Along with other prisoners, Otto was ordered to burn the bodies. Otto witnessed his brother Yulios sent to his death. Otto used his fluency in German to survive encounters with SS officers, and was later transferred to Birkenau, where he took part in the construction of prisoners' barracks and the crematorium. He also witnessed mass gassings there. In July 1942, Otto's brother Aladar arrived on a transport with his wife and daughter. Only when Otto, whose weight was then 30 kilograms, sang a family childhood song did Aladar recognize him. A few days later, Aladar and his family were murdered. On January 18, 1945, as Auschwitz was evacuated, Otto was loaded on a train headed for Austria together with Polish prisoners. He jumped from the speeding train on Czech territory, and played dead. He then found refuge at the home of Czech farmers, with whom he stayed until the end of the war. In 1947, Otto immigrated to Mandatory Palestine. After being detained at Atlit, he joined the Haganah and fought in the War of Independence. In Israel, Otto was reunited with his brother Alexander, who had immigrated in 1938. Otto and his wife Bracha live in Herzliya.

Otto Dov Pressburger BY Rafat Zrieq ISRAEL
HERZLIYA, ISRAEL, 2022

RACHEL LEVI MASHIACH was born in 1936 in Bulgaria. In 1941, Bulgaria allied with Nazi Germany, and the Bulgarian government announced racial laws and restrictions aimed at its Jewish citizens. The Nazis demanded that Bulgaria deport its Jews to death camps. Neighbors came to the aid of Rachel, her sister Rina, and their parents Angela and Moshe, and the family was able to remain in Sofia. Bulgarian authorities faced resistance from ordinary citizens and from the Bulgarian Orthodox Church. Senior church officials Patriarch Cyril and Prelate Stephan I refused to cooperate with the Nazis. In 1943, when the Jews of the city of Plovdiv were rounded up, destined to be deported, Patriarch Cyril joined them, declaring that he would go where they would go. That message was conveyed to Tsar Boris III of Bulgaria. The Jews of Plovdiv were released, and the deportations of Bulgaria's Jews were called off. Instead, many were subjected to forced labor, but survived. The Jews from Greece, Thrace and Macedonia who had fallen under the Bulgarian regime during World War II were deported to death camps. When the war ended, Rachel's father, Moshe, returned from the forced labor camp, and the family was reunited. In 1948, they immigrated to the newly independent Israel. Patriarch Cyril and Stefan I of Bulgaria have been recognized as Righteous Among the Nations. Rachel is pictured with daughter Shlomit and Shahar, 11, Rachel's youngest grandson, taking part in a massive demonstration in Tel Aviv, supporting democracy in Israel and protesting against efforts to weaken it.

Rachel Masiach BY Jim Hollander USA
TEL AVIV, ISRAEL, 2023

MALKA RENDEL was born in Hungary in 1927. Malka's mother, Sara, who was widowed before the war, provided for a family of eight. The Germans entered their town of Nagyecsed in 1944, and the Jews were deported to the Mátészalka Ghetto. Three weeks later Malka and her family were crammed into a cattle car headed for the Auschwitz extermination camp, a journey which lasted six days. On arrival, during the Selektion, in which Nazi officers chose which inmates would be sent to immediate execution and which would be spared for forced labor, Malka and her sisters, Miriam and Rachel, were separated from their mother and their extended family. Her mother gave Malka two cookies, and her last words to the older sisters were, "Take care of Malka." Three months later, Malka and her sisters were sent to the Płaszów concentration camp. There they labored in a quarry where prisoners were constantly being killed by falling rocks. Returned to Auschwitz after the winter, they were sent to Neustadt, to a factory for weaving parachutes. As the Red Army approached, Malka and her sisters were forced on a death march, during which those who collapsed were shot. At night, to survive, the sisters hugged each other. The three were transferred to Bergen-Belsen camp, where Miriam and Rachel died. Malka cries when she remembers how their bodies were thrown through a window onto a pile of corpses. 'They gave me their bread. If I hadn't eaten it, maybe they would have survived. Only when I roll up my sleeve and look at the number on my arm, it proves to me that it did happen.' After liberation, Malka was hospitalized in Sweden. Upon her recovery, she and other refugees boarded a ship to Mandatory Palestine. The British police redirected the ship to detention camps in Cyprus, where Malka continued studying Hebrew. In Israel she became a Hebrew teacher to new immigrants, and married Yehoshua. They have three daughters, eleven grandchildren, 36 great-grandchildren and one great-great-grandson.

Malka Rendel BY Anat Saragusti ISRAEL
TEL AVIV, 2023

RYFKA FINKELSTEIN was born in 1928 in Korytnica, Poland, the fourth of five children. In June 1941, Korytnica was occupied by Nazi Germany. The Nazis, with the cooperation of the Ukrainian police, established ghettos, Jewish schools were discontinued, and the Jews were ordered to wear the yellow Star of David. Ryfka recalls, 'My mother did so much better than my father and sisters. She died a natural death. I wished in the time of the war that I could die. I would like to go to sleep and never wake up.' On May 25, 1942, the Gestapo and Ukrainian police surrounded the Korytnica Ghetto, rounding up young Jewish men and women under the pretext of sending them to work. Early that morning, before the roundup, Ryfka's father asked her to sneak out and fetch some lima beans from a gentile neighbor. "The less you're home, the better," he said. When she reached the neighbor's home, she could hear shooting in the town. The gentile woman went into Korytnica to find out what happened. She returned and said, "Ryfka, you don't have anybody left." The Jews of Korytnica had been led to the forest edge and shot. Ryfka was told to take off her shoes and coat and run toward the fields and meadows. While running, Ryfka came to a crossroads and met her brother Anshel, who hadn't been home at the time of the roundup. They began to realize their father and sisters were among the murdered Jews.

Ryfka and Anshel spent the next two years moving from one hiding place to another. They survived thanks to the rare acts of kindness from farmers they encountered. 'One man, Mitke, started giving us food every evening,' Ryfka recalls. 'Others would give me a piece of bread. That kept us alive. Anyone helping a Jew in any way could have been killed themselves.' Ryfka and Anshel slept inside haystacks and never ventured out in daylight. 'We were all alone in the world.' Liberation came in 1944, when the brother and sister escaped into the woods and joined the Russian partisans who were fleeing towards the advancing Red Army lines. They were crossing the Turiya River when Ryfka's strength began to flag, but she could hear her father's voice urging her forward, "*Noch a bissele*" (Yiddish),"a little more," to freedom. In 1964, Ryfka and her brother Anshel learned that their brother Leyve survived the Holocaust as a partisan and soldier in the Soviet Army. Ryfka emigrated to the USA in 1950 with her husband Jacob, a Holocaust survivor whose family perished in the Sobibor death camp. The Finkelsteins settled in New Jersey with their four children and ran a chicken business. Ryfka, 94, told her photographer, 'I am happy that I wasn't caught by police or by Germans. I'm happy that I wasn't killed…dying, I wanted to die, but I didn't want to be killed. I did survive. I looked life straight in the face. It's good to be alive.'

Ryfka Finkelstein BY Sara Bennett USA
CHERRY HILL, NEW JERSEY, USA, 2023

Chaim Grosbein was born in 1937 in Dołhinów, Poland (today Belarus). In July 1941, Nazi Germany occupied Dołhinów, and the town's Jews were forced into the ghetto. In 1942, Chaim's father and cousin were sent to forced labor, where they were murdered by the Nazis. During an Aktion, a military roundup operation in the ghetto, Chaim, his mother and three siblings hid in a pit. The pit was discovered, but by chance, Chaim and his cousin Rishka went undetected. They were the only survivors. Searching for help, the two children found their aunt, Dvosia, who took them into hiding on the edge of the ghetto. During the next Aktion, they escaped to the partisans in the woods. The partisans tried to smuggle out the Jews behind enemy lines, but they were ambushed by the Germans, and Chaim was shot in the leg. His Aunt Dvosia carried him on her back until she was no longer able. Chaim was later found by Russian partisans, and their Jewish doctor operated on him without anesthesia. The partisans then retreated from the area. Chaim was left alone. He slept in ditches and hunted for food and water for two long years, occasionally herding cattle for the farmers in the villages. Chaim fled to a partisan camp. From there, he was sent first to a Belarussian orphanage and, later, was drafted into the Red Army. When the war ended, he learned that only Aunt Dvosia and another aunt had survived. In 1960, Chaim immigrated to Israel. In 1965, he married **Aliza**. Three years after Aliza was born in 1939 in Rovno, Poland (today Ukraine), her family attempted to escape. Her mother was caught and executed by the Nazis. 'My father paid all he owned to save his children. I was raised as a Christian on a farm and despite us being children, we were forced to hard physical labor. When war ended, my father returned for his children, and I refused to leave the Christian family.' In 1962, Aliza, already an experienced nurse, immigrated to Israel. On Yom HaShoah, 2016, Chaim lit a memorial torch in the ceremony in Yad Vashem, Jerusalem.

Chaim & Aliza Grosbein BY Tomer Neuberg ISRAEL
MODI'IN, ISRAEL, 2023

Gizella Lefkovits BY *Avner Shahaf* ISRAEL

HERZLIYA, ISRAEL, 2023

Gizella Lefkovits was born in Hungary in 1924. Following the Nazi invasion in the spring of 1944, Gizella and her family were deported from their home in Nyirtass and were confined to the Kisvárda Ghetto, in the area around the synagogue. A few weeks later, the Nazis rounded up all the Jews, loading them onto cattle trains bound for Auschwitz. Gizella recalls every detail of that three-day journey, the cries and screams and the gasping for some air. 'People were collapsing all around me, many died in the wagons.' She describes the first Selektion, when SS officer and physician Josef Mengele would choose which of the new arrivals would be sent to forced labor, and which to immediate execution. She remembers him pointing with his stick, determining 'who to live and who to die.' She and her five sisters held on to each other while they were being separated from their parents and brother, never to be seen again. 'My sisters and me were ordered to the showers and we were afraid to undress. The gas chambers were already known.' Eventually they were forced to undress, and their hair was shaved off, but all Gizella could think about was where her parents were. Gizella remembers having asked again and again for her mother. The guard of their block then pointed to the smoke rising from the crematorium chimneys. For six months, the six sisters looked after each other, surviving the daily Selektions. They were shipped to forced labor, digging anti-tank trenches in the front lines at the border of Poland and Germany. As the Allied forces were advancing, the sisters were forced by the Nazis on a death march away from the front lines, inland. The sisters helped each other along the frozen roads, not allowing each other to show any sign of weakness, knowing that this would be a death sentence and that they would be shot. They marched for an entire week, crossing empty villages and deserted farms, where the Nazis stopped at night. It was in one of those farms that the sisters decided to hide in a haystack. The following morning, an SS guard poked his bayonet into the large stacks of hay, injuring Gizella's youngest sister, who saved all of her sisters by not making a sound. The sisters emerged from the hay 24 hours later. Thirsty, they threw themselves on the snow. The Red Army was advancing, and in a matter of days the sisters were liberated. They returned to Hungary, where Gizella met her future husband, Nandor. In 1949, they immigrated to Israel, created a family and rebuilt their lives. 'For many years I was silent, I was ashamed I stayed alive.' Gizella, 99 years old, lights Sabbath candles in the apartment where she lives, independent and on her own. One of the two candlesticks is lit every Friday for her mother who perished in Auschwitz.

Leonid & Zina Bernshtein BY Ricki Rosen USA/ISRAEL

BAT YAM, ISRAEL, 2023

LEONID BERNSHTEIN was born in Kherson, Ukraine, in 1939. His wife ZINA was born in 1941, in the Dubno Ghetto, Poland (today Ukraine). She was an infant when the Nazis came into Dubno, rounded up the ghetto's Jews and marched them all out of the town, bound for extermination. Zina's father threw Zina into the crowd, and the baby was caught by a Polish woman, Maria Ostrovska, who used to work for Zina's grandparents. Maria took care of Zina throughout the war, often hiding her in the basement among sacks of potatoes. Zina became Halina Ostrovska and was raised as a Christian child. After the war, Maria revealed to Zina her Jewish identity. She told her that her parents and grandparents had been killed by the Nazis. Zina was sent to a Jewish orphanage in Lodz after Maria was rewarded financially by an American organization searching for surviving Jewish children. Zina spent three years at the orphanage. She recovered from tuberculosis, and was adopted in 1949 by a renowned Jewish professor from Warsaw, Berl Mark. Zina recalls how happy she was to finally have a home, but could never call her adoptive parents, "Mother and Father." In 1941, Leonid's father, a Red Army officer, was killed. Leonid's mother fled with her two boys toward the Urals near Siberia. They were aboard a train when German forces carried out a bombing attack. In the commotion, Leonid's six-year-old brother ran into the forest. Three days passed before his mother was able to locate him. In 1946, they moved to Poland, where Leonid fell in love with tennis and became a young prodigy in the Polish sports scene. In 1957, Leonid and his family immigrated to Israel, and he began a lifetime career of playing and coaching tennis and ping pong. He was the second-ranked Israeli national tennis champion in the 1970s. Leonid met Zina in 1963 in Israel, and a month later they were married. The couple created a family in Bat Yam, near the sea. Leonid says that Zina never felt truly loved and kissed until the day they met.

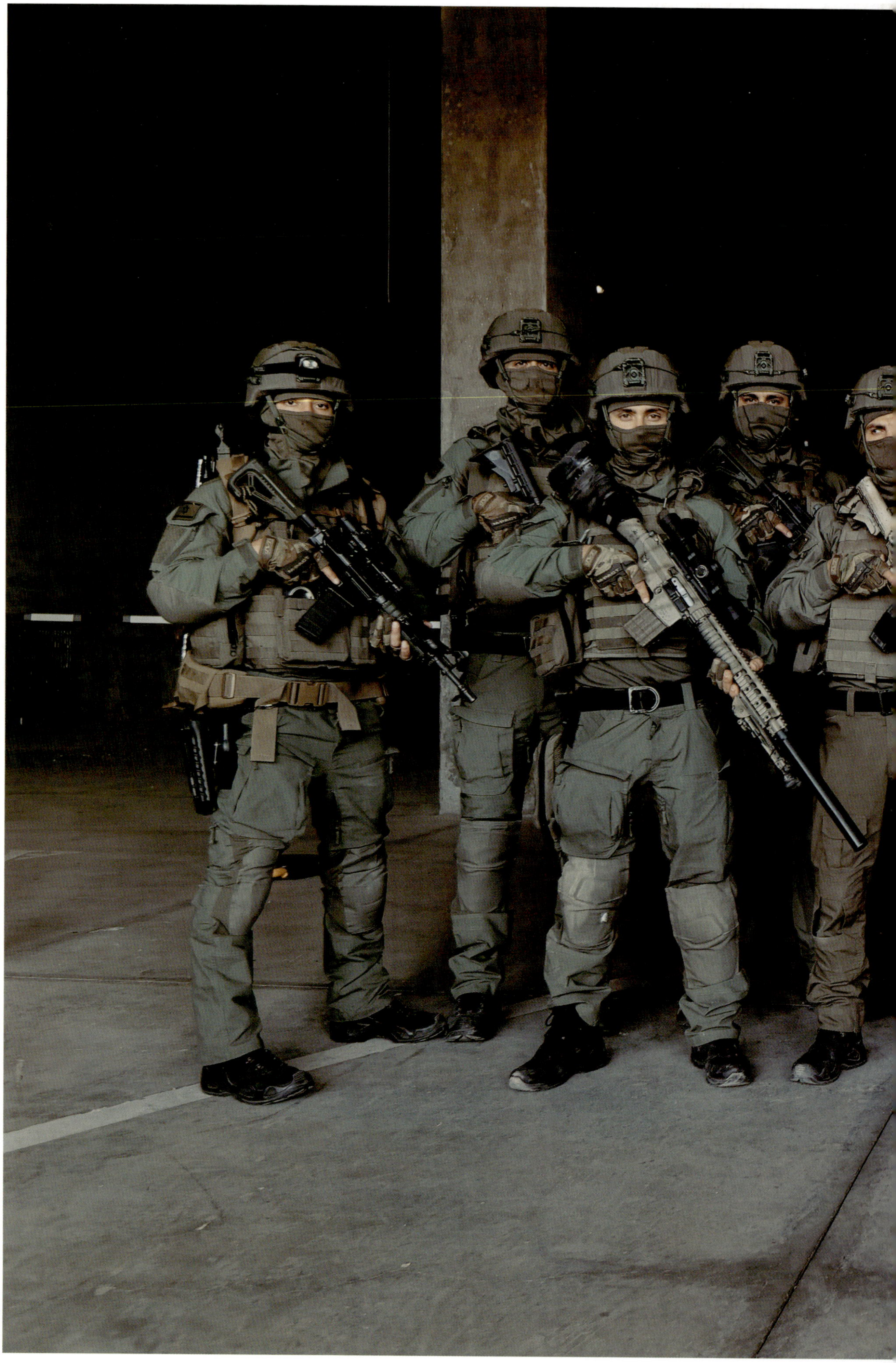

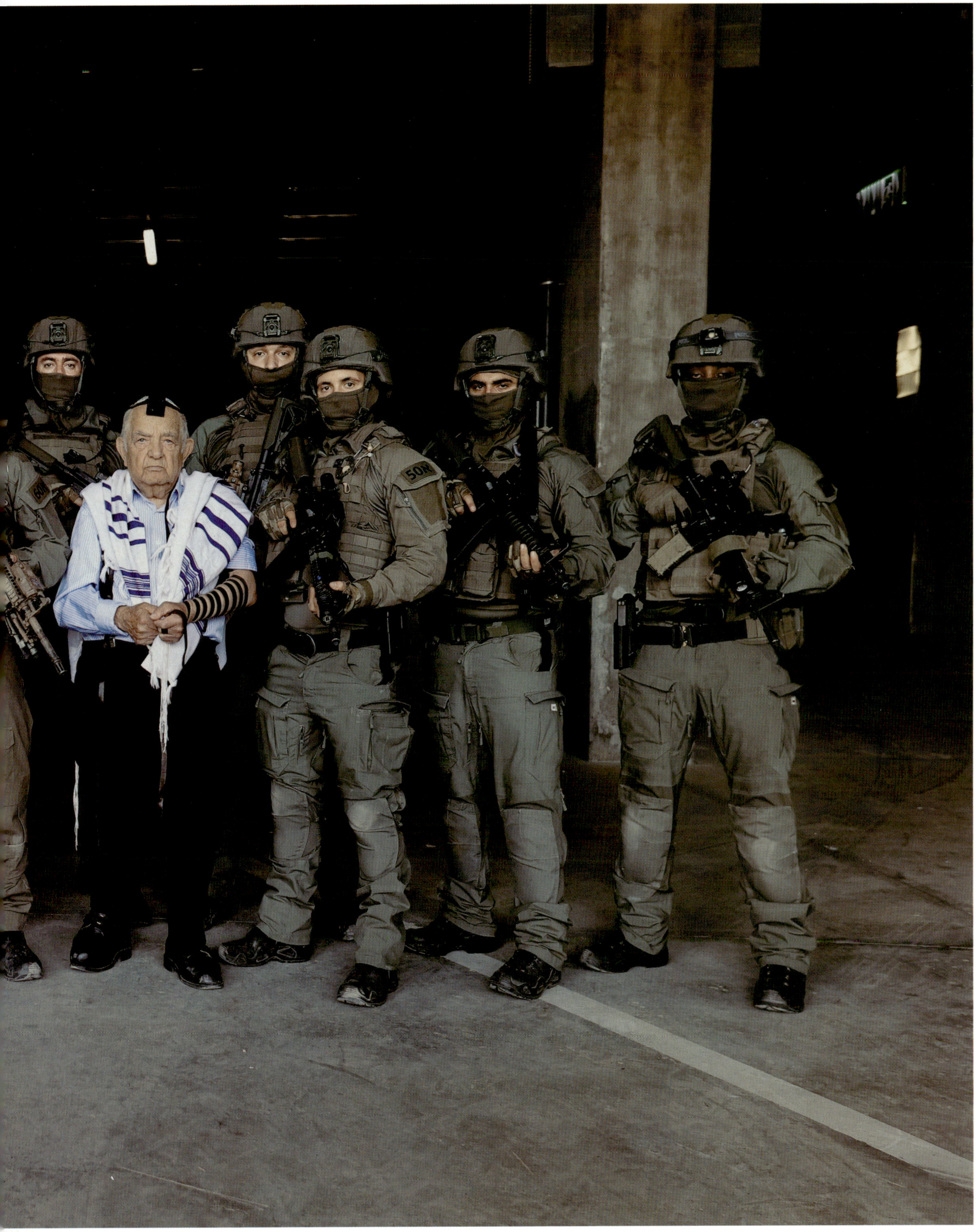

YECHEZKEL HERSHTIK was born in Romania in 1931. The seventh of nine siblings, Yechezkel, who was born with a disability, recalls how the family was expelled to the Nalacz Ghetto. 'The ghetto in Nalacz was surrounded by walls and a Nazi military camp. Jewish families were placed there and assigned a small sleeping area.' From there the family was transferred to other labor camps, where they endured four years of hunger, slavery and oppression. Yechezkel's older brothers were taken to forced labor camps. Three of his brothers perished in the labor camps. When Yechezkel was 12, he remembers stopping on a bridge as they were marched from the Romanian camp of Sacel to the camp of Iliora. They lit candles along the wall of the bridge, said the Hanukkah prayers, and then continued on their way. 'One day we were ordered to prepare to move to another camp in Germany. We already knew about the extermination of the Jews, and everybody burst out crying. That night we heard a voice that woke us all up. Father said it is time and we must get ready, but the voice was of his friend from the ghetto, screaming "We survived! We survived!" Father did not believe him at first. They hugged, and his friend shouted that Nazi Germany had surrendered to the Russians. The camp courtyard was filled with the joy of liberation, but father warned us that beyond the walls there was still a camp of disgruntled German troops, and he asked everyone to be silent. The next day, joy was replaced by apprehension. No one knew what to do. We are free, and there is nowhere to go, no one to take care of us. There is nothing to eat, nothing to drink. And there is a fear that the Germans will return to take revenge.' The surviving members of the Hershtik family decided to emigrate to Mandatory Palestine. Yechezkel received his certificate to immigrate only when he turned 16. In 1947, accompanied by his youngest sister, they boarded a boat for Palestine. But the British Army, under government orders to restrict Jewish immigration to Palestine, redirected the ship to a detention camp in Cyprus. The next year, just days before Israel was declared a state, Yechezkel arrived at Haifa port. Yechezkel would marry and create a family. Recently widowed, he was "adopted" by the undercover unit of the Jerusalem Police, which has a custom to "adopt" lonely Holocaust survivors, keep them company and assist with their needs. 'It was my dream to feel protected,' says Yechezkel, 'not only in the labor camp during the war, but as a child fearing to walk down the street because I'm a Jew.' For his photograph, Yechezkel donned phylacteries and wrapped himself in a tallit prayer shawl, as symbols of his dream having come true.

Yechezkel Hershtik BY Oren Cohen ISRAEL
JERUSALEM, 2022

HEDY BOHM was born in Transylvania in 1928. An only child, Hedy attended an all-girls Jewish school until tenth grade. In April 1944, Hedy and her family were sent to the Oradea Ghetto, and later deported to Auschwitz-Birkenau. They were then separated. 'As long as I was with my parents, I felt safe. But on arrival, when we had to get off, within moments, my father was gone. My mother was gone.' Hedy assumed that her parents were alive, enduring the torments of the camp, as she was. For months, she slept on dirt floors in crowded barracks with thousands of other Jewish women. In August 1944, she was relocated to a forced labor camp, where she spent the remainder of the war, producing military equipment for the Germans. Hedy was liberated by American forces in April 1945. After the war, Hedy learned that her parents were murdered soon after they had arrived in Auschwitz. In December 1947, she married Imre Bohm and the two obtained a visa to Canada. They arrived in Toronto in August 1948, built a family and a small shoe business. Hedy was widowed in 1992, and started a new life in Holocaust education.

Hedy Bohm BY Ziv Koren ISRAEL
OŚWIĘCIM-AUSCHWITZ, POLAND, 2023

Arek Hersh was born in Poland in 1928. He was one of five children in an Orthodox Jewish family. In 1939, Nazi Germany occupied Poland and began the immediate persecution of the Jews. Arek witnessed Jews being dragged from their homes and beaten in the streets. His own father was among them. Arek's family was deported to the Chelmno death camp, and Arek, then 11, was sent to forced labor. Arek was later placed in the orphanage of the Lodz Ghetto until its liquidation by the Nazis. Arek and the children were rounded up and loaded onto a cattle train bound for Auschwitz. During the notorious Nazi Selektion in Auschwitz, in which many of the arrivals were separated out and sent to be murdered, Arek took advantage of a moment of SS distraction, and swapped queues. This saved his life. His friends from the orphanage, including his first love, were sent to their deaths. Arek witnessed Nazis experimenting with gas, as prisoners were shuffled into a van. The van's exhaust fumes were then piped into the vehicle. Arek recalls having to deal with the horror of death which surrounded him for years through many transfers from camp to camp. Arek was forced on a death march to Buchenwald, and later shipped to Theresienstadt. On May 8, 1945, he was liberated by the Russians. By May 14, he was on a Lancaster bomber headed for England. He was enrolled in the Windermere program, which Briton Leonard Montefiore had set up for Jewish orphans of the Nazi death camps. Arek and his sister Mania were the only members of their family to survive. In 1948, Arek volunteered to fight in Israel's War of Independence. After the war, he returned to the UK, where he lives with his wife Jean. He did not speak about his experiences until 1995. In 2009, he was awarded an MBE for his voluntary service to Holocaust education.

Arek Hersh BY Ziv Koren ISRAEL
OŚWIĘCIM-AUSCHWITZ, POLAND, 2023

Nate Leipciger was born in Poland in 1928. When he was eleven years old, the family was forced to leave their home in Chorzów and move into the Sosnowiec Ghetto. The family was later deported to Auschwitz, separating Nate from his mother and sister. He would never see them again. Twice his father saved Nate from death. Nate recalls how, when he stood in the queue for the gas chamber, his father pulled him out and smuggled him back into the barracks. Later, when the Nazis were about to send his father to forced labor in Germany, his father convinced a Nazi officer that Nate was a useful electrician. The officer allowed Nate to accompany his father to forced labor. They were later incarcerated in the concentration camps of Fünfteichen, Gross-Rosen and Flossenbürg, before ending up at Waldlager V, part of the Mühldorf camp complex and a sub-camp of the Dachau concentration camp. Nate and his father were liberated by American soldiers on May 2, 1945. Three years later, they immigrated to Canada, where Nate attended high school and earned a degree in engineering. He married Bernice, and the couple created a large family. Nate has participated 18 times in the March of the Living, from Auschwitz to Birkenau. Nate also guided Canadian Prime Minister Justin Trudeau through the Auschwitz camp.

Nate Leipciger BY Ziv Koren ISRAEL
OŚWIĘCIM–AUSCHWITZ, POLAND, 2023

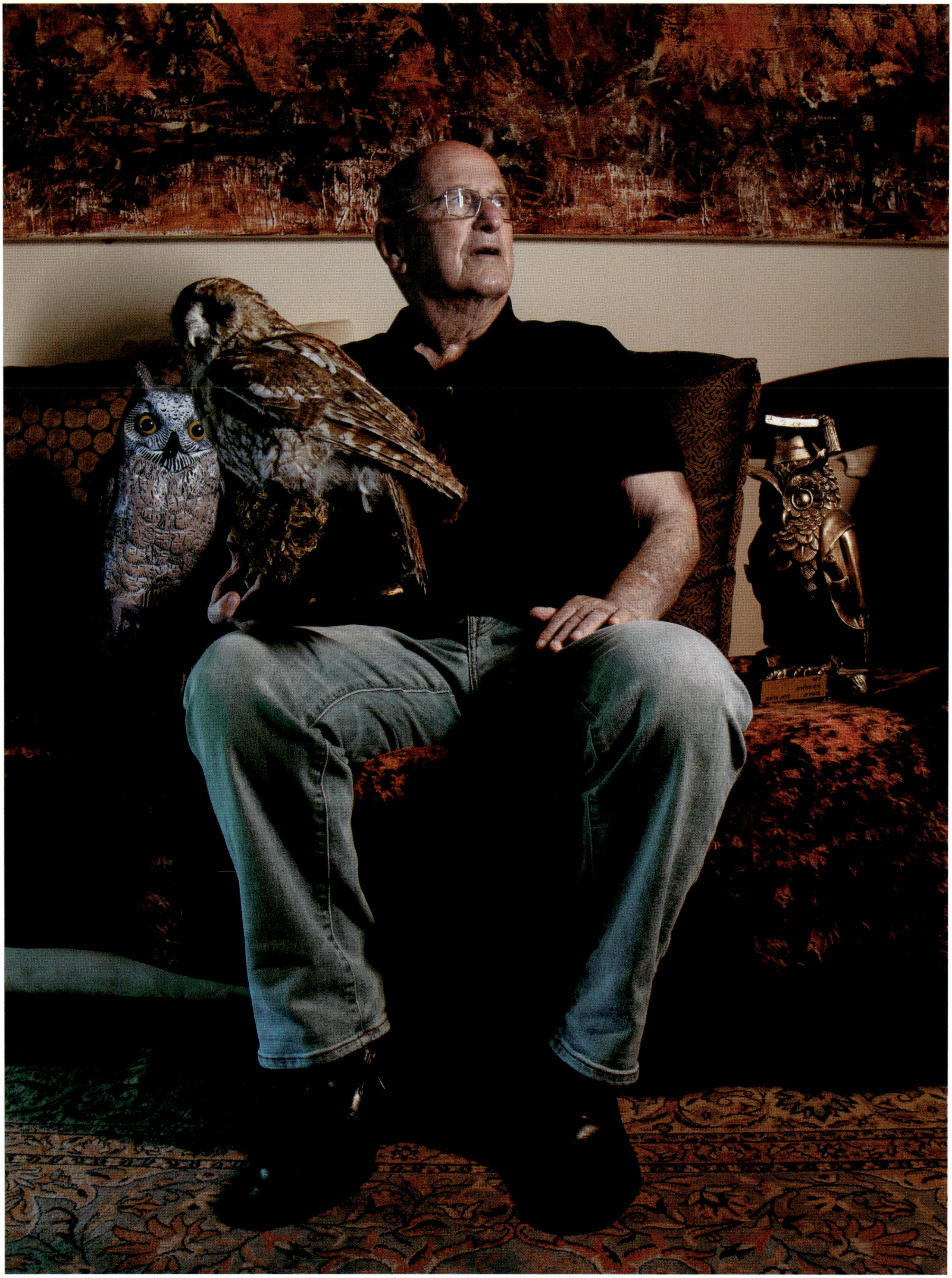

Yossi Peled was born Jeffke Mendelevich in Belgium in 1941, during WWII. 'At the age of six months, I was handed over to a Christian family in Belgium, and I had a good childhood.' Yossi was raised as a Christian child. 'Every Sunday we went to church, and it was festive and very impressive with the sounds of the organ that accompanied the prayers,' he recalls. 'We wouldn't go to sleep without praying to Jesus, but then suddenly I had to detach myself from all that and start living as a Jew. One day, when I was playing in the garden of our country house, near Antwerp, my Christian father called me inside. There sat a tiny woman in the center of the living room and without any prior preparation my father said to me: "We are not your parents; this is your mother!" 'The world crushed all at once,' recalled Yossi. 'That unfortunate woman, one of the victims of the infamous Dr. Mengele's experiments, in Block 10 in Auschwitz, finally met the baby she left behind, and I didn't let her kiss me or touch me.' Yossi had to say goodbye to his adoptive parents. 'My whole life then was one of a child abandoned again and again. My real mother was unable to raise me due to her poor physical condition. She had to hand me over to a large Jewish orphanage in Antwerp and I adapted to life there, but after the establishment of the state, I was brought to Israel with other orphans on the ship *Kedma*. From Haifa we were taken to the youth village of Nitsanim. One day, out of nowhere, a man I didn't know introduced himself as my mother's brother and said, "You're coming with me!" I was taken to Kibbutz Negba, where I learned to defend myself from those who called children who came from "there" like me, "soaps" [a derogatory term for Holocaust survivors]. Negba was a symbol of heroism. Its residents had stopped the Egyptian army during the War of Independence. The fathers of the children who studied with me were known as heroes, while my father was burned in Auschwitz.' Only years later did Yossi fully understand the sacrifice which his mother and mothers like her had made during the Holocaust, and he calls them the real heroes. All of Yossi's family except his mother died in Auschwitz concentration camp. Yossi served in the Israel Defense Forces for 30 years, in the Six-Day War, in the War of Attrition, in the Yom Kippur War and in the First Lebanon War. Yossi became an avid collector of owls after his late Chief of Staff, Chaim Bar-Lev, gave him an owl to express his appreciation for Yossi's wisdom and foresight, commenting Yossi thought during the day and acted during the night, like an owl. Yossi's final military position was as a major general heading the IDF's Northern Command. He later turned to politics, serving briefly as a cabinet minister.

Yossi Peled BY Ira Anner ISRAEL
TEL AVIV, ISRAEL, 2023

László Roth was born in 1920 in Romania. At the age of 21 he began studying composition and conducting in the Budapest music academy, but he was forced to quit in 1943 due to antisemitic proclamations. László and his parents were forced into the Budapest Ghetto. In 1944, the entire family was shipped to Auschwitz, with most being sent to their deaths upon arrival. In Auschwitz, László was forced for weeks to remove bodies from the crematorium. Later, he was sent with his father to the Mauthausen camp, where László was forced to serve in the camp's orchestra as an accordion player as prisoners marched to their deaths. He was later transferred to Ebensee camp, where he was released by US soldiers. László and his father were the sole survivors in his family. László had a rich musical career as both a composer and conductor before emigrating to Israel in 1960, and rose to worldwide fame. At age 103, László Roth holds the self-made notebook of scrap cloth and paper made during his time in the Auschwitz extermination and death camp, in which he wrote the music he had composed in his head and has kept it all these years.

László Roth by Nissim Sellam FRANCE

BAT YAM, ISRAEL, 2023

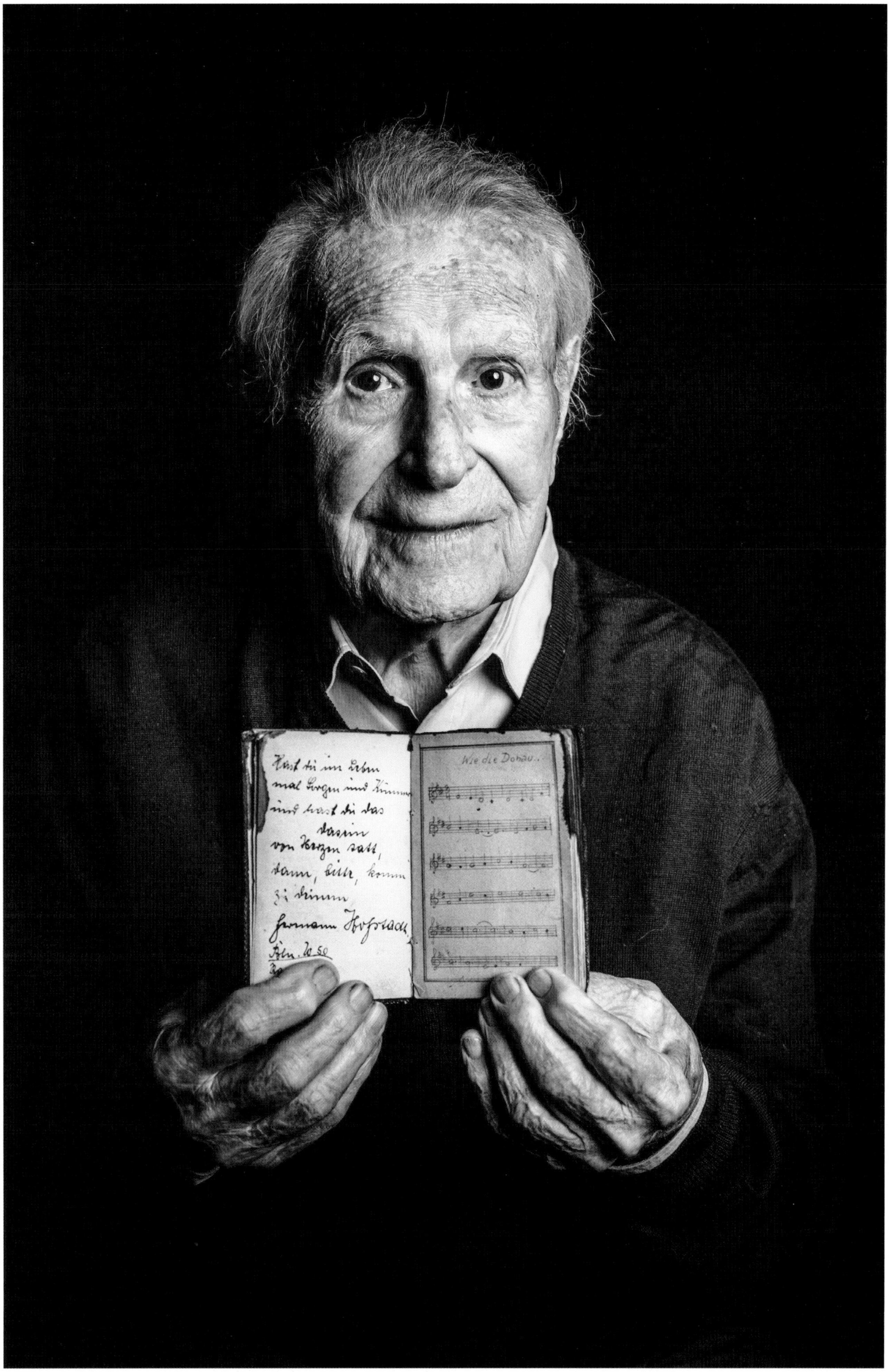
Wie die Donau..

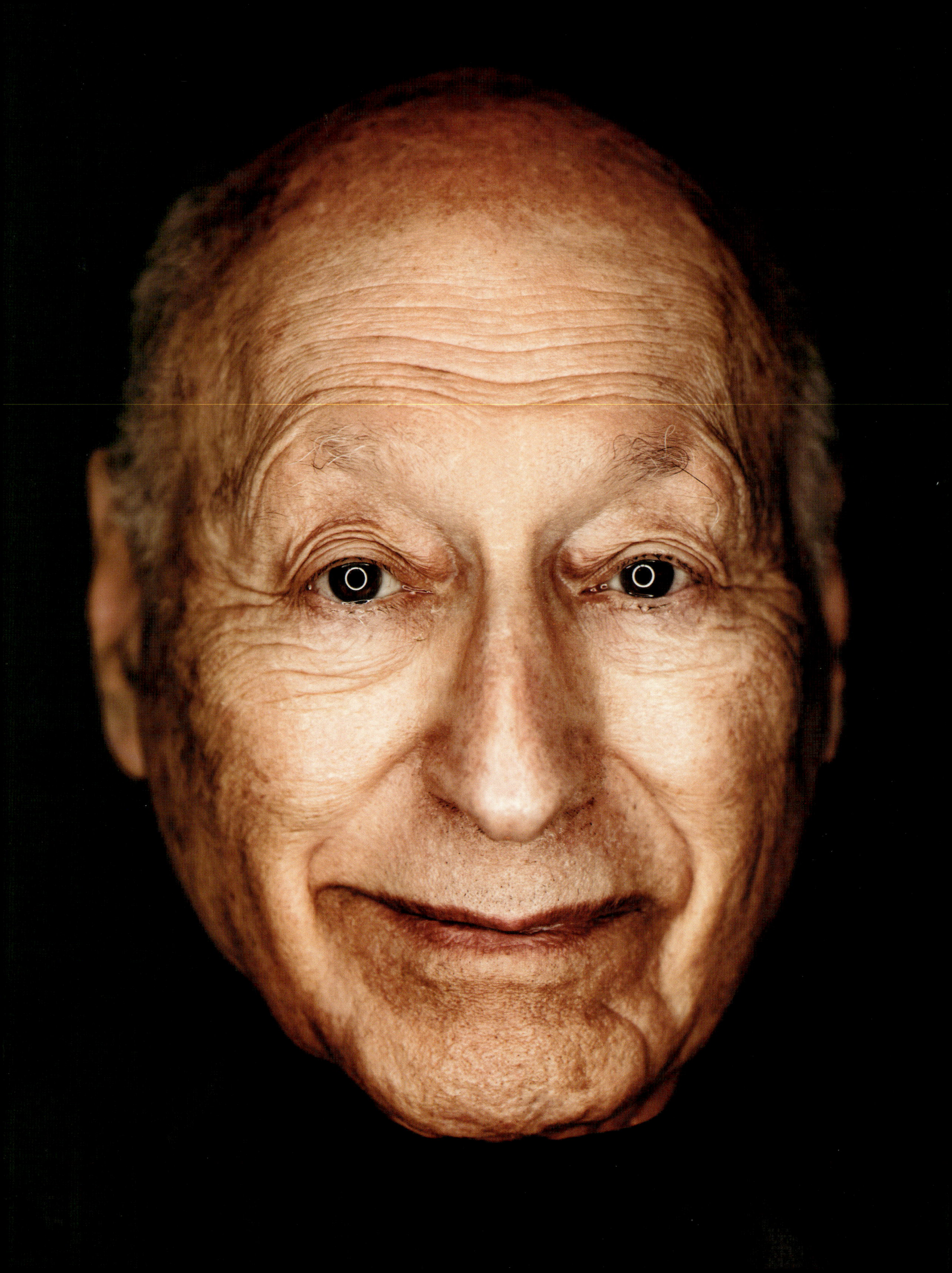

RALPH J. PREISS was born in 1930 in Breslau, Germany (today Wrocław, Poland), the only child of Margot and Harry Preiss, a physician. 'After Hitler came to power, Jews could not go to public school with other German children. It became illegal for Jews to own pets. Our dog, Axel, was taken away from us, a beautiful German Boxer who I loved very much. Hitler took away the German citizenship of all Jews, and even though my father or my grandfather had probably delivered every child living in our town, my father was no longer allowed to treat non-Jews. He began frantically to look for escape to any country that would take us.' As a doctor, Harry was approved for refuge status in the Philippines. Philippine President Manuel Quezon saved more than 1,200 Jews from Germany and Austria, making the Philippines an unlikely haven as most nations closed their doors to Jewish refugees. While waiting for their visas to come through, Ralph witnessed Kristallnacht, or the "Night of Broken Glass," during which mobs destroyed synagogues throughout Germany. He recalls, 'I was home alone with my grandmother. She woke me and bundled me hastily to our attic air raid shelter. I heard people shouting outside the house and banging on our wooden shutters. This was followed by breaking glass as the shutters were torn from their hinges and stones thrown through our windows. I was terrified. This breaking of glass went on for what seemed like hours. Then gunshots rang out. Our neighbor, a Christian school teacher whose son I admired for his snappy German Boy Scout uniform, had shot into the air to scare away the Nazi hoodlums that attacked our house. Later, from my bedroom window, I saw our synagogue was in flames. The Gestapo arrived to arrest my father but he was away, and he went into hiding until our departure.' Ralph and his parents left Germany for the Philippines in January 1939, seven months before the outbreak of World War II. But war came to the Preiss family when Japan invaded the Philippines. Having an expired German passport, even one marked with a red "J" for Jude, permitted them to live outside the concentration camps set up by the Japanese during the war. The family survived liberation by joining Filipino guerillas on Mount Banahaw for three months. Ralph recalls, 'I stayed one step ahead of the Japanese until the Americans liberated us.' After high school in the Philippines, Ralph obtained a US visa in 1949 and attended MIT in Cambridge to study engineering. He pioneered automated diagnostics in computers at IBM's Poughkeepsie lab, working there his entire career. He and his wife Marcia had four daughters. Marcia's wedding dress, made of piña cloth from the Philippines, has been worn by three generations of the family.

Ralph J. Preiss BY **Mark Mann** SCOTLAND
NEW YORK CITY, USA, 2023

Moshe Ridler BY Moshe Ridler ISRAEL
KIBBUTZ HOLIT, ISRAEL, 2021

Moshe Ridler was born in Romania in 1931. He was nine years old when Romania aligned with Nazi Germany and the Jews of the town of Hertsa were rounded up for deportation. Moshe, his mother and a young sister were sent to a concentration camp in Transnistria. His father Zelig was sent to a forced labor camp near Odesa and his older sister, Feige, to a work camp in Ukraine. After his mother and sister perished in the camp, he joined other youths who were set to escape, and they succeeded. Moshe kept running all night till he collapsed in the fields and woke up in the home of a Ukrainian family. The family sheltered him. He became a shepherd and part of their family, helping them with farm work till the war ended. Moshe decided to return to his hometown and search for relatives. He was seated on the steps of the local synagogue when his father appeared and later, they were reunited with his older sister. In 1951, Moshe moved to Israel and became a police detective. Later he worked with the Jewish agency helping Ethiopian new immigrants in absorption centers. Five years ago, Moshe moved to Kibbutz Holit on the border with Gaza and Egypt to be near his daughter Pnina, who lived in the kibbutz. They hired an assistant, Petrov Busco, from Moldova who could communicate with Moshe in Romanian. Moshe became known as the grandfather of Holit, a tiny kibbutz of some 200 members. Moshe met last with his family on September 30, 2023. His 18 grandchildren and great-grandchildren, he used to say, are his greatest pride. On October 7, 2023, Hamas terrorists infiltrated southern Israel, murdering some 1,200 people, including over 320 Israeli soldiers. They breached the fence around the Gaza Strip in 29 places and took back into Gaza some 240 hostages from Israel and 25 other countries. Israel immediately declared war on Hamas. Moshe's daughter Pnina was visiting relatives that day when early morning sirens sounded all over Israel, and rockets from the Gaza Strip began to rain down on Israeli communities. Soon she learned that armed Hamas terrorists from Gaza invaded also into Kibbutz Holit and were rampaging through the tiny kibbutz, going from house to house with grenade launchers and shooting at everyone. Moshe and his caregiver Petrov were told to hide in the safe room and lock the steel door. It is the last that Pnina heard from them. It took a few more hours before Pnina heard that Israeli soldiers were evacuating people under gunfire. The terrorists shot a rocket propelled grenade at Moshe's house, and it caught on fire. The following night Pnina was notified that Moshe and Petrov were murdered. Moshe's remains were found in the safe room and Petrov's at the entrance to the house. Hamas murdered 13 members of this tiny community where mothers were shot dead in front of their children. Pnina hopes her father's death was quick and he did not suffer. His remains were identified on October 17, ten days after the attack, and he was laid to rest near his late wife near Tel Aviv. Pnina says they will return and rebuild Holit. "We are not going to give up." Her father Moshe did not.

RUTH HARAN was born in Bucharest, Romania, in 1935. Romania established antisemitic laws and carried out a massive torturous campaign against the Jews even before it became an ally of Nazi Germany in 1940. Ruth's father, a Jewish doctor from Poland, was deported and found employment in a hospital in Odessa. Ruth's mother, a Romanian Jew, fled with her three children and was reunited with her husband in Odessa just before Axis troops set siege to the city. Ruth's family, along with tens of thousands of Jews, fled Odessa in 1941. Odessa surrendered and over 80,000 remaining Jews were massacred. Ruth, who was seven years old at the time, recalls the fear and starvation during their escape and also the bombings by the approaching Nazis. They fled across the Soviet lines and Ruth's father, the doctor who treated the many wounded and sick throughout their escape, kept their family safe and together. They set out on the long and arduous road to Uzbekistan, by foot and on train. Ruth recalls the typhoid epidemic among the fleeing refugees, which her father treated but which later took his life. After the war they traveled to Kishinev and in 1947, Ruth, her mother and siblings immigrated illegally to Mandatory Palestine. Israel was declared a state in 1948, and Ruth's life flourished. Even so, it was never easy. Over the years, two members of Ruth's family were killed in Israel's wars. Eight decades after the Holocaust, Ruth is reliving her childhood horrors as destruction and death of loved ones are devastating the 88-year-old great-grandmother's life. Five years ago, after her husband passed away, Ruth moved to Kibbutz Be'eri to be near her son Avshalom. At the time she was dealing with a bout of cancer. She described her life in Be'eri as beautiful; she was surrounded by love, care and beautiful fields her kibbutz cultivated. Handymen and farmers from Gaza, just down the road, returned to work in the kibbutz some time ago and there was hope for peace, she says. On October 7, 2023, Hamas assaulted and carried out a massacre in the Israeli communities of southern Israel. This time Ruth was all alone. She awoke that morning with the incoming barrages of rockets and kept calling her son Avshalom who lived next door. She tried her daughter-in-law; she tried her grandchildren but got no response. Through her window she noticed armed men on the front lawn and soon there was a knock on her door. Ruth opened the door to a group of armed men who burst into her home and forced her into her safe room. Her life was spared when they were called by another and left her trembling indoors. For 15 long hours she was hiding in her home. She does not remember where but not in the safe room, she says. She emerged once and saw bodies on the lawn nearby and she ran back inside. It was already nighttime when Israeli soldiers rescued her. As they were leading her to safety, she witnessed death everywhere with burned-down and still smoldering homes. Ruth was taken to a nearby field with other kibbutz members who survived the massacre. They huddled together for hours under gunfire and there she learned that the terrorists had gone from house to house executing people. Her neighbors were sobbing and telling each other of the murder, rape and the slaughter of babies and children. 'It is a Shoah. Only in Shoah are babies brutally murdered out of pleasure, women, pregnant women, killed or raped, homes burned,' Ruth says, sobbing. Only days later was she notified that her son Avshalom, 66, was among the dead. Ruth says he was killed while trying to reach her home. His cell phone, which she had tried to call all day, was answered by someone in Gaza. Seven members of her family, including her daughter, grandchildren and great-grandchildren, aged three and eight, were kidnapped to Gaza. 'They murdered my son, they took my family to Gaza… release them!' cries Ruth, insisting, 'I will return to my kibbutz, we will rebuild.'

Ruth Haran BY Rina Castelnuovo ISRAEL
BE'ER SHEVA, ISRAEL, 2023

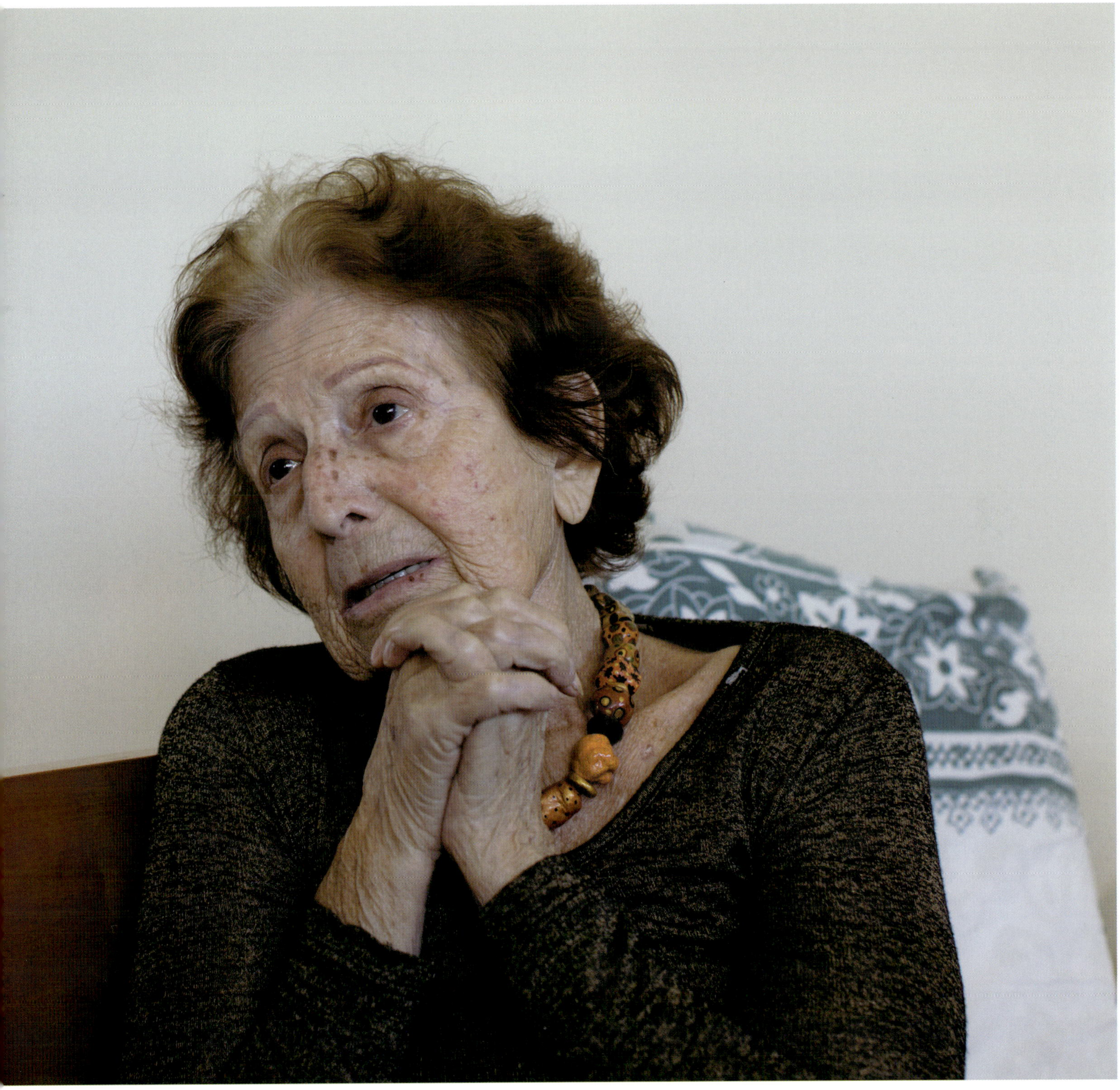

Acknowledgments

Special thanks to:

Advocate Naomi Assia and Lili Haber, daughters of Jacob & Yona Leser. Yona survived three death camps. Jacob was rescued by Oskar Schindler.

Tsafrir Abayov	Max Hirshfeld	Moshe Rosenzeig
Zvi Agmon	Alexandra Hollander	Romina & Lali Rothschild
Efrat Amrani	Mikella Hollander	Hadas Ruso
Maya Anner	Oliver Holmes	Jonathan Russo
Colette Avital	Edith Ilan	Jorg Schierenbeck
Ariel Bart	Dtto. Edmondo Illi	Ilan Schwarz
Rea Ben-David	Anna-Patricia Kahn	Gil Shechter
Gladys Bendahan	Gisela Kayser	Yaniv Shezifi
Frank Bengfort	Yuval Keshet	Daniel Shlomo
Gigi Benson	Françoise Kirkland	Erez Shoham
Alon Bernstein	Ziv Koren	Enrique Shore
Nella Cassouto	Dina Kraft	Armin Smailovic
Liya Chechik	Eyal Landesman	Jeffrey Smith
Howard & Lise Cohen	Jean-Luc Landier	Hila Smolansky
Igal Cohen	Dr. Alexandra Lavastine	Sharon Soffer
Randy Cole	Galia Levinovich	Ami Steinitz
Peter Dench	Jean-Francois Leroy	Hans-Rudolf Strasser
Ruth Diskin	Ariane Littman	Eva Strenger
Shai Doron	Grzegorz Litynski	Shir Tamuz
Ido Efek	Anat Negev	Ronit Tern
Moshe & Elisheva Farjon	Nadav Neuhaus	Anat Tzur
Debbie Findling	Ido Ofek	Lisa Usdan
Tova Fish-Rosenberg	Rami Ozeri	Harry Wall
Kobi Frig	Keshet Partem	Maurice Weiss
Brain Gale	Judah Passow	Lauren Winfield
Esti Goldwasser	Imri Perel	Christian Wolf
Nina Gomiashvili	Monika Plhal	
Ilan Greenfield	Irina Pozhidaeva	
Deborah Greyson	Kezia Raffel Pride	
David Grossman	Yaara Raz Hakla	
Tamar Herzberg	Patrick Roberts	
Ronne & Donald Hess	Emily Rogers	

The Jerusalem Biennale / הביאנלה של ירושלים